ORRIN PORTER ROCKWELL

ORRIN PORTER ROCKWELL
1813–1878

ORRIN PORTER ROCKWELL

Man of God
Son of Thunder

By Harold Schindler

Illustrated by DALE BRYNER

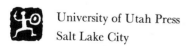

University of Utah Press
Salt Lake City

VOLUME FIFTEEN OF THE UNIVERSITY OF UTAH
PUBLICATIONS IN THE AMERICAN WEST, UNDER THE EDITORIAL DIRECTION
OF THE AMERICAN WEST CENTER

University of Utah Press, Salt Lake City 84112
© 1966 by Harold Schindler

Second edition © 1983 by Harold Schindler
First paperback edition 1993
4

Printed in the United States of America.

Library of Congress Cataloguing in Publication Data

Schindler, Harold, 1929–
    Orrin Porter Rockwell: man of God, son of thunder.

    Bibliography: p.
    Includes index.
    1. Rockwell, Orrin Porter, 1813–1878. 2. Mormons —
United States — Biography. I. Title.
BX8695.R6S32   1983   289.3'3 [B]   82-23747
ISBN 0-87480-440-X

The paper in this book meets the standards for permanence and durability
established by the Committee on Production Guidelines for Book Longevity of the
Council on Library Resources.

To Orrin Porter Rockwell,

> *whose life on the American frontier deserves more than a legacy of hypocrisy and scorn . . .*

to my wife, Benita,

> *who shared her husband with a ghost . . .*

and to Carolyn, Steve, and Jeffrey . . .

this book is affectionately dedicated.

CONTENTS

PORTRAITS

PREFACE

Because the *Salt Lake Tribune* did not publish on Mondays in 1878, thirty-six hours passed before the then-rabidly anti-Mormon newspaper was able to trumpet in mock despair: PORTER ROCKWELL THE CHIEF OF THE DANITE BAND SHUFFLES OFF IN A STABLE — AND CHEATS THE HANGMAN OF A WORTHY CANDIDATE. Elsewhere in the *Tribune*'s columns an editorial informed its Gentile readers that Rockwell killed unsuspecting travelers for their booty, he killed other members of the Church of Jesus Christ of Latter-day Saints "who held secrets that menaced the safety of their fellow criminals in the priesthood," he killed apostates "who dared to wag their tongues about the wrongs they had endured," and he killed "mere sojourners in Zion . . . to keep his hand in." All of these crimes amounted to a staggering total, the editorial clucked, adding: "It is estimated he participated in at least a hundred murders for the Church, none of which he ever divulged."

That Rockwell neglected to confess this wholesale slaughter during his lifetime did not deter the newspaper from reeling off one unsubstantiated accusation after another in his obituary of June 11, 1878. But having been the vortex of controversy while he lived, it seems, somehow, only fitting that he would be as well after his passing. Rockwell's past has been distorted to incredible extremes by writers on two continents who transformed his name into a synonym for terror. "The Destroying Angel," his contemporaries called him; he led the "Danites," a secret society of Mormon assassins, they said.

When Rockwell died, his church eulogized him as a "natural born pioneer" and devout Latter-day Saint; yet in succeeding years his deeds were quietly pushed deep into the mustier reaches of Mormon history. Porter Rockwell became a skeleton in the closet, a figurative but spacious cubicle he shared with a number of friends — John D. Lee and Bill Hickman, to name but two. Historically, only an instant has flickered by since Rockwell spurred one of his magnificent stallions across the plains; still, so little is known of him that authors content themselves with echoing apocrypha surrounding his adventures. And with each repetition a new stamp of authenticity is imprinted on the legend of the Destroying Angel of Mormondom.

Well then, what kind of man *was* Orrin Porter Rockwell?

Was he, as his obituary charges, a man who would calmly kill unsuspecting travelers for booty, who would deal out death to "mere sojourners" simply "to keep his hand in"? Is this concept consistent with the widely accepted image of Rockwell as a fanatic who would murder fellow Mormons to safeguard church secrets, or kill apostates for any of several reasons? And is this consistent with his reputation as an often well-liked and largely orthodox member of the church? The obvious difficulty, of course, in drawing a clear and distinct picture of the man is that history has left us with at least two different Rockwells: the stalwart Mormon pioneer and western frontiersman, and the malign, sinister figure of anti-Mormon legend.

Through years of searching the crevices of Rockwell's past for hidden clues to the truth, I found him to be shrouded in ambiguity and contradiction. Now that I have uncovered all I can of him, much of the ambiguity and mystery remain. Insofar as the record is recoverable, this is what it contains, and it is now left for you to decide how these facts are to be assessed, for good or for ill. After reading this biography a good many church members will tend to feel that Rockwell led an essentially blameless life and in the course of time became a victim of his own legend, stemming from the Boggs shooting of 1842. A good many non-Mormons may take an exactly opposite view. And members of the Reorganized Church (followers of Joseph Smith III) may tend to feel that there was nothing wrong with Rockwell, really, but that he was corrupted by Brigham Young after reaching Utah.

A very large part of his story is clearly lost in time. Rockwell is dead, and he went without ever having set down on paper a connected account of his life, to say nothing of the controversial incidents in it. (Perhaps it is just as well; who would have believed him?) Evidence exists that in his later years he approached a friend, Mrs. Elizabeth D. E. Roundy, and asked her to chronicle his life. That history — if it was written — has never come to light. Her manuscript may yet turn up in an attic or a trunk; until then, I offer this as a substitute. It was my intention to piece together the tale Rockwell might have dictated to Mrs. Roundy in 1873. Wherever possible I have used primary sources; in some instances it was necessary to consult works considered anti-Mormon. Since an account of Rockwell's life must be the history of a myth, a folk legend, not less than the history of a man, the possible bias of an authority is in a sense immaterial for such a book as this. I have used dubious sources where necessary with the greatest of care and (good, I hope) judgment. In recreating Rockwell's checkered career, I have drawn on pioneer diaries and journals, memoirs, court records, letters, newspaper articles, and unpublished manuscripts as well as books of the period. Of all the volumes of Western Americana available, no reliable work on Rockwell has existed. This book was written to fill that vacuum.

One publication, *The Destroying Angels of Mormondom* — its author, "Achilles," effectively concealed behind the mask of anonymity — appeared in California in 1878 and calls for a word of comment here. Purporting to be a "Sketch of the Life of Orrin Porter Rockwell, the Late Danite Chief," the monograph's entire forty-five pages are devoted to heaping blame on the Mormon for virtually every bloody deed perpetrated west of the Mississippi. Achilles proclaimed it to be Rockwell's confession. A perusal of its pages, however, indicates that Achilles borrowed liberally from contemporaries; his narrative relies heavily on information found in at least three books available in California during the 1870s: John H. Beadle's *Life in Utah, or the Mysteries and Crimes of Mormonism* (Philadelphia, 1870); William A. Hickman's *Brigham's Destroying Angel* (New York, 1872); and Nelson Slater's *Fruits of Mormonism* (Coloma, California, 1851).

In fairness to the mysterious "Achilles," there are several areas in which he offers previously unpublished particulars, all lacking corroboration yet disturbingly convincing. The account of the shooting of the McRae brothers is an excellent example. Here he provides details during a time in Great Salt Lake City when the settlement's only newspaper, the *Deseret News*, had temporarily suspended publication because of a paper shortage. Achilles' statements in this matter are confirmed by diaries of the period. Perhaps one day Achilles' identity will be discovered, which may answer many perplexing questions. [AUTHOR'S NOTE: Several months after *Orrin Porter Rockwell; Man of God, Son of Thunder*, had gone to press, I chanced across a story in the *Salt Lake Herald* (see August 6, 1878) in which Achilles is identified as Samuel D. Sirrine. And so, Achilles' past and his motives may yet be called to account by inquisitive minds. — H.S., 1971]

In the search for Rockwell data I incurred debts of gratitude for assistance, and moral support during frequent periods of frustration, which are far too numerous to mention. But several cannot go unrecognized. Consequently, I wish especially to extend my deepest appreciation to: Chad J. Flake and Donald T. Schmidt at Brigham Young University Library; Dr. Everett L. Cooley, director, and his staff at the Utah State Historical Society; the staff at the LDS Church Historian's Office; and the countless researchers at the Library of Congress and the National

Archives, unknown to me by name, who helped in tracking Rockwell's cold trail.

Sam Weller, for his friendship and constant efforts to obtain fresh material pertinent to this biography; and David L. Bigler, whose propensity for rescuing long-forgotten diaries and journals is without equal.

Mrs. Juanita Brooks, a source of inspiration, whose wise counsel and encouragement have done much to stoke the fires of enthusiasm throughout The Quest.

Dale L. Morgan, whose thoughtful criticisms and words of advice I esteem as coming from one of the finest and most remarkable historians and scholars the West will ever be fortunate enough to call its own.

But in the final analysis, responsibility for what is set down here — including errors of fact and judgment, which inescapably creep into a book of this size despite every precaution — is mine and mine alone to shoulder.

For those members of my church who may feel that I have wrongly opened forbidden doors, I offer these words of the late Brigham H. Roberts, assistant church historian, scholar, and member of the First Council of The Seventy:

> We need not follow our researches in any spirit of fear and trembling. We desire only to ascertain the truth; nothing but the truth will endure; and the ascertainment of the truth and the proclamation of the truth in any given case, or upon any subject, will do no harm to the work of the Lord which is itself truth. . . .*

— Harold Schindler
October 1966

* *New Witnesses for God* (Salt Lake City, 1909), Vol. III, p. 503.

PREFACE TO THE SECOND EDITION

Can sixteen years really have gone by since *Orrin Porter Rockwell: Man of God, Son of Thunder*, turned out to face the public? The swift passage of time is frightening. I thought that, once written, Rockwell's biography would find its place wherever history saw fit and we might part company. But we have never really been able to cut the cord, he and I. If this Man of God, Son of Thunder could speak for himself, I have no doubt he would whisper, "Leave it be, can't ye?" But having disturbed his rest once, and so roughly, I am haunted by the possibility that what has been laid bare for all to see and judge may do him an injustice through neglect. So he has never been far from my thoughts and is always the first consideration in any examination or perusal of new material.

When in 1966 the University of Utah Press stepped forward to publish my manuscript it was a brave decision and not one taken lightly. But from the first, the book's acceptance was wide, warm, and genuine. For this I am elated, grateful, and pleased. Its publishing history over these sixteen years has encompassed six printings and now a second edition, revised and enlarged. Through the exceptional editing of Trudy McMurrin and the incomparable typographical skills of Donald M. Henriksen, I have been privileged not only to hone and refine the rough edges of the earlier work, but to indulge myself in adding what new information I chose without measurably disturbing the general harmony of the biography.

Much of the new material in this second edition has been fitted into footnotes, and while most of it is supplemental, it is there to flesh out the individuals and events of Orrin Porter Rockwell's world. Not all of it is startling, by any means, nor does it always involve him directly. But the research, in my mind, goes far toward illuminating the mores of those unsettled times. Some new descriptive narrative has been inserted in the passages pertaining to the fight at Crooked River and the attack on Haun's Mill to provide a better understanding of the turbulence which engulfed members of the early church and shaped their thinking and attitudes in coping with day-to-day survival.

Occasional changes have been made to clarify footnotes. Sometimes these revisions have been small, but always, to my thinking, important. Thus Dale L. Morgan is given proper credit for his part in the discovery in 1966 of the mass of affidavits and petitions filed by Mormons seeking redress for persecutions in Missouri — documents which scholars had been attempting to recover for more than a century. Morgan's uncanny ability to reason through complicated and often contradictory situations and his genius for comprehending human behavior have not yet been fully appreciated; his preeminence as an historian and scholar still remains largely unrecognized.

I have tempered some documentation to afford a bit of elbowroom for the future. So, a note concerning the pioneer trek has been revised to spell out the specific contributions of William Clayton, Orson Pratt, and Appleton Milo Harmon to the creation of the "roadometer," yet omit crediting Mormons with the first use of such a device because of likely evidence to the contrary.

There is additional detail on the shooting of Frank Worrell of the Carthage Greys, the attempted murder of John Tobin, and the tangled business arrangement involving Orrin Porter Rockwell in the ownership of the Hot Springs Brewery Hotel.

And for the first time, an outside source, *The New York Times*, has been found which not only substantiates the existence of the Aiken party, but provides vital new information on the identities and backgrounds of its ill-fated members.

Using contemporary newspaper accounts, I have enlarged on the implications of Joseph Smith's high military rank as lieutenant general of the Nauvoo Legion. I also took advantage of the opportunity to discuss "mountain fever," the malady which incapacitated so many overland travelers, including Brigham Young. The chapter on the Utah Expedition now tells of the bloodied in that so-called "bloodless" war and mentions the role played by two youngsters who went on to adventure and notoriety in their own right — William F. Cody and James Butler Hickok. I have also given John Riggs Murdock his due as the west's most extraordinary wagonmaster.

In the first edition I chose to omit an incident involving Rockwell and Vice President of the United States Schuyler Colfax because I could find no evidence of its truth. Then, years later, while I was browsing among volumes in a used book store, an 1886 biography of Colfax fell open, and — serendipity. The anecdote is now part of this edition. The most recent sidelight to Orrin Porter Rockwell's story occurred during the Bicentennial celebration when the State of Missouri rescinded Gov. Lilburn W. Boggs's 1838 "Extermination Order."

This second edition also contains an expanded bibliography, and a greatly amplified index. Through a redesigned text, much added material has been accommodated in only a few more pages, footnotes have been set in larger type for easier reading, and still all the illustrations from the first edition have been retained.

That brings me to "Achilles," the mysterious tale-teller and self-proclaimed purveyor of Rockwell's "confession." Alas, he continues to elude close examination. Readers of earlier printings of the first edition may remember that his true identity was brought to light quite by accident, through a few sentences in *The Salt Lake Herald* of August 6, 1878. Under the heading "The Life of Porter Rockwell," the item read:

> Some days ago we announced the appearance in San Francisco, of a book entitled "the Life and Confessions of O. P. Rockwell," etc., and suggested that ex-District Attorney Howard might have had something to do with it. We have since learned that the author of the work, who signs himself, "Achilles," is Samuel D. Sirrine, a person whose name has figured in rather disgraceful connection in this territory during late years. The book seems to be regarded in its true light, that is, as a fraud, hence it finds little sale. It has been taken off the railroad trains, where it did not pay the newsboys for handling it.

And so Achilles stands unmasked. But an Achilles by any other name remains an enigma; Samuel D. Sirrine he may be, but Sirrine is as much a mystery as his pseudonym. *The Mountaineer* for September 8, 1860, has him as a juror in the lawsuit of *Brigham Young* vs. *Peter K. Dotson* (in the matter of the destruction of certain engraved plates in President Young's office). Sirrine seems to drop from public view until February 1865, when he is named a member of the committee to plan the Utah celebration of President Lincoln's inaugural. And, finally, the following year, the *Deseret News* for October 31, 1866, records Sirrine as one of the coroner's jury in the J. K. Robinson inquest. So much for Samuel D. Sirrine. At least we know that he wasn't one of the more notorious members of Utah society, thus placing him, temporarily at least, beyond the argument that his purported "confession" of Orrin Porter Rockwell was a matter of revenge. Sirrine must shoulder the responsibility solely on the basis of having sought mere money for his enterprise.

We are left with the hope that future research, perhaps more energetically applied, will tell the tale on Achilles.

I have been encouraged to satisfy my abiding passion for "gee whiz" notes, those trivial but interesting asides which adorn the luncheon conversation of historians but seem never to find their way into books. Actually, no persuasion was necessary and I sprinkled these oddments with

Chapter One

VALLEY OF THE BIG BLUE

As the barge labored its way along the ice-choked Erie Canal toward Buffalo, New York, seventeen-year-old Orrin Porter Rockwell separated himself from the other youngsters at the rail and hunched against a packing case roped to the deck. Even it offered little protection from the biting March wind that slashed at his eyes and cheeks. Great floes, piled twenty feet thick, clogged the harbor, squeezing a profusion of obscenity from the pilot. Finally, the old tub crunched against a frozen pier and its passengers transferred to a side-wheel steamer. There they learned that their journey might be delayed as long as two weeks until warmer weather opened navigation along Lake Erie to Ohio. The listeners chorused a groan. Their predicament was uniformly discomforting since the group was comprised of Mormons, eighty members of the sect en route to Kirtland, Ohio, to join Joseph Smith, Jr., their prophet, seer, and revelator.

No sooner had the announcement been made than Orrin Porter Rockwell bounded down the slick gangplank to shore. He was followed immediately by several whooping youngsters who were equally as tired of the overcrowded canal barge which had been their place of confinement for most of a week.

"Porter! You come back here this minute and bring the rest of those rowdies with you — or we'll leave the lot of you behind!" Lucy Mack Smith spoke with the authority of a woman used to having her own way. And after all, the mother of the prophet was to be obeyed; her word was law. The boy, embarrassed at having been singled out for criticism, returned to the steamer without a murmur. His companions, finding themselves suddenly leaderless, followed suit.

Mother Smith addressed the Mormon women in stern, almost exasperated, tones: "How many times must I tell you to watch out for your children? Don't you realize I can't be responsible for them? There are too many other problems to be solved without worrying about a pack of rascally youngsters."

This shipboard incident near Buffalo in 1831 is one of the earliest mentions of Orrin Porter Rockwell by a contemporary.[1] Genealogical records of the Church of Jesus Christ of Latter-day Saints offer only the sketchiest details of Porter's childhood. He was born in Belcher, Hampshire County, Massachusetts, on June 28, 1813, to Orin and Sarah Witt Rockwell, the second of nine sons and daughters.[2] He was named after his father (with an extra *r* in Orrin) and his paternal grandmother, Irene Porter. The Rockwells were solid New Englanders who could trace their roots back through family members in Windsor, Connecticut, to Deacon William Rockwell of York, England. It was the Deacon himself who brought the Rockwell name to America. Through a jumble of ancestral lines, Orrin Porter Rockwell was related to Joseph Smith, Jr., for Irene Porter was descended from John Porter and Ann White, progenitors of the Mormon prophet. And through the same complicated network of family branches, Porter was a distant cousin of a young boy named Abraham Lincoln.[3]

In Porter's fourth year the Rockwells moved from Belcher to Manchester, New York. Two years later, in 1819, Joseph Smith, Sr., gathered his family and left Palmyra, New York; he, too, resettled in Manchester, just a mile from the Rockwells.[4] Before long the two households became firm friends.[5] Porter, along with his parents, was a frequent visitor at the Smith home, and it was on these occasions in 1829 that he begged to stay

[1] As related by Lucy Mack Smith in *Biographical Sketches of Joseph Smith the Prophet, and His Progenitors for many Generations* (Liverpool, 1853), p. 179.

[2] The others were Caroline, Peter, Emily, Electa, Alvira, Merritt, Horace, and Mary. See *Deseret News*, August 31, 1935; "Records of Early Church Families," *Utah Genealogical and Historical Magazine* (Salt Lake City, 1935), Vol. XXVI, p. 154; and *Biographical History of Northeastern Ohio, Embracing the Counties of Ashtabula, Geauga and Lake* (Chicago, 1893), p. 684.

[3] *Deseret News*, August 31, 1935. Rockwell also was connected to Ulysses S. Grant, Grover Cleveland, Wilford Woodruff, and Daniel H. Wells.

[4] Mrs. M. C. R. [Caroline] Smith's affidavit in *Naked Truths About Mormonism* (Oakland, California), Vol. I, No. 2, April 1888.

[5] It was in the home of Hyrum Smith that Parley P. Pratt met Orrin Porter Rockwell's mother when Pratt first sought out Joseph Smith. See "Discourse by Parley P. Pratt," of September 7, 1856, in *Deseret News*, December 24, 1856.

up late, if only "to keep the pine torch burning" so that he could listen to Joseph relate for the thousandth time the startling events leading to his discovery of the Golden Plates in the Hill Cumorah.[6]

Orrin sat enthralled as Joseph explained how an angel of God had appeared and directed him to the golden record of the Nephites hidden beneath Cumorah's surface. The hill, a prominent local landmark, was on the outskirts of Palmyra. Written in "Reformed Egyptian," Joseph said, the plates bore the history of an ancient people who flourished in North America during the time of Christ. To Porter, whose backwoods childhood had unfolded during a period rampant with freewheeling revivalism and religious upheaval, the thoughts of such adventure and romantic mysticism sent his mind reeling with delight as Joseph described the Urim and Thummim which enabled him to read the sacred writings. They were two stones, he said, set in silver bows and fastened to a breastplate. When he wore the Urim and Thummim the device magically deciphered the characters on the Golden Plates, Joseph told his transfixed audience. But that was not all. Joseph explained that he had been commanded by God to publish the translation to "bring forth and establish the cause of Zion." [7]

Eager to aid his friend in this wonderful task, Porter worked at odd jobs — picking berries and cutting firewood after the chores at home were finished — to raise money for the printing of Joseph's book.[8] Then, in March of 1830, the undertaking was accomplished and the Book of Mormon placed on sale in Palmyra.[9] Reaction to its appearance was immediate and violent. Critics fired a fusillade of invective. In anger and indignation they called Joseph an imposter, a faker, a liar, and an opportunist

[6] Parts of Mrs. Elizabeth D. E. Roundy's letter to the LDS Church Historian in which she explained that Rockwell had asked her to write his history were extracted without attribution in an article on Rockwell for the *Deseret News* "Church Section" of August 31, 1935. Several incidents in Porter's life were mentioned in the letter and subsequently incorporated in the newspaper story. This was one of them.

[7] Revelation given to Joseph Smith, Jr., and Oliver Cowdery at Harmony, Pennsylvania, in April 1829 in *Doctrine and Covenants of the Church of the Latter Day Saints, Carefully Selected From the Revelations of God, and Compiled by Joseph Smith, Jr., Oliver Cowdery, Sidney Rigdon, Frederick G. Williams* (Kirtland, Ohio, 1835).

[8] Roundy letter and *Deseret News*, August 31, 1935.

[9] Porter's sister, Mrs. M. C. R. [Caroline] Smith, claimed in a sworn statement to Arthur B. Deming that her father "copied the 'Book of Mormon' for the printer, or part of it." See her affidavit in *Naked Truths About Mormonism*, Vol. I, No. 2, April 1888.

4

who used a peepstone to bilk unwary souls into subsidizing searches for buried treasure.[10] These accusations and more were hurled at the twenty-five-year-old Vermonter who later would claim he had seen the face of God.[11] Unmindful of the storm of words which raged around him, Joseph, his two brothers, Hyrum and Samuel, Oliver Cowdery, Peter Whitmer, Jr., and David Whitmer, formally organized the Church of Jesus Christ on April 6, 1830.

Porter idolized Joseph. The young prophet was everything his youthful companion wanted to be. Joseph was tall for his time and handsome, with a vibrant personality; he was an eloquent speaker who held audiences in his palm. Porter, conversely, was of average height and tended to be slightly stocky. His face was broad and round; in later years he would be described as resembling a "rugged, mastiff-like, English ruffian." His manner was quiet, almost shy. In all, the two men were as opposite as the poles of a magnet. Yet, typically, they were attracted to each other. But there was something deeper than mere adulation on Rockwell's part; both he and Joseph had suffered great personal tragedy early in life, and the circumstances were strikingly parallel. As a boy, Joseph had injured his leg and an inept country practitioner had removed a small piece of bone in setting the fracture. Consequently, the youngster walked with a perceptible limp, one he was fated to carry through life. At the age of ten Rockwell also fractured a leg. In his case, too, a young Palmyra doctor botched the job of straightening it and left the boy with one leg shorter than the other.[12] If anything, their mutual handicap served to strengthen

[10] Joseph's adventures with a peepstone have been widely publicized, and there is little need to expand on them here. For his money-digging activities see Eber D. Howe, *Mormonism Unvailed* (Painesville, Ohio, 1834), pp. 234, 237, 240. For a description of his use of the stone in the Book of Mormon translation, see David Whitmer, *An Address to All Believers in Christ* (Richmond, Missouri, 1887), pp. 30-31, 37. There is evidence that Mrs. Rockwell (Porter's mother) had been told by Joseph that treasure was buried near the Rockwell home and that she spent considerable time searching for it without success. See C. M. Stafford affidavit in *Naked Truths About Mormonism*, Vol. I, No. 2, April 1888.

[11] In 1833, Joseph, in recounting his childhood for the church's official history, would tell of a vision "in the 16th year of my age" in which the Lord had appeared and forgiven him of his sins. See Paul R. Cheesman, "An Analysis of the Accounts Relating Joseph Smith's Early Visions," M.A. thesis, Brigham Young University, 1965, p. 129. This version would seem to be the earliest written account of the "First Vision." There is no evidence that Joseph mentioned the experience prior to 1833.

[12] Mrs. M. C. R. [Caroline] Smith's affidavit in *Naked Truths About Mormonism*, Vol. I, No. 2, April 1888.

their friendship. Joseph's leg kept him from serving in the militia; Porter's lameness prevented him from working the land.

Once formal organization of what was to become known as the Mormon Church was completed, Joseph called a meeting of his followers, exhorting them to throw off the shackles of other religious connections and join him. "[S]everal persons . . . became convinced of the truth and came forward shortly after, and were received into the Church; among the rest, my own father and mother were baptized, to my great joy and consolation; and about the same time, Martin Harris and Orrin Porter Rockwell." [13]

With her son setting the example, Mrs. Rockwell stepped forward and permitted Joseph to baptize her.[14] In succeeding days three other Rockwells — Peter, Caroline, and Electa — joined the new converts.[15] Porter's father hesitated. Two years would pass before the elder Rockwell would accept the mantle of Mormonism.[16] The family attended services with the Fayette Branch in Seneca County, New York, until 1831, when they followed Lucy Mack Smith to Kirtland.[17] Joseph had preceded them in response to a revelation.[18]

Again there are no records extant to show whether the Rockwells stopped at Kirtland, for after leaving the steamship at Fairport, Ohio, the family drops from sight until the fall of that year, when they settled in the Big Blue district of Jackson County, Missouri, some twelve miles west of

[13] Joseph Smith, Jr., *History of the Church of Jesus Christ of Latter-day Saints. Period I. History of Joseph Smith, the Prophet, by Himself.* Introduction and notes by B. H. Roberts (Salt Lake City, 1902–1912), six volumes, Vol. I, p. 79. Hereafter cited as *History of the Church.*

[14] C. M. Stafford, Orrin Porter Rockwell's brother-in-law, said in an affidavit that Mrs. Rockwell was baptized on the same day Joseph Smith's parents underwent the ritual of total immersion. See affidavit in *Naked Truths About Mormonism,* Vol. I, No. 2, April 1888. Sarah Witt Rockwell received a patriarchal blessing from John Smith in Nauvoo on July 2, 1845. See Patriarchal Blessings, Vol. IX, p. 272, No. 820, on file in the LDS Church Historical Department.

[15] *History of the Church,* Vol. I, p. 86.

[16] Mrs. M. C. R. [Caroline] Smith's affidavit in *Naked Truths About Mormonism,* Vol. I, No. 2, April 1888. Orin Rockwell received a patriarchal blessing from Joseph Smith, Sr., in Caldwell County, Missouri, on January 20, 1839. See Patriarchal Blessings, Vol. IX, p. 272, No. 819.

[17] According to the *Deseret News,* August 31, 1935, and Nauvoo Temple records, Sarah Witt Rockwell was baptized for forty-five of her own and her husband's relatives in ceremonies at Nauvoo, a record at the time.

[18] Smith, *Biographical Sketches,* p. 171; *Doctrine and Covenants,* revelation given to Joseph Smith, Jr., and Sidney Rigdon in December 1830.

Independence.[19] It is more than probable that Porter and his parents journeyed to Kirtland, if only to see Joseph again. The Fayette group arrived in the Ohio community in May and was greeted by Edward Partridge, a bishop assigned to find them temporary quarters until permanent homes could be constructed.[20] Any plans the Rockwells may have had for settling in Kirtland would have been discarded almost at once, for Joseph announced that he had been divinely instructed to begin gathering the Saints in western Missouri.[21] In fact, he and several elders in the church were leaving immediately. The Rockwells were included in the advance company and their arrival in Jackson County can be placed with the Colesville Branch at July's end,[22] when flatboats brought them up the Missouri to the mouth of the Big Blue River.[23]

On August 2, 1831, Joseph wrote, "I assisted the Colesville branch of the church to lay the first log, for a house, as a foundation of Zion in Kaw township. . . . The log was carried and placed by twelve men, in honor of the twelve tribes of Israel." The next day the prophet selected a site for a temple, about three-quarters of a mile west of the courthouse in Independence, a brawling frontier town of ramshackle cabins occupied by a strange assortment of rough, tough Missourians, few of whom had ever seen the inside of a schoolhouse. This then was to become the holy city of Zion, the New Jerusalem, Joseph said.[24]

What Porter Rockwell saw when he stood on the high ground near the Big Blue was land much different from the timbered Eastern states of his childhood. Here the prairie sprawled to the horizon, with flowers occasionally splashing a daub of color on the rich black soil. Thick stands of trees clustered along the riverbank and sheltered a variety of game from deer to beaver. Sidney Rigdon, Joseph's most influential friend and advisor, wrote of the area: "It produces in abundance, wheat, corn, sweet potatoes, cotton and many other common agricultural products. Horses, cattle and hogs, though of an inferior breed, are tolerably plentiful and

---

[19] *Utah Genealogical and Historical Magazine*, Vol. XXVI, p. 154.

[20] *History of the Church*, Vol. I, pp. 173–74; *Doctrine and Covenants*, revelation given to Joseph Smith, Jr., in May 1831.

[21] Ibid., pp. 177–79; revelation of June 1831.

[22] Ibid., p. 191.

[23] Emily M. Austin, *Mormonism; or Life Among the Mormons* (Madison, Wisconsin, 1882), p. 65.

[24] *The Pearl of Great Price, Being a Choice Selection From the Revelations, Translations, and Narrations of Joseph Smith* (Liverpool, 1851), The Book of Moses, Chapter 7, Verse 62.

seem nearly to raise themselves by grazing in the vast prairie range in summer, and feeding upon the bottoms in winter." [25]

To many of the travel-weary Saints the new land may have seemed a paradise; others, perhaps, were disappointed. But all of the Jackson County Mormons would come to regret having set foot on Missouri soil.

A week after the log-laying ceremony, Joseph, in company with ten elders, left Independence Landing for Kirtland, where other church matters needed his attention. One of the prophet's first decisions upon returning to Ohio, however, concerned the purchase of a press and type "for the purpose of establishing and publishing a monthly paper at Independence . . . to be called the *Evening and Morning Star*." Independence's first newspaper would be edited by W. W. Phelps, a Mormon.

The Jackson County Saints, meanwhile, were occupied with the problem at hand — that of establishing a productive colony. Soon work commenced on several settlements scattered over a wide area. Under the guidance of seven high priests—Oliver Cowdery, John Whitmer, Edward Partridge, W. W. Phelps, John Corrill, Sidney Gilbert, and Isaac Morley — the church members purchased land from the federal government at a standard rate of $1.25 an acre. It was too late in the season for crops, but the industrious Mormons prepared the ground for cultivation and saw to it that enough hay was on hand to feed the livestock until spring. The fall and winter months saw permanent cabins raised in every settlement; some of the little sod homes were quite comfortable that first winter. Food consisted mainly of beef and a little bread made of coarse meal produced by rubbing ears of corn on a tin grater.

When he wasn't busy working on his cabin, Porter Rockwell spent most of his time with another family of Saints, the Isaac Beebes, who had settled in Independence. Isaac and Olive Beebe, it seemed, had a comely daughter of eighteen who was attracted to the intense young man. The winter was cold and the nights long. Luana Beebe had reached marriageable age, and her parents agreed that young Mr. Rockwell appeared to be a fellow with good prospects. The formalities thus observed, Orrin Porter Rockwell and Luana Beebe were married February 2, 1832; it was the first Mormon wedding in Jackson County and hundreds of Saints took a welcome respite from their labors to attend the festivities. [26]

[25] *Church Encyclopaedia*, Book I, edited by Andrew Jenson (Salt Lake City, 1889), containing Volumes V, VI, VII, and VIII of *The Historical Record*, a monthly periodical, p. 631. Hereafter cited as *Church Encyclopaedia*.

[26] "A List of Saints in Jackson County," compiled by Thomas Bullock, on file in the LDS Church Historical Department in Salt Lake City, mentions the ceremony.

By the summer of that year Zion had grown to include nearly nine hundred church members. Porter's home was a central meeting place for the high priests and elders in their discussions of church affairs,[27] and Porter himself had become an integral part of the community's way of life by operating a ferry on the Big Blue with his father — an enterprise which led subsequently to a minor skirmish with the law.[28] Between his duties at home and work at the ferry, he had little time to spare on nonessentials. High on the list of unacquired skills was "book larnin'." To his death, Rockwell failed to master the rudiments of reading and writing.

The rapid influx of Saints to Jackson County proved both a boon and a bane to the church, for as word spread that Zion had been located, members began wildly speculating in land. Soon a real estate frenzy swept the settlements. An appeal from the high priests for Joseph to move to Missouri and ease the situation met with cool response from Ohio: "Brother Joseph will not settle in Zion until she repent, and purify herself." It was only after the Jackson County Saints expressed "sincere and humble repentance" in an epistle to the Kirtland authorities that the atmosphere cleared.

The third anniversary of the founding of the church was marked by a conference at Porter's ferry on the Big Blue.[29] It was a big day for Orrin Porter Rockwell — business was good, he and Luana were happy, all seemed serene. But the serenity was destined to end; for even as the Saints gave thanks for their blessings, the "old settlers" of Jackson County were scheming to drive "the damned Mormons" out of the county.

From the beginning the Missourians had resented what they considered an encroachment upon their land by a sect of crack-brained religious zealots. They also looked with suspicion upon anyone who worked as hard as the enterprising Saints. The Missourians had listened apprehensively as the Mormons pretentiously boasted that God had given them the land, that it was their divine inheritance and would someday be entirely free of Gentiles, as non-Mormons were labeled. Such continued declarations by the Saints had the twofold effect of frightening and anger-

---

[27] Journal History (Church of Jesus Christ of Latter-day Saints Historical Department, Salt Lake City), September 27, 1832. The Journal History is a daily account of the activities of the LDS Church, incorporating transcripts of letters, journal excerpts, editorial notations, and other material, published and unpublished.

[28] A grand jury convened February 20, 1833, on a presentment against Orrin Porter Rockwell "for keeping a ferry without a license," was discharged when it failed to return a true bill. See Record B, pp. 197–98, Circuit Court, Independence, Missouri.

[29] *History of the Church*, Vol. I, p. 336.

ing their neighbors. As early as the spring of 1832, the first signs of trouble bubbled to the surface when several Mormon homes were stoned and their occupants harassed by nightriding marauders. Later the same year a haystack owned by the church was burned and nearby cabins were fired upon. Then, in mid-April of 1833, some three hundred Missourians gathered in Independence to work out a plan that would rid them of Mormons once and for all. The settlers let their natural enthusiasm for whiskey get the best of them, however, and the meeting degenerated into a free-for-all. June passed without incident, but in July Editor Phelps unwittingly set off a powder keg, and the resulting blast jarred Jackson County to its taproots.

The *Evening and Morning Star* had been established primarily to publish Joseph's doctrine and spread the gospel and principles of the church in Missouri. It was not strange, therefore, that sooner or later Phelps would touch upon a subject close to the hearts of all Missourians—the Negro. In an article entitled "Free People of Color," the editor carefully explained: "To prevent any misunderstanding among the churches abroad, respecting free people of color, who may think of coming to the western boundaries of Missouri, as members of the church, we quote the following clauses from the Laws of Missouri . . . ." Phelps pointed out that Missouri statutes prohibited entry of blacks into the state without proof of citizenship from another state. He added: "So long as we have no special rule in the church, as to people of color, let prudence guide, and while they, as well as we, are in the hands of a merciful God, we say: Shun every appearance of evil." The Missourians pounced on the article as encouraging free blacks to enter the state as members of the Mormon Church, and, they howled, Phelps was showing them how to do it legally! Crying "Abolitionism," the settlers angrily denounced the editor and claimed free Negroes would "pollute" their slaves. Phelps, realizing he had loosed a lightning bolt, hurried to mollify the seething populace. Rushing into print an extra which proclaimed his earlier story had been "misunderstood," he hastened to explain, "our intention was not only to stop free people of color from emigrating to this state, but to prevent them from being admitted as members of the church." [30]

Unfortunately for the Mormons the damage was done. The old settlers met to deal with this "important crisis . . . as regards our civil so-

[30] *Evening and Morning Star*, Vol. II, No. 14, July 1833, p. 109, and EXTRA, July 16, 1833.

ciety" and issued a manifesto declaring that the Missourians intended to "rid our society, 'peaceably if we can, forcibly if we must,' . . . [of these] deluded fanatics." [31]

On July 20 a dozen or so hard-faced men en route to Independence boarded the ferry on the Big Blue. While young Rockwell and his father poled the lumbering raft across, they overheard their passengers boasting that before the sun had set they would destroy the Mormon printing office which published the *Evening and Morning Star*. About dusk the party reappeared at the landing for the return journey. Fixing the Rockwells with a cold, unblinking stare, one of the men growled, "We tore up Phelps's press and gave a couple of your friends a tar and feathering. Unless you want a taste of the same, you'll chuck the Mormons. Understand?" Ashore, the men refused to pay their passage.[32] It was not until later that Rockwell learned the details of the trouble in Independence.

A crowd numbering nearly five hundred furious Missourians from miles around congregated at the courthouse and handed down an ultimatum — Jackson County Mormons were to cease all future settlement of the area; those already settled were to indicate in writing their intention to leave the county; the editor of the *Evening and Morning Star* was to close his shop and discontinue the business of printing in Jackson County; all other Mormon stores and shops were to close; and Mormon leaders

---

[31] Ibid., No. 15, December 1833, p. 114.

[32] As described by Orrin Porter Rockwell in an affidavit contained in evidence submitted by the Church of Jesus Christ of Latter-day Saints to the U.S. House of Representatives on May 10 and 21, 1842 (previously presented to the Senate Judiciary Committee, 26th Congress, 1st Session, December 2, 1839–July 21, 1840), to substantiate claims against the State of Missouri for damages allegedly inflicted by residents of that state against the Mormons from 1833 to 1838. Hereafter cited as Rockwell affidavit to House of Representatives.

With publication of the first edition of *Orrin Porter Rockwell*, the collection of Mormon affidavits and petitions — lost to public view for 126 years — was brought to light for the first time since Joseph Smith, Jr., left the documents in the care of Elias Higbee with instructions to press the matter to a conclusion in Congress. The papers now are catalogued as TG233, Records of the U.S. House of Representatives, filed in Boxes 141 and 142 of the Library of Congress Collection (five folders containing some 400 pages). The collection was discovered in 1966 after a long and frustrating search. Dale L. Morgan, western historian and scholar, thought that the manuscripts could have fallen into the bureaucratic hopper in those early days and been smothered in official procedure. Acting on his hunch, I located the packet in the House archives. Through the gracious cooperation of Utah Senator Wallace F. Bennett, the documents were released from their century-long storage, transferred to the Library of Congress in June 1966 and now are accessible to researchers.

were to use their influence in preventing further immigration to the county.

Finally, the Missourians warned, "Those who fail to comply with these requisitions, be referred to those of their brethren who have the gifts of divination, and of unknown tongues, to inform them of the lot that awaits them." [33] In plain language the old settlers were telling their Mormon neighbors they meant business. A committee of twelve was appointed to serve notice on the Saints while the rest waited at the courthouse.

Confronted by this sudden turn of events, the high priests informed the delegation that Mormon authorities in Kirtland would have to be told of the situation before any decision could be made; they asked the committee for three months in which to prepare a reply. When the courthouse crowd heard of the high priests' refusal to answer the ultimatum immediately, pandemonium broke loose. In a matter of minutes the gathering erupted into a mob thirsting for Mormon blood. Armed with what weapons they could find, the Missourians stormed Editor Phelps's home, where the printing press was located. After forcing the Phelps family into the street, they began destroying the house and tearing the press apart. Surging toward the residence of Edward Partridge, they dragged the bishop to the courthouse grounds, stripped him of his hat, coat, and vest, and smeared him from head to foot with tar and feathers. Another Mormon,

[33] *Western Monitor*, Fayette, Missouri, August 2, 1833, as quoted in *Church Encyclopaedia*, p. 639.

Charles Allen, was caught by the mobbers minutes later and similarly abused.[34]

Several Saints who escaped the settlers' wrath later said that Lieutenant Governor Lilburn W. Boggs had strolled through the ruins of the Phelps house and remarked aloud for Mormon ears, "You now know what our Jackson boys can do, and you must leave the country." It was this attitude that was to earn Boggs the enduring hatred of all members of the church; he was destined to be their most dedicated enemy, a Nero who sought to scourge them from the earth.

Three days after the mob action in town, a small army of Missourians — riding under a red banner symbolizing blood[35] — flourished a deadly arsenal of weapons, from whips to rifles, and galloped into Independence with a public warning to all Saints in Jackson County. They promised to flog every Mormon on sight and burn church crops until the Saints came to terms. The sudden and coordinated display of force accomplished its purpose; the Mormon leaders agreed to move their families and half the remaining Saints from the county by January 1, 1834, with the others to leave by the following April. In turn, the Missourians pledged no further violence as long as the Mormons complied with the stipulations of their removal.

Immediately after the treaty was signed, Oliver Cowdery left Independence for Ohio to discuss the crisis with the church presidency. At the same time the first Mormon evacuees attempted to move into nearby Van Buren County, but the settlers there organized to drive them back. From Kirtland came word for the Jackson County Saints not to dispose of their lands or property, nor to abandon their homes — except those individuals who had actually signed the agreement with the Missourians.

On September 28 the Saints petitioned Governor Daniel Dunklin to "raise by express proclamation, or otherwise, a sufficient number of troops, who, with us, may be empowered to defend our rights, that we may sue for damages for the loss of property, for abuse, for defamation, as to ourselves, and if advisable try for treason against the government; that the law of the land may not be defiled, or nullified, but peace be restored to

[34] The attack on Mormons in Independence is described in detail in *Times and Seasons*, Vol. 1, No. 2, December 1839, pp. 17–20, and John P. Greene, *Facts Relative to the Expulsion of the Mormons from the State of Missouri, Under the "Exterminating Order"* (Cincinnati, 1839), pp. 10–11.

[35] Greene, *Expulsion of the Mormons*, p. 11; *Church Encyclopaedia*, p. 640.

our country." [36] The petition was signed by Edward Partridge and nearly all of the Jackson County Saints, including Orrin Porter Rockwell.

In forwarding the document to Governor Dunklin the Mormons acted in good faith, for they knew many prominent members of the county government had not only encouraged the mob but in some cases actually had joined in violent demonstrations against the church. The settlers' manifesto, for example, was signed by the county clerk, the Indian agent, the postmaster, a judge, an attorney, two justices of the peace, and the county constable, among others.

Governor Dunklin answered the petition on October 19. He offered sympathy, but suggested the Saints take their grievances to court. [37] His decision to refuse aid to the Mormons was influenced to a great extent by his lieutenant, Boggs, who made no secret of his animosity toward the church. Acting on Dunklin's advice, the Saints retained the legal firm of Wood, Reese, Doniphan and Atchison to represent them for a fee of $1,000. [38] One of the partners in the firm, Alexander Doniphan, was later to play an important part in Rockwell's life.

With the news that the Mormons planned to appeal to the courts for redress, the Missourians flared into action. On the night of October 31 they swooped down on the Big Blue settlement and began an eight-day nightmare of blood and carnage ending on the banks of the Missouri River with the cowed inhabitants fleeing for their lives. It was an experience which etched itself deeply into Orrin Porter Rockwell's memory, and from it came a vow he kept to his death — Rockwell would meet violence with violence; in the years to come his skill with a gun would become legendary.

But as the Jackson County drama played out, Rockwell was unarmed and defenseless against the overwhelming strength of the marauding settlers. Stories of what occurred in those final days at the Big Blue and other Mormon settlements have survived the years in vivid detail. [39]

[36] *History of the Church*, Vol. I, p. 415.

[37] Dunklin's animosity toward the Saints, while not so flagrant as Boggs's, was there nevertheless. In a private letter to a friend written some months later, Dunklin confided, "I have no regard for the Mormons as a separate people; & have an utter contempt for them as a religious sect . . . ." See his letter to Joel H. Haden, August 15, 1834, Western Historical Manuscripts Collection, University of Missouri.

[38] *History of the Church*, Vol. I, pp. 424–25.

[39] For eyewitness Mormon accounts of the Jackson County War see David Pettegrew, "History and Journal," MS, pp. 16–25; Lyman Wight's testimony in "History of Joseph Smith," *Deseret News*, December 24 and 31, 1856. The Missouri view-

Between forty and fifty armed mobbers descended on the Blue and un-roofed nearly a dozen homes before the Saints fully comprehended their desperate situation. Ignoring the screams of their victims, the raiders flogged and clubbed two Mormon men — Rockwell's brother-in-law, George, and a neighbor, Hiram Page. A band of two-score men called young Beebe out of his house at gunpoint in the middle of the night and "beat him inhumanly with guns and whips." [40] Since few of the Saints had weapons, those who could attempted to escape in the darkness. The unlucky ones were scourged and battered mercilessly. When the mob came to the house of David Whitmer, a raider pulled the young Mor-mon's wife from the crude home by her hair while his companions demol-ished the dwelling. [41] Before the attack was over at least thirteen houses had been unroofed and thrown down in the Whitmer settlement of the county.

Their fury spent, the Missourians rode off, jubilant in victory, shout-ing terrible threats of death and annihilation to the bleeding survivors. The nightriders left terrified Mormon women groping in the darkness for husbands and sons; everywhere cries of pain and anguish echoed from the rubble of what had been their homes. [42]

Another assault was planned for the following night, but this time the Saints were prepared. The attack was meant for the Colesville branch located on the prairie about fourteen miles from Independence. While posting guards around the settlement, Parley P. Pratt, a high priest, sur-prised two raiders sent in advance as spies. Though they clubbed him viciously, Pratt was able to sound the alarm and the pair were caught. Now alert that trouble was in the wind, the Mormons held the spies hos-tage. They were released in the morning when the expected invasion failed to materialize, a circumstance attributed to the capture of the two men. [43]

The Saints in Independence were having their problems, too. A gang of Missourians roamed the city, destroying Mormon homes and pillaging

---

point can be found in *History of Jackson County, Missouri* (Kansas City, 1881), pp. 250–69.

[40] Lyman Wight testimony, *Deseret News*, December 24, 1856.

[41] Rockwell affidavit to House of Representatives. Others whose homes were destroyed on this occasion included Stephen Chase, George Beebe, Hiram Page, and Peter Whitmer.

[42] *History of the Church*, Vol. I, pp. 426–27.

[43] Parley Parker Pratt, *Autobiography*, edited by Parley P. Pratt, Jr. (New York, 1874), p. 103.

their property. One of the mob, Richard McCarty, caught red-handed in the act of looting a Mormon shop, was hauled before a justice of the peace by the outraged owner and some friends. Unfortunately, the magistrate chanced to be one of the signers of the settlers' manifesto and he refused to issue a complaint against McCarty. Instead, the justice recognized the Missourian's counterclaim of false arrest and ordered the Mormons who caught him jailed. John Corrill, one of the defendants trapped in this snare, commented bitterly that, "Although we could not obtain a warrant against him for breaking open the store, yet he had gotten one for us for catching him at it." [44]

Events now moved swiftly. A party of raiders from west of the Blue met a group from Independence and joined forces for an assault against the Big Blue settlement. Under cover of darkness, the horsemen descended on the small community from all sides. Rockwell was busy at the ferry when a band of men, stripped to the waist and hideously smeared with paint, Indian-fashion, reined up at his father's home, which stood near his own, and commanded the elder Rockwell to come forth. [45] Visibly shaken by the sight which confronted her, Mrs. Rockwell told the raiders she was home alone with the children. Hot words passed among several men in the party. "We're wasting time. Pull the house down, and let's be on with it!" shouted one. "No! We'll catch him on our way back," snapped another, apparently the leader. With a final insult to Rockwell's mother and his sister Electa, the marauders vanished into the night to join the orgy of destruction. [46]

In the ensuing frenzy a Mormon bullet found its mark in the thigh of one of the painted raiders, and the Missourians went berserk. They tore the roof from one home and discovered David Bennett, bedridden and helpless. As he begged for mercy they lashed him, shot him through the head — the ball slicing deeply across the top of his skull — and left him for dead. Again the Mormons fled to save themselves.

Both Porter's home and that of his father were surrounded by whooping riders. Quickly, in the manner of men experienced in their work, they

---

[44] *Times and Seasons*, Vol. 1, No. 3, January 1840, p. 34; *History of the Church*, Vol. I, p. 428n.

[45] Rockwell affidavit to House of Representatives.

[46] Although the affidavit does not mention Electa by name, she was the oldest (seventeen) remaining unmarried daughter. Both older girls, Emily and Caroline, had settled in Ohio with their husbands, Christopher Stafford and M. C. Smith, respectively, before this date.

looped ropes over the eaves of the two squat log buildings and, tying the ends to saddle pommels, spurred their horses forward. A wrenching crack, like a breaking limb, and the father's cabin was unroofed, its bare walls standing shamefully, obscenely, violated in the moonlight. No sooner had the sound died away than the second roof came crashing to the ground. Luana Rockwell, frightened nearly out of her wits, huddled in a corner of the dwelling while Missourians pulled her possessions from the house. Next door, Electa implored the men not to destroy their household goods.

A knife flashed from its scabbard, blade glittering. "Get the hell from under foot, or it's this across the throat!" hissed a painted figure.[47]

As swiftly as they had come, the horsemen disappeared. David Pettegrew, a neighbor whose home had somehow escaped damage, described the scene at Orrin Porter Rockwell's cabin: "[The raiders] stopped at Brother Rockwell's who kept the ferry, though the river was fordable at the time. . . . They threw his house down, or all they could, cut open feather beds, destroyed all of his furniture, and all they could lay hands on. Sick as I was, I mustered strength enough to go over to Brother Rockwell's the next morning, and saw the destruction by the mob."[48]

While the settlement reeled under the onslaught, the streets of Independence had become a no-man's land. At the height of the violence, two Mormon delegations sought peace warrants to halt the outrages before all members of the church were massacred, but their entreaties were brushed aside by unfriendly circuit judges; the Saints prepared to rally what remained of their shattered ranks for a last-ditch stand against the demoniac Missourians.

Whispers filtered through Jackson County on Sunday, November 3, that "Monday would be a bloody day." As dawn broke, raiders rode to the Big Blue and commandeered Rockwell's ferry at gunpoint.[49] Outnumbered and facing rifles, the Mormons had no choice but to obey. A half-dozen armed Missourians held the ferry landing while the remainder headed for Wilson's grocery, a predetermined rendezvous for Jackson County settlers who were forming for a final push against the Saints. At the store, two youngsters told the Missourians that nineteen Mormons were marching to the aid of Saints at the Big Blue. Five minutes later fifty settlers were riding to head off the reinforcements.

[47] Rockwell affidavit to House of Representatives.
[48] Pettegrew, "History and Journal," p. 19.
[49] *History of the Church*, Vol. I, pp. 429–31; *Church Encyclopaedia*, pp. 643–44.

They intercepted the marchers on the outskirts of Independence, but the Mormons vanished into nearby fields at the first sight of the superior force. Dismounting, the Missourians turned their horses into the church-owned fields in an attempt to flush their quarry. Neighboring Mormon women and children were threatened with torture and death on the spot unless they pointed out the hunted men. So preoccupied were the mobbers, they were unaware until the last moment that a strong party of Mormons had slipped up on them. Led by David Whitmer, thirty men armed with seventeen guns charged the Missourians.

Caught by surprise, the raiders stood rooted in their tracks until one shouted at his companions, "Fire, Goddamn ye, fire!" Scattered shots then provoked a withering volley from the advancing Mormons. Two Missourians screamed and fell mortally wounded; their companions fled. The victims later were identified as Thomas Linville and Hugh L. Brazeale. Earlier, Rockwell had heard Brazeale, a lawyer, boast, "With ten fellows, I will wade to my knees in blood, but what I will drive the Mormons from Jackson County." [50] The Saints counted four of their number killed and another seriously wounded.

Later that night, the settlers, humiliated at having been routed by a numerically smaller force, dispatched riders throughout the countryside to spread the lie that Indians had surrounded Independence, that the Mormons had stormed the town, and that the two parties were allied to destroy all Missourians caught in the attack.[51] It was a desperate maneuver to draw the governor into calling the militia against the Saints.

In Independence Sidney Gilbert, John Corill, and Isaac Morley, jailed on McCarty's false arrest charges, were released under guard from their cells to confer with other Mormon leaders; any hope of preventing a full-scale collision rested with the three prisoners. After futile, time-consuming discussions, the three were returned to jail. It was nearly two o'clock on the morning of November 5 when the prisoners and guards approached the courthouse and found a half-dozen ruffians waiting for them. Ignoring a warning from the sheriff to move on, the Missourians drew guns. Morley and Corill dove for cover, but Gilbert stood his ground despite a pair of pistols pointed directly at him. Both weapons miraculously misfired. Unnerved, the gunmen fled. Again the three Mormons were imprisoned, but this time for their own protection. They were released about sunrise.

[50] Rockwell affidavit to House of Representatives.
[51] *History of the Church*, Vol. I, pp. 429–31; *Church Encyclopaedia*, pp. 643–44.

Meanwhile, the false stories of a besieged Independence were having their effect. Seizing the opportunity to rid himself and the county of Mormons, Lieutenant Governor Boggs encouraged Governor Dunklin to sound a call for the Jackson County militia commanded by Colonel Thomas Pitcher, a man scarcely able to carry the banner of impartiality since he, too, was a signatory of the settlers' manifesto.

Word that Corrill, Gilbert, and Morley were behind bars and in danger spread like wildfire through the nearby branches of the church, and by noon some two hundred Saints had volunteered to ride to Independence and deliver their brethren from the clutches of the enemy. At the head of the small army was Lyman Wight, a huge bear of a man who later would become an apostle to Joseph Smith.

Wight's volunteers encountered Pitcher's militia on the road skirting Independence, and the Mormon chieftain, believing the governor had sent troops to arrest the mob, agreed to meet the militia commander and talk peace terms. Unfortunately, Wight the Warrior was no match for Pitcher the Bargainer. Explaining that Corrill and his two companions had been freed, the colonel allowed that all the difficulties of the past had been a mistake growing out of prejudice against Joseph Smith. He suggested that the Saints, beginning with Wight's men, turn their arms over to the militia and go home.

Here Wight made a costly blunder; he believed Pitcher to be sincere. The Mormon later said he had agreed that the Saints would surrender their guns if Pitcher would disarm the settlers as well. "To this the colonel cheerfully agreed, and pledged his honor with that of Lieutenant Governor Boggs. . . ." [52] Wight failed to take into account, however, that Pitcher might not value a promise made to a man he considered a "deluded fanatic."

Once the Mormons laid down their arms, the Jackson County settlers paused to breathe an audible sigh of relief, then unhesitatingly plunged into a wholesale looting of church settlements. Knowing the Saints were now completely helpless and at their mercy, the Missourians swarmed over the Big Blue district — their favorite target — the Whitmer settlement, the Prairie branch, and all the rest, destroying homes and threatening instant death unless the Mormons packed and left. It was a harrowing ordeal for the nearly twelve hundred Jackson County Saints.

[52] Affidavit of Lyman Wight, officially subscribed to before the municipal court of Nauvoo, Illinois, July 1, 1843. See *Latter-day Saints Millennial Star* (Liverpool, 1840 et seq.), Vol. XXI, p. 506; *History of the Church*, Vol. I, p. 435n; and the *Deseret News*, December 24, 1856.

Families were separated in the confusion; the sick and feeble perished in the November cold, but the Saints, clutching their meager possessions, pulled out. Still the Missourians were dissatisfied. The exodus was much too slow to suit them. As a reminder of the fate awaiting those who tarried, riders thundered down on unarmed Mormons and flogged them into insensibility. Some escaped the beatings only to be shot for defying their assailants.

Such were the scenes unfolding around Orrin Porter Rockwell as he helped his wife gather their belongings and prepare for the journey north across the Missouri River to Clay County. As the Saints trudged from Jackson, driven by those they had called neighbor, it was with a belief that God was trying the faith of His flock.

Their shameful treatment at the hands of the Jackson settlers was a memory never to be forgotten; the ordeal would be chronicled in the history of their church for all who followed to remember. Even now, as they turned their eyes toward a new land, many Mormons were vowing that someday there would be a reckoning. Rockwell was no exception.

Lyman Wight, who now found himself wanted in three counties, saw "one hundred and ninety women and children driven thirty miles across the prairie, with three decrepit men only in their company; . . . the ground thinly crusted with sleet, and I could easily follow on their trail by the blood that flowed from their lacerated feet on the stubble of the burnt prairie!" [53] A marked man, Wight was forced to keep a constant watch for roving bands of Missourians. "I was chased by one of these gangs across an open prairie five miles, without being overtaken, and lay three weeks in the woods, and was three days and nights without food," he wrote.

[53] *History of the Church*, Vol. III, p. 439; *Millennial Star*, Vol. XXI, p. 506.

By Thursday, November 7, the shores of the Missouri River were lined for miles with evacuees. Nearly a thousand Saints were waiting their turn on the ferry which would take them across to Clay County.[54] Wagons, clothing, and other property were scattered in great heaps up and down the shore. Hastily-rigged tents crowded the area; tight clusters of women and children huddled around campfires to warm their chilled bodies, while the men searched for food and firewood. Torrential rain forced the ferry to halt its shuttle runs until the boiling river permitted safe crossing. Many families used the opportunity to locate missing members.

When word reached Joseph Smith that his church had been driven from Zion, and when he had been told of Boggs's perfidy, the prophet wrote:

> [I]t was the design and craft of this man [Boggs] to rob an innocent people of their arms by stratagem, and leave more than one thousand defenseless men, women and children to be driven from their homes among strangers in a strange land to seek shelter from the stormy blast of winter. All earth and hell cannot deny that a baser knave, a greater traitor, and a more wholesale butcher, or murderer of mankind ever went untried, unpunished and unhung — since hanging is the popular method of execution among the Gentiles in all countries professing Christianity, instead of blood for blood, according to the law of heaven.[55]

"Blood for Blood!" Boggs now occupied a position in the Mormon saga as their greatest oppressor, a responsibility he accepted with unstinting energy. Jackson County provided Orrin Porter Rockwell with reason enough to hate this man, but their paths were destined to cross again in a most violent manner.

As the struggle for survival continued on the Missouri River's broad shoreline, the bedraggled Saints desperately sought a sign, something to let them know they had not been forsaken by their Lord. Early on the morning of November 13, 1833, their prayers were fulfilled, or so they thought. The heavens produced a pyrotechnic display which amazed and delighted the demoralized Mormons.

Parley P. Pratt watched the fantastic phenomenon from the tiny doorway of his riverbank hut:

> [A]ll the firmament seemed enveloped in splendid fireworks, as if every star in the broad expanse had been hurled from its course, and

---

[54] Austin, *Life Among the Mormons*, p. 72.
[55] *History of the Church*, Vol. I, pp. 434–35.

sent lawless through the wilds of ether. Thousands of bright meteors were shooting through space in every direction, with long trains of light following in their course. This lasted for several hours, and was closed only by the dawn of the rising sun. Every heart was filled with joy at this majestic display of signs and wonders, showing the near approach of the coming of the Son of God.[56]

And so a meteor shower taken for a godly sign revitalized the dejected, hunted, and persecuted Saints. They found new strength to continue, to resettle, and once again to establish their faith until the time came when they could return to Jackson County and reclaim their divine heritage. Orrin Porter Rockwell crossed the river into northern Missouri to start a new life on the other side.

[56] An illustration and discussion of this astronomical phenomenon can be found in John Majors, *Common Sense; or Thoughts of a Plain Man, in Regard to Several Things of Importance* (n.p., 1878), pp. 34–35.

Chapter Two

THE SONS OF DAN

SPRING OF 1838 FOUND ROCKWELL in the small Mormon settlement of Far West in Caldwell County, Missouri. The town had grown swiftly since its founding two years earlier by W. W. Phelps and John Whitmer, who, as trustees for the church, laid out its boundaries. Nearly one hundred and fifty log cabins comprised the village, including four dry goods stores, nine family groceries, a half-dozen blacksmith shops, and two hotels.[1] More important, a temple site had been located and the foundation excavated in the center of the mile-square community. In selecting a spot for Far West, the church had chosen an isolated area in the western portion of the county, where the Saints would not be disturbed by outsiders. The parcel, established as Caldwell County, was expressly set aside by the Missouri General Assembly as a haven for the refugees from Jackson County and for members of the Kirtland branch emigrating to Missouri.

Much had transpired in the four years since the Mormons had been pushed from their lands across the Missouri River. The Rockwells, like many Jackson County Saints, first sought sanctuary in Clay County.[2] There they had lived in comparative peace, but as before it came to an

---

[1] For an excellent description of Far West during this period, see *History of Caldwell and Livingston Counties, Missouri* (St. Louis, 1886), pp. 120–22.

[2] Chapman Duncan, "Biography." MS, pp. 8–9, 39; Rockwell affidavit to House of Representatives. One of those who crossed into Clay County, Emily M. Austin, Newel Knight's sister-in-law, left a vivid picture of the hardships suffered by members of the faith: ". . . The Colesville church, together with twenty or thirty other branches of the Mormon Church, had already arrived [on the northern side] and more were on their way . . . we lived in tents until winter set in, and did our cooking in the wind and storms. Log heaps were our parlor stoves, and the cold, wet ground our velvet carpets, and the crying of little children our piano forte; while the shivering, sick people hovered over the burning log piles here and there, some begging for cold water and others for hot coffee or tea . . . ." Austin, *Life Among the Mormons*, pp. 72–73.

end.[3] Clay County's settlers tolerated the Mormons for barely three years before demanding their removal. Again the Negro question figured prominently in the decision; the Saints primarily were Easterners and non-slavers, which excited deep and abiding prejudice in a community where slavery was practiced and protected. So once more the Mormons packed up their now pitifully meager belongings and in 1836 moved on to Caldwell County.[4]

For Orrin Porter Rockwell the time had been spent caring for his growing family; he and Luana now had two daughters, Emily and Caroline.[5] But he had watched with deep interest the fluctuating fortunes of the church to which he had dedicated his life.

Rockwell had heard of the debacle of Zion's Camp, when Joseph, encouraged by the fiery Lyman Wight, rallied two hundred and four men to his side and marched to free Jackson County from the Gentile curse, thereby securing "the redemption of Zion." The expedition ended in dismal failure. A cholera epidemic swept the ranks and killed fourteen Saints despite a revelation to Joseph that "all victory and glory is brought to pass unto you through your diligence, faithfulness and prayers . . . ." The Lord was trying the faith of His flock, Joseph explained.

---

[3] Occasionally the Saints' antagonists ventured across the river after them. One such visit, ostensibly a peace mission, the Missourians came to regret. After Jackson County settlers seized land and property owned by Mormons they baldly attempted to obtain legal title as well. It was toward this end that the settlers sent a committee of twelve across the river to Clay County to deal with the Saints. The date was June 15, 1834. On the return trip, having been rebuffed, the Missourians boarded the ferry and at once became embroiled in a heated argument over their unsuccessful efforts at negotiation. While they were so engaged the ferry sprang a leak and sank. Seven of the committee drowned. Joseph Smith commented, "The angel of God saw fit to sink the boat . . . ." *History of the Church*, Vol. II, pp. 99–100. Mrs. Austin, however, said the Saints "took off a plank and bored several places in the bottom of the boat and placed the plank back as before." Austin, *Life Among the Mormons*, p. 82. See also *History of Jackson County*, pp. 262–63; *History of Caldwell and Livingston Counties*, p. 116; and Majors, *Common Sense*, pp. 30–31.

[4] The Rockwells settled in Caldwell County in the latter part of 1836, but Porter's sister Electa married a Clay County resident, S. M. Ousley, in Clay on January 11, 1837. See *History of Santa Clara County, California* (San Francisco, 1881), p. 622, and *History of Santa Clara County, California* (Los Angeles, 1922), p. 407.

[5] Records in the Genealogical Society of Utah, Salt Lake City, show that Emily was born "about 1835," but the correct date is January 31, 1833, and Caroline Stewart Rockwell "about 1837." Both were named after Porter's sisters. (Emily A. Tyrrell of Esmaralda [sic] County, Nevada, is named in an indenture dated August 7, 1880, selling her interest as heir to the estate of Orrin Porter Rockwell, deceased.)

And Rockwell remembered the great apostasy at Kirtland when a group of prominent members of the priesthood had openly rebelled against Joseph's leadership and branded him not only a false prophet, but an adulterer and thief as well. Sweeping renunciations of Mormonism had followed one of Joseph's most serious setbacks, failure of the Kirtland Safety Society. What began as an effort to establish a banking system in the Ohio community ended in financial disaster, which culminated in the prophet's flight to Far West to escape the wrath of those who had been wiped out. Despite these ill-fated episodes, Rockwell's faith remained unshaken, and he joined his Missouri brethren in the belief that Joseph's troubles in Kirtland were merely the Lord's way of moving the prophet to his rightful realm in Far West. With an eager enthusiasm the Saints laid plans for the future.

But there were dark clouds on the horizon, for discontent was brewing within the church hierarchy because of the Kirtland dissenters. A number of those who had rebelled in Ohio were now in Caldwell County and their presence was a stench in the nostrils of many Mormons, who regarded them as traitors to the faith. A couple of the original Jackson County Saints had fallen from favor, too. After due consideration, the High Council decided on a course of action aimed to remove these undesirables. Charges first were filed against John Whitmer and W. W. Phelps for misuse of church funds; both men were excommunicated. Oliver Cowdery was next to fall; his crimes: "Urging vexatious law suits against the brethren, falsely insinuating that Joseph was guilty of adultery, and . . . being involved in the bogus [counterfeiting] business." [6] Two days later David Whitmer and Lyman E. Johnson were disfellowshiped for unchristian-like conduct.

The resolute manner in which the purge was carried out reflected a change in the attitude of a majority of Saints. They were becoming acutely aware of the advantage in the strategic use of force. Since formation of the church in 1830 the Mormons had met with aggression of one sort or another at every turn, but now, as they became entrenched in Far West with Joseph at their head, it was with a resolve to be pushed no farther.

All that was necessary to ignite this tinder-like atmosphere was a bit of flint, and it arrived in the person of Sidney Rigdon, crusty, bombastic, vengeful, and a master manipulator of behind-the-scenes intrigues. When

[6] *History of the Church*, Vol. III, pp. 16–17.

he and his family drove into Far West on April 4, 1838, Rigdon was first surprised, then infuriated, to find the dissenters still living among the Saints. This was a personal matter with him — the five men represented a final obstacle to his ambition of becoming the undisputed second power in the church. It was, therefore, with great reluctance that he turned his attention even briefly from the dissenters, long enough to consider a problem of more pressing urgency.

It had taken little more than a year for the Mormons to become unwelcome in Caldwell County. As in Jackson they constantly annoyed the Gentiles with stories of revelations and divine inheritance until finally the Caldwell settlers determined to free themselves of this nuisance. When a now-familiar pattern of antagonism began to take shape, the First Presidency — Joseph, Rigdon, and Joseph's brother, Hyrum — gave the situation anxious thought.

With both factions maneuvering for position, the stage was set in typically melodramatic fashion for the villain to make an appearance. It was not a person but a concept which touched off the explosion in Caldwell County, however. And this concept — which created the image of nightriding Mormon demons — was fated to forever taint the church's history. In early June a number of Far West Saints met to discuss possible alternatives in dealing with the dissenters. According to Reed Peck, who was prominent in Mormon affairs at the time, "a proposition was made and supported by some as being the best policy to kill these men that they would not be capable of injuring the church. All their measures were strenuously opposed by John Corrill and T. B. Marsh one of the twelve apostles of the church and in consequence nothing could be effected until the matter was taken up publicly by the presidency the Sunday following (June 17th) in the presence of a large congregation . . . ." [7]

Sidney Rigdon was the man of the hour that Sabbath morning as he mounted the speaker's stand in the town square and exhorted his listeners

[7] Reed Peck, "Mormons So Called" (Quincy, Adams County, Illinois: September 18, 1839), MS, pp. 22–23. This manuscript, a narrative written in faded, but entirely legible, ink in a journal of 152 numbered pages, was intended, according to its author, "as a correct statement of the difficulties of that [Mormon] people in Jackson county." The manuscript was copied verbatim in November 1943 by Dale L. Morgan from the original then in possession of Fawn M. Brodie, who had previously purchased it from two descendants (granddaughters) of Reed Peck living in Bainbridge, N.Y. Other details concerning the history of the manuscript can be found in a preface accompanying the Morgan typescript. Citations set forth here refer to the pagination in the original.

to crush dissension and apostasy with cruel determination. Later his harangue would be remembered as "Sidney's Salt Sermon." Selecting for his oration the theme, "Ye Are the Salt of the Earth," Rigdon, in a thinly-veiled threat to the dissenters, warned: "If the salt have lost [its] savour, wherewith shall it be salted? It is thenceforth good for nothing, but to be cast out, and to be trodden under foot of men." [8] Again Peck fills in the details of Rigdon's rhetoric:

> From this Scripture [Rigdon] undertook to prove that when men embrace the gospel and afterwards lose their faith, it is the duty of the Saints to trample them under their feet He informed the people that they have a set of men among them that have dissented from the church and were doing all in their power to destroy the presidency, laying plans to take their lives &c., accused them of counterfeiting lying cheating and numerous other crimes and called on the people to rise en masse and rid the county of such a nuisance He said it is the duty of this people to trample them into the earth and if the county cannot be freed from them any other way I will assist to trample them down or to erect a gallows on the square of Far West and hang them up as they did the gamblers at Vicksburgh and it would be an act at which the angels would smile with approbation.[9]

At the risk of his personal safety, John Corrill sought out John Whit-mer and warned him that trouble was in the air. But the former church historian, unconvinced the Saints would turn on him, refused to flee Far West. Instead, he approached Joseph and asked what could be done to calm the storm of ill-feeling aroused by Rigdon's enflaming speech. The prophet brought up the subject of Whitmer's large Far West holdings and reminded him that they had been purchased with church funds while

---

[8] James H. Hunt, *Mormonism; Embracing the Origin, Rise and Progress of the Sect, With an Examination of the Book of Mormon; also, Their Troubles in Missouri, and Final Expulsion from the State* (St. Louis, 1844), pp. 165–66; T. B. H. Stenhouse, *The Rocky Mountain Saints: A Full and Complete History of the Mormons, from the First Vision of Joseph Smith to the Last Courtship of Brigham Young* (New York, 1873), p. 78n; B. H. Roberts, *Comprehensive History of the Church of Jesus Christ of Latter-day Saints* (Salt Lake City, 1930), six volumes, Vol. I, p. 438; Peck, "Mormons So Called," pp. 23–24. The scripture comes from Matthew 5:13.

[9] Peck, "Mormons So Called," pp. 24–25. Peck, incidentally, places the date of the Salt Sermon at June 17, 1838, while John Whitmer, in the suppressed Chapter XX of his "History of the Church of the Latter-day Saints From 1831–1846," published by the Reorganized Church of Jesus Christ of Latter Day Saints in its *Journal of History* (Independence, Missouri, 1908), Vol. I, says the date was June 19. It would appear that Peck's date is correct since the seventeenth was a Sunday.

Whitmer and Phelps were acting as church trustees. "Place the property into the hands of the bishop and high council to be disposed of according to the laws of the church, and things will quiet down," Joseph suggested.[10] But Whitmer rebelled, replying that he preferred to control his own property and be governed by the laws of the land. "Now you wish to pin me down to the law," the prophet retorted indignantly and ended the conversation.

The following day the dissenters were handed an ultimatum, drafted by Rigdon, demanding that they pack and leave Far West in three days or "we will use the means in our power to cause you to depart; for go you shall."[11] Failure to heed the warning would result in a "more fatal calamity." Eighty-three of Caldwell County's most influential residents had signed the document. Rockwell's mark was in sixty-ninth place. In its entirety, the roster comprised a veritable "Who's Who" of Mormondom.[12] In turgid prose, the ultimatum accused the dissenters of a variety of transgressions against the church and the Saints of Caldwell County:

> . . . until it is no longer to be endured; neither will they endure it any longer, having exhausted all the patience they have, and conceive that to bear any longer is a vice instead of a virtue. . . . Neither think, gentlemen, that, in so saying, we are trifling with either you or ourselves; for we are not. There are no threats from you — no fear of losing our lives by you, or by anything you can say or do, will restrain us; for out of the county you shall go, and no power shall save you. And you shall have three days after you receive this communication *to you*, including twenty-four hours in each day, for you to depart with your fami-

[10] John Whitmer's testimony in *Document Containing the Correspondence, Orders, etc., in Relation to the Disturbances With the Mormons; and the Evidence Given Before the Hon. Austin A. King, Judge of the Fifth Judicial Circuit of the State of Missouri, at the Court-House in Richmond, In a Criminal Court of Inquiry, Begun November 12, 1838, On the Trial of Joseph Smith, Jr., and Others, for High Treason and Other Crimes Against the State* (Published by order of the General Assembly, Fayette, Missouri, 1841), pp. 138–39.

[11] Ibid., Dr. Sampson Avard's testimony, p. 103.

[12] In all probability, the eighty-three signers of the ultimatum comprised the charter members of the Danite Society, which grew to number at the most three hundred men. Ebenezer Robinson, a close associate of Joseph's during these troubled times, said, "The above manifesto was signed by 83 determined men. Among the names we recognize some of the members of the High Council, and others holding high positions in the church, including that of Hyrum Smith, one of the first Presidency." Robinson himself was one of the letter's signatories. See his "Items of Personal History of the Editor," *The Return* (Davis City, Iowa, October, 1889), Vol. I, p. 147.

lies peaceably; which you may do undisturbed by any person; but in that time, if you do not depart, we will use the means in our power to cause you to depart; for go you shall.

We will have no more promises to reform, as you have already done, and in every instance violated your promise, and regarded not the covenant which you had made, but put both it and us at defiance. We have solemnly warned you, and that in the most determined manner, that if you did not cease that course of wanton abuse of the citizens of this county, that vengeance would overtake you sooner or later, and that when it did come it would be as furious as the mountain torrent, and as terrible as the beating tempest; but you have affected to despise our warnings, and pass them off with a sneer, or a grin, or a threat and pursued your former course; and vengeance sleepeth not, neither does it slumber; and unless you heed us this time, and attend to our request, it will overtake you at an hour when you do not expect, and at a day when you do not look for it; and for you there shall be no escape; for there is but one decree for you, which is depart, depart, or a more fatal calamity shall befall you.

. . . Oliver Cowdery, David Whitmer and Lyman E. Johnson, united with a gang of counterfeiters, thieves, liars and blacklegs of the deepest dye, to deceive, cheat and defraud the saints out of their property, by every art and stratagem which wickedness could invent; . . . and John Whitmer and William W. Phelps were assisting to prepare the way to throw confusion among the saints of Far West. . . . For the insult, if nothing else, and your threatening to shoot us if we offered to molest you, we will put you from the county of Caldwell: so help us God.[13]

Realizing the peril of their situation, the dissenters sought legal aid. Cowdery, the Whitmers, and Johnson rode to Liberty, in Clay County, to consult attorneys. When they returned, the families of Cowdery and Johnson had been cast out in the street with all their belongings.[14] The entire episode came as a shock to Oliver Cowdery. "I never dreamed [Rigdon] would influence the Prophet . . . into the formation of a secret band at

---

[13] *Correspondence, Orders, etc.*, pp. 103–6. John Whitmer denied the allegations; he maintained the ultimatum was an act of reprisal for refusing to obey Joseph. According to Whitmer, "Smith called a council of the leaders together, in which council he stated that any person who said a word against the heads of the Church, should be driven over these prairies as a chased deer by a pack of hounds, having an illusion to the Gideonites [Danites], as they were termed, to justify themselves in their wicked designs. Thus on the 19th of June, 1838, they preached a sermon called the salt sermon, in which these Gideonites understood that they should drive the dissenters, as they termed those who believed not in their secret bands, in fornication, adultery or midnight machinations." See Whitmer, "History of the Church," unpublished Chapter XX.

[14] Whitmer, "History of the Church," unpublished Chapter XX.

Far West, committed to depredations upon Gentiles and the actual assassination of apostates from the church." [15]

Emboldened by their success in chasing off the dissenters, the Saints sought to improve on the technique responsible for such a swift, clean victory. Soon secret meetings were conducted in Far West. To those not permitted to attend, it was obvious something out of the ordinary was in progress among the male members of the church. Reed Peck provides this look behind the bolted doors and shuttered windows:

> Ignorant of the nature of these meetings I attend[ed] one about the last of June and heared [sic] a full disclosure of its object — Jared Carter Geo. W. Robinson and Sampson Avard, under the instruction of the presidency, had formed a Secret military Society, called the "daughter of Zion" and were holding meetings to initiate members. The principles taught by Sampson A[v]ard as Spokesman, were that "As the Lord had raised up a prophet in these last days like unto Moses it shall be the duty of this band to obey him in all things, and whatever he requires you shall perform being ready to give up life and property for the advancement of The Cause. When any thing is to be performed no member Shall have the privilege of judging whether it would be right or wrong but shall engage in its accomplishment and trust God for the result.
>
> ["] It is not our business or place to know what is required by God, but he will inform us by means of the prophet and we must perform.
>
> ["] If any one of you See a member of the band in difficulty in the Surrounding country contending for instance with an enemy, you shall extricate him even if in the wrong if you have to do with his adversary as Moses did with the Egyptian put him under the Sand and both pack off to Far West and we will take care of the matter ourselves. No person shall be suffered to speak evil or disrespectfully of the presidency. The secret signs and purposes of the Society are not to be revealed on pain of death." . . .[16]

Peck also disclosed that the society was commanded by Jared Carter, who for purposes of anonymity was referred to obliquely as "the terrible brother of Gideon" (because it was known that Jared Carter had a brother named Gideon). For a time the society itself was known as the Brother of Gideon, but it eventually underwent the first of several name changes. Jared Carter also carried the impressive title of "Captain General of the Lord's Hosts." His subalterns, according to Peck, were Major General

---

[15] Oliver Cowdery, *Defence in a Rehearsal of My Grounds for Separating Myself from the Latter Day Saints* (Norton, Ohio, 1839), p. 2.

[16] Peck, "Mormons So Called," pp. 38–41.

Sampson Avard, who did most of the talking for the brotherhood, Brigadier General C. P. Lott, and Colonel George W. Robinson. Other high-ranking officers in the society included a lieutenant colonel, a major, a secretary of war, and an adjutant, plus captains of hundreds, fifties, and tens.[17] Ironically, Peck, who so opposed the principles and objectives of the secret organization, was stunned to find himself named adjutant by virtue of his experience in that office in the 59th Regiment of Missouri Militia.

Agreeing on a suitable name for the band was an exercise in indecision. Several ideas were discussed and discarded, among them this scriptural offering from Micah 4:13: *Arise and thresh, O daughter of Zion; for I will make thine horn iron, and I will make thy hoofs brass; and thou shalt beat in pieces many people; and I will consecrate their gain unto the Lord, and their substance unto the Lord of the whole earth.* This suggested "Daughter of Zion," which was used briefly. But there was a certain incongruity with the bearded and rough men who comprised the society's ranks and the appellative was dropped, joining other rejects, "Destroying Angels," "Big Fan," and the "Thresher."

---

[17] A clue as to the table of organization within the society can be found in the *Elders' Journal of the Church of Latter Day Saints* (Far West, Missouri), Vol. I, p. 60, which describes the protocol to be followed during the Fourth of July parade staged two weeks after the brotherhood was formed. ". . . that Reynolds Cahoon, be marshal of the day, and Col. George M. Hinkle and Major Jefferson Hunt, be assistant marshals. . . . that George W. Robinson act as Colonel for the day; Philo Dibble, as Lieut. Colonel; Seymour Brunson as Major, and Reed Peck as Adjutant. . . . that Jared Carter, Sampson Avard, and Cornelius P. Lott, act as Generals, before whom the military band shall pass in review. . . ."

Peck soon found that the ferociously militant talk of the society's leadership was having an alarming effect on the members. "The blood of my best friend must flow by my own hands if I would be a faithful Danite should the prophet command it," he wrote, and to make his point, Peck reported the extent to which some of the group were willing to go: "Said A McRae in my hearing 'If Joseph should tell me to kill Vanburen [*sic*] in his presidential chair I would immediately start and do my best to assassinate him let the consequences be as they would. — ' " Peck, "Mormons So Called," pp. 41–42. Such intensity could not fail to agitate jealousy between the priesthood and the warriors. And when Jared Carter's reckless ambition was challenged, even his exalted position could not prevent his swift fall from favor, but it may have saved his life. "In the fore part of July [1838] the 'brother of Gideon' or Jared Carter capt Genl of the Danites having complained to Joseph Smith of some observations made by Sidney Rigdon in a Sermon was tried for finding fault with one of the presidency and deprived of his Station and Elias Higbee was appointed in his stead. . . . [D. B.] Huntington also Said that on his trial Carter came within a fingers point of losing his head." Ibid., pp. 47–49.

Finally, Genesis 49:17 provided: *Dan shall be a serpent by the way, an adder in the path, that biteth the horse heels, so that his rider shall fall backward.*[18] From this came "The Sons of Dan," or more commonly, "Danites." In time Gentiles would corrupt it to "Damnites." So was born the dread brotherhood whose very mention struck terror in the hearts of men for forty years, long after its driving force, Avard, had been forgotten.

Joseph denied any knowledge of the Danites until their existence was disclosed in a court of law. And then he placed the blame for the organization squarely on Avard's shoulders. "When a knowledge of Avard's rascality came to the Presidency of the Church," Joseph wrote, "he was cut off from the Church, and every means proper used to destroy his influence, at which he was highly incensed, and went about whispering his evil insinuations, but finding every effort unavailing, he again turned conspirator, and sought to make friends with the mob." [19]

Under oath in court Avard insisted that Joseph was the "prime mover and organizer of this Danite Band." [20] He swore that commanders of the society's fifties and hundreds appeared before the First Presidency and heard the prophet say, "it is necessary this band should be bound together by a covenant, that those who reveal the secrets of the society shall be put to death." [21] Such threats notwithstanding, there were a few Mormons

[18] John Hyde, Jr., *Mormonism: Its Leaders and Designs* (New York, 1857), pp. 104–5. See also Robinson, "Items of Personal History of the Editor," *The Return*, Vol. I (October, 1889), p. 145. Robinson was a high-ranking officer in the society.

Nearly two decades later, on July 5, 1857, Brigham Young in a speech at the Bowery in Great Salt Lake City said, "If men come here and do not behave themselves, they will not only find the Danites, whom they talk so much about, biting the horses' heels, but the scoundrels will find something biting *their* heels. In my plain remarks I merely call things by their right names." *Journal of Discourses, by Brigham Young, President of the Church of Jesus Christ of Latter-day Saints, His Two Counselors, and the Twelve Apostles, and Others* (Liverpool, 1854–1886), twenty-six volumes, Vol. V, p. 6. See also the *Deseret News*, July 15, 1857.

[19] *History of the Church*, Vol. III, p. 181. Avard was not excommunicated until March 17, 1839, four months after Joseph was brought to trial; ibid., p. 284. Sampson Avard's role in the Danite Band and its action against the dissenters is doubly interesting in light of a letter written November 18, 1835, by Orson Pratt to Oliver Cowdery, later a principal figure in the dissenting group. Pratt wrote he had baptized three persons in Freedom, Pennsylvania, ". . . one of which (Sampson Avard) I ordained an elder, he formerly had belonged to the Campbellites, and had preached among them. . . . May the Lord bless elder Avard and send some one of his servants to assist him." *Latter Day Saints Messenger and Advocate*, Vol. II, No. 2, November 1835, pp. 223–24.

[20] Avard's testimony, in *Correspondence, Orders, etc.*, pp. 97–102.

[21] Ibid., p. 97.

who dared expose the mysteries of the Sons of Dan; others did so unwittingly by confiding in journals and diaries. Whether anyone was sacrificed for this indiscretion is a question unanswered.

Of all who joined the order, no one suffered the notoriety of membership more than did Orrin Porter Rockwell. Indeed, he went to his grave branded with the inglorious title of Danite chieftain[22] — an unworthy and unfounded appellation. It is not only pertinent but necessary to explore more thoroughly the inner workings of the society, particularly its significance and scope within the church.[23]

[22] William A. [Bill] Hickman also was proclaimed chief of the Danites in the title of his published confession, *Brigham's Destroying Angel; Being the Life, Confession, and Startling Disclosures of the Notorious Bill Hickman, the Danite Chief of Utah* (New York, 1872). This sobriquet, however, was entirely the invention of J. H. Beadle, under whose guiding hand the manuscript was printed. Nowhere in his confession does Hickman call himself the Danite chief, or for that matter refer at all to the Sons of Dan. Beadle's preoccupation with Danites was due in great measure to the unquestioning acceptance in the East of blood-curdling stories about Mormon assassins.

[23] One of the great controversies surrounding the Sons of Dan concerns the question of whether or not Joseph knew and approved of its existence prior to the society's public exposure in November 1838. The point is relevant because if his denials of such knowledge are true, it marked the only occasion in Orrin Porter Rockwell's life when he strayed from the dictates of the church by entering into an unauthorized doctrinal venture. His close relationship with and devoted obedience to the prophet make it inconceivable that he would have failed to inform Joseph of the Danites. Even so, the prophet's absolute grip on the church precludes the possibility that Avard could have carried out an undertaking of such magnitude in secret. Finally, the argument presents itself that the prophet probably encouraged the organization, since it played a dual role of preventing a recurrence of the Kirtland rebellion by uncovering potential apostates almost immediately, while at the same time protecting the Mormons against their Gentile enemies.

Lending credence to this conjecture is the testimony of three Mormon witnesses who admitted under oath that Joseph addressed the society during at least one of its meetings. John Corrill, a prominent Saint during the Jackson County persecutions, described a gathering of the Sons of Dan at which the entire First Presidency was introduced to officers of the order and "pronounced blessings on each of them." Corrill added that Joseph arose and "made some general remarks . . . relating [to] the oppressions [members] had suffered, and [said] they wanted to be prepared for further events." *Correspondence, Orders, etc.*, Corrill's testimony, p. 111. Reed Peck, adjutant of the band, substantiated Corrill's statements on this point; ibid., Peck's testimony, p. 117. And John Cleminson added, "Dr. Avard called on Joseph Smith, jr., who gave them a pledge, that if they [the First Presidency] led them into difficulty he would give them his head for a foot-ball, and that it was the will of God these things should be so. The teacher and active agent of the society was Dr. Avard and his teachings were approved of by the presidency." Ibid., Cleminson's testimony, p. 114.

Joseph himself, speaking at a special city council meeting in Nauvoo, Illinois, January 3, 1844, acknowledged, "The Danite system . . . was a term made use of by

William Swartzell, an Ohio convert to the church, described a Danite session held July 14, 1838, prior to his initiation into its ranks: "Sentinels, armed with pistols, swords, and guns, were posted on the outskirts of the grove, while the [Danites], as they were called, occupied the centre. . . . After the meeting adjourned, brother Thayer said to me, 'Ah! brother Swartzell, you should have been at the meeting; you should have heard all about the [Danite] business, for brother Joseph preached, and brother Hiram, and brother Rigdon.' "[24]

Other Mormons in Far West were writing of their experiences with the band. Luman Andros Shurtliff explained: "I was invited to unite with a society called the Danite society. It was got up for our personal defense, also for the protection of our families, property and religion. Signs and pass words were given by which members could know the other wherever they met, night or day. All members must [resolve] difficulties if he had any with a member of the society, before he could be received." [25]

Swartzell had something to say about the signs and passwords. He wrote in his journal that having once been initiated he was charged never to betray his trust as a Danite, and that Lyman Wight, swinging a lead-weighted cowhide blackjack from his wrist,

> next informed us that he would give us a *sign* "whereby ye may know each other anywhere (either by day or by night,) and if a brother be in distress. It is thus: To clap the right hand to the right thigh, and then raise it quick to the right temple, the thumb extending behind the ear." He then gave us the pass-word — which was to be spoken at the moment of giving the hand of fellowship — "*Who be you?*" Answer — "*Anama.*" "This word, anama," he further informed us,

some of the brethren in Far West, and grew out of an expression I made use of when the brethren were preparing to defend themselves from the Missouri mob, in reference to the stealing of Macaiah's images (Judges, Chapter 18) — If the enemy comes, the Danites will be after them, meaning the brethren in self-defense." *History of the Church*, Vol. VI, p. 165.

Rigdon in later years acknowledged the existence of the secret society, but maintained that neither he nor Joseph had actually been a member of the brotherhood. He admitted that the purpose behind its inception was mutual protection by Mormons in Missouri. For Rigdon's statement see ibid., Vol. III, pp. 453–54.

[24] William Swartzell, *Mormonism Exposed, Being a Journal of a Residence in Missouri From the 28th of May to the 20th of August, 1838* (Pekin, Ohio, 1840), pp. 17–18. In discussing the Sons of Dan, Swartzell used the word "Daranites."

[25] Luman Andros Shurtliff, "Biographical Sketch," MS, p. 33.

"is, by interpretation, a *friend*. This then is the sign to distinguish ourselves from all other people under heaven." [26]

This initiation, Swartzell wrote, permitted him to embrace the mysteries of Daniteism and become "*a man of God and a son of Thunder!*" [27] Another Saint, Allen Joseph Stout, remembered, "The church organized under captains tens, fifties, one hundreds and one thousands. This made the inhabitants [Missourians] mad to see us making ready to defend ourselfs. They call[ed] our organization the 'Danite Band.' I belonged to the 3rd fifty led by Reynolds Cahoon." [28]

Perhaps the most eloquent description of the society's effect on the Missourians was recorded by Oliver B. Huntington, who served "as an apprentice in the divine brotherly union." He later committed his thoughts to paper:

> This society of Danites was condemned by the public like the rest of Mormonism; and there was a great [hue and cry] about the Danites, all over the county and among the army; but who and what they were no one was any wiser for anything they heard; and as many stories were in circulation, the most horrid and awfully distorted opinions their minds could imagine, and they all thought that every depridation was committed by the Danites; Danites, awful Danites; every mobber was afraid of the thoughts of one of them awful men.
> And if they were to see a man of their own acquaintance, and were told in confidence he was a Danite, they would even shun his company and conversation. Such being their opinion and belief of the Danites, and we knowing it, concluded to make the best of it. So every mysterious trick and bold adventure which had been transacted, was planned upon them . . . .[29]

These then were the Sons of Dan, the culmination of Avard's ambitious scheming, and the Mormon answer to Missouri persecution. It was with meticulous care that Avard and Rigdon chose the words of the cove-

---

[26] Swartzell, *Mormonism Exposed*, pp. 22–23. Compare with John D. Lee, *Mormonism Unveiled; Including the Remarkable Life and Confessions of the Late Mormon Bishop John D. Lee* (St. Louis, 1877), pp. 57–58.

[27] Swartzell, *Mormonism Exposed*, p. 21.

[28] Allen Joseph Stout, "Journal," MS, p. 7.

[29] Oliver Boardman Huntington, "Journal," MSS, two volumes, Vol. I, p. 36.

nant to which each initiate bound himself. Listen with Orrin Porter Rockwell as the satanic Avard intones the blood oath:[30]

> In the name of Jesus Christ, the Son of God, I now promise and swear, truly, faithfully, and without reserve, that I will serve the Lord with a perfect heart and a willing mind, dedicating myself, wholly, and unreservedly, in my person and effects, to the upbuilding of His kingdom on earth, according to His revealed will. I furthermore promise and swear that I will regard the First President of the Church of Jesus Christ of Latter Day Saints, as the supreme head of the Church on earth, and obey him the same as the Supreme God, in all written revelations given under the solemnities of a "Thus saith the Lord," and that I will always uphold the Presidency, right or wrong. I furthermore promise and swear that I will never touch a daughter of Adam, unless she is given me of the Lord. I furthermore promise and swear that no Gentile shall ever be admitted to the secrets of this holy institution or participate in its blessings. I furthermore promise and swear that I will assist the Daughter of Zion [Sons of Dan] in the utter destruction of apostates, and that I will assist in setting up the kingdom of Daniel in these last days, by the power of the Highest and the sword of His might. I furthermore promise and swear that I will never communicate the secrets of this degree to any person in the known world, except it be to a true and lawful brother, binding myself under no less a penalty than that of having my blood shed. So help me God and keep me faithful.[31]

Obviously this is not a vow Rockwell would have treated lightly. Once his word was pledged, it was a matter as final as the grave. The Danite oath may have been a major reason for his unswerving and absolute obedience to church authorities in the years after Joseph's death. A Danite constitution was composed, and Sampson Avard summoned his captains.[32] When all were present, Avard began: "My brethren, as you

---

[30] Legend has it that Rockwell later succeeded to the leadership of the society, but this is highly unlikely. See William Hall, *The Abominations of Mormonism Exposed; Containing Many Facts and Doctrines Concerning That Singular People, During Seven Years' Membership With Them; From 1840 to 1847* (Cincinnati, 1852), p. 118.

[31] See John C. Bennett, *The History of the Saints; an Exposé of Joe Smith and Mormonism* (Boston, 1842), p. 267; Achilles, *The Destroying Angels of Mormondom, or a Sketch of the Life of Orrin Porter Rockwell, the Late Danite Chief* (San Francisco, 1878), pp. 8–9. Achilles follows Bennett's version closely, except for a twist in the final line, which Bennett says should include, ". . . I hold my life as the forfeiture, in a cauldron of boiling oil." Achilles' version is used here.

[32] For complete text of the Danite Constitution, see *Correspondence, Orders, etc.*, pp. 101–2, and Robinson, "Items of Personal History of the Editor," *The Return* (October 1889), Vol. I, pp. 145–46.

have been chosen to be our leading men, our captains to rule over this last kingdom of Jesus Christ — and you have been organized after the ancient order — I have called upon you here today to teach you, and instruct you in the things that pertain to your duty, and show you what your privileges are, and what they soon will be."

Avard was pleased to see his audience listening absorbedly. "Know ye not, brethren, that it soon will be your privilege to take your respective companies and go out on a scout on the borders of the settlements, and take to yourselves spoils of the goods of the ungodly Gentiles?" He paused to lend his words impact.

"For it is written, the riches of the Gentiles shall be consecrated to my people, the house of Israel; and thus you will waste away the Gentiles by robbing and plundering them of their property; and in this way we will build up the kingdom of God, and roll forth the little stone that Daniel saw cut out of the mountain without hands, and roll forth until it filled the whole earth. For this is the very way that God destines to build up His kingdom in the last days. If any of us should be recognized, who can harm us? For we will stand by each other and defend one another in all things." Then, grinning, Avard said, "If our enemies swear against us, we can swear also."

This last remark brought low muttering from the gathering. The Danite leader shouted, "Why do you startle at this, brethren? As the Lord liveth, I would swear to a lie to clear any of you; and if this would not do, I would put them or him under the sand as Moses did the Egyptian; and in this way we will consecrate much unto the Lord, and build up His kingdom; and who can stand against us?"

Avard had been pacing back and forth in front of the captains during his tirade. Now he halted; in a low deliberate tone, he said, "And if any of us transgress, we will deal with him amongst ourselves." There was no mistaking the meaning of his words. Avard paused, watching the captains exchange surprised glances. "If any one of this Danite Society reveals any of these things, I will put him where the dogs *cannot bite him*!" [33]

No sooner had he spoken than a half-dozen men in the throng were on their feet shouting that what Avard was teaching conflicted with the doctrines of the church and constituted criminal acts as well. Brushing aside their protestations, the Danite leader argued, "There are no laws executed in justice! Besides, this is a different dispensation — and the scriptures teach that the kingdom of God will put down all other kingdoms, and the

[33] *History of the Church*, Vol. III, pp. 180–81.

Lord Himself will reign — His laws alone are the laws which will exist!''

When John Corrill described Sampson Avard as the most perfect villain he had ever seen, his character analysis was excellent; but for all of Avard's savage talk, he was the first to abandon the Mormon cause and act the traitor.[34] Daniteism would cost the church many members in the months to come; among those who rebelled because of its sinister workings was Corrill.

Avard acted like a man possessed. Gorged with new-found power and authority, he doggedly sought out malcontents heard criticizing the church presidency. Paradoxically, one of his first victims was Danite Captain General Jared Carter, who was guilty of speaking against Sidney Rigdon. For his effrontery, Carter was summarily booted from office and very nearly lost his life in the bargain.[35] For Avard it was an opportunity to clear the field of a competitor, and he quickly sounded a muster call for the purpose of announcing the disciplinary action. He concluded with an explanation of what he would do to others opposing church decisions: "When I meet one damning and cursing the presidency, I can damn them as well as he; and if he will drink, I will get a bowl of brandy and get him half-drunk. Then, taking him by the arm into the woods or brush, I will be into his guts in a minute and put him under the sod." [36]

July 4, 1838, found Far West bustling with activity as the Saints prepared for a day of speeches and celebration. A multitude assembled around the liberty pole near the temple site, and after an opening prayer and hymn, Sidney Rigdon took the rostrum. His sermon began mildly enough, but before long he launched into a full-scale attack on Gentiles. A superb orator, Rigdon played on the emotions of his listeners with a skill and deftness even Joseph admired. Then, with a smooth finesse born of years in the pulpit, the gaunt, hatchet-faced second elder brought his

[34] Lorenzo Dow Young was another who pegged Avard as a rogue. As early as the Kirtland days, this younger brother of Brigham Young felt that Avard was "a dishonest hypocritical man," and told Sidney Rigdon, "Give Dr. Avard time and he will prove my estimate of his character correct." See James Amasa Little, "Biography of Lorenzo Dow Young," edited by J. Cecil Alter, *Utah Historical Quarterly*, Vol. XIV (1946), p. 52.

[35] "Elias Higbee was appointed in his stead," Peck, "Mormons So Called," pp. 47–49.

[36] *Correspondence, Orders, etc.*, Reed Peck's testimony, p. 120; see also Peck, "Mormons So Called," pp. 49–50.

exhortation to a close with what amounted to a Mormon Declaration of Independence. Rigdon spat out the words:

We take God and all the holy angels to witness this day that we warn all men in the name of Jesus Christ, to come on us no more for ever. The man, or the set of men, who attempts it does so at the expense of their lives. And the mob that comes on us to disturb us, it shall be between us and them a war of *extermination*, for we will follow them till *the last drop of blood is spilled*, or else they will have to exterminate us; for we will carry the seat of war to *their own houses* and their own *families*, and one part or the other shall be utterly destroyed. Remember it, then, all men! . . .

No man shall be at liberty to come into our streets, to threaten us with mobs, for if he does he shall atone for it before he leaves the place, neither shall he be at liberty to vilify and slander any of us, for suffer it we will not in this place. . . .Neither will we indulge any man or set of men in instituting vexatious law suits against us, to cheat us out of our just rights; if they attempt it, we say *woe* be unto them. We this day, then, proclaim ourselves free, with a purpose and a determination that can never be broken. No, never! No, never! No, never![37]

His words were drowned in the roar from his audience. In a single voice they shouted, "Amen! Amen! Amen!" until it seemed to roll like thunder across the Missouri countryside. A newcomer to Far West and to Mormonism, John D. Lee, thought to himself, "When he closed his oration, I believed the Mormons could successfully resist the world." [38]

In this frenetic atmosphere, Rockwell, during a conference conducted in Far West two days later, was ordained a deacon[39] — the first step in the priesthood of the Mormon Church.[40]

---

[37] Stenhouse, *Rocky Mountain Saints*, p. 78; Swartzell, *Mormonism Exposed*, p. 16.

[38] Lee, *Mormonism Unveiled*, p. 63. While Lee reflected the emotion of the moment, the outburst of militancy was not altogether welcomed by every member of the church. John Corrill, by nature a contemplative man, had already taken his doubts to the First Presidency. When whispers reached him that Avard was considering scattering poison, pestilence, and disease among the settlers and "make them think it was judgments sent from God . . . I accused Smith and Rigden [sic] of it, but they both denied it promptly." Still, Corrill worried, "some individuals went so far as to state, that they would kill any person, if the presidency would say it was the will of God; for these things were necessary sometimes to save the church from corruption and destruction."

[39] "Answers to Questions," *Improvement Era*, Vol. V (February 1901), p. 309.

[40] The offices of teacher and priest follow in the Aaronic, or lesser priesthood of the church.

On July 8 Joseph announced a revelation dealing with the consecration to the church of all surplus property not necessary for the support of the individual. Rigdon explained that if the Saints did not offer their surplus to the Lord by "laying it down at the feet of the apostles," they would eventually be compelled to "consecrate and yield it up to the Gentiles." [41] Sampson Avard reacted to the revelation by threatening all Mormons who hesitated to follow the Lord's counsel. "All persons who attempt to deceive and retain property that should be given up will meet with the fate of Ananias and Saphira, who were *killed by Peter*," he confided to John Corrill and Reed Peck.[42] No available records show whether Rockwell consecrated a surplus, but by the end of the month most of the Saints were turning in their worldly goods in obedience to the prophet and his revelation.

While this was transpiring, the Gentile population was busily electioneering in Caldwell County, and William Swartzell, recognizing the potential of a solid Mormon vote, wrote in his journal:

> Twenty [Saints] drove off some of the Missourians from their improvements with cow-hides. The brethren are determined to have all the lands and property that they can lay their hands upon. Said I to brother Thayer, "They [the Missourians] will be friends with the brethren until the election is over, and then look out that they don't make them smoke, for driving the citizens off of their lands. This will be kept quiet until after the election: then will come hard times." "But," said brother Thayer, "the land is ours, and we will either have actual settlers upon it, or we will take it by the sword." [43]

Swartzell called the turn correctly, for the pent-up bitterness of the Missourians erupted on the very day of the election at Gallatin in nearby Daviess County. Nearly three hundred Gentiles were gathered at the polls when a number of Mormons arrived on August 6 to cast their ballots. John D. Lee, still a stranger to many of the Saints, watched the proceedings as he lounged on the grass a short distance away. A drunken bully named Dick Weldon approached a Mormon and knocked him to the ground. When another Mormon came to the aid of his companion, a half-dozen settlers attacked him.[44] One Mormon, Riley Stewart, clubbed Wel-

---

[41] Lee, *Mormonism Unveiled*, p. 61.

[42] Peck, "Mormons So Called," pp. 50–51. Italics in original.

[43] Swartzell, *Mormonism Exposed*, pp. 27–28.

[44] *An Appeal to the American People: Being An Account of the Persecutions of the Church of Latter Day Saints; and of the Barbarities Inflicted on Them by the*

don across the head with a piece of cordwood and fractured his skull. "Immediately the fight became general," Lee said.

Stewart flashed the Danite sign of distress and Lee, with several other Sons of Dan, hastily grabbed at a pile of oak hearts stacked nearby and leaped into battle. In the confusion Lee came within a hair of braining one of his confederates, when, as he raised his cudgel, the intended victim "gave the sign" and Lee pulled back. Suddenly the donnybrook was over; the Missourians were in complete rout. Said Lee, "I felt the power of God nerve my arm for the fray. It helps a man a great deal in a fight to know that God is on his side."

Word of the encounter, garbled and distorted, spread swiftly. On the day following, Swartzell noted:

> . . . an express arrived from Gallatin [reporting] that the Missourians had raised a mob against the brethren, and killed two of them, and would not permit them to be buried. There was a great fight on the election ground in Gallatin. Trouble has began in earnest — for stabbing with knives, throwing of stones, clubs, staves, &c., is the order of the day, in every direction. . . . As soon as this news was known, an express was immediately sent to Far West, and 180 armed brethren assembled at Adam-on-Diammon,[45] for the purpose of resisting an attack that was hourly expected.[46]

When the express rider galloped into Far West, Joseph had rallied twenty or so men and headed for Daviess County. While they were on the road the group met a second Mormon contingent, and the entire party congregated at Lyman Wight's home for a war council. Here Joseph found several Saints who had been involved in the Gallatin election fracas and "received the cheering intelligence that none of the brethren were killed, although several were badly wounded."

Early the next morning, August 8, Joseph, Lyman Wight, and fifteen men were scouting the countryside when they reined up at the home of Adam Black, a justice of the peace and one of the original settlers of Daviess County. Black, Joseph was convinced, had agitated the Missourians to assault Adam-ondi-Ahman and drive the Mormons out. The

---

Inhabitants of the State of Missouri (Cincinnati, 1840), pp. 17–24. See also Lee, *Mormonism Unveiled*, pp. 58–60.

[45] Adam-ondi-Ahman was organized as a "stake of Zion" on June 28, 1838, by Joseph Smith. It was located four miles above Gallatin on the north side of the Grand River. Contemporary writers frequently misspelled the name.

[46] Swartzell, *Mormonism Exposed*, p. 28.

prophet's object was to force the magistrate to sign an agreement binding him to deal fairly with the Saints. But Black felt the demand was an affront to his judicial dignity. Why, he asked, had he been singled out for such discourteous treatment? Wight, who spoke for the group, answered that he intended to see all civil and military officers in the county follow suit. Those who declined to sign would be shot down, he said casually.[17] Black was handed a prepared paper; he refused to affix his name to it.

At this the group wheeled and rode off, only to return a half-hour later with reinforcements; more than one hundred and fifty Danites breathing vengeance against "mobocrats" surrounded the small home.[18] Now Sampson Avard was in command. "Sign this!" he ordered Black. "Refuse and you'll be cut down."

Despite his fear, the justice was adamant. He offered, however, to prepare his own agreement, and the Mormons could "damn well take it or leave it." They took it. With a sigh of relief, the badly shaken magistrate wrote: "I, Adam Black, a Justice of the Peace of Daviess county, do hereby Sertify to the people, coled Mormin, that he is bound to suport the Constitution of this State, and of the United State, and he is not attached to any mob, nor will not attach himself to any such people, and so long as they will not molest me, I will not molest them. This is the 8th day of August, 1838." [19]

This invasion of Black's home further inflamed the Missourians. Affidavits were issued in all directions, with charges and counter-charges flying on both sides as hostility between the two factions deepened. In quick order a warrant was sworn against the prophet and Lyman Wight for threatening the justice's life; the two were bound over for trial after posting $500 bond. But, certain the Mormon leaders would resist the warrant, settlers from eleven counties organized to take them by force, and Lilburn W. Boggs, now governor of Missouri, called out four hundred mounted militiamen as a "precautionary measure."

Knowing the Mormon camps were ill-equipped for a fight, the Missourians felt sure that they could push the Saints from the state with little effort. But the situation changed abruptly when Joseph sent a raiding

[17] Accounts of this meeting differ widely. Compare *History of the Church,* Vol. III, pp. 59–60; Swartzell, *Mormonism Exposed,* pp. 29–30; and *Correspondence, Orders, etc.,* pp. 15, 159–63.

[18] Peck, "Mormons So Called," pp. 63–64; *Correspondence, Orders, etc.,* pp. 161–62.

[19] *History of the Church,* Vol. III, pp. 59–60.

party to intercept a shipment of guns and ammunition intended for Gentiles in Daviess County. "This was a glorious day, indeed," the prophet exulted. "The plans of the mob were frustrated in losing their guns, and all their efforts appear to be blasted." Joseph found himself crowing prematurely. By stealing the supply wagon the Mormons brought Boggs in his wrath down on them like an angry hornet. The governor, who had been looking for just such an excuse to act, issued orders to militia commanders declaring a state of insurrection in Daviess and Caldwell counties; they were instructed to march on the Mormons and crush the uprising.

There were other troubles. Missouri rowdies were terrorizing the Mormon residents of DeWitt, a riverport landing fifty miles below Far West. Joseph ordered the community fortified to thwart a threatened attack. On October 2 the Missourians placed DeWitt under siege; the following day the settlement of Adam-ondi-Ahman was raided by a mob which left a trail of flogged Mormons lashed to trees. The sight of their mutilated brethren sent the Saints into blind fury. With Lyman Wight sounding the war cry, the Mormons girded for battle.

It was too late to save DeWitt. Under the stranglehold applied by the Missourians, the beleaguered population soon caved in. Salvaging what they could, the Saints loaded their wagons and were permitted to evacuate the town on October 12. They headed for Far West, only to find Joseph organizing another march in defense of Adam-ondi-Ahman. Again he had waited too long. The relief column found the settlement a smoking ruin, homes burned and livestock stampeded. The reinforcements cursed in frustration when they learned two Mormons had been taken prisoner and ridden out of the settlement on a cannon while their captors boasted they would drive the church from Daviess to Caldwell and "from Caldwell to Hell." They taunted, "the Mormons shall find no quarter, but at the cannon's mouth!" [50]

In retaliation Danites struck at Gallatin and two other towns, Millport and Grindstone Fork. The three onslaughts occurred simultaneously and had a crushing impact on the Missourians, who were unaccustomed to Mormon resistance. When Captains Lyman Wight, David W. Patten, and Seymour Brunson rode into Far West at the head of their companies, the sight of wagonloads of plunder was offensive to a number of the less

[50] "Petition of the Mormons to Congress," December 21, 1840, *House Document No. 22*, 26th Congress, 2d Session, p. 81.

aggressively inclined Saints. That night they gathered their families and abandoned the settlement.

Among the defectors were two of Joseph's most trusted followers, Thomas B. Marsh and Orson Hyde, both members of the Council of Twelve Apostles. The two men fled to nearby Richmond and blurted out everything they knew. Marsh signed an affidavit which Joseph later described as "all the vilest slanders, aspersions, lies and calumnies towards myself and the church, that his wicked heart could invent." According to Marsh:

> Joseph Smith, the prophet, had preached, in which he said, that all the Mormons who refused to take up arms, if necessary in difficulties with the citizens, should be shot or otherwise put to death. . . . I thought it most prudent to go . . . . a company of about eighty of the Mormons, commanded by a man fictitiously named Capt. Fearnaught,[51] marched to Gallatin. They returned and said they had run off from Gallatin twenty or thirty men, and had taken Gallatin — had taken one prisoner, and another had joined the company. I afterwards learned from the Mormons that they had burnt Gallatin, and that it was done by the aforesaid company that marched there. . . . They have among them a company consisting of all that are considered true Mormons, called the Danites, who have taken an oath to support the heads of the church in all things that they say or do, whether right or wrong . . . .
>
> I am informed by the Mormons that they had a meeting at Far West, at which they appointed a company of twelve, by the name of the Destruction Company, for the purpose of burning and destroying . . . and if the people of Clay and Ray [counties] made any movements against them, this destroying company were to burn Liberty and Richmond. . . . they passed a decree that no Mormon dissenter should leave Caldwell county alive . . . . Avard proposed to start a pestilence among the Gentiles . . . by poisoning their corn, fruit &c., and saying it was the work of the Lord . . . .
>
> The plan of said Smith, the prophet, is to take this State, and he professes to his people to intend taking the United States, and ulti-

[51] "Captain Fearnaught" was David W. Patten, an apostle. Danite leaders assumed fictitious names to protect their identities. Reed Peck testified that Jonathan Dunham, a Danite captain of Fifty, was known as "Captain Blackhawk." See *Correspondence, Orders, etc.*, p. 119, and *Senate Document 189*, 26th Congress, 2d Session, 1840, p. 20. George Hinkle was "The Thunderbolt," and Lyman Wight, "The Intrepid." "Captain Bull of the Regulators," a company of twelve men in Far West, was King Follett. See *Senate Document 189*, ibid.

mately the whole world. . . . I have heard the prophet say that he should yet tread down his enemies, and walk over their dead bodies; that if he was not let alone he would be a second Mahomet to this generation, and that he would make it one gore of blood from the Rocky Mountains to the Atlantic Ocean; that like Mahomet, whose motto, in treating for peace, was "the Alcoran, or the Sword," so should it be eventually with us, "Joseph Smith or the Sword. . . ." [52]

Orson Hyde backed up Marsh's story with a second affidavit attesting simply that, ". . . most of the statements in the foregoing disclosure of Thomas B. Marsh, I know to be true, the remainder I believe to be true." [53] When word of the apostasy reached Sidney Rigdon, he was apoplectic with rage. Any further desertions, he screamed, would be met with instant death "and all the burial he shall have will be in a turkey buzzard's guts." [54] While Joseph was wrestling with these problems, the Missourians razed Mormon homes wherever they found them.

A militia captain named Samuel Bogart, in civilian life a Methodist minister, blustered that once he combined forces with Cornelius Gilliam at Crooked River, they would shower Far West with "thunder and lightning."

When Joseph received an express reporting "a party of the enemy were plundering houses, carrying off prisoners, killing cattle and ordering families out of their homes on pain of having them burned over their heads," he asked for volunteers to ride with David Patten "to surprise and scatter Bogart's forces camped at Crooked River, retake the prisoners and prevent the threatened attack on Far West."

Sixty men saddled up and followed "Captain Fearnaught" to the river. Perhaps Orrin Porter Rockwell was one of them; the names of this small company, except for a mere handful, have gone unchronicled. They arrived at the scene an hour before dawn. Leaving their horses under a ten-man guard, the main body took up strategic positions along the embankment. It was during this maneuver that a sentry spotted a Mormon silhouetted against the grey dawn sky. The guard fired and downed Pat-

[52] For the complete text of Marsh's affidavit, see *Correspondence, Orders, etc.*, pp. 57–59. A condensed version can be found in *History of the Church*, Vol. III, p. 167.

[53] Ibid.

[54] *Correspondence, Orders, etc.*, Phelps's testimony, p. 124.

terson O'Banion, one of the Far West Saints. John D. Lee later said Patten's raiders were composed primarily of Danites,[55] and at the sound of the shot Patten shouted the Jewish battle cry, "The sword of God and Gideon!" [56] Then he ordered, "Charge, Danites! Charge!" and plunged into the thick of the fight. Garbed in a white greatcoat, the Mormon captain made an excellent target for Bogart's sharpshooters. A rifle ball smashed into his hip and penetrated his bladder in a mortal wound. Although he gushed blood with every step, the apostle led his men forward for several minutes before falling. With each gasping breath he continued to encourage his followers to charge. At his side, Parley P. Pratt pressed all the harder. "Being on the eve of victory, I dared not stop to look after his fate, or that of others, but rushed into the enemy's camp."

With the crack of the first shot ripping through the morning mist, Lorenzo Dow Young was startled to see O'Banion, who was but a step ahead, fall heavily to the ground. Young and his captain, John P. Greene, carried the mortally wounded Mormon to the side of the road, "asked the Lord to preserve his life, laid him down, put a man to care for him, ran on and took our place again."

As the fighting became heated, Young and his comrades scattered. Near the riverbank Bogart's militia broke like flushed quail. "I snapped my gun twice at a man in a white blanket coat, and while engaged in repriming, he got out of range." A tall, powerful Missourian sprang from cover under the embankment and rushed at Robert Thompson waving a heavy sword and crying, "Run you devils or die!"

"Brother Thompson was also armed with a sword, but was a small man, and poorly calculated to withstand the heavy blows of the Missourian," said Young. "He defended himself well, but his enemy was forcing him back towards a log over which he would doubtless soon have fallen and been slain. I ran to his aid and leveled my gun within two feet of his antagonist, but it again missed fire."

The Missourian now turned on Young and with slashing blows pushed him to the river's edge. The Mormon was trapped; to move was to risk toppling from the vertical bank eight or ten feet to the water. The Missourian raised his blade, summoning all his energy into a final killing stroke. For an instant he wavered and Young delivered him a furious

[55] When Joseph girded for the defense of his settlements, he organized non-Danite church members into a force variously called the Army of Israel and the Host of Israel. Not all Mormons were Sons of Dan.

[56] *History of Caldwell and Livingston Counties*, p. 130.

smash with the breech of his musket. The gun "parted at the handle, sending the butt some distance from me, and bending the barrel (as it was afterwards ascertained) ten inches. As my enemy fell his sword dropped from his grasp; I seized it and dealt him three desperate blows on the neck! At the same time John P. Green[e], the captain of my ten, came up and reported that Colonel Patten was killed. . . ." [57]

Bogart's men faltered under the ferocity of the surprise attack and broke toward the river, hoping for the safety of the opposite shore. "The firing now ceased," Pratt said, "And the wilderness resounded with the watchword, 'God and Liberty!' " As a ranking Mormon on the field now that Patten had fallen, Pratt counted their losses.[58] "I turned to Gideon Carter, who was lying on his face, and saw him die. His face was so marred and disfigured with wounds and blood that I did not recognize him then, but learned afterwards that we had mistaken him for one of the enemy, and left him on the ground by mistake."

As the sun's rays lighted the battlefield, Parley Pratt searched for Captain Fearnaught and found him. "He could speak, but was lying on his side, pale and almost dying." Pratt ordered a captured wagon brought up and the casualties placed in it. "This done," he said, "our whole troop mounted the horses we had taken and formed in front and rear of the wagon which bore the wounded." Two of the three Mormon prisoners Bogart had captured the day before had made good their escape during the fighting; the third was shot down while running to the Mormon lines, but later recovered.

A rider was dispatched to Far West with news of the triumph. Five miles from the settlement a relief party met the column with a surgeon, the Danite Dr. Sampson Avard. Patten died that evening. John D. Lee, who had been with Lyman Wight's company at Far West when the Crooked River fracas broke out, looked with horror on the body of the

---

[57] Little, "Biography of Lorenzo Dow Young," edited by J. Cecil Alter, *Utah Historical Quarterly*, Vol. XIV (1946), pp. 54–55. This recollection of the fight at Crooked River is one of the most detailed and lively first-hand accounts on record.

[58] Apparently leadership of the Mormon force fell to C. C. Rich. According to Junius F. Wells, writing in *The Contributor*, Vol. V, No. 3, December 1883, "At the battle of Crooked River, when David Patten fell mortally wounded, and while bullets were flying thick and fast, [Brother Rich] laid down his sword in the heat of the battle and administered the ordinance of laying on hands to the dying hero; after which, he resumed the sword, assumed command, and the battle of Crooked River was won by the Saints" (pp. 114–15).

fallen apostle. If Captain Fearnaught could be killed, what Mormon could claim immunity from Gentile gunfire?

"I had considered that I was *bullet proof*, that no Gentile ball could ever harm me, or any Saint, and I had believed that a Danite could not be killed by Gentile hands," Lee wrote. He added mournfully, "I thought one Danite could chase a thousand Gentiles, and two could put ten thousand to flight. Alas! my dream of security was over." Lee's attitude reflected the shroud of gloom which settled over Far West in the wake of Crooked River.[59]

Although three Mormons were killed and Bogart counted one of his men dead in the skirmish, reports of the encounter were outrageously distorted by the time they reached the ears of Lilburn W. Boggs. One message from a group of settlers frantically asserted that Bogart's entire company had been wiped out by Mormons who at that very moment were supposed to be marching on Richmond. "We know not the hour or the minute we will be laid in ashes — our county is ruined — for God's sake give us assistance as quick as possible," they pleaded.[60] Twenty-four hours after the Crooked River fight, Boggs, armed with the affidavits of Marsh and Hyde plus complaints from frightened settlers describing a wholesale Mormon rebellion, ordered two thousand militiamen from five divisions into the field against Joseph Smith and his Latter-day Saints.

Then Boggs received a message confirming an earlier report of Bogart's defeat but compounding the rumors of a massacre and a mythical attack on Richmond. This latest communiqué was based entirely on the unsubstantiated report of one of Bogart's men who claimed that ten of his comrades had been slaughtered by Danites and the rest captured. Erroneous as it was, this report prompted Boggs to issue his infamous "Exterminating Order" of October 27 to General John B. Clark. In

---

[59] Other Mormon accounts of the battle can be found in Pratt, *Autobiography*, pp. 177–80; Lee, *Mormonism Unveiled*, pp. 73–75; *History of the Church*, Vol. III, pp. 170–71. An excellent impartial report is contained in *History of Caldwell and Livingston Counties*, pp. 129–31.

[60] This letter to Governor Boggs from Sashiel Woods and Joseph Dickson, residents of Carrollton, Missouri, twenty-five miles west of Richmond, can be found in *History of the Church*, Vol. III, pp. 168–69, and *Correspondence, Orders, etc.*, p. 60. It is interesting that the date of the letter, October 24, 1838, is the day *prior* to the actual battle; it suggests that either the letter simply was misdated, or Wood and Dickson had heard the Mormons were moving against Bogart and sent the message in anticipation of the clash in a gamble intended to pressure Boggs into executive action.

effect, the order challenged Sidney Rigdon's Fourth of July address in which Rigdon had defied the Gentiles and threatened a "war of extermination." It was more than coincidence that Boggs chose that particular word in his instructions to General Clark. The complete order read:

> Sir — Since the order of this morning to you, directing you to cause four hundred mounted men to be raised within your Division, I have received by Amos Rees Esq. of Ray county and Wiley C. Williams Esq. one of my aids [*sic*], information of the most appalling character, which entirely changes the face of things, and places the Mormons in the attitude of an open and avowed defiance of the laws, and of having made war upon the people of this State. Your orders are, therefore, to hasten your operations with all possible speed. *The Mormons must be treated as enemies, and must be exterminated or driven from the State if necessary for the public peace — their outrages are beyond all description.*[61] If you can increase your force, you are authorized to do so to any extent you may consider necessary. I have just issued orders to Major-General Willock, of Marion county, to raise five hundred men, and to march them to the northern part of Daviess, and there to unite with General Doniphan, of Clay, who has been ordered with five hundred men to proceed to the same point for the purpose of intercepting the retreat of the Mormons to the north. They have been directed to communicate with you by express, you can also communicate with them if you find it necessary. Instead therefore of proceeding as at first directed to reinstate the citizens of Daviess in their homes, you will proceed immediately to Richmond and then operate against the Mormons. Brigadier-General Parks, of Ray, has been ordered to have four hundred of his Brigade in readiness to join you at Richmond. The whole force will be placed under your command.
>
> I am very respectfully,
your ob't serv't
[s] L. W. Boggs, Commander-in-Chief[62]

Strangely, the iron fist which Boggs so quickly ungloved was in direct contrast to his passive attitude during the five years the Mormons were

---

[61] Italics supplied.

[62] The Exterminating Order is included in *Correspondence, Orders, etc.*, p. 61. *History of the Church*, Vol. III, p. 175, contains the order, but the language has been changed slightly. This extraordinary document, Executive Order 44, with its murderous implications, remained on the books until 1976, when it was called to the attention of Governor Christopher S. Bond by a group of Missouri citizens. Gov. Bond rescinded the infamous Boggs order in the "spirit of the American Bicentennial," as an apology to the Mormon people and to close a dark chapter in Missouri history; see *Deseret News*, June 26, 1976.

being battered from pillar to post by the Missourians. With the Saints now on the offensive, Boggs donned the cloak of public protector; his intense dislike for all things Mormon had not dimmed since the early days in Jackson County.[63]

With the fall of DeWitt, many of the outlying Mormon settlements had been abandoned and their inhabitants relocated in Far West and Adam-ondi-Ahman to prepare for further attacks. Scouts hourly reported troops massing in several areas, and Joseph ordered food and ammunition readied for a prolonged siege. Some Saints were reluctant to abandon their property to renegades unfettered by military control. One such Mormon was Jacob Haun, owner of a small mill on the north bank of Shoal Creek, sixteen miles from Far West. Joseph was discussing Far West fortifications with Lyman Wight and John D. Lee when Haun approached and asked counsel regarding the evacuation of his settlement, which consisted of the mill, a blacksmith shop, and a half-dozen homes. Some thirty families were living there, Haun explained, and if they left, the Gentiles would burn everything to the ground.

"You had much better lose your property than your lives," Joseph said. "One can be replaced, the other cannot." But Haun argued that the best plan would be for the settlers to move into the mill and use the blacksmith shop as a fort to ward off an assault.

"You are at liberty to do so if you think best," the prophet said, and returned to the conversation with Wight and Lee.

On October 30, Joseph's wisdom, in this matter at least, was to be tragically borne out. A band of Missourians (possibly as many as two hundred and forty), comprising three companies of Livingston County citizens led by Captains Nehemiah Comstock, William O. Jennings, and William Gee, collected under the command of Colonel Thomas Jennings, an old militia officer, and rode on Haun's Mill. As the column moved forward word passed along its ranks: "Shoot at every thing wearing breeches, and shoot to kill."

The scene was like an autumn painting. "It was four o'clock in the afternoon; the sun hung low and red in a beautiful Indian summer sky." From the timber north and west of the mill the Missourians burst onto

[63] Boggs's successful 1836 gubernatorial campaign included an anti-Mormon position. Despite Mormon opinion, Boggs was highly esteemed in Missouri and later in California for his efficient and resourceful leadership. In 1842 he won a seat in the Missouri State Senate.

the settlement. Wholly surprised, the Mormons were thrown into complete confusion; they had no chance. Eighteen were slain, among them a ten-year-old boy, Sardius Smith, whose piteous pleas to be spared were answered with, "Nits make lice." The man who spoke then shot the child's brains out.

One settler, Isaac Laney, fled toward the blacksmith shop. He was caught in a shower of lead which pierced his body through and through, but miraculously he survived the onslaught. Wilford Woodruff later confided in his journal, "Brother Laney showed me eleven bullet holes in his body. There were twenty-seven in his shirt, seven in his pantaloons, and his coat was literally cut to pieces. One ball entered one arm-pit and came out at the other. Another entered his back and came out at the breast. A ball passed through each hip, each leg and each arm. All these shots were received while he was running for life, and, strange as it may appear, though he had also one of his ribs broken, he was able to outrun his enemies, and his life was saved." [64]

That same afternoon the militia approached Far West and camped in plain view of the Saints. At dawn of October 31, a delegation of Mormons met with militia commanders under a flag of truce and were told that Joseph, Rigdon, Wight, Pratt, and others were to give themselves as hostages while treaty negotiations were under way. Reed Peck, one of the delegates selected by the First Presidency to "beg like a dog for peace," [65]

[64] For a full story of the Haun's Mill slaughter, compare *History of Caldwell and Livingston Counties*, pp. 145–59; *Times and Seasons*, Vol. 1, No. 10 (August 1840), pp. 145–50; *History of the Church*, Vol. III, pp. 183–87; Lee, *Mormonism Unveiled*, pp. 79–81, and *Church Encyclopaedia*, pp. 671–84. By far the best single account of the massacre comes from the pen of Major Reburn S. Holcombe. Holcombe, a prolific writer and author of the best of the Missouri county histories. Holcombe, over the pseudonym *Burr Joyce*, prepared a report on Haun's Mill after consulting official documents, studying affidavits of witnesses, and examining statements made by actual participants. His findings appeared in the *St. Louis Globe-Democrat*, October 6, 1887, and were reprinted as part of Rollin J. Britton's series "Early Days on Grand River and the Mormon War," in *The Missouri Historical Review*, Columbia, Missouri, Vol. XIII, No. 3 (April 1919), pp. 298–305. Wilford Woodruff's recollections are in his autobiography published in serial form in *Tullidge's Quarterly Magazine*, Edward W. Tullidge, editor and proprietor, Vol. III (Salt Lake City, 1885), p. 123, and in *Wilford Woodruff, History of His Life and Labors as recorded in his Daily Journals*, edited by Matthias F. Cowley (Salt Lake City, 1909), p. 103.

[65] Peck, "Mormons So Called," p. 103. See also John Corrill, *A Brief History of the Church of Christ of Latter Day Saints (Commonly Called Mormons); Including An Account Of Their Doctrine and Discipline; With the Reasons of the Author For Leaving the Church* (St. Louis, Missouri, 1839), p. 41. Joseph told Corrill that he would rather spend twenty years in prison or die himself than have his people exterminated.

informed the church leaders of the stipulation, and they agreed, since the army outnumbered the Mormons five to one. Joseph later denied that he had surrendered, claiming his capture was an act of treachery perpetrated by Colonel George M. Hinkle, the ranking Mormon officer at Far West.[66]

When Joseph and his companions failed to appear by the appointed hour, the militia was ordered to move forward. The Mormon forces, unaware of the secret bargaining on the part of their leaders, rushed to the breastworks to defend the settlement. Each Saint tied a white handkerchief around his forehead as a distinguishing feature against being confused with a Missourian when the fighting came to close quarters. Mormon drums rolled a warning through Far West, and a trumpet sounded the final call to arms. Here and there along the barricade could be seen the grim faces of Saints determined to die for their religion. Among them were Hosea Stout, Charles C. Rich, John D. Lee, and Orrin Porter Rockwell.

Lee was hunched down behind a fallen log, his cap-box open and lead balls arranged on the ground by his side. "I never had a doubt of being able to defeat the Gentile Army," he said.

[66] Corrill, in his *Brief History of the Church*, p. 41, says, ". . . although the Mormons have accused us of giving up their leaders by intrigue, yet Smith himself was the first man that agreed to the proposal." Hinkle was expelled from the church and by his former brethren forever held in contempt, cursed as a traitor and Judas. He moved to Iowa and, resolute in his view that he had been made a scapegoat, published his side in *The Ensign*, Buffalo, Scott County, Iowa Territory, Vol. I, No. 2 (August 1844). Hinkle steadfastly insisted that all on the battlefield would have been put to the sword if Joseph had not been delivered to the militia. When Boggs issued his orders to Gen. John B. Clark, the Governor was flirting with genocide, perhaps even closer than he could have believed. Clark's astonishing arrogance in his speech to the defeated Mormons reveals how dangerously precarious their position was, or would have been, had not Hinkle acted as he did. Said Clark:

The order of the Governor to me was, that you should be exterminated, and not allowed to remain in the State. And had not your leaders been given up, and the terms of the treaty complied with, before this time your families would have been destroyed and your houses in ashes. There is a discretionary power vested in my hands, which, considering your circumstances, I shall exercise for a season. You are indebted to me for this clemency. I do not say that you shall go now, but you must not think of staying here another season, or of putting in crops; for the moment you do this the citizens will be upon you, and if I am called here again in case of your non-compliance with the treaty made, do not think that I shall act as I have done now. You need not expect any mercy, but *extermination*, for I am determined that the Governor's order shall be executed. As for your leaders, do not think, do not imagine for a moment, do not let it enter into your minds that they will be delivered and restored to you again, for their fate is fixed, the die is cast, their doom is sealed. . . .

Tullidge, *History of Salt Lake City*, Appendix, Biographies, p. 4.

52

"It seemed like nothing could prevent the effusion of blood should the Militia come within reach of the Mormon rifles," wrote Reed Peck. But at the last moment Joseph stepped forward and gave himself up. He was arrested immediately, and with Rigdon, Wight, Pratt, and George W. Robinson, charged with high treason against the state.

From defender to defender word spread through the Mormon bastion that Joseph had surrendered and that the remaining Saints would be expected to lay down their arms within hours. Those who had participated in the fight at Crooked River, suspecting that they would be tried as criminals, fled into the night. It is more than probable that Rockwell was with this group of twenty-seven fugitives, not caring to submit himself to the tender mercies of the Missourians who had treated him so savagely in Jackson County.

With the backbone of Mormon resistance broken, the militia easily disarmed the Far West defenders. Joseph, meanwhile, with Rigdon and the others, was sentenced to be executed on the morning of November 2. When Lyman Wight was told of his fate the barrel-chested giant roared, "Shoot and be damned!" General Alexander Doniphan, a militia commander and one of the attorneys who had come to the aid of the Saints in Jackson county five years earlier, balked at the sentence and declared he would have nothing to do with "cold-blooded murder." As a consequence of Doniphan's threat to remove his brigade from the scene, Joseph and the others were instead transported under heavy guard to Independence to stand trial.

Defeat was galling for the Saints as they trudged single file between a cordon of grinning militiamen to the Far West liberty pole where four months earlier Sidney Rigdon had defied the world with his Declaration of Independence. There, at a writing desk, stark and unreal in the center of the square, the Mormons silently relinquished their weapons and signed a surrender document. Its terms were harsh and demanding. John D. Lee, who gave up a Kentucky rifle, two pistols, and a sword, described the articles of capitulation:

> We were to give a deed to all of our real estate, and to give a bill of sale of all our personal property, to pay the expenses of the war that had been inaugurated against us; that a committee of twelve should

be appointed, one for Far West and one for Adam-on-Diamond, who were to be the sole judges of what would be necessary to remove each family out of the State, and all of the Mormons were to leave Missouri by the first of April, A.D. 1839, and all the rest of the property of the Mormons was to be taken by the Missouri troops to pay the expenses of the war.

When the committee had examined into affairs and made the assignment of property that the Mormons were to retain, a pass would be given by the committee to each person as an evidence that he had gone through an investigation both as to his conduct and property. The prisoners at Far West were to be retained and not allowed to return home until the committee had reported and given the certificate that all charges had been met and satisfied.[67]

In plain and simple language, the Mormons were to be picked clean and kicked out of Missouri.[68] The church's leaders were led in chains to the courtroom of Judge Austin A. King in Missouri's Fifth Judicial District to join some forty other Mormon prisoners awaiting trial. They faced the bench and were arraigned variously on charges of "several crimes of high treason against the state, murder, arson, burglary, robbery and larceny." To the dismay of the defendants, the first witness called by the prosecution was someone they all knew — Dr. Sampson Avard, flushed out of hiding and anxious to save his neck. When he was through talking, the Danite chieftain was followed to the stand by John Corrill, Reed Peck, W. W. Phelps, and other Mormons who testified to the existence of the Sons of Dan and its machinations.[69] Morris Phelps admitted attend-

[67] Lee, *Mormonism Unveiled*, pp. 83–84.

[68] Missouri reaction to the surrender was reflected by the militia's behavior when it located the loot accumulated in Danite raids. Oliver Boardman Huntington described the scene this way: ". . . we came to see them pick out personal property from the confused mass that filled and surrounded the plunder house, for every man thought the property he lost was the best, or at least every one nearly took and claimed the best he saw, that was of the kind he had; so that the poorest property was left to them that came last, and it came like to have ended in an uncivil war." Huntington, "Journal," Vol. I, p. 37.

[69] All testimony heard in Judge King's court can be found in *Correspondence, Orders, etc.*, pp. 97–151. Also included are the documents which passed between Governor Boggs and the Missouri Militia commanders in regard to the Mormon situation during the period June to November 1838. This also was published as *Senate Document No. 189*, 26th Congress, 2d Session, 1841. Sampson Avard impressed Peter H. Burnett, a spectator at the Richmond Court proceedings, as a "very eccentric genius, fluent, imaginative, sarcastic, and very quick in replying to questions put by the prisoner's counsel." Burnett, himself a lawyer, represented Mormon defendants who were bound over to Clay County Court. His observations and im-

ing two Danite meetings; John Cleminson acknowledged under oath he had been a Danite and had heard Rigdon's Salt Sermon. He added that he had been told by fellow Mormons of their complicity in the attack on Gallatin. Mormons who attempted to testify for the defense were discouraged — at gunpoint. And, Joseph protested, except for a few witnesses with courage, the accused Saints were denied due process of law. Most of the defendants were released or admitted to bail when the perplexed judge was unable to pinpoint laws prohibiting membership in a society such as the Sons of Dan.

Allen Joseph Stout wrote in his journal: "The only crime that was proved against me was that of being a Danite which was sworn to by Sampson Avard; but since they could find no law on the case, I was set at liberty and returned home."

Joseph, Hyrum, Rigdon, Lyman Wight, and Alexander McRae, along with Caleb Baldwin, an old friend of Rockwell's from the Big Blue, were remanded to Liberty Jail in Clay County to await "further trial." Shortly after the first of December the prisoners were herded into a large, heavy wagon, fitted with a high box to hide them from sight, and removed to Clay County. When the rig rattled to a halt in front of the jail, Joseph was the last to enter the bleak prison. He hesitated for a moment, turned to a crowd of curious onlookers, and smiled.

"Good afternoon, gentlemen," he said, and passed out of view.

Since it was evening the prophet's remark caused an uneasy stir among the jittery citizens who construed it to be a threat that he would be free by morning. Actually, Liberty Jail was to be Joseph's home for the next five months. While the prophet and his fellow captives were being led to their cells, the Mormon committees in charge of evacuation in Far West and Adam-ondi-Ahman were struggling to complete arrangements for the removal of the church from Missouri before the April deadline.

A whispered fear that the Danites were regrouping to seek vengeance in a final act of hostility before leaving Missouri caused a new wave of anxiety among the Gentiles, but all remained quiet, except for the indiscriminate plundering of Mormon homes. Pillaging became so prevalent that two hundred and forty Far West Saints signed a pact pledging aid in conducting their brethren out of reach of Boggs's Exterminating Order. Affixed to the covenant, which implied defiance to the Missouri deadline

---

pressions concerning Joseph Smith, Lyman Wight, and others are included in Peter Burnett, *Recollections and Opinions of an Old Pioneer* (New York, 1880), pp. 63, 65–68. Burnett later would become the first governor of California.

if necessary, were the signatures of such Mormon stalwarts as Brigham Young, Heber C. Kimball, John D. Lee, and Orrin Porter Rockwell.[70]

While the committee was engrossed in the problem of transporting the Saints, Rockwell had decided the coast was clear and busied himself carrying messages between Far West and Liberty Jail. Although Joseph was a prisoner, he was kept up to the minute on church affairs being conducted in his absence. As days passed into months, public opinion against the Mormons underwent a subtle change. With the fighting at an end, most of the Missouri populace turned its thoughts elsewhere, and except for the most rabid, hard-core anti-Mormons, the Saints found the atmosphere almost friendly. So much so that when Joseph failed in a jailbreak attempt his captors treated the matter lightly. The abortive effort occurred shortly after Rockwell managed to smuggle tools to the captives. Fired with enthusiasm, they quickly bent to the task of gouging a hole through the cell wall, but their "auger handles gave out" on the final stone to freedom. Consequently, during one of Rockwell's regular visits to deliver food[71] Joseph told him of their plight and suggested he concentrate on slipping in some replacement handles as soon as possible. Rockwell's eagerness to comply proved disastrous; he aroused the suspicions of the sheriff and the escape attempt was discovered.

"It was a fine breach," Joseph chuckled, "and cost the county a round sum." [72]

A second bid for freedom fell through when the prophet and his companions bolted from their quarters during a visiting period only to be thwarted when the jailer and a guard slammed a cell door in their faces. Then, in early April 1839, the prisoners were returned to Gallatin to appear before a grand jury. On April 12 the panel returned a true bill against Joseph, Hyrum, Wight, McRae, and Baldwin for "murder, treason, burglary, arson, larceny, theft and stealing." Rigdon had previously been admitted to bail and had fled Missouri to join church members at Quincy, Illinois.

Quite unexpectedly, three days later the court ordered a change of venue and the five Mormons were placed in the custody of Sheriff William Morgan to be transferred to Boone County for sentencing. It was

[70] *History of the Church*, Vol. III, pp. 251–54; *Church Encyclopaedia*, pp. 713–14. In many cases the "signatures" were no more than X's witnessed by fellow Mormons. Such was Rockwell's case.

[71] *History of the Church*, Vol. III, p. 257.

[72] Ibid., p. 292.

apparent that the move was being made in a deliberate maneuver to provide the prisoners with a chance to make a break. While many Missourians still pressured to have the Mormons hanged, several officials in high places, perhaps Boggs himself, had come to the realization that an "escape" would be convenient to all concerned, since the fugitives certainly would leave the state at the first opportunity, and it was unlikely that they would return, with a grand jury indictment hanging over their heads. Accordingly, Sheriff Morgan and his guards conveniently became intoxicated during the ride to Boone County.[73] Late that night the five prisoners galloped across the border into Illinois.

With the Mormon prophet out of their grasp, the enraged Missouri population completely razed church settlements in Daviess, Clay, Caldwell, and Ray counties, shooting livestock, firing homes, and stealing everything left behind. The handful of remaining Saints hastily packed what they could and made tracks for Illinois.

Little love was lost between Illinoisians and their Missouri neighbors, and when the story of the Mormon expulsion spread across the state line, the people of the town of Quincy were quick to offer solace and hospitality. They also extended a blanket invitation for the Saints to resettle in Illinois, a suggestion the Mormons eagerly accepted. Had Joseph not said, ". . . the Saints ought to lay hold of every door that shall seem to be opened unto them, to obtain a foothold on the earth . . ."?[74]

Exhausted and hungry, Joseph Smith, Hyrum Smith, Lyman Wight, Alexander McRae, and Caleb Baldwin rode into Quincy on April 22. "Thank God we have been delivered," the prophet said as his family and friends ran to embrace him. Among them was Orrin Porter Rockwell.

[73] On his return to Gallatin, Sheriff Morgan was attacked by fellow-citizens for his part in the escape and run out of town on a rail. A few weeks later Ebenezer Robinson saw the sheriff in Quincy. The lawman was talking to Joseph and being paid for the horses he had provided in the getaway. Robinson, "Items of Personal History of the Editor," *The Return*, Vol. II (April 1890), p. 243.

[74] *History of the Church*, Vol. III, p. 298.

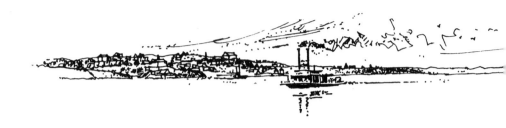

Chapter Three

THE CITY OF JOSEPH

WITH THE CLEAN, FRESH BREATH of freedom in his lungs, Joseph swiftly regained his good spirits and plunged with enthusiasm into the staggering job of rebuilding his uprooted church in this new land of Illinois. After an initial council meeting to establish the order of things, he scrutinized available property in the surrounding countryside and decided to purchase two parcels of farm acreage in the tiny hamlet of Commerce in Hancock County. It was a wilderness area, covered with trees and brush. Undaunted, Joseph said, "Commerce was so unhealthful, very few could live there;[1] but believing that it might become a healthful place by the blessing of heaven to the Saints, and no more eligible place presenting itself, I considered it wisdom to make an attempt to build up a city."[2]

Again, as in Far West, the Mormons bent to the task of hauling timber, clearing enormous tracts of ground, and apportioning lots for cabins. Within a year two hundred and fifty blockhouses, hewn log homes of the period, rose in Commerce. Even the name had changed with the topography, for now the village became known as "Nauvoo." One thousand acres had been neatly laid out in blocks and lots to make room for the rapidly expanding Mormon community. But all the while the Saints keenly felt the nagging burden of poverty; most families were penniless, living off the charity of their more fortunate brethren. At the height of this new crisis, Joseph resolved upon a bold venture, one he knew stood little chance of success. He planned to draft a petition to the President of the United States asking the federal government to reimburse the church for damages suffered at the hands of its Missouri persecutors. Who was better qualified to personally present such an important appeal in Wash-

---

[1] The unpleasant conditions existing in Commerce may have been a contributing factor in the death of Orrin Porter Rockwell's father, who passed away on September 22, 1839; *Times and Seasons*, Vol. 1, No. 2 (December 1839), p. 32.

[2] *History of the Church*, Vol. III, p. 375.

ington than the prophet himself? The High Council agreed and so voted on October 28, 1839.

Orrin Porter Rockwell was asked to join Joseph's party, which included Sidney Rigdon, Elias Higbee, a Mormon lawyer, and Dr. R. D. Foster.[3] Rockwell's presence was desirable in case any Missourians chanced upon them. The five men left Nauvoo in a two-horse carriage the following day and headed for the capital, stopping only to pick up additional documents and to preach an occasional impromptu sermon. When the journey proved too much for Rigdon's fragile health, he and Rockwell stayed behind with Foster at Columbus, Ohio, and were instructed to follow at a more leisurely pace in the carriage while Joseph and Higbee transferred to a coach.[4]

Once in Washington, Joseph made arrangements for an audience with President Martin Van Buren. The chief executive listened perfunctorily to the Mormon plea for succor, then said, "Gentlemen, your cause is just, but I can do nothing for you. If I take up for you I shall lose the vote of Missouri."[5] Van Buren's remark provided the Saints with an

[3] Ibid., Vol. IV, p. 19.

[4] Rigdon, Rockwell, and Foster took the opportunity to visit Andrew L. Lamoreaux in Dayton, Ohio. Lamoreaux so testified at the Nauvoo trial of Dr. R. D. Foster in the *Expositor* affair; see *Millennial Star*, Vol. XXIII, p. 770.

[5] Although there is no mistaking Van Buren's position in regard to the Mormon question, some confusion exists as to exactly how the President expressed himself. Joseph, for instance, gives two versions of Van Buren's reply. The first is in a letter dated December 5, 1839, to his brother, Hyrum, in which the prophet makes no mention of Van Buren's admission that, "Your cause is just"; the second is in the February 6, 1840, entry in his journal, in which the latter phrase is included. See *History of the Church*, Vol. IV, pp. 39–40, 80. Andrew Jenson, assistant church historian, resolves the discrepancy by creating a later interview between Joseph and the President. See *Church Encyclopaedia*, pp. 474, 476. However, I can find evidence of only one meeting between the two men, that which took place November 29, 1839. The quotation used above is taken from the prophet's journal entry in *History of the Church*, Vol. IV, p. 80.

undeniably effective piece of propaganda for more than a hundred years.

Despite Van Buren's natural reluctance to deal with a politically unpopular cause, Joseph was determined to confront members of Congress with the Mormon claims, if for nothing else than to arouse public sympathy for the church. He wrote Nauvoo and called for as many signed affidavits from Missouri Saints as the High Council could muster in a short time. While he waited for the statements, the prophet visited Philadelphia, where he was joined by Rockwell and Higbee; Rigdon stayed in the nation's capital to regain his health. Shortly after the new year the documents arrived, along with a message that the High Council had voted to care for the families of the delegation while it was in Washington.

Joseph added Rockwell's testimony to the stack of papers and, with a list of claims from four hundred and ninety-one Saints, amounting to $1,381,044, presented the papers to a congressional committee for consideration. Included were Joseph's demands for $100,000 in damages to personal property, Rockwell's request for $2,000, and his father's claim for $3,000.[6] For all of Joseph's exertions, the committee failed to act and the dejected delegation returned to Illinois, leaving Higbee to press the matter to a conclusion.

After a brief stop to visit his sister Caroline and her husband, M. C. Smith, at Hamden, Ohio, Rockwell arrived home in early March 1840, to see his infant son, born two days before he had left Nauvoo with the prophet. The five-month-old boy was named Orrin DeWitt Rockwell.[7]

---

[6] *Senate Document 247*, 26th Congress, 1st Session, December 2, 1839–July 21, 1840, reports the Committee of the Judiciary found against the Mormon appeal and ordered the mass of evidence returned to the delegation. But Higbee, in pressing the matter, submitted the documents to the House of Representatives and they can be found in the National Archives under 1842. Rockwell's affidavit is dated February 3, 1840, and was sworn before B. K. Morsell, District of Columbia justice of the peace. It is signed "Oren P. (his [X] mark) Rockwell." See also *History of the Church*, Vol. IV, p. 81, and Journal History, November 29, 1839.

[7] *Utah Genealogical and Historical Magazine*, Vol. XXVI, pp. 155–56. In later years the youngster legally changed his name to Orrin Porter Rockwell, Jr.

On April 8, the third day of the Saints' tenth annual conference, the Mormons were told that the Senate Judiciary Committee had announced that it had no Constitutional right to interfere in the dispute between the church and the state of Missouri. In a lengthy resolution passed by the High Council, Joseph, Rigdon, and Higbee were instructed to, "continue to use their endeavors to obtain redress for a suffering people. And if all hopes of obtaining satisfaction for the injuries done us be entirely blasted, that they then appeal our case to the Court of Heaven, believing that the Great Jehovah, who rules over the destiny of nations, and who notices the falling sparrows, will undoubtedly redress our wrongs, and ere long avenge us of our adversaries." [8]

To Rockwell, sitting in the conference gathering, the words *avenge* and *adversaries* had particular significance. The adversary of all Mormons abused at the hands of Missourians was symbolized by one man — Lilburn W. Boggs — who soon would be out of office and, his term completed, divested of official authority. It was something to think about.

The years had wrought a great change in Rockwell. Gone was the naive, unaffected youth of Jackson County; in two months he would reach his twenty-seventh birthday. Always reserved and close-mouthed, his persecution by Gentiles had made him even more reticent. The Missouri apostasies had embittered him, and although he was friendly, he chose companions with care, rarely discussing church or personal affairs with others, save Joseph. Those who enjoyed his limited confidences also gained his loyalty.

Rockwell had hardened in mind and body; heavy muscle bunched in his shoulders, his chest was broad and deep as a keg, and the lines in his face, especially the little crow's-feet around the eyes, gave his countenance a strangely intense quality. Even Rockwell's small hands, which he despised because of their almost effeminate appearance, had strengthened and calloused. A thick beard, black as licorice, covered his cheeks from ear to ear. He wore the usual broadcloth coat, homespun trousers, wide-brimmed hat, and boots of the frontier. There was a characteristic above all others, however, which irritated Rockwell without end — his voice. In moments of anger it reached a shrill falsetto, intensifying his fury. Because of this he learned to control his temper beyond the limits of other men.

If Rockwell had developed any unusual abilities since his childhood, even his enemies would have been quick to agree that two accomplish-

[8] *History of the Church*, Vol. IV, p. 108.

ments stood out above the rest — his deadly accuracy with either a rifle or a pistol, and his uncanny way with horses. These gained for him a wide and envied reputation among border citizens who respected little else in a man.

While Rockwell carved out a new home for his family, another personality moved into the Mormon limelight, a man who was to rattle the church to its very foundation, Dr. John C. Bennett, an ambitious and unscrupulous rogue,[9] had weaseled his way into Joseph's confidence after a lengthy correspondence in which the "brigadier general of the Invincible Dragoons of Illinois" had pleaded:

> Wealth is no material object with me. I desire to be happy, and am fully satisfied that I can enjoy myself better with your people, with my present views and feelings, than with any other. I hope that time will soon come when your people will become my people, and your God my God.
>
> At the time of your peril and bitter persecution in Missouri, you are aware I proffered you my utmost energies, and had not the conflict terminated so speedily, I should have been with you then. God be thanked for your rescue from the hand of a savage, but cowardly foe![10]

Bennett made his appearance in Nauvoo in August of 1840, was baptized, and within two months was appointed lobbyist to the Illinois Legislature, where he urged the passage of a bill seeking incorporation of Nauvoo. As a result of his dangling the prize of a solid Mormon voting bloc (by now the Saints knew full well how to apply political pressure) before both Democrats and Whigs, the measure passed and was signed by Governor Thomas Carlin. The act chartered the City of Nauvoo, permitted organization of the Nauvoo Legion, and authorized establishment of the University of the City of Nauvoo. Bennett was exultant: "Illinois has acquitted herself with honor . . . . Every power we asked has been granted, every request gratified, every desire fulfilled." [11] There was good reason to rejoice; the Nauvoo City Charter was an extraordinary document, indeed.[12]

[9] Thomas Ford, *History of Illinois* (Chicago, 1854), p. 263.

[10] *History of the Church*, Vol. IV, pp. 169–70.

[11] Bennett's letter to *Times and Seasons*, Vol. 2, No. 5 (January 1841), p. 266.

[12] A capsule commentary on the unusual aspects of the charter can be found in *Historical Encyclopedia of Illinois*, edited by Newton Bateman, J. Seymour Currey, and Paul Selby, and *History of Hancock County*, edited by Charles J. Scofield (Chicago, 1921), three volumes, Vol. II, pp. 834–35 (hereafter cited as Scofield, *History of Hancock County*).

It permitted, among other things, a city council, including a mayor, four aldermen, and nine councilmen, empowered to pass any ordinance not in conflict with state or federal constitutions. The mayor and aldermen formed the Municipal Court, having the power of justices of the peace and the right to issue writs of habeas corpus in all cases involving city ordinances. In allowing the Nauvoo Legion, the act specified that, "The said Legion shall perform the same amount of military duty as is now or may be hereafter required of the regular militia of the State, and shall be at the disposal of the Mayor in executing the laws and ordinances of the city corporation . . . and shall be entitled to their proportion of the public arms . . . ."

The Legislature, in its desire to curry Mormon favor, had placed in Joseph's hands the legal and military power with which to institute a secular dictatorship unmatched in any other city in the land. Bennett was well paid for his labors on behalf of his newly-found brethren; in the first municipal election held February 1, 1841, he was named mayor of Nauvoo. Joseph, Hyrum, and Rigdon were elected councilmen. In his inaugural address, Bennett, slipping with remarkable ease into his new role as a Mormon leader and "Joab, General in Israel," emphasized to the citizens of Nauvoo that, "Nothing is more necessary to the preservation of order and the supremacy of the laws, than the perfect organization of our military forces, under a uniform and rigid discipline and approved judicious drill; and to this end I desire to see all the departments and cohorts of the Legion put in immediate requisition. The Legion should be all powerful, panoplied with justice and equity, to consummate the designs of its projectors . . . ." [13]

Bennett was permitted the title of mayor, a figurehead position at most, since the Saints obeyed only the prophet, but when it came to running the Legion, the highest office — lieutenant general — went to Joseph. [14] Under his orders the organization was divided into two co-

[13] *History of the Church*, Vol. IV, p. 291.

[14] Previous to Joseph's appointment, the only other military leader to hold such a high rank had been George Washington. Much has been said since then by experts arguing on both sides regarding Joseph's Legion rank and its relationship to the federal service, but clearly it was a matter of concern at the time. S. Francis, editor of the *Sangamo Journal*, published a lengthy editorial critical of the Illinois Legislature for currying favor with the Mormons by agreeing to certain provisions in the City Charter. "They gave him power and he is to give them votes," the editor complained. One of the criticisms dealt with Joseph's Nauvoo Legion rank,

which makes him the highest military officer in the United States, and when in the service of the United States, he will command all its armies. Gen. Washing-

horts — cavalry in the first, infantry in the second. The State of Illinois turned over three pieces of cannon and two hundred and fifty stands of rifle and pistol, the Legion's "proportion of the public arms." It was a subsidy which put the Mormons back in the military business.

Despite the now-rising fortunes of the church, Joseph still was troubled. Missouri authorities constantly threatened him with writs of extradition, and bounty hunters, eager to collect on the prophet's head, regularly made attempts to spirit him across the Mississippi. Their dogged determination finally prompted Joseph to pick forty men "from the old tried veterans of the cause" as protectors of the church hierarchy.

Even a bodyguard could not prevent sheriffs' deputies from arresting Joseph when he least expected it — immediately after a conference with Governor Carlin. But the prophet was not to be outdone; he quickly sought a writ of habeas corpus challenging the legality of the Missouri decree and took it before Stephen A. Douglas, a judge of the Illinois Supreme Court on circuit duty, who ruled the Missouri warrant faulty and ordered the Mormon leader released.

About this time, Joseph angrily prophesied that Lilburn Boggs would "die by violent hands within a year." And in a fit of pique he added that Governor Carlin would die in a ditch.[15] According to later statements

---

ton was appointed Lieutenant General after the revolution, but since his resignation the office has remained vacant in the army of the United States, and thus Joe Smith is believed to be the only officer of that rank now in this country. He is certainly the superior of all the militia officers of Illinois, and in service will rank above them all. Although some question his right to command Gen. Scott, if called into the service of the United States, yet it is the opinion of experienced military men with whom we have conferred, that there is no doubt upon this point, as no rule is better understood or more clearly settled in our country, than that, when a regular and militia officer are acting together in the United States service, if of the same grade the former takes precedence, but if the militia officer is of superior rank, he is entitled to the command; and thus, as Lieutenant General is higher than Major General and the latter is the highest office in the army of the United States, there can be no doubt, that when in the service of the United States, Lieutenant General Joseph Smith will command her armies.

As reported in *The Wasp*, Nauvoo, Hancock County, Illinois, June 18, 1842. Brigham Young was of the same opinion. In later years, when an historian reminded him that, after Washington, Joseph was the first man in America to hold the rank of Lieutenant General, and that Brigham himself was the next, Young remarked, "I was never much of a military man. The commission has since been abrogated by the State of Illinois, but if Joseph had lived when the war [with Mexico] broke out, he would have become commander-in-chief of the United States armies." See Edward Tullidge, *Life of Brigham Young* (New York, 1876), pp. 30–31.

[15] Word of the prophecy ultimately reached Carlin, who questioned Joseph about it in a letter dated June 30, 1842, after an attempt had been made on Boggs's life. See *History of the Church*, Vol. V, p. 50.

made by Bennett, the prophet had more to say about Boggs: "The exterminator should be exterminated and the Destroying Angel will do it by the right hand of his power. I say it," Joseph added, "in the name of the Lord God!" [16] Bennett also claimed that the prophet had declared in a First Presidency meeting, "The Destroying Angel will do the work; when God speaks, His voice must be obeyed."

For Rockwell, Joseph's words recalled the Danite oath of 1838: "I furthermore promise and swear that I will regard the First President of the [church] . . . as the supreme head of the Church on earth, and obey him the same as the Supreme God, in all written revelations given under the solemnities of a "Thus saith the Lord." [17]

In the past it had not been considered improper for members of the church to assist in fulfilling prophecies. One classic example concerned a revelation received by Joseph on July 8, 1838, which commanded the Council of Twelve Apostles to take leave of the Saints at the temple site in Far West on April 26, 1839, for a mission "over the great waters." Nothing could have been more explicit. Yet, to the consternation of the prophet and his followers, as the date drew near they found themselves extremely unwelcome anywhere in the Far West area. How then was the revelation to be fulfilled? The apostles conducted a clandestine conference at the appointed location at night. Thus, they considered the conditions of Joseph's prediction satisfied. [18]

Therefore, in February of 1842, when Orrin Porter Rockwell gathered up his family to visit Independence so that Luana, eight months pregnant with their fourth child, could be with her parents, Bennett, so he says, was not surprised at Joseph's explanation that Rockwell had gone to "fulfill prophecy." [19] Once in Independence, Rockwell set out to find work until such time as the baby was born, after which he planned to return to Nauvoo. His natural faculty with horses stood him in good stead; a Missourian named Ward offered him a job caring for a valuable stallion. [20]

---

[16] Bennett, *History of the Saints*, p. 281.

[17] "The using of the name of God is allowed only on judicial occasions, when a curse is laid upon some individual, as that of Joseph upon Governor Boggs, who had one fulminated against him . . . ." J. W. Gunnison, *The Mormons, or Latter-day Saints in the Valley of the Great Salt Lake* (Philadelphia, 1852), pp. 73–74.

[18] Jenson, *Church Encyclopaedia*, pp. 466–67.

[19] Bennett, *History of the Saints*, p. 282.

[20] Abstract of the Census of 1840, Jackson County, Mo., MS, p. 52, lists a farmer named Cyrus Ward as a resident of the county.

Since Jackson County settlers still harbored a hatred for Mormons, Rockwell used an assumed name while in the area; he called himself Brown.[21] On March 25 the baby came and was named Sarah for Rockwell's mother.[22]

[21] William F. Switzler, *Illustrated History of Missouri From 1541 to 1877* (St. Louis, 1879), p. 251.

[22] Genealogical records of the Church of Jesus Christ of Latter-day Saints show that the infant was born in "1840/1841," but this is an error.

Chapter Four

THE DESTROYING ANGEL

A CREATURE OF HABIT, Lilburn W. Boggs invariably retired to his study after dinner and spent a quiet hour assiduously reading his newspaper. This diversion from an otherwise busy day of campaigning for the Missouri Senate was particularly enjoyable on the night of May 6, 1842, because of a driving rain which splashed at the window behind his chair and emphasized the snug atmosphere of his favorite room. At his feet, the former governor's daughter, six-year-old Minnie, was kneeling beside a cradle, rocking her infant sister to sleep. Mrs. Boggs and the rest of the family were occupied in clearing the dinner table.

Suddenly the roar of a pistol in counterpoint to shattering glass resounded through the house. In the dining room, Mrs. Boggs was doubly startled to hear Minnie shrieking. A son, William, ran to the study and found his father slumped backward against his chair with blood spurting in huge gouts from several wounds in his head and neck; the pungent smell of black powder pervaded the room. Mrs. Boggs, fighting hysteria, clutched the sobbing Minnie to her breast and choked back tears as her fingers probed the child's body for signs of injury. William ran to the window, but the slashing rain made it impossible to see for more than a few feet. Ignoring the storm, he ran for help while his mother attempted to stanch the blood from her husband's fearsome wounds.[1]

Judge Samuel H. Woodson, a neighbor, was the first outsider on the scene; and moments later, when Sheriff J. H. Reynolds arrived with a doctor (the first of four that night), Boggs was unconscious and near

---

[1] Lyman L. Palmer, *History of Napa and Lake Counties, California* (San Francisco, 1881), p. 380; *History of the Church*, Vol. V, p. 15. After his term as governor came to a close in November 1840, Boggs returned to the mercantile business in partnership with a son. He was thus engaged when the attempt on his life was made. For an excellent and most interesting biographical brief of this key figure in early Mormon history, see Palmer, this note, pp. 373–86. Once moved to Independence, Boggs lived on South Spring Street, a few blocks from the public square. See William Southern, Jr., *Messages and Proclamations of the Governor of Missouri*, Vol. I (1922), pp. 305–6.

death. An examination showed that he had been struck four times by large buckshot; two balls had penetrated his skull and lodged in the left lobe of the brain; a third had buried itself in the thick muscles of his neck; and the fourth had pierced the hollow of his neck, entered his mouth through the back of his throat, and been swallowed with blood as his head hung limply against the back of the chair.[2] Reynolds counted thirteen other buckshot imbedded in the woodwork around the room; all had somehow missed Minnie, who had been in a direct line with her father and the window. The would-be assassin was more than likely unaware of the girl's presence, the large chair blocking his vision.

Outside the house a crowd gathered at first report of the shooting and now numbered nearly two hundred persons; one of the spectators searching the spot where the gunman had stood found traces of footprints in the mud, and in a partially-filled puddle discovered a gun. Sheriff Reynolds studied the firearm carefully, but was unable to detect any identifying mark. It was a "large German holster pistol, chambered for four shots," he observed. Three of the barrels were loaded with buckshot instead of single balls.[3] Reynolds surmised that the recoil of such a heavy charge had kicked the pistol from the gunman's grasp, and failing to find it in the rain, the assassin had fled. While the sheriff mulled these thoughts in his mind, a storekeeper named Uhlinger[4] recognized the weapon as one stolen from his shop.[5]

[2] Details of the Boggs shooting are taken from Palmer, *History of Napa and Lake Counties, California,* pp. 380–81, and William M. Boggs, "Sketch of Lilburn W. Boggs," *Missouri Historical Review,* Vol. IV (January 1910), pp. 106–8.

[3] The gun was probably a pepperbox pistol manufactured in Suhl, Germany, introduced in 1835 and sold extensively in the United States. Loading pistols with shot instead of a single ball was not an unusual practice during this period.

[4] Census of 1850, Jackson County, Missouri, [abstracted], p. 129, lists a Philip Uhlinger as a resident.

[5] Boggs, "Sketch of Lilburn W. Boggs," p. 108; *Jeffersonian Republican,* May 14, 1842.

"I thought the niggers had taken it, but that hired man of Ward's — the one who used to work with the stallion — he came in to look at it just before it turned up missing!" the storekeeper said.[6]

Grateful for a genuine lead, Reynolds began looking for the hired hand, "to ask some questions," but the man was nowhere to be found. It was not long before the sheriff determined that Mr. Brown, the suspect, was Orrin Porter Rockwell.

Eight days after the shooting, a steamboat pulled into Nauvoo from St. Louis[7] and Rockwell disembarked.[8] The following morning, May 15, a Sunday, Joseph spoke at a meeting in the center of town and told the congregation he had received word from Missouri that Boggs had been murdered.[9] The audible gasp which escaped the crowd was interpreted by some as a cheer; certainly a majority of the Mormons suppressed an urge to celebrate openly. Their sentiments were perhaps best described by "Vortex," a contributor to the Nauvoo newspaper, The Wasp: "Boggs is undoubtedly killed according to report; but who did the noble deed remains to be found out."[10]

The report was premature. Despite the severity of his wounds, Boggs clung stubbornly to life and was slowly gaining, though he had been given up for dead by his family and a cluster of physicians, one of whom was his brother, Dr. Joseph O. Boggs.[11] With early accounts of the shooting

[6] Boggs, "Sketch of Lilburn W. Boggs," p. 108.

[7] It was reported that a man of Rockwell's description boarded a boat for St. Louis at a landing "just below Independence" the morning after the assassination attempt; see Hunt, *Mormonism*, p. 296.

[8] Bennett, *History of the Saints*, p. 282, says Rockwell arrived in Nauvoo "the day before the report reached there." Joseph first mentioned the attempt on May 15, 1842. There was no direct passage from Independence; passengers transferred at St. Louis.

[9] In *History of the Church*, Vol. V, p. 9, Joseph refers to the *attempted* assassination of Boggs on this date, yet a week later, in an article for *The Wasp*, the prophet spoke of Boggs as dead. The error is a probable result of the editing of Joseph's papers for inclusion in the *History of the Church*.

[10] *The Wasp*, May 28, 1842. Vortex, who more than likely was William Smith, editor of the paper, was responding to an item in the *Burlington Hawkeye* which reported that a Mormon was suspected of the shooting. The *Hawkeye* article was reprinted in *The Wasp* alongside the Vortex letter. See also Oliver H. Olney, *The Absurdities of Mormonism Portrayed, a Brief Sketch* (Hancock County, Illinois, 1843), p. 19. Olney says word of the assassination "went through the city [Nauvoo] as if a great prophesy had been fullfiled [sic]."

[11] Palmer, *History of Napa and Lake Counties, California*, p. 381. The presence of four doctors at Boggs's home on the night of the shooting undoubtedly was re-

came a renewed interest in Joseph's prophecy of death for the former Missouri governor. Said the *Quincy Whig* of May 21, "Lilburn W. Boggs, late governor of Missouri, was assassinated...by an unknown hand...." The paper continued:

> The governor was alive on the seventh, but no hopes are entertained of his recovery. A man was suspected, and is probably arrested before this. There are several rumors in circulation in regard to the horrid affair; one of which throws the crime upon the Mormons, from the fact, we suppose, that Mr. Boggs was governor at the time, and in no small degree instrumental in driving them from the state. Smith, too, the Mormon Prophet, as we understand, prophesied, a year or so ago, his death by violent means. Hence there is plenty of foundation for rumor.

Joseph saw to it that the printer's devil at *The Wasp* offices worked overtime, for in the next edition the prophet had an item aimed at the *Whig*: ". . . you have done me manifest injustice in ascribing to me a prediction of the demise of Lilburn W. Boggs . . . by violent hands. Boggs was a candidate for the state senate, and, I presume, fell by the hand of a political opponent, with 'his hands and face yet dripping with the blood of murder;' but he died not through my instrumentality. . . ."

On top of this clamor over the shooting came the biting voice of John C. Bennett, who, having resigned his position as mayor because "his whoredoms and abominations were fast coming to light," [12] began sniping at Joseph from a multitude of directions. The prophet, meanwhile, deemed it wise to assume the mayor's office himself.

Determined to destroy Joseph for publicly disgracing him, Bennett composed a series of sensational letters for publication in the *Sangamo Journal* exposing the prophet and his secret doctrine of spiritual wifery,

---

sponsible for the saving of his life. Boggs regained his strength in time to take the oath as state senator. He died, with two buckshot still in him, at his California farm on March 19, 1861, nineteen years later. Dr. Boggs, who lived in Westport, Missouri, is said to have remarked of his brother, "Lilburn had more sense after he lost part of his brains than before . . . !" *Messages and Proclamations of the Governors of Missouri*, p. 305.

[12] These are Joseph's words as written in *History of the Church*, Vol. V, p. 12. Bennett had accused the prophet of granting him permission to "hold illicit intercourse with women." Bennett later retracted his statement, but in his book said he did so only after Joseph held a gun to his head and threatened to make "cat-fish bait" of him or turn him over "to the Danites for execution." See Bennett, *History of the Saints*, p. 287.

among other things.[13] He also told what he knew of the Boggs affair. Bennett said Rockwell had been sent to kill the man on Joseph's orders. "In the spring of the year Smith offered a reward of five hundred dollars to any man who would secretly assassinate Governor Boggs." [14] And after the attempt was made, Bennett related, "Smith said to me, speaking of Governor Boggs, 'The *Destroying Angel* has done the work, as I predicted, but Rockwell was not the man who shot; the Angel did it.' " When this statement circulated, Orrin Porter Rockwell found himself with a sobriquet little to his liking. He had become, in the eyes of many, "The Destroying Angel." [15]

Even the stoical Rockwell was vexed by the deadly gossip Bennett's correspondence had evoked, and he was determined to put a stop to it. Seeking out the loquacious apostate in nearby Carthage, Rockwell brushed past three visitors in Bennett's parlor and confronted his antagonist with the stories being spread in Nauvoo. It took some moments for Bennett to overcome his surprise at the unexpected appearance of a man he knew to be a Danite, but in typical fashion the erstwhile soul-brother of the Saints attempted to bluster his way out of the unpleasant situation; he found Rockwell was not to be sidetracked. Gesturing at the trio of strangers, he

---

[13] Although Bennett's disclosures regarding plural or celestial marriage were emphatically denied at the time, the doctrine later was made public with an admission that it had been practiced extensively for years. Spiritual wifery was caught in the harsh glare of the public spotlight again two years later in Massachusetts, adding credence to Bennett's exposé. See John Hardy, *History of the Trials of Elder John Hardy, Before the Church of "Latter Day Saints" in Boston, For Slander in Saying that G. J. Adams, S. Brannan and William Smith, Were Licentious Characters* (Boston, 1844).

[14] Bennett, *History of the Saints*, p. 281. A rogue named Joseph H. Jackson claimed that Joseph had offered him $3,000 to kill Boggs; see his *A Narrative of the Adventures and Experience of Joseph H. Jackson; Disclosing the Depths of Mormon Villainy Practiced in Nauvoo* (Warsaw, Illinois, 1844), p. 7, and the *Warsaw Signal*, June 5, 1844.

[15] See Thomas Gregg, *The Prophet of Palmyra* (New York, 1890), p. 198, and Fitz Hugh Ludlow, "Among the Mormons," *The Atlantic Monthly*, Vol. XIII (April 1864), p. 492. The lurid nickname gained widespread acceptance when whispers implicated Rockwell in the brutal slaying of another Mormon, John Stephenson, on June 2, 1842. An account of the murder can be found in the *Sangamo Journal*, July 15, 1842. For statements connecting Rockwell to the crime, see Charles W. Dilke, *Greater Britain: A Record of Travel in English-Speaking Countries During 1866 and 1867* (London, 1868), two volumes, Vol. I, p. 184.

asked Bennett for a private conversation, and was answered with, "If you have anything to say, you can say it in front of them!" [16]

"It's a personal affair," Rockwell retorted.

After a moment's hesitation Bennett led the way to another room.

Once they were alone, Rockwell turned to his accuser. "Doctor, you don't know who your friends are. I'm not your enemy and I don't want you using my name in your publications!"

"Joe Smith and *all* of his friends are my personal enemies," Bennett snapped in reply.

Rockwell's tone hardened: "I've been told you said Joseph gave me fifty dollars and a wagon for shooting Boggs." Without waiting for an answer, Rockwell continued, "Now hear me well, Doctor Bennett. I can— and I will — whip any man who tells a cursed lie like that about me. Now! did you say it or not?"

Bennett ran his tongue over his lips and thought for a moment. "No, I didn't say that. I said — and I'll tell it to your face — you left Nauvoo about two months before Boggs was shot. And, you came back the day before the report of the attempted assassination reached here; two persons in Nauvoo said you told them you had been in Boggs's neighborhood."

"Oh, I was there all right," Rockwell said curtly. "But if I shot Boggs, they have got to prove it. I never did an act I was ashamed of, and I do not fear to go anywhere that I have ever been. I've done nothing criminal!"

Startled by the sudden outburst, Bennett hastily concurred. "Certainly they've got to prove it. I know nothing of what you did, I wasn't there."

Before Bennett could say more, Rockwell interjected: "If you say that Joseph Smith paid me to shoot Boggs — I'll be back!" [17] There was no mistaking the implication. Satisfied that Bennett understood him, Rockwell marched from the room. In Nauvoo, Rockwell clambered into his elegant new carriage and whipped the fine team forward. It was true the equipage had been a gift from Joseph upon Rockwell's return from Missouri; the prophet said he gave the present to his friend, "to enable him to convey passengers from the steamboat landing to the temple and back." [18]

Whether Orrin Porter Rockwell fired the shot which nearly snuffed out the life of Lilburn W. Boggs is a matter for conjecture; certainly con-

---

[16] "Affidavit of John C. Bennett," sworn before Samuel Marshall, justice of the peace, Hancock County, Illinois, July 7, 1842; published in *The Wasp*, July 27, 1842, and Bennett, *History of the Saints*, p. 283.

[17] Ibid. The conversation is recounted by Bennett in his affidavit.

[18] Bennett, *History of the Saints*, p. 285.

temporary writers — and their successors — eagerly picked up the cry and blamed him for the deed, if for no other reason than it made good reading. One of Rockwell's virtues was his unalloyed veracity; he did not lie.[19] With this in mind, it is significant that no evidence has been found to show that he refuted the charge; he denied only that Joseph had ordered the crime. On the other hand, at least two people claimed he admitted the assassination attempt. According to one, Rockwell in later years told General Patrick E. Connor in Utah, "I shot through the window and thought I had killed him, but I had only wounded him; I was damned sorry that I had not killed the son of a bitch!"[20] The other, Mormon apostate William Hall, said he heard Rockwell boast of the shooting,[21] and William Law, a member of the First Presidency, asserted in an interview that Joseph told him of sending Rockwell to murder Boggs.[22] Since Law, who repudiated the church during the Nauvoo period, waited forty years to make the statement, his testimony is suspect.

If Rockwell did fire the fateful shot, it would appear the decision was of his own making; he had no love for Boggs, and in Rockwell's eyes the man had sinned against the church in ordering the expulsion of the Saints from Missouri. It also is possible that Rockwell felt he was performing a religious duty as a member of the priesthood in fulfilling Joseph's prophecy.[23] In any event, only Rockwell knew the truth of the matter, and he took that with him to the grave.

When Rockwell left Independence, he left Luana behind with her parents to return when she pleased. He, meanwhile, took up residence in

[19] George W. Bean, *Autobiography*, compiled by Flora Diana Bean Horne (Salt Lake City, 1945), p. 175.

[20] Wilhelm W. Wyl [Wymetal], *Mormon Portraits, Joseph Smith the Prophet, His Family and His Friends* (Salt Lake City, 1886), p. 255.

[21] Hall, *Abominations of Mormonism Exposed*, p. 30. Hall also stated, "The fact of Rockwell shooting Boggs is not kept as a secret among Mormons, it is universally known."

[22] Wilhelm W. Wymetal interview with William Law, published in the *Salt Lake Tribune*, July 31, 1887. Another disfellowshiped Mormon, John Whitmer, said Joseph had ordered the killing. See the suppressed Chapter XXI of Whitmer, *History of the Church*.

[23] Governor Thomas Carlin, writing to Joseph in regard to the prophecy of death, said, "I have seen your denial published in *The Wasp*, of the prediction, attributed to you, of the death (or assassination) of Governor Boggs; be that true or false, nothing has contributed more towards fixing the belief upon the public mind, that you had made such prediction, than the repeated statements of a portion of

the tavern-hotel of a captain in the Nauvoo Legion named Amos Davis.[24] Davis's inn also provided a more convenient headquarters for Rockwell from which to operate his carriage taxi service. Some said he took the job only as a subterfuge for his true purpose — spying on newcomers to the city for the prophet.

After the *Sangamo Journal* began printing Bennett's letters attacking the Mormon prophet, the apostate physician became convinced that efforts would be made to silence him permanently. He feared, too, that Rockwell would, in the parlance of the Mormons, "use him up," if he persisted in linking him with the assassination attempt. How much longer Rockwell would have tolerated Bennett's highly colored and entirely assumptive stories[25] is a moot question, for without warning, on the morning of August 8, Rockwell found himself under arrest for "assault with intent to kill Lilburn W. Boggs." Deputy sheriffs, acting on an order from Governor Carlin, who possessed an affidavit from Boggs blaming Rock-

---

your followers, that the manner of his death had been revealed to you, and their exultation that it needs must be fulfilled." The governor's letter is indicative of the widespread circulation Joseph's prophecy had gained, and its influence on the Mormons; see *History of the Church*, Vol. V, p. 50.

[24] Bennett, *History of the Saints*, p. 285.

[25] The measure of Bennett's evidence can be found in his *Affidavit*, in which he tells Rockwell: "Certainly they have got to prove it on you, if you did shoot him [Boggs]; I know nothing of what you did, as I was not there. I only know the circumstances, and from them I draw my own inferences, and the public will theirs . . . ." Bennett's inferences are explained in his *History of the Saints*, p. 286: "I feel . . . certain . . . that Rockwell, as a member of the Daughter of Zion, acted as the *conductor* or *guide*; and that, one of the twelve composing the Destroying Angel, assisted by Rockwell, did the deed. *This is the amount of what I know in relation to this unfortunate transaction.*" [Italics supplied.]

W. Wyl [Wilhelm W. Wymetal] included in his book an interview with Mrs. Sarah M. Pratt, widow of the apostle Orson Pratt, in which she stated: "One evening Dr. Bennett called at my house and asked me to lend him my husband's rifle. This was an excellent arm, brought from England by Orson Pratt; it was known to be the best rifle in that part of the country. I asked him what he wanted the rifle for, and he said: 'Don't be so loud; Rockwell is outside — Joseph wants it; I shall tell you later.' . . . I suspected some foul play, and refused to give him the rifle, stating that I dared not dispose of it in the absence of my husband. Bennett went away, and when the news came that Gov. Boggs had been shot at and all but killed, Bennett came and told me that he had wanted the rifle of my husband for 'that job,' and that Joseph had sent him to get it." Wyl, *Mormon Portraits*, pp. 33–34. This tale can be discounted entirely, since Bennett himself would never have let the opportunity pass of reporting to the world in his book, written forty years earlier, that he had absolute knowledge of Joseph's hand in a plot to kill Boggs and that he, Bennett, had been the agent used to procure a murder weapon.

well for the crime, also arrested Joseph as an accessory "before the fact."[26] The arrests were more of Bennett's work; when he failed to bring the Mormon Church crashing down around the prophet's head with his accusations of adultery, Bennett had contacted Boggs, recovering in his Independence home, and confided his "inferences" in regard to the shooting. On the strength of these disclosures, the invalid Boggs swore to the following affidavit:

> State of Missouri, county of Jackson: This day personally appeared before me, Samuel Weston, a justice of the peace, within and for the county of Jackson, the subscriber, Lilburn W. Boggs, who being duly sworn doth depose and say that on the night of the 6th day of May [1842], while sitting in his dwelling, in the town of Independence, in the county of Jackson, he was shot with intent to kill, and that his life was despaired of for several days, and that he believes and has good reason to believe from evidence and information now in his possession, that O. P. Rockwell, a citizen or resident of the state of Illinois, is the person who shot him[27] on the night aforesaid, and the said deponent hereby applies to the Governor of the State of Illinois, to deliver the said O. P. Rockwell to some person authorized to receive him and convey him to the county aforesaid, there to be dealt with according to law.[28]

Only a man of Boggs's influence could have gained anything on such flimsy testimony. But in Rockwell's case, "good reason to believe" his

---

[26] *The Wasp*, August 13, 1842. The newspaper commented: "As to Mr. Rockwell it is said he can prove that he was in Nauvoo the day after the aforesaid assault on Ex-Governor Boggs, is said to have been committed in Independence, Mo., a distance of at least 300 miles." This sentence was deleted when the article was rewritten in *History of the Church*, Vol. V, pp. 86–87, as Joseph's journal entry for the day.

[27] Much has been written of Boggs's true feelings in regard to the attempt on his life. Mormon writers suggest the former governor had made a number of Gentile enemies, so many in fact, that to insinuate that the church was to blame was typical of his bigotry. Even though the controversy over the near assassination will never be resolved, one thing can be stated as a certainty — Boggs sincerely believed his attacker was a Mormon. In 1846, when he journeyed west, he confided to his traveling companions that he understood the Saints were headed in the same direction and confessed he feared for his life because they had made an earlier attempt to kill him. See letter from Charles T. Stanton to Sidney Stanton, dated July 12, 1846, published in the *New York Herald*, November 4, 1846, quoted in *Overland in 1846, Diaries and Letters of the California–Oregon Trail*, edited by Dale Morgan (Georgetown, California, 1963), two volumes, Vol. II, p. 614.

[28] *History of the Church*, Vol. V, p. 67.

guilt was sufficient for Governor Carlin to grant a writ of extradition.[29] They underestimated Joseph Smith's resourcefulness, however. Under the city charter the prophet was permitted to seek a writ of habeas corpus in the Municipal Court of Nauvoo. This he did, but the deputies refused to comply with the writ, demanding a hearing on the Missouri order, and returned to Carlin for instructions. The lawmen left their two prisoners in the custody of the Nauvoo city marshal. Once the deputies were out of sight, Joseph and Rockwell "went about our business."[30]

Joseph knew that sooner or later the sheriffs would return. Deciding discretion was the better part of valor, he crossed the Mississippi River to an island between Nauvoo and Montrose, Iowa, and immediately called a council meeting. From Rockwell he learned of a rumor that a warrant had been issued by the governor of Iowa for their arrest and extradition to Missouri. The rumor proved groundless, but the council was of the opinion that Rockwell should leave the state until things calmed down.[31] Joseph, it was decided, would continue to remain near Nauvoo, sheltered by trusted Mormons.

On August 14 Wilson Law, major general of the Nauvoo Legion in Bennett's stead, was told by Joseph that if he should be captured by Missourians, the Legion, "forthwith, without delay, regardless of life or death [is to] rescue me out of their hands."[32] The prophet went even further and ordered: ". . . that whenever any mob force, or violence is used on any citizen [of Nauvoo], or that belongeth thereunto, you will see that the force or violence, is immediately dispersed and brought to punishment; or meet it, or contest it, at the point of the sword with firm, undaunted and unyielding valor . . . ."[33]

Law was told to secrete several guns in strategic places around the city in case Joseph needed one in a hurry. Law replied, "One of them is in the stone shop by the Nauvoo house. One I expect to get put into Mr. Ivins' barn, and the others I cannot get under lock and key in any place I know of yet, but I will have them taken the best care of that I can."

[29] Justin Butterfield, United States Attorney for the District of Illinois, wrote a learned treatise on habeas corpus as it applied to Joseph Smith and Orrin Porter Rockwell in this case in a letter to Sidney Rigdon, October 20, 1842. The essay was considered of such importance that it was printed in its entirety in *The Wasp*, December 17, 1842.

[30] *History of the Church*, Vol. V, p. 87.

[31] B. H. Roberts, *The Rise and Fall of Nauvoo* (Salt Lake City, 1900), p. 145.

[32] *History of the Church*, Vol. V, p. 93.

[33] Ibid.

Since Boggs had used influence in getting requisitions from two states for the prophet, Joseph decided to apply a little pressure himself. In an editorial in the church's Illinois newspaper, *Times and Seasons*, August 15, 1842, the public was informed that: "Missouri, frantic with rage, and not yet filled with blood, wishes now to follow her bleeding victims to their exile, and satiate herself with blood." Decrying the Missouri warrant, the editorial went on to explain that Joseph had not been in Independence but in Nauvoo on the day Boggs was wounded; "Nor can it be proved that he has been in the state of Missouri for the last three years." As for Rockwell, the newspaper announced, "it is reported that he is gone there [Missouri] to prove himself clear, but we should think that Missouri is the last place to go for *justice*; we don't think she is capable of administering it to the Mormons . . . ."

Rockwell was not on his way to Missouri; quite the contrary, he was trying to put as many miles between himself and that state as possible until the clamor for his arrest subsided. In this respect he was to be disappointed, for already a reward of $1,300 was being offered for his apprehension and delivery to Independence.[34] A similar amount was posted for Joseph. In time, the sum for Rockwell's capture alone would reach $3,000.[35] As Rockwell made his way east, Wilson Law urged Joseph to leave his hiding place in Iowa and return to Nauvoo where he could be quartered in safety, moving frequently to avoid discovery. Law argued that there was no reason why the prophet could not stay in the city unmolested; his presence would serve to ease the anxieties felt by Mormons concerned over Joseph's welfare. "And why should it be otherwise," Law said, "when the Lord's anointed is hunted like a lion of the forest, by the most wicked and oppressive generation that has ever been since the days of our Savior." Joseph was convinced. He returned to Nauvoo on the night of August 18.

With Rockwell on the run and Joseph forced underground in his own city, John C. Bennett bent all his powers to keep them on the defensive. Dissatisfied with the inability of Missouri lawmen to snare the Mormon fugitives, he pressed the Boggs family to insist on action. Bennett wrote Joseph O. Boggs, asking if legal proceedings had been slowed because of some doubt as to Joseph's complicity; if so, Bennett suggested, he was prepared to offer additional "evidence," if necessary. His concern was

[34] Ibid., p. 92.

[35] Boggs, "Sketch of Lilburn W. Boggs," *Missouri Historical Review*, Vol. IV, p. 108.

unwarranted; the next mail brought him this answer: "We have now no doubt of the guilt of Smith and Rockwell. Rockwell is known here, and was seen in Platte county for several days preceding the shooting of my brother. When he was arrested [August 8], he told the messenger that he could prove that he was seven miles north of Independence on the night that Governor Boggs was shot. This only confirms the suspicions against him." [36]

Mollified, John C. Bennett left the field of combat. But he found it difficult to completely disconnect himself from the excitement of Mormonism. Joining the ill-starred cause of James J. Strang, who claimed to be Joseph Smith's rightful successor, Bennett quickly assumed the role of second counselor in the First Presidency. But even in the Strang movement his penchant for teaching "unauthorized doctrine" proved to be his undoing; he was cut off in the summer of 1847. In retirement, Bennett became a poultry farmer. His greatest achievements were yet to come — creation of a new strain of chicken, the Plymouth Rock, and organization of the first poultry show in America.[37]

[36] Bennett, *History of the Saints*, p. 286. Dr. Boggs's allusion to Rockwell's alibi for the night of the shooting could indicate that Rockwell had planned to use Luana's parents as witnesses.

It is appropriate here to point out that while Dr. Boggs appears convinced of Rockwell's guilt and gives the impression the Mormon was under suspicion from the first, eight days after the shooting a citizens' committee comprised of Samuel D. Lucas, ex-Gov. Boggs's close friend and political advisor and a militia major-general during the turmoil in Jackson County, S. H. Woodson, Wilson Roberts, John King, and Lewis Jones, advertised in the *Jeffersonian Republican* (Jefferson City, Missouri), May 14, 1842, a $500 reward for the arrest and conviction of: "A spare, well built man, about 5 feet 8 inches high, thin visage, pale complexion, regular features, keen, black eye, and remarkably long, slender hand; had on when last seen, a half worn brown or grey beaverteen frock coat, a warm cloth vest, boots considerably worn, and dark drab, smooth cast broad brim hat. He landed at Owen's landing, Jackson county, off the steamboat Rowena, on the 27th day of April, and departed on the same boat, on the 29th of the same month, for Lexington, Mo., and on the evening of the assassination, was seen in the vicinity of Independence — which with many other corroborating circumstances, leaves no doubt of his guilt. When first in Independence he called himself Tompkins, and professed to be a silver-smith by occupation. He is quite talkative, and has the appearance of an eastern man. He is about 38 or 40 years of age." Despite the committee's conviction that Tompkins was the malefactor, the *Jeffersonian Republican*, May 21, 1842, reported that the "professed silversmith" had been "fully acquitted and exculpated from all suspicion." See Monte B. McLaws: "The Attempted Assassination of Missouri's Ex-Governor, Lilburn W. Boggs," *Missouri Historical Review*, Vol. LX (October 1965), pp. 50–62.

[37] For more on John Cook Bennett consult Dale L. Morgan, "A Bibliography of the Church of Jesus Christ of Latter Day Saints [Strangite]," *Western Humanities*

Despite the inconvenience of remaining in seclusion when his very personality resisted confinement, Joseph continued his work with only slight hindrance. Yet his bubbling spirit suffered, and he frequently found himself in the depths of melancholy. On one such occasion the prophet fought depression by busying himself with temporal matters of his spiritual kingdom. These included such mundane chores as logging entries into his Book of the Law of The Lord. Here were recorded Joseph's faithful friends "of such as have stood by me in every hour of peril, for these fifteen long years past." High on the list of devoted followers the prophet penned the name of Orrin Porter Rockwell, "who is now a fellow-wanderer with myself, an exile from his home, because of the murderous deed, and infernal, fiendish dispositions of the indefatigable and unrelenting hand of the Missourians. He is an innocent and a noble boy. May God Almighty deliver him from the hands of his pursuers. He was an innocent and noble child and my soul loves him. Let this be recorded for ever and ever. Let the blessings of salvation and honor be his portion." [38]

Depressed, Rockwell journeyed to Philadelphia after unsuccessfully searching for work in Indiana and Ohio, but his real wish was to return home to be with his children. For some time prior to his flight from Illinois, Luana had been cooling toward him, feeling that his devotion to Joseph and the church surpassed his affection for her. Faced with a choice, Rockwell put his wife aside and out of his mind. She left him. The children, as was Mormon custom, stayed within the church; Rockwell had turned them over to the care of his mother. Now, in a strange

---

Review, Vol. V (Winter, 1950–51), pp. 40–41, and Ralph V. Chamberlin, *The University of Utah, A History of Its First Hundred Years, 1850 to 1950* (Salt Lake City, 1960), pp. 577–78. Morgan describes Bennett as "something of a wayward genius," and Chamberlin points out that he had a marked interest in founding colleges. Among his other accomplishments Bennett excelled in mathematics and acquired a knowledge of the classical languages. Yet, this man, who consistently rose to positions of leadership and prominence in whatever he undertook, persisted in his ventures into organized religion in expounding what can only be described as a doctrine of free love. Bennett's role in the poultry world, during the dawning of "the century of the chicken," is extolled by Page Smith and Charles Daniel in *The Chicken Book, Being An Inquiry Into The Rise And Fall, Use and Abuse, Triumph And Tragedy of Gallus Domesticus* (Boston–Toronto, 1975), p. 207. The Boston Poultry Show held in November 1849 was Bennett's inspiration and attracted more than ten thousand spectators "through the Public Gardens to inspect 1,023 birds of all breeds and varieties." Further, the authors remarked, ". . . what July 4, 1776, and George Washington are to Americans in their capacity as citizens of the Republic, November 14, 1849, and Dr. John Bennett are to all Americans infatuated with chickens."

[38] *History of the Church*, Vol. V, p. 125.

city, the youngsters were uppermost in his thoughts. At first opportunity, he sought out a Pennsylvania Mormon he could trust to act as his amanuensis. Shortly thereafter, Joseph received the following letter dated December 1, 1842:

> DEAR BROTHER JOSEPH SMITH — I am requested by our friend Orrin Porter to drop a few lines informing you that he is in this place [Philadelphia]. His health is good, but his spirits are depressed, caused by his being unable to obtain employment of any kind. He has applied in different parts of the city and country, but all without success, as farmers can get persons to work from sunrise till dark for merely what they eat.
>
> He is most anxious to hear from you, and wishes you to see his mother and the children and write all the particulars, how matters and things are, and what the prospects are. I pity him from the bottom of my heart. His lot in life seems marked with sorrow, bitterness and care. He is a noble, generous friend. But you know his worth; any comments from me would be superfluous. He will wait in this place until he hears from you. Please write immediately, as it will be a source of great comfort to him to hear [from you].
>
> If Joseph is not home Brother Whitney will be kind enough to write. [The letter was superscribed to Newel K. Whitney for transmittal to the prophet.] He [Rockwell] says every other one [Mormon] he has come across has been afraid of their shadows . . . . Answer this as soon as received.
>
> Yours truly,
/s/ S. Armstrong
for Orrin Porter[39]

Joseph's reply to his friend's entreaty, if any, cannot be found.[40] Ironically, nothing would have better suited the purposes of both men than to have their situations reversed at that moment. While Rockwell struggled with recurring pangs of homesickness, Joseph contemplated a change of scenery — Wisconsin, perhaps. He discarded the idea, however, when a new governor, Thomas Ford, was elected to succeed Carlin. Ford, an affable but ineffectual leader, inherited a state government torn by indecision, incompetence, and corruption, teetering on the edge of bankruptcy. Among other serious difficulties facing the new chief executive,

---

[39] *Millennial Star*, Vol. XX, p. 215.

[40] A diligent search of the Journal History, Joseph's correspondence for the period, and other letterbooks in the LDS Church Historical Department in Salt Lake City failed to unearth any answer to the Armstrong letter.

he was forced to cope with such problems as: "A debt of near fourteen millions of dollars had been contracted for the canal, railroads, and other purposes. The currency of the State had been annihilated; there was not over two or three hundred thousand dollars in good money in the pockets of the whole people, which occasioned a general inability to pay taxes." [41] With his energies thus occupied, Ford was not in the least anxious to engage in unnecessary controversies involving religious groups or niggling Missouri warrants. After voicing an opinion that Boggs's writ for Joseph was illegal, Ford neatly sidestepped further entanglement by expressing doubt that he had authority to interfere with the actions of his predecessor. He suggested that the entire matter be placed before the Circuit Court of Illinois for a decision. Joseph agreed.

Prophesying, "In the name of the Lord, I shall not go to Missouri — dead or alive!" Joseph took the precaution of ordering a contingent of Mormons to Springfield in case the verdict went against him. He need not have bothered. Judge Nathaniel Pope held that Boggs's affidavit had been drafted in legal language so nebulous as to be worthless. He also contended that Boggs's opinions were not "authority," that the evidence referred to in the affidavit had not been included, and that Boggs's suspicions were "light and unsatisfactory." Commenting on his decision, Judge Pope explained: "The proceedings in this affair, from the affidavit to the arrest, afford a lesson to governors and judges whose action may hereafter be invoked in cases of this character." The magistrate then ordered the Mormon prophet discharged from arrest.[42]

It was an exuberant Joseph Smith who returned to Nauvoo on January 10, 1843, cheered by his elated followers. In celebration of his victory, the prophet issued a dinner invitation to the Council of Twelve Apostles. Brigham Young, president of the council, took the opportunity to declare a day of thanksgiving on the part of the Saints for the deliverance of their leader. Brigham added in his proclamation that Joseph "has been recently obliged to expend large sums of money in procuring his release from unjust persecution, leaving him destitute . . . ." The apostle suggested that collections be taken for the prophet's benefit. "*A word to the wise is sufficient*," Young concluded.[43]

[41] Ford, *History of Illinois*, p. 278.

[42] Proceedings of Joseph's hearing before Judge Pope are reported in *The Wasp*, January 28, 1843, and *History of the Church*, Vol. V, pp. 220–44.

[43] *History of the Church*, Vol. V, p. 249; italics supplied.

Eight hundred and fifty miles to the east, a despondent, weary Rockwell shut his carpetbag and trudged out of his cheaply furnished Philadelphia room on another search for work. By February, a month later, he had scoured New Jersey from one end to the other without a flicker of success. Disgusted with the role of fugitive, Rockwell threw caution to the winds, faced about, and stepped out toward Nauvoo and home — Boggs and his warrants be damned! With the few dollars he had left, he headed for the Erie Canal.

On March 4, 1843, a big paddle-wheeler splashed to a shuddering standstill at the St. Louis riverboat landing. Rockwell walked down the gangplank and gazed across the river toward Illinois. He would board a ferry and be back among his friends in a few days. So engrossed was he that he did not notice the stranger approach.

"Orrin Porter Rockwell, I arrest you on a charge of assault with intent to kill Lilburn W. Boggs — just keep your hands right there where I can see them — the reward poster says 'Dead or Alive.' "

Chapter Five

LEG IRONS AND VERMIN

ROCKWELL CURSED HIMSELF FOR A FOOL. After nine years of constant vigil against Missourians, he had let himself be caught in broad daylight like a country clod. The man named Fox jammed the snout of a pistol against the small of Rockwell's back and motioned him forward; a second man walked quickly from the shadows of a warehouse doorway to join them. Elias Parker cast a nervous glance at Fox's prisoner. "That's him, that's Rockwell!" [1]

Under Fox's watchful eye and steady gun hand, the Mormon was herded before a St. Louis magistrate, where Parker swore that their captive was the O. P. Rockwell named in Missouri reward posters as Boggs's assailant. The judge ordered Rockwell tossed into the county jail until arrangements could be made to transfer him to Independence for trial. Fox chained a pair of iron shackles to Rockwell's ankles; he was taking no chance of losing the famous Destroying Angel, the man every bounty hunter in three states was licking his lips to catch. Three thousand dollars was too much money to risk in a moment of carelessness, and from what Fox had heard of his quarry, Rockwell was no man to take for granted. In Nauvoo, Joseph, upon hearing of his friend's capture, prophesied "in the name of the Lord Jesus Christ, that Orrin Porter Rockwell will get away honorably from the Missourians." [2] But for Rockwell, prophesying was one thing, getting away honorably was something else again.

---

[1] Details of Rockwell's arrest, imprisonment, and subsequent release used here are, except where otherwise noted, taken from his own account in *Millennial Star*, Vol. XXII, pp. 517–20 and 535–36.

[2] *History of the Church*, Vol. V, p. 305.

He was confined to a cell for two days before Fox returned for him — and then in the middle of the night. Hampered by his leg irons, Rockwell had difficulty climbing into a stagecoach waiting in front of the jail. He was roughly shoved into the presence of seven other passengers, two of them women, and dumped unceremoniously into a jump seat. Sullen stares greeted his appearance, and several men muttered angrily about having to accompany a "Mormon assassin" to Independence. Scarcely had the coach jogged into motion when Rockwell was punched sharply in the back by one of the men sitting behind him. Again and again the jabs came, until finally Rockwell broke the tight-lipped silence which had marked his demeanor since the afternoon of his capture. "It's dark and I can't see you, but you're no gentleman," he said grimly. One of the women leaned over and whispered something to Rockwell's antagonist; the harassment ceased.

Clattering across the countryside that night and all the next day, the coach paused only to change horses before halting, well after sundown, at a roadside inn for a brief rest. The respite was gratefully accepted by the passengers, stiff and sore from the long miles in the cramped, over-crowded coach. While the others consoled themselves in exchanging critical observations concerning overland travel, Fox busied himself checking Rockwell's shackles for the dozenth time. The stage driver made his way to the bar for "a drop of something to cut the dust"; he succeeded in the short time at hand in swallowing enough "Missouri white lightnin' " to reduce an ordinary man to complete stupefaction. But somehow he managed to board the Concord and assume his position behind the reins. When the coach lurched forward, it had trouble keeping the road. Less than a mile passed beneath its wheels before the driver guided his lead span directly into a tree, stunning the animals, overturning the coach, and shearing its kingpin bolt in the bargain.

Manacled as he was, Rockwell extricated himself from the vehicle, crawled into the boot, located a spare bolt, and succeeded in replacing the damaged pin in the black of night. The other passengers helped right the stage and planted the unconcerned driver back in his seat. Once the horses had regained their senses, the coach again set out. Inside the Concord, Rockwell dozed peacefully, but in the next moment was catapulted from his seat and sent flying against the two men opposite him. All was chaos within the coach as it veered crazily, then crashed with bone-snapping force into an embankment.

84

Again Rockwell surveyed the situation. The carriage was wedged against the hillside, but had sustained little actual damage. Glancing at the driver, dead drunk and unconscious, Rockwell turned to his fellow travelers and offered to drive if he were unshackled. Fox protested, but the others, anxious to continue their journey, shouted him down.

Encumbered by his chains, which Fox flatly refused to remove, Rockwell climbed into the driver's seat. He managed to ease the understandably skittish horses forward and coax them to the next station on the Osage River, where Fox saw to it that his prisoner was lodged securely in the Jefferson City jail until a new driver could be found to finish the run. This done, the pair rode on to Boonville, where two days later they overtook an army officer who had begun the trip with them at St. Louis but who had ridden ahead from Jefferson City. The three men completed the passage to Independence together.

Sheriff Reynolds was waiting at the stage station when the coach wheeled in. Motioning to the army officer, the lawman ordered, "Come with me, Rockwell." Then, addressing the Mormon, "Did he give you any trouble?" Fox interrupted. "That one isn't Rockwell, this one is!" Unabashed, Reynolds quipped, "I swear, the other fellow looks guiltier than any of you." The sheriff guided Rockwell and his captor through a crowd gathered at the stage office. Shouts of, "Hang him. Hang the Mormon!" encouraged others: "String him up! Save the county some money!" But Reynolds was able to keep them in check until he placed Rockwell under lock and key.

Days passed before he finally was taken before a justice of the peace, but not until he had faced another mob at the courthouse. This time the Missourians were armed with hickory clubs. Again they threatened a lynching, and again Reynolds and his deputies succeeded in scattering them. While the lawman dealt with leaders of the mob, youngsters ran from the crowd to kick and spit at the chained man.

Inside the courtroom, Fox was the state's star witness. He told the justice that Rockwell denied having been in Missouri for at least five years, a statement which brought the prisoner shouting from his chair: "That's a damn lie. Everybody knows I've been in Independence off and on during that time." His outburst was cut short by the angry bang of the judge's gavel. Rockwell in later years was convinced he had been the victim of a conspiracy. "Fox lied so that he and Elias Parker could get their hands on the reward money." The magistrate chose to believe Fox and ordered Rockwell remanded to district court "without bail" — a safety measure, he said, since he feared the townspeople would hang the Mormon if he were permitted to walk free in the city.

Flanked by deputies, Rockwell was led to the cell which was to be his home during the daylight hours. By night he languished in a basement dungeon. A pile of foul-smelling, urine-soaked straw served as his bed; he was not permitted a fire. Each day the routine was repeated without variation — at nightfall, the dungeon; at daybreak, the second-floor cell. "For eighteen days," Rockwell recalled, "I shook from the cold. Finally I got permission to buy some charcoal which I put into an old kettle and lighted. When that was gone, they wouldn't let me have more."

As he studied his dismal surroundings and wondered if the prophet knew he had been captured, Rockwell regretted having given up his weapons to the two men who had approached him in the St. Louis jail. They had identified themselves as Joseph Wood and R. S. Blennarhasset. Both claimed to be lawyers; Wood said he was an apostate Mormon. The two suggested that Rockwell turn his property over to them for "safekeeping." Otherwise it would be confiscated by Sheriff Reynolds, they said. With no one else to rely on, Rockwell had reluctantly told Fox to give the men his pair of pistols, a bowie knife, and his watch; it was the last Rockwell would ever see of the two "lawyers" or his belongings.[3]

In the days and weeks that followed, Rockwell was given a few old newspapers to peruse, which his occasional cellmates read aloud to him. He also found amusement in watching people stroll by on the street below his daylight quarters. Once in a while he would receive a small basket of food from a friendly family living near a corner of the jail. One day their small Negro servant girl pushed a Missouri whipstock through the grated window, along with a ball of twine. In a rare burst of good humor, Rockwell tied the string to the whip handle and "baited it with a chunk of corn-dodger[4] hard enough to knock down a nigger." He poked the makeshift fishing pole through the bars and commenced angling for "pukes." [5] Unaccustomed to seeing pieces of corn bread dangling from the sky at eye-level, passing Missourians were puzzled, then chagrined to discover they were being made the butt of a joke. The daughters of a minister liv-

---

[3] In *History of the Church*, Vol. V, p. 307, Joseph mentions receiving a letter from "R. S. Blennarhasset, Esq., St. Louis, dated 7th instant, concerning Orrin Porter Rockwell; which I immediately answered." No trace of this letter or Joseph's reply has been found in the LDS Church Historical Department.

[4] A type of corn meal bread.

[5] An Illinois slang term for a Missourian. See Ford, *History of Illinois*, pp. 68–69.

ing directly across the narrow road from the jail laughingly inquired of Rockwell if he had felt any bites.

"Nope," the Mormon roared, "but I've had some glorious nibbles."

A few weeks after Rockwell's arrest, Joseph thought he had struck upon a way to free his friend. Several days earlier a tall, refined-looking man had ridden into Nauvoo and quietly taken lodgings. Once settled he had asked for and received, after being relieved of his weapons, an introduction to Joseph Smith. The stranger identified himself as Joseph H. Jackson and confessed to being a wanted man from Macon, Georgia. He had come to Nauvoo, he explained, for protection from the law. While Joseph digested this information and studied his visitor, Jackson leaned back in his chair and stared at the ceiling. "I can get Rockwell free," he said.

Joseph H. Jackson was playing a deadly game, one which could well cost his life. He had nerve and imagination, this man, but he was a completely amoral adventurer. He had come to the City of Joseph with a dual purpose: to spy for Harmon T. Wilson, a Carthage constable,[6] ostensibly to gather damaging evidence against the Mormons, and to gain what he could as an ally of the Saints using the protection afforded by Wilson's authority. Once he captured Joseph's interest, Jackson hinted that he had influence and powerful friends in Missouri and that freeing Rockwell would be a simple matter for a man of his talents and connections. Jackson later told Wilson that Joseph responded by offering him $3,000 to effect Rockwell's release and "kill old Boggs" in the bargain.[7] Jackson, outfitted by the prophet with a horse, bridle, and saddle, said Joseph urged him to hurry:

> "Now go and perform in the name of God, and let the little fellow out of jail, for my heart bleeds for him." . . . [I went to Missouri] for the purpose of seeing Rockwell, and that I might give a straight account of myself. I found him with a pair of shackles on, and a lion-skin overcoat; looked rather uncouth. There were, however, so many in prison at this time, that I had no opportunity to converse with him. My hope was, that by representing myself as being in the employ of Joe [Smith], and convincing him of that fact, to draw from him a confession that

[6] Jackson claimed he sought revenge on the Mormons for an attempt on his life made in Nauvoo.

[7] Jackson, *Narrative*, p. 7, and *Warsaw Signal*, June 5, 1844.

might be useful for the purposes which Harmon T. Wilson and myself had in view.[8]

Jackson's perfidy eventually was discovered, but not until he had caused great mischief within the church. The prophet ultimately came to the realization that if Rockwell were to be freed, it would have to be without his help. Joseph was powerless to act in Illinois and unable to enter Missouri without risking his life. It was therefore with serious misgivings that Joseph reconciled himself to putting Rockwell's unhappy predicament from his mind.

April had given way to May before Rockwell experienced a break in the dull monotony of his jail routine; a new prisoner, under suspicion of stealing United States Treasury bonds,[9] was placed in the same cell with him to await a hearing.[10] Unlike most maximum security inmates,

[8] Jackson, *Narrative*, pp. 7–8.

[9] In later recounting his jail adventures, Rockwell identified his cellmate as a counterfeiter. The man, "Watson," was for a short time a member of Sir William Drummond Stewart's planned hunting expedition to the Rocky Mountains, but was arrested at Stewart's Camp William some two miles outside Westport, Missouri. Charges were lodged against him for stealing and altering United States bonds; it is likely that Rockwell was entirely unaware of his new companion's background. See letter from Matthew C. Field to the *New Orleans Daily Picayune*, June 7, 1843. See also Matthew C. Field, *Prairie and Mountain Sketches*, collected by Clyde and Mae Reed Porter, edited by Kate L. Gregg and John Francis McDermott (Norman, Oklahoma, 1957), pp. 18–19.

[10] Matthew C. Field, one-time actor and in 1843 an assistant editor of the *Picayune*, also was a member of the Stewart hunting party and had befriended "Watson." After the young man's arrest, Field and a few friends visited him in Independence Jail where they also met Rockwell, who had become a celebrity of sorts. Here is Field's account:

> . . . He is a man of fair proportions and good looks, apparently about twenty-eight or thirty. His eye has in it something between cunning and insanity, but you look in vain for any indication of the desperate and determined villain. He was laughing joyously during the whole period of our visit and replied in a merry and nonsensical manner, which we were told had marked him ever since his arrest; whether assumed or not, it may, perhaps, be difficult to determine. One of our companions from St. Louis who was present on the occasion bears the precise cognomen of the Mormon Prophet, Joseph Smith, and we presented him before Rockwell as the "Great Latter Day Saint," *junior*, at which the Mormon prisoner laughed prodigiously; but his cunning, roving eye was scanning intently everybody present, and it seemed clear that there was no soul in the merriment he affected. He was heavily ironed and when we moved to go, he quietly descended to his cell with his only companion, Watson. The Mormons, who were supposed to have been gathered about Independence, to effect the release of this man, have either dispersed or are carrying on their operations so secretly as to excite no attention, for little mention is now made of the subject.

Field to the *Picayune*, June 7, 1843; Field, *Prairie and Mountain Sketches*, pp. 19–20.

the new arrival, by some oversight, had been permitted to retain his belongings, a circumstance which commanded the Mormon's immediate and undivided attention. After exchanging the usual amenities, Rockwell, with a forced nonchalance, inquired as to the possible contents of his cell-mate's saddlebags. In answer the man casually relinquished the pouches and busied himself bunching a straw pallet. Quickly emptying the bags on the cell floor, Rockwell pawed through the contraband with excited anticipation as his new companion watched in amused curiosity. Rockwell could hardly keep from shouting when he discovered several gunflints and fire steels among the newcomer's possessions. He grabbed a steel and began furiously filing away at the links on his leg irons. As he worked, Rockwell rapidly sketched a plan of escape for the stranger's benefit. That night the Negro servant girl was called to the cell window and presented with a bank note by the jail's latest tenant. She returned later and slipped a knife through the grating. Two days passed before Rockwell succeeded in severing the last link on his shackles. The two men now were ready to make a break!

It was nearly dusk when the jailer came to pick up the supper dishes. He was paying little attention to his prisoners, when suddenly they pushed past him and sprinted into the corridor. Rockwell turned, slammed the oaken door, shot the bolt, and gave the key a twist. For good measure he tossed the key through a nearby window opening on the jailyard garden. Scrambling down the stairway, the two men bumped squarely into the turnkey's wife. "We've only locked him in; he's not hurt!" Rockwell shouted as he ran by.

The fugitives fled through a back door into the yard and came face-to-face with a twelve-foot-high board fence. Rockwell made a running leap at it, clutched the top, and after an agonizing moment of uncertainty, pulled himself over. He had covered only a short distance when he heard his companion call out, "I can't make it — help me over!" Rockwell cast a quick look about, ran back and lifted the prisoner to the fence top by his shirt collar.

Confinement during the past weeks had taken its toll; the unfamiliar fresh air soon made the Mormon's head reel. Sucking wind noisily, he slackened his pace, but by now the jailer's cries for help had attracted passers-by, who summoned the sheriff. Rallying his deputies, Reynolds easily overtook the panting Rockwell and within minutes had captured the second man. "If I hadn't stopped to help him," Rockwell gasped, "I would've been free."

Embarrassed by the jailbreak, Reynolds lost his temper and pushed Rockwell into the gathering crowd of angry spectators. "There he is, god damn him! Do what you damn please with him!" the lawman shouted.

Smallwood Nowland, a notorious Mormon-hater, stepped forward and prodded the crowd. "Somebody get a rope." A Mexican, emboldened by Nowland's harangue, reached out for the prisoner but quickly retreated when Rockwell turned on him. "Touch me and I'll mash your damned face in!"

Sobered by the crowd's violent reaction, Reynolds pulled Rockwell away and marched both prisoners back to their cell, the crowd following until the room and hallway were choked with spectators. Rockwell surrendered the fire steels he had used, but as he fumbled through the saddle bags for them, his hands felt a small buckskin pouch filled with pistol balls. He palmed the shot bag without being discovered; if others intended a hanging, at least a few would feel the weight of the lead-filled pouch across their faces. Rockwell had no sooner tucked the bag into his belt than Reynolds caught sight of a rope being passed over the heads of the crowd toward the prisoners.

"There'll be no lynching!" Reynolds shouted. He barked an order and the deputies pulled their pistols. Cocking hammers echoed through the small cell, dampening the mob fervor. Once in control of the situation, Reynolds ordered the jail cleared of spectators.

To ensure against another escape, the sheriff ordered Rockwell taken to the basement dungeon and chained; this time the irons were fastened from his right ankle to his left wrist and from his left ankle to his right wrist. So manacled, the man was unable to straighten to a standing position. He later recalled, "When they put those irons on my wrists, they were so small they could hardly close them. My wrists swelled they were so tight. But in eighteen days I could slip the irons up and turn them around my arm at the elbow."

If Rockwell's food had been poor before, what followed could only be described as hog slop. His diet consisted of cold corn-dodger and scraps of meat left from the jailer's dinner. At first he refused to eat, hoping the quality of food would improve, but to his frustration he found that whatever remained of his uneaten meal of the day was returned the following evening. As the weeks passed the once husky Mormon wasted away until he was little more than an apparition. His hair grew long and shaggy, infested with vermin from his dank, tomb-like cell; his beard became matted with sweat and dirt; his eyes sank into the dark hollows of his face. Only the glitter of his gaze betrayed the intensity of his inner spirit.

Reynolds was unconcerned. Prior to the escape attempt, the sheriff had written Joseph a letter:

> Sir, At the request of Orrin Porter Rockwell, who is now confined to our jail, I write you a few lines concerning his affairs. He is held to bail in the sum of $5,000, and wishes some of his friends to bail him out. He also wishes some friend to bring his clothes to him. He is in good health and pretty good spirits. My own opinion is, after conversing with several persons here, that it would not be safe for any of Mr. Rockwell's friends to come here, not withstanding I have written the above at his request; neither do I think bail would be taken (unless it was some responsible person well known here as a resident of this State). Any letter for Mr. Rockwell, (post-paid) with authority expressed on the back for me to open it, will be handed to him without delay. In the meantime he will be humanely treated and dealt with kindly until discharged by due process of law.[11]

Reynolds' concept of humane treatment apparently had undergone a radical change in the month since he had penned the letter to Nauvoo. The sheriff had been receiving a quantity of mail over the past weeks from the Mormon stronghold in Illinois. Written by certain of Joseph's enemies, the letters informed Reynolds that the prophet placed unquestioned confidence in Rockwell. The possibility that he had the key to Joseph Smith's downfall locked in his basement intrigued the Missouri lawman to the point of his offering the prisoner a deal.

"Get Smith out on the prairie where we can lay our hands on him and you can name your pile," Reynolds propositioned. "Whatever it is, Jackson County will raise it." Rockwell studied his captor in silence, then grinned in his grimy beard. "I'll see you all damned first — and then I won't."

It was a reply Reynolds had half expected. He sneered at his chained captive. "Then you can rot. We'll get him without you."

While Rockwell struggled with the problem of warning Joseph that danger threatened, Reynolds prepared to make good his boast to capture the prophet. According to Reynolds' Nauvoo informants, Joseph was planning a trip to Dixon, Illinois, to preach. That would be the place to snare him, Reynolds decided. It was a location far from Nauvoo and his bodyguards. The sheriff's only concern was whether or not his intelligence

---

[11] *Millennial Star*, Vol. XX, p. 806; the letter was dated April 7, 1843.

was correct. A slip-up would put the prophet on his guard, and Reynolds knew another opportunity to net him might not offer itself.

Joseph arrived in Dixon on the 23rd of June. He had put up with some relatives named Wasson and was in the backyard of their home when two men identifying themselves as Mormon elders asked Mrs. Wasson if they could see "Brother Joseph." The two "elders" were Reynolds and the Carthage constable Harmon T. Wilson in disguise. It was Wilson who spotted their man. Pressing a cocked pistol against Joseph's chest, Reynolds warned, "God damn you, if you stir, I'll shoot." [12]

Once the prophet was under arrest Reynolds had planned to spirit him across the river into Missouri before word of his capture leaked out. But the two officers were seen by a Mormon, Stephen Markham, as they pulled their weapons, and Markham hurried off to obtain a writ of habeas corpus. Meanwhile, Joseph managed with the aid of friends in Dixon to swear out a complaint against the two lawmen for assault and threatening his life, whereupon the surprised officers found themselves under arrest. The following morning, in a desperate effort to stall for time until help arrived, Joseph swore out a second complaint charging Reynolds and Wilson with false imprisonment and claiming $10,000 in damages. By now the situation had become hopelessly confused; no one knew who was arresting whom.

Reynolds and Wilson were able to obtain a writ of habeas corpus and once again ordered Joseph to head for Missouri. The party had gone as far as Pawpaw Grove when, much to the consternation of his captors, the prophet abruptly accepted an invitation to preach to the local citizenry. The sight of a large crowd gathering did little to quiet their rattled nerves, and Reynolds made the mistake of ordering the congregation to disperse. His words had less than the desired effect, for David Town, an aged country squire, tottered forward with the aid of a huge hickory walking stick and exploded in Reynolds' face. "You damned infernal puke! We'll learn you to come down here and interrupt gentlemen." Waving his cane at a nearby chair, he yelled, "Sit down there and sit still. Don't open your head till General Smith gets through talking!"

When Reynolds started to protest, Town cut him short. "If you never learned manners in Missouri, we'll teach you that gentlemen are not to be

[12] *Times and Seasons*, Vol. IV, No. 16 (July 1843), p. 242; *History of the Church*, Vol. V, p. 440. Joseph D. Wasson was Emma Smith's nephew.

imposed upon by a nigger-driver! You can't kidnap men here, as you do in Missouri; and if you attempt it here, there's a committee in this grove that will sit on your case; and, sir, it is the highest tribunal in the United States, as *from its decision there is no appeal!*" [13]

Reynolds quietly took the chair and listened in stony silence as Joseph spoke for an hour and a half on the merits of his marriage. As it turned out, the prophet's delaying tactics proved successful. The retinue was forced to return to Dixon when a magistrate was unavailable in Pawpaw Grove. Joseph subsequently was joined by more than one hundred of his toughest Nauvoo Legionnaires. At this juncture it was the prophet's wish that they proceed to Nauvoo; under the circumstances, Reynolds and Wilson were in a poor position to disagree. Once in his stronghold, Joseph was master of the situation. He quickly obtained a writ of habeas corpus from the Municipal Court and was ordered released from custody. Shaken to the core by their experience, the two lawmen left Nauvoo without their man — but threatened to return at the head of the state militia. His request for military assistance was denied by Governor Ford, however, and Reynolds departed for Independence.

When Rockwell in his dungeon heard of the sheriff's ignominious defeat, he breathed a sigh of relief while his thoughts drifted back to a

[13] *History of the Church*, Vol. V, p. 445. David Town was the leader of a committee which had protected settlers on public domain from being victimized by land speculators; his remarks to Sheriff Reynolds alluded to the verdict of lynch justice. Italics in original. Some idea of just how emotional the Mormon issue had become between the citizens of Illinois and Missouri can be formed from a letter written July 23, 1843, by J. Hall of Independence to "a respectable lawyer" of Dixon, Illinois, in which Hall confides, "Missouri will have Jo Smith for trial or impose as powerful restrictions as the Constitution will allow upon the intercourse of the citizens of Illinois in Missouri. If the governor of Illinois is so imbecile as to allow his warrant to be disregarded by the Mormons, and permit the Prophet to go at large, then let him be impeached, and a new, honorable, energetic man will be placed in his stead. I have it from a high source that Missouri will hold the whole state responsible for the treatment of our messenger [Reynolds], and for the delivery of the Prophet." Hall also had some comments about Missouri justice and Orrin Porter Rockwell: "I will now give you an impartial opinion of the prejudices against Rockwell here, and my opinion of his guilt. There is not a man in this community [Independence] but believes him guilty. There is a chain of circumstances against him so strong that no rational man can doubt his guilt. I was at Boggs' house two minutes after the deed; it is in sight of mine; and the incidiousness [*sic*] of the offense renders it difficult to restrain the citizens from hanging him up without judge or jury. So far, however, we have succeeded in quelling it; but should he be discharged upon trial, *the power of man cannot save him.*" Ibid., p. 539. Italics supplied.

strange incident which had occurred shortly after Reynolds had left for
Illinois to carry out his scheme:

> . . . [knowing] they were after him [Joseph], and no means under
> heaven of giving him any information, my anxiety became so intense,
> knowing their determination to kill him, that my flesh twitched upon
> my bones. I could not help it; twitch it would. While undergoing this
> sensation, I heard a dove alight on the window in the upper room in
> the jail, and commence cooing, and then went off. In a short time, he
> came back to the window, where a pane was broken; he crept through
> between the bars of iron, which were about two and a half inches apart.
> I saw it fly around the trap-door several times; it did not alight, but
> continued cooing until it crept through the bars again, and flew out
> through the broken window.
>
> I relate this, as it was the only occurrence of the kind that hap-
> pened during my long and weary imprisonment; but it proved a com-
> fort to me; the twitching of my flesh ceased, and I was fully satisfied
> from that moment that they would not get Joseph into Missouri, and
> that I should regain my freedom. . . .[14]

Months passed before finally, in August, Rockwell was unchained and
brought before Judge John F. Ryland's Circuit Court, where he was told
that a grand jury had refused to bring an indictment against him. Rockwell's elation at hearing the news was short-lived; the judge informed him
that a true bill had been returned by the grand jury for "escaping jail," [15]
to which Rockwell immediately entered a plea of not guilty. Since he was
penniless, the Mormon was permitted to select an attorney from those
gathered in the courtroom on other matters. "Take your choice," the
judge said.

Scanning the room Rockwell noticed a familiar face, that of Alexander Doniphan, the man who had represented the Saints in their legal
difficulties during the old Jackson County days, the same man who had
headed a militia column against the Mormons in the final stand at Far
West.

"How about him?" Rockwell asked, pointing to the attorney.

At this Doniphan stood and, addressing the court, explained that he
was crowded with work and suggested that there were other young lawyers equally as capable of handling Rockwell's case. Brushing aside Doni-

---

[14] *Millennial Star*, Vol. XXII, p. 535.

[15] Circuit Court Records, Jackson County, Missouri, August Term, Book E,
1843, p. 166.

phan's objections, the judge told the defendant he could consider himself represented by counsel. Doniphan shrugged and told his new client he would do what he could but promised nothing. Rockwell was returned to his cell to contemplate his absurd quandary: He was free of one charge, only to be tried for escaping jail when the law admitted he should not have been jailed at all. Three days later Doniphan visited Rockwell and explained that Judge Ryland had granted a change of venue to Clay County where, the attorney hoped, a trial could be conducted with less prejudice against Mormons.[16]

When the sheriff's two deputies came to transfer Rockwell to Liberty Jail in Clay, they made it abundantly clear that it was a task they considered most unpleasant. There was talk around Independence of mob violence if Rockwell was removed from his cell, and the deputies were dismayed at the prospect of protecting the prisoner from their friends and neighbors. Ignoring orders to hurry, Rockwell, who had been denied a change of linen for five months, took the opportunity to shed himself of his rags — and the pests with which he shared them. "I'll wear a clean shirt to Clay if it costs me my life," he announced.

Once dressed, the Mormon was herded to a "very hard-trotting horse with a miserable poor saddle." He sat tight-lipped as his ankles were roped together beneath the animal and his hands lashed behind his back. Risking no chance of alerting Rockwell's enemies, the trio galloped the six miles to the ferry which would take them across the Missouri River into Clay. They arrived in time to see the boat dock on the opposite shore and discharge several men who made straight for the woods. Rockwell and his two guardians exchanged wary glances as the ferryman explained that his previous fares were planning to "hew timber" — a difficult task without axes, and the mysterious men had not been carrying any tools.

[16] Ibid., pp. 196–98.

Keeping a careful watch, the party — which now numbered four with the addition of a stranger who had joined them aboard the ferry — trotted along the tree-lined trail to Liberty. An uneasy stillness pervaded the forest, heightening the suspicions of Rockwell and the two officers. Cautiously they quickened their pace. The quartet was a full three miles into the woods when they first heard the sound of crackling underbrush and men forcing through a back trail. In a breath the deputies whipped their mounts to a full gallop and raced down the road; Rockwell lurched in the saddle as one of the lawmen reached over and landed a stinging crop lash across the flank of his horse. Only when they were safely out of the woods did the riders rein up their foaming animals. The thoroughly frightened stranger listened apprehensively as his companions told him of their mission, then gasped out a story of having overheard several toughs in an Independence saloon plotting to waylay "a Mormon" in the thick timber of the Missouri bottomlands. The scheme had apparently backfired when the conspirators spotted the stranger, who could have identified them, in the company of the law and its prisoner.

Rockwell's transfer to Clay County was in vain, however, for the local magistrate denied him a trial on the basis of a discrepancy in the legal papers ordering the change of venue.[17] After ten days in Liberty Jail, Rockwell was returned to Independence, escaping a second attempt on his life when his escort of guards changed the route at the last minute. In his old cell once again, the routine of past months repeated itself — leg irons and foul food for the next sixty days, until the latter part of October. He now had been in custody for seven months, most of it in chains.

October held a surprise for Rockwell, however: His mother came to visit him unexpectedly. Fearing that their conversation would be overheard, the two huddled in a corner of his dungeon room and spoke in whispers, Rockwell self-consciously attempting to conceal the irons which shackled him, his mother sobbing at the sight of her son's emaciated figure. She committed each word to memory as he carefully phrased a message for Joseph. That very night, distraught and shaken by her experience, Mrs. Rockwell struck out for Illinois, determined to obtain the prophet's aid in freeing her son.

Arriving in Nauvoo, she had little difficulty in seeing Joseph, and her message prompted the prophet to call a special conference of the Saints.[18]

---

[17] Fifth Judicial District Court of Missouri, Record Book G, No. 4, p. 228.

[18] *History of the Church*, Vol. VI, p. 47, and Wandle Mace, "Journal." MS, p. 89.

Bad weather kept many church members indoors on October 6, the day scheduled for the conference. Consequently a one-day postponement in the proceedings was ordered. The session opened with the usual ceremonies, followed by a brief address from Joseph regarding the purpose of the gathering; it was, he said, to discuss Sidney Rigdon and his posture within the church leadership. When Rigdon heard this he was permitted a short preliminary discourse. This done, Joseph again took the speaker's stand and announced that he was dissatisfied with Rigdon's service as a counselor in the First Presidency.

"We have had no material benefit from his labors or counsels since our escape from Missouri," Joseph said.

After a pause, he recited several complaints in respect to Rigdon's management of the mails as Nauvoo's postmaster. Building his case logically, strongly, Joseph heaped it on; he accused his counselor of secretly corresponding with Bennett, ex-Governor Carlin, Sheriff Reynolds, and others in a treacherous maneuver designed to have Joseph arrested or killed, thereby placing Rigdon in the position of First Elder of the church. Carefully measuring the response of his stunned audience, Joseph shouted that Rigdon had deliberately delayed an important document in the mails to hinder the prophet's legal battles. Then he dropped the bomb: Orrin Porter Rockwell's mother, Joseph explained, had returned from Independence with information from Rockwell himself that Rigdon had masterminded Reynolds' attempted arrest and capture of the prophet at Dixon![19] The disclosure threw the meeting into pandemonium. Joseph was grim-faced as he took his seat.

A hush of anticipation cloaked the gathering as Rigdon made his way to the stand. Surprised as he was at Joseph's sudden concentrated attack, Sidney Rigdon was not easily cast aside. His entire life had been spent fighting for one thing or another, and as he shuffled to the rostrum the old man's mind was working with an agility which his frail appearance belied. Opening his defense to Joseph's barrage of charges, Rigdon admitted that a legal document had been delayed, but only because of his illness, he said. He vigorously denied that he had exchanged letters with either Bennett or Reynolds, and he disclaimed any participation or implication in the Dixon incident. At this point in his rebuttal, Rigdon was interrupted by a sudden downpour, and the conference adjourned until the following day. Resuming the stand on the morning of October 8, Rigdon pleaded with the Saints to consider his past relationship with the prophet; he reminded

[19] *History of the Church*, Vol. VI, pp. 47–48.

them that he, too, had shared the trials of Kirtland and Far West and had settled Commerce when it was no more than a swamp. Rigdon's eloquence stood him in good stead; realizing that his impassioned address had excited sympathies in certain of the congregation, Rigdon, with great emotion, turned away and took his seat.

Joseph rose to emphasize his disgust with Rigdon and sat down in anger when several leading members of the church hierarchy came to Rigdon's defense. A motion by William Marks, president of the High Council, that Rigdon be permitted to retain his position as counselor in the First Presidency was seconded by none other than Joseph's brother and patriarch in the church, Hyrum.

The prophet glowered when the Saints approved the motion. He said, *"I have thrown him off my shoulders, and you have again put him on me. You may carry him, but I will not!"* [20]

At the conclusion of the conference, Joseph set out to fulfill his promise to Mrs. Rockwell. Astride his horse, Jo Duncan,[21] the prophet rode to the site of the temple, where workmen were preparing to leave for the day; he waved for them to wait.

"Boys, has Bonaparte any friends in the French Army?" he asked cryptically.[22] Their curiosity aroused, the laborers clustered around the prophet. "For two hundred dollars Porter Rockwell can be released from prison and as I have not sufficient money I need your help." Those who had cash in their pockets turned it over; the others went to their homes for whatever they could spare. Joseph shortly obtained the $200 he had asked for. In later days Rockwell would say, "My mother . . . came to see me and brought me $100, whereby I was enabled to fee Mr. Doniphan for his services."

In his dungeon, Rockwell was contemplating another escape. He had been able, despite his shackles, to remove the stovepipe connecting to the upstairs main floor. Stripping off his clothes, he shoved the garments through the hole and inched his way into the opening in the 14-inch-thick

<hr />

[20] Ibid., p. 49. Italics in original.

[21] Joseph Duncan, governor of Illinois from 1836 to 1838, was the Whig candidate for that same office in 1842 on a bitterly anti-Mormon platform. He was defeated by Thomas Ford, prompting Joseph Smith to comment, "God was asked not to let Joe Duncan be governor, and it was so." Naming his horse after the one-time chief executive was the prophet's way of ridiculing his antagonist.

[22] Related in Mace, "Journal," p. 92.

logs which formed the floor of the upper room. Even in his emaciated condition, Rockwell's shoulders scraped against the sides as he wiggled through the stovepipe hole and into the room. After a quick examination of the inside door, he pulled the handle from a water pail and managed to manipulate the bolt into an open position, but for all his efforts he was unable to open the outside door — the last obstacle to freedom. Failing in this bid for escape, Rockwell wormed his way back into the dungeon and replaced the stovepipe. He would try again another day.

Twenty-four hours later he retraced his route and once more came up against the outer door, which would not yield. He struggled with the lock deep into the night until finally he collapsed exhausted on the floor, to be discovered the following morning by jail personnel. Rockwell's daring attempt caused a great excitement; for punishment he was doubly chained, tossed back into the dungeon, and his meals halved.

Several nights later Doniphan came to see him. A special term of court had been called and would convene in a matter of days. "Meantime, you stay out of trouble and don't give up hope," he said. Two weeks passed before Rockwell's name came up on the calendar. Gaunt, his clothes in tatters, the Mormon eyed the judge warily. It was not Ryland who looked down on him this time, but Austin A. King, the magistrate who had held a hearing on the Saints at Richmond five years before.[23] Rockwell repeated his plea of not guilty, and a jury was impanelled to hear the case. Doniphan attempted to show that the charge of jailbreak was unfounded because under Missouri law an integral part of the crime consisted of breaking a lock, a door, or a wall, none of which Rockwell had done. King, however, ruled that walking through an open door also fell within the limits of the law as defined by him. After careful consideration of the facts, the jury brought in a verdict of guilty — and assessed the punishment at "five minutes confinement in the County Jail." [24]

Even the "five minutes" stretched into five hours while Judge King and Sheriff Reynolds attempted to bring further charges against Rockwell. Frustrated, they were forced to order his release. Shortly before eight o'clock on the morning of December 13, 1843, Orrin Porter Rockwell walked out of Independence Jail, a free man for the first time in nine months.

[23] Fifth Judicial District Court of Missouri, Record Book G, No. 4, p. 236. King was a rabid Mormon-hater because he had lost a brother-in-law, Hugh Brazeale, in the Jackson County war.

[24] Ibid.

His release was one thing; getting back to Nauvoo was another. As Doniphan explained it, Rockwell would have to move across country on foot, avoiding traveled roads in the daylight and maintaining a sharp lookout at night. Rumors were circulating in Jackson County that the Destroying Angel would never leave Missouri alive. Accompanied by his mother, Rockwell started on his homeward journey before noon. Their first stop was at the home of a widow, where Rockwell ate his first meal outside of a cell in months. Dusk found them at the home of a friend, where they were able to borrow $4.00. Here Rockwell decided it would be safer to travel alone. Choosing two return routes, he sent his mother on one and he took the second. Scarcely had they parted company when he heard the sound of horses. Dodging behind a tree, Rockwell watched as two riders galloped by. "He hasn't been gone many minutes; we'll soon overtake him," one man shouted to the other.

Convinced now that he was still a hunted man, Rockwell took to the fields and kept well away from the main roads. By nightfall he had covered twenty-five miles. The following day he passed Crooked River and stopped at a farm to rest and buy food. Examining his feet, Rockwell found he had walked the skin off his soles. After breakfast the next morning, he paid his host fifty cents and was permitted to ride a horse for the next fourteen miles.

Rockwell's line of march took him to the scene of the Haun's Mill massacre, where he stopped briefly to contemplate the tragedy and pledge his word to someday avenge the deaths of his fellow Mormons. By now his feet were raw and bleeding freely, so much so that he was unable to continue under his own power. As he considered his plight, a fellow-traveler came strolling down the road. After some little haggling, the stranger agreed to carry Rockwell on his back the rest of the day for seventy-five cents.

Good fortune joined him, and as night closed in Rockwell reached friendly territory. Even so, his months in prison and his experience with Reynolds had taught him to be doubly careful. With the effects of confinement effectively concealing his identity, Rockwell remained cautiously silent after entering the home of a family who in better days had known him well. Leaving fifty cents for supper, a bed, breakfast, and the use of a horse for the next twelve miles, Rockwell continued his journey at dawn. Thirty miles farther he was forced to stop and "recruit" his feet. He halted for three days before he was again able to travel, and then only on horseback. Mile after mile passed as Rockwell trudged on. "Twenty-five miles by horse and walked the same day twenty-five miles," he later related. It would have been an amazing exploit for a healthy man; it was phenomenal for a man in Rockwell's condition. But determination kept him moving. Forty miles more and he was able to rest; then he hired another man to carry him to Montrose, Iowa, "to which place I was three days in going." His ordeal was nearly at an end. Rockwell paid the last of his $4.00 at the Mississippi ferry and crossed into Illinois. From there he slowly made his way to Nauvoo and Joseph's Mansion House. It was Christmas Day when he arrived.

Fifty couples had accepted the prophet's invitation to dine and dance at his home, celebrating not only the Christmas season, but also Joseph's victories over the forces against him. He had been three times arrested and three times acquitted during the year on charges preferred by the state of Missouri. Bennett had been defeated. And Joseph had successfully weathered the storm of controversy surrounding the doctrine of plural marriage.

Most important, Joseph had secretly decided to become a candidate for the presidency of the United States.

Suddenly the festivities were interrupted by a noisy scuffle at the front door. Members of Joseph's Life Guard were struggling furiously to control what they thought to be a drunken Missourian who was punching and jabbing in every direction. The prophet, resplendent in his Legion costume, pushed through the crowd to the center of the disturbance and ordered the guards to throw the intruder out forcibly. As Joseph turned to walk way he was caught by something familiar in the filthy, disheveled specter of a man whose hair dangled in greasy snarls down his shoulders. For a moment Joseph looked the creature full in the face. It was grinning at him.

"To my great surprise and joy untold," he wrote, "I discovered it was my long-tried, warm, but cruelly persecuted friend, Orrin Porter Rockwell, just arrived from nearly a year's imprisonment, without conviction, in Missouri." [25] For Joseph, his friend's appearance was the fulfillment of his prophecy of March 15 that Rockwell would "honorably escape" the clutches of the Missourians.

Rockwell was the center of attention, and after partaking of a glass of the wine which flowed so freely at the festivities, he sat down with Joseph and a knot of church dignitaries to recount his trials since fleeing Nauvoo.

[25] *History of the Church*, Vol. VI, pp. 134–35.

At the conclusion of the story, the prophet sat silent for several minutes; then, placing his arm around his friend's shoulder, announced for all to hear: "I prophesy, in the name of the Lord, that you — Orrin Porter Rockwell — so long as ye shall remain loyal and true to thy faith, need fear no enemy. Cut not thy hair and no bullet or blade can harm thee!" [26]

Joseph's pronouncement astonished the revelers. They were witnesses to the word of God offering protection from violent death to one of their brethren in a land where a natural demise was unusual. The man known as the Destroying Angel now was the subject of a prophecy which would lionize him as the Samson of the Mormon Church. It mattered little what others thought of Joseph's declaration. Only Rockwell's reaction was important, for it was he who would face "bullet and blade." Rockwell took the prophecy to heart, and except for a single incident, he was destined to wear his locks unshorn for the remainder of his life . . . *and his enemies were powerless against him.*[27]

[26] The story of Joseph's prophecy to Rockwell spread throughout Nauvoo within days, but the prophet's exact words were never recorded. Rockwell himself mentioned the prophecy to his friends and family on many occasions. A journal notation made the following morning which refers to the incident can be found in James Jepson, "Memories and Experiences." MS, pp. 9–10. For additional evidence see Stenhouse, *Rocky Mountain Saints*, p. 140n; Bean, *Autobiography*, p. 175, and Mrs. Elizabeth D. E. Roundy's letter to the LDS Church explaining her part in writing Rockwell's life history at his request. Letter on file in the LDS Church Historical Department.

[27] From this day forward through thirty-five violent years in which Rockwell encountered hostile Indians, desperadoes, and other characters on the western scene, he managed to avoid a single physical injury at the hands of another man.

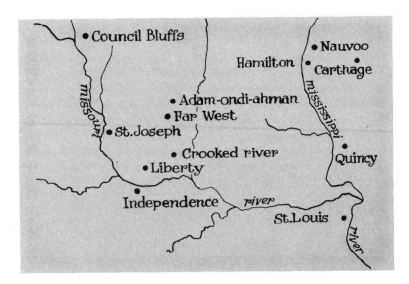

Chapter Six

"THE DEED IS DONE BEFORE THIS TIME"

ROCKWELL'S TRIUMPHANT RETURN from the dungeons of Missouri was greeted by his fellow Saints as a splendid victory of good over evil, a deliverance from the jaws of death suggestive of Old Testament heroes. The *Nauvoo Neighbor*[1] assailed his treatment:

> This demagoguery and political corruption has caused an innocent man to be immolated in a Missouri dungeon for upwards of eight months, without the slightest evidence of his guilt, or even the most remote evidence of crime leading to his committal. He was.taken without process, and committed to jail upon mere supposition, and finally acquitted without any shadow of proof having been adduced from beginning to end. This is the way that Missouri treats free-born American citizens, and they can obtain no redress. . . .[2]

While the *Neighbor* and other newspapers traded volleys over his case, Rockwell began thinking about the future. Here, too, Joseph had plans. In a city where liquor was controlled by the mayor, what better business to be in than tavern-keeping? As a matter of fact, Joseph mused as he glanced at Rockwell's shoulder-length hair, Nauvoo could also use a barbershop. If the two enterprises were combined, the operator of such an establishment would surely make money, especially since the prophet could not hope to accommodate every visitor to the city at his new Mansion House barroom. The idea appealed to Rockwell, and it suited Joseph's plans as well. Consequently, a choice lot directly across the street from the Mansion House was set aside for the purpose, and work was ordered begun on a building to house the saloon and barbershop. In the meantime, Joseph suggested that Rockwell practice his bar-tending at the Mansion House.

---

[1] *The Wasp* was enlarged and its name changed to the *Nauvoo Neighbor* on May 3, 1843.

[2] December 27, 1843.

Emma, Joseph's wife, had been away in St. Louis on a furniture-buying trip. She returned to find the main room filled with guests, the majority of whom were crowded the length of a bright new counter upon which was displayed a variety of liquors; a scrubbed and combed Rockwell held forth behind the bar, busily filling glasses. Emma held her tongue until the visitors had departed, then flew into a tirade. "Joseph, what is the meaning of that bar in this house!" [3]

Dumbfounded by her outburst, Joseph stammered an explanation, only to be cut short. "How does it look for the spiritual head of a religious body to be keeping a hotel in which a room is fitted out as a liquor-selling establishment?"

"But Emma," Joseph pleaded, "All taverns have bars. And this will only be for a short while. It is only being done for Porter's benefit, not mine. He was forced to leave his home—and he was jailed on the charges made against us, while I went free. I am obliged to help him, don't you understand that?"

His words fell on deaf ears.

"Well, Joseph, the furniture and the other goods I have purchased for the house will come, and you can have some other person look after things here. As for me, I will take my children and go across to the old house and stay there, for I will not have them raised under such conditions as this arrangement imposes upon us, nor have them mingle with the kind of men who frequent such a place."

"But Emma —" Joseph interjected.

"You are at liberty to make your own choice. Either that bar goes out of the house, or we will!" she said firmly. Joseph answered without hesitation. "Very well, Emma, I will have it removed at once."

Rockwell, after hearing the prophet's embarrassed recital of his argument with Emma, understood Joseph's dilemma. Declining an apology, he helped Joseph remove the tavern paraphernalia from the house. But now Joseph had another idea. It was just as well that his friend was not tied down; ever since Rockwell's information regarding a conspiracy against the prophet had reached Nauvoo, Joseph had been troubled. As yet he had not been able to identify the plotters, and his life was not safe

[3] This incident is described in detail by Joseph's son, who witnessed the argument between his parents. See *Joseph Smith III and The Restoration*, edited by Mary Audentia Smith Anderson and condensed by Bertha Audentia Anderson Holmes (Independence, 1952), pp. 74–76. See also Gilbert Belnap, "Journal." MS, p. 30.

as long as they were at large. For some time Joseph had been seeking someone he could trust, a person whose loyalty was beyond question and who was equal to the task of protecting him. Since the prophet's very nature rebelled against seclusion, he was continually exposed to an unanticipated act of treachery by a disgruntled disciple. Perhaps Rockwell detected a note of sadness in Joseph's voice, perhaps not. But when the prophet asked him to be his personal bodyguard, Rockwell looked at his friend, and quietly said, "Your enemies are my enemies, Joseph." [4] The conversation ended on a handshake.

[4] If rumors bruited about Nauvoo were true, Orrin Porter Rockwell meant just what he said. It was whispered that he and Joseph Smith had drowned an elderly Mormon woman who gossiped openly about the prophet's private life and was embarrassing high officials of the church with her disclosures.

In *Mormon Portraits*, pp. 47–49, Wilhelm W. Wymetal relates a tale told him by "old Richard Rushton, the faithful steward of the 'Nauvoo Mansion,'" in regard to this alleged murder. According to Wymetal, Rushton was a witness to a conversation between Rockwell and Joseph immediately after the slaying. Wymetal first quotes Rushton as saying that the prophet held a council meeting in his room and decided that the woman "must be silenced at all hazards." After describing the drowning in detail, Wymetal continues, "In less than five minutes after the ceasing of the screams from the drowning victim, the prophet, O. P. Rockwell and two others rushed wildly into the hotel [Mansion House]. The prophet was dripping wet. He was loudly expostulating with 'Port' and the others: 'You should not have drowned her; she couldn't have done us much harm.' 'We had to do it,' was the response [presumably from Rockwell], 'for your safety and our own, as well as for the good of the church. She can't harm us now.' 'I am very sorry;' said the prophet, 'if I had thought of it a few minutes sooner, you wouldn't have drowned Sister - - - - - - -.'" Wymetal gave no reason for suppressing the victim's identity.

Word of such an incident apparently gained wide circulation in the city, for the editors of *Times and Seasons* said in an editorial regarding Joseph's presidential candidacy, ". . . we are not going to either 'murder ex-Governor Boggs' . . . nor 'walk on the water'; nor '*drown a woman*' . . . nor '*marry spiritual wives*' . . . ." See *Times and Seasons*, Vol. V, No. 4 (February 1844), p. 441. Italics supplied. Wymetal made a final effort to obtain evidence of the alleged killing in an interview with William Law, published in the *Salt Lake Tribune*, July 31, 1887. He asked: "Have you ever heard of the old woman that was drowned in the interest of the church?" Law replied: "I have heard of a woman put aside. They said she had been brought over the [Mississippi] river and buried on an island near the shore or on the other shore near the water. But at the time I did not believe a word of rumors of this kind, and did not investigate them."

It should be noted here that Wymetal's obvious attempts to discredit the Mormons place his work under suspicion.

An interesting sidelight on Rockwell's service as Joseph's bodyguard came many years after Porter's death when a patriarch, in bestowing a blessing on Rockwell's fourth wife, Christine, described her husband as one of God's noble sons, and added, "The Lord has been merciful unto him in doing the good deeds that he did, in protecting the life of the Prophet Joseph. The Lord will pass by all his weaknesses, and all is right with him." *Deseret News*, August 31, 1935.

One problem long nagging at the prophet concerned the rapidly tarnishing reputation of Nauvoo the Beautiful. Reports of wholesale thievery continued to spiral despite Joseph's denunciations, and the city had gained for itself the unenviable distinction of having become a haven for freebooters and coiners from up and down the Mississippi. There were whispers of dark deeds in Nauvoo, of men disappearing from the streets without a trace, of bodies dumped into the river at night. Such transactions were disturbing to Joseph; he wanted outsiders to leave the city with a favorable impression of the Mormons. But since the Missouri period he had been unable to completely control the Saints in taking what they pleased. Three years earlier he had addressed a conference and ordered all debts between church members wiped out. At that time he had explained:

> I wish you all to know that because you were justified in taking property from your enemies while engaged in war in Missouri, which was needed to support you, there is now a different condition of things existing. We are no longer at war, and you must stop stealing. When the right time comes we will go in force and take the whole State of Missouri. It belongs to us as our inheritance; but I want no more petty stealing. A man that will steal petty articles from his enemies, will, when occasion offers, steal from his brethren too. Now I command you that you that have stolen, must steal no more. . . .[5]

His counsel had gone unheeded; therefore, Joseph determined to organize a police department to handle the situation, and on December 29, 1843, he announced the forty men who would comprise it.[6] The names necessarily included many of the prophet's Life Guards, but the coincidence provoked talk that Daniteism had come to Nauvoo.

In a burst of energy the city's new constables pursued their duties until Joseph was swamped with cases in Mayor's Court. His decision to polish the face of Nauvoo to its old luster and unmask his secret enemies as well

[5] Lee, *Mormonism Unveiled*, p. 111. Members of a bandit gang uncovered in the town of Ramus, east of Nauvoo, in November of 1841 confessed to being Mormons and told arresting officers they had been sustained in their criminal activities by leaders of the church as long as their victims were Gentiles. See *History of the Church*, Vol. IV, pp. 453–54, 460–67. Ford, in *History of Illinois*, p. 329, felt the reports were exaggerated.

[6] *History of the Church*, Vol. VI, p. 149. Stealing was an important topic of discussion during sessions of the church's April 6, 1843, conference. See Hyrum Smith's remarks in conference minutes published in *Times and Seasons*, Vol. IV, No. 12 (May 1843), pp. 183–84. Compare with affidavits published in ibid., Vol. 3, No. 3 (December 1841), pp. 615–18, reprinted in *The Wasp*, March 29, 1843.

was aired publicly in a speech to the police force; some of the "dirty linen" washed clearly illustrated the depths to which the city had fallen. Joseph had charged the officers to:

> Have the ordinances of the city always in your possession, and study them, and ferret out all grogshops, gambling-houses, brothels, and disorderly conduct; and if a transgressor resists, cuff his ears. If anyone lifts a weapon or presents a pistol at you, take his life, if need be, to preserve your own; but enforce the ordinances, and preserve the peace of the city, and take care of your own lives. Let no horses be taken away out of the city, or anything else stolen, if you can help it. . . .
>
> There are speculators in this State who are wanting to sell revolving pistols to us, in order to fight the Missourians, and at the same time inciting the Missourians to fight us. Don't buy: it would be better to buy ploughshares and raise corn with them.
>
> My life is more in danger from some little dough-head of a fool in this city than from all my numerous and inveterate enemies abroad. I am exposed to far greater danger from traitors among ourselves than from enemies without, although my life has been sought for many years by the civil and military authorities, priests and people of Missouri; and if I can escape from the ungrateful treachery of assassins, I can live as Caesar might have lived, were it not for a right-hand Brutus. I have had pretended friends betray me.
>
> All the enemies upon the face of the earth may roar and exert all their power to bring about my death, but they can accomplish nothing, unless some who are among us and enjoy our society, have been with us in our councils, participated in our confidence, taken us by the hand, called us brother, saluted us with a kiss, join with our enemies, turn our virtues into faults, and, by falsehood and deceit, stir up their wrath and indignation against us, and bring their united vengeance upon our heads. All the hue-and-cry of the chief priests and elders against the Savior, could not bring down the wrath of the Jewish nation upon His head, and thereby cause the crucifixion of the Son of God, until Judas said unto them, "Whomsoever I shall kiss, he is the man; hold him fast." Judas was one of the Twelve Apostles, even their treasurer, and dipt with their Master in the dish, and through his treachery, the crucifixion was brought about; and *we have a Judas in our midst.*[7]

Joseph ended his impassioned sermon by pronouncing a blessing on the forty officers, after which his brother Hyrum spoke briefly. The prophet then admonished the men that if anyone should offer them a bribe, the city, in return for the culprit, would pay twice the amount

[7] *History of the Church*, Vol. VI, pp. 150–52. Italics in the original.

offered. No sooner had Joseph's remarks filtered through the city than rumors sprang up that the police were under secret instruction to kill the man he had described as the "dough-head of a fool." For the most part the stories merely provided grist for the Nauvoo gossip mill, but one man, William Law, Joseph's second counselor, was extremely agitated by them. For some months there had been a widening breach between the prophet and his subordinate for a variety of reasons, the most important of which concerned Law's wife, whom, it was said, Joseph had attempted to seduce into becoming one of his spiritual wives.[8] Law and his brother Wilson, a major-general in the Nauvoo Legion, were fast becoming disenchanted with Joseph's leadership and had joined several other discontented Mormons who were convinced he was a false prophet and imposter.

William Law's concern over the "secret instructions" he believed had been given to the police drove him to confront Hyrum Smith and report his suspicion that Joseph had ordered Law "put out of the way."[9] Hyrum, in turn, went to Joseph and repeated the counselor's accusation. Again Joseph was master of the situation; he called a special meeting of the city council to hear Law's complaint and stifle the damaging gossip.

When Law faced the prophet with the allegation in front of the city council and assembled policemen, Joseph dramatically asked the officers to signify whether they had been presented with a secret oath. "On conditions I have had no private conversation with any of you, rise up and change the breech of your gun upwards." Every policeman stood and reversed the position of his firearm. Law sat quietly surveying the scene while awaiting the arrival of the man who had told him of the secret orders.

Eli Norton, the witness, admitted that his information had been second-hand and that it had come through one of the policemen. Under close questioning by the prophet, Norton broke down and named the man, Daniel Carn. Law took over the questioning. "Did you not understand from Brother Carn that he was suspicious of some person near Joseph being a dough-head and that person was myself?"

"He mentioned a dough-head as being very near Joseph," Norton replied, "and he guessed you was the man." The witness paused, then added, "I thought it might be that Daniteism was not done with."

Daniel Carn was sworn in and promptly testified that he had assumed

[8] Lee, *Mormonism Unveiled*, p. 147; Ford, *History of Illinois*, p. 322.

[9] *History of the Church*, Vol. VI, pp. 162–63.

from Joseph's remarks that Law was the Judas, but he denied receiving any secret orders. Carn's testimony was enough to bring an end to the hearing. Satisfied that the matter was closed, Joseph addressed the gathering to clear up the references made to the Sons of Dan. "The Danite system alluded to by Norton never had any existence," he said. "It was a term made use of by some of the brethren in Far West, and grew out of an expression I made use of when the brethren were preparing to defend themselves from the Missouri mob . . . ." [10]

At the conclusion of the meeting, Law announced that he believed the rumors were groundless and that he would stand by Joseph to the death. The scene became highly emotional when Law grabbed the prophet's hand and shook it for all to see; their friends pounded the two men on the back and the hearing ended on a high note. But Law would soon come to regret his words and actions that day.

Meanwhile, Joseph's reference to a "dough-head" continued to cause trouble. When policemen kindled a fire near the home of William Marks, president of the High Council — one of the men they had been ordered to protect — Marks complained to Joseph that he was to be the victim of an assassin's bullet, and the fire had been started to make him a better target. "Another tempest in a teapot," the prophet said in disgust, but he ordered a second special council meeting to hear out the frightened man. As before, the session ended in a profusion of handshaking and pledges of unwavering loyalty. In the privacy of his home, Joseph reflected on the proceedings of the day:

> What can be the matter with these men? Is it that the wicked flee when no man pursueth, that hit pigeons always flutter, that drowning men catch at straws, or that Presidents Law and Marks are absolutely traitors to the church, that my remarks should produce such an excitement in their minds. Can it be possible that the traitor whom Porter Rockwell reports to me as being in correspondence with my Missouri enemies, is one of my quorum? The people in the town were astonished, almost every man saying to his neighbor, "Is it possible that Brother Law or Brother Marks is a traitor, and would deliver Brother Joseph into the hands of his enemies in Missouri?" If not, what can be the meaning of all this? "The righteous are bold as a lion." [11]

After a few days the waves of apprehension subsided, and Joseph buried himself in work. By the end of the month he cast secrecy aside and

---

[10] Ibid., p. 165. Joseph's statement here is a complete reversal of his earlier denials that he had known anything of the Danite Band. See chapter two, note 23.

[11] Ibid., p. 170.

announced that the Saints could not lend their support to either Van Buren or Clay in the coming elections; therefore, "we will have an independent electoral ticket, and . . . Joseph Smith [will] be a candidate for the next Presidency!"

While the prophet was engaged in the details of his platform and planning his campaign, strange intrigues were unfolding in Nauvoo. Joseph's first intimation of what was transpiring came when two Mormons approached him with word that the Laws, Chauncey L. Higbee, Chauncey's brother, Francis, Dr. Robert D. Foster, and Joseph H. Jackson, who had dropped the cloak of spy and openly turned against the Mormon prophet, were conspiring to kill Joseph and had boasted that "not a Smith would be alive in two months." A second source confirmed the story. Joseph was only too well acquainted with the plotters and appreciated that he was dealing with desperate men. He ordered his agents to attend the secret sessions being conducted by the conspirators and to report the proceedings to him.[12] The prophet's bearded bodyguard was constantly at his side, ever vigilant, alert to any attempt on his life. Rockwell was a dark and menacing figure as he hovered in the background, ready to act at the first sign of trouble.

Calling his most trusted followers within the High Council, the Legion, and the police together for a series of strategy meetings, Joseph laid out a plan of action.[13] First reports from the informers indicated that Foster was planning to make public an accusation that Joseph had attempted to seduce Foster's wife under the doctrine of plural marriage. To thwart such a move the prophet obtained an affidavit from Mrs. Foster denying that he had ever been guilty of an immoral or indecent act toward her. Then, on March 24, 1844, at a gathering of Saints near the temple site, Joseph unleashed a scathing indictment against the conspirators, hoping to frighten them out of their plans, or at least to lessen the shock of an exposé by seizing the initiative:

> I have been informed . . . that a conspiracy is got up in this place for the purpose of taking the life of President Joseph Smith, his family, and all the Smith family, and the heads of the church. . . . And the lies that C. L. Higbee has hatched up as a foundation to work upon are — he says I had men's heads cut off in Missouri, and that I had a

[12] Ibid., p. 280 and 280n. See also Horace Cummings, "Conspiracy of Nauvoo," *The Contributor*, Vol. V (April 1884), pp. 251–60.

[13] Representing these groups within the church were Orrin Porter Rockwell, Sidney Rigdon, Willard Richards, George Miller, William Marks, and others.

sword run through the hearts of the people that I wanted to kill and put out of the way. I won't swear out a warrant against them, for I don't fear any of them; they would not scare off an old setting hen. I intend to publish all the iniquity that I know of them. If I am guilty, I am ready to bear it. . . .[14]

In succeeding days the conspirators discovered that they were being kept under close scrutiny. The Higbee brothers were arrested for assaulting police officers. Although they were acquitted, Chauncey, an attorney, was fined $10 for using abusive language and insulting the city marshal in the performance of his duty. He retaliated by filing a complaint of false imprisonment against the marshal and two officers. When the case was heard the court found the charge was "originated in a malicious and vexatious suit" by a "very disorderly person"; it was quashed, the officers were discharged, and Higbee was ordered to pay court costs.

Foster, himself a Nauvoo magistrate, was arrested, taken before another justice of the peace, and fined $10 for a violation of the city's gambling ordinances. Then on April 13, Joseph and Foster engaged in a spirited exchange at a city council meeting which ended with the prophet preferring before the High Council a charge against Foster of "unchristianlike conduct in general, for abusing my character privily, for throwing out slanderous insinuations against me, for conspiring against my peace and safety, for conspiring against my life, for conspiring against the peace of my family, and for lying." [15]

No Mormon could hope to survive such an onslaught of accusations from Joseph Smith. Foster was summarily excommunicated along with William Law, Law's wife, Jane, and Wilson Law.[16]

Then occurred an incident which very nearly cost the prophet his life. It began when a Mormon, Augustine Spencer, became embroiled in an argument with his brother, Orson, a Nauvoo alderman. On hearing of the dispute, Joseph, as mayor, ordered the arrest of Augustine Spencer on an assault charge. Before the city marshal could serve the warrant, Joseph and Rockwell located the wanted man in the office of an attorney and informed Spencer that he was under arrest. Rockwell went for the marshal, but Spencer refused to accompany him to the mayor's office. "Get some help and take him out of here whether he wants to go or not," Joseph said.

[14] *History of the Church*, Vol. VI, p. 272.
[15] Ibid., p. 333.
[16] Ibid., p. 341.

J. P. Greene, the marshal, stepped to the street and stopped the first passers-by he saw, ordering them as citizens to aid in removing the prisoner from the law office. Unfortunately, Greene had made a poor choice of helpers; he had stopped Chauncey Higbee, Foster, and Foster's brother, Charles. Before Greene fully comprehended what was happening, the three men showered him with invective, shouting that they would see the mayor and the city damned before lending him any assistance.

At the first outburst Joseph turned to the perplexed marshal and ordered him to place the trio under arrest for refusing to assist a city officer in the discharge of his duty. His words were greeted by an explosion of curses from the three men. For the husky prophet of the Lord such abuse was intolerable. Grabbing a Foster in each hand he slammed the two brothers against a wall, but Charles Foster, anticipating such a move, pulled a double-barreled pistol from his coat and swung it toward Joseph. Rockwell leaped forward and smashed his fist against Foster's forearm, sending the gun flying across the room.

Insane with rage, his arm dangling loosely at his side, Foster screamed at the prophet, "Goddamn you, goddamn you — I would have killed you!" The sight of his sobbing brother shocked Robert Foster into a stream of profanity. "I would be favored of God for the privilege of ridding the world of such a tyrant," he yelled at Joseph.[17]

The three men were herded to Joseph's office where he fined them each $100. They immediately appealed the case to municipal court, and trial was called for the next day, April 27. Before the matter could be heard, Joseph pulled Robert Foster aside and asked him not to continue his public denunciations, but Foster met the request with bitter charges that Joseph had revived the Sons of Dan in Nauvoo and had been guilty of adulterous conduct. He cut the conversation short by accusing Joseph of being a false prophet.

Court adjourned for the weekend without Foster's trial. Joseph made a final effort to silence his antagonist, but it met with failure as before. Foster offered to meet the prophet in public debate with the proceedings to be published in newspapers outside Nauvoo; Joseph countered with an offer that if Foster would shut his mouth a settlement agreeable to both

[17] An account of the affair as described by the marshal was published in the *Nauvoo Neighbor*, May 1, 1844.

parties would be published in the *Nauvoo Neighbor*. Foster scornfully rejected the proposal. It was Joseph who settled the question: "I have done my duty; the skirts of my garments are free from your blood. I have made the last overtures of peace to you and deliver you into the hands of God!" The prophet shook his garments in a symbolic emphasis of his words. When court convened, Foster's case was transferred to the jurisdiction of an alderman's court by Joseph's order and eventually dismissed.

In the midst of this turmoil came Thomas A. Lyne, a New York tragedian, who proposed to stage a few plays for the pleasure of the Mormons. Joseph seized the chance to lay aside his cares for a few hours and ordered the Saints to provide Lyne with whatever assistance he needed. One of the suggested productions was *Pizarro*, a popular romantic drama. When the curtain rose on opening night, who should appear in the role of Davina, "a Spanish soldier," but Orrin Porter Rockwell.[18] It was his most magnificent hour, poised with an unfamiliar spear clenched tightly in a fist more accustomed to a gun butt; he became hopelessly stagestruck. Joseph attended every performance of each of the half-dozen plays on the bill with the enthusiasm of a first-nighter. His booming laughter resounded throughout the Masonic Hall, filled to capacity with Mormons, few of whom had seen a theatrical production before.

But the escape from reality was all too fleeting, and Joseph returned to the prodigious task of being a prophet. The Laws, Foster, and the Higbees had organized a new church with William Law as "prophet," a maneuver which prompted Brigham Young to comment, " 'Tis the same old story over again — 'The doctrine is right, but Joseph is a fallen prophet.' "

On May 7 a large crate was delivered to Foster's home in Nauvoo, an occurrence Joseph recorded in his history: "An opposition press arrives at Dr. Foster's." The *Nauvoo Expositor* was about to make its debut. Within a few days the conspirators were circulating among the citizens a prospectus of the new publication to be issued on Friday of each week and,

> devoted to a general diffusion of useful knowledge, and its columns open for the admission of all courteous communications of a Religious, Moral, Social, Literary, or Political character, without taking a decided stand in favor of either of the great Political parties of the country. A part of its columns will be devoted to a few primary objects, which the Publishers deem of vital importance to the public welfare.
>
> Their particular locality gives them a knowledge of the many *gross abuses exercised under the pretended authorities of the Nauvoo City*

[18] Journal History, September 15, 1868.

113

Charter, by the legislative authorities of said city; and the insupportable *oppressions* of the *Ministerial* powers in carrying out the unjust, illegal, and unconstitutional ordinances of the same. The publishers, therefore, deem it a sacred duty they owe to their country and their fellow citizens, to advocate through the columns of the *Expositor*, the UNCONDITIONAL REPEAL OF THE NAUVOO CITY CHARTER; to restrain and correct the abuses of the *Unit Power*; to ward off the Iron Rod which is held over the devoted heads of the citizens of Nauvoo and the surrounding country; to advocate unmitigated *disobedience* to *Political Revelations*, and to censure and decry gross moral imperfections wherever found, either in the Plebian, Patrician, or *self-constituted* MONARCH . . . .[19]

With the newspaper, the conspirators planned to attack Joseph in his most vulnerable spot — the soft underbelly of public opinion. Joseph had always recognized the need for a newspaper as a sounding board for his doctrine; now this powerful force was being turned on him in the city where his grip was strongest. Yet there was little he could do until the first issue was published; then perhaps there would be reason to act.

Now, more frequently than ever before, Joseph sought the seclusion of the open prairie. His companion on these brief riding excursions was his friend and protector. The two spoke for hours in the solitude of the untrammeled wilderness.[20] Occasionally, as in their youth, the two men raced their fine horses across the grass. Joseph seemed to be increasingly preoccupied, and close friends were quick to notice that Rockwell was rarely more than a shout from the prophet's side.

William Law's testimony in Carthage before a grand jury resulted in a true bill against Joseph on charges of adultery. No sooner had the prophet absorbed this news than he learned that Foster was adding his testimony that Joseph had illegally sworn out a complaint against another man. The prophet countered by sending Rockwell to Carthage to charge Foster with perjury, a decision which stirred the usually reticent Hyrum to caution his brother against speaking so freely of the conspirators as to make it actionable in court. Joseph answered impatiently, "Six months will not roll over your head before they will swear twelve as palpable lies about you as they have me!"

[19] The prospectus was reprinted in the *Nauvoo Expositor*, June 7, 1844. Italics and capitals in original.

[20] *History of the Church*, Vol. VI, pp. 399, 424.

Rockwell returned from Carthage and reported that he had been unsuccessful in lodging the complaint, since the grand jury had adjourned. Before it had recessed, however, Joseph H. Jackson had joined Law and Foster in making allegations against the prophet, and Francis Higbee had sworn so vehemently that Joseph was guilty of receiving stolen goods that his testimony was rejected.

At first Joseph thought it might be best to make himself scarce to avoid writs for his arrest, but in considering the matter he decided that he might be able to defeat the conspirators in court. With Rockwell and several others, he rode to Carthage to demand that the circuit court investigate the indictments against him. Arriving at a place called Hamilton's Hotel, Joseph found that his enemies were staying there as well. Surprisingly, they treated him with mild accord, except for Jackson, who loaded his pistols in public and swore he would have the satisfaction of killing both Joseph and Hyrum.[21] The case was deferred until the following term, and the prophet's retinue prepared for their homeward journey. Chauncey Higbee, seeing Rockwell in the hotel, made an insulting remark about Joseph and was knocked senseless by the bodyguard. When word of the incident reached the prophet he commented dryly that Rockwell had resented Higbee's language "nobly as a friend ought to do."[22]

On the first Friday in June the *Nauvoo Expositor* made its appearance. The paper stirred a violent reaction among the Saints, who read in its columns an exposé of spiritual wifery reminiscent of the Bennett scandal. Further, the *Expositor*'s accusations struck home with a greater force than had the Bennett letters since the Laws were held in greater esteem. After a weekend of hasty consultations, Joseph called a session of the city council Monday morning, June 10, and pushed through an ordinance prohibiting libel on penalty of a $500 fine and six months in jail.[23]

Armed with the decree, the prophet called on the council to consider

[21] Gregg, *The Prophet of Palmyra*, pp. 296–97, says of this man, "If half of Jackson's statements were true, the prophet and some of his abettors should have been hung; if not true, Jackson himself should have been hung — in either case without benefit of clergy." On the Sunday after his appearance in Carthage, Joseph preached from the stand in Nauvoo on the subject of persecution; and in the course of the sermon, Joseph H. Jackson's name came up: "Jackson has committed murder, robbery and perjury," Smith said, "and I can prove it by half-a-dozen witnesses . . . . [N]ow [Jackson] threatens my life." Unfortunately for history, Joseph did not choose to expand on Jackson that morning. See *Millennial Star*, Vol. XXIII, p. 673.

[22] *History of the Church*, Vol. VI, p. 414.

[23] *Nauvoo Neighbor*, June 12, 1844.

the *Expositor* matter and asked for testimony in regard to the reputations of the newspaper's publishers. An appropriate number of witnesses were heard, including Rockwell, each of whom told the council of various misdeeds of the conspirators. This done, a motion was made and carried that under the new libel law the *Nauvoo Expositor* be deemed a public nuisance. Accordingly, the mayor was ordered by the city council to "cause said printing establishment and papers to be removed without delay." It was unnecessary to ask Joseph to act promptly; he issued the following order to the city marshal:

> You are here commanded to destroy the printing press from whence issues the *Nauvoo Expositor*, and pi the type of said printing establishment in the street, and burn all the *Expositors* and libelous handbills found in said establishment; and if resistance be offered to your execution of this order by the owners or others, demolish the house; and if anyone threatens you or the Mayor or the officers of the city, arrest those who threaten you, and fail not to execute this order without delay, and make due return hereon.[24]

To ensure that there would be no mistakes, Joseph joined the posse which formed to carry out the marshal's order.[25] When they arrived that night at the *Expositor* office, Foster and Chauncey Higbee met them at the door and refused to surrender the key to the shop. At a signal from the prophet, Rockwell kicked the door from its hinges and the posse entered. Seven men pulled the press into the street and smashed its bed beyond repair. The type was pied and battered, the chases were dumped on the remains of the press, and the entire pile of metal was soaked in coal oil and set aflame. Marshal Greene reported to the city council that: "The within-named press and type is destroyed and pied according to order, on this 10th day of June, 1844, at about 8 o'clock p.m."

Even Joseph was unprepared for the uproar which swept Hancock County in the wake of the *Expositor* affair. Once Foster and the others made public what had occurred in Nauvoo, Joseph's precipitous decision to wipe out the newspaper aroused a wave of controversy. Illinoisians

[24] Ibid., June 19, 1844; *History of the Church*, Vol. VI, p. 448.
[25] Lee, *Mormonism Unveiled*, pp. 153–54.

were very sensitive about what happened to newspapers in their state. They still carried a bad taste in their mouths from an incident of seven years before, an episode which left them with a special understanding of the constitutional right of freedom of the press.

In 1837 the Rev. Elijah Lovejoy, a Presbyterian minister, had attempted to establish an abolitionist newspaper in Alton, Illinois, after being driven from St. Louis for the same reason. Alton residents forbade such a press until the minister promised to operate a religious organ only and omit the slavery question from his columns. But after a few impressions had been published, it was evident that the paper's sympathies were violently abolitionist. When Lovejoy denied that he had made a policy pledge to the contrary, a mob dumped the press and fonts of type into the Mississippi River. Undaunted, the minister and his sympathizers purchased another; when it arrived in Alton a mob attacked the warehouse in which the press was stored. In the confusion, shots were fired and Lovejoy suffered a fatal wound.[26] Criticism aimed at Illinois made the state an object of scorn and ridicule throughout the nation, and its citizens were anxious not to repeat their mistake. In fact, the liberal attitude toward the state's newspapers which followed Lovejoy's death had become a source of pride to Illinoisians, a badge of honor which they jealously guarded against stain. But the Mormon prophet's act in destroying the *Expositor* placed them in the intolerable position of having again violated freedom of the press — and the citizenry was quick to react. Gentiles in Hancock County called a mass meeting at Carthage to place the blame squarely on the Saints and demonstrate the outrage of the Illinois population against the Mormons.

While this was taking place, Foster and his group were swearing out complaints against those who had participated in the destruction of the *Expositor*, demanding their arrests on charges of committing a riot. High on the list named by the conspirators were Joseph, Hyrum, Greene, and Rockwell. A writ was served on the Mormons, but Joseph petitioned for a habeas corpus hearing in Nauvoo and ramrodded through a decision which discharged him from the Carthage warrant and forced the complainant, Chauncey Higbee, to pay court costs.[27]

Indignation meetings at nearby Warsaw and Carthage attracted large crowds of fanatical anti-Mormons who organized an association to deal

[26] Ford, *History of Illinois,* pp. 234–45.

[27] *History of the Church,* Vol. VI, pp. 454–58. Rockwell was one of Joseph's most effective witnesses at the hearing. His testimony is on p. 457.

with their unwanted neighbors. They passed resolutions stressing the duty of every good citizen to "put an immediate stop to the career of the mad prophet and his demoniac coadjutors." [28] One consequence of the gatherings was the selection of a deputation to Governor Ford in Springfield requesting that he invoke executive powers against Joseph. Apprised of the situation, the prophet attempted to take the sting out of the Carthage reports by sending the governor a message explaining his movements in ordering the *Expositor* abated as a nuisance. The communication convinced Ford that he must visit Nauvoo himself and survey the situation firsthand.

Anticipating trouble, Joseph heeded his legal advisors and permitted himself and the others named in Higbee's complaint to be arrested and brought before a friendly magistrate for trial. It was considered wise not to rely entirely on the habeas corpus hearing. Like actors in a play, the principals mouthed the appropriate words on cue, and the judge nodded sagely. Within a matter of hours the entire slate of defendants was discharged.[29]

Now Joseph had another problem: Word was spreading through the city that a mob was forming in Carthage to march on Nauvoo and give the prophet a taste of lynch justice. Quickly he called for the Legion to be held in readiness as a precautionary measure. So there would be no confusion as to authority if Nauvoo were attacked, Joseph issued an order proclaiming martial law. Donning his general's uniform, he reviewed the Legion's cohorts as they marched past the Mansion House. For ninety minutes he spoke to the Legionnaires, at one point shouting, "Will you all stand by me to the death, and sustain at the peril of your lives, the laws of our country, and the liberties and privileges which our fathers have transmitted unto us, sealed with their sacred blood?"

The answer came as a thunderclap over the City of Joseph: "Aye!"

"It is well. If you had not done it, I would have gone out there," he said, gesturing to the west, "and would have raised up a mightier people." Drawing his sword, he thrust the blade to the sky. "I call God and angels to witness that I have unsheathed my sword with a firm and unalterable

---

[28] The minutes of the mass meeting were published in the *Warsaw Signal*, June 19, 1844.

[29] Proceedings of the trial can be found in *History of the Church*, Vol. VI, pp. 488–91. See also Ford, *History of Illinois*, p. 324. Esquire Daniel H. Wells, before whom the trial was held, later joined the church and rose to lieutenant-general of the Nauvoo Legion in Utah.

determination that this people shall have their legal rights, and be protected from mob violence, or my blood shall be spilt upon the ground like water, and my body consigned to the silent tomb." [30]

Of all Joseph's words, those were to be the most prophetic; in ten days he would be dead, his blood "spilt upon the ground like water." As the prophet concluded his last address to the Legion, only Rockwell had cause to pay any particular attention to the platform on which Joseph was standing. It was the unfinished structure of what was to have been the barbershop and tavern Joseph had promised him on his return from Independence Jail.

Thomas Ford, governor of Illinois, arrived in Carthage June 21 and requested Joseph to send a delegation to a conference in Carthage that day "to avert the evils of war." The prophet appointed three men, arming them with affidavits outlining the Mormon view of the situation; he also asked the chief executive to visit Nauvoo and converse with him privately. When his emissaries returned, Joseph learned that Ford sided with the anti-Mormon society and expected the prophet to journey at once to Carthage and allay public excitement by "proving the Mormons wished to be governed by law." Joseph knew his cause was lost. To enter Carthage might well cost his life.

Summoning Rockwell and several others, Joseph announced his decision to abandon Nauvoo and strike out for "the Rocky Mountains." "We will cross the river tonight," he said. It was nine o'clock when Hyrum Smith stepped from the Mansion House. He was followed minutes later by Joseph, who bade a tearful farewell to his family. Holding a handkerchief to his face, the prophet walked silently into the night. The hands on Joseph's pocket watch stood nearly at midnight when he, Hyrum, and Willard Richards knocked on Rockwell's door. By prearrangement, Rockwell had obtained a boat; leaky though it was, the craft stood ready and waiting on the riverbank for its passengers. Caught by the emotion of the moment, Rockwell grasped Joseph's hand firmly. They had decided the day before that Rockwell would be the guide for their precarious journey into the mountains.

While his three passengers bailed for all they were worth, Rockwell pulled hard on the little skiff's oars against a blustering wind which threatened to swamp them at any moment. Finally they reached the safety of the far shore, and while Joseph planned their next move, Rockwell re-

[30] *History of the Church*, Vol. VI, p. 499.

turned to Illinois for horses which he intended to smuggle across the river the next day so they could start for "the Great Basin in the Rocky Mountains." [31]

In Nauvoo the population faced an angry posse. The Mormons were told that the Gentiles would level the city unless Joseph was turned over to them. For many, the warnings recalled with a shudder the dark days of Missouri. Governor Ford explained that the prophet could expect safe conduct and absolute protection if he surrendered. Strangely, it was Emma, Joseph's wife, who faltered first, but she soon was joined by others who feared for their lives and property. Such was the situation as Rockwell found it when he rode into the city that morning. Emma prevailed upon him to carry a message to her husband and begged Rockwell to try and change the prophet's mind. One of the Saints in favor of Joseph's surrender, Reynolds Cahoon, accompanied Rockwell across the river to plead personally with the prophet. Cahoon told Joseph of the posse's threats and explained that Ford had pledged himself to Joseph's safety. But Joseph had been in too many tight spots to believe promises made by Gentiles; he remained adamant in his decision to head west. "I know my business," he said. Cahoon angrily accused him of cowardice. "You always said if the church would stick to you, you would stick to the church; now trouble comes and you are the first to run!" [32]

Chagrined, Joseph replied, "If my life is of no value to my friends it is of none to myself." He turned to Rockwell, "What shall I do?"

"You are the oldest and ought to know best; and as you make your bed, I will lie with you," the bodyguard answered, his jaw set firmly.

Joseph turned. "Brother Hyrum, you are the oldest, what shall we do?"

Looking even more gaunt and haggard under the pressure of the moment, Hyrum squared his shoulders and answered, "Let us go back and give ourselves up, and see the thing out."

Joseph pondered for what seemed an hour, then with a shrug said, "If you go back I will go with you, but we shall be butchered."

"No, no; let us go back and put our trust in God, and we shall not be harmed. The Lord is in it. If we live or have to die, we will be reconciled to our fate," Hyrum expostulated.

Joseph smiled at his brother's simple logic. "All right, Brother Cahoon, if you'll tell Captain Davis to have the boat made ready we will return to

[31] Ibid., p. 548.

[32] Mace, "Journal," p. 144.

Nauvoo." The prophet's features mirrored his inner anxieties; it was as if a shroud had settled over his soul. While walking to the riverbank, Joseph and Rockwell lagged behind. Ignoring shouts from the rest of the party to quicken the pace, Joseph muttered, "It is of no use to hurry, for we are going back to be slaughtered. If only I could speak to the Saints once more."

"If that is what you wish, I will get them together. You can speak by starlight," Rockwell said.[33]

But the others brushed the idea aside as a foolish whim and hurried Joseph across the river and into Nauvoo where Emma urged him to write to Ford immediately, accepting his surrender offer. Thus on June 24 Joseph began a journey to what he felt might be his death. To his escort he remarked, "*I am going like a lamb to the slaughter, but I am calm as a summer's morning. I have a conscience void of offense toward God and toward all men. If they take my life I shall die an innocent man, and my blood shall cry from the ground for vengeance, and it shall be said of me, 'He was murdered in cold blood!'* "[34]

Their entry into Carthage shortly before midnight was saluted by shouts of derision from militia, primarily Carthage Greys clustered in the public square.

"Goddamn you, old Joe, we've got you now," yelled one man. Another joined the chorus of angry jeers: "Clear the way and let us have a view of Joe Smith, the prophet of God! He has seen the last of Nauvoo. We'll use him up now, and kill all the damned Mormons!"[35]

These taunts convinced Joseph he had been right in ordering Rockwell to stay behind in Nauvoo, for if mob rule erupted only a trusted lieutenant could be counted on to respond quickly in bringing Mormon troops to the prophet's side in time to prevent his harm. Upon surrendering, Joseph and Hyrum were told that they would face treason charges as a consequence of the prophet's martial law proclamation in Nauvoo. Anxious to show the populace that the Mormon prophet had given himself up, Governor Ford called for a review of the Illinois militia and paraded the prisoners before the soldiers. That afternoon Joseph hastily scribbled a note to Emma describing the events of the day. He also sent a message to Rockwell emphasizing the danger of the bodyguard making an appear-

[33] *History of the Church*, Vol. VI, p. 551; Jenson, *Church Encyclopaedia*, p. 560.

[34] *History of the Church*, Vol. VI, p. 555. Italics in original.

[35] Ibid., p. 559.

ance in Carthage. "Stay in Nauvoo and do not suffer yourself to be delivered into the hands of your enemies, or be taken prisoner by anyone!" [36] It was imperative that Rockwell remain close to the Legion. Disobedience to Joseph's wishes could cost the prophet his life, and Joseph was not sure how his fearless friend would respond when he learned of the bloodthirsty attitude of the militia. The last thing Joseph wanted at the moment was for Rockwell to charge into Carthage with guns blazing.

Later in the day Joseph, Hyrum, and thirteen others named on the riot complaint were taken before a magistrate; all were released on bail except Joseph and Hyrum, who were remanded to Carthage Jail. When Ford finally granted Joseph an interview, the prophet detailed the events which had unfolded in Nauvoo during the weeks previous. He concluded with a demand that Ford "deliver us from this place, and rescue us from this outrage that is sought to be practiced upon us by a set of infamous scoundrels." But the governor hesitated to provoke the wrath of the non-Mormon citizenry by such direct action. He avoided an answer by changing the subject, suggesting that perhaps he would make a personal visit to Nauvoo. The remark brought an immediate plea from Joseph that he be permitted to accompany the governor. Joseph knew that once within the Nauvoo city limits he was safe. Sensing the urgency in the prophet's voice, Ford abruptly ended the interview. "I do not know that I shall go tomorrow to Nauvoo, but if I do," he said, "I will take you along."

Alone in his cell Joseph was filled with a feeling of gloom he could not dispel. He felt that Ford was a weak man and was certain that under the slightest additional pressure the governor would crumble. His promises of protection would collapse with him. "I have a good deal of anxiety about my safety since I left Nauvoo, which I never had before when I was under arrest. I could not help those feelings and they have depressed me," Joseph remarked.

His fears were well founded. Even as he brooded, evidence was being uncovered in Nauvoo pointing to a well-organized plot directed at the Mormons. It happened that Rockwell spotted one of the conspirators, Francis Higbee, on the street and accused him of scheming to kill the prophet. Higbee made the mistake of cursing Rockwell and was sent sprawling. In the brief scuffle Higbee's hat fell to the dirt and a letter sailed from its lining. When Higbee scrambled for the paper, a second punch flattened him. Rockwell, deciding the letter might be important

[36] Ibid., p. 565.

and unable to read it himself, took the document before the High Council where it was found to be a message telling Higbee that seventy men waited on the Iowa side of the river for a signal to attack Nauvoo.[37] The raid fizzled, and Rockwell's fight with Higbee was credited with having upset the enemy applecart.

Because Ford had permitted Joseph to use the debtor's apartment in jail and allowed several of the prophet's friends access to him, it was possible to smuggle messages out of Carthage. Realizing time was precious, Joseph dictated a note to Major General Jonathan Dunham ordering him to call out the Legion and march on the jail immediately. Dunham received the communication in Nauvoo but failed to carry out the command.[38] One of the Legionnaires, Allen Stout, said, "Dunham did not let a single man or mortal know that he had received such orders and we were kept in the city under arms not knowing but all was well." [39]

Shortly before four o'clock in the afternoon of June 26, the Smith brothers were ordered before a Carthage judge to be heard on the treason charges. Expecting to be massacred at any moment as they passed through the massed Carthage Greys guarding the jail, Joseph struck upon a bold plan. Scanning the crowd, he selected the most savage anti-Mormon he could find and locked arms with him. Hyrum snared the other arm and the two forced their reluctant companion to accompany them to the courtroom through the gauntlet of glowering Gentiles.

After an hour or more of legal wrangling a motion by the defendants to continue the case until morning was granted. Again the Smiths were thrust into jail, but their friends were forced to leave one by one until finally only Willard Richards and John Taylor remained in the cell with the prisoners. Earlier visitors had managed to smuggle pistols to the two brothers, a circumstance which aroused Hyrum's normally pacifistic nature.

"I hate to use such things or to see them used," he complained sadly.

[37] *History of the Church of Jesus Christ of Latter-day Saints. Period II. Apostolic Interregnum. From the Manuscript History of Brigham Young and Other Original Documents.* A one-volume addition to *Period I.* Introduction and notes by B. H. Roberts (Salt Lake City, 1932), p. 130. Hereafter cited as *History of the Church*, Vol. VII.

[38] Dunham's act came to light after the martyrdom when Joseph's order was found in a Nauvoo street and read. Stenhouse, *Rocky Mountain Saints*, p. 164n, says Dunham was sent on a mission a year later and died of "dysentery."

[39] Allen Joseph Stout, "Journal," p. 13.

Joseph was more realistic. "So do I," he observed, shoving a pepperbox pistol into his waistband, "but we may have to defend ourselves."

Despite his promise, Ford left for Nauvoo without Joseph on the morning of June 27, leaving as a jail guard a detachment of the vicious Carthage Greys. The Mormons immediately sensed a plot. John P. Greene hurried to overtake Ford's party.

"If you leave now, with only the Greys guarding the jail, then this is no more than a conspiracy to kill those two men," he told the governor angrily.

Ford smiled. "Marshal Greene, you are too enthusiastic."

With that, Ford's entourage moved out for Nauvoo. He took with him a contingent of troops friendly to the Mormons; the remainder of the militiamen he ordered disbanded. Eight men were on duty at the jail, with the main body of Greys camped on the public square a quarter of a mile distant. It was shortly after five o'clock in the afternoon when Joseph, Hyrum, Richards, and Taylor finished dinner. Retiring to the cell, they sent for a bottle of wine, some pipes, and two small papers of tobacco with which to pass the time.[40] Their guard, hearing a voice downstairs call him, left the Mormons. A moment later sounds of a struggle were heard, followed by a cry of surrender. Several firearms were triggered in quick succession. Richards jumped to the window and saw a mob of armed men milling about the jail grounds. The Carthage Greys on guard duty pointed their rifles in the air, fired them, and stepped aside.[41] This act apparently was a signal for the intruders to open fire on the cell from the outside while others ran into the building and mounted the stairs.

At the first sound of shooting, Joseph and Hyrum grabbed their pistols; Taylor and Richards reached for their canes and sprang to the door to prevent anyone from entering. Bullets whistled up the stairway as the attackers pressed toward the debtor's apartment. Taylor and Richards knocked aside several guns as they poked through the partially opened door. Hyrum had fired a shot directly through the panel when a bullet smashed into his face.

"I am a dead man!" he screamed, and pitched to the floor. A hail of lead struck him as he fell; one ball entered his left side and passed through his body with such force that it destroyed the watch he wore in his vest

---

[40] *History of the Church*, Vol. VI, p. 616; Jenson, *Church Encyclopaedia*, p. 569.

[41] This was only a token effort at resistance, and even it was a sham, for the rifles had been unloaded and charged with blanks by the previous contingent of guards. Scofield, *History of Hancock County*, Vol. II, p. 847.

124

pocket. Another shot grazed his chest, pierced his throat, and entered his head. A fourth bullet shattered his left leg.

Joseph reached around the doorjamb and fired all six barrels of his pepperbox. A steady stream of bullets sprayed the room. Swinging canes wildly, Taylor and Richards fractured gunhands left and right as men attempted to force their way into the tiny cell. By sheer weight of numbers the attackers succeeded in bursting through the door. The trapped Mormons were visibly shaken by the sight; the mobbers had smeared their faces with gunpowder to protect their identities, and the effect was staggering. With the realization that resistance was useless, Taylor made for the window. A pistol ball caught him in the left thigh and he fell across the sill. But a rifle shot from outside tore into his vestpocket watch and hurled him back into the room. He struggled to stand and was wounded twice more, one ball striking his left forearm, the second smashing his left knee. Barely conscious, Taylor managed to roll under a bed in the corner of the room. While he lay there, a fifth bullet plowed into his left hip, mangling the flesh terribly. Blood literally washed the floor.

No sooner had Taylor been thrust from the window by the outside shot than Joseph sprang to the sill. Silhouetted in the opening, he made an excellent target for the mob. Two shots from the undefended doorway struck the prophet in the back, a third bullet, from outside, entered his chest. Joseph screamed out, "O Lord. My God!" and plunged to earth. He struck the ground on his left side.

"He's leaped the window!" cried one of the men inside the jail, and the painted gunmen ran out to where he had fallen.

Inside the blood-splattered cell, one man stood alone amid the carnage. Willard Richards, bleeding slightly from a nick on the lobe of his left ear from a bullet, had been forgotten by the attackers almost at the moment he had thought himself a dead man. From the window he watched the crowd gather around Joseph. Richards did not witness what took place outside the jail in the next few minutes, and many of the facts became distorted in the confusion which followed. But apparently a man, barefoot and bareheaded, without a coat, his shirtsleeves rolled above his elbows, his pants above his knees, pushed through the mob. He propped the prophet against the south side of the well curb a few feet from the jail wall. Four men then were ordered to finish what they had started. Standing eight feet from their victim, they fired their muskets simultaneously into Joseph. A slight tremor shook his body; he pitched forward on his face, dead.

The barefoot man again stepped forward, this time with a bowie knife in hand. He intended to sever Joseph's head and collect the considerable bounty said to be offered for it.[42] Suddenly the sun flashed through the clouds and bathed the bizarre scene in an eerie light.[43] This so startled the mobbers that they paused momentarily in the slaughter. Someone remembered Taylor and Richards back in the jail, and several raiders turned to finish their bloody deed. Expecting to be shot at any instant, Richards had stepped from the window moments before and prepared to flee when Taylor called to him from under the bed.

"Take me," he cried out piteously.

Richards caught Taylor under the arm and pulled him to a dungeon room. Stretching the horribly wounded man on the floor, Richards covered him with straw.

"This is a hard case to lay you on the floor, but if your wounds are not fatal, I want you to live to tell the story," Richards explained quickly.[44]

He then stood to meet his death; he could hear men running up the stairs, then excited conversation as they found the dead body of Hyrum. From outside the prison came anxious shouts.

"The Mormons are coming! The Mormons are coming!"

Panic seized the milling crowd, and general confusion reigned as the mobbers broke and fled. Richards all at once found himself alone, surrounded by an almost appalling silence. Wearily he brushed away the straw which covered Taylor and made him comfortable before going for

[42] There is some question regarding the validity of this version. Mormon accounts of the martyrdom generally report that in one way or another the prophet's body was the object of a final outrage by the mobbers; either it was riddled by bullets or an attempt was made at decapitation. For example, see Jenson, *Church Encyclopaedia*, p. 571. But members of both the Carthage Greys and the mob steadfastly denied that Joseph's body was propped up and used for a target after his leap from the window — or that an effort was made to behead him. See Scofield, *History of Hancock County*, Vol. II, pp. 845–47, which contains statements from William R. Hamilton, a Carthage Grey, and "J. H. S.," one of the mob.

On the other hand, both Richards and Taylor agree that Joseph was shot three times as he crouched in the window. Yet, a later examination of his body disclosed that five bullets had struck him; *History of the Church*, Vol. VI, p. 627. One can only conclude that Joseph was shot again after his fall to the ground.

[43] As described by William M. Daniels, who said he was an eyewitness and later published his story as: *A Correct Account of the Murder of Generals Joseph and Hyrum Smith, at Carthage, on the 27th Day of June, 1844* (Nauvoo, Illinois, 1845), p. 15. B. H. Roberts in *Comprehensive History of the Church*, Vol. II, pp. 332–34, completely discredits Daniels' version.

[44] Jenson, *Church Encyclopaedia*, p. 572.

help. Taylor's watch was shattered where it had been hit. The hands pointed to five o'clock, sixteen minutes and twenty-six seconds, an hour which would live in infamy for the Mormons.

While the Carthage drama was being enacted, Governor Ford stood on the platform in Nauvoo telling the Saints, "A great crime has been done by destroying the *Expositor* press and placing the city under martial law, and a severe atonement must be made, so prepare your minds for the emergency."

An angry murmur ran through the crowd, but Ford continued: "Depend upon it, a little more misbehavior from the citizens, and the torch, which is already lighted, will be applied, and the city may be reduced to ashes, and extermination would inevitably follow; and it gives me great pain to think that there is danger of so many innocent women and children being exterminated."

Ford's continued use of the word exterminate caused many Mormons to exchange ominous glances.

"If anything of a serious character," he was saying, "should befall the lives or property of the persons who are prosecuting your leaders, you will be held responsible." [45] Satisfied that he had made his point, Ford stepped from the platform and joined his party.

Rockwell, who had listened to the governor with keen interest, sat in his room for a long time that evening, lost in thought. For the first time in his stormy life he was genuinely worried; there had been no word from Joseph, and it bothered him. Then, too, there was the matter of Ford's conduct. Rockwell had not liked the governor's repeated emphasis on "atonement" and "extermination." On top of that, an incident earlier in the day had puzzled him greatly. Just before Ford addressed the Saints he had closeted himself with members of his escort in a suite of rooms in the Mansion House. Prior to his arrival, the apartment had been the scene of a meeting between Rockwell, the Nauvoo Legion staff, and the High Council, in which they discussed the note Rockwell had taken from Francis Higbee. But Ford's appearance had interrupted the session, and the participants quickly dispersed. In his haste Rockwell left his hat behind and discovered the oversight only after Ford had taken the suite.

Unaware that the rooms were occupied, the Mormon walked in on the governor while he was in deep conversation with several of his retinue.

45 *History of the Church*, Vol. VI, p. 623.

One man was finishing a speech, and, gesturing with his hand, he concluded: "The deed is done before this time." [46] At the sight of Rockwell the speaker blanched and stood silent; an uneasy quiet fell over the group as the prophet's bodyguard walked to the rack and picked up his hat. The remark had perplexed Rockwell at the time, but he shrugged it off. Now, as he lay stretched out on his bed, fitting the pieces together in an effort to make order out of confusion, things made less sense than before.

Late that night Rockwell saddled his horse and rode out of Nauvoo on the Carthage road. Here he met George D. Grant bearing news of the attack on the jail. Rockwell listened in disbelief as Grant blurted out what he knew of the killings. The breathless rider concluded his message by describing the Carthage Greys firing their weapons skyward.

"Who was in charge of the troops?" Rockwell asked.

"Worrell. Frank Worrell," came the reply.

Anson Call was one of the Nauvoo Temple guards on the morning of June 28. The tour of duty had been uneventful and Call was preparing to leave when he heard the rhythmic hoofbeats of a horse being ridden hard. The voice which bellowed through the night air was unmistakably Porter Rockwell's, but Call quickly sensed an unusual urgency in the throaty roar. He was unable to make out the words until Rockwell had closed the gap by nearly two of Nauvoo's lengthy city blocks.

"*Joseph is killed — they have killed him! Goddamn them! They have killed him!*" [47]

[46] Affidavit of Orrin Porter Rockwell made April 14, 1856, in Great Salt Lake City before Salt Lake County Recorder Thomas Bullock, ibid., pp. 588–89.

[47] Anson Call, "Life and Record," MS, p. 27.

Chapter Seven

A PROPHET AVENGED

THREE MILES FROM NAUVOO, Ford and his party had intercepted Grant and another messenger heading for the Mormon city with the first report of the murders.[1] Fearing an outbreak on the part of the Saints, the governor ordered the riders to accompany him as far as Grant's home on the outskirts of Carthage from where he could issue orders to evacuate the town and remove all the county records and documents. This done, Ford proceeded to Carthage and permitted Grant to continue to Nauvoo. The governor's anxiety over a Mormon rebellion was needless; Willard Richards had sent a message to the High Council ordering the Legion to "stay at home and be prepared for an attack from Missouri mobbers."

Early on the morning of the twenty-eighth, Richards brought the bodies of the prophet and his brother into Nauvoo. A crowd of some ten thousand had assembled to meet them. Weeping men and women lined the streets four deep, their sobs mingled with cries for revenge. Allen Stout penned in his journal the emotion of that day:

Their dead bodies were brought to Nauvoo, where I saw their beloved forms reposing in the arms of death, which gave me such feelings as I

[1] Ford in *History of Illinois*, pp. 354–55, described the prophet's assassination in these words:

Thus fell Joe Smith, the most successful imposter in modern times; a man who, though ignorant and coarse, had some great natural parts which fitted him for temporary success, but which were so obscured and counteracted by the inherent corruption and vices of his nature that he never could succeed in establishing a system of policy which looked to permanent success in the future. His lusts, his love of money and power, always set him to studying present gratification and convenience rather than the remote consequences of his plans. It seems that no power of intellect can save a corrupt man from this error. . . . It must not be supposed that the pretended prophet practiced the tricks of a common imposter; that he was a dark and gloomy person with a long beard, a grave and severe aspect, and a reserved and saintly carriage of his person; on the contrary, he was full of levity, even to boyish romping; dressed like a dandy, and at times drank like a sailor and swore like a pirate. He could, as occasion required, be exceedingly meek in his deportment; and then again rough and boisterous as a highway robber; being always able to satisfy his followers of the propriety of his conduct. He always quailed before power and was arrogant to weakness. . . .

am not able to describe. But I there and then resolved in my mind that I would never let an opportunity slip unimproved of avenging their blood upon the head of the enemies of the church of Jesus Christ. I felt as though I could not live; I knew not how to contain myself, and when I see one of the men who persuaded them to give up to be tried, I feel like cutting their throats yet. And I hope to live to avenge their blood; but if I do not I will teach my children and children's children to the fourth generation as long as there is one descendant of the murderers upon the earth.[2]

After the martyrs to the Mormon cause had been viewed by the multitude, the Mansion House was cleared of mourners, and a select group of elders planned the funeral. The coffins were removed from their outer pine boxes and locked in a bedroom until they could be transferred unnoticed. Sand was placed in the boxes and they, in turn, were taken to the cemetery and interred with great ceremony. Toward midnight, the secret group removed the coffins containing the bodies from the Mansion bedroom and carried them under guard to the still uncompleted Nauvoo House; there they buried the caskets in the basement as a precautionary measure against desecration of the graves by enemies of the church.

Within days of the Carthage attack the Mormons were in possession of a complete roster of the Carthage Greys as well as a list of every man believed to have participated in the mob. The information came from various sources, including eventually Jacob B. Backenstos, newly-elected sheriff of Hancock County and a Mormon sympathizer.[3] Willard Richards added to the roll the names of Joseph H. Jackson, the Laws, the Higbees, and the Fosters, all of whom he had seen in the mob at the jail.

When the Saints failed to march against Carthage, the anti-Mormons

[2] Allen Joseph Stout, "Journal," pp. 13–14.

[3] It was alleged by some that Backenstos was, in fact, a Mormon. It was certain, at least, that his brother had married a niece of Joseph Smith. Ford, *History of Illinois*, p. 408; *History of the Church*, Vol. VI, p. 43.

quickly seized the initiative and bombarded the governor with demands to oust the church from Illinois. Ford was caught between two forces. While the Mormon-haters were agitating for action, the Saints were clamoring for the murderers of their prophet to be brought to justice.

"The anti-Mormons ask me to violate the constitution, which I am sworn to support, by erecting myself into a military despot and exiling the Mormons. The Mormons, on their part, in their newspapers invite me to assume absolute power by taking a summary vengeance upon their enemies, by shooting fifty or a hundred of them without judge or jury." Ford's decision was typical of the manner in which he set about solving thorny issues of the Mormon question during his tenure in office — he did nothing.

The Saints now were faced with a problem which threatened their very existence — who was to assume leadership of the church? With both Joseph and Hyrum dead, Sidney Rigdon was the sole remaining member of the First Presidency, and he was in Pittsburgh campaigning for the prophet's election to the White House. The twelve apostles were scattered to the winds on mission assignments, and the church was without direction in the confusion which followed Joseph's assassination. To stem the disorder which prevailed in the city, Richards, Taylor, who was recovering from his wounds, and W. W. Phelps issued a statement asking the Saints to calmly await the arrival of the apostles, who had been called home.

Sidney Rigdon arrived in Nauvoo on August 3 and immediately conferred with an attorney. He avoided a confrontation with members of the Council of Twelve Apostles the following day, a Sunday, and instead addressed the six thousand or so Saints assembled for services. Rigdon quickly announced that he had seen a vision.[4] A guardian must be ap-

[4] Orson Hyde, *Speech of Elder Orson Hyde, Delivered Before the High Priests' Quorum, in Nauvoo, April 27th, 1845, Upon the Course and Conduct of Mr. Sidney*

pointed to rule the church, he said. And he was just the man for the job, he added. Another day passed and Rigdon told the now-angry apostles — there were only five in the city — that he did not expect the brethren to select a guardian at once, but "to have a prayer meeting and interchange of thought and feeling, and warm up each other's hearts." Meanwhile, he would be available should anyone wish to speak to him on the subject. Rigdon's heart cooled somewhat when Brigham Young disembarked at the steamboat landing fresh from his eastern mission. Young was the one man clever and ruthless enough to lock horns with the wily Rigdon — and Rigdon knew it.

While the church authorities were embroiled in this power struggle, one man had paid little heed to what was happening. Porter Rockwell contented himself with standing on the fringe of the turmoil and looking on. He already knew what he would do — just what Joseph would have wanted him to do. The Saints remembered how the prophet had come to despise Rigdon, how he had told them in conference he would have no more to do with his counselor. Now Rigdon was attempting to gain a position he had coveted all the time he had been a member of the presidency. Rockwell knew how the Saints would vote, if it came to a vote. He had reminded his friends of the prophet's words: "I have thrown him off my shoulders . . . ." This time Rigdon would stay off. It remained only for Brigham Young to quash Rigdon once and for all.

Young was more than equal to the task. As president of the Council of Twelve Apostles, he made a stirring speech to the Saints of Nauvoo at a special conference on August 8. It was so potent in its delivery that many Mormons went away believing they had heard the voice of their martyred prophet.[5] "Do you want a church properly organized," Young

---

Rigdon, and Upon the Merits of His Claims to the Presidency of the Church of Jesus Christ of Latter-Day Saints (Liverpool, 1845), p. 12.

[5] Several Mormons described this phenomenon. See Jenson, *Church Encyclopaedia*, p. 27, and Lee, *Mormonism Unveiled*, p. 155. Lee says, "Just then Brigham Young arose and roared like a young lion, imitating the style and voice of Joseph, the Prophet. Many of the brethren declared that they saw the mantle of Joseph fall upon him. I myself, at the time, imagined that I saw and heard a strong resemblance to the Prophet in him . . . ." Lee, however, was only repeating hearsay, for he did not arrive in Nauvoo from his mission to Kentucky until August 20, 1844. Anson Call, "Life and Record," p. 30, wrote: "It was Joseph's voice and Joseph's gestures through the entire discourse." See also statements of George Q. Cannon in Tullidge, *Life of Brigham Young*, pp. 115–16; and Wilford Woodruff in the *Deseret News*, March 12, 1892.

asked his massive audience, "or do you want a spokesman to be chief cook and bottle-washer?"

When the conference came to a close, Sidney Rigdon was a broken man, the membership had voted to support the apostles and had agreed as well to name trustees-in-trust and to continue paying a tithe until the temple was constructed. All that remained to make Rigdon's humiliation complete was his excommunication, a formality not long in coming. On September 8, 1844, after a High Council trial, Sidney Rigdon was "delivered over to the buffetings of Satan in the name of the Lord."

Disturbing reports reached Nauvoo of a "wolf-hunt," planned by the anti-Mormons for the purpose of burning out the Saints and killing their leaders. It was thought that the scheme was purely retaliatory in response to an increasing number of thefts plaguing the Gentile population, crimes which were laid at the feet of the Mormons. The underlying reason, however, was the approaching election. The Whig party, badly used by the Saints in the election of 1840, was emphatic in its desire to prevent the Mormons from balloting again. At the same time, the Democrats, willing and anxious for Mormon votes, were reluctant to risk the party's popularity by catering to them. It was a situation which prompted Ford to remark, "Such being the odious character of the Mormons, the hatred of the common people against them, and such being the pusillanimity of leading men in fearing to encounter it," his Democratic friends "quailed under the tempest." [6]

To be on the safe side, Brigham Young ordered the Legion to again begin regular drills. He also opened an arsenal. If mobs came, Young wanted the Mormons ready to fight. To meet his challenge, the anti-Mormons invited militia captains in neighboring counties, including Missouri and Iowa, to join in the so-called wolf-hunt. It was to be a turkey shoot — with Mormons as targets. Then, in the midst of this charged atmosphere, Ford intervened to stymie the Gentiles. A volunteer army of five hundred men commanded by Brigadier General J. J. Hardin routed arriving militia groups, whose leaders ran off to Missouri. "The Carthage Greys fled almost in a body, taking their arms with them," Ford said.

The months to follow were filled with accusations and recriminations between the Mormons and the "anti's," each charging the other with the

[6] Ford, *History of Illinois*, p. 364.

blackest of deeds — even murder.[7] Week after week the *Nauvoo Neighbor* and the *Warsaw Signal* traded insults, and occasionally the name Porter Rockwell was splashed across pages of the opposition press.[8] Finally the Saints issued a proclamation denouncing the *Warsaw Signal*, the *Alton Telegraph*, and the *Quincy Whig* for engaging in "the circulation of falsehood," and declared that "to prevent further depredations in our city, by lawless desperadoes from abroad, we approve the raising of 500 police by this city." [9] It was too late to close the barn door; Nauvoo had already become the most lawless city on the river. At a Seventies meeting called to study the problem, Brigham Young presented a novel point of view:

> When men have come into our midst who were as corrupt as the devil himself, many have supposed it would have been better to have cut their throats with a feather and exposed their sink of corruption, and

[7] Some of the murders attributed to the Mormons during this period are discussed in Lee, *Mormonism Unveiled*, pp. 158–60. Thomas Gregg, a resident of the area, laid the blame for outrages in and around Nauvoo on the Danite Band. See Gregg, *History of Hancock County, Illinois, Together With an Outline History of the State and a Digest of State Law* (Chicago, 1880), p. 272.

[8] Rockwell was mentioned in the *Burlington Hawkeye and Iowa Patriot* (Burlington, Iowa), as being a "very suspicious" character around Nauvoo and was accused of soliciting help in a proposed burglary. Quoted in Bennett, *History of the Saints*, p. 92.

Robert H. Birch, accused of complicity in the murder of Colonel George Davenport, a retired fur trader, at his Rock Island, Illinois, home on July 4, 1845, confessed that the plot to rob the aged victim was hatched in Nauvoo. "The first council for arranging the robbery . . . was held in Joseph Smith's old council chamber in Nauvoo. [William] Fox, John and Aaron Long, Jack Redden, and Hodges, O. P. Rockwell, John Ray, Wm. Louther, myself and several others . . . were present . . . . Fox said . . . [we] would get as much as thirty or forty thousand dollars. They all thought . . . it best to rake the old fellow down. Rockwell remarked that it was best for us to monopolize the business, as there was enough of us to raise all the good sights [potential thefts] we could find." Edward Bonney, *The Banditti of the Prairies; A Tale of the Mississippi Valley* (Chicago, 1850), p. 202. *The Illinois State Register*, October 31, 1845, published a paragraph from the *Missouri Reporter*, October 23, 1845, about Birch, one of the men arrested for the murder of Colonel Davenport, saying that Jack Redden had killed "Arvine Hodges" and Brigham Young was privy to it. See also *Illinois State Register*, November 14, 21, 1845, and January 9, 1846, for reports of the execution of the condemned men, the appeal of John Baxter, who was arrested with them and later freed; and a long letter from Edward Bonney explaining his part in bringing the gang to justice.

For more on the Mormons during this period see J. M. Reid, *Sketches and Anecdotes of the Old Settlers and Newcomers, the Mormon Bandits and Danite Band* (Keokuk, Iowa, 1876).

[9] *Times and Seasons*, Vol. VI, No. 1 (January 1845), pp. 773–75.

let them go to hell where they belonged, than to have borne with them as Brother Joseph Smith did; but this course would meet with a conflicting argument. To stop a man in his career would be taking away his agency . . . . If they were cut off from the earth they might with propriety come up in the day of judgment and say we took away their agency, which if we had let alone, they would have repented of their sins and redeemed a part of their time. The presidents of seventies should be men of wisdom and know how to save men instead of destroying them . . . .[10]

To add to their woes, the Saints suddenly found their highly prized city charter pulled out from over them by an act of the Illinois Legislature.[11] Under general law, Nauvoo was now permitted only justice of peace courts, none higher. By revoking the charter, the Legislature hoped to break the back of the Municipal Court which Joseph had used to such advantage. Thus the Saints were stripped of their power to issue writs of habeas corpus. With their ability to fend off legal warrants so severely restricted, the Saints began to panic. The church's steamer, *Maid of Iowa*, marked an unexpected surge in fares from Nauvoo due to an unexpected number of Mormons called to missions rather than face writs of arrest.[12] Aware that it was only a matter of time before an open clash between the Saints and the anti-Mormons, Young stepped up the work on the temple and the Nauvoo House in an effort to complete the two projects before the collision occurred. Then came the greatest disappointment of all.

On May 19, 1845, members of the Carthage mob were brought to trial for the murders of Joseph and Hyrum Smith. The proceedings commanded the undivided attention of Mormon and Gentile alike in western Illinois and Missouri. In its own way the case had resolved itself to a showdown between the two forces. As the prosecution progressed, daily reports were carried to Nauvoo, where each nugget of testimony was digested, interpreted, and argued with passionate interest. Rockwell was particularly concerned with evidence elicited from Frank Worrell, the

---

[10] *History of the Church*, Vol. VII, pp. 366–67. At this same meeting Elder Joseph Young criticized the Seventies when he said, "There are brethren in these quorums and even presidents who are connected with a body of those consecrating thieves, who pretend to say that they have a right to consecrate from the Gentiles, but such will steal from their brethren as well as others.'

[11] A report on the Nauvoo Charter debate was carried in the *Illinois State Register*, January 17, 1845.

[12] *History of the Church*, Vol. VII, p. 380.

Carthage Grey lieutenant. Worrell had flatly refused to answer a question put forth by the prosecution as to whether the rifles carried by the Greys on the night of the attack had been loaded with blanks. The sullen young officer informed the court that any answer he gave would incriminate him. After twelve days of testimony and cross-examination, the defendants were acquitted,[13] provoking unrestrained celebration among the anti-Mormons and causing Brigham Young to comment caustically that the verdict was reached despite "the court, attorneys, jury and bystanders being all fully satisfied of their guilt." [14]

Indignation boiled over Nauvoo with the fury of a storm at sea. In their anger the Saints neglected the tight-knit security which had been their protection for so many years. Now Gentiles infiltrated the population with ease, seeing and hearing things which in the past had been concealed from outsiders. One of the first victims of this reckless indifference was Rockwell. He was seized by Carthage authorities, who held a warrant for his arrest on counterfeiting charges. But before the sheriff could manacle his prize, Rockwell escaped.[15]

The mood in Hancock County grew more and more uncertain. Before his death, Joseph had organized the secret Council of Fifty, an exclusive body of men charged with being the legislature of the Kingdom of God (which included the church). It was also known as the General Council and was presented with the task of finding a new home for the Saints, preferably in the far west.[16]

---

[13] Accused of the crime were Colonel Levi Williams, a minister; Thomas C. Sharp, editor of the *Warsaw Signal*; Jacob C. Davis, attorney and state senator; Mark Aldrich, captain of a Hancock County militia company; and William N. Grover, attorney. Four others: John Allen, William Voras or Voorhees, John Wills, and William Gallaher, were indicted, but avoided arrest and were never brought to trial; little is known of their backgrounds. The best work on the court proceedings is Dallin H. Oaks and Marvin S. Hill, *Carthage Conspiracy; The Trial of the Accused Assassins of Joseph Smith* (Urbana, Illinois; Chicago; London, 1975).

[14] *History of the Church*, Vol. VII, p. 420. There apparently was little doubt on the part of the public as to the guilt of the defendants. According to John Hay, "The Mormon Prophet's Tragedy," *The Atlantic Monthly*, Vol. XXIV (1869), p. 678, the prosecutor failed to prove his case. There may be some analogy in Rockwell's acquittal in Missouri.

[15] *History of the Church*, Vol. VII, p. 428.

[16] Joseph formed the nucleus of this unique body on March 11, 1844, as a policy-making organization for the church. Membership was considered a high honor and the nature of the council's responsibilities demanded talents as varied as the problems with which it dealt. (Unschooled as he was, Rockwell gained a seat in the council because of his knowledge and capabilities in the field and his reputation

Young frequently availed himself of the combined experience of council membership to discuss various possibilities for resettlement. Consequently, on September 9 the Fifty reached a momentous decision — to send a company of men to the Valley of the Great Salt Lake west of the Rockies to determine the wisdom of establishing a new Zion in that distant land.[17] The same night, an anti-Mormon meeting in the nearby

as a man of great courage.) Council members often held positions of authority in other church, civic, and political areas, and in this way were able to exert a wide measure of influence. At the time of its inception, Joseph observed in his journal: ". . . I organized [a] special council, to take into consideration the subject matter contained in the above letters [regarding the Southwest as a new location for the church], and also the best policy for this people to adopt to obtain their rights from the nation and insure protection for themselves and children; and to secure a resting place in the mountains, or some uninhabited region, where we can enjoy the liberty of conscience guaranteed to us by the Constitution of our country." *History of the Church*, Vol. VI, pp. 260–61. In "History of Brigham Young," *Millennial Star*, Vol. XXVI, p. 328, Young says several of the members of the council were non-Mormons. It has been suspected by some historians that Daniel H. Wells, a Nauvoo justice of the peace, had been called to join the body before his actual conversion in 1846, and that Colonel Thomas L. Kane enjoyed the privileges of membership. Young also said of the secret group: "We prepared several memorials to Congress for the redress of our grievances, and used every available means to inform ourselves of the unoccupied territory open to settlers.

"We held a number of sessions, and investigated the principles upon which our national government is founded; and the true foundation and principles of all governments."

The west was never very far from Joseph Smith's thoughts in these troubled times. As early as April 1844, he had received assurances from Orson Hyde in Washington, D.C., that Congress, while reluctant to set Oregon territory aside for particular individuals, would not as a body oppose a Mormon migration to that region. Stephen A. Douglas had supplied Hyde with a map of Oregon and a report on explorations of the country between the Missouri River and the Rocky Mountains along the Kansas and great Platte rivers by Lieut. John C. Frémont. "Judge D says the [report] is a public document, and [he] will frank it to [Joseph Smith]," Hyde wrote. *Millennial Star*, Vol. XXIII, p. 519.

A study of the council and its role in the Kingdom of God can be found in James R. Clark, "The Kingdom of God, the Council of Fifty and the State of Deseret," *Utah Historical Quarterly*, Vol. XXVI (April 1958), pp. 131–48.

[17] Prior to his death Joseph had ordered a company under the command of James Emmett to journey to the Missouri River and plant crops in preparation for the mass Mormon migration west. The expedition encountered delays, but finally undertook its mission in May 1845, nearly a year after the martyrdom. The effort was a disaster, and the company, riddled with dissension, returned. William Decatur Kartchner, "Expedition of the Emmett Company." MS. For an excellent treatment of this obscure venture see "The Reminiscences of James Holt; A Narrative of the Emmett Company," edited by Dale L. Morgan, *Utah Historical Quarterly*, Vol. XXIII (1955), pp. 1–33, 151–79.

community of Green Plains, south of Warsaw, was fired upon. Enraged, the anti-Mormons vowed vengeance on Nauvoo, while Young futilely protested that the entire matter had been staged by Gentiles as an excuse to declare open warfare.

His denials were ignored; the anti-Mormons put the countryside to the torch. The Mormon settlements in Yelrome, Morley, and Lima were swiftly reduced to cinders. Once again hideously painted raiders led by Levi Williams rode into the night to terrorize the Saints. Williams swore he would leave a trail of burned Mormon homes all the way to Nauvoo—and set a match to that city, too.

Jacob Backenstos, the county sheriff, hastened to Warsaw to raise a posse and capture the marauders. But sentiment against the Saints ran high, and he was unable to recruit a single volunteer. By September 15 the Mormons counted forty-four homes destroyed. After his failure to muster a posse in Warsaw, Backenstos rode to his home in Carthage, only to be driven out by a committee of seething Illinoisians who accused him of siding with the Mormons. Returning to Warsaw, the sheriff spent the night with friends who warned him of a plot against his life. Thus alerted, Backenstos was doubly careful as he drove his carriage back to Carthage the next morning.

Lieutenant Frank Worrell of the Carthage Greys was flanked by two companions as he nudged his horse along the Warsaw road on the morning of September 16. Behind the three riders came five other men in a light rig and a two-horse wagon containing their rifles.[18] As they approached the Nauvoo road, Worrell pointed to a carriage nearing the crossroads in front of them. "It's that damn Backenstos," he shouted, spurring forward.

Backenstos had been eying the riders closely as they drew nearer, and when the lead horseman suddenly slapped his mount to a gallop, the sheriff laid on the whip and urged his own animal to top speed. Having the advantage of a two-hundred-yard lead, Backenstos disappeared over the brow of a hill before the rider could overtake him.

As it happened, Rockwell and another Mormon, Return Jackson Red-

[18] From contemporary newspaper accounts four of the Worrell party can be identified as James Stewart, James D. Burnes, John Harper, and Fountain McQuary. See *Warsaw Signal*, October 15, 1845; and *Illinois State Register*, December 19, 1845.

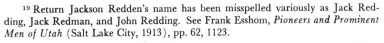

den,[19] were watering their horses near a railroad siding when they spotted Backenstos charging straight at them. His pursuers were still out of sight beyond the rise. Rockwell and Redden, who had been assisting burned-out Mormon families in moving their possessions, sensed trouble and reached for their guns. The sheriff pulled hard on the reins and jerked to a stop in a cloud of dust. Backenstos sputtered in his haste to get the words out; he ordered the two Mormons to protect him "in the name of the state of Illinois, County of Hancock," from the "mob" at his heels.[20] "Don't worry," Rockwell said, "We've got our pistols and two rifles."

No sooner had he spoken than two horsemen appeared on the crest of the hill and raced down on them. Worrell was well ahead of the closest man; the other had been thrown when his horse stumbled. Once the two were within hailing distance the sheriff shouted an order to stop. In answer, Worrell reached for his pistol. Before he could bring the gun to bear, a ball from Rockwell's rifle tore into his abdomen and catapulted Worrell from the saddle. At the sound of the shot the second rider frantically wheeled his horse and galloped to the wagon and buggy now arriving on the scene. The men gazed in disbelief at Worrell's crumpled form on the ground. Under Rockwell's cold gaze they gathered up their wounded leader and carried him to the wagon; he died before they reached Warsaw.[21]

---

[19] Return Jackson Redden's name has been misspelled variously as Jack Redding, Jack Redman, and John Redding. See Frank Esshom, *Pioneers and Prominent Men of Utah* (Salt Lake City, 1913), pp. 62, 1123.

[20] *History of the Church*, Vol. VII, p. 446. See also letter from George Miller to the *Northern Islander* (Beaver Island, Lake Michigan), dated June 28, 1855, published September 6, 1855.

[21] Another Mormon, Peter Wilson Conover, was a witness to the shooting. "Rockwell fired and the man jumped four feet in the air and rolled away from his horse dead." Conover, "Autobiography," MS, p. 20. See also Gregg, *History of Hancock County*, pp. 340–41. The water hole at the siding was a busy place that morning. Four teamsters who were there, Edward Johnson, Calvin and Josiah Miles, and Gilbert D. Goldsmith, appeared as witnesses at the sheriff's trial for murder. They testified that he had called out to the pursuing horsemen, "Go back, go back, peaceably!" and that one of the riders had leveled a gun at Backenstos, when a rifle was fired from the brush, taking effect upon Worrell. *Illinois State Register*, December 19, 1845. In an affidavit sworn September 22, 1845, and published in the *Warsaw Signal*, October 15, 1845, John Harper, one of Worrell's party, said that Backenstos was seen coming in his buggy "and we thought he knew us, for he left the road and took through the prairie as fast as he could push his horse, and we took after him; but he run until he came to a branch where there was a group of Mormons in the brush." Harper stated that Backenstos "could not have shot Worrell, for he

Turning to Redden, Rockwell remarked matter-of-factly, "I aimed for his belt buckle."

A Mormon farmer, Jacob Baum, on whose property Rockwell and Redden had halted for water, came running to see what the shooting was about. Rockwell was slipping the rifle into his saddle boot as Baum approached.

"What happened?" Baum asked.

"I got him," Rockwell explained.

"Got who?"

"Worrell. I was afraid my rifle couldn't reach him, but it did, thank God." [22]

A shaken Backenstos accompanied Rockwell and Redden to Nauvoo and sought out Brigham Young. He had sent the Mormon leader a message asking for help in providing a posse and now pressed for an answer. Young replied by offering Backenstos the services of two thousand men of the Nauvoo Legion.[23] With the sheriff and Rockwell[24] leading them, the Legionnaires swept across Hancock County routing anti-Mormons from their homes, causing many to flee into Missouri and Iowa.[25] House-burnings continued, but now Gentile property went up in flames as Backenstos' army tipped the scales of power. In a frenzy, the *Warsaw Signal* unleashed a vicious tirade against "Napoleon Backenstos," and

---

was 100 or 150 yards off, and had nothing but a pistol; it was a yager or musket fired from the bushes, for it was an ounce ball and went through him. Worrell was put into the wagon & died in my lap in one half-hour . . . ."

[22] Bean, *Autobiography*, p. 175. Baum's conversation with Rockwell here is exactly as the farmer repeated it to his son-in-law, George W. Bean.

For another version of the shooting, see Hall, *Abominations of Mormonism Exposed*, p. 28. "The death of John Worrell, about this time, caused a deep sensation. He was riding on the highway, some six miles from Carthage. The sheriff . . . I think, M'Intosh [Backenstos] by name, was called a Jack Mormon, because he had been elected by Mormon influence. [He] and Porter Rockwell, the man who shot Gov. Boggs . . . espied Mr. Worrell coming up the road . . . . They immediately got behind a copse of hazel, and as he came up, Rockwell fired and Worrell fell . . . ."

Backenstos' report of the affair was published as his "Proclamation II" reprinted in the *Nauvoo Neighbor* on September 17 and 24 and October 1, 1845.

[23] *History of the Church*, Vol. VII, p. 445.

[24] Journal History, September 18, 1845. According to George Miller in a letter to the *Northern Islander* dated June 28, 1855, and published September 6, 1855, Rockwell was a confidential courier between Backenstos and Brigham Young during these hectic days.

[25] Ford, *History of Illinois*, p. 408.

called on the anti-Mormons to arm and seek "Revenge! Revenge!" for Worrell's death.

News of the potential civil war reached Governor Ford at Jacksonville where, in a conference with state leaders, it was decided to send Judge Stephen A. Douglas, General Hardin, Attorney General T. A. McDougal, and Major W. B. Warren with four hundred troops to Hancock County to put an end to lawlessness on both sides. Describing the situation, Ford wrote: "During the ascendency of the sheriff and the absence of the anti-Mormons from their houses the people who had been burnt out of their houses assembled in Nauvoo, from whence, with many others, they sallied forth and ravaged the country, stealing and plundering whatever was convenient to carry or drive away." [26]

Among other things, the governor's committee entered Nauvoo to search for the bodies of two men believed murdered by the Mormons.[27] As General Hardin and Judge Douglas examined the Mansion House stables for some sign of the missing men, Almon W. Babbitt, a Mormon attorney, grumbled, "You must think we are fools to bury dead men in a stable when it is so easy to throw them into the Mississippi a few rods away." [28]

Brigham Young met the committee in council on October 1 and announced that the Saints had decided to abandon Illinois to the devil and migrate West, perhaps to Oregon or even Vancouver Island. This unexpected news met with the hearty approval of the four representatives. They were convinced that,

> affairs have reached such a crisis, that it has become impossible for your church to remain in this country. . . . Should you not [leave], we are satisfied, however much we may deprecate violence and bloodshed, that violent measures will be resorted to, to compel your removal, which will result in most disastrous consequences to yourselves and your opponents, and that the end will be your expulsion from the state.

[26] Ibid., p. 409.

[27] According to Ford, *History of Illinois*, p. 409, the victims were two men named Daubenheyer and Wilcox. In *Proceedings of a Convention, Held at Carthage, in Hancock County, Ill., on Tuesday and Wednesday, October 1st and 2nd, 1845* (Quincy, 1845), p. 9, the editors of the *Quincy Whig* commented bitterly that "[Andrew] Daubenhayer's body subsequently was found [in Nauvoo] with a musket ball through the back of his head." Phineas Wilcox ". . . lies probably at the bottom of the Mississippi, 'food for the catfish,' as the Mormon Prophet has often threatened should be the fate of those who opposed his power."

[28] *History of the Church*, Vol. VII, p. 448.

We think that steps should be taken by you to make it apparent
that you are actually preparing to remove in the spring. . . .[29]

Now that the Saints had, in effect, knuckled under to the pressure of
popular opinion, the emboldened anti-Mormons screamed all the louder.
In particular they clamored for action in the Worrell shooting. Exasperated by the carping criticism of *Warsaw Signal* editorials, General Hardin
finally ordered the arrest of Backenstos on charges of first-degree murder
and demanded that the Mormons deliver Rockwell to stand trial as well.
The general's threat to "unroof every house in Nauvoo" unless his commands were obeyed was greeted with cold disdain by the populace.[30]
Backenstos managed a change of venue to Peoria and was acquitted in the
relative serenity of a non-partisan courtroom. Rockwell, meanwhile, remained out of sight until interest in his arrest waned.

Since Joseph's death Rockwell's attitude had undergone a striking
change; no longer reticent, he was now aggressive, even belligerent, and
his behavior became the cause of some little consternation to the Mormon
hierarchy. He boasted openly that with Joseph's death, the Gentile mob
had eliminated the only man who could control him. As if to emphasize
his words, Rockwell took a plural wife — at gunpoint. Prior to his arrest
in 1843 on charges of assault on Governor Boggs, Rockwell had taken up
residence in a tavern operated by Amos Davis, a Nauvoo Legion captain.
It was this officer's wife of whom Rockwell had become enamored. How
long the affair had been blooming is not a matter of record, but he did
acknowledge the lady publicly early in December of 1845.[31] Because of

[29] Ibid., pp. 450–51.

[30] Journal History, October 9, 1845; *History of the Church*, Vol. VII, p. 481.

[31] Concerning this, Hall, *Abominations of Mormonism Exposed*, p. 28, says, in
discussing the Worrell affair, "The reward given by Brigham Young to Rockwell for
this service was punctually paid. It was no less than the wife of a Mr. Davis, a
merchant of Nauvoo, whom he obtained through Young, and brought her into the
temple, and according to the spiritual wife system, she was *sealed up to him* for time
and eternity. Thus Rockwell perpetrated the double crime of murder and adultery."
Ford, *History of Illinois*, pp. 356–57, also has something to say about Mrs.
Davis: "It is a notorious fact that a desperado by the name of Rockwell, having
attracted the affections of a pretty woman, the wife of a Mormon merchant, took
her from her husband by force of arms to live with him in adultery. But whilst she
was so living notoriously in adultery with a Mormon bully, in the same city with her
husband, she was freely admitted to the best society in the place, to all the gay
assemblies, where she and her husband frequently met in the same dance."

his notoriety the matter did not pass unnoticed. Said the *Warsaw Signal* of December 10:

> O. P. ROCKWELL — This delectable specimen of humanity, who was once the peculiar pet of Joe Smith and has since been regarded as the main champion of Zion in the Holy City, who some time since refused to bury his own child,[32] but suffered it to be done at public expense, who was during the late difficulties Gen. Napoleon Backenstos' principal aid-de-camp, and rode by his side while making valiant charges on unarmed and unresisting men, this same O. P. Rockwell, the assassin of Governor Boggs, has taken to himself a wife — not his own wife, for be it remembered that he cast off the woman that law regarded as his wife long since; but he has appropriated to himself the wife of Amos Davis. It is generally the case that when a wife leave her husband to live with a seducer, they elope and settle in a place where they are not known; but there is no necessity for such a step in the Holy Nauvoo. So fashionable is it for the Heads of the church to appropriate the wives of other men to their own purposes, that it is regarded as no crime for one man to steal the companion of his neighbor and live with her in open unconcealed adultery. What a beautiful moral code is Mormonism!

Not long after the article appeared, word spread through Nauvoo that a widow had been "used up" for her life savings. In reporting the particulars, the *Warsaw Signal* commented: "Another suspicious feature of this matter is that some of the Saints accuse Amos Davis (who has lately become very unpopular in Nauvoo, because he would not tamely submit to an outrage from O. P. Rockwell) of the murder. This is evidently done for the purpose of running Davis out of the City, he being in the way of the Mormon pet, Rockwell." [33]

The *Signal*'s conjecture to the contrary, Davis did not depart from Nauvoo, a display of courage which placed him in a delicate and dangerous position, for one morning there appeared at his door the person of Mrs. Davis — in company with Rockwell. The humiliated tavernkeeper watched incredulously as his wife casually gathered together her belongings; Rockwell stood to one side and conspicuously inspected the trigger mechanism on his pistol. Scarcely had the couple closed the door on the hapless husband than word of the incident flashed through the streets of

---

[32] Some members of the Rockwell family remember being told a baby girl died in childbirth, but no records seem to exist which would show the date or place of birth.

[33] *Warsaw Signal*, December 24, 1845.

the city. By nightfall every gossip in town had told the story in detail several times.[34]

While Rockwell engaged in his rather public courtship, Brigham Young and the Council of Fifty were in difficulty. The church leader and eight apostles had been named in federal complaints charging them with counterfeiting United States coin.[35] After several unsuccessful attempts to arrest Young, Governor Ford used the situation to hasten the Saints' hegira from Illinois.[36] Since he considered it impolitic to have the apostles jailed, thereby retarding the exodus, Ford wrote a letter to Backenstos, knowing it would find its way into Young's hands, in which he presented misleading information to the effect that because of the outstanding warrants the federal government probably would attempt to prevent the Saints from leaving Nauvoo.[37] The scheme worked just as Ford had anticipated. Already laboring at a feverish pace, the Mormons redoubled efforts to evacuate their city. Hundreds of Saints received endowments in the partially finished temple from apostles who struggled round the clock to perform the ordinances. All Mormon houses in the city, including the temple itself, were converted into workshops where by spring more than twelve thousand wagons would be constructed for the journey ahead. Word that nearly all of Nauvoo was up for sale attracted speculators from far and wide. Overnight, houses, farms, livestock, and personal property went on the auction block.

Mormons who had worked for more than five years on their homes and in fields sacrificed everything for hard cash. Some, like John D. Lee, refused to be stampeded and balked at the ridiculous offers made by greedy bargain-hunters and land pirates. "My large house, costing me $8,000 (in Salt Lake City it would have been worth $50,000), I was offered $800 for. My fanaticism would not allow me to take that for it. I locked it up, selling only one stove out of it, for which I received eight

[34] Ibid., see also Hall, *Abominations of Mormonism Exposed*, p. 28. Hall says Rockwell occasionally entered Davis' inn with Mrs. Davis on his arm and the husband "did not dare refuse to deal or he would have been assassinated . . . ."

[35] *History of the Church*, Vol. VII, p. 549. *The Springfield Journal*, December 25, 1845, reported that twelve bills of indictment had been found against "prominent" Mormons for counterfeiting U.S. and Mexican coins.

[36] When a U.S. marshal attempted to arrest Young on the warrant, another Mormon, William Miller, duped the lawman into believing he was Young. This became known as the "Bogus Brigham Incident." *History of the Church*, Vol. VII, pp. 549–51.

[37] Admitted by the governor in Ford, *History of Illinois*, p. 413.

yards of cloth. The building, with its twenty-seven rooms, I turned over to the committee, to be sold to help the poor away. The committee informed me afterwards that they had sold the house for $12.50." [38]

When Orrin Porter Rockwell received his endowments in temple ceremonies on January 5, 1846, he may have been accompanied by the former Mrs. Davis, as William Hall suggests, but Luana Beebe Rockwell was not at his side. That is a certainty. She had been endowed three days before. Then too, on January 14 Luana married and was sealed in the temple[39] to Alpheus Cutler,[40] president of the High Council and one of the men selected to oversee construction of the Nauvoo Temple. Rockwell's children also were sealed to Cutler. In the midst of this disorder in his life, Rockwell continued to figure in the news. A St. Louis newspaper published an erroneous account that he had been "stabbed in Nauvoo by a man named Davis, whose wife he had appropriated to himself." [41]

His temple work completed, Rockwell joined the endless columns of Mormons ferrying the Mississippi for the long march across Iowa.[42] Plagued by freezing temperatures and lack of food, the Camp of Israel, as the migration called itself, pushed forward toward the Missouri River.

---

[38] Lee, *Mormonism Unveiled*, p. 175.

[39] Archives Records, Genealogical Society of Utah, Salt Lake City. In Mormon practice, "sealing" is an ordinance uniting for eternity husbands, wives, and children in the sacred bonds of the family.

[40] Not long after the death of Joseph Smith, Cutler announced that he had seen a vision in which he was authorized to reorganize the church "when he should see two half-moons with their backs together in the sky." In 1853 Cutler reported that he had seen the moons and the time was at hand for him to form "the true church." Proselyting in Winter Quarters, he was successful in convincing forty families to join him rather than journey west to Utah. They settled in Fisher Grove, Fremont County, Iowa. Cutler called this splinter group The True Church of Latter-day Saints. He denounced polygamy, tithing, and Brigham Young, teaching that Joseph Smith was the only true prophet of God. Cutler died in 1864. Luana Beebe came to Utah after 1878 and lived in Juab County with a son by her marriage to Rockwell. She died March 6, 1897, and was buried in Provo City Cemetery. The legend on her headstone proudly identifies her as "Luana Hart Beebe, Wife of O. P. Rockwell."

[41] *St. Louis Daily New Era*, February 18, 1846.

[42] Just when he was ordained to the higher or Melchizedek Priesthood is not known, but that Rockwell did progress to the office of elder during the Nauvoo period is verified by William Hall, who received his endowments in the Nauvoo Temple and reported that Rockwell was a participant in the dramatic ceremony, a privilege not accorded a member of the lesser, or Aaronic Priesthood. Hall said, "In the midst of this harmony the serpent came in. This part was *characteristically* represented by the celebrated Porter Rockwell, notorious for shooting Boggs and Worrell." Hall, *Abominations of Mormonism Exposed*, p. 48, carries a full description.

At the same time in New York another group of two hundred and fifty Mormons crowded aboard the rickety ship *Brooklyn*, chartered by the ambitious Sam Brannan, and headed for the sunny shores of California by way of Cape Horn.

In Nauvoo, the Council of Fifty, desiring some method of communication between the city and the Camp of Israel, selected Rockwell to carry messages between the two points. With Rockwell as messenger, the risk of losing dispatches to Gentile marauders was substantially reduced. Consequently, between March and May of 1846 he made five trips across Iowa.[43] All proved uneventful but the last. Arriving in Nauvoo on the seventh of May, Rockwell had paused briefly at a local inn. Here word reached him that an old enemy, Chauncey Higbee, had slipped into the city a few days before under the protective wing of Sheriff Backenstos, who had guaranteed the apostate safety during his stay. When Backenstos had offered to defend the one-time conspirator, neither he nor Higbee had planned on encountering Rockwell. The circumstances were described in the May 6 issue of the *Quincy Whig*:

> On Saturday evening last, six of the riflemen, viz.: John Archer, James Evans, John Carlin, H. C. Bush, E. B. Wood, and J. W. Burns, arrived here from Nauvoo, having in custody O. P. Rockwell, widely known in Hancock as an outlaw that has long been sheltered by Joe Smith and the Mormons. The excitement when the fact was made known that Rockwell was actually in the city, was sufficient to draw a large crowd in the vicinity of the jail, and he was almost instantly put under lock and key before any number of the people had an opportunity of seeing him. The charge upon which he is now arrested is for the murder of Franklin A. Worrell, and we understand there are several other writs against him for divers other crimes and misdemeanors. In person, he is of small stature, with a countenance and appearance that denotes a "hard case." He surrendered after a short parley with the officers, and at the time, had he been disposed, might have made a desperate resistance, as he had taken refuge in an upper room which could be approached only by a long and narrow stair-way, and he had any number of shooting irons and other deadly weapons in abundance, on and about his person. He was apprehended at the instance of Backenstos, who was present and assisted in his capture.

Rockwell's career of crime is familiar to those who have heard or read of Mormon proceedings in Hancock. He was Joe Smith's right hand man, and stood ready to execute any order of Joe's however criminal. He it was, who was confined for a long period in Missouri,

---

[43] Journal History, March 14 and 31, April 2 and 19, and May 8, 1846.

on the charge of attempting to assassinate Gov. Boggs of that State; and it has been charged that he was *despatched* on that mission by Joe, to fulfill an imperious prophecy which Smith had previously made concerning the duration of life of the said Governor. He also is said to be privy to the most of the iniquity and particularly the counterfeiting which has been going on in the Holy City, in times past; and it is further said, was raised by Joe Smith from a boy, and tutored by his master in all the ways of sin and wickedness until the one came to a violent death, and the other now stands on the verge of the gallows.

Rockwell has been a perfect desperado — reckless and ruffianly to the last extreme. A few days since one of the Higbees had occasion to visit Nauvoo on business. Upon Backenstos assuring him that he should be protected while he remained, he prolonged his stay for one or two days. Rockwell, hearing of his presence in the city, followed him about, threatening his life, firing pistols over his head, etc., until it became apparent that Backenstos could not much longer protect him; thereupon a messenger was despatched to Maj. Warren asking for a force to arrest him. The riflemen above spoken of, volunteered for the purpose, and the result is the outlaw is now in our jail.

The day or two previous to his arrest, he was roaming about the streets of Nauvoo, with his weapons belted around him, swearing that the troops were now disbanded — that he intended to regulate the county, and openly boasted that he had killed Worrell, and that there were more in the county that he intended to serve in the same way. The fact is, the fellow had so long been suffered to run at large in violation of the law, that he began to think he could continue his career with impunity. But he is now in the hands of the law, and we leave justice to take its course.

When the militiamen disarmed Rockwell they found weapons enough in his stronghold to fire seventy-one rounds without reloading, plus an array of knives.[44] The unexpected ease with which Rockwell was captured puzzled many people,[45] as did the lodging of an eight-month-old charge against him — since Backenstos already had stood trial and been acquitted of the shooting.[46] On the surface it seemed the redoubtable Mormon had gotten himself into a real mess; even leaders of the church

[44] *Daily Missouri Republican*, May 5, 1846.

[45] Upon learning of Rockwell's arrest, Hosea Stout commented, ". . . I suspect that there has been some treachery used by some or he could not have been taken as it seems to me." Hosea Stout, "Journal." MSS, eight volumes, Vol. 2, p. 226; also published as *On The Mormon Frontier: The Diary of Hosea Stout, 1844–1861*, edited by Juanita Brooks (Salt Lake City, 1965), two volumes, Vol. 1, p. 160.

[46] Said the *Burlington Hawkeye*, May 7, 1846, "This is a new move which we do not understand."

in Nauvoo took the pulpit to proclaim that his arrest was just.[47] But his capture was in fact a carefully hatched plan to temporarily divert the attention of the anti-Mormon party and gain precious time for the Saints.[48] Because Backenstos was prepared to testify that he had ordered Rockwell to shoot Worrell, church authorities were of the opinion that an impartial jury would not return a guilty verdict. Rockwell had agreed to face trial on first-degree murder charges, but the plan involved obtaining a change of venue to a court more favorable to the Saints.[49] (If he were tried in Hancock County nothing could save him.) As soon as the jailer turned the cell key behind Rockwell, wheels were put in motion to change jurisdiction in the case; this was done through the church's lawyer, Almon W. Babbitt. But even as Babbitt was drawing up the legal papers, additional charges of counterfeiting and passing bogus money were filed against the prisoner.[50] Ultimately, the request for a change of venue to Galena, one hundred and fifty miles to the north in Daviess County, was granted — and not a moment too soon.[51] A grand jury handed down an indictment against Rockwell by the first of June and ordered him to appear for trial the following month.[52] Babbitt, after relieving his client of a gold watch

[47] The *Quincy Whig*, May 13, 1846, editorialized:

It is stated, that the leading Mormons have cast him [Rockwell] off, and say that his arrest was right and proper. They proclaimed from their stand the Sunday succeeding his arrest, that he was a dangerous man, and should be taken care of — and that Backenstos should not be censured by the Mormons for the part he took in his arrest. We have heard it stated that Rockwell would not have given himself up so readily, were it not for a promise that he should have the assistance of friends and legal counsel — but when the leaders had seen him secure in the toils of the law, they turn their backs upon him and leave him to his fate. As bad as Rockwell is — and as deeply involved as he is in crime — there are others among the Saints who are equally involved with him, and who have found as low, if not lower depth in crime. He was, doubtless, but the instrument of others in much of the iniquity he practised, and in visiting upon him a punishment, it is to be lamented that his accomplices should not bear a share of it.

A year and a half earlier, in reporting a fist fight involving Rockwell, the *Sangamo Journal*, October 10, 1844, had noted, "The Mormons are very afraid of Rockwell, and his overhearing spirit is making him exceedingly troublesome to them."

[48] Hall, *Abominations of Mormonism Exposed*, p. 29, claimed that Rockwell turned himself in to Backenstos so the two men could split a $2,000 reward offered for the Mormon's capture.

[49] *The People's Daily Organ*, May 5, 1846, and *Missouri Whig*, May 14, 1846.

[50] *Warsaw Signal*, May 6, 1846.

[51] *St. Louis American*, May 30, 1846; *St. Louis Daily New Era*, June 1, 1846.

[52] *Missouri Whig*, June 4, 1846; *St. Louis American*, June 17, 1846.

as a fee for his services, subpoenaed his star witness, Sheriff Backenstos, and Rockwell was promptly freed.[53] Apparently the counterfeiting charges were dismissed at the same time.

With the slate wiped clean, Rockwell made straight for Nauvoo to pack his belongings and join the main body of Saints gathering on the east bank of the Missouri. It was in the City of Joseph that he met an old friend, Joseph Smith III, thirteen-year-old son of the dead prophet. Their meeting in the gentle glow of a summer evening was filled with emotion. Many years later Smith described the encounter:

> . . . extending my hand, [Rockwell] shook it warmly, put an arm affectionately around my shoulders, and said, with much emotion, "Oh, Joseph, Joseph! They have killed the only friend I have ever had!" He wept like a boy. We spoke but little, for even then an air of suspicion had crept abroad in the city, and whoever was friendly to my mother or her family was under surveillance. I tried to comfort him, but to my astonishment he said, "Joseph, you had best go back. I am glad you came to meet me, but it is best that you are not seen with me. It can do me no good and it may bring harm to you." [54]

When Orrin Porter Rockwell kicked the dust of Illinois from his heels and spurred his horse toward Iowa, he left behind a kaleidoscope of memories — persecutions suffered at the hands of Missouri settlers, the secret rides of the Danite Band, a wife and four children, a "plural wife," and a year spent in jails. It would have been typical if he had not given Nauvoo a backward glance as he rode west.

[53] *Quincy Whig*, August 26, 1846.
[54] *Joseph Smith III and the Restoration*, pp. 76–77.

Chapter Eight

THE PLAINSMAN

WHEN ROCKWELL RODE INTO THE COUNCIL BLUFFS ENCAMPMENT on the eastern bank of the Missouri he was just in time to assist Brigham Young and several other high-ranking members of the church in administering to William Clayton, clerk of the Camp of Israel, who was suffering the ravages of fever. Weak as he was, Clayton managed to write in his journal the next morning: "The brethren all laid hands on me and rebuked my disease in the name of the Lord, President Young being mouth. I immediately felt easier and slept well all night being the first sleep I had had of any account for three days and nights." [1]

Later Rockwell related his experiences in Galena to the apostles and members of the Council of Fifty,[2] after which he met briefly with Young and was told it would be his responsibility to carry messages between the widely scattered string of Mormon camps stretching across Iowa.[3] Young also explained that some five hundred men from the church had enlisted in a "Mormon Battalion" under the command of Colonel Stephen W. Kearny, and were on the march for New Mexico. It was arranged that battalion members would join the church somewhere in the Rockies. Since Rockwell had been languishing in jail when the call for men came he was spared the necessity of signing up for the campaign.[4]

[1] William Clayton, *William Clayton's Journal, A Daily Record of the Journey of the Original Company of "Mormon" Pioneers from Nauvoo, Illinois, to the Valley of the Great Salt Lake* (Salt Lake City, 1921), pp. 61-62. Hereafter cited as *Clayton Journal*.

[2] Journal History, August 19, 1846.

[3] There were Mormon camps at Richardson's Point, Chariton River, Locust Creek, Garden Grove, Mt. Pisgah, Council Bluffs, Council Point, and Winter Quarters.

[4] The *Quincy Whig*, July 29, 1846, greeted formation of the battalion with the lament: "Five hundred Mormons are to be taken into the American Army! Where is Backenstos? Where is Orrin P. Rockwell?" Backenstos became an Army officer in 1846, and as captain of the 2d Division, 1st Brigade, Illinois Mounted Rifles, was

On August 22, 1846, Young called a meeting of the Council Bluffs camp and disclosed that he had received word that a force of Missourians planned to attack and seize members of the Council of Twelve Apostles. "Clean your rifles, keep your ammunition ready, pray for your families and keep your dogs tied up at night," Young warned.[5] To be on the safe side, the church leader decided that he and the six apostles in camp should cross the river into Indian territory. To ensure his personal safety, Young took Rockwell along as a bodyguard. According to the church's Journal History:

> About 1 p.m. Pres. Young, Elders Heber C. Kimball, Willard Richards accompanied by Orrin P. Rockwell, Wm. H. Kimball and Emeline Free[6] started in Bro. Kimball's carriage, and Elder Orson Pratt, Wilford Woodruff, Geo. A. Smith, Amasa M. Lyman and Bro. James M. Flake in his carriage, for Council Point, Iowa, arrived at the Cold Spring thirty five minutes past four, crossed the Missouri River about 6, and arrived at Father Morley's at Council Point about eight. After supper the president chatted till about eleven and retired.[7]

During the carriage ride, Rockwell told Young of Babbitt's demand for his watch as a legal fee. The president had little enough respect for the lawyer, whom he considered vain and pompous; as soon as time permitted he fired off a letter to the trustees-in-trust at Nauvoo: "The council wish you to consider the church property in Nauvoo sufficient to meet all expense incurred in the late imprisonment and release of O. P. Rockwell, and we wish you to forward Bro. Rockwell's watch to the council by the bearer, Charles Kennedy, the watch which was taken by Mr. Babbitt as an attorney fee." [8]

wounded in the battle of Chapultepec, was twice brevetted for gallantry and meritorious conduct in the war with Mexico, marched to Oregon with the Mounted Rifles in 1849, and committed suicide there in 1857. See *Daily Alta California*, October 12, 1857. The adventurer Joseph H. Jackson also volunteered for service in the war against Mexico. He died in Vera Cruz in May 1847. See *The Iowa Statesman*, June 25, 1847.

[5] *Clayton Journal*, p. 63.

[6] Emmeline Free was one of Young's spiritual wives. The spelling of the name in Journal History is incorrect.

[7] Journal History, August 22, 1846.

[8] Ibid., August 25, 1846.

Satisfied that the report of an impending Missouri attack was false, Young ordered the small party to return to Council Bluffs. Released temporarily from dogging Young's footsteps, Rockwell took time to scout Winter Quarters, the river's west bank encampment.[9] From his vantage point, Rockwell could see the tents of Council Bluffs with their occupants busily fashioning boats and rafts for the trip across; the river bottom was gorged with cattle and wagons making their way to the opposite bank. On the west shore things were moving at the same pace, but one shocking sight struck Rockwell full force — the number of graves dotting the hillside. (More than six hundred deaths would eventually be counted among the Saints, due largely to malarial fever which flourished in the stinking yellow pools of the river bottom.) Brigham Young knew if the Saints remained for any protracted period under prevailing conditions, the fever would pick them off one by one. But the immediate problem was surviving the winter season now fast approaching. Calling together a council of the Omaha chiefs on whose land the Mormons were bivouacked, Young extracted an agreement, which met with the approval of the local Indian agent, allowing the Saints to stay for as long as two years, with rights to firewood and timber. In return the tribes were permitted to borrow Mormon teams for plowing and harvest. By year's end, hunger and disease had taken a devastating toll among the Saints, and the Council of Fifty worked desperately to complete plans for the first migration west.

In a special council meeting on December 29, 1846, it was agreed to send out an advance group of pioneers charged with the two-fold responsibility of locating a new Zion in the Rocky Mountains and blazing an adequate trail for the main body of Mormons to follow.[10] One hundred and forty-three men, three women, and two children eventually comprised this company, led by Brigham Young himself. Rockwell was attached to the tenth group of Ten, captained by Appleton Milo Harmon, and appointed scout and chief hunter for the pioneers. The party was to leave at the first sign of spring. In the meantime, Rockwell rode to a Mormon camp on the Niobrara River with dispatches from Young, a chore which occupied him until mid-February.[11]

A cold, numbing wind whistled through Winter Quarters on the morning of April 14, 1847, as the advance company pointed its lead team

[9] Now the site of Florence, Nebraska.

[10] Journal History, December 29, 1846.

[11] Details of this trip to the Niobrara can be found in Erastus Snow, "Journal." MSS, eight volumes, Book 3, pp. 56–57.

west and moved out. Once they had crossed the Elk Horn River, thirty-five miles distant, Young called the company together and organized it into two groups under the leadership of Stephen Markham and A. P. Rockwood, who would report directly to Young. As the pioneers again rolled forward, Rockwell and another Mormon, J. C. Little, returned to Winter Quarters to fetch one last mail.

When the two caught up with the pioneers three days later, they were accompanied by Return Jackson Redden and a fourth man, Tom Brown.[12] Their small cargo of letters quickly disappeared in a flurry of outstretched hands. Rockwell added a couple of surprises. Turning to Willard Richards, he handed over the reins of a mare which had bolted from the Richards wagon east of the Elk Horn. The sharp-eyed scout had spotted the animal and run her down near the river. For William Clayton, he had a small package containing, to the clerk's delight, "some few fish hooks . . . a ball of fish line and three pencils . . . ."

With such natural frontiersmen as Rockwell, Redden, Howard Egan, and Brown as scouts, the pioneers were amply prepared for trouble as they pushed their way into Indian country. Rigid discipline was enforced from dawn to dusk. Each morning at five a bugle blared out breakfast call, and by seven the company was on the move. All wagons were drawn in a half-circle at sunset with the horses secured in the perimeter; the bugle sounded again at eight-thirty and every man returned to his wagon for prayer. All lights were out by nine.[13] The first Indian scare came on April 26, when night guards discovered a half-dozen savages crawling toward the camp about 3:30 in the morning. A volley of rifle fire succeeded in driving the intruders off before they could steal the horses, but

[12] Tom Brown's appearance with the Mormons is indeed curious. He was suspected of complicity in the murder of one John Miller in Montrose, Iowa, and was sought by bounty-hunter Edward Bonney, who later described Brown's exploits in his *Banditti of the Prairies*, p. 43ff. Other diarists, Appleton Milo Harmon, Erastus Snow, Howard Egan, and Norton Jacob, reported this man's arrival in camp. Brown later was included in Mormon records as Nathaniel Thomas Brown. He was killed by an unidentified man at Winter Quarters in 1848. Not only was he a baptized Mormon, but he was apparently a church member in good standing until his death. See Andrew Jenson, *Latter-Day Saint Biographical Encyclopedia* (Salt Lake City, 1901–1936), four volumes, Vol. IV, p. 695. See also Gregg, *History of Hancock County*, p. 337.

[13] Wm. M. Egan, ed., *Pioneering the West, 1846–1878; Major Howard Egan's Diary, also Thrilling Experiences of Pre-Frontier Life Among Indians; Their Traits, Civil and Savage, and Part of Autobiography, Inter-Related to His Father's, by Howard R. Egan* (Richmond, Utah, 1917), pp. 23–24.

tension in the company heightened with the realization that they were now in hostile territory.[14]

Despite added precautions throughout the camp, Willard Richards' skittish mare succeeded in running away again, and Rockwell organized a small party to search for the missing animal. He and three others — Tom Brown, Joseph Mathews, and John Eldridge — backtracked the trail for telltale signs of the mare, until by afternoon they had reached the site of their April 26 camp where the Indian alarm had been sounded. Near the Elk Horn Rockwell spotted a movement in the grass at the foot of a nearby slope, "Probably a wolf," said Brown. Dropping the reins, Rockwell guided his stallion with his knees and carefully eased his rifle from its saddle boot.

He raised the weapon to his eye ("One less wolf is one less wolf"), and fifteen Pawnees, naked save for breechclouts, exploded from the grass. Each carried a bow, arrows, and a rifle. Quickly the four Mormons brought their guns to bear, but they held fire on a command from Rockwell. Halting some fifty yards away, the Indians eyed the riders warily, then slowly advanced in a half-crouch. Rockwell waved them back with the muzzle of his rifle.

"Bacco, bacco," one Pawnee whined, arm outstretched. His companions took up the chant and continued their furtive approach. One reached Mathews' horse. The brave begged for tobacco, but his eyes were on the horse's bridle. Mathews cocked his pistol and pointed it at the Indian's head. Scowling, the Pawnee retreated. Meanwhile, the others were gesturing for the whites to follow them to the river, but Rockwell shook his head. The four men turned their horses and rode slowly away. Before they had gone fifty yards the Indians opened fire. Pulling hard on the reins, Rockwell spun his mount and raked the animal's flanks with his spurs. Seeing the angry Mormon charging down on them, the Pawnees sprinted for the river bottom and vanished.[15] The scouting party reined in at the pioneer camp late that night and reported the incident to Young.

By early May the pioneers had crossed the Wood River. Along the Platte the prairie was green with grass and discordant with wild geese. Here and there were dark piles of buffalo dung. "But none very recent," complained William Clayton, who had been contemplating the pleasures of a buffalo steak. The Mormons soon found an excellent use for these

[14] Ibid., pp. 29–30; *Clayton Journal*, p. 104.
[15] This skirmish is described in both the *Clayton Journal*, pp. 109–10, and Egan, *Pioneering the West*, p. 30.

154

buffalo "chips" for they made a fine fire, and suddenly the pioneers took an active interest in the droppings of plains cattle.

One morning the scouts spotted a large herd nearby. After a frenzied few minutes of tangled harnesses and clashing tempers, every Mormon with a horse gave chase. The rest of the company watched from the wagons with lively anticipation. Amid the swirling dust and noisy confusion one man maneuvered his pony expertly through the milling animals to close dangerously time and time again until a clear shot presented itself. Twice his rifle cracked, and twice buffalo tumbled from the herd. By now the other hunters had stopped to watch this display of horsemanship and sharpshooting. Once more the rider plunged into the surging mass and again his rifle roared crisp and clean through the rumble of pounding hooves. "Port got a cow that time," one Mormon shouted to another.

So magnificent was his performance that Rockwell was applauded by the Saints watching from the wagons. Then came his supreme moment. During the long nights around the campfire the hunters had argued that a buffalo could not be stopped by a frontal shot in the skull, and now Rockwell found himself in a position to settle the question. Jockeying his horse near a huge bull until he was within a rod of the animal, Rockwell poked his rifle at the center of the great shaggy head and fired.[16]

That night over a buffalo steak feast, Rockwell recounted the episode. "The ball just stirred up a little dust is all. That old bull shook his head like he was brushing off a fly and kept right on coming. I had to move pretty fast to get out of his way. Somebody else got him." William Clayton took time out two days later to examine the bull's skull. "I found where Porter shot at his head. The ball made a small hole, barely cutting through the outer surface or grain of the hide which was near an inch long."

Scattered bands of Indians were now being reported at frequent intervals, prompting Brigham Young to order defense drills with increasing regularity, while he occupied his spare moments with a spyglass, scanning the horizon for signs of trouble. By now an accomplished buffalo hunter, Rockwell kept the camp well supplied with fresh meat as the train plodded onward; the last thing he concerned himself about was Brother Brigham's spyglass.

[16] *Clayton Journal*, p. 120.

On the morning of May 6, Young was attempting to separate the camp herd from a number of wandering buffalo when he discovered that his prized possession, the spyglass, was missing. The church leader's distress was complete when he realized the instrument could have been lost anywhere along twenty miles of trail. Young hastily ordered a search party to comb the back trail and placed Rockwell in command. The scout set out, and, Clayton wrote, "About four p.m., Porter and the others returned, having found the spy glass which was a source of joy to all the brethren." [17]

Where once the pioneers welcomed buffalo, they came to detest the huge animals blandly grazing in the company's path. After a buffalo herd finished feeding there was little grass left for the livestock. Wrote Appleton Milo Harmon in his journal for May 8: "At this time I could stand on my wagon and see more than ten thousand buffalo. This was possible because the plain was perfectly black with them on both sides of the [Platte] river and on the bluff, on our right, which slopes off gradually and presents its south side to our view. O. P. Rockwell killed a two-year-old heifer which was good."

A trail of dead buffalo punctuated Rockwell's route as he scouted the terrain ahead of the pioneers. On the morning of May 22 he galloped into camp to tell Young that he had seen Chimney Rock; the Mormons had traveled more than four hundred miles since leaving Council Bluffs.[18] Pushing on, the pioneers camped opposite Scotts Bluff, some twenty miles beyond Chimney Rock, and sat down to a hearty meal of antelope, which had fallen under Rockwell's deadly aim. To relieve the boredom of their

[17] Clayton's remark about the recovery of Young's spyglass bringing "joy to all the brethren" seems to indicate that the church leader's behavior was anything but pleasurable to the pioneers while the instrument was missing. Certainly the entire incident was blown out of proportion in that no fewer than three diaries mention the matter in detail. See *Clayton Journal*, pp. 134–35; Egan, *Pioneering the West*, p. 35; and Appleton Milo Harmon, *Appleton Milo Harmon Goes West*, edited by Maybelle Harmon Anderson (Berkeley, 1946), p. 18. This should not be confused with Harmon's manuscript diary, which appears in later citations.

[18] William Clayton suggested and Orson Pratt designed an odometer attachment for a wagon wheel so that distances traveled each day could be accurately measured. Appleton M. Harmon, the camp carpenter, did the actual construction work. Clayton published his findings in *The Latter-day Saints' Emigrants' Guide: Being a Table of Distances, Showing all the Springs, Creeks, Rivers, Hills, Mountains, Camping Places, and all other Notable Places, from Council Bluffs, to the Valley of the Great Salt Lake* (St. Louis, 1848).

journey the pioneers entertained themselves by conducting mock trials after dinner. High-ranking Mormons were hailed before a "court" and made to answer a variety of "charges," much to the glee of their brethren. One such trial is documented by a penciled note to Rockwell which read:

Pioneer Camp, Wednesday, May 26, 1847.

To Marshall O. P. Rockwell:

Sir — You are hereby commanded to bring, wherever found, the body of Col. George Mills,[19] before the Right Reverend Bishop [Edson] Whipple, at his Quarters, there to answer to the following charge, viz.: — That of emitting in meeting on Sunday last, a sound, *a posteriori*, (from his seat of honor) somewhat resembling the rumble of distant thunder, or the heavy discharge of artillery, thereby endangering the steadiness of the olfactory nerves of those present, as well as diverting their minds from the discourse of the speaker.[20]

This levity among the pioneers aroused Brigham Young's stern disapproval; for some time he had felt that the small band of Mormons was losing its religious zeal and would soon be destroyed by a "mean, low, groveling, covetous, quarrelsome spirit." After blistering the Saints for "acting the nigger night after night," Young threatened to turn the company around and head back to Council Bluffs unless the pioneers repented their "wickedness."

I understand there are several in this camp who do not belong to the church. I am the man who will stand up for them and protect them in all their rights. And they shall not trample on our rights nor on the priesthood. They shall reverence and acknowledge the name of God and His priesthood, and if they set up their heads and seek to introduce iniquity into this camp and to trample on the priesthood, I swear to them, they shall never go back to tell the tale. I will leave them where they will be safe.[21]

---

[19] Stephen Markham's name was scratched out here and Mills's substituted.

[20] The original of this note is in the LDS Church Historical Department. A photographic copy is in my possession and another is in the files of the Utah State Historical Society. The note is unsigned. Italics in the original. See also the trial of James Davenport "for blockading the highway and turning ladies out of their course." *Clayton Journal*, p. 176. Clayton remarks, "We have many such trials in the camp which are amusing enough and tend among other things to pass away the time cheerfully during leisure moments."

[21] Brigham Young's harangue on this occasion can be found in the *Clayton Journal*, pp. 189–97, and Egan, *Pioneering the West*, pp. 52–57.

Thoroughly subdued and chagrined, the company abandoned its usual campfire joviality that night, retiring instead to the wagons. The next day chanced to be a Sunday, and Council of Fifty members, dressed in priestly raiment, withdrew to the bluffs near camp to offer prayers for the safety of the pioneers, those they had left behind, and men of the Mormon Battalion.[22] Albert Carrington and Rockwell, having no garments with them, stood guard over the ceremony to prevent interruption.[23] "I have never noticed the brethren so still and sober on a Sunday since we started," William Clayton was moved to comment.

A fine cool morning greeted the pioneers on May 31, and hitting the trail shortly after eight o'clock, they struck a wagon road from Fort Laramie (to Fort Pierre?) shortly thereafter. The fort itself came into view on the afternoon of the following day. Halting briefly opposite old Fort Platte, which had been abandoned the previous year, the company proceeded two miles and pulled up across from Fort Laramie.[24] On hand to welcome the new arrivals was the fort's manager, a doughty Frenchman named James Bordeaux, who extended every courtesy and offered them the meager hospitality of his oasis in the desert.

After exchanging introductions, the trader informed the Saints that when their old nemesis Lilburn W. Boggs had passed ahead of them the summer before, he had left a warning for Bordeaux to keep a sharp eye on his horses and cattle around Mormons.[25] "I wasn't worried," the Frenchman laughed. "Nothing could be worse than the company Boggs was in."

[22] Clayton also referred to the Council of Fifty as the Council of the Kingdom of God or the Council of the K. of G. He noted members were "Brigham Young, Heber C. Kimball, Willard Richards, Orson Pratt . . . myself . . . and Porter Rockwell." See *Clayton Journal*, pp. 202–3.

[23] Ibid.

[24] Established in 1834 by William Sublette as Fort William, the post was renamed Fort John when rebuilt in 1841, and that was its proper name until it was sold to the U.S. Army in 1849, at which time it was officially named Fort Laramie, after one Jacques LaRamie, or Loremy, a free trapper killed by Indians in the vicinity in 1821. Fort Laramie was the major station of its kind on the overland route.

[25] En route to California, Boggs stopped at Fort Laramie on June 29, 1846. See *James Clyman, American Frontiersman, 1792–1881*, edited by Charles L. Camp (San Francisco, 1928), p. 230. This completely refutes the prevailing myth that Rockwell and Boggs were thrown together on the same ferry crossing the Platte River. According to that tale, Rockwell pretended the raft was out of control, thereby frightening the ex-governor out of his wits. Boggs was in California before the Mormons settled in at Winter Quarters, in 1846. Also see Morgan, *Overland in 1846*, Vol. II, pp. 550, 559, 682, 714.

Adjourning to his office, Bordeaux explained that the pioneers would not be able to travel more than four miles on the north side of the river before reaching bluffs he described as unsurmountable to loaded wagons (though such a road was worked out in 1849–50). He offered the Mormons an answer and an alternative: For $15 he would sell a flatboat which would carry two wagons at once, or he would ferry them across for $18. The Saints decided to purchase the flatboat outright. Business concluded, the pioneers toured the trading post. Again Clayton provides a description:

> A pair of moccasins are worth a dollar, a lariat a dollar, a pound of tobacco a dollar and a half, and a gallon of whiskey $32.00. They have no sugar, coffee or spices as their spring stores have not yet arrived. They have lately sent to Fort Pierre, 600 bales of robes with ten robes in each bale. Their wagons have been gone forty-five days, etc. The blacksmith shop lies on the south side of the western entrance. There are dwellings inside the fort beside that of Mr. Bordeau's. The south end is divided off and occupied for stables, etc.[26]

On the morning of June 3 the first division of the pioneer camp began ferrying across the swift North Platte, averaging a wagon every fifteen minutes. Those on the south bank took advantage of the delay to set up a blacksmith shop and repair damaged equipment. Rockwell amused himself by bargaining with the canny Frenchman, a diversion which proved stimulating for both parties since the Mormon was no stranger to the intricacies of frontier horse-trading. After interminable haggling, appropriately sprinkled with expressions of outrage and indignation from the participants, Rockwell gave Bordeaux an Indian pony for "two cows and calves, one heifer, two pair of moccasin shoes, and two lariats."[27]

A piercing blast on the bugle snapped the pioneers awake the next morning, and after an hour for breakfast the company resumed its westward push. The ensuing week found the party above the Black Hills faced once again with the task of crossing the North Platte. The spring thaw had swollen the river to a depth of fifteen feet; one hundred yards of bone-crushing current separated the shorelines. It was with a noticeable lack of enthusiasm that the Mormons attacked the problem of transporting the company to the opposite bank.

[26] *Clayton Journal*, pp. 210–11.

[27] Appleton Milo Harmon, "Diary." MS, p. 275.

Here a train of Missourians overtook the pioneers and hesitantly asked if the Mormons would cross their wagons as well. In exchange they would pay a dollar and a half a load, acceptable in flour at the rate of two and a half dollars per hundred pounds. "We made $34 in provisions," Clayton rejoiced, "which is a great blessing to the camp inasmuch as a number of the brethren have had no bread stuff for some days." [28] Brigham Young was quick to see that a ferry here on the North Platte could easily become an enterprise profitable to the church; he detailed nine men to remain at the location with their pioneer-built rafts and charge other emigrants a crossing toll until the next company of Mormons arrived in some six weeks.

Two days of hard driving brought the company to Independence Rock and the good grass of the Sweetwater Valley, then to Pacific Springs, two miles west of South Pass, where the Saints met the gregarious Moses (Black) Harris, mountain man, scout, and trapper.[29] Harris had guided a party as far as the Springs and was hoping to sign on as pilot to some wagon train headed west. From him the Saints learned more about their intended destination, the Valley of the Great Salt Lake. Harris, like others the Mormons consulted, was disappointingly pessimistic about the land. "It's as barren as the back of your hand," he said, "and as fertile." Before he and the Saints parted company, Harris presented them with a file of California newspapers, among which were numbers of the *California Star*, published in Yerba Buena by Sam Brannan, leader of the Mormon detachment which had voyaged to the coast in the ship *Brooklyn*.[30] Harris' parting bit of advice to Brigham Young was to urge the emigrants to change course to Cache Valley near the Bear River Mountains and establish a colony there, where water and timber abounded.

Mid-afternoon of June 28 found the company on the California trail when suddenly they came upon three trappers making their way toward Fort Laramie. By unique coincidence the leader of the small party was Jim Bridger, the very man Young wished to see, for few whites knew the West as well as the wily mountain man. Bridger may have been the first white man to see the Great Salt Lake and taste its saline waters. "Old

[28] *Clayton Journal*, pp. 234–35.

[29] Harris was a crony of other now-legendary fur trappers of the West, notably Jim Bridger, Hugh Glass, Jedediah Smith, and Thomas Fitzpatrick.

[30] Brannan and his party had landed at Yerba Buena, the future San Francisco, on July 31, 1846. He put their printing press into operation and soon became the town's leading citizen.

Gabe" consented to spend the night with the pioneers and tell them about the valley they sought to settle. That evening in camp near the Little Sandy, members of the Council of Twelve Apostles, with Brigham Young and several other influential Mormons, including Rockwell, sat with Bridger in absorbed silence as he described what lay ahead. Clayton summarized the trapper's narrative:

> We will find better grass as we proceed farther on. . . . There have been nearly a hundred wagons gone on the Hastings route through Weber's Fork. . . . From Bridger's fort to the salt lake, Hastings said was about one hundred miles. [Bridger] has been through fifty times but can form no correct idea of the distance. . . . In the Bear River valley there is oak timber, sugar trees, cottonwood, pine and maple. . . . There is no timber on the Utah Lake only on the streams which empty into it. . . . The Utah tribe of Indians inhabit the region around the Utah Lake and are a bad people. . . . The soil is good and likely to produce corn were it not for the excessive cold nights which he thinks would prevent the growth of corn. . . . The Indians south of the Utah Lake raise as good corn, wheat, and pumpkins as were ever raised in old Kentucky. . . .[31]

Jim Bridger and the Mormons said goodbye on June 29. The Saints, pressing on with renewed vigor, made twenty-three miles by nightfall. The last day of the month found them at the Green River, its swollen current impossible to ford. Here several members of the company fell victim to mountain fever, an illness characterized by chills, fever, nausea, and vomiting which entirely incapacitated its sufferers.[32] While the Saints were

[31] *Clayton Journal*, pp. 274–78.

[32] "Mountain fever" was a popular generic name applied to various febrile affections, intermittent, remittent, and typhoid which attacked mountaineers, Indians, emigrants, and soldiers with equal ferocity. There were two distinct classes of "mountain fever." The first, a milder form, was described by trappers as a kind of "seasoning" to mountain air which affected them most frequently in the spring when following the rivers to their mountain sources to trap beaver. The trappers also claimed that the Indians were subject to the same disease when roaming through the mountains in the spring. It was thought to be a fever of acclimation. The second variety was severe, but responded to quinine. It was believed by a number of Army doctors to be malarial

occupied in treating the sick and hewing timber for makeshift ferries, Rockwell and his scouts warned of approaching horses. To the surprise of everyone, Sam Brannan and two companions came galloping into the encampment, having ridden all the way from Yerba Buena to intercept the Mormons and tell Brigham Young of the magnificent potentialities of California.[33] But for all his eloquence Brannan was unable to divert Young from his decision to settle the Great Salt Lake Valley.

Once across the Green, the pioneers resumed their march. By July 5 they were in sight of the Bear River (Uinta) Mountains to the southwest, and after camping on Black's Fork they followed the stream past Ham's Fork until on July 7 they arrived at Fort Bridger. According to Clayton: "Bridger's Fort is composed of two double log houses about forty feet long each and joined by a pen for horses about ten feet high constructed by placing poles upright in the ground close together, which is all the appear-

---

in nature and contracted through bad water supplies in the Fort Laramie, Fort Kearny, and river crossings areas. But it is more likely that the fever was carried by livestock and transmitted by the hordes of mosquitoes along the trail.

[33] Brannan and his party had crossed the Sierra Nevada and were among the first to view the remains of members of the Donner–Reed train who had perished the previous winter.

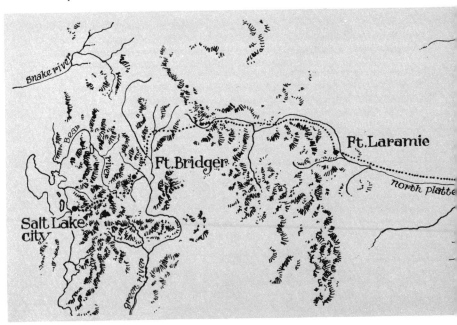

ance of a fort in sight. There are several Indian lodges close by and a full
crop of young children playing around the door. These Indians are said to
be of the Snake tribe, the Utahs inhabiting beyond the mountains. . . ." [34]
Despite its meager facilities, the fort provided most Saints with the opportunity of firing up the forge to repair damaged wagon wheels and replace
shoes on their weary animals. Others, like Howard Egan, spent the time
bartering. Two rifles brought him nineteen deerskins, three elk hides, and
moccasin-making material.

Taking the Hastings Cutoff, the Mormons once more rolled onward
and crossed Muddy Fork, camping within two miles of Bear River, where
on July 10 they were visited by Miles Goodyear, a slight, wiry, red-haired
Connecticut Yankee whom Bridger had mentioned as a farmer "in the
Bear River Valley." (Goodyear was settled at Ogden in the Great Salt
Lake region.) Goodyear painted a picture of the valley "more favorable
than some we have heard," wrote Clayton, "but we have an idea he is
anxious to have us make a road to his place through selfish motives." [35]

[34] *Clayton Journal*, pp. 285–86.

[35] Ibid., p. 289. For more on Goodyear, see J. Roderic Korns, "West From
Fort Bridger. The Pioneering of the Immigrant Trails Across Utah 1846–1850.

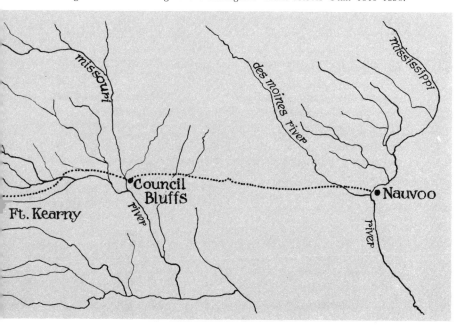

While most of the company oiled their gun stocks and shoes and filled tar buckets from "an oil spring about a mile south of camp," Rockwell, J. C. Little, and others joined Goodyear on a scouting expedition of the route he suggested the Mormons follow. Rockwell later reported to Young that Goodyear's trail was too rough for wagons and far off course. Nevertheless, the camp voted to follow the route. A choice was permitted the Saints, Clayton said, "so that none may have room to murmur at the twelve hereafter." [36]

As the pioneer company approached the threshold of what was to become their new home, Brigham Young was stricken with mountain fever. On July 12 he ordered the main body of Mormons to move on while he fell behind with a few wagons. Heeding his instructions, the company whipped the oxen forward, camping that night at the mouth of Echo Canyon; nearby Return Jackson Redden discovered a shell-like cave which was named in his honor.[37] From this point it was decided to send ahead to Weber Canyon an advance party of twenty-three wagons under the leadership of Orson Pratt in an effort to find a pass which would take the Mormons through to the valley; Rockwell was to be scout for the group. Word from the rear reassured the anxious Saints that although Brigham Young had spent the previous night "insensible and raving," he apparently had passed a crisis and was improving every hour.

Forty-two men set out under Pratt on July 13 to locate the route used by the Donner–Reed company the previous year. Ravines, steep slopes, and heavy underbrush blocked their path, forcing them to literally hack out a passage with axes and shovels. Rockwell rode back to the main wagon train on July 16 to report that the trail had been discovered and the advance company was clearing it at that very moment.

Ignoring rattlesnakes and rockslides, the Pratt party managed to reach East Canyon, followed a ravine west, and finally crossed to the summit of Big Mountain. Descending the precipitous slope with wheels double-locked to prevent the wagons from hurtling to destruction, the men followed the Donner–Reed trail over Little Mountain and halted a mile below its summit on July 21. That afternoon Orson Pratt and Erastus

Original Diaries and Journals," edited and with introductions, *Utah Historical Quarterly*, XIX (Salt Lake City, 1951), pp. 122–23, 194–95; and Dale L. Morgan, "Miles Goodyear and the Founding of Ogden," *Utah Historical Quarterly*, XXI (July–October 1953).

[36] *Clayton Journal*, p. 290.

[37] This landmark later became known as Cache Cave.

Snow rode down what later was named Emigration Canyon and first entered the valley they had come more than a thousand miles to settle.[38]

Rockwell had brought word to the advance party from the still-ailing Young instructing Pratt to "turn a little north" when he entered the valley and "put in seed of all kinds, a small quantity of each to try the soil." Accordingly, the next morning Pratt selected a half-dozen men to accompany him on a mission to "seek out a suitable place" for the planting. He chose Rockwell, George A. Smith, John Pack, Joseph Mathews, J. C. Little, and John Brown.[39] It is likely that Orrin Porter Rockwell, in his capacity as scout, was the first member of this pioneer group to penetrate the new Zion.

Pack and Mathews returned on July 23 to announce their findings to Brigham Young while the remainder of Pratt's party stayed in the valley to await the main company of pioneers, which had started down Emigration Canyon that very morning. Shortly before noon of July 24, 1847, the last wagons of the first Mormon migration, conveying Brigham Young, rolled out of the canyon into the valley.

[38] As Pratt described the moment: "After issuing from the mountains among which we had been shut up for many days, and beholding in a moment such an extensive scenery open before us, we could not refrain from a shout of joy which almost involuntarily escaped from our lips the moment this grand and lovely scenery was within our view." "Extracts From Orson Pratt's Private Journal," *Millennial Star*, Vol. XII, p. 178.

[39] *Clayton Journal*, p. 308.

Chapter Nine

ZION

IT WAS WITH MIXED EMOTIONS that the Mormon pioneers surveyed the Great Salt Lake Valley sprawling nakedly before them, a treeless crust, parched as an elk hide, with only an occasional ribbon of grass to break the monotony for as far as the eye could see; the iron-hard soil literally snapped the blade of the first plow to test it. In the distance the Great Salt Lake shimmered mirage-like and the Oquirrh Mountains pushed skyward to meet the lowering sun. For those in the company who measured this against the hardships of the journey it was a welcome sight. Apostle Wilford Woodruff spoke of it as "a glorious valley," while others, for whom the memory of Illinois and Iowa woodlands remained fresh, called their new home less attractive names. Perhaps the two most dejected members of the pioneer group were women, Harriet Page Wheeler Young, wife of Brigham Young, and Ellen Sanders Kimball, wife of Heber C. Kimball. Mrs. Young looked at her surroundings in disillusion and cried, "Weak and weary as I am, I would rather go a thousand miles farther than remain in such a forsaken place as this." Mrs. Kimball nodded in agreement. There may have been other complaints, but the Mormons had precious little time to contemplate the scenery; much needed to be done if the main migration was to have food when it arrived.

Almost immediately the wagons were unloaded and a detail sent to dam up a rushing stream which wound its way through the camp. Rockwell was sent out to scout the neighboring mountains.

For the next week the pioneer camp was a whirlwind of activity as the Saints raised shelters, began a city survey, named landmarks, and greeted the arrival of a company of Mississippi Saints and a sick detachment of the Mormon Battalion under command of Captain James Brown. On August 2 the Council of Fifty resolved to send Rockwell and three members of the Battalion as an escort for Apostle Ezra T. Benson on a return journey to meet the main company of Mormon emigrants. Benson carried a letter from the council to Charles C. Rich explaining the situation in the valley and asking Rich for a camp roll listing wagons, livestock, a report on the general health of his people, and his location. The apostle and his bodyguard rode out of the pioneer camp about noon and headed up Emigration Canyon along the trail the Saints had so recently etched into the land. It was two weeks before they met advance riders of the main migration at Deer Creek in present Wyoming. Continuing east, Benson passed companies of the migration with regularity until he hailed the party captained by Rich near the Platte about August 19.

While Rockwell and his apostolic charge rode back on the trail, Sam Brannan argued futilely with Brigham Young to abandon the idea of colonizing what he believed to be no more than a desert wasteland and join him in returning to California. Young adamantly refused to listen.

Brannan finally packed his saddlebags in disgust. "You're making a mistake," he warned Young. "California's the promised land, not this forsaken place." With that he slammed a boot heel into his horse's flank and headed west with Captain James Brown of the Mormon Battalion.[1] If there remained a doubt that the Mormons intended to stay in the valley it was soon dispelled, for on August 22 a council agreed upon a name for its settlement — Great Salt Lake City of the Great Basin of North America. The preliminaries attended to, Young now prepared to return to Winter Quarters, where he planned to personally oversee the task of organizing a mass migration of Mormons to the new Zion.

Four days later, as Young's caravan of 107 persons, 71 horses, and 49 mules halted for a rest at Redden's Cave, up galloped Ezra Benson on the return leg of his ride to Charles C. Rich's company. Rockwell was several miles behind, having taken time to scout side trails and river fords. Benson told Young that he and Rockwell had left the nearest company of approaching Saints at Independence Rock the previous Sunday and that all Mormon companies on the plains were within one hundred miles of each other as instructed. The apostle also reported that the emigrants had lost a great many cattle through sickness, and a number of horses to Indians, but otherwise were in satisfactory condition.[2] Pleased with the news, Young waited until Rockwell rode up, then asked the scout to accompany his party as hunter until they encountered the main body of oncoming Saints.

During the next few days the caravan was annoyed by unseasonably heavy rain mixed with snow and bone-chilling temperatures. To make matters worse, provisions ran out; only Rockwell's rifle kept the Saints in food. The man was inexhaustible. Once, while the others slept, he backtracked the trail to Fort Bridger and returned before they awakened;[3] then he led the way to Ham's Fork. He rode nearly forty miles that day alone, without rest. When Indians struck the Mormon remuda and drove off fifty horses, Rockwell was in the saddle and hot after the raiders before the rest of the camp had rubbed the sleep from their eyes. He succeeded in recapturing eight of the precious animals — a sufficient accomplish-

[1] They carried a power of attorney from each member of the Pueblo Detachment of the Battalion to collect the balance of pay due for services, since the unit's term of enlistment had expired July 16.

[2] Journal History, August 29, 1847.

[3] Egan, *Pioneering the West*, p. 134.

ment when contending with Crows.[4] Indians became so troublesome to the company that Howard Egan, a handy man with a gun, was forced to suspend his nightly journal notes in order to maintain a twenty-four hour watch on the camp and livestock. (A band of two hundred Sioux warriors tried to stampede the remainder of the horses at Big Timber Creek on September 21, but the Saints reached their weapons in time to repel the attack.) After taking Young's company down to the Sweetwater, Rockwell was told by Brigham that he was free to return to the valley.

During his absence from Great Salt Lake City, Rockwell's interests were vigilantly protected. While he was with Brigham Young, the council had agreed that "Orrin P. Rockwell, in consideration of services rendered, be rewarded equally with those who worked on the wall of the fort . . . ."[5] His value to the colony again was reflected in council decision when a week later that august body authorized "Thomas Williams, Ebenezer Hanks and Charles Shumway to trade with the Indians in behalf of the people for the time being. Orrin P. Rockwell is permitted to trade with the Indians at his pleasure." In view of Brigham Young's insistence that the Indians be managed with consummate diplomacy until the Saints could safely entrench themselves in their new home, the terms of Rockwell's appointment were a signal compliment to the man. But as he prepared to attend to his newly acquired avocation, events were shaping to send him off on another long and dangerous journey, one which would nearly cost him his life.

Jefferson Hunt, a lean, stern-faced Kentuckian, was a captain in the Mormon Battalion, recently from California. When Hunt rode into Great Salt Lake City from Sutter's Fort in October, he looked at the bleak array of adobe huts comprising the "fort" and, like Sam Brannan before him, mentally compared the scene with the lovely country he had left behind. But more than that, Hunt was troubled by the obvious lack of food supplies in the valley. Wagon after wagon would be pouring through Emigration Canyon within weeks and by spring the population would reach an estimated two thousand persons, yet provisions were dwindling at an alarming rate. Unless livestock, seed, grape cuttings, and grain were

[4] Journal History, September 9, 1847.

[5] Ibid., October 5, 1847. This action was taken by the High Council. It had been decided that no Council of Fifty sessions would be convened until Brigham Young's return from Winter Quarters.

brought into the valley, the Mormons faced bitter privation.[6] Hunt approached the High Council[7] to offer a possible solution. He suggested that he be permitted to lead a small company of picked men to California, there to purchase whatever the church needed. Since winter snows would prohibit travel by the northern route through the Sierra Nevada, Hunt recommended that the party explore a southern route to the Pacific. His enthusiasm for the venture made a favorable impression on the council. The Spaniards were known to have cut a trail in the area in 1776; then too, Frémont had come north by this route in 1844.

After careful consideration the council agreed to Hunt's plan and on November 15 announced that Asahel A. Lathrop, Orrin Porter Rockwell, and Elijah K. Fuller would make the journey as emissaries of the church to purchase "cows, mules, mares, wheat and seeds" at their discretion. Lathrop was to be the expedition's religious leader; Hunt would be in temporal command, with Rockwell's duties confined to scouting and hunting. The remainder of the party included Fuller, William Peacock, Joseph M. Davis, Eli Harvey Pierce, Thurston Larson, James Hirons, Jake Workman, Jackson Workman, James Shaw, John Y. Greene, Elias F. Pearson, William B. Cornogg, Jefferson Hunt's sons, Gilbert and John, and his adopted son, Peter Nease.

An epistle to the Saints in California was composed under the council's direction and placed in Lathrop's keeping; portions pertinent to the exploration read as follows:

> It seemeth good to us to write you a few words of council and advice by our trusty and confidential brethren, Asahel A. Lathrop, Orrin P. Rockwell and Elijah K. Fuller, who in company with others are going to California this winter to obtain seeds and animals to bring to this, our city . . . .
>
> You will be advised and counseled by our confidential brothers, Asahel A. Lathrop, Orrin P. Rockwell, and Elijah K. Fuller, whom we hereby authorize and fully empower as our representatives to trade and make all contracts in our behalf, and in behalf of this people for our mutual benefit and prosperity . . . .
>
> We counsel all of you not to re-enlist as soldiers . . . . But as fast as you are liberated from your previous engagements, and as your cir-

---

[6] The "Second Company" of 1847 was supposed to bring provisions enough for the first year. Hunt's concern had longer range objectives.

[7] The High Council was organized by acclamation of the pioneers during the August 22 meeting.

cumstances will permit repair to this place, bring with you all you can of things that will be of value.[8]

The reference to re-enlisting held a special significance for Hunt. When he had been mustered out in August, government officials, pleased with the exemplary service of the Mormon Battalion, had sent a message to Brigham Young through Hunt asking the Mormon leader to supply another military unit as a garrison for Los Angeles — this was the council's answer to the request. Rockwell was also charged with a task incidental to the journey; to collect whatever mail awaited the Saints in California.

Pleasant weather prevailed on the morning of November 18 as the party rode out of Great Salt Lake City. By week's end they had passed Mountain Meadows and descended the Santa Clara and Virgin rivers into present Nevada. In planning the expedition, Hunt estimated that the journey would take a month and carried supplies sufficient for that period. But when the provisions were exhausted, two hundred long miles still stretched between the Mormons and their destination. None of the eighteen in the party is known to have kept a journal of that eventful exploration, but in 1905 John Hunt recalled the adventure he had experienced as a boy of fourteen.[9] "We found the directions very hard to follow, and lost the trail so often, and spent so much time hunting it again, that we finally ran out of provisions before we had reached the vicinity of Las Vegas," John Hunt related. Despite Rockwell's prowess as a scout and tracker and Jefferson Hunt's experience in the desert, the party was faced with a clear choice — eat its horses or starve.

Three of the animals were butchered and consumed by the desperate company; "the first we killed at Mountain Spring, just beyond Vegas, the next at Amargose springs, and the final one near the Mojave river." Two of the mounts belonged to Greene, the third to Cornogg. When the eighteen had left Great Salt Lake City it was with a saddle horse each and twenty pack animals; now, near present Barstow, the Mormons realized they could go no farther without aid. Weak and exhausted, Rockwell went in search of game while two volunteers, Shaw and Cornogg, took the best horses and struck out ahead. John Hunt remembered, "They sent

[8] Journal History, November 16, 1847.

[9] Hunt described the trip in an article for the *Deseret News*, October 7, 1905, p. 27.

a Mexican to us with beef and fresh mounts, and we moved on again, arriving at the Chino ranch after forty-five days on the trail."

Rancho Santa Ana del Chino, a sprawling layout near San Bernardino owned by Isaac Williams, seemed like heaven to the half-starved Mormons as they stumbled out of the mountains on Christmas Eve of 1847.[10] The two youngsters, John Hunt and Peter Nease, were able to walk only by holding onto mules' tails for support.[11] On sighting the rancho they dropped in their tracks and cried. Williams turned his house over to the little company until they had regained their strength. He furnished them with milk and flour for some six weeks.

When recovered from his ordeal, Lathrop purchased two hundred cows for six dollars a head, pack mules, mares, and forty bulls. Williams had offered to provide "all the bulls you can drive off" without charge. Lathrop was confident the mission was a success. But here on the sunny southern rancho something occurred between Hunt and Rockwell. Exactly what the friction was or what caused it is lost to history, but in the end Rockwell refused to return in Hunt's company. The two men may have argued about the wisdom of driving cattle across the route they had just traveled; Rockwell more than likely advised against taking a herd over the forbidding southern trail. Whatever the reason, Hunt started the company back on February 14, 1848, reaching Great Salt Lake City three months later. All but one bull had perished from thirst, half the cattle had died on the drive, and the party had been plagued by Indians.[12]

In California, while Sam Brannan was waving his hat in the air and running down the crude streets of San Francisco with a bottle of yellow dust, screaming at the top of his lungs, "Gold! Gold! Gold from the

[10] For further description of this famous emigrant stopping place, see *Annual Publications of the Historical Society of Southern California* (Los Angeles, 1934), Vol. XVI, pp. 1–5.

[11] *Deseret News*, October 7, 1905, p. 27.

[12] Ibid.

American River," [13] Orrin Porter Rockwell was contemplating his return to the land of Zion. He and James Shaw inquired about carrying a mail on their trip back, but before the military would permit it, the following communication passed between Lieutenant William Tecumseh Sherman of Monterey and Colonel Jonathan D. Stevenson at Ciudad de Los Angeles: [14]

> In relation to trusting a mail to Mr. Rockwell for the United States I am directed to say that at this time there is not sufficient necessity to make up a public mail for the United States — I send, however, one package addressed to the Adjutant General of the Army, Washington, D.C., which Col. Mason directs be entrusted to Mr. Rockwell, who will be paid by the Acting Quarter Master at Los Angeles whatever may be considered by him sufficient compensation for delivering said package at any post office in the United States. . . .[15]

Rockwell lost his opportunity to collect a few extra dollars when the military in California decided to deliver their own mail. He and Shaw moved on to San Diego where they met a group of discharged Mormon Battalion men under the command of Daniel Davis, and accepted an offer to guide the ex-soldiers to Great Salt Lake City "the fastest way possible." To Rockwell that could only mean the southern route. The twenty-five veterans and their pilots started out from Rancho Santa Ana del Chino with a single wagon, the first to make the passage north, and one hundred and thirty-five mules.[16] They left on April 12.

Following the "Spanish Trail" out of the ranch, the company inched its way through Cajon Pass, across the torrid Mojave Desert to Las Vegas, the Virgin River, Beaver Creek, Salt Creek, the Spanish Fork River, and finally Great Salt Lake City. Their arrival is noted in the church's Journal History on the morning of June 5.

Rockwell had been in the settlement only a few days before he was

[13] Hubert Howe Bancroft, *History of California* (San Francisco, 1886–1890), seven volumes, Vol. VI, p. 56.

[14] The letter was dated January 25, 1848.

[15] Frank Alfred Golder, *The March of the Mormon Battalion, from Council Bluffs to California, taken from the Journal of Henry Standage* (New York, 1928), pp. 260–64. See also Journal History, January 25, 1848.

[16] Described in Henry G. Boyle, "Diary." MS, p. 41. See also Journal History, June 5, 1848, p. 6; Jenson, *Church Encyclopaedia*, p. 934; and Daniel Tyler, *A Concise History of the Mormon Battalion in the Mexican War, 1846–1847* (Salt Lake City, 1881), pp. 331–32.

asked to ride out and meet Brigham Young, returning to Zion with 1,229 souls, 397 wagons, and a tremendous trail herd. The western plains literally crawled with Mormons, since Heber C. Kimball and Willard Richards, too, were leading large parties to the valley. Jefferson Hunt was sent from the valley with a message for Young on the very afternoon of Rockwell's triumphal entry into the city, triumphal in that he and Shaw, unlike Hunt, had brought every animal safely through the grueling fifty-five day journey. The message informed Young that, ". . . in general the brethren are in pretty good spirits. As it always has been, some few are disaffected and have got what we call the California fever. . . . Orrin P. Rockwell has just arrived from California, in company with Capt. Davis,

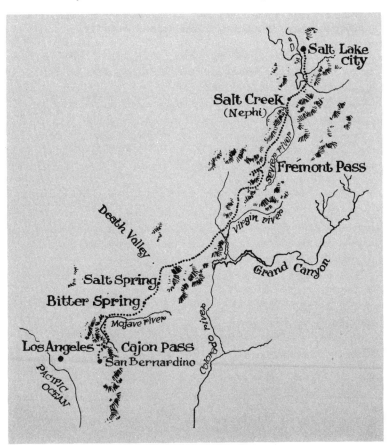

and after he rests a few days intends to go to meet you; if so, we will write you again." [17]

But before the scout could leave for his rendezvous with Young, there was a personal matter to settle; the High Council required that he explain why he had failed to escort Hunt on his return to Zion. Responsibility for the devastating loss of livestock which resulted was Rockwell's, since he, not Hunt, had been selected to guide the party. Under the circumstances, Rockwell felt obliged to state his case publicly; this he did on June 11.[18] That Sabbath morning he spoke earnestly in his own defense; what he said is not recorded, but he persuaded the congregation and the council of his good faith on the mission. This accomplished, he was free to meet the oncoming migration.

On July 20 Rockwell and three companions, Lewis Robison, Quincy Scofield, and Horace Alexander, jogged into "Separation Encampment" (so named by John D. Lee), about forty miles west of Scotts Bluff, and met Lee's company preparing to ford the Platte.[19] After sharing lunch at the Lee table, the four men mounted and galloped to the group commanded by Brigham Young at the rear of the lengthy caravan.[20] During his conversation with the church leader, Rockwell learned for the first time that Young had been named "prophet, seer and revelator" of the church at a conference session in Iowa on December 27, 1847.[21]

Brigham Young's succession to the highest position in the church, vacant since the death of Joseph Smith, was a mere formality. He had been the recognized leader of the Mormons since the martyrdom. This new action, however, once again created a First Presidency, with Heber C. Kimball and Willard Richards as Young's counselors.

Rockwell and the three who had ridden with him from the valley rejoined Lee's company the following morning. It was decided that

[17] *Journal History*, June 9, 1848.

[18] From the journal of Patty Bartlett Sessions in Claire Noall, "Mormon Midwives," *Utah Historical Quarterly*, Vol. X (1942), p. 103.

[19] *A Mormon Chronicle: The Diaries of John D. Lee, 1848–1876*, edited and annotated by Robert Glass Cleland and Juanita Brooks (San Marino, California, 1955), two volumes, Vol. I, pp. 63–64.

[20] Ibid. Journal History, July 20, 1848.

[21] The conference lasted from December 24 to 27, 1847, but it was only on the last day that action taken by the Council of Twelve Apostles on December 5, naming the First Presidency, was ratified.

Quincy Scofield would stay behind and drive a team while the others rode ahead as scouts. For the next two weeks Rockwell, Robison, and Alexander scanned the plains until their eyes ached, always alert for a sudden attack by Indians.[22] When a relief train from the valley brought extra oxen to the emigrants, Young busied himself in doling the animals out to those who needed them the most. Here occurred an incident indicative of his absolute authority over the Saints. John D. Lee described it this way:

> Pres. B.Y. at 8 o'clock the morning before [August 5] stopped a co. that [was] in possession [of] several yoke of catle, converted to their own use, that had been sent from the valley for the benefit of the cos. at the discretion of Pres. B.Y. Said to the man that the catle were the Lord's & that he was Boss of these Prairies & would dictate the Teams & see that the poor were not left behind & that he had from three to 4 yoke of la[r]ge catle on his waggons, when there were many waggons of the same size & weight with one yoke & perhaps a yoke of cows. This is not equality, neither is it bearing each other['s] burden. . . . I am not willing to have you go ahead with more team then what is necessary . . . .[23]

Marking an easier ford across the Platte, Rockwell pushed ahead to meet a party of Saints coming to help the new arrivals through the mountain passes between Fort Bridger and the valley. Rockwell briefed their captain, Isaac Haight, on the relative position of the approaching companies, then raced back with word that relief was on the way. Haight found the Mormons stalled at the Sweetwater, fighting thirst, sickness, bad weather, and broken-down teams. The added hardships seemed only to increase Brigham Young's determination to reach the valley straightaway, and he refused to slacken the pace. When fever claimed one of Lee's wives, Young would not permit burial to slow the train down. Wrote Lee, "About 2 P.M. Squire Wills [Daniel H. Wells], O. P. Rockwell & G. D. Grant was sent by Pres. B.Y. to see if J. D. Lee wanted help & insisted on his roling out the next morning." [24]

[22] Howard Egan and Thomas Ricks had been wounded in a brief clash with an Indian raiding party on the Elk Horn River June 6. See Egan, *Pioneering the West*, p. 140, and *A Mormon Chronicle*, Vol. I, pp. 39–40. Egan was struck by a bullet in the right wrist, and Ricks suffered a near-fatal back wound.

[23] *A Mormon Chronicle*, Vol. I, pp. 68–69.

[24] Ibid., p. 75. The date was September 3, 1848.

By September 15 the Mormons were four days from the valley; Rockwell stayed with Young's company[25] and entered Great Salt Lake City on September 20 to the cheers of the population, which had turned out to greet the emigrants. There now were more than two thousand Saints in Zion.

A mountain of work awaited Young, matters such as the allocation of lots within the city, the suggested cutting down of every tree within thirty miles for timber, and the proposed construction of a wall around the block set aside for a temple site. While attending to these incidentals, the new prophet found time to speak on the gold craze, badgering the brethren thus: "If we were to go to San Francisco and dig up chunks of gold, or find it here in the valley, it would ruin us. Many want to unite Babylon and Zion, but it is the love of money that hurts them. If we find gold and silver, we are in bondage directly. To talk of going away from this valley for anything is like vinegar to my eyes. They who love the world have not their affections placed upon the Lord." [26]

Daily now, the Council of Fifty met from dawn to dusk determining proper arrangement and allocation of the "inheritances," those parcels of land given free to church members as their share in Zion. The tedious process of distribution began early in October and continued for more than two weeks. But Rockwell, perhaps because of his frequent travels and the circumstance that he had no family to settle, was not among those provided with an inheritance lot.[27] Later he claimed nearly a section of land on the southern outskirts of the city, but for now at least, the property dole was not a concern of his.[28]

[25] Journal History, September 15, 1848; and Isaac C. Haight, Journal. MS., September 19, 1848.

[26] Ibid., October 1, 1848.

[27] Book A2, Salt Lake County Abstracts, Plats and Surveys, shows original owners of all pioneer lots issued as inheritances during this period. Rockwell's name does not appear. He is shown, however, on December 19, 1866, to have paid $7,500 to Wells Fargo & Co. for Lot 3, Block 73, Plat A, containing one and a quarter acres and located on the east side of 2nd East Street midway between South Temple and 1st South streets. See Abstracts, Plats and Surveys, Book A2, p. 73; Salt Lake County Deeds and Transfers, Book C, pp. 579–80.

[28] He sold Lot 2, Block 1, and Lot 1, Block 2, containing 319 acres, in the Hot Springs Survey to Thomas S. Williams and Charles Mogo on August 14, 1858. The price was $66.66. See Salt Lake County Deeds and Transfers, Book A, p. 423. A land certificate issued by the territorial surveyor on July 14, 1859, shows that Rockwell also owned Lot 2, Block 2, containing 212 acres, in the Hot Springs Survey. See Salt Lake County Deeds and Transfers, Book B, p. 46.

During this period of relative inactivity, Rockwell accepted frequent invitations to dine at the home of Mrs. Catharine Woolley, a new arrival who was repaying him for a slab of buffalo meat he had given her when they had chanced to meet near the Sweetwater a month and a half earlier.[29] Meanwhile, his name was being mentioned by the Council of Fifty for another mission to California and extra duty on the home front.[30] He, Lee, and George D. Grant were named to a committee responsible for managing and superintending the roundup of cattle and horses scattered over the valley before they fell prey to coyotes and cougars.

A general apathy brought on by the fatigue of the previous months quickly caught Brigham Young's stern eye, causing him to comment sharply, "If there is not fire and thunder in this committee we will try to put it in them!"[31] To no one's surprise, the remark had its desired effect; Rockwell, Lee, and Grant, along with two others, spent the next seven days diligently herding livestock. They were too diligent, apparently. In fact, the committee's eagerness to put "fire and thunder" in its work came in for stinging criticism from Mormons living outside the fort. According to Lee: "This move like many others, though designed for the good & general interes[t] of the People, was not without opposition, for some who had not sufficient interest to Join in the drive had their catle drove off to the Fort, and therby were pu[t] to trouble, having to Seperate their stock & take them home again, murmering as they went. One Albon Pouell & Jos. Rollins used harsh and unbecoming language to A. Lyman & some more of the commity. . . ."[32]

When the abuse continued, the committee members asked to be relieved of responsibility, but Young denied the request, explaining, "Natural feelings would say let them and their cattle go to Hell, but duty says if they do not take care of their cattle, we must do it for them."[33] Since the primary purpose of the roundup was to protect the livestock from predators, it was suggested that a hunt be called and all available men in the valley sent out to destroy rapacious birds and animals roaming the

[29] See the Journal of Catharine E. Mehring Woolley, entries of September 20 and October 15, 1848, as extracted by J. Cecil Alter, "In the Beginning," *Salt Lake Tribune*, January 10, 1935.

[30] Journal History, November 26, 1848.

[31] *A Mormon Chronicle*, Vol. I, p. 81.

[32] Ibid.

[33] Ibid., p. 82.

region. The Council of Fifty thought the idea sound and named John D. Lee and John Pack captains of the hunt. Rockwell found himself on Pack's team with ninety-three others. By March 1849, the war of extermination had accounted for some fifteen thousand predators.

In early January Rockwell took nine of the brethren to Utah Valley for the purpose of determining its value as a secondary stock range, since feed near the fort was under eight inches of snow and many cattle were dying from cold and hunger.[34] After four days the party returned. John D. Lee outlined their findings as presented to the Council of Fifty: ". . . comitty returned & reported unfavorable. Said that the Snow was almost as deep in the Eutauh Valley as it was here & almost impassible for weak catle to get there on account of the Snow drifts. Snow North was reported to be 18 inches deep. Catle Suffering. The owners were advised to drive them South. . . ."[35]

Two months later Rockwell was set apart to help operate the Mormon ferry on the north fork of the Platte during the spring migration,[36] and on March 12, 1849, in the first public election held in the Great Salt Lake Valley, he was named a deputy marshal[37] for the provisional State of Deseret.[38] All of these matters had been resolved beforehand in the interminable meetings of the Council of Fifty. None of the council's handiwork was intended to be made public, as an incident involving Rockwell made terribly clear. At a session of the Fifty on March 31, Return Jackson Redden complained that he had been warned to leave the valley or be murdered; he pointed to John Pack as the council member who had threatened him. Rockwell and Heber C. Kimball testified that Redden had repeated Pack's statement to them. Pack was summarily called to account for violating his covenants in revealing the council's secrets; it was understood that proceedings of the Fifty were sacrosanct, and any infraction would be received with great displeasure. Consequently, when

[34] Journal History, January 6, 1849; Bean, *Autobiography*, p. 49.

[35] *A Mormon Chronicle*, Vol. I, p. 86.

[36] Ibid., p. 99; Journal History, March 3, 1849.

[37] *A Mormon Chronicle*, Vol. I, p. 99; Journal History, March 12, 1849. Curiously, Rockwell was made a deputy sheriff after Utah was organized as a Territory on September 9, 1850, and apparently held the appointment for life.

[38] For a penetrating look at this remarkable attempt at self-government, read Dale L. Morgan's monograph on "The State of Deseret," *Utah Historical Quarterly*, Vol. VIII (April, July, October 1940), pp. 65–239. A less detailed treatment can be found in Clark, "The Kingdom of God, the Council of Fifty and the State of Deseret," *Utah Historical Quarterly*, Vol. XXVI, pp. 142–48.

Pack made his appearance before the body, prevailing sentiment held that he should be "pushed over the rim of the basin." And when Pack tried to evade a direct reply to the accusation, Brigham Young angrily denounced him for "not having the wisdom to keep secrets of this council locked up in his breast." [39] Suddenly aware of his precarious position, Pack quickly admitted his error. Weeping, he beseeched his judges for an opportunity to redeem himself, "If I don't prove true, deal with me as you think proper, even if it is to cut my head off!" [40] To Pack's immense relief, he was given another chance. The episode moved Brigham Young to observe, "Members of this council should be men of firmness and integrity, and the things that belong to this council should be as safe as though they were locked in the silent vaults of Eternity." Before the Fifty adjourned that day, Redden also was spared.

Turning its attention elsewhere, the council released Rockwell from his call to the Platte ferry and instead assigned him to accompany Amasa Lyman to California. Apostle Lyman was to carry an epistle to the Saints there and collect tithing. Rockwell's return mission included delivering a mail and acting as guide for any Mormons wishing to reach the valley.[41] Rockwell, Lyman, and a company of men planned to leave by the northern route via Fort Hall as soon as weather permitted; until then Brigham Young had another chore for his best scout. Thirty Mormons sent to Utah Valley to establish a settlement were having trouble with their neighbors,

[39] *A Mormon Chronicle*, Vol. I, p. 103. Brigham Young's remark here strongly supports the conclusion that the Council of Fifty had determined to do away with Redden.

[40] The resolute manner in which the Fifty dealt with their serious problems is described by John D. Lee in his discussion of the case of Ira E. West, a Nauvoo Mormon who had fallen from favor (ibid., p. 98). Lee explained that West had "forfeited his Head, but the difficulty was how he should be disposed of." Some members of the YTFIF (Fifty spelled backwards), as Lee chose to call it, suggested that West should be publicly executed, while others thought it wiser to "dispose of him privately." Lee did not record West's ultimate fate, but the Journal History for March 4, 1849, explains that West and another offender were to be offered for public sale "that they may be made to work until they have paid the fines now due from them."

[41] *A Mormon Chronicle*, Vol. I, p. 104; Journal History, March 31, 1849.

180

the Timpanogos Utes. The Indians depended on Utah Lake for fish and were reluctant to share their land with whites. Young was determined that the Saints would colonize the valley, yet he hesitated to start a war with the Utes; they would be far more valuable as allies.[42] So, he called on Rockwell and eighteen-year-old George W. Bean, a youngster who already had acquired a smattering of Ute, to placate the tribes.

Rockwell and Bean were well aware that the Utes had been seen wearing warpaint on several raids. With this in mind, the two Mormons started out "cautiously and prayerfully." Bean refused to carry a firearm of any kind in treating with Indians, though his companion was amply fortified with a pair of revolvers, a rifle, and a very sharp bowie knife. Bean had a youngster's admiration for his intrepid partner:

> Orrin Porter Rockwell, as I knew him, was a diamond in the rough. It was great to know his inner self. His honest loyalty to church, country and friends was deep and lasting. He abhorred deceit and intrigue as did I. He knew the need and power of prayer, and did I. He was above average height, quick in movement, with strong arms and chest, and gray eyes — cool and searching. He was always well armed since his Nauvoo experiences, although the Prophet Joseph told him to wear his hair long and he would never be killed by an enemy. He held to that promise and on many occasions when he stayed over night with me, my wife Elizabeth would plait or braid his hair and Porter would comb it into a flair next morning, which emphasized his high forehead, and his aristocratic air. He raised thoroughbred horses and drove a fine team . . . . His mouth was expressive of his moods, whether jovial, reckless, worried, or pleasant. . . . His humor made his stories click. In our missionary work, he was humble and earnest. We spent many years of dangerous and worthwhile service together in teaching the Red Men the Gospel of Jesus Christ and of their origin and duties, and in aiding the officials of Government to subdue and punish outlaws. . . .[43]

Rockwell and Bean rode to within a half-mile of the Ute encampment nestled at the foot of the rugged Wasatch Mountains and reined up. Bean

---

[42] An earlier scrap with the Indians demonstrated the futility of employing force to control the tribes. In late February and early March of 1849 a contingent of militia was dispatched to deal with a small band of Ute cattle thieves near Provo to please the Ute leader, Little Chief, who had asked Brigham Young to "kill them mean Ewtes." But once the renegades were cornered, Little Chief interceded on their behalf and in the end cursed the Mormons whose help he had requisitioned. A first-hand account of this episode can be found in Huntington, "Journal," Vol. II, pp. 52–55, 333–40.

[43] Bean, *Autobiography*, pp. 175–76.

spoke first: "If we both ride in, we'll be killed." The older man nodded in assent.

"George," Rockwell said after a moment of thought, "You go into the camp alone. You know the language and maybe some of the Indians. Your personality is better than mine, too. I'll hide in these willows, ready to rush to you when you give the signal."

"Brother Brigham sent us with a message of peace and a 'God bless you.' I'll have nothing to fear in the camp," the youngster replied.[44]

He straightened in the saddle, nudged his horse, and rode toward the distant teepees. The boy was able to make out a number of warriors gyrating around a huge bonfire, its flames licking at the night sky while squaws thumped out a rhythmic accompaniment on a variety of tom-toms. A warning shout silenced the drumming in mid-beat. Three warriors yelped the alarm in a single voice as they spotted the lone rider approaching. Dashing out, they pulled the young Mormon from the saddle and then quickly lashed his wrists behind his back using rawhide thongs. With a Ute brave on each arm and a third bringing up the rear, Bean was roughly shoved to a buffalo robe and motioned to stand fast.

For two hours the boy was taunted by warriors who boasted of their victories over the whites and spat in his face. They grinned sardonically and described what they would do to the "Mormonee" for stealing their hunting grounds. Each time the boy attempted an answer he was clubbed. When the braves tired of this sport they contemptuously turned Bean over to the squaws, more vicious by far than the men. Forty or more sniggering women bunched in a circle around the captive and poked him with sharp sticks; occasionally one whipped a stinging blow across his face, another jabbed at his eyes. Then, through the red haze clouding his vision, Bean saw two braves shoulder their way toward him. He recognized them as Sowiette, leader of the Ute Nation, and Walkara, a cunning and dangerous subchieftain. Walkara looked on in disdain as Sowiette spoke to the captive: "Now you talk!"

Bean's six-foot frame towered over the two Indians as he first motioned for his hands to be untied, then, through puffed lips, delivered his message of peace from Brigham Young. Finishing, the boy looked to Sowiette for an answer. The chief grunted his approval, remarking his satisfaction that the Mormon leader recognized his power over the tribes, and telling Bean he was free to leave. Rubbing his aching wrists, the boy

[44] Ibid., p. 53.

explained that he had a friend waiting for him in the willows on the perimeter of the camp. Bean told them the man also spoke for Brigham Young and suggested that the two Indian chiefs meet him.

Rockwell had given Bean up for dead an hour before and was waiting for daylight to scout the camp at close range when he first heard the approaching hoofbeats. Drawing a revolver, the scout felt certain he could snap off at least two shots before making a run for it. He crouched quietly in the willows and squinted into the darkness. The last sound he expected to hear was Bean's voice. "Porter, it's me — hold your fire, everything's all right."

With a sigh of relief Rockwell eased the hammer of his pistol gently forward and stuffed the heavy handgun into his coat pocket. Hearing Rockwell's pledge of peace, Sowiette agreed to halt his raids and resume trade with the Saints. Walkara stood sullenly silent. Daybreak found the two Mormons galloping back to Great Salt Lake City, where Brigham Young awaited their report.[45] His pleasure at the success of their mission was such that he bestowed upon the two men authority to speak in his name to any and all tribes in the Great Basin whenever necessary.

[45] Bean describes this incident in ibid., pp. 53–54.

Chapter Ten

SAM BRANNAN

THE TIME HAD DRAWN NEAR for Orrin Porter Rockwell to lead Amasa Lyman and his party to California. On April 11, 1849, the First Presidency and the Council of Twelve Apostles gathered at Lorenzo D. Young's home and blessed Rockwell for his western mission. Then that elite group transacted another piece of business, a proceeding which has yet to be explained. According to the Journal History entry for that date, "They also deliberated on the abduction of Orrin P. Rockwell's daughter by Hiram Gates and Levi Fifield.[1] Judge Heber C. Kimball issued his first warrant to the marshal, for the arrest of those two men, on charges of kidnaping and signed the document on his knee."

When Rockwell and Lyman struck out for California, the apostle carried a letter from Brigham Young to Sam Brannan in San Francisco. Brannan's enthusiasm for the church had been on the wane ever since his

---

[1] Few documents are available to shed light on the kidnapping or its outcome. However, there is strong evidence that Hiram Gates, with Levi Fifield's help, eloped with sixteen-year-old Emily Amanda Rockwell to California. Fifield had marched to San Diego with the Mormon Battalion and worked his way north to Sutter's Fort, where he was blacksmithing when James Marshall brought news of the discovery of gold in the Sutter mill tailrace. Fifield returned to Great Salt Lake Valley, but the memory of sunny California apparently was too much for him; before he could enjoy being home, he guided Gates and his bride to the gold fields. Mrs. Carole Gates Sorensen, in her privately published *Henry Gates Family of Upper Canada, 1791–1981, With Genealogy of Allied Families* (n.p., 1981), traced Hiram Gates and Emily to Greenwood Valley in 1849. Marshal Horace Eldredge's signal lack of success in arresting Gates and Fifield before their flight to California may have played an important part in Rockwell's change in assignment from the Platte River ferry to escorting Amasa Lyman to California. Hiram died in early September 1850. Emily was left with his two sons by another wife. Not long afterwards the boys, Thomas, sixteen, and Solomon, fourteen, were killed by Indians. Emily subsequently married Henry W. Brizzee (another Mormon Battalion veteran) and later still married David Tyrrell. Emily Amanda Rockwell Gates Brizzee Tyrrell died April 9, 1909, and is buried near Grouse Creek, Utah.

disagreement with Young on the location of Zion, but this had not deterred him from collecting the tithes of California Mormons.[2] The money failed to reach Great Salt Lake City, and there seemed to be a question regarding Brannan's use of the funds. Some said the tithes had permitted him to develop and indulge a taste for oysters and rare wine. After asking for $10,000 "at least," to settle tithes, Brigham's letter continued:

> If you want to continue to prosper, do not forget the Lord's treasury, lest He forget you; for with the liberal; the Lord is liberal. And when you have settled with the treasury, I want you to remember, that, Bro. Brigham has long been destitute of a home and suffered heavy losses and incurred great expense in searching out a location and planting the church in this place, and he wants you to send him a present of twenty thousand dollars in gold dust, to help him in his labors. This is but a trifle when gold is so plenty, but it will do me much good at this time.
>
> I hope that Bro. Brannan will remember that, when he has complied with my request, my council will not be equal with me unless you send $20,000 more to be divided between Bros. Kimball and Richards, who like myself are straitened; *a hint to the wise is sufficient*,[3] so when this is accomplished, you will have our united blessing, and our hearts will exclaim "God bless Bro. Brannan and give him four fold, for all he has given us."
>
> Now Bro. Brannan if you will deal justly with your fellows and deal out with liberal heart and open hands, making a righteous use of all your money, the Lord is willing you should accumulate the rich treasures of the earth and the good things of time in abundance; but should you withhold, when the Lord says give; your hopes and pleasing prospects will be blasted in an hour you think not of — and no arm can save.[4]

Brigham's stern tone and its implications for unpleasantness should Brannan decide to be difficult provide a good reason for having Rock-

[2] William Tecumseh Sherman, then a lieutenant, was visiting Mormon Island in July of 1848 and overheard a conversation between "Clark of Clark's Point" and Colonel Richard Barnes Mason, military commander and acting civil governor of California, who was inspecting the "diggings." "Governor, what business has Sam Brannan to collect the tithes here?" asked Clark. Answered Mason, "Brannan has a perfect right to collect the tax, if you Mormons are fool enough to pay it." See General William T. Sherman, *Memoirs* (New York, 1875), two volumes, Vol. I, p. 53.

[3] Compare this phrase with the language used by Brigham Young in his thanksgiving proclamation of January 10, 1843, near the close of chapter four, above, this book. Italics are mine.

[4] Journal History, April 5, 1849, pp. 3–4.

well on hand when Amasa Lyman delivered the letter. This in itself may have been the factor which prompted his change of mission assignments from the Platte River ferry. Brannan was headstrong and stubborn, and Young's instructions regarding the tithes offered very little room for negotiation.

The Mormon party trotted out of Great Salt Lake City on April 13.[5] Ahead lay swollen rivers, deep snow, sub-zero temperatures, and hostile Indians. After fording the Weber River and the Bear, they struck northwest to intersect the California Trail near City of Rocks. When the party reached the Sierra, deep snow still blocked its way, but four tortuous days later the small band pushed over the lofty summit to arrive at Sutter's Fort on May 25.[6]

Rockwell headed straight for the "diggings," while Amasa Lyman tended to spreading the gospel among the Californians. Lyman soon discovered that the American River had dampened the religious ardor of many of his brethren, for he gathered only meager tithes from Mormons who preferred the gold pan to the collection plate. By July he had accumulated little more than $4,000 in a region abounding in wealth, and by year's end he had crisscrossed the goldfields with indifferent success.

Rockwell fared better. During his leisure moments the scout had taken pan in hand and sifted the river's sand for its secret treasures; an hour's effort was enough to convince him that the most accessible money was not in the claims, but in the pockets of those who worked them. Before long Rockwell went into business. He opened a saloon at Murderer's Bar,[7] an inn at Buckeye Flat, and a "half-way" house near Mormon Island on the American River.[8] In 1849 a main street crowded

[5] Eliza Marie Partridge (Smith) Lyman, "Autobiography and Diary, 1820–1885." MS, p. 37; Eliza R. Snow, "Diary." MS, April 13, 1849.

[6] Amasa Lyman to J. H. Flanigan, April 11, 1850, in *Millennial Star*, Vol. XII, pp. 214–15.

[7] Address to the California Historical Society by Wendell Robie of Auburn, California, on March 10, 1955; reprinted as "Murderer's Bar and Gold Rush on the Middlefork," *The Pony Express*, Vol. XXV (July 1958), p. 5.

[8] According to Achilles, *Destroying Angels of Mormondom*, p. 14, Rockwell kept "between Sacramento and Mormon Island . . . the 'Half-way House.' Here he practiced rifle shooting, and made a great deal of money at matches." See also Nelson Slater, *Fruits of Mormonism* (Coloma, California, 1851), pp. 77n–78n; Joseph Cain and Arieh C. Brower, *Mormon Way-Bill, To The Gold Mines from the Pacific Springs* (G.S.L. City, Deseret, 1851), pp. 16–17, and Paolo Sioli, *Historical Souvenir of El Dorado County, California* (Oakland, 1883), p. 201.

with makeshift buildings of all descriptions made up Murderer's Bar. Rockwell ran the Round Tent Saloon amid this confusion and hauled in whisky from Sacramento by pack train. Arriving at a hill overlooking the bar, he would loose a blast on a bugle carried for the purpose, and his partner at the Round Tent, Jack Smith, would reply by firing a signal shot to miners up and down the river that "business" was about to begin.[9] There is good reason to believe that "Jack Smith" may have been Judson Stoddard, a fellow Mormon and close friend of Rockwell's. Shortly after Christmas Lyman told Rockwell that the time had come to visit Brannan and settle affairs with him. It was January 8, 1850, when the apostle and his escort confronted the California Saint in Brannan's fashionable San Francisco home.[10] The meeting began politely with the three men exchanging handshakes and customary greetings; then Lyman came to the point. "We've come for the Lord's money," he said.

The dialogue between Brannan and Lyman over the question of tithes has been buried in fiction, but Brannan's reply to the apostle's request has survived in substance: "Give me a receipt from the Lord — and you can have the money!" [11]

Lyman and Rockwell returned to Sacramento, but within a month Lyman retraced his steps to board a ship headed for San Pedro. He visited Brannan once more to offer him an opportunity to reconsider, but was again rebuffed.[12] Lyman then sailed to San Pedro to meet Charles C.

[9] "Murderer's Bar and Gold Rush on the Middlefork," *Pony Express,* Vol. XXV, p. 5.

[10] Amasa Lyman, "Journal, 1848–1850." MS, January 8, 1850.

[11] Lyman, in a subsequent letter to Young, said: "Bro. Samuel Brannan has disclaimed all connexion with the church . . . ." Journal History, July 23, 1850. No actual account of the confrontation between Lyman, Rockwell, and Brannan is extant, but popular and contemporary versions agree that Brannan demanded a receipt signed by God. See Asbury Harpending, *The Great Diamond Hoax and Other Stirring Incidents In The Life of Asbury Harpending,* edited by James H. Wilkins (San Francisco, 1913), p. 169. More than a year passed before Brigham Young could tend to the Californian. Meeting in San Francisco on September 1, 1851, Parley P. Pratt brought the matter up for consideration by the local Mormon mission branch. ". . . Fellowship was then withdrawn from Samuel Brannan by an unanimous vote for a general course of unchristianlike conduct, neglect of duty, and for combining with lawless assemblies to commit murder and other crimes." "A Mormon Mission to California in 1851, From the Diary of Parley Parker Pratt," edited by Reva Holdaway Stanley and Charles L. Camp, *California Historical Quarterly,* Vol. XIV (June 1935), p. 176. (The remark about murder is a reference to the 1851 Vigilance Committee with which Brannan became associated.)

[12] Lyman, "Journal," February 3, 1850.

Rich, also on a mission assignment for the church, and the two apostles journeyed up the coast to the goldfields, joining Rockwell at Mormon Tavern on May 19.[13] Twelve days later in Sacramento, Lyman wrote in his journal: "Heard of the death of J. M. Flake[14] which was caused by falling from his mule May 22. Died May 23."[15] The next entry on May 31 reads, "Traveled to Mormon tavern there meet with Capt. [Jefferson] Hunt and O. P. [Rockwell]." While Lyman and Rich pursued their missionary duties, Rockwell looked after the hotel and saloon he operated under the alias of James B. Brown.[16] He was aware that his old enemy, Lilburn W. Boggs, now alcalde of Sonoma, knew of his presence in California, and Rockwell was convinced that the former governor planned to have him ambushed at the first opportunity.[17] To thwart any such attempt on his life, Rockwell used a different name, armed himself with a brace of revolvers, kept a pair of duelling pistols loaded with buckshot, and had a trained dog constantly at his side.[18] There were those,

[13] Ibid., May 19, 1850. Mormon Tavern was another of the many inns operated in the diggings by Mormons.

[14] James M. Flake had guided Charles C. Rich and his party to southern California from Great Salt Lake City the previous October.

[15] Rumor accused Rockwell of murdering Flake, but here Lyman confirms that the guide's death was accidental. See also "Extracts from the Journal of Henry W. Bigler," *Utah Historical Quarterly*, Vol. V (1932), p. 138.

[16] Slater, *Fruits of Mormonism*, pp. 77n–78n, says: "[Rockwell] spent the last season [1850] in California under the assumed name of Brown, and kept a tavern on the road between Sacramento and Placerville, about thirty miles distant from the former place . . . ." Achilles, *Destroying Angels of Mormondom*, p. 14, adds: "[Rockwell] came to California, and, under an assumed name, calling himself James B. Brown, settled in what is now Sacramento County, between Sacramento and Mormon Island, and kept, for several years, the 'Half-way House.'" Louisa Barnes Pratt, "The Journal of Louisa Barnes Pratt," *Heart Throbs of the West*, Vol. VIII (1947), p. 256, provides this revealing entry under the date of July 16, 1850: "Camped in an oak grove near Brown's, a fictitious name for Porter Rockwell." Mrs. Pratt, wife of Addison Pratt, was Caroline Barnes Crosby's sister and a member of the Crosby wagon train. Rockwell's use of the alias "James B. Brown" was more than mere fancy on his part; it was the same name he used in Independence in the months preceding the attempt on Lilburn W. Boggs's life. See Switzler, *Illustrated History of Missouri*, p. 251.

[17] John M. Letts, *California Illustrated: Including a Description of the Panama and Nicaragua Routes. By a Returned Californian* (New York, 1852), p. 95.

[18] Ibid. Letts says he knew Rockwell under the name "Scofield" during this period. John Fitzgerald, Holladay, Utah, recalls his uncle, Willard B. Ennis, Draper, Utah, telling of Rockwell's dog, a small white animal that rode behind Rockwell on his horse, occasionally placing his paws on Rockwell's shoulder to look forward, but more often perched on the horse's rump. "Uncle Willard also spoke of the dog hav-

however, who shared the secret of his identity. Mission-bound Saints passing through the goldfields on their way to the islands of the Pacific were asked not to divulge his real name, and in return his trading post–saloon was recommended to Mormon travelers as a place to get a square deal. Eighteen-year-old Thomas J. Orr, Jr., was one of those early travelers attracted to California by the promise of gold. His family left Provo in time to reach Deer Creek near Pleasant Valley by the first week in July of 1850. Young Orr remembered:

> . . . A man was keeping a trading post there and father had known him in Illinois and at Salt Lake. Father recognized him and called him by name, Porter Rockwell. He was alarmed and told father to call him Brown in the future because he was one of Brigham Young's destroying angels and his life wouldn't be worth much if people discovered his real identity. Father asked Brown where he thought the best place to settle and was told it was no use going further and that place was as good as any to locate. . . .[19]

One wagon train of missionaries heading for the Sandwich Islands included several of Rockwell's friends. Jonathan Crosby and his wife Caroline arrived at the diggings in mid-July and were debating where to trade when they spotted Rockwell hawking whisky to a crowd of miners.[20] Rounding up other members of the train, Crosby "went on to where Porter Rokwel & an other man in Co. were keeping a licquer shop, we camped a day & sold our teems & waggons to P. Rockwell. . . . but we had the use of them to take us to Sacramento & Porter send a man along to take the teems back." [21]

With the coming of August, Amasa Lyman made preparations for his return to Great Salt Lake City, a circumstance which offered Rockwell a change for a week or two from the drudgery of ramrodding his whisky pack train. He joined C. C. Rich's company in escorting Lyman and his men for nearly two hundred miles through the Indian-infested Humboldt Valley, then returned to the Round Tent and Half-way

---

ing been trained to lick Rockwell's face rather than barking to sound the alarm after dark while Rockwell was sleeping."

[19] Caroline Barnes Crosby, "Journal," MS, July 17, 1850; Jonathan Crosby, "Biographical Sketch," MS, July 17, 1850. *Life History of Thomas Orr Jr., Pioneer Stories of California and Utah*, edited by Lillie Jane Orr Taylor (n.p., 1930), p. 21.

[20] Caroline Barnes Crosby, "Journal," July 17, 1850; Jonathan Crosby, "Biographical Sketch," July 17, 1850.

[21] Jonathan Crosby, op. cit.

House.[22] Things moved smoothly for the quiet Mormon until one day when another trading post operator, an ex-Battalion member, challenged him to a shooting contest.

In their brief hours of relaxation, the forty-niners found little amusement outside of the marathon drinking bouts and continual free-for-alls which provided the entertainment for every camp in the mines. Consequently, when word spread that "Brown" and Boyd Stewart were going to shoot at targets for a prize of $1,000, Half-way House found itself playing host to hundreds of garrulous miners. Stewart hailed from Columbia, California, and had distinguished himself during the Mormon Battalion march by his inability to stay out of trouble.[23] He knew who "Brown" really was, a detail Rockwell came to regret.

The rifle match took place in the afternoon, and when the scores were tallied, "Brown" was declared winner, and the $1,000 in dust and nuggets was turned over to him. This was all the reason necessary for a celebration, and before an hour had passed the plaza at Half-way House had become the scene of perhaps the wildest whiskyfest ever staged in the goldfields. Stewart, stung by defeat, turned to the drunken mob and shouted Rockwell's identity for all to hear. Not a few men in the horde of miners were Missourians and Illinoisians by birth; many others harbored grievances over their treatment by Mormons in Zion. In their stupor, they shouted threats of reprisal against the man they knew as The Destroying Angel and surged forward to offer him a taste of camp justice. According to Achilles, it was only with a great deal of luck that Rockwell managed to avoid being caught and hanged.[24]

[22] Journal History, September 29, 1850.

[23] Once, for failing to salute an officer in the middle of the night, Stewart was tied to a slow wagon and forced to march behind it in the heat of the day while wearing a full knapsack. On another occasion an officer ordered him chained to a stack of rifles during sleeping hours for an infraction of regulations. See Pettegrew, "History and Journal," pp. 81, 90.

[24] After Rockwell had successfully given them the slip, Achilles (*Destroying Angels of Mormondom*, p. 14) says the crowd at the Half-way House "imagined,

C. C. Rich was now ready to set out for Utah. With fifty men, and Rockwell for a guide, he moved out on the northern route September 5. For nearly four hundred miles the company was dogged by Indians, who kept the camp on edge by sniping at nightguards and hazing the livestock. One night several braves managed to belly their way into the remuda and stampede a number of horses, several of which belonged to Rockwell. In retaliation, the scout and two others invaded an Indian encampment and ran off with a string of ponies. Hastily pitching camp at the height of a sandstorm which caught them in the Carson Sink, the men awoke the next morning to find half the animals gone and waterholes filled with sand. In one of the holes were the bodies of three white men, murdered and horribly mutilated by Indians.[25]

Goudy E. Hogan, a young Mormon who had tried his luck in the goldfields and was now returning home, described Rockwell as "a well known brave man." He gave this account of an Indian whose courage cost his life when he tried to trick the wily scout: "While on guard one night there came a large Indian walking into camp with his gun on his shoulder making out he was a relief guard. As Porter spoke to him he run, at this said Rockwell fired 2 shots with his dragoon pistol. In the morning we found the intruder about 300 yards from camp lying dead on his face." [26] Thirty-seven days after leaving California, Rockwell led the Rich party into Great Salt Lake City.

In the nineteen months Orrin Porter Rockwell had been away, Zion had changed. The Saints were prospering in the Gold Rush. The first issues of a new Mormon newspaper, the *Deseret News*, were off the press, and five Mormon mills were working around the clock grinding flour which sold for $25 a hundredweight to Gentiles swarming into the city for the final push to California. Always ready to bargain, the Saints traded horses, harnesses, and wagons from the travelers for a fraction of their original cost. In short, the once-desolate valley had blossomed into

naturally enough, that [Rockwell] had been assassinated." Achilles claims that Rockwell made a great deal of money in shooting matches during this period. After the shooting match and ensuing drama, Stewart was dispatched by church authorities on a mission to Oregon. *Deseret News*, November 16, 1850. (In later years, the *Deseret News* of February 5, 1862, listed him as a delinquent taxpayer of the Seventh Ward.)

[25] Journal History, November 12, 1850. Rich reported that the victims included Hiram Gates's sons Thomas and Solomon.

[26] Goudy E. Hogan, "History." MS, p. 21.

a major supply point for emigrants trekking westward.²⁷ Many of the Gentiles were baptized into the church as well. As the population of Zion burgeoned, so did Rockwell's notoriety. His activities were a prominent topic of conversation among visitors, and his exploits had become so exaggerated in the retelling that Rockwell was fast becoming a legend in his own time.²⁸

He already was being accused of murder in Utah. A company of gold-seekers, caught in the valley by the lateness of the season, related the strange tale that during the previous summer Rockwell had decapitated a luckless emigrant believed to have been in the mob at Carthage Jail.²⁹ But there were no Gentile emigrants in Utah until June of 1849, and Rockwell had left for California with Lyman in April. Nevertheless, after spending the winter of 1850–51 in Ogden, a Gentile named Nelson Slater continued to the goldfields the following spring convinced that he and his fellow-travelers had been victimized by the Mormons. On his arrival in Coloma, Slater wrote the experiences of his company for publication, splashing the details of Rockwell's alleged crime about for all to see.

²⁷ For an excellent description of the city at the peak of the Gold Rush see George A. Smith's letter to Orson Pratt, dated July 31, 1850, published in the *Millennial Star*, Vol. XII, pp. 349–50.

²⁸ William P. Bennett, *The Sky-Sifter* ([Gold Hill, Nevada], 1892), pp. 285–86, tells of Bennett's search for an aunt in Great Salt Lake City and his attempt to conceal her intended flight from Utah and Mormonism by using Rockwell's name. Bennett explains: "[I] went up to take another look at Mrs. [Alice] Bardsley's cabin to see . . . if she had been missed, and if so, whether her disappearance was making any noise. I found half the women of the neighborhood there. . . . As there was much wondering and a vast deal of 'cackling,' I said: 'You will all do well to keep your mouths shut. There has been a "revelation." The old lady has long been sick; she was troubled with a disease known as apostacy, but she will now soon be cured. She has gone on a little trip for her health with Porter Rockwell (the leader of the Destroying Angels), so you see that the less you say the better.' . . . Mention of the name of Porter Rockwell had sent a chill to every heart." According to Bennett, the incident occurred between July 14 and 22, 1850.

²⁹ Slater, *Fruits of Mormonism*, pp. 78–79, says: "[The unidentified victim] was pursued by three mormons, Mr. Scott, the sheriff; Porter Rockwell, the Danite already mentioned; and one other man. The emigrant saw his pursuers coming after him, and ran his horse, being aware of their intention. Discovering that he was likely to be overtaken, he turned off from the road to get among willow bushes. The mormons came up to him, and without trial, judge, or jury, they cut off his head." It was commonly believed that Missourians were severely dealt with in Utah. See "Who Killed the Smiths," *Naked Truths About Mormonism*, Vol. I, No. 2 (April 1888).

Chapter Eleven

PEACEPIPES AND GUNSMOKE

FOR THE NEXT FIVE YEARS Rockwell's duties kept him closer to home. His energies now were directed toward improving the delicate relationship between the Mormons and neighboring Indians who resented white intrusion on their tribal lands. Unwittingly the Saints had squatted in a valley which for ages had been a great neutral ground, the traditional battlefield where generations of Ute and Shoshone met to settle their differences. Young's Indian policy was simple: feed an Indian rather than fight him. But occasionally circumstances demanded stern measures; consequently, Rockwell's methods varied — from the peacepipe to the smoking muzzle of his pistol.

On his return from California, Rockwell had been told to keep an eye on the Great Basin tribes and maintain peace in Brigham Young's name. Some months earlier a long string of skirmishes with Indians had culminated in a full-scale battle at Fort Utah on the Provo River, with the Timpanogos Utes being crushed in the encounter. Now the Saints were determined to squelch the isolated, but irritating, raids perpetrated by small bands of Utes and Gosiutes, who were intent upon driving the white man from the valley, or at least upon causing him the greatest discomfiture possible. For Rockwell, the months passed uneventfully until April of 1851, when a dozen warriors attacked a settlement in Tooele Valley, west of Great Salt Lake City.[1] A Gentile emigrant subsequently lost his life because Rockwell misjudged Indian behavior. It was an error he did not repeat.

The victim, Lorenzo D. Custer of Akron, Ohio, became involved when Apostle Ezra T. Benson proposed to construct a sawmill in the Tooele area and employed a group of snowbound emigrants headed by Custer to raise a mill dam under contract calling for payment of $1,000.

---

[1] Prior to this date, from February 19 to 27, 1851, Rockwell had been called to serve with elements of the Nauvoo Legion in tracking down emigrant thieves, with negligible results. See payroll records of Captain William H. Kimball's Life Guards, Military Records Section, Utah State Archives.

Custer, it happened, had come west in the same wagon train with Nelson Slater, who later claimed the Ohioan had never been fully paid by Benson.[2] According to Slater:

> The work was done . . . and accepted, but it was found that the dam needed to be two or three feet higher than was specified in the contract. Mr. Benson told them if they would raise the dam that much higher, he would pay them for the additional labor in proportion to the other. They raised the dam and completed the work. The raising of the dam amounted to about $200, making with the first contract $1200. On this amount the company received $700. No reason was assigned for the non-payment of the balance. No fault was found with the work. The debt remains unpaid, and probably always will. Mr. Custer was shot by the Indians just before starting for California.[3]

The job was completed and Custer was waiting for his remaining $500 in pay when a band of Indians swooped out of the hills and ran off with the settlement's horses. Rockwell was summoned to lead a company of men (among them Custer) after the thieves.[4] Riding swiftly, the posse followed the trail to Rush Lake, but lost the sign in a jumble of tracks created by several Indian families camped on the east shore. Rockwell ordered thirty warriors taken prisoner from the circle of teepees, and headed them back to Tooele for questioning.[5]

[2] Slater was no stranger to Mormonism. As far back as 1838 he had organized a school, the Western Reserve Teachers' Seminary, in the Kirtland Temple after the Saints moved to Missouri. Both he and Custer were natives of Ohio. See C. G. Crary, *Pioneer and Personal Reminiscences* (Marshalltown, Iowa, 1893), p. 35.

[3] Slater, *Fruits of Mormonism*, p. 37. Benson's advertisement for men to work on the mill dam was first published in the *Deseret News* for August 24, 1850.

[4] Written orders from Daniel H. Wells to Captain [P. R.] Wright, dated April 21, 1851. Military Records Section, Utah State Archives.

[5] Edward W. Tullidge, *Tullidge's Histories, Vol. II, Containing the History of all the Northern, Eastern and Western Counties of Utah; Also the Counties of Southern Idaho* (Salt Lake City, 1889), p. 83. Hereafter cited as *Tullidge's His-*

As the disgruntled braves mounted their ponies, one of the Gentiles in the posse, W. R. Dickinson, was disturbed to discover that they were not being told to surrender their weapons. With a worried frown he sidled his horse against Rockwell's and pointed out the apparent oversight.

> . . . I toald the Captain Purtie Rockwell, Mormon, who came from Callafornia last fall to take thir guns a way. He said Dam them let them pack thre oan guns. They went a long easy well untill sunset they began to get uneasy scaterd in all Directions w [k]ept them strait as we could untill Moon lite & by 9 oclock we wair with in a boute a quarter of a mile of the settlement they bega to scatter a gain. Custer who spured his horse to git Rounde them he then puild his revolver pointed at the ingine Shot a nother ingine got Custer. I shot the ingine that shot Custer we then laid Custer on the horse and wente to the settlement Brought Him to town the day and burid Him and quit. . . .[6]

Perhaps he felt it was a trifling detail, but Rockwell's report to Brigham Young made no mention of his decision to allow the Indians to keep their guns.

> We have been out [he explained] about eighteen miles from the saw mill and found 30 Indians whom we ordered to go to the settlement. Some of them hurried ahead and under guard reached the settlement before the rest. While the remainder were coming up, and a short distance from the settlement, some reluctance on the part of the Indians to come in was shown. One of the Indians fired upon Mr. Custer, who

tories. See also Peter Gottfredson, *History of Indian Depredations in Utah* (Salt Lake City, 1919), p. 38.

[6] Letter from Dickinson to his "folkes," dated May 29, 1851, from "State of Deserett, Salt Lake City." Typescript copy in Utah State Historical Society Library.

fell from his horse, instantly dead. Mr. Custer's pistol was found, one barrel discharged and three caps bursted [misfired]. The Indians then made their escape with the exception of four who are now with us as prisoners, whom I intend to take along with us as guides. We shall start again to-day and wish to have William H. Kimball raise as many men as he can to come on our trail with Judson Stoddard. Word will be left behind us of our movements, so that the company will understand the route. The body of Mr. Custer will be sent into the City this morning.[7]

With the four captives leading the way, the posse scoured the countryside for both Custer's killers and the raiding party with the stolen horses. It was a futile effort; the Utes led the company in circles until Rockwell's patience was exhausted, and he called a halt in Skull Valley. Pitching camp, the men ate a cold dinner before making a final search for the horse thieves. They returned empty-handed and bone-weary twenty-four hours later. After consulting with several other elders in the posse, Rockwell decided to end the chase and return to Tooele, but first he intended to deal with the prisoners. Deeming it unwise to turn the four loose "to commit more depredations and perhaps shed the blood of some useful citizen . . . they were sacrificed to the natural instincts of self-defence." [8] At a signal from Rockwell, the four Utes were shot to death, their bodies dumped into shallow graves scooped from the desert sand. There was irony in the executions; Skull Valley was by tradition a sacred Indian burial ground.

In early June Rockwell was called to Brigham Young's office to discuss the state of affairs existing among the tribes in the Basin area, and it is likely that the name of Jim Bridger popped up a time or two.[9] For more than a year Young had suspected the wily mountain man of fomenting the Indian uprising at Fort Utah. He also believed that Bridger was actively engaged in selling arms and ammunition to Walkara's warlike Utes. Rockwell fitted out a pack train and disappeared into the moun-

[7] Journal History, April 23, 1850. This letter, signed "O. P. Rockwell," is incorrectly recorded. It should have been entered under April 23, 1851. Because the original, which ought to be on file in the LDS Church Historical Department, cannot be located, it is not possible to determine Rockwell's amanuensis (he himself could not write). See also Journal History for April 22, 1851.

[8] *Tullidge's Histories*, p. 84; Hosea Stout, "Journal," Vol. 4, p. 283; Brooks, *On The Mormon Frontier*, Vol. II, p. 398; and Gottfredson, *Indian Depredations*, p. 39.

[9] Journal History, June 3, 1851.

tains to assess the situation. In the months to follow he ranged far and wide, constantly probing for signs of unrest or brewing trouble. When the snows came to the peaks of the Wasatch and Oquirrh mountains, Rockwell came down to the settlement. For a time he tended to personal affairs, which had been sorely neglected for nearly two seasons. Whenever he could Rockwell sought out the company of John Neff, a Mormon several years his senior who had become a close friend. Frequently, he and Neff were invited to dine at the home of Mrs. Woolley, the woman whom Rockwell had befriended on the plains in 1848. On these occasions Neff was accompanied by his wife and his daughter, Mary Ann, a girl of twenty-two who had caught Rockwell's eye. Though sixteen years her senior, Rockwell was as healthy as a buffalo and rock-hard from his outdoor life. To Mary Ann Neff he was a man of adventure and dauntless determination. In comparison to other men in Great Salt Lake City, Orrin Porter Rockwell stood head and shoulders above the crowd. Rockwell's ties to the Neff family strengthened in November of 1851 when he and John Neff "obtained the land claim and privileges to the first canyon south of Mill Creek from James Rollings." [10]

As the new year dawned, the Journal History records that Elder Rockwell was called upon to officiate in the sacred ceremonies of endowment — a duty collateral to his position as a member of the Melchizedek Priesthood.[11] This is one of the few times that he was asked to fulfill his priestly obligations in the Endowment House.

Rockwell's movements for the next twelve months are vague, but he apparently spent a great deal of time with the Indians. Then, on January 19, 1853, Great Salt Lake City's enterprising group of thespians proudly announced the opening of what was to be the first dramatic performance presented in the brand new Social Hall. In honor of their martyred prophet they selected Joseph's favorite production, *Pizarro*, for the curtain-raiser. Prominently displayed on the roll of players was a bit of nostalgic casting — Rockwell as Davina, the Spanish soldier, whom he had essayed

[10] Ibid., November 20, 1851. Now known as Neff's Canyon.

[11] Ibid., January 3, 1852: "Thos. Bullock engaged in the endowment rooms. Heber C. Kimball, superintending; Geo. A. Smith, Thos. Bullock, Wm. C. Staines, Orrin P. Rockwell, W. W. Phelps, Samuel L. Sprague, Zerubbabel Snow officiating." Two years later the Saints completed an Endowment House to be used for the purpose of administering these secret ordinances of the church, but in the interim the rites were performed in the President's office located between the soon-to-be-constructed Beehive and Lion houses.

so well in Nauvoo's Masonic Hall nine years before.[12] But time had taken its toll; he bobbled the part. Addressing a fellow actor portraying "the Old Peruvian," Rockwell delivered the line: "Another word, grey-headed ruffian, and I shall strike!" Then, turning to the prompter, in a whisper which carried over the hall, he asked nervously, "Shall I stick him?"[13] The ad-lib convulsed the audience, delaying the performance several minutes.

In the spring of the year Rockwell took a herd of horses to Carson Valley.[14] While he was gone, Indian troubles broke out anew in Zion. Near the small community of Springville, fifty miles to the south of Great Salt Lake City, Mrs. James Ivie traded a Ute squaw three pints of flour for three large trout. This innocent bit of barter on July 17, 1853, ultimately cost the lives of thirty whites and as many Indians. Two Ute braves approached the Ivie cabin a few minutes later, and one, seeing what the squaw had done, began beating her, shouting that she had made a bad exchange. Ivie, busy digging a well on his property, heard the commotion and saw the squaw run into the cabin for refuge. He attempted to stop the Indian from following her.

Enraged at the interference, the Ute picked up his rifle and tried to shoot the farmer, who grabbed the weapon by the barrel. In the struggle the rifle broke in their hands; the Indian held the stock, Ivie the gun barrel. With all the strength he could muster Ivie clubbed the brave across the head, crushing his skull. While the scuffle was in progress, the second Ute strung his bow and sent an arrow at Ivie, grazing him as it passed through his buckskin shirt. Before the Indian could fit another shaft, the Mormon pivoted and pole-axed him. The Ute pitched across the body of his dying comrade.

In the melee, the Ivies had ignored the squaw, and now, as the settler stood gasping for breath, the Indian woman padded through the cabin doorway with a length of cordwood gripped in her hands. Ivie heard his wife's warning scream and turned. The squaw smashed him across the face, tearing a deep gash in his upper lip, a scar he would carry the rest of his life. As he reeled under the blow, Ivie managed to swing the rifle

[12] Orson F. Whitney, *History of Utah* (Salt Lake City, 1892–1904), four volumes, Vol. I, p. 502.

[13] Ibid., p. 501n.

[14] *Daily Alta California*, July 6, 1853, says he accompanied "Cogswell's Train of 20 wagons."

barrel in a last whipping arc and felt it connect solidly. The squaw collapsed in a heap.

No sooner had Ivie landed the final blow than Joseph Kelly, a leading Springville citizen, arrived on the scene.[15] Kelly quickly sized up the situation. "You'd better take your wife and child and get out of here and into town before Walker[16] hears about this," he told the dazed settler. After the Ivies had departed, Kelly worked to revive the three unconscious Utes. The squaw and the second brave finally came around, but the warrior Ivie had struck first remained in a coma and died within a few hours.

When word reached Walkara of the fracas, the war chief flew into a rage, vowing to soak the land in blood for Ivie's meddling in matters which did not concern him.[17] Thus, Walkara began a war which would drag on for ten months and see a score of Mormon settlements abandoned in favor of stronger, better-protected communities like Fort Utah and Great Salt Lake City — all for three trout and three pints of flour.

While the Utes smeared on their warpaint, Brigham Young was giving serious thought to ridding the Saints of another irritant — Jim Bridger. Convinced that the mountain man represented the primary source of his Indian troubles, Young had come to a decision. He knew that Bridger would never leave the territory voluntarily. (The old trapper had been in the country far longer than the Saints.) That left the church leader with a single alternative. Writing out a warrant for Bridger's arrest, he

[15] This account of the episode which ignited the Walker War is related in detail by George McKenzie in Gottfredson, *Indian Depredations*, pp. 43–45. Compare with Bean, *Autobiography*, p. 90. Bean says the Indian did not die.

[16] Walkara was known by the whites as Chief Walker.

[17] Walkara later told a Mormon emissary that it should have made no difference to Ivie if the squaw had been killed. The chief added that had a Mormon woman been involved, Ivie would have been justified in interfering. See report of Major Nelson Higgins to Adjutant General James Ferguson, dated March 16, 1854, in the Military Records Section, Utah State Archives. To make a bad situation worse, the dead brave (Showeneshockitz) was Walkara's cousin.

199

told William A. (Bill) Hickman to serve it.[18] Hickman — gunfighter, trouble-shooter, and bodyguard to Brigham Young — called a posse of one hundred and fifty men to ride on Fort Bridger, arrest the famous fur trapper and trader, and "capture his ammunition and destroy all his liquors."[19] But the wily Bridger proved he was nobody's fool. When the Mormons arrived, "Old Gabe" had flown the coop. In the face of overwhelming force he had left behind all he owned — his land and his cattle. But as far as the posse was concerned the march was not a total loss. According to Hickman: "No ammunition was found, but the whisky and rum, of which he [Bridger] had a good stock, was destroyed by doses; the sheriff, most of his officers, the doctor and chaplain of the company, all aided in carrying out the orders, and worked so hard day and night that they were exhausted — not being able to stand up. But the privates, poor fellows! were rationed, and did not do so much."[20]

Bridger made his way to Fort Laramie, where he poured out his tale of sorrow and woe to all present.[21] Even as he told his story the Mormons

[18] Nelson Winch Green, *Fifteen Years Among the Mormons, Being the Narrative of Mrs. Mary Ettie V. Smith* (New York, 1860), pp. 343–44, says of William A. Hickman: "The darkest annals of the world can scarcely furnish a more terrible record, than would the simple biography of a few of these Danite leaders. When that record is written, the names of Porter Rockwell, Wm. Hickman, Hiram Clawson, Captain James Brown, John and Wiley Norton, James Furguson, Robert Burton, and others, whose names I do not recollect, will be found linked with the most cruel and bloody acts, that have ever disgraced humanity.

"Rockwell was the leader of this [Danite] band at Nauvoo; but Wm. Hickman is now supposed to fill that post; having won this distinction, by his daring and success. It is said, that his soul knows no pity; and he fears no law but the Prophet's will. It was this man who won for his band the title now proudly borne by them; viz., 'Destroying Angels.'" Bonney, *Banditti of the Prairies*, p. 218, described Hickman as "one of the most notorious rascals unhung. A fugitive from justice for several larcenies committed in the county of Lee [Iowa]."

[19] Hickman, *Brigham's Destroying Angel*, p. 91.

[20] Ibid., p. 92.

[21] Randolph B. Marcy, *Thirty Years of Army Life on the Border* (New York, 1866), p. 401. Marcy was among those who saw Bridger at Fort Laramie then. Said the captain: ". . . [The Mormons] came to his place [Fort Bridger] with a force of 'avenging angels,' and forced him to make his escape to the woods in order to save his life. He remained secreted for several days, and, through the assistance of his Indian wife, was enabled to elude the search of the *Danites*, and make his way to Fort Laramie, leaving all his cattle and other property in possession of the Mormons." Thomas Flint, "Diary of Dr. Thomas Flint," *Annual Publications of the Historical Society of Southern California*, Vol. XII (1923), p. 97, relates: [August 27, 1853] ". . . White went to the Fort [Bridger] for ammunition but found the Fort

were leaving for Zion. Making a short detour to the nearby Green River, the posse settled a dispute between a group of fellow Mormons and a crowd of mountain men over the right to operate a ferry. Hickman's men solved the argument, he says, by "shooting two or three mountaineers" and threatening the others with arrest.[22] When the foray to Fort Bridger was over, Hickman commented, "The property that was taken went to pay a few officers, and, as was said, the expenses of the *posse*; but, poor fellows, I never knew of one of them getting a dollar. It went to pay tithing; and, finally, all was gobbled up and turned over to the church . . . ."[23]

With Bridger out of the way,[24] Young paid full attention to Walkara and his war parties, a problem which worsened each day as the Indians, screaming for Mormon scalps, came charging out of the mountains in a succession of raids that left a gory wake of butchered settlers across the valley.[25] On top of this came an incident unrelated to the Walker War:

in possession of the territorial officer. Mormons who had 24 hours before driven old man Bridger out and taken possession."

New York Daily Times, Saturday, November 12, 1853, carries notice from the *St. Louis Republican*, November 5, 1853, that Bridger was a week out of Westport, Missouri, and had been picked up at Devil's Gate by the October mail stage from Salt Lake City.

When Bridger returned once more to the Great Basin a year and a half later to reclaim his property, it was a singular coincidence that his traveling companions for a time would be William M. F. Magraw and W. W. Drummond. The *New York Times*, July 3, 1855, copied from the *St. Louis Democrat*, June 29, 1855, this item of news: "McGraw has returned from Blue River, having accompanied so far the outgoing mail for the present month. There went as passengers Judge Drummond, recently appointed as associate justice of Utah Territory, accompanied by his lady, and Bridger, the mountain trader, with his Indian wife and child. Mr. Bridger is going for the purpose of resuming possession of his trading post on Black's Fork, from which he was summarily ejected by the Mormons a year or two since. . . ." As we shall see, both Magraw and Drummond would become two of Mormondom's most determined antagonists.

[22] Hickman, *Brigham's Destroying Angel*, p. 93.

[23] Ibid.

[24] Mrs. Mary Ettie V. Smith in Green, *Fifteen Years Among the Mormons*, p. 368, implies that the posse murdered Bridger. She says: "What was his fate, or that of his family, none but the few 'Danites,' who were engaged in that 'mission,' can tell; and for some reason, the same men who had spoken freely to me of other crimes, were silent upon this point. When asked what became of him, they did not know. . . . and now the fate of Bridger is seldom mentioned." Mrs. Smith's conclusions concerning Jim Bridger were wide of the mark. The mountain man returned to his fort with a survey party on November 1, 1853. He died a natural death in Missouri July 17, 1881.

[25] Accounts of various incidents of the Walker War can be found in Gottfredson, *Indian Depredations*, pp. 43–83.

201

the Gunnison Massacre on October 26. In one terrifying attack, Captain John W. Gunnison and seven members of his Pacific Railroad surveying expedition were murdered by Pahvant braves at a camp on the Sevier River thirty-five miles from Fillmore.[26] In retaliation for the slayings of two tribesmen by a company of Missouri emigrants, the Pahvants had wiped out the topographical party and mutilated their bodies. The massacre sent a wave of revulsion through the territory, and oddly enough seemed to ease the friction between the Mormons and Walkara. After a few token raids, Walkara made it known that he would sit in council with the whites. Brigham Young sent Rockwell and George Bean to parley with the war chief. Young was determined to stop the fighting, which had cost the Saints dearly in lives and property.

[26] Because a year earlier Captain Gunnison had published *History of the Mormons* — a thoughtful and critically fair book, but considered in some quarters as unfriendly to the Saints — rumors were abroad that Mormons had somehow had a hand in his death. See Hubert Howe Bancroft, *History of Utah*, 1540–1887 (San Francisco, 1890), pp. 470–71n.

Mrs. Mary Ettie V. Smith, for instance, offers the "facts" of the tragedy in Green, *Fifteen Years Among the Mormons*, p. 318, when she asserts: "I have heard the circumstances of this atrocious murder discussed frequently at Great Salt Lake, by the Heads of the Church, and by the Prophet, and others. In all these cases, it was exultingly claimed by them, and unquestioned in well informed circles among us, that Capt. Gunnison and his party were murdered by the 'Danites,' disguised as Indians, by, and with the knowledge and 'counsel' of the Prophet. It was, however, believed by some that the massacre was perpetrated by the Indians in fact, but instigated by the Prophet — all parties agreeing in this, that it was done for the good of the Church, which justified the act. My belief is, that the first theory is the true one."

Some authors have wandered even farther in their assumptions. Charles Kelly and Hoffman Birney, *Holy Murder, the Story of Porter Rockwell* (New York, 1934), p. 109, at least do not pretend to use fact when they write: "Again and again Porter and the Danites have been accused of inspiring or participating in the massacre of the government surveying party, commanded by Captain J. W. Gunnison . . . . The

Rockwell made ready. Most of the past few months had been spent improving canyon property.[27] A change would be welcome. Rockwell's last public task had come when he and a party of Mormons were named to a committee for selecting a proper penitentiary site.[28] After a dull two weeks of inspecting locations in American Fork, Provo, Springville, Spanish Fork, Payson, Nephi, and Fillmore, the committee decided that the prison should be built "four and a half miles [east of] the city of Great Salt Lake . . . ." The penitentiary so built was used until March 12, 1951.

Now, in April of 1854, Rockwell, with Bean, listened closely as Brigham Young outlined their mission. They were told to meet Walkara near Beaver and present him with a letter penned by Young outlining proposals for peace. In case the chieftain proved difficult, the Mormons would have presents for him. Young's words were somber as he finished his instructions. "You must make peace with Walker. And you must see that he stays off the warpath for at least a year — no matter if it costs $10,000. Our people have suffered much during this war of his and they need at least a season to raise crops." [29]

Rockwell, Bean, and Amos Neff found Walkara trading with a mountain man named (James?) Waters near Parowan. With Young's stern words still echoing in their ears, the three Mormons attached themselves to the train and followed it to New Harmony, where the church's Southern Indian Mission was clearing land for a fort. All the while they urged

---

atrocity was charged to the Indians — Goshutes of the band headed by Kanosh — but to this day [1934] gossip in Utah alleges that Rockwell and the Danites participated in the slaughter."

For the Indian version of the Gunnison massacre — why it occurred and who participated — consult Josiah F. Gibbs, "Gunnison Massacre — 1853 — Millard County, Utah — Indian Mareer's Version of the Tragedy — 1894," *Utah Historical Quarterly*, Vol. I (July 1928), pp. 67–75. See also Call, "Life and Record," pp. 46–49.

[27] A petition by Rockwell and Franklin Neff was granted March 22, 1853, for rights to the first "kanyon south of Millcreek," to erect a tollgate and to charge 20 cents a load for firewood and fence poles and 50 cents a load for sawn timber "as soon as they commence making a road."

[28] Utah Executive Papers, 1850–1855, Territorial Secretary Correspondence; Almon W. Babbitt to James Guthrie, Secretary of the Treasury, December 17, 1853, Utah State Archives; Journal History, November 28, 1853, and *Deseret News*, December 4, 1853.

[29] Bean, *Autobiography*, p. 94.

the chief to return with them to Great Salt Lake City and meet with Brigham Young. Thomas D. Brown, recorder of the mission, chronicled their efforts: "Porter Rockwell, Bean, Neph . . . met Walker and the train on the Beaver and were using Watter's influence as well as their own to induce Walker to accompany them to Gt. Salt Lake City to have an interview with Govr. Young. Walker declined, urging as an excuse, that he wished to remain at home till his wheat was sown. Here interpreter Bean and Walker had two long 'talks.' " [30]

It was during one of these long "talks" that the hot-tempered Walkara finally gave vent to his emotions. The chief had been surly and indignant when Bean had offered him gifts on behalf of Young, and at one point in the negotiations, Walkara, anxious to demonstrate his prowess and importance, began swaggering around the conference circle. Gradually he closed in on a lesser chief named Beaverads, hunkered down next to Bean.

"This is how we treat our enemies!" He slashed with a knife at Beaverads before the startled Indian could move, and sliced the keen blade across his face. Blood spurted from the terrible wound and streamed between Beaverads' fingers as he clawed at the gash to squeeze off the burning pain.

Taken aback by the unexpected attack, the two Mormons sat dumbfounded as Walkara moved to whip the knife across Beaverads' other cheek. But his victim rolled to one side, regained his feet and grabbed at a nearby rifle. At the same instant, Rockwell lunged at Walkara while Bean jerked the gun from Beaverads' grasp. Under Rockwell's determined grip, Walkara dropped the knife.

Bean shouted a jumble of words in Ute to both chiefs. Walkara responded with a grunt and, rubbing his wrist, turned a baleful eye on the Mormon who had subdued him. Beaverads snarled invective at his attacker and stubbornly pulled at the rifle with his free hand, the other still pressed tightly against his bleeding face. Bean held the weapon out of reach and butted Beaverads with the stump of his left elbow (he had lost the arm in a cannon accident at Fort Utah in 1849) until the Ute backed off.

Speaking rapidly, Bean berated Walkara for his unmannerly conduct in the presence of guests. He was careful not to overplay his role as peacemaker — a wrong word and Walkara might order his braves back into

[30] Thomas D. Brown, "Journal of the Southern Indian Mission." MS, April 26, 1854.

the mountains, and the war would continue indefinitely. "You have plenty of presents from Brigham Young — why not show Walkara's generosity; give some gifts to Beaverads."

Phlegmatically, the chief thrust several trinkets at the wounded leader of the Beaver clan. Bean poked Beaverads and he grudgingly accepted the offering. Rockwell breathed a sigh of relief; he had not relished the prospect of fighting his way out of the encampment. Bean took the opportunity to lead the talk back to the objective. "The result of the visit with Walker was a tentative arrangement to meet him in company with President Young at Upper Chicken Creek in fifteen days, and if plenty of beef cattle, flour, and Indian goods were brought, then all might be well, otherwise not. This was afterwards all fulfilled." [31]

Bean motioned to Rockwell and the two men rode out of the camp to rejoin Neff at Waters' wagon. Walkara haughtily turned his back on Beaverads and strode to his tent.

May 3, 1854, was an important day in the life of Orrin Porter Rockwell, for on that morning in the parlor of Brigham Young's new home, the Neff clan had gathered to witness the marriage of this rough and ready frontiersman to Mary Ann, whom he had been courting for some time. The ceremony was performed by Brigham himself. [32]

There was no lengthy honeymoon. Twenty-four hours after the vows had been exchanged, Brigham Young's company pulled out of the city on its yearly visit south. The entourage included eighty-two men, fourteen women, and five children in thirty-four wagons. In the twenty-fifth wagon sat Rockwell, Bean, and Amos Neff. [33]

Reaching Nephi at sunset, the party decided to stay overnight and continue to Chicken Creek the next day. Rockwell, Bean, and Neff arose at daybreak and tended to the task of hitching their team. Perhaps assur-

[31] The whole account is related in Bean, *Autobiography*, pp. 93–94.

[32] "A Record of Marriages (Solemnized) (Alphabetically Arranged) 1853–1856," p. 36.

[33] Journal History, May 10, 1854.

ing Bean that everything would be "all wheat," [34] Rockwell took along some liquor. Recalls Bean:

> President Young and party having stayed at Nephi over night, reached Walker's Camp before eleven o'clock, bringing a load of flour, and a dozen of beef cattle. O. P. Rockwell and myself preceded the President's party a few minutes, just long enough for Porter to slip a bottle of whiskey into the Old Chief's hands, about half of which went down his throat instanter, as it were, and when President Young arrived, Walker was half drunk and sulky. He would not talk nor allow Dimick Huntington [the interpreter] to say a word, and finally ordered him away from his lodge (tent). [35]

Angered by the rebuke, Brigham spun on his heel and shouted for wagonmasters to move out, but Walkara forbade it, saying he must stay the night. Only his anxious desire for peace prevented Young from marching out of the camp. Reluctantly, he countermanded his order to leave. The change in plans gave Rockwell the opportunity to correct the mess he had made of the peace parley. He told Young that Walkara's child was ill and the Ute chief was distracted by worry over the youngster's condition. That night the church president (and Governor) administered to the sick boy; by morning the child showed signs of improving. Jubilant — and sober — Walkara agreed to accompany the Mormons as far south as New Harmony.

---

[34] "Wheat" was an expression coined by Rockwell. It suggested that everything was fine. Kelly and Birney, *Holy Murder*, p. 23, theorized that Rockwell's use of the word came from the phrase, "Separating the tares from the wheat," as it pertained to the activities of the Danites. The assumption, however, has no foundation in fact. See also Samuel Bowles, *Across the Continent; A Summer's Journey to The Rocky Mountains, the Mormons, and the Pacific States, with Speaker Colfax* (Springfield, 1866), p. 129; and Achilles, *Destroying Angels of Mormondom*, pp. 21–22. Volney King, a resident of Millard County, tells in his journel of an incident in which a band of organized horse thieves was being hunted by separate posses from Millard and neighboring communities. As two of the groups closed in they in turn were surprised by Porter Rockwell and deputies from Salt Lake County on the same trail. The parties concerned, each unaware that the others were lawmen, prepared for a fight. "The officer in charge of the S L Party . . . called out All Wheat All Wheat & O P Rockwells slang word was too well known by all through the country not to know who used it. & the excitement soon subsided & all three parties then joined & finally the outlaws were captured, & their band completely broken up . . . ." See Volney King, "Millard County, 1851–1875," *Utah Humanities Review*, Vol. I, No. 4 (October 1947), pp. 381–82.

[35] Bean, *Autobiography*, pp. 94–95. For the names of the Mormons in Brigham Young's party at this meeting see Journal History, May 11, 1854.

As they rode along, Young told the Ute he would send Rockwell and Bean back to Great Salt Lake City for additional trade goods, thus saving the tribe the inconvenience of the journey. An ulterior motive prompted Brigham to offer this suggestion: He did not like the thought of the unpredictable chief and his braves strolling the streets of Zion. In this, Young was following his own counsel. A month before, in the course of the church's twenty-fourth annual conference, he had cautioned, "Never let [Indians] come into your houses, as the whites did in Utah [County]. There they would let them lounge upon their beds . . . . When their familiarities became oppressive to the whites, and they desired them to leave their houses, it made them angry . . . . this is the true cause of the Indian difficulties in Utah." [36]

Young parted with Walkara at Chicken Creek on a promise that Rockwell and Bean would meet him a fortnight later at Nephi with all the provisions he would need.[37] To show his good faith, the church leader exchanged blankets for horses he knew had been stolen from Mormons. The trade pleased Walkara.[38]

When told of his new assignment, Rockwell asked for the help of two men from the Southern Indian Mission in establishing the trade caravan. "John Lott and John Murdock are just the boys," Young answered.[39]

One of the members of Young's party was S. N. Carvalho, an artist who had accompanied Colonel John C. Frémont's fifth expedition as far as Parowan and remained for several months with the Mormons while recovering from frostbite and near-starvation. After sketching Walkara's rugged features, Carvalho retired to his wagon and wrote in his journal: "[Governor Young] has appointed the following gentlemen to take up a

[36] *Journal of Discourses*, Vol. VI, pp. 328–29.

[37] Journal History, May 11, 1854.

[38] Ibid., May 12, 1854. See also Bean, *Autobiography*, p. 95.

[39] Brown, "Journal of the Southern Indian Mission," May 21, 1854. Brigham Young's ability to judge character is well illustrated here. He recognized early in the Utah experience the developing skill of John Riggs Murdock as a wagonmaster. By the time of the transcontinental railroad, Murdock's reputation on the plains was unequaled. By 1869 he had made eleven round trips and brought through five large trains of emigrants — more emigrants to the territory by wagon than were brought by any other leader. Murdock had carried mail to and from Independence, Missouri, and made unprecedented short time; had brought trains of merchandise for Livingston & Bell in the early days; and had gone with an escort to Omaha with Thomas L. Kane, President Buchanan's commissioner, in 1858, completing the round trip of 2,120 miles, with the same animals, in forty-two traveling days! See *Tullidge's Quarterly Magazine*, Vol. II, No. 1 (April 1882), p. 57.

permanent residence with Walkara's band of Utahs, viz.: Porter Rockwell, James A. Bean, interpreter; John Murdoch, and John Lott. These persons will follow them in their wanderings, and will, most probably, prevent many depredations and murders." [40]

Brigham Young's satisfaction with his visit to the Indian camp was frustratingly short-lived. Hard on his return to Great Salt Lake City came word that Walkara was making ready for war. The chief, after leaving Young at Chicken Creek, rode to Nephi and discovered the settlers raising a wall around the colony in accordance with Young's earlier instructions. Walkara demanded that the work stop at once and ranted that the whites had proven they could not be trusted. The Mormons, he said, treated for peace with one hand while with the other they raised a wall to keep the Indians out.

Acting with utmost speed, Brigham Young wrote a letter to the chief and had Rockwell carry it to Nephi with the trade caravan. Rockwell, accompanied by Bean and Neff, found Walkara camped near the partially constructed enclosure. He had harangued the settlers over their "treachery" until he was blind with rage.[41]

"When the wall is done, then what will you do?" he challenged. "If Walkara comes to you for food, will you throw a biscuit over your wall to him like a dog or a slave?" [42]

Walkara reminded the Nephi colonists that "he had given Brigham and the Mormons the privilege of settling on these lands and jointly occupying them with the Indians, using land, water, grass, timber together as brothers, but if 'Whites' separated and fenced off their settlements, they would have to stay inside and the Indians outside — no more getting wood and grass for the 'Whites' if they continued the wall business." [43]

Bean unfolded Brigham Young's letter and began reading aloud. In the note Young expressed his surprise that Walkara had so soon forgotten him — forgotten, too, the good time they had traveling together. He acted

<hr/>

[40] Entry for May 21, 1854, in S. N. Carvalho, *Incidents of Travel and Adventure in the Far West; with Col. Frémont's Last Expedition* (New York, 1857), pp. 213–14.

[41] Major George W. Bradley to Lieutenant General Daniel H. Wells, June 17, 1854, Military Records Section, Utah State Archives. A resident of Nephi, Andrew Love, wrote in his journal, "He [Walkara] feels to trample under foot the authority of Brigham. So Brother Walker's end is fast approaching." See Andrew Love, "Journal." MS, p. 45.

[42] Bean, *Autobiography*, p. 96.

[43] Ibid.

foolishly, Young wrote. The building of the walls was the Lord's work and the Mormons were His people; Walkara was to mind his own business, and the people would do the same. The letter ended on a note of warning: If Walkara troubled the Lord's chosen any more, he would suffer for it.[44]

> At this point [Bean says] Walker snatched the letter from my hand in the greatest rage and trampled it under his feet, and then struck into a boastful tirade, saying that he would let Brigham Young know that he had lived before he came here and he had fought the Sioux, the Snakes, the Arapahoes, and Cheyennes, and the Crow Indian tribes — that his scars were all in front, and not on his back, and if he said so War would commence this very day, and finally ordered his Camps to move instantly. At this there was a great scattering of the crowd around us, and a howl of grief from the squaws, and a pulling down of lodges. The boys and young "Bucks" gathered in the ponies and packed the tents, etc. This was hastily carried on for thirty minutes, and the ground was clear and the whole cavalcade moved toward Salt Creek Canyon.[45]

In thirty minutes the tribe was on its way, the campsite barren of tents, dogs, and ponies. Yet, fifty warriors lingered — to deal with their visitors. They encircled the white emissaries. Several of the braves chanted boasts of their exploits as they closed in on the three men. Battiese, Tintic, and Bear-Scratch, old sub-chiefs of the Ute clans, recounted aloud their coups of the Walker War. A number of younger warriors whooped noisily, snapping percussion caps on their empty rifles, the explosives popping like firecrackers around the Mormons. Other braves twanged their bowstrings in a steady rhythm, all the while drawing closer. Walkara watched stoically.

Bean snatched the torn letter from the dirt. "I will leave and tell Brigham how you have treated his words of counsel." Rockwell caught Neff's eye and motioned him toward their horses. Their audacity surprised Walkara and he became excited. "No! You won't go and get the Mor-

[44] Ibid., pp. 97–98; Journal History, June 23, 1854.
[45] Bean, *Autobiography*, p. 98.

mons after us again! And the trade goods — they belong to us now. We have need for them." [46]

Neff gingerly held the reins of the two riding horses in one hand, firmly gripping the bit of the lead wagon team with the other. He was ready to move at a signal from Rockwell. Then came the unexpected. One of Walkara's lieutenants, Washear (Squash), pushed his way through the knot of warriors and spoke up. "Walkara talks like a fool. I was with Poorets [Bean][47] when Brigham gave him the letter and Brigham was not mad, but talked straight and he wants you to do right and not act foolish." [48]

Washear's outburst caused a minor sensation. First to react was Walkara, who began arguing loudly against trusting the Mormons. Soon the two Indians were shouting at each other at the top of their lungs. Other braves gathered around and injected their opinions. In the bedlam the three Mormons slipped away and succeeded in reaching Nephi unnoticed. Inside the settlement Rockwell rounded up an armed escort and prepared to take the trade goods back to Great Salt Lake City, but a sentry's alarm sent him running to the wall. In the direction of the Indian campsite Rockwell could see Walkara on foot, accompanied by his boy, with Washear leading the war chief's horse. Bean and Rockwell went out to meet them. Walkara apologized for the trouble, explaining that Washear had convinced him that his suspicions of the Nephi Mormons were groundless.

Bean accepted the apology and agreed to continue trading. He, Rockwell, and Neff then proceeded to Ephraim where they spent the next five days bartering with the Utes. The Mormons survived several stormy bouts with Walkara's greed and were forced to purchase eight Indian children slaves or see them butchered by their Ute captors.[49]

In his report to Brigham Young, Bean explained:

On Monday [June 20, 1854] he [Walkara] packed us off for S. L. City and wanted a letter from Brigham Young to take to the Mexicans, clearing him of all blame in killing two Spaniards, who were murdered back of Sanpete.[50]

[46] Ibid., p. 99.

[47] "Poorets" in the Ute tongue means "one-armed man."

[48] Bean, *Autobiography*, p. 99.

[49] Ibid., p. 100.

[50] As early as November of 1851 the *Deseret News* was reporting the fact that more than a score of Mexicans had entered Utah Territory and were trading horses

Walker formerly wanted us to go with him to the Navajoes and see the Indians but now he don't want us to go with him for fear the Mexicans should kill us, and that we should know how he traded with them.

Tintic, Uinta and other Indians are mad with Walker and quarreled with him at Nephi. Tintic said to Walker, "It was calling them squaws, not to let them trade for themselves," and he said he was no squaw last summer, when he made the Mormons run from Summit and Willow Creeks.[51] The Mormons need not be afraid of him now since Walker called him and all the rest of the Indians "squaws.". . .

Walker demanded a squaw at Allred's Settlement while he staid there and wanted them to levy a tax and pay to him in gold and silver.[52]

Walker said Brigham did not know how to use a chief like him, for when he came down [from the mountains] Brigham would not allow him a squaw to sleep with like the Moquitches and Navajoes.

Grosepene, Sanpitch, Washear and a great many of the Indians have a venereal disease which they got of the Navajoes.[53]

With the Indian war at an end and some semblance of peace restored among the tribes, Rockwell returned to his bride. But in a matter of weeks he was back on the trail. This time Brigham Young sent him to visit the Shoshone clans of the northeast, near Fort Bridger. Outfitting a pack train with several thousands of dollars in goods, he set off for the trading post to meet James S. Brown, a member of the Mormon party credited with discovering the gold at Sutter's Mill in 1848.[54] Brown, who had been among the tribes, described his encounter with Rockwell:

On the 14th [of July] I began a journey [from Fort Supply] back to Green River, but met Porter Rockwell at Fort Bridger. He had a license from Governor Brigham Young for me to trade with the Indians; also some two or three thousand dollars' worth of Indian goods for me to market. At that time there was no opportunity to

<hr />

for Indian slaves and guns. They held licenses signed by James Calhoun, governor and superintendent of Indian Affairs in New Mexico, purporting to authorize trading in Utah. On April 23, 1853, Brigham Young issued a proclamation prohibiting such dealings with tribes in Utah. See U.S. State Department, Territorial Papers, Utah Series, April 30, 1853–December 24, 1859, National Archives.

[51] See Gottfredson, *Indian Depredations*, pp. 56–58, for details of these raids.

[52] Spring City, Sanpete County.

[53] Journal History, June 23, 1854, pp. 1–2.

[54] James S. Brown, *California Gold, An Authentic History of the First Find* (Oakland, 1894).

trade, as the Indians had disposed of their robes, pelts and furs for the season, so we sent the goods to Fort Supply and had them stored there.

I accompanied Rockwell to Salt Lake City, arriving there on July 19. We reported conditions to the governor, who received us very kindly, and approved of what we had done. . . .[55]

On the last day of August, Lieutenant Colonel Edward Jenner Steptoe rode into Great Salt Lake City at the head of three hundred troops to take over as military governor of Utah. Brigham Young's term was about to expire and Steptoe had been ordered to maintain peace and quiet until President Franklin Pierce could appoint a successor to the Mormon prophet. While there may have existed some indecision in the mind of President Pierce as to who was best suited to occupy the governor's chair, Brigham Young's thinking in the matter was as clear as a mountain stream. Speaking in the Tabernacle two months earlier, the church leader had said, "We have got a Territorial Government, and I am and will be Governor, *and no power can hinder it, until the Lord Almighty says, 'Brigham, you need not be Governor any longer'* . . . ."[56]

A collision between federal and church powers was avoided when the problem resolved itself in December. Under questionable circumstances, Steptoe declined a Presidential appointment as governor and underlined his refusal by signing a petition with other powerful Utahns urging Pierce to reappoint Young to the office.[57] The petition was granted. Brigham Young later remarked, "If the gallant gentleman [Steptoe] who is now in our midst had received the commission of governor of this territory, as was reported, and had accepted it, I would have taken off my hat and honored the appointment . . . ."

It was in this climate that Steptoe attempted to carry out his two secondary objectives: one, to fully investigate the murder of his comrade-in-arms, Gunnison; the other, to locate and chart a shorter, more practical route south of the Great Salt Lake to Carson Valley. In both matters

[55] James S. Brown, *Life of a Pioneer, Being an Autobiography* (Salt Lake City, 1900), pp. 345–46.

[56] *Journal of Discourses*, Vol. I, p. 187.

[57] Some writers insist that Steptoe was compromised into signing the petition through a scheme hatched by Brigham Young. Mrs. C. V. Waite, *The Mormon Prophet and His Harem* (Chicago, 1867), pp. 27–28, explains the intrigue in detail. J. H. Beadle, *Life in Utah, or the Mysteries and Crimes of Mormonism* (Philadelphia, 1870), p. 171, repeats Mrs. Waite's story.

he solicited the advice of Brigham Young, who assigned Bean and Rockwell to treat with the Pahvants for the surrender of Gunnison's killers and called Oliver Boardman Huntington to work with Steptoe on the exploration problem.

Rockwell, Bean, and a big Frenchman named Nicholas Janise were hired by the federal government at $5 a day while they negotiated with the Pahvant chief, Kanosh.[58] There were complications, the Mormons learned. In their first meeting with Kanosh they were told of the mistreatment of his tribesmen by a party of Missouri emigrants, an incident which provoked the Gunnison attack. As the talks continued, the Mormons realized that Kanosh had no intention of revealing the culprits responsible for the massacre, but they patiently waited for the chief to make the first move. Kanosh, for his part, called several tribal councils to decide what compensation could be offered for the murder of the eight whites. In retrospect, Bean wrote:

> It is laughable to think of our first trip in a Government outfit Ambulance and four good mules, expecting to bring the criminals back with us. It required many trips, and finally, Kanosh, Parashont and all the Chiefs agreed to give up the number. Eight Indians were surrendered on certain conditions, just after New Year, 1855. We were accompanied to Fillmore by Major John L. Reynolds and twenty men, to receive and safely convey the prisoners to Salt Lake City, where the troops were all comfortably housed for the winter.
>
> Kanosh and his friends had the number on hand — but such a turn-out of "murderers" was never before seen: one squaw, for the Mormon killed; one old blind fellow, one foolish chap, one outsider, that had no friends, another old sick fellow, and three little boys, ten to thirteen years old, made up the number. . . . This group shocked us all. Kanosh said it was the best he could do without a fight, as the Indians were determined to shield the Chief Braves who participated,[59] as they felt justified pretty much in the killing because of the treatment some of them had received from Emigrants going to California. . . . so the Soldiers took charge of the Prisoners, right in the midst of fifty or more half hostile Braves all blacked and painted, armed and being continually harangued by Sub Chiefs. We made the journey back to Salt Lake City and the prisoners were guarded by the soldiers until court time. . . .

[58] Bean, *Autobiography*, p. 110.

[59] Gibbs named the Pahvant braves in his "Gunnison Massacre, etc.," *Utah Historical Quarterly*, Vol. I (July 1928), p. 72.

When Steptoe saw the "prisoners" he was furious, but his hands were tied and he was forced to accept the situation.[60]

Although Rockwell's responsibility in the matter was officially at an end, he was not without problems as far as Indians were concerned. During the months of dickering with the Pahvants, and while Rockwell's attention was occupied, Ute braves were causing him trouble closer to home. On October 26 he placed the following advertisement in the *Deseret News*:

$15.00 Reward

STOLEN (Supposed by the Indians) about the middle of August last, from John Neff's Mill, on Mill Creek, a dark bay or light brown French Mare, six years old, black legs, brown head and neck, heavy mane and tail, saddle and cinch marks, paces and trots — Whoever will bring said mare to me will have the above reward, and any one giving information of her whereabouts, will be liberally rewarded.

O. P. Rockwell

While Rockwell was catching his breath and spending some welcome time at home with Mary Ann, Oliver Boardman Huntington was experiencing difficulties in another part of the territory. Since Rockwell was destined to become caught up in subsequent events, it is of some interest to follow Huntington's adventures as an explorer.

On September 14 Steptoe had written a letter to Colonel S. Cooper, United States adjutant general, and informed him that, "I have employed two citizens of this place [Great Salt Lake City] and an Indian, to pass over Captain [R.M.] Morris' new route to Carson's Valley and return this fall. One of them will thus be qualified to guide us next spring. They are also to observe for a still nearer route, or 'cut-off,' which there is good reason to believe may be found." [61]

The "two citizens and an Indian" mentioned by the colonel were Huntington; his nephew, Clark Allen Huntington, who signed on as an interpreter; and a young Ute named Natsab. All three were ordered to return to Great Salt Lake City upon completion of their mission. They

---

[60] Bean, *Autobiography*, pp. 110–12. Steptoe did little to endear himself to the settlers in Fillmore during the trial. Bean hints obliquely that "Several disgraceful occurrences took place with certain Government officials, soldiers and squaws of Chief Ammon's Camp." See Bean, p. 112. But Andrew Love is more specific; he says that Steptoe and Almon W. Babbitt were drunk in court. Love, "Journal," p. 70.

[61] Steptoe to Cooper, September 14, 1854, Office of Indian Affairs, National Archives.

were to be accompanied by Colonel John Reese, whose home was in Carson Valley, and two of Reese's friends, a man named Willis and another named Davis, who had "been to California, made a raise, returned to the States and now was making his way west again with a very fleet race-horse in hope of opening another stake by gambling." [62] On the outskirts of the city the six men were joined by eleven deserters from Steptoe's command "content to sail under the Mormon flag as far as Carson."

Toward the end of September the party found itself west of Ruby Valley when, as the men sat around the campfire eating dinner, seven painted Indians abruptly rode into the bivouac from all sides. [63] After some confusion, Huntington's nephew determined that the leader could understand Snake but stubbornly refused to answer questions; instead, the chief poked around and through the wagons, eyeing the whites menacingly. Huntington was perceptibly worried. He was sure the chief also spoke English, but he was at a loss as to how to make the warrior give himself away. Then came an unforeseen twist of fate:

> As soon as the interpreter and I were done eating, we walked around the horses after cautioning the men. While drawing the animals a little nearer camp he asked me if I had noticed a secret sign, a strange motion, the Indian made as he shook hands with us, and he showed it to me, stating he believed these Indians were of the tribe and party who had done so many murders on the Humboldt among the California gold seekers, and that he believed they were banded with whites by secret oaths, signs and pass-words. [64] Immediately after he told this I felt a strange but bright sensation come over my mind and I could see with my heart, or my spirit could see without my

[62] O. B. Huntington, "A Trip to Carson Valley," *Eventful Narratives* (Salt Lake City, 1887), p. 78.

[63] According to Huntington, about September 29, "We dug a little dust and washed it out and found several rubies, one very large and fine. We therefore called the place Ruby Valley." Ibid., p. 80.

[64] Huntington subsequently identified the Indian as Bloody Chief and the band as Snakes of the White Knife clan. See Huntington, "Journal," Vol. II, p. 84. The White Knives were so-called because "of white men being connected with them and their being so completely armed with almost every description of weapon. . . ." Jacob H. Holeman, Indian Agent for Utah Territory, in report to Luke Lea, Commissioner of Indian Affairs, "Utah Expedition," *House Executive Document No. 71*, 35th Congress, 1st Session, 1858, p. 141. It was also reported that the clan used white obsidian in making arrow points. Office of Indian Affairs, *House Executive Document No. 1* (1856), p. 778. See also "A Memoir on the Indians of Utah Territory," by Garland Hurt, in Captain J. H. Simpson, *Report of Explorations Across the Great Basin of the Territory of Utah, for a Wagon-Route from Camp Floyd to Genoa, in Carson Valley* (Washington, D.C., 1876), p. 461.

eyes.[65] I told him we would leave the horses and go quickly to camp, where he should go up to the Indian (the chief), give him the same sign he had given us, and that we would be safe among them.

He did this and the effect was astonishing. The Indian shook hands and hugged him heartily.

I gave further instruction to the interpreter what to say about a certain man whom we knew lived on the Humboldt River, where so much murdering had been done, and with whom I went to school in Nauvoo. Every word had its effect as I anticipated and the chief understood that this man who lived on the Humboldt,[66] and whom many believed to be the cause of the murdering done for money and plunder, was our friend from boyhood . . . .[67]

Without further trouble except for the inconvenience of having to feed Indians, Huntington's company pushed on and sighted Carson on October 15. After a short stay Huntington and his nephew — the Indian guide Natsab had gone ahead — departed for home; they arrived twenty-three days later on November 25. In Great Salt Lake City Huntington

[65] Huntington described this sensation as the spirit of the Holy Ghost controlling his mind. It may be, too, that he remembered the secret Danite handshake and grip revealed to him in Missouri in 1838, as outlined in chapter two.

[66] Kelly and Birney, *Holy Murder*, pp. 116–17, suggest that the "man on the Humboldt" was Return Jackson Redden, who had moved to that region to live. They cite letters from Indian Agent Jacob H. Holeman to Commissioner of Indian Affairs Luke Lea, dated May 2 and 8, 1852, in which Holeman reports that a local Mormon had received a letter from a friend in Carson Valley "and [the friend planned] to plunder and rob the emigrants. He advises [Thomas S.?] Williams . . . to paint the horns of his cattle, so that he may be known, as they do not wish to molest the brethren." Later Holeman wrote, "I have since learned that the individual who made the communication to Mr. Williams is a notorious character, by the name of 'Reading,' and although he was once a member of the Mormon Church, he is now held by them in utter contempt . . . ." Both letters can be found in "Utah Expedition," *House Executive Document No. 71*, 35th Congress, 1st Session, 1858. Redden was in the Carson area in 1852 (he gave the name to Jack's Valley), but the man Oliver B. Huntington alluded to was Alpheus Haws, a hellion whose father, Peter, had on one occasion aroused the ire of Brigham Young for dealing in counterfeit coin. Huntington crossed paths with Haws in 1899 in California: "We visited Alpheus Haws, the man who, in 1854 had the Indians on Humboldt River and in Ruby Valley Banded together with secret signs and pass word, like the robbers of old, and he laid a plan to murder me and my traveling partners explorers at south end of Ruby Valley . . . . We chatted together like other men but he could not hold his eyes on mine — was uneasy under my gaze for he had sought my life yet I felt no bitterness towards him . . . ." Huntington, "Journal," Vol. II, p. 441. A lively account of banditry along the Humboldt River during this period can be found in Dale L. Morgan, *The Humboldt; Highroad of the West* (New York, 1943), pp. 213–21.

[67] Huntington, *Eventful Narratives*, p. 81.

handed Steptoe a detailed account of the journey and a rough map of the trail. He told the officer that a military command could move with ease on the road and save between 150 and 200 miles.[68] Steptoe made up his mind to take the troops across the new route at the first opportunity; later he changed his plans. Captain Rufus Ingalls, Steptoe's quartermaster, explained why in a letter to the Quartermaster General dated August 25, 1855:

> As spring approached, however, the chief Mormon [Huntington], who had agreed to act as guide, became rather restive, and evinced an unwillingness to go, which caused the Colonel to distrust him, and shook his confidence in the report he had made of the road. As a matter of security, another party was organized under "Porter Rockwell," a Mormon, but a man of strong mind and independent spirit, a capital guide and fearless prairie-man. He went out as far as the great desert tracts lying southwest of the lake, and very nearly on a level with it, and found that at *that season*[69] they could not be passed over, "unless with wings," and returned. It proved fortunate that we did not undertake the march with O. B. Huntington as guide. The march would have been disastrous; though Rockwell and others are of the opinion that by going on a line some thirty miles farther south, along the foot of mountains seen in that direction, a fine road can be laid out, avoiding in a great degree, the desert.
> I believe such to be the case myself. . . .[70]

Beyond the fact that Huntington was reluctant to make the grueling journey to Carson again and risk another meeting with the Indians, Steptoe may have been irritated with the guide for aiding deserters in escaping the territory, another reason for rejecting the Mormon's report of the new route. In any event, by selecting Rockwell for the task of piloting the command, the colonel acknowledged a man he already knew to be capable and dependable.

For Rockwell the call to duty came at an inopportune time; Mary Ann was heavy with child. The baby was born March 11, 1855, in John Neff's Mill Creek Canyon home and was named Mary Amanda Rockwell.[71] Two weeks later the child's father started west with George Bean,

---

[68] Huntington's report can be found in the *Deseret News*, December 7, 1854.

[69] Italics in original.

[70] Captain Rufus Ingalls to Major General Thomas S. Jesup, in "Report to the Quartermaster General," *Senate Executive Document No. 1*, 34th Congress, 1st Session, 1855, p. 161. See also Captain J. H. Simpson, *Report*, pp. 24–25.

[71] *Utah Genealogical and Historical Magazine*, Vol. XXVI, p. 156.

George W. Boyd, Peter W. Conover, and John Nebeker, all Mormons.[72] From Steptoe's Government Station at Rush Lake the small party of trailblazers headed through what is now Johnson's Pass, across Skull Valley, past Granite Mountain — a craggy knob protruding from the Salt Desert — striking the old Hastings wagon road at the east edge of the desert.[73] They loaded up with fresh water at Granite Mountain and slogged across a sea of clinging salt mud directly in the face of a blinding sandstorm. Frigid fingers of wind tore the packs from the mules and drenched the men in an icy brine. When they finally reached Redden's Springs on the west shore of the desert, the party was numb with cold, each man caked with a stiff crust of salt.

Sheltered by swamp tules at the springs, the Mormons suffered through the night until the storm had spent itself on the empty salt plain. When morning came Rockwell made up his mind to skirt the edge of the desert on a southeasterly tack in returning to Rush Valley. The following day the party discovered several large springs used for burial by Indian tribes in the vicinity. Examining the largest pool, the Mormons were startled to see "six Indian bodies standing bolt upright and crusted over with the salty deposit in this [spring], giving them the appearance of mummies." [74] After the initial shock had passed, the whites came to the conclusion that heavy stones had been lashed to the ankles of the dead men to keep them perpendicular in the water. Rockwell and Bean both thought they saw other corpses submerged beneath the six.

Resuming their journey, the party struck a trail scouted in the fall of 1853 by Lieutenant E. G. Beckwith, attached to Gunnison's ill-fated expedition.[75] Rockwell followed the route for a distance and found the salt marshes near the Sevier impassable. The sloughs farther south and east were equally bad. Returning to camp with his report, the scout concluded that a wagon load was impossible for at least two months and decided to head back to the city to turn his findings over to Steptoe.

When the colonel learned of the obstacles awaiting him on the projected cutoff, he revised his orders so that the line of march would be along the established northern route to Sacramento. From there the

[72] Bean, *Autobiography*, p. 113.

[73] Ibid.

[74] Ibid., p. 114.

[75] Because Captain R. M. Morris, in charge of a mounted rifle escort, was in the Beckwith detachment and was the ranking officer, Steptoe referred to the trail as the "Morris route," despite the fact that he did not command the mission.

troops would proceed to Benecia, some miles to the southwest. With Rockwell in the lead, commanding the princely wage of $5 a day, the standard government rate for guides, Lieutenant Colonel Edward Jenner Steptoe rode out of the land of Mormons, never to return.[76]

Once in California, Rockwell separated himself from army service and visited his old haunts of the gold rush days. In San Francisco Joseph L. Heywood, who had named Rockwell his deputy in 1849 when the State of Deseret was organized, wrote to a fellow Mormon, George A. Smith. His letter was copied into the *Deseret News*: ". . . O. P. Rockwell calls upon me occasionally. He accompanied Col. Steptoe's command to Bernecia [*sic*]. . . ." [77] And he made a brief visit to his sister Electa. (The Ousley family had moved to Gilroy in Santa Clara County just two years before.)

During this final trip to California Rockwell met the widow and family of Don Carlos Smith, brother of the martyred prophet. Many years later in Salt Lake City Rockwell would tell Mrs. Elizabeth D. E. Roundy the story of that meeting. In her words:

> When he saw [Don Carlos' widow], she was just recovering from typhoid fever, in consequence of which, her hair had all fallen off.

[76] Steptoe's decision to disregard Huntington's findings was viewed by the Mormon with some bitterness. A degree of animosity appears to have existed between Rockwell and the Huntingtons prior to this incident, for Oliver Boardman Huntington wrote in his journal on April 29, 1855: "Steptoe with his troops left the City . . . for California by the north route having been turned from their purpose of going the desert west route, by O. P. Rockwell and Geo. Been who were sent out to explore a portion of the route and pronounced it impassable, more as enemies to our family than friends to improvements." Huntington, "Journal," Vol. II, p. 96.

[77] *Deseret News*, September 19, 1855. The letter is dated July 25, 1855.

Porter wore his hair long, as he said the Prophet had told him that if he wore his hair long his enemies should not have the power over him neither should he be overcome by evil. When he met Sister Smith he had no gold dust or money to give her, so he had his hair cut to make her a wig and from that time he said that he could not control the desire for strong drink, nor the habit of swearing.[78]

In San Francisco, Rockwell bumped into Nathaniel V. Jones, a Mormon elder returning from a church mission in Calcutta, and the two struck out for Utah together. Rockwell and Jones, with others headed east, left Carson on September 22. In thirteen days they were riding down the streets of Great Salt Lake City.[79]

When Rockwell walked into his home on the afternoon of his return, he had a visitor; John Bennion was waiting to ask his permission to build a cabin and graze a herd of cattle in Rush Valley.[80] Rockwell's control over the valley extended to grazing rights, but Bennion was told to see Bill Hickman on the matter of building a cabin there.

Word reached Rockwell that a pair of French scientists who had preceded him across the central route to visit Utah were camped on the outskirts of the city prior to setting off for a return to California by the southern route. Jules Remy and Julius Brenchley, both wounded, had stumbled into the city with barely the clothes on their backs and given a harrowing account of being attacked by Shoshone in Carson Valley while gathering rock samples and botanical specimens as they made their way

[78] Mrs. Roundy's letter is in the LDS Church Historical Department. Excerpts were published in the "Church Section" of the *Deseret News*, August 31, 1935. How Don Carlos Smith's widow, Agnes, turned up in California after her husband's death in Nauvoo is related in Josephine Dewitt Rhodehamel and Raymund Francis Wood, *Ina Coolbrith, Librarian and Laureate of California* (Provo, 1973), pp. 24–25. Agnes Moulton Coolbrith Smith had remarried (to William Pickett) and emigrated to San Francisco in the early 1850s. One of her daughters by the first marriage (Josephine Donna Smith), took the name Ina Coolbrith and was to become California's first poet laureate.

[79] *Deseret News*, October 10, 1855.

[80] John Bennion, "Journal." MSS, five volumes, Book I, p. 18. [After Rockwell's return from California in 1850, he had settled in a remote area north of newly created Weber County. His location first was known as Porter's Spring, then Three-Mile Creek, and finally Perry, a name it still bears, though now the town is in Box Elder County. Upon his marriage to Mary Ann, Rockwell had built a home near the mouth of Neff's Canyon on the valley's east bench, and it was here that Bennion came to call. See U.S. Population Census, Seventh (1850), Utah; and "Box Elder County," *Heart Throbs of the West*, Vol. IX (1948), p. 241].

to Zion. Remy had been struck in five places by buckshot; Brenchley suffered an arrow wound in the neck.

When the two intrepid adventurers sought an audience with Brigham Young, the Mormon leader regarded them with suspicion. "He was fully justified from our strange demeanor, our beggarly costumes, our inability to prove by any written documents the truth of our assertions," Remy said.[81] In fact, Young had spread the word that the scientists bore all the earmarks of being assassins. But it turned out for the best; a Mormon recognized Remy and vouched for his character. Brigham Young then graciously welcomed his two renowned visitors. Once having been accepted as friendly, the scientists further ensured their well-being within the community by placing an article in the *Deseret News* describing their predicament and explaining their intention to "visit the natural curiosities of the Lake and environs," then to "direct their course to the South," to California.[82]

Now, fully recovered from their ordeal, the two Frenchmen were camped at Big Cottonwood while they packed their gear for the ride west. Out of curiosity more than anything else, Rockwell determined to visit them. When he reined up, the scout found that many of the city's prominent citizens had the same idea. Carriages were clustered around the camp, and nearly a score of horses were picketed nearby. Rockwell's arrival on October 25 was greeted by shouts of welcome from all parties, and a gallon of whisky made its appearance.[83] Several decks of cards and a chessboard were pulled from saddlebags, and soon the encampment was a hub of boisterous activity. Raucous songs burst forth and continued through the night until the rising sun reminded the revelers of the hour. One by one the visitors took their leave, until Rockwell alone remained. He offered to stay and help the two scientists break camp. Remy later penned this profile of the rough and rugged Mormon:

> Rockwell is a person sufficiently well known in the history of the Mormons for us to bestow a word on him. He is a man without much education, and of very ordinary intelligence, but at the same time extremely amiable and polite, with exceedingly distinguished and graceful manners. He has an imposing look, with a dash of the aristocratic in it, which is also perceptible in his small, plump, fair, and

[81] Jules Remy, *A Journey to Great-Salt-Lake City* (London, 1861), two volumes, Vol. I, p. 204.

[82] *Deseret News*, October 3, 1855.

[83] Remy, *A Journey to Great-Salt-Lake City*, Vol. II, p. 311.

well-made hands. He has been accused, on no evidence — and many still persist in accusing him — of having, in May, 1842, fired a pistol at Governor L. W. Boggs, of Missouri: We will not attempt to settle the question either one way or the other. Rockwell is a man as vehement in his hatred as in his friendship. His attachment to Joseph Smith may have impelled him to desire and compass the death of one of the greatest enemies of the Mormons. Fanaticism and affection may have directed Rockwell's arm in this criminal act, and it is by no means impossible that the Church will one day revere him on this account . . . .

What appears clear to us is, that Rockwell is incapable of doing wrong except under the impression that he is doing right; so persuaded are we of this, that we would trust him with life and property without any hesitation. He is a lion in a lamb's skin, that we admit; but a brave and generous lion, full of heart and greatness, capable of the grandest devotedness, ready to sacrifice himself in behalf of any one who has gained his esteem, without exception of sect or person, whether Jews, Pagans, Mussulmans, or Mormons. He is of the stuff from which heroes are wrought, and if the blood of heroes can be inferred from the expression of the face, or the qualities of the heart, one would swear there were traces of a lofty origin in him. It is he who is ever at hand where there is a perilous service to be accomplished, a crime to be avenged, a sacrifice to be made which can be of advantage to the oppressed.

He it was who at Carson Valley wished to put himself at the head of a company of volunteers for the purpose of avenging our reported death; and yet we were entire strangers to him then; but our boldness, our rashness possibly, in exposing ourselves alone in the desert, had touched him, and won for us a place in his affection. He proposed to escort us as far as California, and had we accepted his offer, he would have accompanied us happy and content, without the remotest thought of any advantage to himself, proud of being able to give us this proof of his sincere regard.[84]

While M. Jules Remy was proud to say Orrin Porter Rockwell was his friend, there were others who felt differently. Branding him an "assassin" who had "acquired a hyena-like taste for blood," another author, the mysterious "Achilles," afterward challenged Rockwell's motives:

One of his peculiarities was manifested in his efforts to make the acquaintance of all Gentiles who might come to the Territory, and ingratiate himself into their favor. While in these movements, he assumed the air of suavity, and yet was simply acting as the spy of the

[84] Ibid., Vol. II, pp. 314–15.

222

magnates of the church. In this capacity, it was his earnest endeavor to suggest investments and induce embarcation in business, always with an eye to benefiting the treasury of the church. He would expatiate eloquently on the beauties of the Territory, the advantages of the various locations, the excellencies of the society, and the generaly propitious opportunities for success afforded by becoming domiciled under the shadow of Zion. In fact, he was a fac-totum of Brigham Young.[85]

As the year 1855 came to a close, Rockwell, now a man of forty-two, was entering the most exciting period of his checkered career — a time in which his name would become synonymous with the mysteries and terrors of Mormonism described in dime novels of the day.

---

[85] Achilles, *Destroying Angels of Mormondom*, pp. 36–37. There is no evidence to substantiate the charges made here.

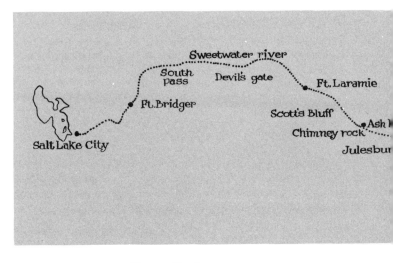

Chapter Twelve

MAIL, MONEY, AND MURDER

BRIGHAM YOUNG WAS DISSATISFIED. For eighteen months he had watched the Gentile firm of Magraw and Hockaday milk the federal government of thousands of dollars through its lucrative contract to carry the mails between Independence and Great Salt Lake City. In the first fourteen months of operation the two partners had succeeded in meeting the schedule just three times.[1] Not only did the contractors average an unimpressive forty days each way, but on several occasions the mail had been lost entirely. An idea was taking shape in Young's mind, and he called Rockwell in to discuss it, for few Mormons knew the plains better. Would it not be possible for the Saints to carry the mail faster, the church leader wondered.

Running through Brigham Young's mind was the concept of a Mormon mail and carrying company to serve the Great Basin region. Such an undertaking, if successful, could monopolize freighting business in the West, since Magraw and Hockaday at their best would prove little competition. He also reckoned that a mail and carrying company would be a popular enterprise in the Territory, even among Gentile residents who frequently expressed their disgust with the present service. Young put his

---

[1] *Deseret News*, September 12, 1855.

Ft. Kearny

Independence

plan to work without delay. On January 9, 1856, a delegation of prominent Utahns addressed the Legislative Assembly and a capacity audience
at Fillmore. Territorial Secretary Almon W. Babbitt made the opening
statement: "We are here to take into consideration the propriety of establishing a daily express line of stages from the Missouri River to California,
via Salt Lake City." [2] Babbitt then lent his endorsement to the proposal.
He was followed to the speaker's stand by such luminaries as Associate
Justice G. P. Stiles, Orson Pratt, Enoch Reese, John S. Fullmer, and
Orrin Porter Rockwell. When it came his turn, the gruff plainsman
explained in simple language that Mormon riders could cut Magraw's
time in half and do it consistently if there were stations along the route.
He took his seat amid a burst of applause.

More meetings followed on January 26 and February 2.[3] At the
latter session Brigham Young dramatically offered to personally equip
and stock three hundred miles of the route, a gesture greeted by a standing ovation.[4] The proposal to organize such a firm was unanimously sus-

[2] Ibid., January 23, 1856; Journal History, January 12, 1856, p. 2.

[3] Rockwell again was called to speak, this time in the Old Tabernacle in Great
Salt Lake City. His appearance prompted the apostate John Hyde to comment:
"Some of the leading spirits of that [Danite] band are still in Salt Lake City. Although they do not maintain their organization, being generally merged into 'Brigham's Life Guards,' yet without the same name, they have performed the same
deeds. O. P. Rockwell, the attempted assassin of Governor Boggs . . . Brigham has
had into the pulpit to address the meetings!" Hyde, *Mormonism*, p. 105.

[4] *Deseret News*, February 6, 1856; Journal History, February 2, 1856.

tained, and the Brigham Young Express and Carrying Company was born. Soon everyone knew it simply as the YX Company. In April a special conference in Great Salt Lake City called nineteen men on missions to construct the necessary supply stations along the thousand-mile route. Meanwhile, pressures were brought to bear in Washington by both Mormons and influential Gentiles to annul the Magraw–Hockaday mail contract — efforts which eventually proved successful.

At the same time, Rockwell prepared to guide a party back to the States. Among those in the wagon train were Almon W. Babbitt and U.S. Marshal Joseph L. Heywood, who had business in Washington; Orson Pratt and Ezra T. Benson, en route to missions in Europe; George A. Smith and John Taylor, who were headed for the Territorial Convention "to urge Utah's claims to be numbered among the Stars." [5] A. O. Smoot was captain of the train; Rockwell was scout, guide, and hunter.

Assembling at Emigration Canyon on April 22, the party awaited the arrival of Brigham Young, who wished to see them off. He rode up shortly before noon, and for the next quarter hour the Mormons knelt as their prophet bestowed a blessing upon them. By midday the journey had begun, with Rockwell a mile or so ahead. The train crossed the Weber River, angled up Echo Canyon, forded the Bear River, and in five days sighted Fort Bridger. Pausing only to rest their animals, the party hit the trail again on the morning of the twenty-eighth — without Rockwell, who was off chasing horses which had strayed during the night. Aware of the importance of spare mounts during the long pull ahead, the travelers were delighted when their scout jogged into camp the following day with the strays in tow; he was saluted by a chorus of cheers.[6]

At Ham's Fork, two days east of Fort Bridger, Smoot thought it time to survey the company's arsenal before proceeding into Indian country; for twenty-one months the Sioux between the Elk Horn River and Fort Laramie had been increasingly troublesome, threatening to fulminate an all-out plains Indian war with the Army, and only now were observing a very uneasy truce.[7] George A. Smith, a colonel in the Mormon militia as

[5] *Deseret News*, April 23, 1856. Some of the others in the party included John A. Ray, Erastus Snow, Chief Justice J. F. Kinney and family, W. I. Appleby, Truman O. Angell, Phineas H. Young, Ira Eldredge, William Miller, and James Ure.

[6] Journal History, June 8, 1856. The entire journey is detailed here by James Ure, clerk of the company.

[7] Ironically, the hostilities broke out over a sore-footed old Mormon cow. The animal had lagged behind a party of Danish Mormon emigrants on the trail near

well as an apostle, called a muster of the thirty-eight members of the company and held inspection.[8] Satisfied that there was sufficient powder and lead for emergencies, Smoot ordered the train to move out. They were ready for Indians, but another enemy was girding to meet them — the weather. Every eye contemplated the thick, leaden clouds bunching overhead. Three days later the camp was aroused from sleep by excited night guards shouting that the horses were freezing. Snowflakes the size of rifle patches came slanting down in the first chilling blast of a full-scale mountain blizzard. Rockwell scrambled from his sleeping bag, bellowing orders as he ran for the horses. Throwing his blankets and bedding across two animals, he yelled for others to do the same; then he led the string of

---

Fort Laramie and limped off toward a circle of Sioux lodges on the North Platte. A Miniconjou brave found the stray and killed it for meat. The emigrants reported their loss to officers at Fort Laramie and continued on. But the next morning, August 19, 1854, a brash brevet second lieutenant, John L. Grattan, just a year out of West Point and awaiting a regular Army commission, assembled a volunteer party for "perilous service." He, a sergeant, twenty-five privates, two musicians, and a civilian interpreter, with two mounted howitzers, rode out to arrest the offender. Lt. Grattan confronted the Miniconjou and demanded his surrender. The Indian refused. Shots were fired and a number of Brulé Sioux who made up the main part of the camp joined the fight, darkening the sky with their arrows. Both cannons were fired, but without effect. Grattan and his men were wiped out. The officer's body, pierced by two dozen arrows — one completely through his head — was found the next day. So mutilated was he that identification was possible only through his pocket watch. Depredations along the Oregon–California trail became more daring and frequent in the weeks and months which followed, until finally, a year later, Brevet Brigadier General William S. Harney was sent out on an expedition to punish the Sioux. Harney engaged the Brulés near Ash Hollow on September 2, 1855, and slaughtered more than eighty Indians, including women and children. The encounter earned for him the nickname "Squaw-killer." Harney called a council of the plains tribes at Fort Pierre, Nebraska Territory, in March 1856, and gained a truce. Such was the situation when the Mormon party came through a month later. The War Department investigation into the death of Lt. John L. Grattan and troops under his command on August 19, 1854, can be found in "Engagement Between United States Troops and Sioux Indians," *House of Representatives Report No. 63*, 33rd Congress, 2d Session, 1855, pp. 1–27. For the Ash Hollow battle, see Gen. Richard C. Drum, "Reminiscences of the Indian Fight at Ash Hollow, 1855," Nebraska State Historical Society, *Collections*, Vol. XVI (1911), pp. 143–50; and Eugene Bandel, *Frontier Life in the Army 1854–1861*, translated by Olga Bandel and Richard Jente; edited by Ralph P. Bieper (Glendale, 1932), pp. 28–35.

[8] A roster of the men and their arms is found in the Journal History, June 8, 1856, p. 5. For example, Rockwell carried two pistols and twenty rounds of ammunition; Marshal Heywood, who appeared to be in charge of the arsenal, carried two pounds of powder and ten pounds of lead; Ezra T. Benson, forty rounds; A. O. Smoot, fifty rounds; Isaac Higbee, fifteen rounds; Erastus Snow, twenty-five rounds.

mounts to a cluster of willows three miles distant for protection and for brush on which to graze.[9]

Fifty-six hours the blizzard raged, the wind piling drifts five and six feet deep. The paralyzing cold and shrieking gale prevented the party from sleeping. The horses were fed flour and biscuits to keep them alive. All but two of the animals survived the storm but they were greatly weakened by the experience. When the snow showed signs of letting up, Rockwell ordered the company to saddle up and push out. Even with his legendary tracking ability the trail was difficult to find in the drifts.

No sooner had the men overcome one natural obstacle than another rose in its place. As long as clouds dulled the snow's dazzling glare, the men stubbornly plodded forward, most of the time leading horses through waist-deep drifts. Fatigued, numb, their senses dulled, the Mormons failed to immediately realize the danger when, as if an unseen switch had been thrown, the landscape burst forth in a blinding brilliance. The sun came out. Shimmering white snow covered the mountains, trees, canyons — everything. The men had been struggling along with scarves swathing their faces, shielding noses and mouths against a wind so cold it froze the tears in their eyes. Suddenly Rockwell barked a warning, "Cover your eyes! Put your neckerchiefs over your eyes!" He had at once recognized that the party stood in imminent peril of being struck snow-blind.

It was early afternoon when the first rays flashed through the clouds, and by dusk most of the men were complaining of eye inflammation. Orson Pratt was the first to be afflicted; soon others exhibited similar symptoms.[10] By morning of the following day, May 7, fully half the company was snowblind, including the indomitable Rockwell. The pain was excruciating. Eyeballs seared in sockets, each movement feeling as if the pupil were grating across a lid impregnated with sand; sudden jabs of fire shot fine lines of blood across the whites. Salty, burning tears flowed constantly. The eye demanded to be rubbed, but rubbing only increased the agony twofold.

Hungry, cold, and exhausted, the men gathered around a flickering campfire that night and, forgetting their tribulations for the moment, listened as Rockwell told of Joseph Smith and the magnificent treasures of the Hill Cumorah.[11]

[9] Ibid., June 8, 1856, p. 7. See also George A. Smith's letter in the *Deseret News*, June 11, 1856, in which he describes portions of the journey.

[10] Journal History, June 8, 1856, pp. 7–8; *Deseret News*, June 11, 1856.

[11] Journal History, June 8, 1856, p. 8. In all probability Rockwell told them the same story he was to pass on to Brigham Young later. It concerned a chest of

With the break of day the company pushed forward through the terrible drifts. At Greasewood Creek came another storm. Farther northeast at Willow Creek the snow measured a foot deep on the ground, but scattered blades of grass poked through the icy white crust. Then dawn of May 12 brought a new alarm: "The horses have run off!" Resolutely, Rockwell and a Mormon named William Wadsworth trudged out after the animals. If they failed to find them, the company most certainly would perish. Hours later the two men returned with six of the runaways. By May 16 the wagon train had reached the LaBonte River, beyond the North Platte and some four hundred and forty miles from their starting point. They pitched camp in a torrential rain. Lamented George A. Smith, "We seem to be blessed with storms of great severity." [12]

Rockwell noticed the grass thickening, prompting Apostle Smith to remark, "It should be the best graze on the prairie for years—if the grasshoppers don't destroy it." There was joy in camp that morning; Rockwell shot a plump antelope, and the company feasted for the first time in days. They had been on the move for nearly a month, fighting snow for the last three weeks. In all this time they had not seen a soul; then overnight there were emigrants everywhere. Fifteen miles west of Fort Kearny on May 29 Smith scribbled in his pocket journal: ". . . have passed trains almost hourly. Yesterday we met about 2000 head of cattle . . . . We have also passed several government trains freighted with corn for General Harney's command . . . . May 30 — We have found the road to-day literally filled with emigrant trains . . . . The rumor is that the Mormon emigration is tremendous; 5000 are said to be fitting up at Omaha city, and as many more in other points." [13]

In less than a week the party reached the sandy banks of the Big Blue, and by June 8 their wagons were rolling into Mormon Grove near Atchison — an amazing ten days ahead of schedule despite the weather. As Rockwell bade each member of the company goodbye, he had the satisfaction of knowing he had brought them through without losing a life, a fact upon which he would perhaps reflect with grim amusement in the months to come. While Rockwell took time to visit a few familiar places

---

money exhumed near the Hill Cumorah during Rockwell's treasure-hunting days. See "Discourse by President Brigham Young," June 17, 1877, *Journal of Discourses*, Vol. XIX, pp. 37–38.

[12] *Deseret News*, June 11, 1856.

[13] *Deseret News*, July 2, 1856. Smith is referring here to the great Mormon experiment, the handcart emigration which nearly ended in complete disaster.

before his return to Zion, one member of the company, Almon W. Babbitt, made straight for Washington.

Although no longer a Mormon in good standing,[14] Babbitt continued to serve Brigham Young as secretary of Utah Territory, a political plum which had fallen into his hands when the former secretary, Benjamin G. Ferris, had unceremoniously quit his post and departed from Utah. Babbitt took the job in 1852 after a pro tem period served by Willard Richards. He enjoyed the prestige of his position, but incurred Young's displeasure by carousing around the nation's capital with the abandon of a French sailor. It was an open secret in Great Salt Lake City that Young considered all the work accomplished by Dr. John M. Bernhisel as territorial delegate to Congress destroyed by Babbitt's free-wheeling caprices.

(In 1851 Babbitt had infuriated the church president with his handling of $20,000 entrusted by Congress for construction of a statehouse at the seat of territorial government in Utah. Stung by his excommunication two months earlier in Kanesville for immorality and intemperance, Babbitt petulantly doled out the appropriation in irritatingly small amounts. To make matters worse, Young suspected that Babbitt was in league with Territorial Secretary Broughton D. Harris in a plan to smuggle $24,000 in gold — earmarked for the expenses of the Utah Legislature — out of Great Salt Lake City.[15] Harris, a headstrong young man of twenty-seven, had clashed with Young over the territorial census which Young, as gov-

[14] Babbitt was disfellowshiped in 1851 for "profanity and intemperance in the streets of Kanesville; and for corrupting the morals of the people . . . by giving them liquor to beguile them from the path of duty and honor. Thus prostituting to the shrine of party zeal, his priestly powers, by which to operate upon the low and deranged passions of men; and for ministering by his priestly office, in things that are forbidden." *Frontier Guardian* (Kanesville), May 2, 1851, and Journal History, May 2, 1851. Babbitt had been cut off from the church once before, in 1840, but had been reinstated.

[15] Journal History, July 23, 1851. At this time Babbitt was serving as delegate to Washington, D.C., from the Provisional State of Deseret, but was not seated. For Harris's account of the dispute with Brigham Young, see Sarah Hollister Harris, *An Unwritten Chapter of Salt Lake 1851–1901* (New York, 1901), pp. 55–56. Mrs. Harris, wife of the secretary, relates that in the fall of 1851 Babbitt attempted to leave the valley with his family, but was halted some 40 miles outside the city by a company of armed men sent to "restrain and take into their possession A. W. Babbett, with his effects, and search his wagons for a sum of money — probably gold — to the amount of twenty-four thousand dollars, and for the seal of the Territory of Utah, and bring the same before the Governor in Great Salt Lake City." Mrs. Harris explains that her husband, upon learning of the incident, informed Brigham Young that he [Harris] still was in possession of the federal funds and intended to leave the city with the money. He did so unharmed, she said.

ernor, had initiated prior to the secretary's arrival. Harris insisted that the undertaking be repeated, and Young firmly refused. Harris remained stubbornly unyielding on the subject and in the end succeeded in returning the gold to the federal treasury.)

After eight weeks in Washington, Babbitt began making arrangements for the homeward journey. Ordering an ox train fitted out with books, stationery, a carpet for the new statehouse, and other supplies required for the approaching Legislative Assembly, he sent it ahead, planning to catch up on the trail in a light, fast buggy. Four teamsters and a Mrs. Wilson and her child made up the company. They had no way of knowing that the Cheyennes and Arapahoes had taken the warpath and were ravaging the plains.[16]

Babbitt spent the next few days occupying himself with details, then set out for Great Salt Lake City, stopping briefly at Cutler's Park in Nebraska Territory where thousands of Mormon emigrants were loading their flimsy handcarts for the trek to Zion. One of the pioneers remembered seeing the Utah secretary that day.

> . . . Almon W. Babbitt, dressed in corduroy pants, woolen overshirt, and felt hat, called as he was passing west. He seemed in high glee, his spirits seemed very elastic, almost mercurial. He had started with one carriage for Salt Lake, with the mail and a considerable amount of money.[17] He was very confident that he should be in Salt Lake within fifteen days. He intended to push through vigorously and sleep on the wind, meaning an airfilled mattress. . . .[18]

Babbitt's "mercurial spirits" would have dampened considerably had he known that at that very moment his ox train was being ripped to pieces by a Cheyenne war party thirty miles east of Fort Kearny. But oblivious to its fate, he and Thomas Sutherland, a shotgun guard, rode out of Cutler's Park, waved a final farewell to the emigrants, and galloped smartly away in the swift little buggy. On August 30, only a day's ride from

---

[16] George Bird Grinnell blamed the Indian excitement and the subsequent Sumner punitive expedition against the Cheyennes in 1857 on the impetuous reaction of the army to an incident in late August 1856, when a Cheyenne party begging tobacco skirmished with a mail wagon driver. See George Bird Grinnell, *The Fighting Cheyennes* (Norman, 1955), p. 113.

[17] Babbitt carried six bank drafts totaling $13,000 plus $1,500 in gold coin. Rumors that he had $20,000 in cash on his person were untrue and possibly had been confused with the 1851 incident involving Secretary Harris.

[18] John Jaques, "Some Reminiscences," *Salt Lake Herald*, December 8, 1878. See also Journal History, November 30, 1856, p. 14.

Kearny, a horrified Babbitt reined up at the remains of his wagon train.[19] Pressing on to the fort, the secretary found that one of his teamsters, Orrin Parrish, had survived the attack unharmed.[20] Parrish said that two of his companions were dead, a third was wounded, the child was slain by Cheyennes and the mother carried off.[21] (Mrs. Wilson's body was found later the same day by troops from the fort; the Indians had killed her when she was unable to keep up with them.)[22]

At the fort, Babbitt found Rockwell outfitting a wagon for Utah. (There were other Mormons at Kearny that day, among them Franklin D. Richards, Daniel Spencer, A. O. Smoot, and James Ferguson.) Rockwell assisted Babbitt in purchasing additional stock and refitting the supply train. This accomplished, Babbitt made a deal with Rockwell to haul the goods to Great Salt Lake City at the rate of fourteen cents a pound for the 5,643 pounds.[23]

[19] Cheyennes had raided the train in retaliation for the loss of ten braves in a skirmish with cavalrymen earlier in the day. "Report of the Secretary of Interior," *House Executive Document No. 1*, 34th Congress, 3rd Session, December 1, 1856, to March 3, 1857, p. 650. Babbitt, on the evening of August 30, after having discovered the ruins of his wagon train, overtook James G. Willie's handcart company at Dry Creek and the Platte River and spent the night. The handcart Mormons had, on the day before, learned from passing Pawnees that Babbitt's wagons had been hit by Cheyennes. Levi Savage, Jr., Journal, MS, August 29–31, 1856. Thomas Sutherland, described by the *New York Times*, May 11, 1857, as a disillusioned Mormon, was in the original group from Great Salt Lake City headed east in May 1856 and could well have been Babbitt's employee. Journal History, June 8, 1856.

[20] This probably is the same Orrin Parrish who became involved in the sensational Potter-Parrish murder case in Springville, March 15, 1857.

[21] *Millennial Star*, Vol. XVIII, p. 686; *Council Bluffs Bugle*, September 9, 1856, and Captain H. W. Wharton's reports to Washington in *Transactions of the Kansas State Historical Society, Embracing the Fifth and Sixth Biennial Reports, 1886–1888* (Topeka, 1890), Vol. IV, pp. 492–93.

[22] "Report of the Secretary of the Interior," *Senate Executive Document No. 5*, 34th Congress, 3rd Session, December 1, 1856, to March 3, 1857, p. 650; "Report of the Secretary of the Interior," *House Executive Document No. 1*, 34th Congress, 3rd Session, December 1, 1856, to March 3, 1857, p. 650.

[23] See affidavit of Orrin Porter Rockwell before W. I. Appleby, clerk of the Supreme Court of the United States for the Territory of Utah, dated February 11, 1857, in Utah Executive Papers, 1856–1858, "Governor (Miscellaneous Correspondence) 1857," Utah State Archives. Here Rockwell is paid $790.02 from the Almon W. Babbitt estate for freighting goods from Fort Kearny to Great Salt Lake City in accordance with an agreement between the two parties made ". . . during the last days of August (precise date not remembered) A.D. One Thousand eight hundred and fifty-six . . . ." A bill of lading is annexed to the affidavit. It shows that Rock-

On September 4 he and Rockwell visited the scene of the ox train raid and there met a Mormon handcart company under command of James G. Willie.[24] The emigrants had just placed the last rock on a cairn over the graves of Babbitt's dead teamsters. In a heavy voice Babbitt told Willie of the attack and alerted him to the dangers ahead; then he and Rockwell returned to the fort.[25]

Despite repeated warnings from the commander at Fort Kearny and efforts by his Mormon friends to dissuade him, Babbitt stubbornly insisted on continuing to Utah alone.[26] The Indians could go to hell for all he cared, he said. Captain H. W. Wharton, in charge of the post, offered the territorial executive a mounted escort if he would wait a few days until a patrol returned, but Babbitt refused to listen, arguing that it would only slow him down.[27] Fully aware of the foolishness in attempting to travel so lightly armed through hostile Indian country, Rockwell tried to reason with Babbitt, urging him to wait until a larger train could be formed, but the secretary had made his decision.[28] To Rockwell he said, "Porter, perhaps the next thing you will hear of me will be in my grave, but I must go on!" [29] No satisfactory explanation has ever come to light regarding Babbitt's seemingly unreasonable haste to reach Utah. (He had carried a one-wagon mail to Utah in 1849, which perhaps established a precedent in his mind.) Nevertheless, with four mules harnessed to the carriage, he, Sutherland, and an extra guard, Frank Rowland[30]

---

well carried thirty-three cases of books marked for federal officials and Brigham Young, two bales of window blinds and fixtures, two rolls of carpeting for the state-house, a case of stationery, and four cases of ink. Utah Executive Papers, 1856–1858, "Secretary of Territory (Miscellaneous Correspondence) 1857," Utah State Archives.

[24] Jaques, "Some Reminiscences," *Salt Lake Herald*, December 29, 1878.

[25] Ibid.

[26] Journal History, October 4, 1856.

[27] Wharton to Major G. Deas, assistant adjutant general, in *Transactions of the Kansas State Historical Society*, Vol. IV, pp. 494–95, and Julia Ann Babbitt, "Letter to the Editor," *New York Herald*, July 25, 1857, reprinted in *The Mormon*, August 1, 1857.

[28] Even a larger train wouldn't have guaranteed Babbitt's safety, however; Franklin D. Richards, who traveled with one of the largest Mormon companies on the prairie that year, reported to Brigham Young that the Indians "came to our company in wolfskins; we could hear them croak to each other and we kept a good guard every night. . . ." Journal History, October 4, 1856.

[29] Ibid.

[30] Rowland may have been the wounded teamster who survived the ox train raid with Parrish.

(James Ferguson had refused the secretary's entreaties to leave the Richards train and join him),[31] rolled out of the fort on September 6.[32]

The next day Babbitt and his guards halted for a rest at Ash Hollow, one hundred and twenty miles from Fort Kearny, having made excellent time. Sutherland went in search of firewood while Babbitt and Rowland stood near the carriage and stretched their legs, stiff from hours of cramped riding. A dozen Cheyenne dog soldiers rode unnoticed to the crest of a ridge above the hollow where Babbitt had halted and stood in plain view for several moments while surveying the scene below.

Abruptly the prairie stillness was shattered by a shrill war cry mingled with the drumming hoofbeats of running Indian ponies as the warriors raced down on the surprised whites. Babbitt sized up the situation in a glance, yelled at Rowland to grab a rifle, and reached for his double-barreled shotgun in the back of the buggy. He fired both charges at the oncoming braves without noticeable effect, then pulled his revolver and shot at the closest Cheyenne. But the canny dog soldier was not to be taken so easily; he crouched low along his pony and the slugs whined harmlessly over his head. Sutherland, realizing they were outnumbered, ran for his life. One Cheyenne, anxious to count first coup, yipped and gave chase. He caught the fleeing man in forty yards and plunged a lance deep into Sutherland's back.

At the carriage Rowland screamed piteously as a volley of arrows struck him. Even as he slumped to the ground the frenzied braves sent shaft after shaft into his body until a score of arrows bristled like quills from his lifeless form. Babbitt was another matter. Pistols empty, he snatched up his shotgun and clubbed several Cheyennes as they closed for the kill. One brave dismounted in the turmoil and worked his way behind

[31] Journal History, October 4, 1856.

[32] Julia Ann Babbitt, *New York Herald*, July 25, 1857; *The Mormon*, August 1, 1857. Shortly before Babbitt left Fort Kearny for Utah he wrote a letter to his brother-in-law Joseph Ellis Johnson, editor of the *Council Bluffs Bugle*. Dated September 1, 1856, the letter explained that Babbitt had arrived from Florence, Nebraska, in two and a half days, "the best time I have Ever Made." He went on to say that he found his train had been destroyed by "Shianns" and his teamsters either killed or wounded, except for Parrish. "My hole train goods, &c. became a Spoil to the Indians," he wrote. The original of this letter is in the possession of Rufus D. Johnson of Washington, Utah, a son of Joseph Ellis Johnson. Mr. Johnson very generously provided me with a copy.

the defiant white man who was crashing blows on Indians left and right. The warrior leaped into the buggy and from this vantage point swung his tomahawk in a short, wicked chop. Babbitt dropped in a bloody heap, his skull split.[33] Drunk with victory, the Cheyennes plundered and fired the carriage, rounded up the mules, and, as a final symbol of their coup, scalped the three bodies.[34]

The Indians rode west in a wide sweep which eventually took them to Fort Laramie. There they approached a French trader and attempted to barter some of the stolen goods.[35] But the Frenchman, recognizing the spoils, feared that they would be reclaimed and refused to deal. He made a mental note of the four mules, a few pieces of jewelry (among which were Babbitt's gold watch and seal ring),[36] and a quantity of gold coin.[37] Confronted by the local Indian agent, Thomas Twiss, and accused of murder, the Cheyennes admitted the slaying and told Twiss they had followed Babbitt's party for nearly two days while waiting for the right

[33] Details of the savage ambush of Babbitt's party were published in the *Council Bluffs Bugle* and reprinted in *The Mormon* for April 18, 1857. See also the *Crescent City Oracle*, May 22, 1856, and the *Millennial Star*, Vol. XIX, p. 443.

[34] According to Captain W. J. Hawley, a Mormon emigrant train leader quoted in *The Mormon*, April 18, 1857, Captain H. W. Wharton at Fort Kearny had recovered a number of Babbitt's papers "and some of his hair." Wharton also found some bones believed to be Babbitt's remains. *Millennial Star*, Vol. XIX, p. 443.

[35] A Mr. Archambeau [Auguste Archambault?], owner of a wagon train out of Green River, passed Ash Hollow and gathered up documents which had been scattered over the prairie, and delivered them to Captain Wharton. In the recovered property were the bank drafts for $13,000. See Wharton to Deas in *Transactions of the Kansas State Historical Society*, Vol. IV, pp. 494–95. Edward Martin's handcart company met the Green River train on September 19, 1856, and was informed of Babbitt's fate; four days later they passed the hollow and found "a little harness, two wheels and the springs of a burnt carriage or buggy . . . ." Jaques, "Some Reminiscences," *Salt Lake Herald*, December 8, 1878. The Green River train had taken most of the remains with it to Fort Kearny, and Wharton's patrol screened the debris for whatever else could be salvaged. Joel Hills Johnson, another of Babbitt's brothers-in-law, accompanied Mrs. Babbitt to Fort Kearny in June of the following year, 1857, and were shown by Captain Wharton "a bundle of papers belonging to the late A. W. Babbitt." Included were five drafts for $1,000 each and a bank note for $8,000, all of which Wharton had been ordered to return to Washington. See Joel Hills Johnson, "Journal." MS, p. 53. See also Joseph L. Heywood, "Diary." MS, p. 30.

[36] *Crescent City Oracle*, May 22, 1856; *Millennial Star*, Vol. XIX, p. 443.

[37] Julia Ann Babbitt, *New York Herald*, July 25, 1857; *The Mormon*, August 1, 1857.

moment to strike. They were certain he would be carrying a great deal of plunder. Babbitt fought "like a grizzly bear," they said.[38]

As far as the army and the federal government were concerned, the attack on the secretary's ox train and the death of Babbitt himself were no more than additional statistics for the growing list of Indian depredations on the plains.[39] But when Orrin Porter Rockwell pulled into Fort Laramie with Franklin D. Richards, Joseph A. Young, James Ferguson, and others on September 19,[40] there were those at the trading post who took one look at Babbitt's stock among Rockwell's five wagons and eleven yoke of oxen and decided the Mormon Destroying Angel had notched another victim, an accusation which eventually would reach Washington.[41]

[38] *Council Bluffs Bugle*, reprinted in *The Mormon*, April 18, 1857.

[39] Captain Wharton at Fort Kearny and Captain William Hoffman, commanding officer at Fort Laramie, were convinced that Babbitt's death was caused by Indians, and both officers said so to the victim's widow when she visited the two posts on a fact-finding mission the following year. See Johnson, "Journal," pp. 50, 53, and *Transactions of the Kansas State Historical Society*, Vol. IV, pp. 494–95.

[40] F. D. Richards and Daniel Spencer, "Journey From Florence to G. S. L. City," *Deseret News*, October 22, 1856.

[41] Achilles, *Destroying Angels of Mormondom*, pp. 16–17, paints a lurid picture of Rockwell's role in Babbitt's death. Uninhibited by evidence, Achilles states:

Upon the departure of Babbitt [from Great Salt Lake City in April], the jealousy of [Brigham] Young was aroused, and Rockwell was sent out on a special mission, which was no more nor less than to kill Babbitt as soon as he could find him. Rockwell joined Babbitt's train, and followed it to the Missouri River. Babbitt was suspicious and wary, and kept close under cover of the train, and for the time baulked the murderous hero of our narrative. Rockwell remained at Atchison until Babbitt returned from Washington. The latter was away about two months, and on his return took a train at Council Bluffs, and proceeded on the north side of the Platte to Fort Kearney. Rockwell left Atchison and intercepted Babbitt at Kearney, where the two trains joined. At this point Babbitt, with his companion, Sutherland, and his teamster, left camp and proceeded on toward Ash Hollow. The night of that day Rockwell and two others — both Danites — left on horseback and overtook Babbitt and his companions while they were in camp, between Fort Kearney and Ash Hollow. As soon as Rockwell and his companions reached camp, they opened fire on Babbitt, which was returned, Rockwell losing his horse at the first volley. Babbitt's companions were met a short distance away, and the Danites, approaching them as friends, killed them with their pistols. Babbitt continued the fight single-handed, and was overpowered and riddled with bullets, after a gallant defence. Rockwell captured the $20,000, and paid it over to Brigham Young on his return to Salt Lake. The Mormons announced that Babbitt and Sutherland were killed by the Indians.

Franklin D. Richards' report to Brigham Young pointed out that Rockwell tried to stop Babbitt from leaving the fort with only two guards. Richards said: ". . . Babbitt felt a foreboding of this [Indian] mischief, he wanted [James] Ferguson and some others to leave me and come with him. Porter tried to stop him, but he would

Indian Agent Twiss was not at Fort Laramie to dispel the rumors and clear Rockwell's name; he was at that moment on his way to Andrew Drips's Trading Post, the agency on the Upper Platte, for a powwow with a delegation of Cheyenne chiefs in relation to the plains war. At this parley the chiefs freely confessed the ox train attack and Babbitt's killing as well as other depredations committed by members of the Cheyenne tribe.[42] Twiss's report of the Indian conference was routinely filed with the Office of Indian Affairs, where it was relegated to the official oblivion of government correspondence. Eight months later, when the President of the United States sent an armed force to Utah to suppress a non-existent "rebellion," one of the underlying reasons for the military expedition was a charge that Babbitt had been murdered by Mormons, not Indians.[43] Had President Buchanan only thought to investigate the accusation, he would have found part of the answer at his fingertips in the Twiss report.

Because heavy snows choked the trail through the mountains, Rockwell thought it best to wait at Fort Laramie until it was safe to go on. It was a wise choice, for handcart companies attempting the final leg of their tortuous journey became snowbound, and scores perished before relief parties from Great Salt Lake could reach them. By October 26 Rockwell had gone as far as Fort Bridger, where he paused to have his oxen shod.[44] He drove his team into Great Salt Lake City on Novem-

---

come. . . . He had about $1,500 in cash, besides papers. The carpet for the statehouse was cut up pretty badly. . . ." Journal History, October 4, 1856.

Further evidence that Mormons were innocent of Babbitt's death is found in the journal of Joel Hills Johnson, Mrs. Babbitt's brother. Johnson, on March 23, 1857, says: "Having been councilled by Pres. Brigham Young to go with my sister Julia Ann Babbitt . . . to Council Bluffs City to transact some business appertaining to the estate and also make what discoveries we could in reference to his death on the plains, I commenced . . . to make the necessary arrangements." Johnson, "Journal," p. 41. It seems unrealistic that Brigham Young would have encouraged an investigation if he had ordered the crime committed.

[42] "Report of the Secretary of the Interior," *Senate Executive Document No. 5*, 34th Congress, 3rd Session, 1856, pp. 650–54; "Report of the Secretary of the Interior," *House Executive Document No. 1*, 34th Congress, 3rd Session, 1856, pp. 650–54.

[43] Resignation of Associate Justice W. W. Drummond, published in the *New York Herald*, April 1, 1857, and *The Mormon*, April 18, 1857. See also "Utah Expedition," *House Executive Document No. 71*, 35th Congress, 1st Session, 1858, pp. 212–14.

[44] Huntington, "Journal." Vol. II, p. 106.

ber 4, having been gone seven months.[45] Again he discovered he was a new father; two months before, on August 5, 1856, Mary Ann had given birth to a daughter, Sarah Rockwell.[46]

While Rockwell had been away the Magraw–Hockaday mail contract had been canceled, and a Mormon, Hiram Kimball, had been awarded the contract on a bid of $23,000 — some $13,000 less than Magraw had asked.[47]

That the Kimball bid was in reality Brigham Young's doing is revealed in a letter dated March 27, 1857, from the church leader to Horace Eldredge, his business representative in St. Louis: "The mail will be carried in the name of Hiram Kimball. This was considered the best course to secure the contract." But the contract specified that service would begin December 1, 1856, and because Magraw still carried the mails, it was not until mid-January that the Mormons learned they had been favored with the contract. Brigham Young moved with amazing speed. He demanded that only the toughest and best riders in the church carry the mails, and that the first run be made within three weeks. The postal service was to be the foundation of the Brigham Young Express and Carrying Company, and it was an enterprise Young meant to hang onto. Hiram Kimball, once a man of affluence in Nauvoo, had fallen on sad days. Since he would receive payment for the mail contract, he was responsible for obtaining its stock and riders. Kimball sought out the most competent men he could find, primarily those with horses capable of making the grueling trips. His first choices were Rockwell and Bill Hickman. After preliminary haggling, Kimball agreed to their terms:[48] Rockwell would carry the mail from Great Salt Lake City to Fort Laramie and Hickman would take it the rest of the way to Independence.[49] Hickman

[45] Journal History, November 4, 1856; and Hosea Stout, "Journal," Vol. 6, p. 48, and Brooks, On The Mormon Frontier, Vol. II, p. 604.

[46] Utah Genealogical and Historical Magazine, Vol. XXVI, p. 156.

[47] Unofficial announcement of the bid award was contained in a letter from John M. Bernhisel in Washington to John Taylor in Great Salt Lake City, published in the Deseret News, January 14, 1857.

[48] Rockwell's consent must have been gained at a steep price, for there had been bad blood between the two. In 1844 Rockwell took exception to something Kimball had said in Nauvoo and gave him a savage beating. In reporting the fight, the Burlington Hawkeye for October 3, 1844, commented, "Two or three Sundays since, O. P. Rockwell and Mr. Kimball had a fist combat, in which Rockwell was victorious and gave Kimball a fine chase through the streets, though Rockwell's shirt was torn off."

[49] Hickman, Brigham's Destroying Angel, p. 113.

later reconsidered his hasty acceptance. His arguments were futile; Brigham Young was unyielding: "No!" he said. "You are the very man; get your bays and roll out; you can go."

"I obeyed reluctantly," Hickman wrote. "I dreaded the trip, knowing I would have to be gone three months or more, suffer many privations, be at a heavy expense, and the way they had things fixed, not make a dollar." [50]

Hickman's dissatisfaction with his end of the bargain was the first seed of a growing discontent in the rough, cruel killer, a nurturing hatred which eventually would set him against his church and friends. But for the time being he did as he was told. Leaving Great Salt Lake City with the first mail on February 8, he arrived at Devil's Gate station a month later and pulled into Independence on April 11, a far cry from the twenty days the trip was expected to have taken. Hickman's premonition of the hardships involved in the journey came true, heavy snow in the mountains had made travel nearly impossible. [51]

Rockwell followed Hickman with a wagonload of supplies, leaving two hundred pounds of flour at Devil's Gate, where the station-keepers were starving, and distributing the remaining provisions among the other express stops along the route. [52] While he was refitting in Independence, Rockwell kept his eyes open for several mules bearing the YX brand known to be missing from one of the stations. Just outside of town he spotted the federal government's Pacific Wagon Road Survey camp and rode in to inquire about the lost livestock. Unfortunately, he was unaware

[50] Ibid.

[51] In Hickman's own words: "We were ten days going the first hundred and thirteen miles, to Fort Bridger, with the best of animals. We were fifteen days on the bleak desert going from Fort Bridger to South Pass. We would travel all day, tramp the snow and lead our animals, which, with great difficulty, we could get to travel very slow. At night we would camp on some knoll that the snow was blown off of, and by a poor sage brush fire cook a camp-kettle of coffee and another of corn, having got out of provisions, all but a sack of corn I had taken along to feed the horses. Several of these nights I thought I would freeze to death, but stood it better than any of the others. . . . We finally got to Independence, men and animals tired out, having been two months and three days making the trip." Ibid., pp. 114, 116.

[52] Deseret News, May 20, 1857. See also Daniel W. Jones, Forty Years Among the Indians, A True Yet Thrilling Narrative of the Author's Experiences Among the Natives (Salt Lake City, 1890), p. 102. A brief account of this mail trip can be found in Joseph M. Tanner, John Riggs Murdock, A Biographical Sketch (Salt Lake City, 1909), pp. 114–20. The mail party left Great Salt Lake City, March 1, 1857.

that the survey party superintendent was none other than William M. F. Magraw, Utah's ex-mail contractor.[53] Magraw recognized Rockwell and, having never forgiven the Saints for their treatment of him, roused the camp, shouting for the teamsters to "grab a rope and string the Mormon bastard up!" A young man of twenty-one jumped forward and protested the order, diverting attention long enough for Rockwell to draw his guns.[54] Nodding thanks to the young man, he carefully backed his horse out of the camp. Seething, Magraw harangued his men to rush the Mormon before he escaped, but not a single teamster was willing to challenge the stranger. Rockwell sank spurs to his horse and struck the trail for Fort Laramie.

Once at the fort his stay was brief, for a Mormon team on the Independence–Laramie run brought in twenty-four sacks of mail for Great Salt Lake City, the first delivery from the East since November 13, 1856. Rockwell's entry into the city on the final leg of the route brought him accolades from the editor of the *Deseret News*:

> . . . and much credit is due to Mr. John Murdock, conductor to Laramie, and to Mr. O. P. Rockwell, conductor from that point to this city, for the perseverance, prudence and energy displayed in the transportation of so large a mail in such good time and condition, especially at a time when the east half of the route was nearly destitute of forage and grain was scarce and high priced. . . . The contents of one sack was slightly damp, but in no wise injured, the carriers having crossed a swollen stream under the impression, from their appearance, that the sacks were waterproof, which is not the case, a fact that it will be well to keep in mind. . . .[55]

A fresh postal delivery in Zion was good news, but what the mail contained was not. From newspapers and periodicals weeks out of date the Mormons learned that Associate Justice W. W. Drummond, who had fled the territory several months earlier, had submitted his resignation to the Attorney General and charged the Church of Jesus Christ of Latter-day

[53] M. M. Long and O. H. O'Neill, "Journals of the Eastern and Central Divisions of the Fort Kearney, South Pass, and Honey Lake Wagon Road, June 4, 1857, to October 8, 1859," Records of the Secretary of the Interior, National Archives.

[54] John I. Ginn, "Mormon and Indian Wars, the Mountain Meadows Massacre and Other Tragedies and Transactions Incident to the Mormon Rebellion of 1857, Together With the Personal Recollections of a Civilian Who Witnessed Many of the Thrilling Scenes Described." MS, p. 15. Hereafter cited as "Mormon and Indian Wars."

[55] *Deseret News*, June 3, 1857.

Saints with an assortment of crimes ranging from simple treason to murder, plain and fancy. Thumbing through the pages of eastern newspapers, the outraged Saints read in angry disbelief Drummond's denunciation of their religion and their leaders:

> In the first place, Brigham Young, the governor of Utah Territory, is the acknowledged head of the [church] . . . and, as such head, the Mormons look to him, and to *him alone*, for the *law* by which they are to be governed; therefore no law of Congress is by them considered binding in any manner. . . . I know that there is a secret oath-bound organization among all the male members of the church to resist the laws of the country, and to acknowledge no law save the law of the "Holy Priesthood," which comes to the people through Brigham Young direct from God; he, Young, being the viceregent of God and Prophet, viz.: successor of Joseph Smith, who was the founder of this blind and treasonable organization. . . .
>
> . . . I am fully aware that there is a set of men, set apart by special order of the church, to take both the lives and property of persons who may question the authority of the Church; the names of whom I will promptly make known at a future time.
>
> . . . the records, papers, &c., of the Supreme Court have been destroyed by order of the Church, with the direct knowledge and approbation of Governor B. Young. . . .
>
> . . . the federal officers are daily compelled to hear the form of the American government traduced, the chief executives of the nation, both living and dead, slandered and abused from the masses, as well as from all the leading members of the Church, in the most vulgar, loathsome, and wicked manner that the evil passions of men can possibly conceive.
>
> . . . that Captain John W. Gunnison, and his party of eight others, were murdered by the Indians in 1853, under the orders, advice, and direction of the Mormons; that my illustrious and distinguished predecessor, Hon. Leonidas Shaver, came to his death by drinking poisoned liquors given to him under the order of the leading men of the Mormon Church in Great Salt Lake City; that the late Secretary of the Territory, A. W. Babbitt, was murdered on the plains by a band of Mormon marauders, under the particular and special order of Brigham Young, Heber C. Kimball, and J. M. Grant, and not by the Indians, as reported by the Mormons themselves, and that they were sent from Salt Lake City for that purpose, and that only; and as members of the Danite Band they were bound to do the will of Brigham Young as the head of the church, or forfeit their own lives. . . .[56]

[56] For Mormon comment, see *The Mormon*, April 18, 1857. Months later when Gentile merchants were leaving Utah for the duration of hostilities, William Bell,

Drummond closed his indictment of the church by suggesting that Brigham Young be replaced as governor and his successor be reinforced by military troops. Until then, he said, "it is noonday madness and folly to attempt to administer the law in that Territory." Drummond's hot words succeeded beyond his wildest expectations in striking a telling blow against the Mormons he so despised. His allegations and the ensuing wave of public resentment against the Saints spawned by misconception and ignorance prompted President Buchanan to order an army to Utah.[57] Even as the Mormons were reading of Drummond's arraignment, the first elements of the Utah Expedition were forming at Fort Leavenworth in Kansas.[58]

Buchanan had acted before first determining whether the accusations were just and without examining the character of the magistrate upon whose veracity he placed such weight. Had he done the latter, the President would have discovered that when Drummond had accepted the federal post in Utah in 1854, he abandoned a wife and family in favor of a Washington, D.C., woman whom he brought West and passed off as

---

partner in the firm of Livingston and Bell, journeyed to California and then to New York. In an interview published by the *New York Herald* on February 23, 1858, Bell refuted Drummond's charges and exonerated the Mormons. He told the *Herald* that Gunnison's men and Babbitt were the victims of Indian attacks; of that, he said, "There is no room for doubt." As for Judge Shaver, Bell, a Gentile member of the Mormon community for seven years, was invited to serve on the coroner's jury investigating that official's death. "There were no grounds for the insinuation of the Judge being poisoned by the Mormons," Bell said. The *Herald* interview was reprinted by the *Deseret News*, May 12, 1858. Drummond's resignation in full can be found in *House Executive Document No. 71*, 35th Congress, 1st Session, 1858, pp. 212–14.

[57] After Drummond's resignation appeared in print the editorial columns of eastern newspapers fairly erupted with letters from outraged, but anonymous, contributors offering first-hand knowledge of insubordinate, even treasonable acts by the church and the "horrors of Mormonism." Written under such pen names as "Goliath" and "The Little Villain" (Drummond himself used the pseudonym of "Amicus Curiae" on occasion), a stream of venom was directed at the Saints. On all sides New York newspapers were inflaming popular opinion, urging Buchanan not to repeat the mistakes of his predecessors who had appointed and retained Brigham Young, that a "firm and fearless man for governor" was wanted, and that "the Mormons will not rebel when they are convinced that they cannot conquer; they will not fight when they understand that the United States will put down their rebellion at whatever cost." See April 1857 issues of the *National Intelligencer*, and *New York Times, Tribune, Sun*, and *Herald*.

[58] President Buchanan's decision to send a military expedition to Utah was made official May 20, 1857, and reported in the *New York Times*, May 21, 1857.

242

Mrs. Drummond. It became commonplace to see her sitting beside him on the bench while court was in progress.[59] Bill Hickman, a practicing attorney by profession, heard of her and boasted that should he have a murder case before Drummond "and he had that woman on the bench, I would kick them both out of the house." The threat reached the judge's ear, and he promptly issued a warrant for Hickman for contempt of court. Said the gunman, "I heard of it when I got in town, and said if he served a writ on me I would horsewhip him. It was not served." [60] Public indignation, both Gentile and Mormon, swelled at this scandalous behavior and finally provoked the judge's flight from Utah. Had Buchanan possessed these facts, the Utah Expedition might never have been.[61]

---

[59] An entire catalogue of Mormon charges against Drummond's character and moral values is outlined in an open letter from W. I. Appleby, who served as clerk of the Supreme Court for Utah Territory, to *The Mormon*, May 23, 1857. Appleby's correspondence with *The Mormon* was reprinted in the *Millennial Star*, Vol. XIX, p. 401, *et seq*. Other exposures of Drummond's misbehavior with the woman Ada Carroll were carried in *The Mormon*, June 13, 20, and July 4, 1857. Jules Remy observed of Drummond, ". . . [he] lives openly with a woman all the world knows not to be his wife." Remy, *A Journey to Great-Salt-Lake City*, Vol. I, p. 208. Remy remembered Drummond as the "magistrate who had the boldness to declare in our presence that 'Money is my God' . . ." Ibid., pp. 208, 469.

For evidence that Drummond had not divorced his wife, see her letter to a sister and brother-in-law, Mr. and Mrs. Silas Richards, in Great Salt Lake City, dated September 4, 1856, and published in the *Deseret News*, May 20, 1857; reprinted in *The Mormon*, July 25, 1857.

[60] Hickman, *Brigham's Destroying Angel*, p. 111.

[61] Before the reader declares this to be a gross oversimplification, it should be understood that I am cognizant of the factors considered by many to have had, in one respect or another, an effect in precipitating the call for troops to Utah. That is to say, I am aware of the pressures brought to bear by the "runaway" federal officials (1851); the constant wrangling between Brigham Young and the territory's Indian agents; William M. F. Magraw's vitriolic "Mr. President" letter of October 3, 1856; Thomas Twiss's complaints in his letter to the Commissioner of Indian Affairs (July 13, 1857); and the public's general abhorrence of the Mormon practice of polygamy. Having examined these influences at length, I am persuaded that while they each contributed to the popular support initially extended to Buchanan's order, the decision itself to send an army was predicated almost entirely on Drummond's vicious and unsubstantiated accusations. In support of this position, see Jules Remy's thoughtful commentary on Drummond's frame of mind after having been publicly reviled for his outrageous conduct with Ada Carroll: "They who desire to ascertain the earliest causes of this costly campaign [the Utah Expedition], must search for them in the illicit union of this magistrate with his charming Ada. The contempt with which he was overwhelmed by all within his jurisdiction when the fact got wind, the spite he felt and the vengeance he chose to take by such means as shame and hatred to dictate to ignoble minds — all this it was, insignificant as it seems,

In New York *The Mormon* began categorically denying Drummond's smear. The newspaper brushed off as pure fabrication the stories of the Gunnison massacre and Judge Shaver's death being Mormon-inspired. Concerning the murder of Almon W. Babbitt, the paper published a letter from his widow absolving the church of any connection with the slaying. "I have not a shadow of suspicion that white men were in anyway concerned in his death. The newspaper story that he was killed by 'Mormons' to the contrary notwithstanding," she wrote after outlining her investigation into the matter.[62]

---

that brought about the crisis by which a nation was led to throw millions to the winds. History, alas! is full of wars which were not a particle wiser." Remy, *A Journey to Great-Salt-Lake City*, Vol. II, p. 343.

By May 1857 Drummond had made his way to Washington, to be "available" for an expected call from Buchanan appointing him governor of Utah Territory, backed by a sufficient military force to depose Brigham Young. The *New York Times* correspondent provided this descriptive account in the issue of May 18, 1857:

> Much interest is excited here by the arrival of Hon. W. W. Drummond, late judge of Utah Territory, who is now a guest of Brown's Hotel. The Judge, who is the "observed of all observed," is, in his personal appearance, very different from [what] the community have generally conceived. In height he is not quite six feet tall. He is well built, possessing evidently a good constitution, with an iron will and a fixed determination of purpose. I find that he is of Scotch-Irish genealogy; reared and educated in the State of Virginia. He removed to Illinois 19 years since, and is now in his 37th year. Today it seems well understood that Judge Drummond will be tendered the office of Governor of Utah . . . and I have it from the judge himself that he will accept upon condition that Gen. Harney is sent into the country with force sufficient to enable the officers to enforce the law. In case Gen. Harney and Judge Drummond go to Utah backed by the government, the Mormons will yield or be compelled to find refuge in another country. They are both cautious but bold men.

Drummond's star burned brightly for only a moment in history; the rise to power and national prominence he so desperately sought did not come. No Territorial governor at the head of U.S. troops would he be. Instead, his fall was swift and crushing. His shame as a profligate and a libertine followed him east, and by 1865 he was convicted of two counts of fraud and divorced as an adulterer. See *Daily* (Salt Lake) *Telegraph*, January 20 and May 25, 1865. Abraham O. Smoot, former mayor of Great Salt Lake City, on business in St. Louis, Missouri, in 1880, was interviewed by a reporter who introduced Smoot to a "seedy person" later identified as W. W. Drummond. The reporter said the former chief justice was a sewing machine company agent. See *Deseret News Weekly*, December 5, 1880. Drummond was arrested on June 28, 1885, and sentenced to a House of Correction for stealing postage stamps in Chicago, and died in a Chicago grogshop on November 20, 1888.

[62] Julia Ann Babbitt, *New York Herald*, July 25, 1857; *The Mormon*, August 1, 1857.

Mrs. Babbitt's brother, Joseph Ellis Johnson, editor of the *Crescent City* (Iowa) *Oracle*, wrote in the issue of May 22, 1857:

> We notice in the letter of resignation, of Hon. W. W. Drummond to Attorney-General Black, that he there, among other very grave charges, asserts that the Hon. A. W. Babbitt was murdered by white men disguised as Indians, by order of the authorities of Utah.[63] In justice to the parties thus maligned, we will state that we have taken much pains to gather all the information possible calculated to throw light upon the death of our relative, Mr. Babbitt, and the particulars connected with the same; and we have not a shadow of doubt but that Indians of the Cheyenne nation murdered him for revenge and plunder. . . .

Through it all, Brigham Young maintained what can best be described as a detached interest. He only shrugged at the furor, for similar

---

[63] This theory of "white Indians" under the control of Brigham Young has been aired before. Waite, *The Mormon Prophet and His Harem*, pp. 24–25, writes:

> In the summer of 1862, Brigham was referring to this [Babbitt] affair, in a tea-table conversation, at which Judge Waite and the writer of this were present. On that occasion, after making some remarks to impress upon the minds of those present the necessity of maintaining friendly relations between the federal officers and the authorities of the church, he used language substantially as follows: "There is no need of any difficulty, and there need be none, if the officers do their duty, and mind their own affairs. If they do not, if they undertake to interfere in affairs that do not concern them, I will not be far off. *There was Almon W. Babbitt. He undertook to quarrel with me, but soon afterwards was killed by Indians.* He lived like a fool, and died like a fool."

Italics in original.

Another author had the same to say. Samuel Bowles, *Our New West; Records of Travel Between the Mississippi River and the Pacific Ocean* (Hartford, 1869), p. 266, commented: ". . . Mr. Babbitt, Secretary of the Territory, had a quarrel with [Brigham] Young, and was murdered." It is more than likely that Bowles merely was repeating Mrs. Waite's statement since he offered no new information.

There are several references to "white Indians" in Utah. William Chandless, *A Visit to Salt Lake; Being a Journey Across the Plains and a Residence in the Mormon Settlements at Utah* (London, 1857), p. 240, says he was speaking to a Utahn in Great Salt Lake City and the man mentioned "that Brigham had a number of sham Indians (white men in disguise) to attack and kill those trying to leave the territory. . . ." According to Richard F. Burton, *The City of the Saints and Across the Rocky Mountains to California* (London, 1861), p. 449, Orrin Porter Rockwell had knowledge of the existence of such a band of men. Burton says that Rockwell advised him of the best route to take out of Utah to "avoid 'white Indians,' the worst of their kind." Stenhouse, *Rocky Mountain Saints*, p. 401n, says: "There is a strong impression among even 'good Mormons,' as well as among the Gentiles . . . that some of the murders of 'apostates' were committed by '*white Indians*,' and in justification of much of that impression the Tabernacle sermons may be cited. There is, besides, much circumstantial evidence to justify the accusation."

attacks had been made in the past by other federal officials — to no avail. The Mormon attitude to such Gentile utterances had always been made abundantly clear by Young's counselor, Jedediah M. Grant, whose fiery tongue won for him the cognomen of "Brigham's Sledgehammer." As far back as March 2, 1856, for instance, in response to denunciatory letters abusive to the church, Grant had taken the Tabernacle rostrum and stormed:

> If they want to send troops here let them come to those who have imported filth and whores, though we can attend to that class without so much expense to the General Government; we can wipe them out cheaply and quickly, for they are only a few in number.
>
> They will threaten us with the U.S. troops! Why your impudence and ignorance would bring a blush to the cheeks of the veriest camp-follower among them. We ask no odds of you, you rotten carcasses, and I am not going to bow one hair's breadth to your influence. I would rather be cut into inch pieces than succumb one particle to such filthiness. . . . If we were to establish a whorehouse on every corner of our streets, as in nearly all other cities outside of Utah, either by law or otherwise, we should doubtless then be considered good fellows.[64]

For all of Jedediah Grant's vituperative oratory, an army had indeed been ordered to Zion, and the Saints were going about their business without a hint of the dark clouds gathering over their promised land. With spring, mountain trails opened and Orrin Porter Rockwell headed east with the July mail. A month earlier John Murdock had covered the distance between Great Salt Lake City and Independence in fifteen days, an average of eighty miles a day; now Rockwell was intent on bettering that time. A hundred miles or so east of Fort Laramie he chanced on A. O. Smoot, mayor of Great Salt Lake City, and a good friend, Judson Stoddard. The two men were pushing YX stock west.

Joining them at Smoot's behest, Rockwell was told of the impending march on Zion by federal troops. Smoot said he had been in Independence and was refused the mail for Utah. Pressing for a reason, the mayor was told by the Independence postmaster that the government had ordered an army to suppress a Mormon rebellion, that Brigham Young had been ousted as governor, and that another governor along with a full complement of federal officials was accompanying the troops to Great Salt Lake City. YX officials in Independence also learned that the Kimball contract had been cancelled abruptly by Congress for the company's

[64] *Journal of Discourses*, Vol. III, pp. 234–35.

failure to begin operations according to the schedule handed down by the Postmaster General.[65] Brigham Young's dream of monopolizing the mail, freight, and passenger service in the Great Basin thus died aborning.

By the time Rockwell, Smoot, and Stoddard reached Fort Laramie, Smoot had made up his mind to send news of the oncoming troops ahead to Brigham Young while the main party continued to drive the livestock. On the evening of July 18, he, Stoddard, and Rockwell hitched two span of the fastest mounts in the YX corral to a light spring wagon and raced for Great Salt Lake City, five hundred and thirteen miles away. With the master hand of Rockwell at the reins, the wagon flew along the trail. Mile after mile passed under the team's churning hooves. Expertly trotting the horses at intervals calculated to conserve their energy, Rockwell coaxed, cajoled, and cursed them into fantastic speeds. Five days and three hours after they had put Fort Laramie behind them, the three dusty and exhausted Mormons galloped into the city — only to find it deserted![66]

Since early morning of that day, July 23, a seemingly endless line of wagons and carriages had inched up Big Cottonwood Canyon to the shores of Silver Lake, an emerald pool captured by the craggy reaches of the Wasatch Mountains some twenty-five miles from the city. Nestled amid the snow-splashed peaks, this vale in the sky was to be the scene of the tenth celebration marking Mormon entry into Great Salt Lake Valley. Light artillery, a detachment of Brigham Young's Life Guards, a platoon of lancers, and a company of infantry, all from the territorial militia, lent a military flavor to the festivities. The air was vibrant with sound as the stirring rhythms of six brass bands echoed from one mountain to another. Nearly twenty-six hundred persons formed a line of march in five hundred vehicles up the twisting canyon trail.

[65] Since the Mormons were not aware until January 1857 that Kimball had been awarded the contract, they could not have commenced service on the stipulated date of December 1, 1856. The contract, then, was obviously annulled for other reasons. Albert G. Browne, correspondent for the *New York Tribune*, writing in *The Atlantic Monthly*, penned an article entitled "The Utah Expedition," Vol. III (1859), p. 367, in which he observed, ". . . The Postmaster General . . . annulled the contract held by certain Mormons for the transportation of the monthly mail to Utah, ostensibly on account of non-performance of the service within the stipulated time, but really because he was satisfied the mails were violated either enroute or after arrival at Salt Lake City." For further commentary regarding suspected Mormon tampering with the mail, see letter dated October 12, 1857, from Colonel Edmund B. Alexander to Brigham Young, Military Records Section, Utah State Archives.

[66] Edward W. Tullidge, *History of Salt Lake City* (Salt Lake City, 1886), p. 157. Letter from A. O. Smoot to Tullidge, dated February 14, 1884, from Provo.

Into this remarkable setting rode the three messengers, Rockwell, Smoot, and Stoddard. With them was Elias Smith, postmaster of Great Salt Lake City, to whom they first had reported the government's refusal to turn over the mails. The quartet arrived at noon and sought out the pavilion tent occupied by Brigham Young. Their report only confirmed what he had been expecting for months. The political climate in the East had made the Mormons an opportune target for a variety of schemers who recognized the "polygamy issue" as a perfect diversion. Young quietly assembled the leading elders in the gathering and conducted a brief council meeting, outlining this latest turn of events. Then the Mormon prophet stepped from his tent to address the assembled Saints.

Solemnly Young repeated a declaration he had made when the pioneers first entered the valley. "Give us ten years of peace, and we will ask no odds of Uncle Sam or the devil," he had said on that day. As he told the multitude before him of the approaching invasion by federal soldiers, he said, "God is with us and the devil has taken me at my word." [67] The church leader then added a prophecy which brought hurrahs from his audience. "In twelve years," he said, "I will either be President of the United States or will dictate who shall be!" [68] On this enthusiastic note the Mormon cavalcade began retracing its steps down the steep canyon road to the city.

On July 26 Heber C. Kimball faced a large gathering of Saints in the Bowery. In typically colorful language, Kimball prepared the Mormons for the days to come. Throughout his oration the crowd chorused "Amen!" Said the angry counselor in conclusion:

> . . . I have been driven five times, been broken up and my goods robbed from me, and I have been afflicted almost to death. . . . I feel to curse my enemies, and when God won't bless them I do not think he will ask me to bless them; if I did it would be to put the poor curses to death who have brought death and destruction on me and

[67] As related in Stenhouse, *Rocky Mountain Saints*, p. 351; Bancroft, *History of Utah*, p. 504; and William Alexander Linn, *The Story of the Mormons* (New York, 1902), p. 483. See also *Deseret News*, September 23, 1857, and *Journal of Discourses*, Vol. V, pp. 226–27.

[68] Stenhouse, *Rocky Mountain Saints*, p. 351; Bancroft, *History of Utah*, p. 505; Linn, *Story of the Mormons*, p. 483. Stenhouse, p. 352n, adds, "The 'twelve years,' and a few more have passed away since Brigham uttered the prediction that he should be President of the United States, and he is today [1873] further away from its fulfilment than he was when he announced to the believing Saints in Cottonwood Cañon this ambition of his soul."

my brethren, upon my wives and my children that I buried on the road between the states and this place. . . . Send 2,500 men here, our brethren, to make a desolation of this people? God Almighty helping me, I will fight until there is not a drop of blood in my veins. Good God! I have wives enough to whip out the United States, for they will whip themselves: Amen.[69]

While Mormon apostles were berating Buchanan's precipitous action, Orrin Porter Rockwell rode wearily home; more than likely his only thought was of a soft bed and the first good night's sleep in nearly five months.

[69] *Deseret News*, August 12, 1857. See also Brigham Young's fiery message to the Saints that day in the Bowery, in which he said: ". . . I guess that James Buchanan has ordered this Expedition to appease the wrath of the angry hounds who are howling around him. . . . Russell and Co. will probably make from eight to ten hundred thousand dollars by freighting the baggage of the Expedition. . . . But woe, woe to that man who comes here unlawfully to interfere with my affairs. Woe, woe to those men who come here to unlawfully meddle with me and this people. . . ." *Journal of Discourses*, Vol. V, pp. 77–78.

Chapter Thirteen

A CALL TO ARMS

Eight companies of the United States Tenth Infantry, the entire Fifth Infantry, and two batteries of artillery, one pulling four six-pound and two twelve-pound howitzers, the other a field battery of four twelve-pounders and two thirty-two-pounder siege cannons, had been on the march along the overland trail toward Utah for nearly two weeks before the first order came down to commanders of the Nauvoo Legion in preparation for the defense of Zion. Lieutenant General Daniel H. Wells outlined the church's official attitude in his directive of August 1, and in something less than the usual curt military vernacular, he explained:

> In such time, when anarchy takes the place of orderly government and mobocratic tyranny usurps the power of rulers, they [the people of the Territory] have left the inalienable right to defend themselves against all aggression upon their constitutional privileges. It is enough that for successive years they have witnessed the desolation of their homes; the barbarous wrath of mobs poured upon their unoffending brethren and sisters . . . . They are not willing to endure longer these unceasing outrages; but if an exterminating war be purposed against them and blood alone can cleanse pollution from the Nation's bulwarks, to the God of our fathers let the appeal be made.
>
> You are instructed to hold your command in readiness to march at the shortest possible notice to any part of the Territory. See that the law is strictly enforced in regard to arms and ammunition, and as far as practicable that each Ten be provided with a good wagon and four horses or mules, as well as the necessary clothing, etc., for a winter campaign. . . .[1]

---

[1] Lieutenant General Daniel H. Wells to district military commanding officers, Nauvoo Legion, August 1, 1857, Military Records Section, Utah State Archives, and Vaux, "The Echo Canyon War," *The Contributor*, Vol. III (1882), p. 177. "Vaux" was Junius F. Wells's pen name; he was Daniel Wells's son.

Shortly thereafter Brigham Young and General Wells selected officers of the Legion to conduct the campaign. Wells, as commanding officer, would answer only to Young. Generals George D. Grant, William H. Kimball, James Ferguson, and Hiram B. Clawson comprised the staff, with Colonels Robert T. Burton, Nathaniel V. Jones, James W. Cummings, Chauncey W. West, Thomas Callister, William B. Pace, Warren S. Snow, Joseph A. Young, and Albert P. Rockwood heading field operations. Since the Mormons planned to engage the troops before they reached the valley, a decision was made to emphasize the use of cavalry as a guerrilla force in harassing military columns and disrupting supply trains. Chosen for this special role were Rockwell, Hickman, and Major Lot Smith.[2] For reasons best known to Wells and Young, both Rockwell and Hickman operated independently of the Legion as captains of ranger companies of one hundred men each. With Smith, the two Mormon guerrilla leaders were accountable only to Wells and Young.[3]

Two "corps of observation" were ordered into the field to keep an eye on the approaching army. One, commanded by Colonel Robert T. Burton, left at once, while the other, a volunteer company led by Captain Andrew Cunningham, went out a month later, ostensibly to found a settlement on the Snake River near Fort Hall. It was known as the "Blackfoot Mission," but its true purpose was to be on the northern route of the Utah Expedition in case the army should detour by way of Soda Springs and Fort Hall — to watch its movements and report.

Still another patrol of a dozen Mormons under Marcellus Monroe was ordered north with instructions to scout Ogden Canyon, traverse the mountains to Bear Lake, move up the Bear River valley, cross the mountains by way of Lost Creek to the Weber, and so to Ogden. The object of their reconnaissance was to familiarize themselves with mountain passes

<hr />

[2] Vaux, "Echo Canyon War," *The Contributor*, Vol. III, pp. 216–17.

[3] Hickman, *Brigham's Destroying Angel*, pp. 123–24. Lot Smith's official title was major of the "1st Battalion of Cavalry." *Deseret News*, April 29, 1857.

in the vicinity and to locate sallying points and places of retreat in the event war became a reality.[4]

Into this sputtering powder keg rode Captain Stewart Van Vliet, assistant quartermaster of the U.S. Army. Displaying an astonishing naïveté, the War Department had assigned Van Vliet to precede the Utah Expedition and determine exactly what forage and fuel would be available for the convenience of the advancing troops upon their arrival. He also was to locate a site near the city suitable for a military post from which the army could control the "rebellious" Mormons. Van Vliet was treated with the utmost courtesy and had no trouble gaining an interview with Brigham Young — a meeting which proved disappointing to the soldier. The captain found his Mormon hosts less docile than expected. He was told in unmistakable terms that the people of Utah considered the approaching Expedition no more than an enemy invading force, and accordingly, no forage or fuel would be sold it. Furthermore, Young added sternly, the soldiers would not be permitted to enter the valley! The Saints did not intend to submit meekly to conquest.[5]

Van Vliet left the city somewhat in sympathy with the Mormons, promising to intercede on his own authority since he suspected that the Expedition's leader, Brigadier General William S. Harney, would be relieved of command. Van Vliet's guess was accurate. Two weeks earlier Harney had been ordered to duty in Kansas, and Colonel Albert Sidney Johnston had been assigned to replace him. So it was that while Van Vliet and Brigham Young were concluding their discussions, Johnston was riding to Fort Leavenworth to take charge of the Utah Expedition.

[4] Roberts, *Comprehensive History*, Vol. IV, pp. 246–47.

[5] The audacious spirit of the Mormons in defiance of federal intervention perhaps can be no better illustrated than by the letter from Adjutant General James Ferguson submitted on the eve of Capt. Van Vliet's departure from Great Salt Lake City. In it, Ferguson asks his antagonists for the means with which to thwart them:

> On behalf of the Militia of the Territory I would feel much obliged by your forwarding to me from the General Department of War one or more copies of the latest and most informed editions of authorized works on Infantry Tactics, Heavy and Light Artillery service — Cavalry Tactics, Fortifications, Regulations for the Army and others as you may judge useful to us. We have received a few copies of *Hardee's Light Infantry and Rifle Drill* which will answer our present needs in that line.
>
> The difficulty in procuring such works so far from the seat of Government furnishes my apology for thus troubling you.
>
> Wishing you all success your desire [*sic*] and rapid promotion in all honorable service.

Brigham Young Letter Book No. 23, September 14, 1857.

On September 16 two companies of cavalry led by Colonel Philip St. George Cooke trotted out of Leavenworth as a guard for the newly appointed governor of Utah, Alfred Cumming, a ponderous Georgian who was taking to Zion a wife, the political acumen acquired as mayor of Atlanta, experience as a superintendent of Indian Affairs, and a wagon crammed with official stationery. Cumming was surrounded by an entourage of federal appointees. A day later Johnston started west with his staff and an escort of forty dragoons. Roughly twelve hundred soldiers were now on the march to the land of the Mormons.

Meanwhile, Van Vliet rode out of the Saints' mountain kingdom; he, too, traveled with a retinue. At his side were Rockwell, Nathaniel V. Jones, and Stephen Taylor, who provided safe conduct for the officer as far as Ham's Fork, one hundred and forty-five miles east of the city.[6] As the captain waved farewell to his three guardians, he was ignorant of the fact that other Mormons were watching his every move. So effectively did they carry out this mission that Van Vliet was under undetected surveillance until he reached the Missouri River. General Wells boasted in later years, "When [Van Vliet] made his report I had men in his camp watching him."[7]

The captain labored many hours over his official report. With painstaking effort he detailed for his superiors a cautious estimate of the situation. Because of the change in command, Van Vliet had been unable to interfere and turn back the troops; thus, he felt an added burden of responsibility in expressing Brigham Young's determination to resist any trespass. A miscalculation on Van Vliet's part could have cost the lives of many men on both sides. In the end he was careful to make plain the adamant Mormon refusal to provide forage or fuel for the army, and he strongly underscored Young's intention to pursue a scorched earth policy.

I told them [the Mormons] that they might prevent the small military force now approaching Utah from getting through the narrow defiles and rugged passes of the mountains this year, but that next season the United States government would send troops sufficient to overcome all opposition. The answer to this was invariably the same: "We are aware that such will be the case; but when those troops arrive they will find Utah a desert. Every house will be burned to the ground,

[6] Journal History, September 14, 1857; *Deseret News*, September 16, 1857. Rockwell was back in the city by September 20, according to the Journal History.

[7] George Alfred Townsend, "Interview With the Mayor of Salt Lake," *The Mormon Trials at Salt Lake City* (New York, 1871), p. 33.

every tree cut down, and every field laid waste. We have three years' provisions on hand, which we will 'cache,' and then take to the mountains and bid defiance to all the powers of the government." . . . The Mormons occupy [Fort Bridger] at present, and also have a settlement about ten miles further up Black's fork [more precisely, on Smith's Fork], called Fort Supply. These two places contain buildings sufficient to cover nearly half the troops now enroute for Utah; but I was informed that they would all be laid in ashes as the army advances. . . ."[8]

By September 21 Colonel Robert T. Burton and his seventy Nauvoo Legionnaires were at Devil's Gate caching the provisions necessary for future operations. His orders also directed him to protect any scattered groups of Saints returning to the valley with remnants of YX property, and to maintain forward observers for intelligence. Burton's instructions were to keep the federal forces in sight at all times and report on their strength and equipment. The following day his outposts sighted elements of the Tenth and Fifth Infantry Regiments which had moved out of Leavenworth on July 18 under the command of Colonel Edmund B. Alexander. Burton camped within a half-mile of the enemy position that night.

Every movement of Alexander's command was reported immediately to General Wells, who established Legion headquarters first at Fort Bridger and then at Cache Cave at the head of Echo Canyon. Information reached Wells swiftly through an ingenious system of Mormon express riders, hardy men astride the fleetest horses in the territory.[9] Anxious to protect the supply columns ahead of his troops, Alexander issued orders for a series of forced marches calculated to take the infantry to Ham's Fork, some twenty miles northeast of Fort Bridger. There the soldiers would await Cooke's cavalry and Colonel Johnston. But the Mormons were of another mind, entertaining little desire for the army to be so near. Minutes after Burton's express reined up at Cache Cave with the news,

[8] Van Vliet to Captain Alfred Pleasanton, assistant adjutant general, Army for Utah. For full text see "Utah Expedition," *House Executive Document No. 71,* 35th Congress, 1st Session, 1858, pp. 24–26. See also Vaux, "Echo Canyon War," *The Contributor,* Vol. III, pp. 147–49.

[9] Junius F. Wells, writing under his pseudonym "Vaux" in *The Contributor,* remarked, "The system of expressing information to and from Salt Lake City by daring hardy men, mounted on mustang horses, was most thorough and safe . . . . There was no movement of the enemy from the time Col. Burton approached them at Devil's Gate, on the Sweetwater that our officers were not speedily apprized of." Vol. III, pp. 178–79.

Wells determined to slow the enemy advance. Wilford Woodruff confided in his journal, "[The Army] will be at Pacific Springs tonight and our brethren will commence operation upon them." [10] The method was simple: Rockwell would lead a raid against the column and run off its mules. Selecting five reliable men, Rockwell set out on the first Mormon action against the United States government.[11] His route was planned to cross the infantry line of march the following night, and with Rockwell's knowledge of the terrain the interception was an absolute certainty. The raiders spotted Alexander's bivouac at Pacific Springs shortly before two o'clock on the morning of September 25 and silently moved into position. Each man checked his guns — and unmuffled the clapper of a huge brass cowbell.

Captain Jesse A. Gove, a Tenth Infantry company commander, was sleeping when Rockwell's signal shot exploded directly behind his tent. The captain instinctively tumbled out of bed at the alarm. "The whole herd of mules stampeded with a terrific rush," Gove wrote his wife. "Herders commenced the halloo and cry, 'Soldiers turn out, we are attacked.' It was an hour when everybody was sound asleep." [12] While Gove groped for his trousers, a young civilian teamster, John I. Ginn, who had bedded down under a wagon, was jarred awake in time to see the six riders charging through camp, firing revolvers, clanging cowbells, and filling the night air with warwhoops. Ginn watched the mules stampede from the remuda. "Here was a plight for a whole regiment to be placed in," he thought, "without a mule to move a wagon." [13]

By the time Gove had pulled on his suspenders, and grabbed his hat, sword, and pistol, "the enemy had disappeared with the mules, our companies were dismissed and we all retired to bed." Rockwell and his raiders had roared through the camp unscathed because they had taken the precaution of maneuvering between tent rows so that any shots fired in their direction placed troops in the facing row in danger.

[10] Wilford Woodruff Journal, MS, September 25, 1857, as recorded in Roberts, *Comprehensive History*, Vol. IV, p. 272n.

[11] Ginn, "Mormon and Indian Wars," p. 7. See also Jesse W. Crosby, "The History and Journal of the Life and Travels of Jesse W. Crosby," *Annals of Wyoming*, Vol. XI (July 1939), p. 211.

[12] Jesse A. Gove, *The Utah Expedition, 1857–1858; Letters of Capt. Jesse A. Gove, 10th Inf., U.S.A., of Concord, N.H., to Mrs. Gove, and Special Correspondence of the New York Herald*, edited by Otis G. Hammond (Concord, N.H., 1928), p. 64.

[13] Ginn, "Mormon and Indian Wars," p. 7.

Colonel Alexander rushed from his tent and called the regimental bugler to sound Stable Call, hoping the stampeding animals would turn. At the moment the gesture seemed futile, but a single stroke of bad luck cost the Mormons their victory, and, ironically it was a cowbell that turned the tide of fortune. Gove explained what occurred in the minutes after the stampede: "The bell mule by the merest accident got caught by the picket rope in a wild sage bush, stopping him, and with him most of the herd stopped." [14]

When Stable Call came blaring through the night, the mules wheeled and headed full speed back to camp to an expected bag of oats. Ginn watched this comedy of errors in wonder. "The mules had come to know this call to eat," he said, "and the clear, ringing notes of the bugle had scarcely died away when the heels of the mules could be heard hitting the road again. Directly they came dashing into camp in a bunch, together with six additional animals wearing saddles and bridles — the whole Mormon mount." [15] A mile away, Rockwell stood transfixed in the center of the trail trying not to believe that the worst had happened. Only moments before, he and another raider had dismounted as the last mule passed, preparing for a rear-guard action in case the troops attempted pursuit. And by the sheerest coincidence, the four other Mormons riding at the head of the milling herd — now thoroughly confused by the tangled bell mule's frantic clanging — had climbed from their saddles to await Rockwell and congratulate themselves. At that very instant the brassy tones of the bugle sounded in the distance, and the mules turned and stampeded back to camp, taking the six Mormon horses with them — to the despair of their owners. [16]

[14] Gove, *Utah Expedition*, p. 65.

[15] Ginn, "Mormon and Indian Wars," p. 7.

[16] Ibid., pp. 7–8. See also Hosea Stout, "Journal," MS, Vol. 7, p. 48, and Brooks, *On The Mormon Frontier*, Vol. II, pp. 638–39. Stout's entry for "Monday 28 Sept 1857. At day light [E. W.] Van Etten and Jesse Jones came into camp on express from the East said that the attempt of our troops to stampede our

Within an hour the small unmounted command had rendezvoused to plan their next move, preferably one designed to extricate them from their predicament. "When I report back," snorted Rockwell, "it'll be on a horse." His men echoed the sentiment. The best plan, Rockwell decided, would be to follow Alexander's troops until they camped the following night, then "borrow" remounts from the army.

Taking to the brush, the raiders made for the Little Sandy three miles below the trail and lay in concealment. The Expedition reached the location about dusk and bivouacked on a grassy flat nearby. From a distance Rockwell could see the tents rising and tired soldiers preparing for bed. Late that night, when the campfires dwindled to warm coals, he ordered his men forward. Stealthily they crept toward the picket lines, carefully keeping themselves between the corral and the stream. Suddenly they heard the whinny of a horse; not ten rods away a string of saddled ponies grazed peacefully. Cutting fifteen of the animals free, the Mormons waded the Little Sandy until safely out of earshot, then, reflecting on their good fortune, mounted and headed for the Big Sandy River, where a strong force of Legion cavalry was headquartered.

It was early morning when the raiders reached their destination, thankful that they had been spared the embarrassment of returning on foot. Rockwell was relaxed in the saddle waiting to report when the cavalry commander stepped from his tent. The Mormon officer took one look at the stolen horses and bellowed, "How in the name of Heaven did you get those animals?" Chagrined, Rockwell explained the abortive mission and its consequences. A look of distress clouded the officer's features. "Those animals belong to us!" he snapped. "They were stolen from a raiding party we sent to the Little Sandy two days ago to cripple Alexander's advance." [17]

Although the Pacific Springs sortie had failed, it set the pattern for

---

enemies animals had proved a failure the animals being tied down or Hobbled with iron hobbles. this happened at the Pacific Springs on Friday night last [.]"

[17] Ginn, "Mormon and Indian Wars," pp. 8–9.

Mormon resistance — a vigorous hit-and-run campaign of harassment against the better-trained but poorly equipped infantry.[18] Supplies were destroyed or stolen, grass and forage burned, horses and mules stampeded, and civilian teamsters terrified by stories of Mormon Danites.[19] Considering Alexander's line of march, General Wells concluded that the troops would chance an advance on Great Salt Lake City through Echo Canyon, the same trail the Saints had used in '47. Orders were posted for Colonel Nathaniel V. Jones to begin construction of fortifications in the nearly twenty-five miles of narrow defile which wound toward Fort Bridger. Jones first set his men carving trenches atop the precipitous walls, then he devised a network of small dams along the canyon to permit a small but deadly flood to sweep the wagon road if necessary. A series of breastworks studded the skyline, and a score of huge boulders were delicately balanced on the canyon rim — should the troops reach this point, they would be crushed beneath an avalanche.[20]

[18] When Colonel Johnston assessed his clothing supplies for 2,500 men he found such items as 8 sashes, 675 pairs of boots, 600 pairs of stockings, and only 723 blankets for troops camped 7,000 feet above sea level in the winter. For the complete inventory see "Utah Expedition," *House Executive Document No. 71*, 35th Congress, 1st Session, 1858, pp. 106–7.

[19] Among the teamsters who had been hired to drive supply wagons in advance of the Army was a boy of eleven, William F. Cody, who three years later would gain fame as a rider for the Pony Express and subsequently become a noted hunter, scout, guide, and Indian fighter. Another young man on the scene as a teamster was James B. Hickok. "Wild Bill" and young Cody became life-long friends. In his autobiography, Cody recalled that Hickok "was ten years my senior — a tall, handsome, magnificently built and powerful young fellow, who could out-run, out-jump, and out-fight any man in the train. He was generally admitted to be the best man physically, in the employ of Russell, Majors & Waddell; and of his bravery there was not a doubt." William F. Cody, *The Life of Hon. William F. Cody, Known As Buffalo Bill, the Famous Hunter, Scout, and Guide* (Hartford, 1879), pp. 69–70.

[20] Because both sides were under orders to shed blood only in self-defense, the so-called Utah War has sometimes been described as a "bloodless campaign." It was not, however, without casualties in the ranks, and the raid at Pacific Springs produced the first of those military statistics. Capt. Gove wrote home: "One man in H Co., Capt. Tracy's died of fright. He had the heart disease, and the sudden fright killed him. Was buried this morning by his company." Gove, *Utah Expedition*, p. 65. Five days later the Nauvoo Legion lost its first "soldier" — shot to death by his best friend. It was at sunset in Echo Canyon. A number of Legion members were fortifying the high crags of the canyon. Hosea Stout entered the circumstances in his diary for Sept. 30: "A man by the name of Frederic Nielsen, a dane and who had been a soldier and good marksman took a yager [rifle] and deliberately took aim at and shot William Simmons through the head. The ball entering his left

While Alexander, disturbed by lack of orders and the delay in Johnston's appearance, trudged on toward a major supply train rendezvous at Ham's Fork, Wells's staff whipped up plans for two large-scale raids intended to leave the Utah Expedition bereft of provisions. The first encounter came September 28 as the infantry plodded southwest from Green River. The column was fat with stocks and stores. In addition to the supplies acquired at the Ham's Fork rendezvous, Alexander had overtaken one wagon train at the Big Sandy and another on the Green. Again the civilian teamster, Ginn, describes the action:

My mess, consisting of nine mounted men (besides a cook) was engaged in driving the beef cattle then with the army. Promptly at dark the Tenth Regiment took the road, followed by the several wagon trains, and we rounded up the beef cattle and started them off. By this time the cattle had become so well trained and so accustomed to following the wagon trains that we had no trouble with them whatever. They would keep close up to the rear of the (corn) train though we might be three miles behind or off the road hunting. On this night we were riding along leisurely, not realizing how rapidly the army was moving on a forced march, so that when we passed through the train on the divide, about midnight, we were fully four miles behind the regiment.

Soon after we passed through it a force of Mormon cavalry under Bill Hickman descended upon it, set fire to the wagons and consumed them and their contents. Hickman soon afterward told me in Salt Lake City that his force stood in a cedar forest half a mile south of the road when the regiment and its wagon trains passed, and that he started to fire the train when he heard horses' hoofs coming up from Green River, when he turned back under cover and waited until a small squad of mounted men (which was myself and my eight companions) passed. The same night or early next morning Hickman's and other Mormon cavalry burned up the two large supply trains [from] Green river and Big Sandy — thus depriving the army of about 500,000 pounds of provisions intended for its maintenance during the long and severe winter then setting in. . . .[21]

Now that the Mormons had struck a solid blow against the army, Wells moved quickly to press the advantage. He sent cohorts of the Legion to ravage the remaining government trains and ordered Forts Bridger and

temple and coming out his right ear. Simmons never spoke [fell over] and expired. What was strange they were both of one Co. and good friends and Nielsen knew the distance was within dead range. Nielsen was put under arrest and the body of Simmons sent home." See also Lorenzo Brown, "Journal" (1823–1900), MS, p. 290.

[21] Ginn, "Mormon and Indian Wars," pp. 9–10.

Supply put to the torch. The scorched earth policy was now a reality. At eight o'clock on the morning of October 1, a Legion company was dispatched to Fort Supply to "thrash, burn, or cache grain" as circumstances dictated.[22] Two days later Rockwell rode into the outpost and ordered everything burned. Moving wagons and horses to a safe distance, the Mormons fired more than a hundred log houses, a sawmill, gristmill, and a threshing machine. The stockade, straw, and grain were set aflame as the last Mormon rode out. One of them, Jesse W. Crosby, recalled, "Owners of the property in several cases begged the privilege of setting fire to their own, which they freely did, thus destroying at once what they had labored for years to build, and that without a word." [23]

His orders carried out, Rockwell raced to Fort Bridger in time to see the last roaring timber of the old trading post crash to the ground in a fountain of sparks visible for miles in the pitch black mountain night. Major Lewis Robison, who had applied the match eight hours before, estimated property loss at $2,000.[24] When Jim Bridger, who had hired on as Alexander's guide, saw the ruins a month later he cursed the Mormons for robbers and thieves, claiming that they had driven him out, stolen his fort, and now finally destroyed it. On the other hand the Saints stoutly denied the trapper's charges, maintaining that they had legally and properly bought out Old Gabe.[25]

Late on the night of October 3 Rockwell and Hickman were sent express to join Major J. D. T. McAllister's company near Black's Fork. Fresh from a council of war with General Wells, Rockwell had specific

[22] Journal History, October 25, 1857, p. 11.

[23] Crosby, "History and Journal, etc.," *Annals of Wyoming*, Vol. XI, pp. 212–13.

[24] Journal History, October 25, 1857, pp. 13, 15.

[25] Until recently the sale of Fort Bridger was a hopeless muddle, but the discovery of certain documents in Salt Lake City tends to verify the Mormon position. If LDS Church records are disregarded as perhaps biased, the first real evidence of the sale is found in Hickman, *Brigham's Destroying Angel*, p. 118, where he says that in 1855 he had "been one of the carriers of the heavy load of gold it took to purchase said place [Fort Bridger] with the stock and goods thereon." According to an indenture located in Salt Lake County Mortgage Records, Book B, pp. 125–27, in the Salt Lake County Recorder's Office, Lewis Robison made a final payment of $4,000 to Louis Vasquez, acting for the firm of Bridger and Vasquez, for the purchase of the fort, its property and improvements, on October 18, 1858. A second indenture in Mortgage Records, Book B, p. 128, dated August 3, 1855, outlines agreement of sale and recognizes the down payment of $4,000. It is signed "Jas (his mark X) Bridger; Louis Vasquez, per H. F. Morrell, agent." There is a very real possibility that the sale was made by Vasquez without Bridger's knowledge.

instructions to recruit forty men from McAllister's command and attempt either to stampede the government cattle at Ham's Fork or fire the forage in the army's path.[26] Henry Ballard, one of the volunteers, detailed the events of the next few days in his journal:

> Oct. 4th: We started again for the Soldiers camp 40 of us led by Orin Porter Rockwell our plan was to drive off their cattle so as to cripple them in their movements but after 8 of us making the attempt we found that all the poor cattle was at the tail end of the camp which covered about 8 miles up and down the river so we had to give it up we then camped the remainder of the night in a large hollow only about one mile from them[.]
>
> Oct. 5th: We started through the hills to get in above them and passed a picket guard and then come over in plain sight of the camp and watered our horses and commenced burning grass only a half mile from their camp O. P. Rockwell posted himself so he could watch the camp and give us Signal they started after us about noon and we retreated into the Mountains till toward evening when we come back got supper and commenced fireing the grass again till it got too wet with dew to burn any longer we then camped at the end of the fire[.]
>
> Oct. 6th: In the morning we saw a picket guard on the hill above which had come there during the night we again commenced our work of fireing till noon when we heard the cannons fireing so we again retreated 9 of us went into the mountains a long way with O. P. Rockwell & Milo Andrews [Andrus] the others only went a short distance to wait till we came back, the 2 brethren went untill they could look down upon the camp and learned they had been placeing their cannon so they could protect their camp . . . .[27]

For the better part of a week Rockwell lay hidden near Alexander's camp, withdrawing only to report to Wells at Legion headquarters. On several occasions the scout edged close enough to eavesdrop on campfire conversations. He heard infantrymen complaining bitterly of raids engineered by Lot Smith in which three government supply trains involving about seventy-five wagons were captured and transformed into a $100,000 bonfire near Green River.[28] Smith's strike had pushed troop

[26] Manuscript History of Brigham Young, p. 715.

[27] Henry Ballard, "Private Journal." MS, pp. 4–5. Compare with Newton Tuttle, "A Territorial Militiaman in the Utah War; Journal of Newton Tuttle," edited by Hamilton Gardner, Utah Historical Quarterly, Vol. XXII (October 1954), pp. 306–7.

[28] Lot Smith's personal account of the victory can be found in Vaux, "Echo Canyon War," The Contributor, Vol. III, pp. 272–74, and Vol. IV (1883), pp. 27–

morale to a new low. Already on strict rations, the soldiers knew that the loss of provisions was a staggering reversal.

Quietly Rockwell vacated his place of concealment and sent a messenger to General Wells apprising him of the rising discontent in Alexander's ranks; as an afterthought Rockwell tacked on a request for food to sustain his ranger company. The Mormon unit had been on short rations since leaving McAllister. A return express brought word that Burton's wandering command would bring up provisions eventually.[29] Rockwell was on the verge of abandoning his position to lead his men in search of victuals when Milo Andrus, an express rider and close friend, managed to reroute a wagonload of rations to the famished guerrillas. Typical of military logistics since time immemorial, Burton's supply detail came rolling up five minutes later. For the first time in a week Rockwell's company crawled out to its posts on full bellies. With the passing of each day the humdrum routine of spying on an indolent enemy grated on Rockwell, who craved a chance to erase the humiliating memory of Pacific Springs. His moment came on October 11 when Bill Hickman rode into camp with news of a huge herd of government cattle grazing unguarded in the vicinity of Camp Winfield, the Expedition's temporary post on Ham's Fork. A week earlier Lot Smith had sacked two wagon trains in the same neighborhood. Rockwell fairly jumped at the opportunity to rustle the stock.

Mustering his men, he set out to scout the terrain, but unexpectedly came across Lot Smith's bivouac five miles above Ham's Fork. Rockwell briefed Smith on the cattle herd and suggested a joint assault on the objective, a proposal to which the young major quickly agreed. Reconnoitering, the two guerrilla leaders found the situation precisely as Hickman

---

29. See also "Utah Expedition," *House Executive Document No. 71*, 35th Congress, 1st Session, 1858, p. 63. Smith's recollection of the Simpson Hollow encounter on October 5, 1857, written years later for *The Contributor*, described the manner in which one of his men suffered a serious gunshot wound. In the minutes after the wagon trains had been put to the torch, Smith said that he expected "at any moment to be overtaken by troops from the camp, and fired my pistol to call in our picket guards. . . . While I was reloading . . . one of the guns . . . was discharged. The heavy ball passed through Orson P. Arnold's thigh, breaking the bone in a fearful manner, struck Philo Dibble in the side of the head, and went through Samuel Bateman's hat just missing his head . . . ." Arnold, suffering greatly, was carried in the night to a mountaineer's camp on Green River 30 miles distant and left until other Legionnaires could move him to Great Salt Lake City for treatment.

[29] Wells to Callister, October 8, 1857, Military Records Section, Utah State Archives, and Journal History, October 25, 1857, p. 17.

had detailed it and retired to devise a plan of action. Ultimately it was decided to use Smith's full command, Rockwell's thirty rangers, plus a picked contingent from Burton's company, bringing the striking force to a hundred strong. Smith's attitude toward his long-haired comrade was one of aloof tolerance. "I did as I pleased," he explained, "and Rockwell, regularly, damned me for it." [30] But united in a common purpose they endured each other. Both men sensed that a successful raid on the army herd could well mean victory for the Mormon cause; without beef the Utah Expedition faced certain starvation during the fast-approaching winter.

As the guerrillas assembled in the hills, Rockwell felt an uneasiness about the lack of sentinels on the livestock. Suspecting a trap, he confided his apprehensions to Smith, who responded with a jeering laugh.

Bristling, Rockwell retorted through tight lips that Alexander had discovered what a "damn fool" Smith was and had planted an ambush for him.

Momentarily taken aback by Rockwell's rebuke, Smith wiped a coat sleeve across his mouth, scratched his bearded chin, and then prodded his horse down the bluff toward the cattle. Fully two-thirds of the Mormon raiders were left behind in the major's haste to reach the herd. Nettled by Smith's reckless action, Rockwell boiled down the slope shouting a string of curses — at the major for riding too fast and at the command for failing to keep up. Out in front by nearly a hundred yards, the two Mormon warriors pounded across the meadow, whipping their horses to greater speed at the sight of infantry picket guards hurrying to drive off the herd.

In later years Lot Smith recalled the guards' panic at the spectacle of a hundred well-armed Mormon cavalrymen exploding into view: "The boys then gave a shout, such as imported steers never heard before, and the latter started away pell mell, trodding many of the poorer under their [hooves] and killing half a dozen of them. The guards were frightened as badly as the cattle and looked pale as death. . . ." [31]

Quickly the raiders separated the livestock into small, easier to handle bunches and moved them out, leaving behind twenty of the poorest animals for the teamsters' food supply. As he was about to leave, Rockwell turned in his saddle and shouted for the wagonmaster, a man he knew

---

[30] Vaux, "Echo Canyon War," *The Contributor*, Vol. IV, p. 48.

[31] Ibid., p. 49. All details of the raid are taken from *Lot Smith's Narrative*, "Echo Canyon War," *The Contributor*, Vol. IV, pp. 48–50.

only as Rupe:[32] "You, Rupe! When you get to camp tell Colonel Alexander that we've stopped playing games. We'll kill every damned blue coat in his command unless he turns our men loose.[33] Do you hear me, Rupe?" Rockwell's features were pulled into the meanest expression he could conjure up for the Gentile.

Lot Smith struggled to keep a straight face when the trembling wagonmaster blanched and came near fainting. "He was the worst frightened man I ever saw," Smith remembered. "When the guards started for camp they ran the three teams until some of the cattle dropped dead, but they never stopped until they got within the lines."

Spurring forward, the two Mormons soon caught up with their men and the rustled herd, which a rapid count showed to number nearly fourteen hundred head. As they rode together through the night reflecting on the events of the day, Rockwell would occasionally let out a chuckle. Even his strait-laced companion was forced to grin at their coup. Twenty-five years later Smith said:

> During the whole of the time while we were engaged driving off this herd and fitting out the guards, a company of two or three hundred soldiers was visible on the bluff. I have never been able to account for their inactivity. They appeared to be interested in our movements, but they made no attempt to interrupt or help us. . . . Rockwell went in with the cattle, very much to my regret. I never found many men like him. I think our officers were afraid that he and I could not get along together. But we could.[34]

At Smith's camp Rockwell changed horses, galloped on to Fort Bridger with news of the successful foray,[35] and then reported directly to General Wells at Cache Cave. He was ordered to return to Smith's command, cut out such steers as were necessary to sustain the Legion, and drive the remainder to Great Salt Lake City. It was October 17 before Rockwell passed the cave again, this time at the head of 624 steers and 4 mules.[36]

---

[32] This would have been James Rupe, general agent for Majors & Russell, assigned to accompany the supply trains.

[33] Vaux, "Echo Canyon War," *The Contributor*, Vol. IV, p. 49. At this point in the hostilities the army had captured three supposed Mormons (two of them Bill Hickman's brothers).

[34] Ibid., pp. 49–50.

[35] Tuttle, "Journal," *Utah Historical Quarterly*, Vol. XXII, p. 309.

[36] Journal History, October 25, 1857, p. 17; Ballard, "Private Journal," p. 7; *New York Times*, December 28, 1857.

Standing in the road, his arms and chin resting on the saddle of his mount, Rockwell glanced up from a brief reverie while his drivers pushed across the Bear River ford. A young man was walking toward him. There was something vaguely familiar about the youth that Rockwell could not quite place; then at once he knew. It was the young fellow who had taken Rockwell's part in the Pacific Wagon Road Company camp near Independence the day Magraw had tried to lynch him.[37] Now, four months later, the youngster had managed to elude Mormon scouts swarming in the mountains and was strolling happily along the road to Great Salt Lake City. Hailing the wanderer, Rockwell learned that his benefactor's name was John I. Ginn, late of the Utah Expedition. Offering his belated thanks, Rockwell listened with amused interest as the young Gentile told of his travels since their last meeting.

Ginn, it seemed, had experienced a change of heart near South Pass, quit the Wagon Road Company at Fort Laramie, and obtained temporary employment as a herdsman with Alexander's regiment rather than risk a winter season in the Rockies under Magraw's questionable leadership.[38] But after the unnerving night raid on the Expedition's mules at Pacific Springs (Rockwell probably smiled at the mention) and Hickman's unopposed attack on the wagons three days later, Ginn and a friend, Joe Franks, saw the handwriting on the wall. When word passed among the troops that Colonel Alexander planned to establish winter quarters at Fort Hall in Oregon Territory if Johnston did not arrive within a certain number of days, the two civilians had decided to part company with the military. Struggling through hip-deep snow toward Mormon lines, Ginn and Franks had been near death when captured by a Legion patrol near Black's Fork. They were taken to Fort Supply and two weeks later permitted under escort to join Rockwell's cattle drive to

[37] Ginn, "Mormon and Indian Wars," p. 15.

[38] Magraw by this time was up to his neck in trouble. The Interior Department was vexed because he had continually dawdled in taking the field and had accumulated excessive debts along the way, the party was on the verge of mutiny, and Magraw stood accused of misconduct by his chief engineer, Frederick W. Lander. The superintendent finally left the company and with 41 other members of the expedition offered his services to Colonel Johnston near Pacific Springs in the march against the Mormons. See "Reports of Fort Kearny, South Pass, Honey Lake Road, 1857–1861," Records of the Secretary of Interior, National Archives. For an excellent treatment of this period in Magraw's career, consult W. Turrentine Jackson, *Wagon Roads West, A Study of Federal Road Surveys and Construction in the Trans-Mississippi West, 1846–1869* (Berkeley, 1952), pp. 191–217.

Great Salt Lake City.[39] Since he was faster afoot than Franks and the mounted guard, Ginn outdistanced them and had reached the main wagon road when Rockwell hailed him.

Years later in his memoirs, Ginn told of the Mormon's genuine affection for him because of the episode in Magraw's camp. Rockwell had listened intently to Ginn's recital and after a few questions, remarked,

> that the ford at Bear River was rough, the current strong and the water cold, and then asked me to mount his mule and ride across to his camp on the opposite bank, remarking that he could jump on behind one of the boys driving the cattle and ride across himself.
>
> I rode across the river and up to the camp fire where four Mormons were cooking supper for the whole command. Recognizing the mule and seeing it in possession of a stranger and a hated Gentile at that, they did not know what to make of it. They were dumfounded, but looked daggers at me, and while I was hitching the mule one of them picked up his gun, brought it to a ready and demanded sharply: "Where did you get that mule?" I told him, when he put down his gun and went on with his cooking. When Porter Rockwell arrived in camp he introduced me to the principal men of his command, and after that I was treated with the greatest respect. After supper Rockwell took myself and Franks to one side and told us they desired to push the cattle a few miles further over that night to Yellow Creek, to the camp of General Wells, the commander in chief of the Mormon army, and promised us a good supper there if we would assist by following behind in the road and pushing up the laggards, while the mounted men would do the flanking and keep the cattle in the road. We did so and got the supper. . . .
>
> The next day [October 17] we moved on with the cattle, Rockwell proffering Franks and myself the finest dinner that could be gotten up in the city if we would help drive the cattle in. We gladly accepted the offer, as we had to follow Uncle Sam's cattle in anyway.
>
> At Cache Cave, at the head of Echo Cañon, we met a Mormon train going out with supplies for their army.[40] Porter Rockwell overhauled it and distributed necessities and luxuries to his own command, giving Franks and myself an equal share with his own men. Passing down Echo Cañon, with its bristling fortifications and great excavations made to flood the road and render it impassable, we

[39] Wells to Callister, October 14, 1857. Military Records Section, Utah State Archives. "Don't keep those teamsters or deserters too long to eat up your rations," Wells cautioned Callister. "You had better send them in with the cattle, in charge of some watchful men, who must be instructed to keep a strict guard on them."

[40] Hosea Stout, "Journal," Vol. 7, p. 55, and Brooks, *On the Mormon Frontier*, Vol. II, p. 642. Stout was in the supply train.

reached its mouth at the Weber river [and] found 1,600 Mormon troops encamped. . . .[41]

The drove of cattle reached the city on October 19, and the two Gentiles were given free rein. Rockwell, who had ridden in the night before, arranged for Ginn to stay at the home of "Mother Taylor," whose son, John, was a member of the Council of Twelve Apostles.[42] According to Ginn, "Rockwell advised me not to put up at the Townsend House (the only hotel then in the city), as there were several Gentiles stopping there, and that they were all under more or less suspicion." [43]

Twenty-one-year-old John I. Ginn had no way of knowing it then, but his Mormon friend had given him some excellent advice. While "Mother Taylor" showed her Gentile boarder his room, Orrin Porter Rockwell delivered the herd to church pasture lands, took his receipt from General Wells to Brigham Young, accounted for each steer, reported on the war situation as he saw it, and went home to his wife and family.

[41] Ginn, "Mormon and Indian Wars," pp. 15–17.

[42] Journal History, October 18, 1857.

[43] Ginn, "Mormon and Indian Wars," p. 17. Franks and Ginn apparently parted company after entering the city. Franks's name next appears the following April on a list of 150 persons who sought safe conduct from Great Salt Lake City under protection of the new territorial governor. See Gove, *Utah Expedition*, p. 291.

Chapter Fourteen

SIX FINE-LOOKING MEN

EARLY IN THE MONTH OF OCTOBER 1857, near Thousand Springs Valley, east of the head of the Humboldt River, a party of six Californians, led by two brothers, John and Tom Aiken, joined a wagon train of Carson Valley Mormons bound for Zion.[1] Riding with the Aikens were Andrew J. "Honesty" Jones,[2] Tuck Wright,[3] John Chapman,[4] and a Colonel

---

[1] Lyman Peters testimony in the *Salt Lake Tribune*, October 12, 1878. Much of what is known of the mysterious Aiken Party came to light during the trial of Sylvanus Collett for the murder of John Aiken. For this reason the court record is of vital importance, but unfortunately no official transcript is known to have survived. In its absence much of the material in this chapter was gleaned from daily accounts published during the trial by the *Tribune*, the *Deseret News*, and the *Salt Lake Herald*. The indictment and collateral court papers can be found in Utah County and Territorial Criminal Records, File 81, 82 (The People vs. O. P. Rockwell et al.), Utah County Clerk's Office, Provo, Utah.

[2] The Aiken brothers and Jones are identified in the *Valley Tan*, April 26, 1859; Ginn, "Mormon and Indian Wars," p. 20; and John Cradlebaugh, *Utah and the Mormons; Speech of Hon. John Cradlebaugh, of Nevada, on the Admission of Utah as a State. Delivered in the House of Representatives, February 7, 1863*, pp. 64–65.

[3] Guy Foote testimony, *Salt Lake Tribune*, October 10, 1878.

[4] Thomas Singleton testimony, ibid.

Eichard,[5] all of Mariposa County in southern California. In marked contrast to the Mormons, the six strangers projected an impressive image, one which suggested a certain gaudy affluence. All were mounted on fine

[5] *Valley Tan*, April 26, 1859. The identities of Colonel Eichard and John Chapman have not been previously established. The names of all six members of the Aiken Party are published here for the first time. Anthony Metcalf, *Ten Years Before the Mast. Shipwrecks and Adventures at Sea! Religious Customs of the People of India and Burman's Empire. How I Became a Mormon and Why I Became an Infidel!* ([Malad City, Idaho, 1888]), p. 36, says the Aiken Party was comprised of a father, a son, and four cousins. Still another account, picked up from California exchanges by the *New York Times*, March 16, 1858, provides a few more facts:

The Placerville *Index* publishes, as from a correspondent in Mariposa, the following information touching the recent murder of five American citizens by the Mormons, as to which alleged event various accounts have already appeared in our columns:

"The party of American citizens recently murdered by the Mormons were from Mariposa County. They were much respected, had many friends in this vicinity, and were useful and worthy members of society. The names of two of the party (brothers) are John and Thomas Aikens. They were formerly from Texas. A Mr. Eichard, another of the party, once kept a livery stable at Agua Frio, a few miles distant from this place. Honesty Jones, still another of the party, was constable of this township in 1854–5. All of them had means, (one of the Aikens $7,000,) [t]he accumulations of years of sweat and honest toil. They left here about the 1st of October last, as they stated, for the purpose of buying cattle for the California market, or if they found prospects unfavorable, with the intention of applying for a contract to furnish Col. Johnston's command with beef and other supplies. Failing in this they designed proceeding to the States. Letters from some of the party were received here about a month since, stating they had been arrested, robbed, and were then confined by the Mormons, ostensibly on the allegation of being spies of the Federal Government, but likely on the real ground of the crime of having money; and doubtless they were afterwards murdered on the principle that 'dead men tell no tales.' A general indignation prevails here at this flagitious outrage, and especially at the manner of the assassination of the two survivors of the *Indian* (!) attack after they had fled for refuge into the Salt Lake settlement. . . ."

horses fitted with silver-tooled Mexican saddles;[6] two or three of the men sported pink leggings, expensive finery for the prairie traveler.[7] John Aiken wore a heavy gold watch on a chain fashioned from dollar gold pieces with each fifth link a two-and-a-half-dollar coin.[8] The Californians were superbly equipped with pack animals, and one, an iron grey mule,[9] attracted as much attention as did John Aiken's white-faced sorrel.[10]

Anyone caring to search the packs would have found playing cards, dice, a faro layout, and a variety of other gaming paraphernalia necessary to the serious pursuit of Lady Luck. In short, the Aiken brothers and their friends were high-rolling gamblers looking for a mark — and they had chosen the men of the Utah Expedition as the likeliest prospects west of the Rockies. Because of this the Californians hesitated to discuss their plans with outsiders. Fully expecting the army to be in Great Salt Lake City by the time the wagon train arrived, the gamblers anticipated a bonanza — two thousand soldiers with money to burn.[11] Their silence was a serious error in judgment, for in explaining only that they intended to "join the army," the six gamblers focused suspicion on themselves long before they reached the Mormon stronghold.[12]

Fifteen miles west of the old Bear River Fort near Blue Springs, the Aiken Party said goodbye to the wagon company and set a course for Box Elder in northern Utah. From there they would follow the main road to the city. The Californians had no way of knowing that a messenger had been dispatched by the wagonmaster alerting the Nauvoo Legion to their presence.[13] Within hours, the unsuspecting travelers were arrested by men of Lot Smith's command in Weber County. Their property confiscated,

[6] Lyman Peters testimony, *Salt Lake Tribune*, October 12, 1878.

[7] Thomas Singleton testimony, ibid., October 10, 1878.

[8] Joseph M. Taylor testimony, ibid., October 11, 1878.

[9] Richard Ivie testimony, ibid.

[10] Guy Foote testimony, ibid.

[11] John R. Young, in a letter to Henry W. Bigler, dated January 31, 1858, indicates that some Saints believed the Californians had come to Utah "with the intention of starting a gambling hall and house of prostitution among the Mormons." See Henry W. Bigler, "Incidents (1857–1858)," a series of reminiscences published in the *Union* (St. George) from August 22 and December 12, 1896. This letter was published on November 21, 1896.

[12] John Ginn to Kirk Anderson, editor of the *Valley Tan*, published April 26, 1859. Ginn's letter was signed "J. J. G."

[13] Ibid.

the gamblers were hustled off to Ogden for questioning.[14] Next morning the prisoners were turned over to Colonel Chauncey West for transfer to Great Salt Lake City, where they were confined in the Townsend House as spies.[15] Mormons not assigned to Legion units in the field were rotated on guard duty over the six men until church authorities could reach a decision in their case.[16] Meanwhile, the captives were permitted some degree of freedom. Under the watchful eye of the sentry at the door, they were allowed visitors. One of the first to avail himself of the opportunity to chat with fellow Gentiles was Rockwell's young friend Ginn. In company with a Mormon, Joe Hunt, Ginn went calling.

> We went down to the hotel, ascended to the second floor and went to the open door of a large room in front of which an armed Mormon sentinel was pacing. Here we found six large, intelligent, manly-looking American mountaineers, somewhat grizzled by age. This was the Aiken party, for the subsequent murder of whom Brigham Young was afterward indicted. The party consisted of John and Thomas Aiken (brothers) who had been old scouts and guides for the army in the Indian wars of early days in California; A. J. Jones, an old grizzly bear hunter in Mariposa county, Cal., where he was well known and universally esteemed as "Honesty Jones," and three others whose names I never learned or have entirely forgotten. We talked with them awhile, and they appeared cheerful and not to apprehend any danger and only temporary detention. . . .[17]

At the time of his capture, Tom Aiken was discovered to be wearing a money belt crammed with gold,[18] and, according to Ginn, this had a

[14] Joseph M. Taylor testimony, *Salt Lake Herald*, October 10, 1878; *Salt Lake Tribune*, October 11, 1878.

[15] Hosea Stout, "Journal," Vol. 7, p. 57; Brooks, *On The Mormon Frontier*, Vol. II, p. 644, relates: ". . . six Cal prisoners taken at Box Elder supposed spies." Journal History, November 3, 1857, states: "Several California prisoners were taken today and brought into this city; they are supposed to be robbers from the mountains." See also Ginn, "Mormon and Indian Wars," p. 20.

[16] Hosea Stout, "Journal," Vol. 7, p. 59; Brooks, *On The Mormon Frontier*, Vol. II, p. 645: ". . . [November 9, 1857] I am guarding the prisoners from Cal."

[17] Ginn, "Mormon and Indian Wars," p. 20.

[18] The actual amount of gold in the Aikens' possession is a matter of controversy. In his testimony at the Collett trial, Guy Foote said Tom Aiken's money belt carried $20 gold pieces six wide completely around his body. See the *Salt Lake Herald* and *Salt Lake Tribune*, October 10, 1878. Ginn, "Mormon and Indian Wars," p. 20, says the sum reached $18,000. Yet, Ginn's letter to Kirk Anderson in the *Valley Tan*, April 26, 1859, claims $8,000. An editor's note by J. H. Beadle in

decided bearing on the fate of the Aiken Party. In his memoirs Ginn recalled that the following conversation took place as he and Hunt were leaving the Townsend House:

"What will the church authorities do with them?" Ginn asked his companion.
"Oh, they will turn them loose," Hunt replied.
"Will they let them go on to the army?"
"No," Hunt said.
"Will they let them return to California?"
"They will let them start back," Hunt replied.
"But will they get through?"
Here Ginn said Hunt replied, "No," with some deliberateness.
"Why not?"
"Because they have too much valuable plunder," Hunt answered.[19]

Ginn wrote that shortly thereafter Brigham Young issued an ultimatum to the Gentile mercantile firms of Gilbert & Gerrish and Livingston, Kinkead & Co. to either depart from the territory or "take their turn in the Mormon army." [20] Both firms chose to leave, and Ginn, with a number of other Gentiles, elected to join them before things became too uncomfortable in Zion. Each man paid a guide fee of $100, furnished his own provisions and bedding, and worked the passage by caring for and driving a team. Only one other formality remained; no one was now privileged to leave Utah Territory (which stretched from the Rockies to the Sierra) without written consent from Brigham Young. Ginn's "passport" read:

John Ingranam Ginn of Ackworth, Georgia, recently a Herdsman for the troops in the "Expedition against Utah" is hereby granted permis-

Hickman, *Brigham's Destroying Angel*, Appendix F, p. 207, estimates the party was worth $25,000 in gold and property. John R. Young writing to Henry W. Bigler, January 31, 1858, reported that the Californians possessed "24 revolvers, four thousand dollars in gold and . . . gambling apparatuses." See Bigler, "Incidents," the *Union*, November 21, 1896.

19 Verbatim conversation from Ginn, "Mormon and Indian Wars," pp. 20–21.

20 John Henry Kinkead was a remarkable young man who entered a wholesale dry goods establishment in St. Louis as a clerk at the age of eighteen and remained until his twenty-third year. He crossed the plains in 1849, and in partnership with J. M. Livingston opened the pioneer mercantile house in Great Salt Lake City known as Livingston and Kinkead. He turned his interests over to William Bell (who also was the city's postmaster) and moved to California in 1854 while Livingston remained. Kinkead continued to prosper and opened a branch in Carson City in 1859. He was active in civic and business affairs, but involved himself only

sion to pass freely and safely through this Territory on his way to California.

> Given under my hand,
> at Great Salt Lake City the
> 3rd day of November A.D. 1857
> [signed] Brigham Young, Governor[21]

Hitching up five light spring wagons, the Gentiles rode out of Great Salt Lake City on November 7 — their goal San Bernardino. John Ginn had no regrets in leaving a land populated by what he believed to be "blood-thirsty fanatics who were daily being taught that it was just as harmless and dutiful an act to kill a Gentile as to kill a venomous snake." [22]

Back at the Townsend House the anxious Californians heard that a decision was near in their case, but nearly two weeks went by before they learned they were free. The gamblers were offered a choice: leave the Territory at once or stay in Great Salt Lake Valley and be welcome. But under no circumstances would they be allowed to contact the army. On November 20, Hosea Stout confided in his journal: "O. P. Rockwell with 3 or four others started with 4 of the prisoners, which we have been guarding for some days, South to escort them through the settlements to Cal via South route. The other two are going to be permitted to go at large and remain till spring and guard dismissed." [23]

---

briefly in politics in 1878 to win election as governor of Nevada. Thomas H. Thompson and Albert A. West, *History of Nevada with Illustrations and Biographical Sketches of Its Prominent Men and Pioneers* (Oakland, 1881), p. 25.

[21] Ginn, "Mormon and Indian Wars," pp. 21–22; Brigham Young Letter Book No. 23, Entries 177, 180.

[22] Ginn, "Mormon and Indian Wars," p. 20. After reaching California, John I. Ginn made his reputation in the booming territory of Nevada as a newspaperman. He was variously editor or publisher of a number of dailies and weeklies in and around Virginia City in the 1870s, a period when frontiering newspapers seemed to blossom like desert flowers in the sun, only to disappear in the cold afternoon of competition. Ginn moved to Texas in later years, settling in El Paso to work on the manuscript of his youthful adventures on the overland trail, memoirs herein cited as Ginn's "Mormon and Indian Wars." In his career as a journalist, Ginn was connected with the Virginia City *Daily Constitution*, 1865; Virginia City *Daily Safeguard*, 1868; Treasure City *White Pine News*, 1870; the Unionville *Silver State*, 1871; Virginia *Evening Chronicle*, 1872; and Virginia City *Daily Independent*, 1874. See Thompson and West, *History of Nevada*, p. 326; Wells Drury, *An Editor on the Comstock Lode* (Palo Alto, 1948), p. 272; and Richard E. Lingenfelter, *1858–1958 The Newspapers of Nevada. A History and Bibliography*, with an introduction by David F. Myrick (San Francisco, 1964), pp. 80, 83, 88, 90, 91, 93.

[23] Hosea Stout, "Journal," Vol. 7, p. 59; Brooks, *On The Mormon Frontier*, Vol. II, p. 645.

All six men of the Aiken Party rode with Rockwell's escort as far as Lehi, where Chapman and Jones, who preferred to remain behind, took their leave. A farmer, Thomas Singleton, overheard one of the four tell Chapman, "Goodbye, John. If you come this way and see our bones bleaching on the plains, bury them." [24] It was the first sign that the Californians were concerned for their lives. Standing there in Lehi's main street, the six gamblers, resplendent in pink leggings and Texas hats, drew admiring glances from the townspeople, who later described them as "fine-lookin' men." Escorting the two Aikens, Tuck Wright, and Colonel Eichard were Rockwell, Sylvanus Collett, and two others, witnesses said. [25] The party headed south that afternoon and stopped overnight in Nephi, Rockwell and his men camping in the public square, the four Californians staying at Timothy Foote's hotel. Foote's son, Guy, looked with envy on the visitors, especially when Tom Aiken pulled off his money belt and asked Mrs. Foote to mend a tear in it. [26] The boy's eyes nearly fell out at the fat stacks of gold double eagles; they were stuffed six deep the length of the belt, he later would say.

Early the next morning, November 21, Rockwell and his men were saddled up and waiting for the Californians in front of the hotel. Wright and Eichard settled their bills individually, while Tom Aiken paid for himself and his brother. The eight men rode south toward the Sevier River. Tom Aiken and Colonel Eichard were never seen again. In the forenoon of the following day, Tuck Wright, bleeding from the head and suffering a bullet wound in the back, shoulder-high, stumbled barefoot and coatless into the hotel. Foote and another Mormon, Reuben Down, helped the injured man inside and made him comfortable. Down noticed that Wright had taken two deep scalp wounds "such as a dull hatchet would make." A doctor probed the bullet hole and extracted a ball of the size fired by a Navy Colt revolver.

---

[24] Thomas Singleton testimony, *Salt Lake Tribune*, October 10, 1878.

[25] Thomas Singleton and Timothy Foote testimony, *Salt Lake Tribune* and *Salt Lake Herald*, October 10, 1878; Richard Ivie testimony, ibid., October 11, 1878; Joseph Skeen testimony, ibid., October 12, 1878. During his trial Collett steadfastly denied being a member of the escort, despite testimony of these witnesses to the contrary. (According to the *Deseret News*, March 19, 1862, Joseph Skeen was an officer in the Mormon Battalion. Rosters, however, list him as Joseph Skein.)

[26] Mrs. Foote testified at Collett's trial that she had never been requested to mend, sew, darn, stitch, or otherwise repair any money belt owned by the Californians. See *Salt Lake Herald, Salt Lake Tribune*, October 15, 1878.

That afternoon Guy Foote, sitting on the hotel porch, was astonished to see John Aiken, bareheaded, barefoot, and splattered with blood, staggering up the street toward him.[27] A hasty examination disclosed that he, too, had been struck twice on the head by a heavy object. Once his wounds had been treated, Aiken told Guy Foote what had occurred, but the youngster was not permitted to repeat the conversation in court, since it constituted hearsay evidence and was inadmissible.

Twenty years later, when Sylvanus Collett was on trial for his life (charged with the murder of John Aiken), two Mormons, Joseph Skeen and his son William, both took the witness stand and testified that Collett had told them the whole story of the Aiken Party. According to William Skeen, Collett had given him a black broad-brimmed hat which Skeen wore with pride despite a four-inch gash in its crown. He later discarded the hat, he testified, when rumors reached him that it had once been the property of one of the Aiken Party. Troubled by the gossip, Skeen asked Collett about it and was told "that he [Collett] had been an escort to the Aiken party from the north, they having been delivered over to Rockwell . . . and himself, with the order to make away with them." [28]

The Skeens, father and son, agreed in substance that Collett gave this account of what transpired after the eight-man party left Nephi: Because the Californians were large and strong, a second group of men had been sent from Nephi south to the Sevier River while the four Gentiles still were asleep at the settlement. When the gamblers and their escort arrived at the river that evening, they camped with the men who had preceded them the night before; the meeting was made to appear accidental.

[27] Guy Foote testimony, *Salt Lake Herald*, October 10, 1878.

[28] William Skeen testimony, *Salt Lake Herald, Salt Lake Tribune*, October 11, 1878.

Owing to considerable Indian activity in the vicinity, the gamblers had no objection to teaming up with a few extra hands.

After dinner the party sat around the campfire singing, when someone shouted that Indians were attacking. The four men who had been sent in advance to act as reinforcements created a confusion to distract the Californians, and at a signal (here the Skeens were in conflict, the father testifying that Collett gave the sign, the son saying it was Rockwell) each of the four men in the escort, having selected a victim in advance, slipped a bar of iron from his sleeve and struck his man on the head. ". . . Collett missed [his] man," William Skeen told the court. In fact, he said, Collett was being badly beaten until Rockwell pulled a revolver and, firing across the campfire, shot Collett's man in the back. The wounded Californian lurched, fell into the brush, and escaped in the darkness.[29] The bodies of the two Aikens and the colonel were thrown into the river; Tom Aiken and Eichard were dead, but the icy water apparently revived John Aiken, who crawled to shore and made his way to Nephi.[30]

(Such was the court testimony of the Skeens, but in his defense Collett denied every word, insisting that he was in the Salmon River region at the time and did not leave the Fort Limhi settlement until "the last of October or the first of November." [31] His traveling companion, Joseph Harker, testified that they left the fort on October 28, 1857, and although Harker could not pinpoint the day of their arrival in Great Salt Lake City, he "thought" they reached the city late in December.) [32]

After the two wounded men were patched up and put to bed in Foote's hotel, Mrs. Frances Cazier, who had watched the drama with interest, noticed Rockwell and three others entering town after dark. The

[29] William and Joseph Skeen testimony, ibid.

[30] Hickman, *Brigham's Destroying Angel*, Appendix F, p. 208. J. H. Beadle, author of the appendix, said that as Aiken pulled himself from the river he heard a voice ask, "Are the damned Gentiles all dead, Port?" and the answer: "All but one — the son of a bitch ran." Compare with Ann Eliza Young, *Wife No. 19* (Hartford, Connecticut, 1876), pp. 272–73.

[31] Sylvanus Collett testimony, *Salt Lake Herald* and *Salt Lake Tribune*, October 15, 1878.

[32] In recent years, Joseph Harker's journal has come to light. In it Harker writes that he left Fort Limhi for Great Salt Lake City on October 28, 1857, arriving at the latter place on November 17, 1857. This would place Collett in the city three days before the Californians were released from custody. See Joseph Harker, "History." MS, p. 39.

next morning she was standing in the doorway of her home adjacent to the Tithing Office and saw Rockwell sitting inside with several other men. At Collett's trial she testified that she had heard a voice say: "Boys, you've made a bad job of it; two got away. Nephi won't be trusted with another job." [33]

Fourteen-year-old Alice Lamb listened to a conversation between several Nephi residents in which the return of Aiken and Wright was discussed and a decision made to lure the two men to another spot and "there to make away with them." [34] Meanwhile, other people in Nephi were hearing and seeing things they would be asked about twenty years later. Guy Foote and Reuben Down had occasion to pass the Tithing Office corral; there they saw horses and pack animals belonging to the Aiken Party.

Four or five days after the two survivors had made their surprise appearance in Nephi, they felt able to travel and announced their intention to return to Great Salt Lake City. When the time came to pay Timothy Foote, both men asked for credit, since neither had any money. Foote refused, with the explanation that Wright possessed a revolver and Aiken still had his gold watch with the fancy coin chain. After a moment's hesitation the Californians offered Foote his choice — the weapon or the watch. The innkeeper took the pistol, a selection which prompted Aiken to lament aloud, "Now we have parted with the last friend we have on earth." [35]

Foote loaned them a horse and buggy and offered Wright, who was coatless, a military jacket. Two youngsters volunteered to drive the wounded gamblers to the city. Shortly before they rode out of the settlement, Rockwell and several men were seen heading north.[36]

The events of the next few hours remain much of a mystery, but William Skeen swore that Collett had boasted of ambushing Wright and Aiken at a place called Willow Creek, eight miles from Nephi. The buggy

[33] Mrs. Frances Cazier testimony, *Salt Lake Herald* and *Salt Lake Tribune*, October 11, 1878.

[34] Her affidavit can be found in Cradlebaugh, *Utah and the Mormons*, pp. 64–66.

[35] Timothy Foote testimony, *Salt Lake Tribune*, October 10, 1878. Foote denied that he had refused the watch in favor of the pistol, but Reuben Down later testified that he had witnessed the transaction and Foote first took the time-piece, then pleaded with Aiken to exchange it for the gun. Foote also denied that Aiken had ever made a statement regarding loss of the pistol as "parting with the last friend on earth."

[36] Reuben Down testimony, ibid., October 11, 1878.

had stopped for water when the door to a nearby herder's shack flew open and a couple of double-barreled shotguns poked out and fired, killing the two men instantly. The bodies were weighted with rocks and thrown in the deep springs bubbling four miles away.[37]

The following day in Nephi, Guy Foote was startled to find the military jacket his father had loaned Tuck Wright lying atop a tool chest on the south porch of the Foote home. Examining the coat, Guy discovered that it was stained with blood; he counted six bullet holes through the high infantry collar and along the shoulder line. Moreover, the boy had passed the stable and had seen the horse the gamblers had borrowed. He showed the coat to Reuben Down, who guessed that there were twenty bullet holes scattered across the back of the garment.

Before long, Aiken Party property was turning up everywhere. Guy Foote saw one of his friends walking around in John Aiken's coat, with what appeared to be a mended bullet hole in the back. A fancy Mexican saddle had been seen near the Foote home. As Rockwell and his men rode back to Great Salt Lake City, they did not go unnoticed. In Provo, Richard Ivie marked the iron grey mule now in possession of the four Mormons as the same animal he had admired in the Aiken Party. George Murdock in Lehi recognized an iron grey mule and a roan pony in the Rockwell outfit as Aiken stock.

The rest of the story is a puzzle, but the known facts would indicate that as Rockwell and his companions continued toward Great Salt Lake City, they were joined, for one reason or another, by A. J. "Honesty" Jones. Perhaps he, too, recognized the mule or some other Aiken gear. Near Point of the Mountain an attempt was made on his life, but Jones

---

[37] Much was made of this during the Collett trial. Timothy Foote admitted that he had recovered two decomposed corpses from the springs a year later. Foote said he assumed they were the bodies of Aiken and Wright. Hammering at this testimony, defense counsel produced several physicians who stated that human bodies would completely dissolve in a year. See testimony of Dr. J. M. Benedict, *Salt Lake Herald*, *Salt Lake Tribune*, October 12, 13, 1878; Dr. W. H. Leach, Dr. Walter R. Pike testimony, ibid., October 13, 1878. Prosecution and defense hinged their cases on corpus delicti. Were the bodies recovered by Foote the remains of Aiken and Wright? That was the crucial point. After deliberating seven hours, on October 16, 1878, the jury brought in a verdict of not guilty.

While little is known of the Aiken affair in Utah today, it was a matter of some notoriety during its time. "The whole world has heard of the destruction of the Aiken Party," quoted in *"Mormonism." A sermon preached by the Rev. T. DeWitt Talmage, D.D., in the Tabernacle, Brooklyn, N.Y., on the 26th of September, 1880* (Brooklyn, 1880), p. 8.

was able to escape with only bruises. He made it across the Jordan River and back to Great Salt Lake City, where he began "telling all that happened, which is making a big stink!" [38]

Bill Hickman, fresh from murder himself, enters the picture at this point.[39] Told that "the boys have made a bad job of trying to put a man away," Hickman says he was ordered to find Jones and "use him up." [40]

[38] Hickman, *Brigham's Destroying Angel*, p. 128. Word of the fate of John Aiken and Tuck Wright spread rapidly. In San Francisco the *Daily Alta California* for January 25, 1858, reported that the Aiken Party had been murdered. Two of them were killed by Indians, the story read, and two others, begging the Saints for protection, "were shot down in the streets in daylight by the people."

[39] In his confession, later published as *Brigham's Destroying Angel*, Hickman admitted the slaying of Richard Yates, a trader caught selling supplies to the Utah Expedition. Confirmation that Yates dealt with the troops is found in Albert Tracy, "Journal of Captain Albert Tracy," edited by J. Cecil Alter and Robert J. Dwyer, *Utah Historical Quarterly*, Vol. XIII (1945), p. 96. A Comanche-fighter and ex-soldier, Daniel W. Jones became a convert to the church after hearing of Mormonism while moving sheep along the Spanish Trail from Santa Fe through Great Salt Lake City to California in 1850. He was acquainted with both Yates and Hickman. Jones was with a company of Mormon troops at Lost Spring,

> about four miles west of Weber valley and ten or twelve miles from Echo
> [when] One very cold morning about sunrise, Hickman and two others came to
> my camp. They seemed almost frozen, shaking and trembling in an unusual
> manner. Hickman asked me if I had any whisky. I told him I had not. He
> then asked if we had coffee. I replied that we had. "Then make us a good
> strong cup." While his coffee was being made, he took me outside and asked
> me if I knew Yates. I told him I did. "Well, we have just buried him."
> He then told about Yates being taken prisoner for tampering with Indians.
> And after talking quite excitedly, he said "We have got away with him, what
> do you think the Old Boss" (meaning Brigham) "will say?" . . . Hickman killed
> Yates for his money and horse the same as any other thief and murderer would
> have done, and then excused himself by telling that he was counseled to do
> these things . . . .

Jones, *Forty Years Among the Indians*, p. 130. The date of Yates's capture can be pinpointed quite readily by an entry in the diary of Hosea Stout: "Sunday 18 Oct 1857 . . . . At dark W A Hickman came in with Mr. Yates a prisoner." (Hosea Stout was named in an 1878 complaint charging him as a co-defendant in the first-degree murder of Richard Yates.)
Yates had come to Utah Territory the previous year (1856) in a small party headed for California. See J. Robert Brown, *Journal of a Trip Across the Plains of the U.S., From Missouri to California, in the Year 1856* (Columbus, Ohio, 1860), p. 76, where Brown says of his traveling companion, ". . . I do believe Yates can outlie any man I ever heard try."

[40] Hickman, *Brigham's Destroying Angel*, p. 128. In recounting the crime, Hickman refers to his victim as a man "whose name I never heard, only he was called Buck." There apparently was some confusion of identities, at least as far as Hickman is concerned. Every member of the Aiken Party can be accounted for except A. J. "Honesty" Jones. His whereabouts after the Californians left Lehi remain a

He was told a man named Dalton had contacted the Californian and offered him sanctuary in his Davis County home. Giving the situation some thought, Hickman got word to Dalton to leave the city with the intended victim just before sundown. He was to drive past the hot springs three miles north of the city — Hickman would do the rest. The details settled, Hickman claims that he and a man named Meacham took up their vigil near the springs. Darkness was closing in when the two heard a wagon approach. Hickman yelled for Dalton to halt, and when the teamster reined up, Hickman fired point-blank at Jones, the bullet smashing into his head.[41] But the California bear-hunter was tougher than expected. Bleeding terribly from his wound, Jones leaped from the wagon only to be pulled to the ground by Meacham, who finished the job with two strokes of his bowie knife.[42] The body was dumped into a shallow ditch along a fence line, and the spot was marked with a white rag. Then, said Hickman:

> We returned to the city to Gen. Grant's, as per agreement, and found him at home with Gen. Kimball, O. P. Rockwell, and somebody else whose name I do not recollect now. They asked if all was right, and I told them it was. They got spades, and we all went back, deepened the ditch, put him in and buried him, returned to Grant's, took some whisky, and separated for the night. The next day Kimball and I went to Brigham Young's, told him that [Jones] was taken care of, and there would be no more stink about his stories. He said he was glad of it. [Jones] was the last one of the Aiken's party, of whom there has been considerable said. I never saw any of them but this man, and him I never saw until I saw him in the wagon that evening.[43]

---

mystery, even though his widow made diligent inquiries concerning him. See *Valley Tan*, April 26, 1859. For these reasons I am convinced the man Hickman knew as "Buck" was in fact "Honesty" Jones.

[41] Hickman, *Brigham's Destroying Angel*, p. 129.

[42] R. N. Baskin, *Reminiscences of Early Utah* ([Salt Lake City], 1914), p. 151. Baskin, a former chief justice of the Utah Supreme Court, was the man before whom Hickman made his confession. (Baskin was U.S. Attorney for Utah at the time.) A calendar of criminal cases pending in April 1872 in the Territorial Court of Utah for the Third Judicial District showed that an indictment had been handed down November 28, 1871, for murder in the first degree in the death of "[No first name] Buck," against Brigham Young, Sen., Wm. A. Hickman, Morris Meacham, Simon Dalton, George D. Grant, O. Porter Rockwell, and Wm. Kimball.

[43] Hickman, *Brigham's Destroying Angel*, pp. 129–30; Baskin, *Reminiscences*, p. 151.

With the last spadeful of dirt on "Honesty" Jones's body, five members of the Aiken Party had been murdered. Only John Chapman, who eventually left the territory for California, survived the visit to Utah.

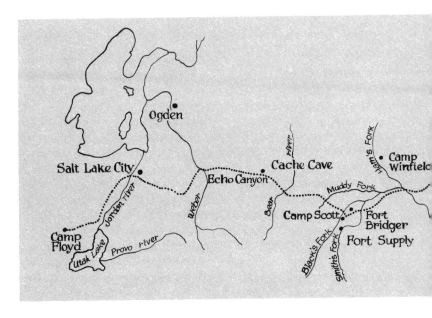

Chapter Fifteen

ZION INVADED

IT WAS EARLY DECEMBER before Orrin Porter Rockwell again turned his thoughts to the troops caught in the mountain fastness. Colonel Albert Sidney Johnston, after a great effort, pushed through South Pass despite heavy snows and reached his command near Black's Fork on November 3. Quickly surveying his position, Johnston ordered the Expedition to Fort Bridger, recognizing that a winter offensive against the Mormon city would be futile. But his movements were misinterpreted by Mormon lookouts and an express rider from Legion headquarters alerted Brigham Young to expect an attack. Against this background, Rockwell was ordered into the mountains to watch the troops, while General Wells hurriedly mustered thirteen hundred men to reinforce Echo Canyon against Johnston's final push to Zion.

But instead of an invasion force, the scout found an army on the verge of complete collapse. Soldiers and cavalry had literally staggered into the gutted ruins of Fort Bridger. There was no spark of fight left in

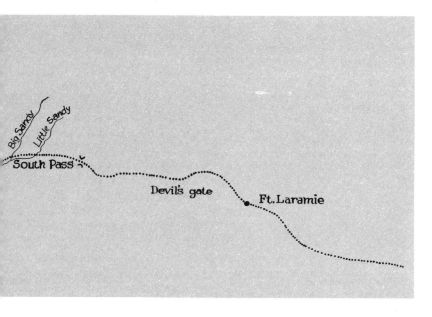

them, only a fierce determination to survive the winter. Carcasses of cattle and mules, frozen in grotesque positions, marked a grisly trail from Ham's Fork to Bridger's trading post. Temperatures sank to sixteen below, wracking hundreds of infantrymen with the tortures of frostbite. Of one hundred and forty-four horses in Johnston's command, only ten survived the journey from Fort Leavenworth. Now, as he examined the blackened remains of Fort Bridger, the colonel realized that it held little strategic value for the Expedition and decided as an alternative to make winter quarters at Black's Fork, a short distance away. The Mormons, meanwhile, made a gradual withdrawal to their fortifications in Echo Canyon and waited for Johnston's next move.

With the immediate danger of attack lessened, men of the Nauvoo Legion were permitted to return to their homes, leaving only a token force in the canyon in case of a surprise thrust by the army.[1] Johnston's pres-

---

[1] This temporary lull provided Rockwell with an opportunity to tend to his other church responsibilities. Once assured that he would have sufficient men and mounts to carry out his military obligations, Rockwell rode to Provo and took the pulpit during a Sabbath service on January 28, 1858, to tell his fellow Saints of the enemy at their door. See William Marsden, "Journal and Diary of William Marsden," *Daughters of Utah Pioneers, Lesson for January, 1951*, p. 157.

ence was of great concern to the men of the Mormon hierarchy, who understood only too well the futility of resisting a full-scale onslaught in the spring. In the end Brigham Young made up his mind to put the city and its surrounding settlements to the torch.

At Camp Scott, the army's winter bivouac on Black's Fork, other momentous decisions were under consideration. Of primary importance to Johnston was the drastic shortage of rations facing his men as a consequence of Lot Smith's raids on government supply trains. With the food situation worsening daily,[2] the colonel ordered Captain Randolph B. Marcy to take a detachment of men across the mountains to New Mexico and bring back horses, mules, and supplies.[3] While Johnston busied himself with military and logistical problems, federal officials in Governor Cumming's party were anything but idle. A crusty federal judge named Delana R. Eckels, whose home at Camp Scott was a hole in the ground, conducted an extraordinary session of the United States District Court on December 30, 1857. A grand jury empanelled by the "court" returned a true bill against twenty Mormons by name and "a multitude of persons (whose names to the Grand Jurors . . . are at present unknown), to the number of one thousand persons or more . . . ."

A glance at the first eight names on the blanket indictment showed Brigham Young, Heber C. Kimball, Daniel H. Wells, John Taylor, George D. Grant, Lot Smith, Porter Rockwell, and William A. Hickman. All were charged with treason, in that they "wickedly, maliciously and traitorously levied war against the United States."[4] Judge Eckels' action, considering his predicament, displayed a surprising optimism. Had he only known, the magistrate could perhaps have ambushed the elusive Rockwell, for the Mormon persisted in scouting the federal camp at close range.[5]

[2] In one foray alone, at Simpson's Hollow, Lot Smith's command destroyed: 2,720 pounds of ham, 92,700 pounds of bacon, 167,900 pounds of flour, 8,910 pounds of coffee, 1,400 pounds of sugar, 13,333 pounds of soap, 800 pounds of sperm candles, 705 pounds of tea, 7,781 pounds of hard bread, and 68,832 pounds of desiccated vegetables. "Utah Expedition," *House Executive Document No. 71*, 35th Congress, 1st Session, 1858, p. 63. For a first-hand account of the privations suffered at Camp Scott, see "The Governor's Lady; A Letter from Camp Scott, 1857," edited by A. R. Mortensen, *Utah Historical Quarterly*, Vol. XXII (April 1954), pp. 165–73.

[3] Details of this remarkable march can be found in Marcy, *Thirty Years of Army Life on the Border*, pp. 224–50.

[4] *New York Weekly Tribune*, March 6, 1858; Journal History, August 30, 1859.

[5] An example of his daring is brought out in this interview: "The redoubtable Porter Rockwell told Mr. [William] Bell that he and his company stood on the

Into this temporary stalemate came a frail, sickly man from southern California who called himself "Dr. Osborne." The mysterious stranger proved to be none other than the celebrated Colonel Thomas L. Kane, Brigham Young's close friend and admirer, come to help the church in its time of need.[6] Kane claimed to be a Gentile, but strong suspicion existed in many quarters that his enthusiasm for Mormonism far surpassed the boundaries of "pure philanthropy," as President Buchanan described it; some went so far as to suggest that Kane had been secretly baptized in Council Bluffs when the Saints first gathered for their westward trek in 1847.[7]

Thrusting himself into the spotlight, Kane intended to act as an emissary between the three forces — Cumming, Johnston, and the Mormons — in Great Salt Lake City. But Kane overplayed his part, and in so doing irreconcilably alienated Colonel Johnston. Captain John W. Phelps, artillery officer for the Expedition, was a witness to their first meeting:

> [Saturday, March 13, 1858] A man calling himself Mr. Kane of Philadelphia . . . bearer of dispatches from Washington, arrived last night from Salt Lake at Fort Bridger. He was so much exhausted that he could hardly announce himself and was helped from his horse. . . . I happened to be at head quarters [Camp Scott] this morning when he came up from Bridgers' [*sic*] Fort. He was a short, dark complected young man and was well mounted. . . . Without looking right or left he moved straight forward to the commanding officer's tent and seemed as if he wished to ride into it instead of stopping out side, so near did he urge his horse to the opening. Some one — probably a servant — knocked and informed the Colonel that some one wished to see him. The Col. was engaged in conversation and did not come out immediately, and this delay when compared with the man's forwardness seemed to look and be felt as a check. Presently the Col. came partly out; being stopped apparently by the man's horse whose head

mountains by the side of which Colonel Alexander was marching his command . . . and so near that they could have thrown rocks upon the troops passing." *New York Herald*, February 23, 1858; Journal History, February 23, 1858; and *Deseret News*, May 12, 1858.

[6] Young's sentiments are expressed in this excerpt: "We shall ever appreciate the good, the generous, the energetic and talented Little Col." Brigham Young to Thomas L. Kane, January 14, 1859. Thomas L. Kane Papers. MSS, Stanford University Library.

[7] Hyde, *Mormonism*, p. 146; Waite, *The Mormon Prophet and His Harem*, p. 52. As noted earlier, some historians feel that there is a strong likelihood that Kane was a member of the Council of Fifty.

was nearly in the opening, and looking up in a crouched attitude, his own head being near the horse's head, said Who are you?

Are you Colonel Johnston, asked the man.

Yes, replied the Colonel.

I am Mr. Kane, said he, from Philadelphia, bearer of dispatches; I ask your permission to see Governor Cummings [sic] first, I'll see you afterwards.

To this the Colonel assented and turned back into his tent. The man immediately turned away saying — I'll see you again Colonel Johnston. — Come on Sergeant.

He seemed to speak with a short breath as if repressing excitement of some kind. . . .

There was an absence of that proper deference due from one of his pretended character to an officer commanding an army of the United States. In his whole bearing he seemed to attach [an] undue importance to his mission whatever it may be.

He went up to the Governor's and has remained there all day without any one knowing what news he has brought. . . .[8]

A solid week of conferences passed before Kane succeeded in persuading Cumming to visit Brigham Young — without government troops — and see for himself that Drummond's charges against the Mormons were untrue. By winning the Georgian over to his side, Kane managed to drive a wedge between the new appointee and the commander of his military escort; Albert Sidney Johnston wanted no less from the Mormons than total submission. But his command could act only as a *posse comitatus* on order of the new governor, who now was thinking strongly in terms of peace. On April 5 Cumming informed Johnston he was prepared to leave for the Mormon capital at once. Despite the colonel's strong warning that he would certainly be poisoned, the governor set out to meet the Rocky Mountain Saints. It was small consolation to Johnston a few days later to learn that he had been brevetted a brigadier general.[9] For a true soldier promotion was gained through action in the field.

[8] John Wolcott Phelps, "Diary." MSS, March 13, 1858.

[9] William Preston Johnston, *The Life of Gen. Albert Sidney Johnston* (New York, 1878), p. 229. He was brevetted November 18, 1857, for "meritorious conduct in the ability, zeal, energy, and prudence displayed by him in command of the

Cumming and Kane barely had settled themselves in the carriage provided for the long journey ahead when a mounted patrol led by Orrin Porter Rockwell materialized out of the night and announced that it was an official escort ordered by Brigham Young to ensure the federal party safe conduct through Mormon lines.[10] Captain Jesse Gove, upon learning the identity of the governor's guardians, grabbed pen and paper in his frigid tent and dashed off a letter of indignation to the East: "This afternoon a man by the name of Gilbert, of the firm of Gilbert, Gerrish & Co., has arrived. He met the Governor in Echo Cañon, with an escort of Mormons under the command of the villain, Porter Rockwell. For shame, that he should have put himself in a position to be so far humiliated by being escorted, more like a prisoner than the chief executive of this territory, by a band of lawless men, led by a notorious murderer and rebel!"[11]

Gove had little to fear; Governor Cumming was being treated with the greatest of care and attention. For his benefit the Mormons had staged something of a show in the gloomy clutches of Echo Canyon. By prearrangement the party stopped at Cache Cave for dinner as guests of the officers of the Nauvoo Legion. When the carriage again rattled forward, the hour was late and the night inky black. Several times during the almost spectral journey through the canyon, hidden sentries challenged the official party and waved the governor on after muted conversation with Rockwell. Splashes of light flared here and there along the sheer walls, and Cumming spotted the silhouettes of riflemen caught for an instant in the light of a campfire. At one point an outpost guard sounded the call to arms and a dozen men surrounded the carriage. Only after Rockwell had spent fifteen minutes explaining the situation was the party allowed to pass on. By the time Cumming reached Weber Station at the west end of the canyon, he guessed that from two to three thousand Mormons manned its fortifications.[12]

---

army in Utah." Francis B. Heitman, *Historical Register and Dictionary of the United States Army, from Its Organization, September 29, 1789, to March 2, 1903* (Washington, 1903), two volumes, Vol. I, pp. 577–78. Johnston resigned May 3, 1861, to join the Confederate Army as a general. He was killed April 6, 1862, in the battle of Shiloh, Tenn.

[10] Bancroft, *History of Utah*, p. 526n; and Cumming to Lewis Cass, Secretary of State, May 2, 1858, U.S. State Department, Territorial Papers, Utah Series, April 30, 1853, to December 24, 1859.

[11] Gove, *Utah Expedition*, p. 147.

[12] Stenhouse, *Rocky Mountain Saints*, pp. 389–90; Bancroft, *History of Utah*, p. 526n; Waite, *The Mormon Prophet and His Harem*, pp. 53–55; and Cumming to Cass, May 2, 1858, U.S. State Department, Territorial Papers, Utah Series.

Had Rockwell been able to read the governor's thoughts, he would have been tremendously pleased. Cumming could not know that he had been the victim of a gigantic hoax, for in truth fewer than one hundred and fifty Mormons occupied the canyon's defenses. Each time the party had been challenged, the sentries raced back to repeat the performance. As for the campfires, they had been lighted and left unguarded, except for the handful of men who had deliberately exposed themselves to Cumming's view. The trick surpassed Brigham Young's expectations; through an elaborate ruse his successor was convinced that an overwhelmingly hostile force faced Johnston's command and that any attempt to penetrate the canyon would be suicidal. Such was Cumming's frame of mind when he accepted the greetings of a Mormon delegation of honor on the outskirts of the city on April 12.

Before the day was over, Brigham Young called on the gentleman from Georgia and turned over to him the executive seal of the Territory of Utah, thus officially recognizing him as governor. Coincidentally, that very day in Washington Buchanan was directing a team of peace commissioners to proceed to Utah with a proclamation of full pardon for all deeds committed during the "war." Its language swept away treason indictments returned by the grand jury at Camp Scott. So long as he accepted the terms, Rockwell, among others, had no need to fear reprisals for military actions during the so-called rebellion.

But Buchanan's declaration of amnesty extended only to the indictments and offered no other promise of immunity. Eventually federal judges would return to Utah and begin asking questions.[13] Their interest in Rockwell would concern itself with several matters to which his name had been linked by gossip and innuendo: the disappearance of the Aiken Party, the attempted murder of John Tobin near the Santa Clara early in 1857, and the brutal slayings of Henry Jones and his mother in Payson on February 27, 1858. Sketchy reports from Gentile informants indicated that the Californians had simply vanished. There was no doubt, however, that an attempt had been made to assassinate Tobin while he was camped on the southern Utah river,[14] and that Jones had been mutilated

[13] Judge John Cradlebaugh, for one, launched into a judicial crusade to ferret out the perpetrators of the Mountain Meadows massacre, the Potter–Parrish homicides in Springville on March 15, 1857, and other sensational crimes alleged to have occurred in 1857–58. Judge Charles E. Sinclair, meanwhile, gave special attention to investigating treason and polygamy.

[14] John Tobin had come to Great Salt Lake City in 1851 as a sergeant with Capt. Howard Stansbury's topographical survey expedition. He met Brigham Young

and admired his daughter Alice. Tobin was an orderly sergeant in Capt. R. M. Morris's command, which served as an escort for Lt. John W. Gunnison. See "Muster Roll of Captain Michael E. Van Buren, Co. A, Regiment of Mounted Rifles, Commanded by Bvt. Gen. Persifor F. Smith, Dec. 31, 1853, to Feb. 28, 1854." Record Group 94, National Archives. After Gunnison's death, the command wintered in Great Salt Lake City. During this time Tobin became enamored of Alice Young and imbued with Mormonism. According to the *New York Times*, May 20, 1857, Tobin embraced the first object of his adoration (Mormonism) and was led to believe that, in the fullness of time, he would be permitted to embrace the second (Alice). After serving out his enlistment, he returned to Utah in the spring of 1856. Tobin told John Hyde that he had begun seeing Alice again, although she was under a written engagement to W. B. Wright, whom Brigham Young had sent off on a mission to the Sandwich Islands. Tobin also insisted (to Hyde) that he had most convincing proof that Alice had "sacrificed her honor" and he had refused to marry her. Brigham Young ordered him put out of the way, Hyde reported, and shortly thereafter Alice Young was quickly given to Hiram B. Clawson. See John Hyde, Jr., *Mormonism: Its Leaders and Designs*, p. 106. For more on Tobin's difficulties with Alice Young, see S. George Ellsworth, *Dear Ellen. Two Mormon Women and Their Letters* (Salt Lake City, 1974), pp. 34, 39.

Col. Peltro, a government surveyor, having determined a line of road for military posts from Fort Leavenworth to Great Salt Lake City, was en route to California to make his report. Tobin joined his party of two other men and Peltro's servant. They stopped at the Santa Clara River and camped at the foot of a perpendicular ledge of rock. About four o'clock on the morning of February 20, 1857, the sleeping men were fired upon from the top of the ledge. Tobin was shot in the head, the bullet entering close under the eye, passing diagonally through his nose and cheek, and lodging in his neck. He was struck by five other bullets and left for dead. His companions ran for cover; one, however, suffered a bullet wound in the back of the neck and another had two fingers shot off. At dawn's light they counted 56 bullet holes in their blankets. Barely alive, Tobin was brought into the Mormon mission at Las Vegas on February 23 by a mail company and then taken on to California, where he later recovered. See *New York Times*, May 20, 1857, and "History of Las Vegas Mission," compiled by Andrew Jenson, in *Nevada State Historical Society Papers*, Vol. V (1926), p. 276. Tobin returned to Utah as proprietor of the Warm Springs baths in 1858, but sold out in 1861 to fulfill a Mormon mission to Scotland. Within a few months he was excommunicated at the Glasgow conference for "adulterous and other unchristian-like conduct." See *The Mountaineer*, Sept. 3, 1859, and *The Millennial Star*, Vol. XXIII (1861), p. 508. In later years an angry Tobin wrote to *The Salt Lake Tribune*, Nov. 12, 1875, that he was the "sole survivor of a Mormon butchery, and Brigham is fearful lest I should visit Salt Lake and explain how three Gentiles were butchered in Santa Clara Canyon in January [*sic*], 1857 . . . ."

Achilles, *Destroying Angels of Mormondom*, pp. 17–18, insists that Rockwell and one of Brigham Young's sons were ordered to put Tobin out of the way, but in February 1857 Rockwell was on the plains helping organize the Y. X. Company. Lee, *Mormonism Unveiled*, pp. 273–74, agrees substantially with Achilles' account of the shooting, but names Joel White and John Willis as the perpetrators. See also Hurt to Forney, December 4, 1859, in *Senate Executive Document No. 42*, 36th Congress, 1st Session, 1860, pp. 94–95.

and put to death after being accused of incest with his mother, who shared his fate.[15]

If Cumming expected to find a city teeming with inhabitants, he was disappointed, for the Mormons had begun their exodus from Zion. Heeding counsel, the Saints gathered up what they could and moved south to Provo, there to await further word from Brigham Young. Cumming was faced with the paradox of being a governor with no one to govern. Once the army made a move to march on the city, the populace would interpret it as a signal to pull out to some undetermined spot in the desert to the southwest and resettle.[16] Thirty thousand Saints were preparing to aban-

---

[15] This incredibly bizarre crime caused a sensation among the Mormons. Henry Jones, according to Achilles, *Destroying Angels of Mormondom*, pp. 18–19, had only recently returned from California when the citizens of Great Salt Lake City spread gossip accusing him of having an unnatural relationship with his mother. Achilles continues:

> Rockwell was despatched to administer justice. Jones was met in a saloon with some friends, and the Chief of the Danites joined the party, and participated in their hilarity. While under the influence of liquor, Rockwell and others enticed Jones out to the suburbs, where they bound and gagged him, and Rockwell castrated him. Jones made out to get home and recovered. Shortly afterwards, he and his mother started by the Southern route to come to California. About seventy miles out from Salt Lake city, they were overtaken at a place called Payson, and encamped in a "dug-out." Rockwell and his party, while they were asleep, entered the "dug-out," and in opening the door awoke Jones, who broke through his assailants and ran for his life. The party then entered and killed his mother, cutting her throat. They then started in pursuit of Jones, and captured him about three miles out, and shot him. They then took his body and carried it back to the "dug-out," and laid it beside his mother, and then pulled the building down upon the bodies, and there they lie to-day.

See also Stenhouse, *Rocky Mountain Saints*, p. 405; Cradlebaugh, *Utah and the Mormons*, p. 64; *Deseret News*, April 6, 1859; Whitney, *History of Utah*, Vol. I, p. 710n; and the *Valley Tan*, April 19, 1859. Under the date, Saturday, 27 Feb 1858, Hosea Stout wrote this matter-of-fact journal entry: "This evening several persons disguised as Indians entered Henry Jones' house and dragged him out of bed with a whore and castrated him by a square and close amputation." Brooks, *On The Mormon Frontier*, Vol. II, p. 653.

[16] Cumming guessed that Mexico would be the intended destination of the Mormons if they carried out their threat to move. On April 25, 1858, he said Brigham Young, addressing the Saints in the Tabernacle, remarked, "I have a good mind to tell a secret right here. I believe I shall tell it anyhow, they say there is a fine country down South there. Sonora, is it; is that your name for it? Do not speak of this out of doors if you please." Cumming to Cass, May 2, 1858. U.S. State Department, Territorial Papers, Utah Series.

Brigham Young's concept of a desert refuge for the Saints during the "move south" was never clearly defined. Best authority on this is Roberts, *Comprehensive History of the Church*, Vol. IV, pp. 360–63.

don what they had labored ten years to build; only a few men stayed behind to light the fires which would reduce the valley to a bowl of ashes.

Reporting to the Secretary of State, Cumming described the hegira and added, "I shall restrain all operations of the military for the present, which will probably enable me to receive from [Buchanan] additional instructions, if he deems it necessary to give them." Cumming's letter was written without knowledge that peace commissioners were at that moment on their way to Camp Scott with a Presidential declaration of amnesty.

Rockwell, whose duty it had been for three weeks to guard Cumming in his tours of the city, was called May 3 to escort the governor back to Camp Scott, a mission completed without incident on May 10.[17]

Accompanied by five soldiers, as many armed teamsters, and a wagon-master, Senator Lazarus W. Powell, former governor of Kentucky, and Major Ben McCullough, of Texas — the President's Peace Commission to Utah — rolled into Camp Scott three weeks later. Announcement of the amnesty brought disappointed groans from the officers and a general outspoken criticism of Buchanan's political machinations. After listening to both Cumming and Johnston in regard to conditions in the territory, the two commissioners decided that the new governor might have been overly enthusiastic in his acceptance of the Mormons. Accordingly, on June 1 they carefully drafted a report to the Secretary of State recommending that Johnston's command — with reinforcements — would guarantee that "this deluded people [will] submit quietly and peacefully to the civil authorities." [18] Senator Powell and Major McCullough met Rockwell's picket guard near the Weber River and were escorted into the city.[19]

With Governor Cumming as a spectator, the commissioners sat down with Brigham Young and other prominent Mormons in the Council House on June 11 and outlined their position. Suddenly the door flew open and Rockwell, his coat pockets sagging under the weight of a pair of Colt revolvers, entered and whispered in Young's ear. The Mormon prophet reddened and, turning to his guests, said sharply, "Senator Powell, are you aware, sir, that those troops are on the move towards the city?"

"It cannot be!" Powell exclaimed, "We were promised by the General that they should not move till after this meeting."

"I have received a despatch that they are on the march for this city.

[17] Journal History, May 10, 1858.
[18] *House Executive Document No. 2*, 35th Congress, 2nd Session, 1858, pp. 165–66.
[19] Jenson, *Church Encyclopaedia*, p. 189.

My messenger would not deceive me!" Young said, his voice trembling in anger.[20]

Rockwell's report of the movements of Johnston's command strikingly demonstrated the astonishing degree to which the Mormons had perfected their spy network and express system. Johnston's sudden decision to march had been prompted by two important developments: Marcy's unexpected early return with provisions from New Mexico, and the arrival of a supply train from Fort Leavenworth. Even so, before his plans reached more than the most preliminary stage,[21] Rockwell learned of them and whipped his horse toward Great Salt Lake City, arriving in three days to make his dramatic appearance at the peace conference.

Brigham Young's immediate reaction to the news was one of hot indignation; he broke off the talks and requested the Council House audience to sing "Zion," a hymn intended to stir the emotions of those present. As the last stanza faded, the two commissioners understood that Young was telling them to stop the army or consider the peace conference closed.[22] But it was too late; word could not reach Johnston in time, and both parties knew it. Yet, the following day Young's attitude underwent a complete reversal. Painfully aware that his Saints were no match for seasoned troops, he resolved to salvage what he could of the situation. The prophet, seer, and revelator asked that the Expedition be barracked outside the city. "They may pass through it, if needs be, but must not quarter less than forty miles from us." [23] It was the final gesture of defeat; the "Utah War" had come to an end.

On June 13 the first elements of Brigadier General Albert Sidney Johnston's Utah Expedition heard the march order and stepped forward, faces west, their destination Zion. As the irregular columns wound through the silent recesses of Echo Canyon, the soldiers studied its fortifications

[20] Tullidge, *History of Salt Lake City*, p. 215; Bancroft, *History of Utah*, p. 532n. Cumming subsequently lodged an official complaint with the Secretary of State that Johnston had given the order to march prior to the agreed date of June 20 and thereby caused great concern at the peace conference. Cumming to Cass, June 18, 1858, U.S. State Department, Territorial Papers, Utah Series.

[21] Tracy, "Journal," *Utah Historical Quarterly*, Vol. XIII, p. 15.

[22] Tullidge, *History of Salt Lake City*, p. 216.

[23] Ibid., p. 217.

with mingled interest and amusement. Captain Albert Tracy instinctively put his finger on the canyon's defensive weaknesses. Mused he:

> ... A singular idea seemed to possess these people, that being regulars, we were necessarily to move in solid and compact bodies to whatever point was most convenient to them to resist us. They little seemed to know or heed the modern system of deploying and skirmishing, or yet the availability of artillery, long before our infantry should be brought under fire. However, with but a beggarly complement of guns upon their own part to respond — the "corrals" of rocks which they had erected by the shelves and gulches and along the ridges of the cliffs, would have been knocked about their ears, and rendered untenable in but a brief time and the way opened for our own light troops from the hills at rear. Once the heights in our possession, all beneath was vain to the Mormons ... .[24]

Tracy was equally surprised at the appearance of Great Salt Lake City. The community, which from a distance he could see was neat and orderly, proved to be a "city of the dead," with its abandoned stores and vacant homes. Heightening the eerie atmosphere was the alien sound of the army's brass band blaring through the empty streets. Here and there the soldiers spotted what Tracy described as " 'destroyers,' of decidedly rough and sinister aspect, left as a police, with orders to fire the city in case we offered to occupy it." [25] On through the deserted community tramped the infantry, past the gabled houses, across the bridge spanning the cocoa waters of the Jordan, south along its banks, then west again. On July 6 the command to halt reverberated through the ranks; the men of the Utah Expedition had reached their destination. The brush-choked spread of land which sprawled before them would soon become Camp Floyd, their new quarters.

The great "move south" ended. The day before, after lengthy conferences with Governor Cumming, Brigham Young had balanced himself on a wagon tongue in Provo and shouted to the thousands of Mormons rendezvoused there that he intended to return to Great Salt Lake City; those who wished were at liberty to follow his example. Within a few hours the tremendous throng had begun the slow journey back. In that seemingly endless procession of Saints were Rockwell, his wife, and their two infant daughters. (Soon there would be another child, for Mary Ann was six months into her third pregnancy.) Now that hostilities were a

[24] Tracy, "Journal," *Utah Historical Quarterly*, Vol. XIII, p. 23.
[25] Ibid., p. 27.

thing of the past, Rockwell intended to devote more time to his family. Gathering up his wife and youngsters, he moved them from the Neff household to a new home near Lehi, where John Orrin Rockwell was born October 23, 1858.[26]

For the first time since the California days, Rockwell began looking around for a money-making enterprise, one which would take the best advantage of the sudden influx of military dollars to the territory. With twenty-five hundred troops stationed at Camp Floyd, Rockwell had warm recollections of the days on the American River when the forty-niners had trampled each other for a demijohn of his whisky. If a half-way house could succeed in the goldfields, it would attract business equally as well in Utah. Once the decision had been made he went about obtaining a suitable location for his establishment. On July 29, 1858, he counted out $500 and purchased from Evan M. Green sixteen acres of real estate at Hot Springs near Point of the Mountain on the road between Great Salt Lake City and Lehi.[27] The trail was traveled by every city-bound trooper in Johnston's Army. Rockwell had it in mind to build a place where a man could buy a glass of homebrew beer,[28] stable his animals, stay overnight, or just stop to pass the time of day. He even had a name in mind; he called it the Hot Springs Brewery Hotel.[29] Once work on

[26] *Utah Genealogical and Historical Magazine*, Vol. XXVI, p. 156.

[27] Utah County Deeds, 1851–1864, Book G, p. 362. Rockwell also owned two other parcels of property near Provo: twenty acres in Lot 4, Block 44 of the American Creek Survey of Meadow Land, and twenty-two acres of Lot 2, Block 2, of Dry Creek, Plat B. See ibid., pp. 169, 308.

[28] Brewing was a necessary talent for a good innkeeper. William Marsden, a clerk in the Utah County Recorder's Office, was Inspector of Spiritous Liquors and Beer for the county. When, in January of 1861, Rockwell decided to sell whisky at the hotel, it was Marsden who issued him a license. See Marsden, "Journal and Diary," p. 174.

[29] Journal History, August 29, 1860. Originally, ownership of the Hot Springs Brewery Hotel was a three-way proposition with Charles Mogo and David H. Burr of the territorial land office operating the hotel and brewery, and Rockwell running the stage station and stables. (He and his family lived on the Dunyon Ranch property near Crystal Springs.) Before long, the partners Mogo and Burr were advertising a "fine lager beer." See *Valley Tan*, November 6, 1858. It was a venture which lasted until July, when Burr pulled up stakes and sold his interest to Robert Hereford, a mountaineer from Bitterroot and Green River country, who had moved to the Salt Lake Valley after the death of his Indian wife the previous winter. (Ibid., July 20, 1859.) But Hereford was no businessman. By mid-January he and Mogo were ready to sell; they put the enterprise up at public auction. (". . . hogs, sows, shoats, mules, oxen, wagons, harness . . . a large and commodious Hotel, a Brewery capable of making 500 gallons of beer per day, a stable and corral and all necessary

the structure had begun, Rockwell put another idea into operation. That night a neighbor penned a letter to Colonel Thomas L. Kane in Philadelphia:

> Mr. J. C. Naile, a friend of mine forwards by today's mail, four several [separate] bids for carrying the Mails of the United States on Routes in this Territory, in which I am interested. Should they reach Washington in time to be considered, and you can render me any service in making these bids successful, it will be a favor that I shall appreciate and remember with gratitude. My health is good and that of my family and of your friends generally in this Territory so far as my knowledge extends.
>
> I remain your faithful and undeviating friend.
>
> O P Rockwell[30]

Rockwell's choice of location for the half-way house proved to be excellent. Situated as it was on two main roads, the inn attracted a large clientele, Mormon and Gentile. With his family near at hand and an income assured, the scout could afford to relax and enjoy a rather uncomplicated existence for the first time since his boyhood. Only once during the year did trouble threaten, but it passed quickly. The territory's new U.S. marshal, a fellow by the name of P. K. Dotson, held a warrant for Rockwell's arrest on murder charges. He was having problems, however, in serving it. In a letter to Judge John Cradlebaugh, associate justice of the Second Judicial District, Dotson poured out his tale of woe:

> I have received from you certain warrants of arrest against many persons, in your Judicial district, charged with murder, including one

---

outhouses." *The Mountaineer*, January 7, 1860.) But the decision to liquidate evidently had not been discussed with the party of the third part, who promptly placed potential bidders on notice that: the undersigned (O. P. Rockwell) is "the rightful owner and possessor of the undivided one-third of said premises, and the sale is without my consent. All persons are hereby warned not to purchase, or in anyway interfere with, said premises, unless they wish to involve themselves in a troublesome and expensive lawsuit, as I am determined to maintain my rights therein." (Ibid.) Hosea Stout, representing Rockwell, negotiated a proper dissolution of partnership satisfactory to all concerned, which allowed Rockwell to occupy the premises and employ Hereford as his barkeep and manager. In October, George A. Smith visited the establishment, noting in his journal that Rockwell had engaged "Miner Frisby, a man lately joined the church," to tend the brewery . . . [and that] "a round sum has been expended there to establish a good brewery. [S]pent the evening with O.P.R. and slept on a wool bed." See "Church Historian's Office Journal," October 20–21, 1860.

[30] Rockwell to Kane, November 20, 1858; Coe Collection (MS 279, Yale University). See also Journal History, November 20, 1858.

against J. D. Lee, John Higbee (a bishop), Hoyte (his counselor), and thirty-six others, for the murder of one hundred and nineteen men, women and children, at Mountain Meadows, also one against Porter Rockwell, John A. Wolf, president of the Seventies . . . for the murder of the Aiken Brothers and two others; one against Lewis Bentz and three others for stealing six mules, the property of the United States. . . .

I regret to inform you that it is not in my power to execute any of these processes, I have made repeated efforts by the aid as well of the military, as of the civil posse, to execute the warrants last alluded to, but without success. So great is the number of persons engaged in the commission of these crimes, and such the feeling of the Mormon Church, and the community in their favor, that I cannot rely on a civil posse to aid me in arresting them. . . . I called on Governor Cumming to make a requisition on the commanding general of this Department for a small number of troops to assist me as a posse. At the same time I made my affidavit to the fact of my utter inability, to execute the warrants without such military aid, which affidavit I left with the governor.

His Excellency, after considering the matter, finally refused to make the requisition. I therefore do not feel warranted in again troubling His Excellency with another application.

On account of the executive right claimed by Gov. Cumming to call for troops to serve as a posse, I do not deem it proper to take the responsibility of making such a requisition myself, until further advised by the government. . . .[31]

Dotson was telling the judge that he had no intention of tackling Rockwell or any other Mormon on his list without soldiers at his side. Certainly, the marshal felt his life expectancy would be protracted that way. With arrest and imprisonment no longer a threat, Rockwell was free to go as he pleased. In July he took time to hunt down Moses Clark,[32] an unsavory character regarded by those who knew him as "the horse-stealer."[33] Somehow Clark had managed to acquire—apparently without benefit of a bill of sale — possession of a mule belonging to Daniel Spencer. Rockwell brought the fugitive in to face trial, and two months later Clark was sentenced to three years at hard labor for his misbehavior.[34]

[31] Journal History, June 3, 1859.

[32] *Deseret News*, September 21, 1859, also refers to him as "Charlie Clark."

[33] Wilford Woodruff to George A. Smith, Journal History, July 12, 1859.

[34] Hosea Stout, "Journal," Vol. 8, p. 21; *On The Mormon Frontier*, Vol. II, p. 703; and the *Deseret News*, September 21, 1859. Clark was granted executive clemency in February 1861, when he chose to remain in his cell rather than join six other convicts in an escape from the territorial prison. Ibid., February 27, 1861.

Chapter Sixteen

OF DEATH AND DYING

Wɪᴛʜ ᴛʜᴇ Uᴛᴀʜ Exᴘᴇᴅɪᴛɪᴏɴ ᴇɴᴛʀᴇɴᴄʜᴇᴅ at Camp Floyd, Brigham Young found his kingdom faced with a peril more fearful than shot and shell. So long as the troops had been contained by weather and terrain, and isolated in the mountains at arm's length, so to speak, the army posed only an implied threat to the safety of the Saints in Zion. But now, perched practically on the city's doorstep, the presence of nearly three thousand unfriendly Gentile soldiers gave the Mormon leadership nightmares. It was not only the sight of cannon which troubled Young and his counselors, but the prospect of a powerful cynical influence festering on the very periphery of Mormon hearth and home — anti-Mormonism simply was too close for comfort. Though the Lion of the Lord preserved an unwavering grip on the church and its people, his wilderness autocracy had come off second best in its confrontation with the outside world. The Utah Expedition soured the theocratic climate overnight; Mormon domination in Utah suffered a hairline fracture, and its enemies meant to widen the breach. Loud, profane soldiers, arm-in-arm with camp followers and civilian teamsters, now caroused the streets in harsh contrast to the almost puritanical peace of years past. Accenting the city's sudden surge of lawlessness brought on by the inevitable squabble for government dollars was the induction of two hundred additional policemen. Alarmed by this unwelcome turn of events, the *Deseret News* muttered editorially that more blood had been shed and more murders committed in the eight months since the Expedition's arrival in the valley than in the previous nine years.

It seemed to many that discharged soldiers were competing with government teamsters for recognition in displays of objectionable conduct. Neither class was subject to a controlling discipline, and both reminded the Mormons of that painful fact at every opportunity. It was said in some quarters that infantrymen were more feared than Indians, and teamsters had made an avocation of stealing government livestock. In fact, Brigham Young was told that rustlers helped themselves to eighty or more mules daily from army corrals.[1] Great Salt Lake City was swiftly earning a reputation as a wide open frontier town.[2]

Horace Greeley, on his way west in the summer of '59, observed of the Mormons: "Formerly they drank little or no liquor; but, since the army came in last year, money and whisky have both been more abundant, and now they drink considerably. More than a thousand barrels of whisky have been sold in this city within the last year, at an average of not less than eight dollars per gallon, making the total cost to consumers over two hundred and fifty thousand dollars, whereof the Mormons have paid at least half."[3]

T. B. H. Stenhouse, a prominent figure in the community, blamed Mormons as well as Gentiles for the degraded state of affairs. "During the summer and fall of 1859," he wrote, "there was a murder committed in Salt Lake City almost every week, and very rarely were the criminals brought to justice." He explained: "The programme of the police authorities seemed to be to give the desperadoes the largest liberty, so that they might, in their drunken carousals, 'kill off each other,' and what they left undone invisible hands readily accomplished."[4]

One such killing, committed by "invisible hands," was blamed on Rockwell, who, it was whispered, did the deed in the spirit of the Refor-

---

[1] Manuscript History of Brigham Young, November 4, 1858, p. 1067.

[2] Some idea of the violent lawlessness which prevailed during this period can be gained from Richard Thomas Ackley, "Across the Plains in 1858," with footnotes by Dale L. Morgan, *Utah Historical Quarterly*, Vol. IX (July, October 1941), pp. 213–25.

[3] Horace Greeley, *An Overland Journey From New York to San Francisco in the Summer of 1859* (New York, 1860), p. 234.

[4] Stenhouse, *Rocky Mountain Saints*, p. 417. Stenhouse was a member of the church for 23 years, laboring as a missionary in England, Scotland, and various parts of Europe. He was for three years president of the Swiss and Italian missions. In Salt Lake City Stenhouse enjoyed a close relationship with members of the general authorities and Brigham Young himself. He was excommunicated in 1869, however, for manifesting a spirit of apostasy.

mation (a fanatic revival of religious subjugation which had swept Zion three years earlier under the zealous direction of Jedediah Grant).[5] In this case the victim, John Gheen, had a curious history in the church, one reaching back to Nauvoo. Those who knew him in the early days claimed that he was a reformed gambler who loaned the church $2,000 in a time of desperate need. In return he was permitted to journey into forbidden Missouri with a pack of playing cards in order to obtain for himself the proper outfit for the impending exodus west.[6] Gheen later turned up at Council Point with two wagonloads of groceries, enough to open a store. In 1848 he became embroiled in a property rights dispute in which he threatened to shoot the first man who crossed his land. Lilace W. Conditt was the unfortunate who called his fellow-Mormon's bluff and was blasted three times through the heart.[7]

A mob of Conditt's friends beat Gheen into a bloody wreck and left him for dead, but he survived to be tried for murder. He was acquitted.[8] Migrating to Utah, Gheen opened a butcher shop in Great Salt Lake City and prospered. Though the years passed uneventfully, Gheen's conscience apparently troubled him over the Conditt shooting. According to rumor, he sought to expiate the crime by offering his life under the doctrine of Blood Atonement. But no one would step forward to "help him," and he lived in misery. Then, for no apparent reason, Gheen began appearing in court. In May of 1858 he brought suit against David J. C. Beck, one of the men responsible for tearing down his fences in Iowa ten years earlier. The jury brought in a verdict favoring Gheen and awarded him $1,500

[5] Discussions of the Reformation and the doctrine of Blood Atonement can be found in Roberts, *Comprehensive History*, Vol. IV, pp. 119–38; Stenhouse, *Rocky Mountain Saints*, pp. 292–308; M. R. Werner, *Brigham Young* (New York, 1925), pp. 398–405.

In many instances Mormon leaders publicly expounded on principles of Blood Atonement. Compare Orson Hyde speech of April 9, 1853, *Journal of Discourses*, Vol. I, p. 73; Brigham Young, February 18, 1855, ibid., Vol. II, p. 186; September 21, 1856, ibid., Vol. IV, pp. 53–54; February 8, 1857, ibid., Vol. IV, pp. 219–20; also published in the *Deseret News*, February 18, 1857; and Orson Pratt, "Repentance," *The Seer*, Vol. II (January 1854), p. 223.

[6] Hall, *Abominations of Mormonism Exposed*, pp. 84–85.

[7] *A Mormon Chronicle*, Vol. I, pp. 19–20. See also Sarah Sturdevant Leavitt, "Memoirs." MS, pp. 49–51. Mrs. Leavitt says Conditt was ill and in a delirium when he wandered onto Gheen's land. The dispute between Gheen and his neighbors concerned proposed construction of a road through his property.

[8] Hosea Stout, "Journal," Vol. 7, p. 81; *On The Mormon Frontier*, Vol. II, p. 659.

in damages.[9] Little more than six months later he charged a Gentile, Frank McNeill, with threatening his life. The court fined McNeill $10 and costs, then charged Gheen with threatening McNeill's life. A guilty plea brought a $10 fine and costs.[10] So matters stood on September 26, 1859, as John Gheen, cardsharp-turned-butcher, walked home from his shop in the quiet of the evening.[11] Minutes later he was dead, a bullet hole, black and ugly, in his forehead. H. F. Maguire, editor of the *Valley Tan*, was one of the first on the scene. In his next edition, Maguire described the affair:

> On last Monday evening, near eight o'clock, two shots were heard discharged upon the corner of Second East Temple and Second South Temple St. Upon repairing to that locality, immediately after the reports, we saw the body of a man stretched out upon the side walk, with the brains oozing from his head. A centre shot had been given, and death must have instantaneously ensued. The deceased was named John Gheen, and had been engaged in the butchering business. His character we hear universally spoken of as good. The circumstances of the death are hidden and vague, mysterious and incomprehensible. The prevailing opinion, we believe, is that the deceased committed suicide, this sentiment being strengthened by the fact that a pistol was found lying by his body; but would it not have been policy if the man was murdered, for the murderer to have dropped his weapon on the body of his victim?[12]

If Editor Maguire smelled something fishy in Gheen's unexpected demise, he was in good company. Hosea Stout, the decedent's attorney, wrote in his journal: ". . . John Gheen was found with a ball hole through his head. It is supposed he committed suicide." And T. B. H. Stenhouse, who also had the benefit of a Mormon's insight into the peculiarities of life in Zion, afterward opined that Gheen was the victim of a friend "who loved him as himself" and spilled his blood in atonement for his "sin unto death."[13] Oddly, no one in civil authority questioned Gheen's violent end. Even the coroner declined to hold an inquest, closing the entire episode without so much as a mention in his register records, this despite the

[9] Ibid.

[10] Hosea Stout, "Journal," Vol. 7, p. 93; *On The Mormon Frontier*, Vol. II, p. 665.

[11] Stenhouse, *Rocky Mountain Saints*, p. 470.

[12] *Valley Tan*, September 28, 1859. The *Deseret News*, September 28, 1859, also reported that two shots were fired.

[13] Stenhouse, *Rocky Mountain Saints*, pp. 470–71.

significant fact that witnesses heard *two* shots before finding Gheen. Equally strange was the location of the wound — the forehead — an unusual target for suicides. At the newspaper office of the pro-Mormon, self-appointed temporal champion of the church, *The Mountaineer*, an editorial also found aspects of Gheen's death peculiar:

> doubts exist in the minds of many, of the practicability of any right-handed man shooting himself from the left side of the skull, the bullet passing through the head in a nearly horizontal line; and the pistol found under him in or near his right hand. The arrival of a certain party from the West, who felt aggrieved with John Gheen, who had also been threatened by the former, is likewise a matter of grave suspicion. I would not, by any means, cast wilfully an imputation on any man, yet it is the gossip of the city . . . . It is suspected that he fell by the hands of another than himself.[14]

To the omniscient Achilles, Gheen's death was but another notch in Orrin Porter Rockwell's gunbutt. The Destroying Angel, he explained, was the man who put the butcher out of the way. The two men were on friendly terms, Achilles said, and,

> a conversation ensued on the sidewalk, under a shade tree . . . . At this point, Rockwell drew his pistol and shot Gean [*sic*] on the spot.
>   There are many residents of California who remember the incident, and will recall the fact of the discovery of the body. Of course, Rockwell was not known in the matter. Gean, when found, had his pistol with him, with one chamber empty, and it was asserted in Mormondom that remorse or a respect for the rules of the Church had prompted him, because of the recollection of the killing of his friend, to perform the bloody atonement, and that he had committed suicide. Such was the general impression everywhere; but an examination of the body showed no stains of fire or powder on the head of the deceased, which of itself precludes the possibility of suicidal act. Porter Rockwell killed this man at the orders of Brigham Young. . . .[15]

Gheen's body was quietly removed to the city cemetery and buried in Potter's Field without further formality. The butcher's death raised scarcely an eyebrow in Zion, where violence of one sort or another was becoming commonplace.

[14] *The Mountaineer*, October 8, 1859.

[15] Achilles, *Destroying Angels of Mormondom*, pp. 30–31. Here again Achilles offers no proof, no persuasive evidence, merely his own unsupported word given anonymously.

During this period two large gangs operated with relative impunity throughout the Territory. Bill Hickman, a ruffian with the temperament of a rattlesnake, headed one faction, while a flashy gambler named Joachim Johnston bossed the opposition.[16] Both gangs were deeply involved in the lucrative business of rustling government livestock for resale at fancy prices in California. About the first week in November, Rockwell was asked by a Mormon freighter to track down thieves who had stolen thirty head of mules from his herd. Acting in his capacity as a deputy sheriff, Rockwell nosed around and found that Johnston's bunch had rustled the mules and at that very moment were headed for Los Angeles on the southern trail. Rockwell started after them, stopping only long enough to recruit the Iron County sheriff in Parowan and a couple of extra posse members. On November 16 the lawmen reined up at John D. Lee's home in Washington.[17] Lee told Rockwell that Johnston, with Lot Huntington, Cub Johnson, Charles Flake, and a youngster named Neibaur — all Mormons — had passed through four days before with a trail herd of one hundred and fifty horses and mules. Riding swiftly, the posse caught up with the gang at Las Vegas and got the drop on them.

Johnston readily admitted hiring men to steal livestock in Great Salt Lake City and Camp Floyd, but insisted that he had never bothered Mormon property. "I didn't think your people would have followed me for stealing from your enemies," he observed caustically.[18] "Government officers robbed me and broke up my place at Camp Floyd, and I am determined to have my revenge." Johnston offered to surrender the herd without resistance on condition that he be permitted to continue to California. Rockwell agreed but insisted that the four Mormons in the gang return to the city to testify against the thieves Johnston had hired.

The episode had a strange sequel. Huntington and his friends later accused Hickman of informing on them, and on Christmas Day the young desperado, himself a fast man with a gun, called Hickman out. Huntington was backed by a half-dozen friends, all well-whiskied. When the

<hr>

[16] His real name, according to Salt Lake City death records, was H. Keitt (Keith?) Johnston. For further reference to organized outlawry in the city see the *Valley Tan*, February 22, 1859. An item in *Valley Tan*, November 23, 1859, suggests that Johnston may have been a Californian named Ashmore and a fugitive from the law.

[17] *A Mormon Chronicle*, Vol. I, p. 222.

[18] Ibid.

shooting stopped, both Hickman and Huntington lay wounded in the streets.[19] (The two subsequently recovered.)

The year 1859 faded into history a week later, moving Hosea Stout to note in his journal: "New Year's Day came and went without anyone being killed, or any ill feeling being manifested."

Whatever calming influence settled on the city lasted but a month for Rockwell, who seemed utterly incapable of exorcising the specter of violence dogging him, even though his energies were focused on the mundane pursuit of private enterprise. For the present at least, the long-haired scout had few plans beyond spending a pleasant winter in the bosom of his family, exerting himself to no greater measure than entertaining overland travelers during stage layovers at his new station at Point of the Mountain.

So it was that Rockwell sat in his favorite rocking chair in one corner of the Hot Springs Brewery Hotel's front room and gazed vacantly out the window; a biting north wind swirled the January snows across the trail in gusts that limited visibility to inches. He hardly noticed the ox team when it pulled up at the hitching rail, and he paid less attention to its driver, a thick-necked bullwhacker named Martin Oats, employed by the federal government as a teamster. As it happened, the foul weather had put Oats in an equally foul mood.

No more than fifteen minutes had passed before Rockwell was jarred from his reverie by a voice urgently calling his name. Running into the barroom, he was startled to see the teamster, Oats, waving a bowie knife at the bartender, Robert Hereford. Oats was shouting that Hereford had called him a thief. Whipping the heavy blade in the bartender's direction, Oats snarled, "I'll cut the heart out of any man who accuses me of stealing." For the first time he glanced at Rockwell. "You're a damned rustler, Mormon. You've stolen cattle from me!"

Unconcerned, Rockwell answered, "I don't know you, and I have no fight with you."

Taking advantage of Oats's diverted attention, Hereford slipped out of the room. Returning with a pair of pistols, he found the teamster and Rockwell locked in a struggle for possession of the knife. Oats had Rockwell by the beard, while the Mormon clenched the teamster's wrist with

---

[19] For details of the gunfight, see the *Deseret News*, December 28, 1859; Hosea Stout, "Journal," Vol. 8, p. 29; *On The Mormon Frontier*, Vol. II, p. 706; Hickman, *Brigham's Destroying Angel*, pp. 145–46; and *A Mormon Chronicle*, Vol. I, p. 234.

one hand and his throat with the other. Pushing a revolver squarely in Oats's face, the bartender ordered him to drop the knife. Hereford kicked the blade across the room and called for two other men lounging in the hotel to remove Oats to his wagon and head him in the direction of Camp Floyd. What followed is described in the *Deseret News* of February 1, 1860:

> . . . Some time after Oats had thus been started off and the two men who escorted him had returned to the hotel, Rockwell mounted his steed and started for Lehi, his place of residence; but before reaching the point where the Camp Floyd road diverges from the road to Lehi, he overtook Oats, who had not made good speed, or had been loitering along by the way for no good and, as Rockwell was passing, he sprang, seized his animal by the bit, and renewed his abuse and threats, whereupon Rockwell, after trying every expedient to make the fellow desist, and giving him proper warning of the consequence that would follow if he did not let him alone, shot the villain: the ball taking effect in the breast, produced almost instantaneous death.
>
> Mr. Rockwell returned to the hotel and informed Mr. Hereford of what he had done, requested him to send out some men and take care of the body and of the dead man's team, and then went to Lehi and gave himself up to the civil authorities.
>
> An investigation of the matter has since been had, and Mr. Rockwell has been honorably acquitted. The result seems to have given general satisfaction to all parties.[20]

Two weeks later, on February 19, Mary Ann Neff Rockwell blessed her husband with another son, David Porter Rockwell.[21] Despite his years (he was now forty-six) Rockwell enjoyed the gift of virility with which all Mormon males seemed endowed. Yet, as he entered that time of life known as middle-age, the scout seemed to flirt with death more than ever. Narrow escapes were becoming common. But Rockwell paid little heed, for he obeyed the prophecy of Joseph and, except for the interval following his benevolence to Don Carlos Smith's widow in California, kept his locks unshorn.

[20] See also the *Valley Tan*, February 1, 1860, and George Laub, "Diary." MS, three volumes, Vol. II, p. 66. Compare Achilles, *Destroying Angels of Mormondom*, p. 28, in which the author discusses the killing of a man named Davidson, allegedly by Rockwell, under circumstances much the same as the Oats incident. Achilles may have confused the identities. See also *The Mountaineer*, February 4, 1860.

[21] *Utah Genealogical and Historical Magazine*, Vol. XXVI, p. 156.

As soon as the weather permitted, Rockwell and a neighbor, Joseph Hollingshead, rode from Lehi to the Santa Clara River to round up the stolen mules they had left to graze the previous November when the Johnston gang was captured. Even this routine chore was to prove dangerous. Driving the herd to Cedar City, they were joined by John D. Lee, who wanted to move several horses to Harmony, a few miles distant. No sooner had the party gotten under way than an Indian express rider arrived with a message for Lee. General Johnston and fifty cavalrymen were on the trail and headed for California, the message warned. Since Lee had figured prominently in the Mountain Meadows massacre and was wanted by federal authorities, he thought it best to stay out of sight.[22]

Lee wrote in his journal: "From this caution I took due Notice & governed myself accordingly. . . . After talking with Rockwell near the grape vine springs, I conceald my Self near the Road & Saw the Train pass, near which quite a No. of Indians had collectd to defend Me provided I Should have fallen into their hands."[23] As Johnston's command came down the trail, the Indians moved into plain view, quietly astride their horses, but with rifles cocked as the soldiers rode by. The air was charged with tension as the two forces closed the distance, but the cavalrymen passed without incident.

Rockwell was less fortunate. A small party of Paiutes approached his company of drovers and grunted a challenge. Before Rockwell could open his mouth, Hollingshead jokingly gestured at the Mormons and announced that they were "Mericats." Scarcely had the words been uttered than the metallic clicking of rifle hammers being thumbed into firing position rattled through the Indian ranks, and the riders found themselves facing a party of very hostile Paiutes. Rockwell shouted, "Kotch Mericat! Kotch Mericat! Mormonee, Mormonee!" (Not American! Mormon!) When the braves hesitated, Rockwell repeated the denial, furiously pushing Hollingshead to the rear of the company.

"John Lee, John Lee. Yauguts, Yauguts!" Rockwell persisted, hoping the warriors would get the message that Lee was his friend and was close by.[24]

---

[22] Mrs. Juanita Brooks has covered this chapter of horrors in Utah history in detail. See *The Mountain Meadows Massacre* (Stanford, 1950, and Norman, Oklahoma, 1962).

[23] *A Mormon Chronicle*, Vol. I, p. 242.

[24] Yauguts is the Ute word for "Crybaby," a name Lee maintained that the Indians had bestowed upon him during the massacre at Mountain Meadows for his show of emotion at the slaughter of women and children.

"That was all that saved them," Lee recalled.[25] Once the danger had been averted, Rockwell paused momentarily to contemplate their narrow escape, paid Lee $10 for feeding the mule herd, then treated Hollingshead to a monumental dressing down for his stupidity.

The last days of March were playing out when Rockwell rode slowly down Whisky Street in Great Salt Lake City after safely herding the mules into the spacious corral behind the Colorado Stables. Attracted by loud laughter from one of the many saloons lining the way, he was surprised to see Joachim Johnston push his hulk through the batwing doors. A giant of a man for his day, the gambler stood well over six feet tall and weighed more than two hundred pounds. If Johnston had a weakness it was his vanity; he delighted in wearing tailored buckskin suits elaborately decorated with flowers and embroidered in brilliant silk. The buttons on his vest were two and a half dollar gold pieces.[26]

Joachim Johnston's boon companion in the City of Saints was an army deserter named Myron Brewer, a disenchanted Mormon with five wives scattered along the trail.[27] Outside of playing fast and loose with the law, Johnston and Brewer had a single common bond — they both hated the military.[28] Out of this hatred came a scheme to counterfeit quartermaster notes drawn on the treasuries at St. Louis and New York. To further their plan, the two men hired a twenty-six-year-old engraver named David McKenzie to make the necessary plates. By coincidence, McKenzie's workshop was located on the floor immediately above the Deseret Store in a building owned by Brigham Young.

Things went well for the two counterfeiters for a while, until a U.S. marshal traced the bogus notes to McKenzie's shop. P. K. Dotson, the same lawman who had tasted galling frustration in attempting to serve Judge Cradlebaugh's murder warrants, perhaps saw an opportunity to avenge his humiliation. He raided the shop, seized the plates, arrested McKenzie, and demanded a full confession. The frightened young man babbled out his story of accepting a job from Brewer, but maintained his own innocence. While he languished in jail, Dotson apprehended Brewer

---

[25] Described by Lee in *A Mormon Chronicle*, Vol. I, p. 242. The incident occurred March 12, 1860.

[26] Stenhouse, *Rocky Mountain Saints*, p. 418n.

[27] Richard Wilds Jones, "Travel Diary." MS, p. 32.

[28] John D. Lee, in *A Mormon Chronicle*, Vol. I, p. 233, portrayed Johnston as "a bitter Enimy to the Troops at camp Floyd."

at Camp Floyd. In his eagerness to avoid prosecution, the deserter shifted blame for the bogus notes to McKenzie and, of all people, Brigham Young. Brewer had guessed correctly that he would be passed off as small potatoes if the authorities believed they could pin a federal crime on the Mormon prophet. With this in mind, Brewer pointed the accusing finger at Young, implying that he was the brain behind the scheme, since the engravings were found on his property in a church-owned store. McKenzie subsequently was fined and imprisoned for his part in the crime, and a counterfeiting charge was lodged against Brigham Young. Governor Cumming refused to permit a writ to be served on him, however, and the matter died there.[29]

On May 17, 1860, Joachim Johnston and Myron Brewer staggered to their boarding house in Great Salt Lake City after a conscientious attempt to drink Zion dry. The two got as far as the corner of East Temple and Second South when gunfire shattered the night silence; both men were killed instantly. A reporter who dashed to the scene wrote:

> Johnston, a prominent member of one of the [outlaw] bands, and a well known government horse and mule thief, and one of the party who lately killed the Indian on the Sevier, arrived from Camp Floyd the evening before and was swaggering about the streets and shops, and without reserve told his business and what he came from Camp Floyd for — his special business being to follow a company that had gone east and steal their mules; but before leaving he intended to take a few scalps; and that his pistols were in first rate order and all was right and that he felt first rate.
> Late in the evening Johnston and Brewer were in one of the stores conversing with some of their acquaintances, and on the way to the place they were boarding, at about eleven o'clock, they were both shot, evidently with guns or muskets loaded with balls and buckshot, which took effect on the left shoulder and side of each, inflicting many wounds, of which they instantly died. . . .[30]

Early the next morning the city marshal and the chief of police announced their verdict: "Johnston and Brewer quarrelled and killed

---

[29] See Stenhouse, *Rocky Mountain Saints*, pp. 410–12; Jones, "Travel Diary," p. 32; Tracy, "Journal," *Utah Historical Quarterly*, Vol. XIII, p. 71; and Linn, *Story of the Mormons*, p. 536.

[30] *Deseret News*, May 23, 1860. Interestingly, the reporter observed that the wounds had been made by "guns or muskets loaded with balls and buckshot," a similarity not to be ignored by students of the attempted assassination of Lilburn W. Boggs.

each other!"[31] In later years Orrin Porter Rockwell was said to have been the assassin who pulled the trigger in the double slaying.[32]

But there was more in Great Salt Lake City to excite the attention than the unspectacular death of a pair of toughs. With the Pony Express a reality, firing the imagination with its swift efficiency and riders of great derring-do, Rockwell's stage station at Point of the Mountain soon became a regular stopping place for settlers eager to hear the latest tidbit of news from east or west. The express was passing regularly either from St. Joseph or Sacramento and carried the mail faster than ever before.

Beginning in mid-August of 1860 the Mormons were privileged for a brief three weeks to play host to an international celebrity — Richard F. Burton, explorer, scholar, raconteur, and invader of forbidden cities. It was Burton who had penetrated Mecca and Medina; now he anticipated adding "the mysteries" of Great Salt Lake City, desert refuge of American polygyny, to his experiences. Little escaped the Briton's marvelously developed powers of observation, and because of this he was quickly disappointed by the unexpected absence of erotica which he had thought engulfed the Mormon practice of plural marriage.

Satisfied that he had seen what there was to see (his notebooks bulged with memoranda), Burton packed and prepared to leave Zion on September 19. But first there was someone he wanted very much to meet — the "chief of the Sons of Dan," Orrin Porter Rockwell (who had been out of the city, freighting a train of 30 to 40 wagons of supplies to Pike's Peak).[33] Calling Rockwell one of the "triumvirate" of the Danites along with "Ephe Hanks and Bill Hickman," the Englishman sat down for an interview with the "notorious" Mormon. Burton's account of the conversation provides one of the most colorful glimpses available of the Mormon Samson.

> Porter Rockwell [he wrote] was a man about fifty,[34] tall and strong, with ample leather leggings overhanging his huge spurs, and the saw-handles of two revolvers peeping from his blouse. His forehead was already a little bald, and he wore his long grizzly locks after

---

[31] Stenhouse, *Rocky Mountain Saints*, p. 418. Stenhouse was moved to comment: "This story was feeble enough, but no one cared to question it: the people had got used to the record of scenes of blood."

[32] Kelly and Birney, *Holy Murder*, p. 198, another allegation unsupported by evidence.

[33] Manuscript History of Brigham Young, August 29, 1860.

[34] Burton's guess was close; Rockwell had turned forty-seven two months earlier.

the ancient fashion of the U.S., plaited and gathered up at the nape of the neck;[35] his brow puckered with frowning wrinkles contrasted curiously with his cool determined grey eye, jolly red face, well touched up with "paint," and his laughing good-humored mouth. He had the manner of a jovial, reckless, devil-may-care English ruffian. The officers called him Porter, and preferred him to the "slimy villains" who will drink with a man and then murder him. After a little preliminary business about a stolen horse, all conducted on the amiable, he pulled out a dollar, and sent to the neighbouring distillery for a bottle of Valley Tan.[36] The *aguardiente* was smuggled in under a cloth, as though we had been respectables in a Moslem country, and we were asked to join him in a "squar' drink," which means spirits without water. The mode of drinking was peculiar. Porter, after the preliminary sputation raised the glass with a cocked little finger to his lips, with the twinkle of the eye ejaculated "Wheat!" that is to say "good," and drained the tumbler to the bottom: we acknowledged his civility with a "here's how," and drank Kentucky-fashion, which in English is midshipman's grog.

Of these "squar' drinks" we had at least four, which, however, did not shake Mr. Rockwell's nerve, and then he sent out for more. Meanwhile he told us his last adventure, how when ascending the kanyon he suddenly found himself covered by two long rifles; how he had thrown himself from his horse, drawn his revolver and crept behind a bush, and how he had dared the enemy to come out and fight like men.[37] . . . When he heard that I was preparing for California he gave me abundant good advice — to carry a double-barrelled gun loaded with buckshot; to "keep my eyes skinned," especially in kanyons and ravines; to make at times a dark camp . . . and never to trust to appearances in an Indian country . . . . I observed that, when thus speaking, Porter's eyes assumed the expression of an old moun-

[35] It would appear that Burton was unfamiliar with the prophecy pertaining to Rockwell's hair.

[36] Homemade whisky distilled in the valley.

[37] This is the only mention of such a fight. An incident which may have a bearing on Rockwell's remark occurred approximately three weeks earlier when a detachment of troops recovered fourteen stolen government cattle from a rustlers' camp on the road to Provo. An Alfred Higgins was arrested, but he later escaped through the aid of an accomplice. Before he was recaptured and sentenced to the penitentiary for grand larceny, Higgins paraded the streets of Provo shouting that he would have his revenge on Rockwell, whom he accused of being an informer. *Deseret News*, September 5, 1860. (Higgins proved to be a slippery character, for on April 30, 1862, he and four other convicts broke out of the penitentiary using keys fashioned from scraps of zinc. Higgins was caught in a mining camp near Malad City some weeks later, but succeeded in escaping again, this time for good. *Deseret News*, May 7, June 11, 1862.)

309

taineer's, ever rolling as if set in quicksilver. For the purpose of avoiding "White Indians," the worst of their kind, he advised me to shun the direct route, which he represented to be about as fit for travelling as h–ll for a powder magazine . . . .[38]

So well did the two men strike it off, that Burton, upon his return to England, sent the rugged westerner a bottle of brandy for his kindness to a passing stranger. Yet Burton also offered Rockwell an injustice; he inadvertently became responsible for a rumor that Rockwell had been killed, and the famous Mormon's demise was solemnly recorded in British newspapers in the autumn of 1860.[39] Rockwell, if indeed he heard the report at all, gave no hint that he was disturbed at being considered among the dear departed.

By early 1861 Rockwell possessed a liquor license and was selling whisky at the inn, which now catered regularly to Overland Stage passengers. Captain Albert Tracy, heading east on furlough, commented on the food at Point of the Mountain: ". . . [took] dinner at a kind of half-way house across the Jordan — and relish[ed] the same, with the appetite of the wayfarer." [40] It would have been interesting to witness the officer's reaction had he discovered the identity of his host.

Over the years Rockwell progressed steadily in the priesthood of his church despite the many sabbath meetings he had been forced to forego because of the press of duty. It was only proper when he began being bothered by a troublesome neighbor in Lehi that he submit the matter to ecclesiastical authority for adjudication, in this case the Council of Seventy to which both he and the neighbor belonged. Had the neighbor been a Gentile, Rockwell might have elected a more simple and direct course of action, one which would have permanently absented his antagonist from the scene. In any event Rockwell and the accused, Israel Evans, appeared before the Seventies on January 26, 1861, at a trial conducted by Brigham Young, a significant indication of Rockwell's prestige, since Young's responsibilities rarely permitted such picayune distractions.[41] After the

[38] This comment, coming from Rockwell, is especially interesting. Burton, *City of the Saints*, pp. 449–50.

[39] Dilke, *Greater Britain*, Vol. I, pp. 184–86.

[40] Tracy, "Journal," *Utah Historical Quarterly*, Vol. XIII, p. 84.

[41] Laub "Diary," Vol. II, p. 83; Charles L. Walker, "Journal." MS, p. 199. An earlier mention of Rockwell's movements in the higher circles of the Melchizedek Priesthood can be found in Edwin Ward Smout, "Journal," MS, p. 8, in which

necessary formalities (Evans was charged by Rockwell with rustling an OP ox and butchering the animal; while John Murdock accused Evans of "abuse"), the council heard all sides of the dispute and reached its verdict. One of those present, George Laub, chronicled the decision: ". . . Evens was disfellow Shiped from the Seventys untill Such times as he gave Full Satisfaction of his doings." [42] Laub added that the decree was handed down by Brigham Young and Heber C. Kimball.

When, in April, the Confederacy fired on Fort Sumter, the news flashed across the nation as fast as the Pony Express could carry it. [43] As early as 1860, when General Johnston had turned over his command to Brevet Colonel Charles F. Smith and taken the southern route out of the territory, the strong smell of secession had permeated the air. Fifteen hundred troops received orders to move to Arizona and New Mexico within three months of Johnston's departure, and by July of the following year the remainder of the Utah Expedition was on its way east. Among the many dispatches pouring into the camp during those final days was one calling for immediate deactivation of the installation, including destruction of surplus powder and ammunition and the sale of government stores. An estimated $4 million in goods reached the auction block and sold for $100,000; $40,000 of which was Brigham Young's as bid in by his business agent, Hiram Clawson. Smaller buyers, like Rockwell's neighbor and amanuensis, J. C. Naile, bid on several buildings, hoping to win their contents as well. So low were the bids that many soldiers angrily threatened to destroy the stores rather than let them fall into Mormon hands for pennies on the dollar. Flour, for instance, which had sold for $25 a sack during the gold rush ten years before, now brought a mere fifty cents. Bacon went for a quarter of a penny a pound, and whisky for twenty-five cents a gallon. [44] Bill Hickman, recognizing a bargain, bought provisions enough to fill ten wagons. All the public buildings and stables in camp sold for a bid of less than $500.

In compliance with orders, the troops destroyed all ordnance and

---

he records that in March 1856 Joseph Young and Rockwell "came to Ogden City for to ordain Seventys."

[42] Laub, "Diary," Vol. II, p. 83.

[43] Elias Smith, editor of the *Deseret News*, recorded in his journal that the Pony Express arrived in the city late in the night of April 20, 1861, eight days after the shelling of Fort Sumter. Editor Smith issued an "Extra" dated April 21.

[44] Hickman, *Brigham's Destroying Angel*, p. 147.

ammunition. Two thousand stands of rifles, for which the Mormons had offered $6 a weapon, were set afire, an act the Saints regarded with hostility. The ill feeling was compounded when soldiers vindictively razed several buildings purchased at auction, prompting Rockwell to complain strongly to Brigham Young of the "depredations" after he learned that the structures were those bought by Naile.[45] Tempers rubbed raw on both sides as the military made final preparations to abandon the camp to its fate. Privately, the troops viewed the demolition of rifles and powder with a sigh of relief; many soldiers had openly expressed the fear that someday they would be faced with their own weapons unless the guns were put to the torch. As one infantryman put it:

> . . . I presume there will be over a million dollars worth of property destroyed, but better destroyed than ever to be used against the government.
> The Mormons seem wrathy at the munitions being destroyed and make threats that we will never reach Fort Leavenworth, there is certainly a crowd of desperadoes in this vicinity at present, headed by the notorious Porter Rockwell . . . .[46]

Obviously the Mormons were not heartbroken to see the army pull up stakes. Hickman, his own larder fattened at government expense, recorded the sentiments of his brethren: "There was rejoicing when the troops left the Territory. They had come here, spent a great quantity of money, and went away without hurting anybody — a victory, of course.[47] Yet, with the soldiers gone the Mormons had few outsiders to blame for acts of violence committed in the valley; now the desperadoes and thieves cursed by the Saints from the Tabernacle pulpit had a home-grown aspect.[48]

For example, on August 31, 1861, Kenneth and Alexander McRae, sons of Alexander McRae, Sr., a close friend of Joseph Smith, were wanted by the law for "robbing an emigrant on the highway of his money

---

[45] Journal History, July 23, 1861. According to one witness, Rockwell went so far as to warn the soldiers that "If they burned anymore barns they would never leave Utah alive." The burning stopped. Orson Twelves, "Early History of Charles Twelves and Family," MS, p. 2.

[46] "Charles A. Scott's Diary of the Utah Expedition, 1857–1861," edited by Robert E. Stowers and John M. Ellis, *Utah Historical Quarterly*, Vol. XXVIII (1960), p. 395, under entry for July 24, 1861.

[47] Hickman, *Brigham's Destroying Angel*, p. 148.

[48] *Journal of Discourses*, Vol. I, pp. 73, 108–9.

and mule." [49] In a matter of hours the sheriff and his deputies closed in on the two brothers in Emigration Canyon and ordered them to surrender. When they ignored the command the two boys were gunned down. [50] No official record remains to show who pulled the trigger, but again Achilles blames Rockwell for shooting "unarmed men."

About twelve miles east of Salt Lake city, the [McRaes] were found, placed under arrest and were disarmed. On the return to Salt Lake city, in a lonely spot in Emigration Canyon, they were shot by Rockwell and the officer, double-barrelled shot-guns being the weapons used. The bodies were placed in a wagon, and taken to the house of their father and mother. They were here taken out and laid in the yard. The horror-stricken mother came out, and in her anguish denounced Rockwell as a murderer and a villain. He retorted upon her by saying, that if she had done her duty, her sons would have been good Saints, and that if she had her deserts, and he did his duty, she would be in the same place that her children were. Rockwell immediately mounted his horse and rode off. It was reported in Salt Lake that the boys attempted to escape from the officers, and were shot in the effort at capture. . . . [51]

And so ended the Brothers McRae. But not all accused badmen were doomed to such a fate in the land of Zion. There also occurred in the year 1861, "about the time the first telegraph lines were strung over Utah," an incident which dramatically illustrated Rockwell's prowess as

[49] The emigrant, John Love, appeared before City Judge Elias Smith and swore out complaints against both McRae boys and two other brothers, Charles and Truelove Manhard, on charges of robbery. See Elias Smith, "Journal," p. 128. The Manhards subsequently were imprisoned, but with three others they managed a spectacular escape from the penitentiary using keys made from pieces of zinc stolen from the workshop. Both brothers turned themselves in to the warden two days later. *Deseret News*, May 7, 1862.

[50] Death Records, Salt Lake City Bureau of Vital Statistics, Certificates 1340 and 1341. Judge Smith wrote in his journal that night, ". . . [the warrant] was returned this evening with the dead bodies of the two accused persons young men aged about 19 & 21 years they having been killed after they were arrested in an attempt to escape." See Smith, "Journal," pp. 128–29; Charles L. Walker, "Journal," p. 249; and Journal History, August 31, 1861, which states tersely: "Kenneth and Alexander McRae were shot by the sheriff and deputies this afternoon. After being arrested on a charge of robbery, they attempted to run away and were killed while fleeing." Oddly, the brothers' gravestones bear the erroneous date of August 30, 1861. See Charles E. Griffin, "History," MS. He was a deputy in the posse and offers details of the arrest, but does not identify the man who actually fired the shots.

[51] Achilles, *Destroying Angels of Mormondom*, pp. 31–32.

313

a manhunter. And not a person was hurt. It all began with Frank Karrick, a well-to-do young freighter who had amassed a neat pile of double eagles hauling goods between Great Salt Lake City and Sacramento. His "fit-out" of twenty teams easily was worth $1,000 each, besides which he had $15,000 more in gold alone. Mr. Karrick was a very successful young man, one who would not give up easily, as subsequent events proved. In essence, these were the circumstances when Karrick rode into his camp, seventy miles south of Great Salt Lake, one night in '61 and paused for a last check of the livestock before turning in.

In two minutes he was shaking his bewildered teamsters awake. "Boys, there's something the matter here," he said, checking off animals as he pushed his way through the corral. Eight mules and a big grey stallion were gone. The nine had a combined worth of at least $4,500. Tracks visible by firelight showed that the stock had been led from the makeshift corral to the trail some distance away. At the first light of day, Karrick was in the saddle and following the stolen animals. A good tracker, he recognized the telltale marks which distinguished his mules and horse from the clutter of impressions in the mouse-colored trail dust. Forty miles from camp, Karrick came upon a confusion of iron shoe prints branching into two distinct and opposing directions. In one batch of tracks he found what he thought was a sign made by one of his mules.

With the search now taking him into unfamiliar country, the freighter was forced into a decision. Galloping back to camp, he buried the $15,000 in gold under cover of darkness. "Since there was no one I could trust," he later explained, "I felt this was the safest way." Remounting, he gave orders for his teamsters to wait until he returned, then made for Great Salt Lake City — his object: to see Brigham Young. Surprisingly, the Gentile had little difficulty in gaining admittance and explaining his predicament.

Satisfied that the stock had been stolen and not merely lost, Young advised Karrick to seek the services of "Port Rockwell."

So it was that later that day Karrick and Rockwell were riding to the spot where the freighter had intercepted the bifurcated trail. From that point on, Rockwell took the lead. Mile after mile passed until the tracks vanished.

"Never mind," Rockwell said, noticing his companion's dismay, "They've only taken the shoes off the mules. We'll just stay on this trail." They rode until nightfall. The next day they pushed all the harder, hoping to catch sight of the rustlers before dusk. Then at sunset Rockwell

314

jogged to the top of a small rise. Barely perceptible in the distance was a drift of dust. He pulled a telescope from his saddlebags.

"Two men . . . some horses . . . and mules — come on!" he said, roweling the flank of his mount. Karrick leaned forward in the saddle and followed. Swiftly the distance between the dust cloud and its two pursuers narrowed, until finally the Mormon and his young companion rode up on two men hunkered near a campfire on the edge of a deep, swift stream. Karrick was delighted to see his mules nibbling at tall grass on the opposite bank.

Rockwell leveled a snub-nosed Colt revolver at the two men.[52] The pair exchanged nervous glances and raised their hands. In ten minutes Karrick had his mules and the big grey stallion tethered. After depositing the rustlers with the sheriff, Rockwell accompanied his freighter friend back to camp, where Karrick exhumed his cache of gold and handed the Mormon $500. Several weeks later the stage from California clattered into Great Salt Lake City and unloaded a nickel-tooled saddle plus a gallon demijohn of Sacramento's finest whisky. Both were marked for Porter Rockwell, compliments of Frank Karrick.

"I heard later that he was vastly more interested in the whisky than in the saddle," Karrick laughed.[53]

New Year's Eve, 1861, at Ephraim Hanks's stage station was like most winter nights in the Wasatch Mountains — frigid, with a wind that could tear the lashes from a man's eyelids. Waiting for the eastbound coach that night was John W. Dawson, late of Indiana and now governor of Utah Territory. Dawson had made his grand entrance into Zion just three weeks before to succeed Governor Cumming as chief executive. In that brief span the Indianan had managed to compromise himself to such an extent that he feared for his life. In fact, at that very moment he was fleeing the Territory, accused of making improper advances toward a re-

---

[52] It was Rockwell's habit to saw the barrels of his pistols to a length of three inches to accommodate the weapons comfortably in the pockets of his coat, since he shunned the use of holsters. In the author's possession is Rockwell's .36 caliber Navy Colt, Serial No. 168832. The barrel and front sight modifications coincide in every respect with those of the Army Colt identified as being Rockwell's, now in possession of the LDS Church.

[53] The events described here were related by Karrick to *Gax*, pseudonym for a special correspondent of the *Salt Lake Herald*, in a dispatch dated July 20, 1885, and published in the *Herald* on July 30, 1885.

spected Mormon widow.[54] While waiting for the stage, the disgraced official was set upon by a gang of drunken hellions, who beat him mercilessly on the pretext of avenging the honor of the lady in question. They left him unconscious and, some said, emasculated.[55]

Charged with committing the outrage were Lot Huntington; Moroni Clawson; John M., Jason, and Wilford Luce; Wood Reynolds; and Isaac Neibaur. Reynolds, it seemed, was related to the offended woman.[56] Warrants were issued for their arrest, and the city police kept an eye open for them. Two weeks passed without incident until Giles Mottin, an Overland Mail Company employee, reported the loss of $800 from a tin box hidden in Townsend's stable, where he worked as a hostler for the stage operation.[57] Suspicion at once centered on Lot Huntington and a friend of his, John P. Smith, as the probable burglars. Judge Elias Smith, who doubled as editor of the *Deseret News*, obliged with warrants for their arrest.

It was now January 14. John Bennion, an old friend of Rockwell's and a comrade-in-arms from the days of the Utah Expedition, tied his mare, Brown Sal by name, to a fence post in West Jordan, then entered the home of his bishop to settle tithing. When he came out shortly after midnight the horse was gone and Bennion was forced to walk four miles home. His son Sam, hearing of the theft, was furious; Brown Sal had the reputation of being one of the finest horses in Zion. Rounding up some of his father's friends for a posse, young Sam, Orson Cutler, and John Irving began tracking the culprits while Sam Bateman went for Rockwell. In Draperville, a settlement south of West Jordan, the five men learned that Huntington and Smith, accompanied by Clawson, had been seen in the vicinity and were heading west.

[54] There is some question regarding Dawson's gallantry in the affair. Several sources insist that he was tricked by scheming Mormon officials. See Stenhouse, *Rocky Mountain Saints*, p. 592; Waite, *The Mormon Prophet and His Harem*, p. 76; and Beadle, *Life in Utah*, p. 201. Others maintain the scandal resulted entirely from Dawson's own actions. See *Deseret News*, January 1, 1862; Tullidge, *History of Salt Lake City*, p. 249; Pomeroy Tucker, *Origin, Rise and Progress of Mormonism* (New York, 1867), p. 239.

[55] Upon reaching Bear River Station Dawson composed a letter to the editor of the *Deseret News* in which he detailed his account of the attack and named his assailants. The statement was dated January 7, 1862. See *Deseret News*, January 22, 1862.

[56] Smith, "Journal," p. 150. She was the widow of Thomas S. Williams.

[57] *Deseret News*, January 15, 1862. A squib in the same issue reported that Reynolds, the Luce boys, and Neibaur were arrested on charges of assaulting Dawson.

Ahead of the posse by a full day, the three suspects, oblivious of the manhunters sniffing at their heels, rode leisurely toward Faust Mail Station, a small outpost twenty-two miles west of Camp Floyd. Huntington, after spotting a large herd of cattle being driven by a friend, Howard R. Egan, son of the pioneer scout, had ridden out alone to eat dinner in the Egan camp. Before bidding his school chum *adiós*, Huntington suggested that the two parties team up at Faust and ride the trail together as far as Ruby Valley, Egan's destination.[58]

By now Rockwell's posse had reached Camp Floyd, where they learned from the Overland Stage agent that the three fugitives had passed through several hours earlier.[59] Accepting an offer to use a stagecoach for the remainder of the chase, the weary riders struck the trail for Faust's, pulling into the secluded station about four o'clock in the morning. Carefully moving the coach out of sight, the four men took positions around the crude log structure and waited for Rockwell's signal. They shivered in the snow and bitter cold until ten in the morning, when the station door opened noisily and the figure of H. J. Faust, station owner, emerged. From his place of concealment Rockwell beckoned to the startled innkeeper, and was told that the three hunted men were at that moment eating breakfast.

"Go back in and tell them to come out with their hands up," Rockwell ordered.

Several minutes ticked off after Faust had closed the door behind him. Then, as Rockwell was contemplating the wisdom of rushing the cabin, Lot Huntington appeared, a heavy cap and ball pistol clenched in his fist. Tall and handsome, the young outlaw moved with a confident swagger. Without bothering to look around, Huntington made straight for the stable and Brown Sal. A warning shout to surrender was ignored. Scrambling from his hiding place, Rockwell shook the numbing cold from his body and ran to the side of the corral adjoining the stable in time to see Huntington pull himself onto the unsaddled stolen mare. Rockwell barked a final warning. Huntington started to squeeze the trigger of his .44 at the instant Rockwell cut loose with a blast from his Colt. The wanted man stiffened convulsively as eight balls tore into his stomach; he slid from the horse and crashed down on a corral rail, one leg catching a

[58] Egan, *Pioneering the West*, p. 217.

[59] *Deseret News*, January 22, 1862, calls Rockwell "one of Sheriff Burton's deputies" and added that he "assumed leadership of the party."

post.[60] Twenty-seven-year-old Lot Huntington dangled grotesquely from the cedar rungs and bled to death.[61]

At the first sound of shooting, Clawson and Smith surrendered without a fight. Huntington's body was placed in the stagecoach, and after stopping at Camp Floyd to telegraph ahead, the posse headed home with its prisoners. A few miles out they intercepted the Egan cattle drive, and Rockwell, recognizing Egan's son, sang out, "Everything all right?" The boy, puzzled at the sight of an unscheduled stagecoach full of heavily armed passengers, answered, "Yeah, so far."

"Good. You be careful and keep a good watch on those cattle."

Only later did young Egan learn that Huntington had planned to rustle his herd and drive it to California.[62]

Four policemen were waiting for the stage when it pulled into Townsend's corral about five o'clock that morning. It was a tired Rockwell who alighted, turned Clawson and Smith over to the law, then led his winded team to the stable. Hardly had he begun to strip the harnesses from the animals than gunfire exploded down the street in the direction the officers had taken with the two captives. Rockwell pulled his revolver and ran toward the sound. He came upon the policeman standing over the lifeless bodies of the prisoners. "Tried to escape," one of the constables explained matter-of-factly.[63]

When word circulated the city of Huntington's death and the subsequent demise of his two cronies, some of the community's citizens exchanged knowing glances. Bill Hickman looked for several minutes upon the body of Huntington, the man who had shot and nearly crippled him two years earlier, then studied the other two corpses. He shrugged off the tale that Clawson and Smith had been killed while escaping. It was "nonsense," he said. "They were both powder-burnt, and one of them was shot in the face. How could that be, and they running?"[64] At the

---

[60] Journal History, January 16, 1862. Significantly, Rockwell fired once and discharged eight buckshot.

[61] Ibid. The entry reads, ". . . with eight slugs cutting the arteries to pieces. . . . He bled to death in four minutes." See also Deseret News, January 22, 1862. Compare Glynn Bennion, "The Best Laid Schemes . . . ," Salt Lake Tribune, March 9, 1924, and George Morris, "Autobiography." MS, p. 89.

[62] Egan, Pioneering the West, p. 218. "If there was a plot laid for me, old Porter burst the bubble and I got through safe," Egan said.

[63] Deseret News, January 22, 1862.

[64] Hickman, Brigham's Destroying Angel, p. 149. Clawson's burial and eventual disinterment turned into the most macabre incident in Mormon history, the appre-

same time, T. B. H. Stenhouse was making a mental note for the book he planned to write:

All the bad and desperate Mormons were not brought to judgment, but the pretext alone was wanting for carrying more extensively into execution the general [police] programme. Resistance to an officer, or the slightest attempt to escape from custody, was eagerly seized, when wanted, as the justification of closing a disreputable career, and in more than one case of this *legal* shooting, there is much doubt if even the trivial excuse was waited for. The Salt Lake police then earned the reputation of affording every desperate prisoner the opportunity of escape, and, if embraced, the officer's ready revolver brought the fugitive to a "halt," and saved the county the expenses of a trial and his subsequent boarding in the penitentiary. A coroner's inquest and cemetery expenses were comparatively light.[65]

Rockwell, Bateman, Irving, and Cutler made their respective ways home; young Sam Bennion jubilantly rode Brown Sal into her stall; and John Bennion, after critically inspecting his recovered mare, that night jotted in his journal: ". . . Samuel R. got home Friday morning about 9 o'clock with the mare saddle and bridle neck strap and chain were missing I brought the sheep down."

---

hension of John Baptiste, the ghoul. This sensational episode is detailed in Dale Morgan, *The Great Salt Lake* (Indianapolis, 1947), pp. 274–82.

[65] Stenhouse, *Rocky Mountain Saints*, p. 419. Italics in the original. In a footnote to the shooting of Moroni Clawson and John P. Smith, Stenhouse comments: "After they reached Salt Lake City, the police, in taking them to the *calaboose*, said that the prisoners tried to escape, and they shot them down. It was believed that the prisoners were walking in front of the officers when the latter quietly put their revolvers to the back of their heads and 'stopped them.'" P. 592n.

Chapter Seventeen

SLAUGHTER AT BEAR RIVER

SUMMER OF 1862 FOUND ROCKWELL wishing he had an extra pair of hands — business was that good. Overland travel had stepped up despite increasing difficulty with Indians, and Colonel Kane's influence in Washington had paid off handsomely, for Rockwell now was a prospering mail contractor with five short-haul routes scattered around the Territory; they alone brought him an annual income of $2,100 — enough to make the hard-working Mormon one of the valley's wealthier citizens, considering his already successful ranching and hotel enterprises.[1] And Rockwell's intense loyalty to the church had brought him great personal honor as well.

After Lot Huntington's death, life settled down long enough for Rockwell to attend the press of his various business interests. He still kept in close touch with Mormon authorities, and his inn was on many a bishop's itinerary. Rockwell entertained Brigham Young whenever circumstances brought him near Point of the Mountain.[2] The two men spent many

[1] The contracts and their annual income included: Route 14601, Brigham City to Logan via Providence, Millville, Hyrum, Wellsville, and Mendon, $350; Route 14603, Cedar City to Santa Clara, $800; Route 14604, Cedar Valley to Gardiner's Mills, $300; Route 14607, Nephi to Manti, $350; and Route 14612, Salt Lake City to Alpine, $300. All were weekly mail runs. See *Deseret News*, December 18, 1861; June 18, 1862.

[2] Journal History, September 4, 1862; September 25, 1862, p. 2.

evening hours discussing "the old days" of Jackson County and Nauvoo. This brief interlude in Rockwell's otherwise violent existence may have been his most enjoyable era, but destiny did not plan a quiet life for Orrin Porter Rockwell.

Shoshone war parties infesting the Overland Mail route had systematically ravaged stage stations between the north fork of the Platte and Fort Bridger since spring. Depredations became almost a daily occurrence. Coaches and mail bags were burned, and drivers were killed or maimed in an uprising that threatened a general disruption of service along the line unless drastic retaliatory measures were taken. After a modicum of preliminary sparring with a group of anxious federal officials in Great Salt Lake City, Brigham Young wired Washington: ". . . the militia of Utah are ready and able . . . to take care of all the Indians, and . . . protect the mail line." [3] Without waiting for a reply, Young ordered Robert T. Burton, a colonel in the Nauvoo Legion, to take the field and protect the eastbound mail coach until further notice.

[3] Tullidge, *History of Salt Lake City*, p. 252; Fred B. Rogers, *Soldiers of the Overland, Being Some Account of the Services of General Patrick Edward Connor & His Volunteers in the Old West* (San Francisco, 1938), p. 17.

Obtaining men for this grueling assignment was one thing, fitting them with mounts was another. It came as no surprise when Rockwell received a letter from the commanding general of the Legion, Daniel H. Wells, "Availing myself of your kind offer of animals I send to you tonight wishing you to have so many as you can spare fit for service in the city Tomorrow Evening or as much sooner as possible. The fact is we want to start a company east by day after tomorrow and can get men much easier than animals. Another fine company is to be got up upon the requisition of Brigham Young which will be further explained to you hereafter. . . ."[4]

Wells's mention of "another fine company" referred to a telegram from the office of President Lincoln authorizing Young to raise, equip, and arm one company of cavalry for a ninety-day period. (Yet, Brigham Young was a private citizen in 1862!) Within the hour Young had issued an order creating the troop. It could not have been mere coincidence that its commander was to be the mountain fox of the Mormon War, Lot Smith.[5] The Saints must have felt a deep satisfaction knowing that Smith's perimeter of responsibility covered the same terrain over which he had stalked government supply trains five years earlier, and that Uncle Sam was again footing the bill. But this time things were different, for Smith, in a complete reversal of his former role, now was charged with protecting United States property at all costs.

Mormon participation in the "police action" against Indian raids was to be temporary, and toward this end Colonel Patrick Edward Connor with seven companies of his Third Regiment of California Volunteers left San Francisco July 12, 1862, for Fort Ruby in the first phase of an operation intended to clear the plains of war parties between Carson Valley, Great Salt Lake City, and Fort Laramie. Leaving a number of men at Fort Ruby, Connor took the main column and struck out for Zion — in the face of Brigham Young's avowal to prevent any federal force from again fouling his promised land with its unwelcome presence. It was this distasteful possibility which had prompted Young to act so swiftly in ordering Burton to protect the stages. He hoped fast action might dissuade the War Department from sending regular troops sorely needed on other battlefields closer to Washington. But Brigham had miscalculated, and Connor was on his way.

[4] Wells to Rockwell, April 28, 1862, Military Records Section, Utah State Archives.

[5] Special Orders No. 3. See Tullidge, *History of Salt Lake City*, p. 255, and the *Deseret News*, May 7, 1862.

Indian outrages, meanwhile, stepped up in frequency. Raiding parties ran off horses in northern Utah counties,[6] six emigrants were murdered near City of Rocks, and twenty-three men had been reported killed near Gravelly Ford on the Humboldt River.[8]

On October 17, 1862, Connor and his men tramped into old Camp Floyd, now renamed Fort Crittenden because former Secretary of War John B. Floyd had defected to the Confederate cause. Three days later, a Sunday, Connor formed his five infantry companies and two troops of cavalry, then gave the march order for the final leg of their arduous journey to Great Salt Lake City. The Volunteers snapped to in their smartest fashion since leaving San Francisco. Word circulated that "the Chief of the Danites" had ridden through the Mormon city offering to bet $500 that the soldiers would never cross the Jordan.[9] When he heard of the threat the bellicose Connor snorted that he would "cross the river Jordan if hell yawned below him." The men arose that morning to find their commanding officer sitting on a log, cleaning and loading his pistols.

All elements of the Great Salt Lake Expedition of the California Volunteers, including stragglers and thirteen men on sick call, marched over the winding muddy stream that afternoon, and on the following morning paraded proudly through the city under the scowling gaze of a silent populace. "With loaded rifles, fixed bayonets and shotted cannon," Connor moved his men to the city's east bench area and pitched tents. From its elevated location, the artillery enjoyed a clear view of the city and a "perfect and unobstructed range of Brigham's residence . . . with their muzzles turned in that direction, the Prophet felt awfully annoyed," T. B. H. Stenhouse recalled. Connor planted the United States flag, creating Camp Douglas in honor of the Little Giant. Contemplating the new military post, Stenhouse said: ". . . certainly no place could have been chosen more offensive to Brigham." [10] Connor unwittingly had

[6] *Deseret News*, August 6, 1862.

[7] Ibid., September 24, 1862. Described in detail in Rogers, *Soldiers of the Overland*, pp. 29–31.

[8] Rogers, *Soldiers of the Overland*, p. 29.

[9] As reported by "Verite," a correspondent for the *San Francisco Evening Bulletin*, reprinted in Tullidge, *History of Salt Lake City*, p. 277, and *Deseret News*, November 12, 1862. No clue was offered as to the identity of the "Chief of the Danites," but it was generally believed that Bill Hickman had made the boast.

[10] Stenhouse, *Rocky Mountain Saints*, p. 603n. Such was the concern over the presence of the soldiers, said Stenhouse, that "The city was in commotion, and rifles, lead and powder, were brought out of their hiding-places. . . . The houses on the

selected a location little more than half a mile from the spot where Young, after his first glimpse of the valley in 1847, had told Wilford Woodruff, "It is enough. This is the right place. Drive on!"

The first three months passed swiftly for the Volunteers; they hacked out a parade ground, molded adobes, cut trees, quarried sandstone, fashioned drainage areas, and generally shaped the foothills into a presentable army garrison. Occasional patrols reported insignificant contact with the Shoshones, and little of consequence was accomplished toward subduing the Indians until the first week in December, when a showdown began taking form.

Major Edward McGarry was detailed to take a detachment of men to the vicinity of the Bear River ferry and engage a band of warriors who had stolen stock from emigrants in the area. The major's scouts captured four braves near the crossing and sent a fifth back to the tribe with a message that unless the stolen animals were returned the prisoners would be shot. When the Shoshones chose to ignore his ultimatum, McGarry resolutely ordered a firing squad. Commented the *Deseret News*:

> . . . the four Indian prisoners, when the time came for their execution, were tied by their hands to the ferry rope and in that condition were shot until they were dead, and then the cords by which they were fastened were cut and the bodies tumbled into the river. It is said that fifty-one shots were fired before life in all of them became extinct,

route which occupied a commanding position where an attack could be made upon the troops were taken possession of, the small cannon were brought out, and the brethren prepared to protect the Prophet. . . . A powerful telescope was placed on top of Brigham's 'Bee-Hive' residence, and every move of the volunteers in Camp Douglas was watched with great care."

which, if so, conclusively proves that the executioners were not good marksmen, or that the unfortunate beings who thus suffered were very tenacious of life.[11]

Within a fortnight settlers from northern Utah were reporting widespread unrest among the Shoshone and Bannock as a result of McGarry's action. If anything, the executions succeeded only in whipping the tribes to a greater ferocity. Travel in the Cache Valley region, at best risky, now became suicidal as raids doubled. At the same time many Mormons heard that young braves of the warrior societies had vowed a "blood for blood" vengeance.[12] In quick succession Indians attacked a small party of miners lost in a snowstorm near Franklin on the Bear River. One man was killed and several others wounded as the whites tried crossing the turbulent river in a flimsy boat fashioned from wagon boxes. Then A. H. Conover came galloping into Great Salt Lake City with a report that two men, George Clayton and Henry Bean, carrying mail and about $1,000 in gold dust, had left Bannock City on November 25 and were last seen in Cache Valley. While checking on their whereabouts, Conover had occasion to question Indians near Portneuf and was told that the missing men had perished in a Shoshone ambush.

One of Colonel Connor's instructions specifically covered protection of mail routes in his area, and the murder of the two dispatch riders was sufficient provocation for the flinty Irishman to move against the hostiles. The call for military intervention became official when U.S. Marshal Isaac L. Gibbs made formal request for troops to aid in arresting certain chief-

[11] *Deseret News*, December 17, 1862.
[12] Ibid., December 31, 1862.

tains believed responsible for other depredations.[13] Reports from settlers, Gibbs said, indicated that the Shoshone leaders—San Pitch, Bear Hunter, Sagwitch, and Pocatello — with several hundred warriors, including Bannock, were at that very moment entrenched near Bear River in a redoubt of breastworks and rifle pits and "ready for a fight." In developing a plan of attack Connor soon realized that his greatest disadvantage centered in the California Volunteers' unfamiliarity with the neighboring country. The colonel understood only too well that no expedition of the size he contemplated could expect to succeed without superior scouting reports and excellent piloting. Clearly Connor would need help from the Mormons; no Gentile was capable of meeting all his requirements. All Connor's inquiries brought him the same answer — Rockwell. Although the colonel believed the scout to be a member of the "Danites" he had heard discussed so often, the choice was unavoidable. On January 22, 1863, Orrin Porter Rockwell put his X on a federal payroll once again: $5 a day and keep. Mustering his troops for the march, Connor was approached by Marshal Gibbs with arrest warrants for the renegade chieftains.

"We won't be needing them," the colonel said. "We do not anticipate taking any prisoners." [14]

Connor's plan was simple. He intended to trick the Indians into thinking that only a small detachment of infantry was being thrown against them; otherwise the red men would break and run. Accordingly, forty soldiers equipped with two howitzers and supply wagons with twelve days' provisions moved out on January 22.[15] Then three days later four cavalry troops with Connor and Rockwell at their head took the trail. To maintain the element of surprise, the infantry was under strict orders to move by day, the cavalry to follow at night, with all units rendezvousing at Bear River. The weather itself proved to be the Indians' greatest ally; by the time the horse soldiers had covered the first sixty-eight miles of that frightful night march, many had fallen victim to frostbite. Merciless winds slashed down on them from the mountain slopes of Cache Valley. Captain Charles H. Hempstead, a member of Connor's staff and later editor

[13] Ibid., January 28, 1863. Marshal Gibbs was acting on an affidavit made by William Bevins, a Salmon River miner, who testified that Shoshones were responsible for the death of his companion, John Smith, near Bear River.

[14] Rogers, *Soldiers of the Overland*, p. 69.

[15] *Deseret News*, January 28, 1863. Deep snows in Cache Valley so hindered the howitzers that they failed to arrive in time to be of service in the ensuing battle.

of the *Union Vedette*, described the tortures of that terrible night as the Volunteers urged their numbed animals forward.[16] "The moistened breath freezing as it left the lips, hung in miniature icicles from beards of brave men. The foam from their steeds stood stark and stiff upon each hair and motion only made it possible for them to endure the biting freezing blast," the captain said. Rockwell, his face wrapped in a heavy muffler, rode along silently. His respect for the California Volunteers increased with every agonizing mile.

Connor's tactical gamble to conceal his true strength from the hostiles was succeeding. The Shoshone chiefs were convinced that they faced only a small number of foot soldiers and chose to stand their ground and fight. Thus, as the mounted columns pushed closer each hour under cover of night, the Indians prepared to fight a military unit they believed to be of less than company size. The Shoshone had excellent reason to be confident of victory, for the tribes were lodged in a deep, fortified ravine some three-quarters of a mile in length. It turned south and opened on the Bear, while its northern mouth disappeared into low foothills. In some areas the ravine was forty feet wide with near perpendicular banks. An open plain flattened to the east about a mile from the river, which gently swung westward to receive the waters of the ravine southwest of the redoubt. On the north and west were hills. The broad expanse in front of the ravine offered the Indians a clear field of fire for several hundred rods. Retreat was possible through the ravine to the northwest and to the river on the south. But before any invader could reach the ravine it was necessary to conquer a succession of steeply rising benches immediately in front of the position. With these natural advantages, the ravine was to have been winter quarters for the Shoshones, a snug and secure retreat against weather and whites alike.

In anticipation of the fight, squaws chopped steps into the solidly frozen embankment, making it possible for the braves to fire and quickly descend to safety while reloading.[17] As they waited for the enemy, the Indians molded rifle balls in lodges scattered along the ravine bottom; in all there were perhaps as many as seventy-five such shelters, some made of brush, others of wagon canvas. Willow branches on the east embankment had been woven into loophole rifle rests for greater accuracy. As

---

[16] Address delivered at dedication ceremonies of the Bear River Battle Memorial at Camp Douglas, reported in the *Union Vedette*, January 30, 1864.

[17] *Deseret News*, February 11, 1863.

the moment for battle drew near, the warriors were unaware that their position was being reported by a scout named Rockwell to a grim Irish colonel several miles away.

Shortly before dawn of January 29, 1863, the cavalry overtook and passed the infantry outside of the small community of Franklin and was first to reach the river. Without hesitation the troopers pushed their mounts into the icy waters. Companies K and M, under command of Captain G. F. Price and Lieutenant Darwin Chase, succeeded in gaining the west bank but had scarcely assembled at the benches when a sniper's shot critically wounded a cavalryman. After considerable difficulty with the chunks of ice swept along by the current, Companies H and A crossed the Bear and joined their comrades. Major McGarry, commanding the cavalry units, ordered his troopers to dismount and deploy as skirmishers, since on horseback they proved vulnerable targets. At this point the Volunteers witnessed a startling sight. As the first rays of sun illuminated the scene, a Shoshone chief in full battle regalia, his legs firmly clamped around a spirited war pony, appeared on the breastworks above, and waving a lance at the soldiers, raced the beautiful animal along the embankment crown. Then, in unmistakable English, from the row of warriors closest to the attacking cavalrymen came the chant, "Fours right, fours left; come on you California sons of bitches!" [18]

The challenge was promptly accepted. Scarcely had the insult been uttered than four companies of incensed troopers scrambled up the slope toward the enemy. In a final gesture of contempt the braves flaunted the dried scalps of white women at the oncoming bluecoats, then retreated behind the embankment to begin the slaughter. In their maddened determination to come to grips with the redmen, the cavalrymen were blind to the deadly muzzles of Indian rifles poking through the willow boughs above them. A single whoop reverberated across the meadow, the signal for a murderous volley of rifle fire and arrows to rake the blue skirmish line. Before the shots could begin to echo, screams of wounded men filled

[18] Ibid. The *Deseret News* correspondent noted stiffly: "On such a polite invitation the word was given to 'advance' . . . ."

This shouted challenge and its unusual phrasing, the existence in the redoubt of fire-steps, "gun-ports," forked-stick rifle rests and other characteristically non-Indian evidence, gives rise to a nagging and persistent question about the Bear River battle: were renegade whites in the ravine with the Shoshones that day? Historians may well ponder how the Indians came to fortify their position in such a non-Indian fashion. While the implications cannot be ignored, no proof of whites being present has yet come to light.

the air, followed instantly by a crackling return fire from the attacking troopers. Word flashed down the line for the Volunteers to save their ammunition until the embankment had been surmounted.

By now the infantry had reached the river, and Connor ordered the cavalry horses sent across to bring them over. Wet and freezing, they joined the fight, bringing all elements of the California command into the battle. Connor instructed McGarry to cross the ravine at the northern end with a detachment and take the Indians in the rear. Here Connor's Californians suffered their heaviest casualties simply because they had underestimated the powerful Shoshone position. In describing the scene later, the *Deseret News* reported that Volunteers "fell like the leaves in autumn." Connor himself was sickened at the sight of his men dropping "thick and fast around me" under the withering fire from the Shoshone redoubt. As for Rockwell, his movements after shooting began were not chronicled, save for the *News* comment that "guides and other [irregulars] . . . went in and had a free fight by way of wiping off all scores with the Indians." [19]

An historian, had one been on the field that day, could not have marked the precise moment at which the tide of battle turned, but the Californians to a man sensed it immediately — an almost imperceptible relaxation on the part of the Indians. It was gone in a breath, but the soldiers knew that something had hurt the enemy deeply. Fighting had raged for nearly an hour when McGarry smashed through the Shoshone position on the north. Indian opposition stiffened, and they returned fire until a full company of skirmishers came to the major's support, catching the braves in a successful enfilading attack from the west which ultimately pushed the hostiles toward the central and lower portions of the ravine. It was this reverse that had been felt along the line. As resistance crumbled, the warriors panicked and ran — directly into a platoon of infantry

[19] Ibid.

stationed at the mouth of the ravine on the south to cut down those who survived the enfilade. Realizing the hopelessness of their situation, the braves fought like demons, but the backbone of opposition along the redoubt had been crushed.

The orgy of bloodletting which followed has no equal in the history of the West — even the butchery at Mountain Meadows pales in comparison. Captain Price, with a small detachment of men from two companies, cut down Indians in every direction. Eight of Price's men fell in five minutes; each time, another trooper stepped into the breach left by his comrade. When resistance finally melted before them the soldiers counted forty-eight braves piled in a single gruesome heap at their feet.[20] Now Connor received word that elements of A Troop had cracked through the enemy front on the east and had entered the ravine at that point. Some of the infantry were so severely frostbitten that they were unable to walk. In many cases only by looking could they tell they held a cartridge in their hands, yet they fought ferociously. Wild yelling from the south told Connor that the Shoshone were making a break for the river. In a rapid-fire sequence of orders the colonel had three lieutenants and their commands mount up and give chase. A quick glance at the sun told the doughty Connor that nearly four hours had passed since the first shot was fired.[21]

Indians spilled from the ravine, and in complete rout broke across the meadow. One brave attempted to escape up the slope of a nearby hill and was shot fourteen times in the back before he could reach the summit.[22] Everywhere it seemed Indians were being methodically gunned down.

When the fighting was over, the colonel counted his losses: killed, 14; wounded, 49; frozen feet, 79 (many of these men would eventually be crippled). On the enemy side of the ledger: killed, 224 (including Bear Hunter, and a sub-chief named Lehi; Pocatello and Sagwitch had missed the battle by a day);[23] wounded, none anyone could find; missing, 80 or

[20] Ibid. See also Connor's report to Lieutenant Colonel R. C. Drum, assistant adjutant general, Department of the Pacific, February 6, 1863. The full text can be found in Tullidge, *History of Salt Lake City*, pp. 284–85.

[21] Connor to Drum, February 6, 1863; in Tullidge, *History of Salt Lake City*, p. 285.

[22] Harmon Zufelt, "The Battle of Bear River," *The Utah Monthly Magazine*, Vol. IX (December 1892), p. 84. Zufelt, a resident of Franklin, said that the soldiers were under orders to kill every Indian they saw.

[23] According to an unidentified eyewitness from Franklin, Indian dead amounted to "three hundred and sixty-eight, besides many wounded, who afterwards died.

more who had reached the river (but probably died in its frigid waters). Spoils totaled 175 horses captured, 70 lodges destroyed, 1,000 bushels of wheat, and large quantities of powder and lead confiscated, plus articles stolen from emigrants and settlers recovered.

Colonel Patrick Edward Connor was satisfied. Indian bands which had terrorized Cache Valley for fifteen years had been dealt a staggering blow, one from which they would never recover. But the Irishman's stunning victory hung by a thread. If he were to save any of his command it was essential to get the men back to Camp Douglas and medical attention as quickly as possible. Even now frostbite was taking a terrible toll, scarcely two score men were fit for guard duty.

Rockwell climbed into his ice-glazed saddle and turned his pony toward Franklin. Once there, he commandeered ten teams and sleighs with which to haul the wounded to Camp Douglas; the dead would be placed in baggage wagons for the trip home.[24] At Farmington, just outside Great Salt Lake City, the troopers transferred to carriages and wagons before continuing their painful journey, arriving at camp on the night of February 2, 1863. On the evening of the following day, quick-stepping hoofbeats heralded the approach of Colonel Connor, who sat proud but weary in a buggy loaned him in one of the Mormon settlements along the way. At his side was the man Connor credited with saving the command through his fast action in acquiring transportation for the troops — Orrin Porter Rockwell, scout, guide, frontiersman, and now Indian-fighter.[25]

About ninety of the slain were women and children." See *Tullidge's Histories*, pp. 367–68. The ravine became known as "Battle Creek." (Sagwitch was shot the following July while in the custody of a detachment of California Volunteers.)

The *Deseret News*, February 4, 1863, remarked that Connor's California Volunteers may have done a "larger amount of Indian killing than ever fell to the lot of any single expedition of which we have any knowledge." And James H. Martineau reported to Brigham Young that Connor's soldiers had killed ninety women and children. ". . . Several squaws were killed because they would not submit quietly to be ravished. Other squaws were ravished in the agonies of death." Manuscript History of Brigham Young, February 7, 1863.

[24] *Deseret News*, February 11, 1863.

[25] See Verite: A series of three letters by this correspondent for the San Francisco *Daily Alta California*, dated February 7 and 9, 1863, described the Bear River Battle in detail. These communications were reprinted in *Tullidge's Quarterly Magazine*, Vol. I (January 1881), p. 194. Compare Richard M. Orton, *Records of California Men in the War of the Rebellion, 1861–1867* (Sacramento, 1890), p. 177; Rogers, *Soldiers of the Overland*, p. 76; and Whitney, *History of Utah*, Vol. II, p. 80n. The arms, mules, horses, ponies, and other property taken from the Indians after the battle were sold at public auction at Camp Douglas. *Deseret News*, February 11, 1863.

Chapter Eighteen

MYTH AND MAN

Not unnaturally, the bloody fight at Bear River brought out in Rockwell and Connor a mutual, if unspoken, understanding. Each admired courage and each had proven himself in the eyes of the other; friendship found in battle ignored words like "Mormon" and "Gentile." [1] If one author is to be believed, Rockwell even confided to Connor that he had indeed attempted the assassination of Lilburn W. Boggs in Missouri. (*"I shot through the window, and thought I had killed him,* but I had

---

[1] If ever strong words passed between this salty army officer and the redoubtable Mormon, it probably would have been over Connor's persistent encouragement of outsiders to exploit Utah's "hidden mineral wealth." The officer's efforts through letters and newspaper articles in the East eventually influenced hordes of prospectors to try their luck in the territory and gained for Connor the reputation of being the "Father of Utah Mining." The last thing Rockwell wanted was some stranger snooping around the mountains in search of gold. In a sermon delivered June 17, 1877, in Farmington, Brigham Young recounted Rockwell's apprehensions that "his mine would be found." According to Young,

> Porter, as we generally call him, came to me one day, saying, "They have struck within four inches of my lode, what shall I do?" He was carried away with the idea that he must do something. I therefore told him to go with the other brethren interested, and make his claim. When he got through talking, I said to him, "Porter you ought to know better; you have seen and heard things which I have not, and are a man of long experience in this Church. I want to tell you one thing; they may strike within four inches of that lode as many times as they have a mind to, and they will not find it." They hunted and hunted, hundreds of them did; and I had the pleasure of laughing at him a little, for when he went there again, he could not find it himself.

Journal of Discourses, Vol. XIX, p. 37.

only wounded him; *I was damned sorry that I had not killed the son of a bitch!"*)[2]

Connor efficiently, and not without a touch of pride, forwarded his report of the Indian engagement to Washington. Meanwhile, trouble festered in the valley. As before, internal strife worsened between the Mormons and the latest crop of federal officials. More than two thousand persons signed a petition to President Lincoln requesting him to remove from office the governor, Stephen S. Harding, and associate justices Charles B. Waite and Thomas J. Drake. A counterpetition was fired off in their defense by officers at Camp Douglas, and recriminations flew for several weeks. The kindling point neared in March 1863, when it seemed certain that a war would ignite between the military camp and the city. Armed volunteers had gathered in consequence of a rumor circulating the community that Connor was planning to arrest Brigham Young. On the evening of March 9[3] Marshal Gibbs served a warrant charging Brigham with violation of an anti-polygamy bill of 1862.[4] Cooperating fully, Young, with several friends intent on seeing that no harm befell their prophet, appeared before Chief Justice J. F. Kinney, who ordered the church president held in lieu of $2,000 bail to insure his appearance at the forthcoming term of Third District Court. Having no funds on his person, the prophet asked his companions to post the required monies. Four men stepped forward to share the burden. Lorenzo D. Young, Enoch Reese, Theodore McKean, and Orrin Porter Rockwell[5] — testifying under oath that they were worth some $20,000[6] — were permitted to sign bonds totaling $5,500 to make the bail.[7] Contrary to whispers prevalent in the city, Colonel Connor had no hand in the matter. Said Stenhouse: ". . . Connor never had orders to arrest Brigham Young, or he would have done so — or tried." [8]

In April Rockwell made a rare appearance in a court of law — but not as a defendant. A month after he had shouldered a share of Brigham

[2] Wyl, *Mormon Portraits*, p. 255. Italics in the original.

[3] Journal History, March 9, 1863.

[4] Tullidge, *History of Salt Lake City*, p. 316. (A grand jury later acquitted Young.)

[5] Journal History, March 9, 1863.

[6] *Deseret News*, March 11, 1863.

[7] Journal History, March 9, 1863.

[8] Stenhouse, *Rocky Mountain Saints*, p. 607n.

Young's bail, Rockwell, in town on a horse-buying trip for the mail service,[9] stopped at the courthouse during a moment of leisure to watch the trial of one Charles Davey, accused of illegally purchasing a soldier's weapons. While the veniremen considered a verdict, the judge proceeded with the calendar. Next on the docket was the matter of Elias Smith, the Mormon newspaper editor, seeking to practice as an attorney at law, who was on hand to take the oath. Since the court was temporarily minus the services of a bailiff while the jury was out, Judge Kinney cast an inquisitive glance around the gallery for a likely substitute. He selected a surprised Rockwell, who reluctantly took his station by the door until released by the magistrate.[10]

Rockwell normally did not loiter near the court, but on this occasion he had been called to the city on an "emergency" two nights before when a message received at Camp Douglas announced that Patrick Edward Connor had been promoted to brigadier general.[11] Overly exuberant members of the California regiment had loaded cannon with powder and fired an eleven-gun salute in their commander's honor. Before the roar of the last howitzer had subsided, Brigham Young was out of bed, dressed, and surrounded by bodyguards. Because of the constant fear that Connor would someday launch an attack against Zion, express riders were dispatched to rally available Mormon fighting men to protect their prophet from this unprovoked artillery bombardment.[12] By the time the Saints fully comprehended the situation, several hundred minutemen had swarmed to the Beehive House for marching orders. Young's embarrassment upon learning the true cause for the cannon fire did nothing to improve relations between the Mormons and troops.

Near mid-April Connor's men again received orders to take the field, this time to track a band of Indians thought responsible for several outrages in the vicinity of Cedar Valley and Spanish Fork Canyon. A patrol led by Captain George F. Price clashed briefly with about fifty braves, killing one warrior and wounding several others. On April 11, a detachment under Lieutenant Francis Honeyman was jumped by a raiding party near Pleasant Grove. The officer retaliated with howitzer fire, but suc-

9 Lyman, "Journal," March 27, 1863.

10 Journal History, April 2, 1863; *Deseret News*, April 8, 1863.

11 *Deseret News*, April 1, 1863.

12 Ibid.

ceeded only in cracking the walls of an adobe house, causing the death of his own coralled mules, and losing seven more to the Indians, who, incidentally, escaped without a scratch.[13] General Connor rode into Pleasant Grove on the night of April 12 to learn firsthand what the Indians were up to. His guide was Rockwell. William H. Seegmiller, a Mormon on his way to an audience with Brigham Young, noticed with deep disgust that Rockwell obviously had taken on an overload of whisky. Later, in conference with Young in Great Salt Lake City, Seegmiller was astonished when Rockwell interrupted the conversation to report, in amazing detail, the Pleasant Grove Indian situation. Said Seegmiller:

> O. Porter Rockwell while at Pleasant Grove was taken to be slightly intoxicated. He was active in moving among the crowd at the soldiers' camp; this all seems very distinct even now, I thought him almost silly with drink and had little respect for him until this interview with President Young. On that occasion he was well dressed in a black broadcloth suit, wore neatly polished shoes and a black silk hat; his language was free and grammatical. I concluded then that Rockwell lived a double life in the interest of his friends and God's cause on the earth. I will ever remember him with esteem.[14]

A final clash between the soldiers and the Indians came on April 15 in Spanish Fork Canyon and lasted the better part of the day. When the smoke cleared, the dragoons had routed the warriors, had captured a large number of horses and mules — even those lost by Lieutenant Honeyman — and had killed thirty or more hostiles. Elated by their hard-fought victory, the tough cavalrymen scalped twenty-seven of the fallen braves and took the hairlocks back to camp with them.[15] In two months the eastern Shoshones sued for peace and signed a treaty at Fort Bridger. The northwestern bands came to terms at Brigham City, and the western clans concluded a pact at Ruby Valley. Peace talks with the Gosiutes and mixed bands of Shoshone stragglers and Bannock followed, with a semblance of tranquility returning to the prairie by autumn. But before these treaties came about, a tragedy occurred in Utah County which profoundly affected Rockwell's private life.

He and Mary Ann had been living quietly at their ranch near Point of the Mountain. She had given birth to another daughter, Letitia, bring-

---

[13] Gottfredson, *Indian Depredations*, pp. 115–17; Rogers, *Soldiers of the Overland*, p. 91.

[14] Gottfredson, *Indian Depredations*, p. 118.

[15] *Deseret News*, April 22, 1863.

ing to five the number of youngsters in the Rockwell home.[16] All the children were a delight to their rough and rugged father, who found relaxation in allowing eight-year-old Mary and six-year-old Sarah to unbraid and comb his long black hair with its streaks of silver. Mary Ann made the home a cheery blend of warmth and comfort in a land and a time when such things meant much. Brigham Young made it a point to visit the family whenever he was in the neighborhood.[17] Among the many who enjoyed Rockwell hospitality were the off-duty drivers of Overland stages which halted daily at the Hot Springs Brewery Hotel.

On June 9 Rockwell sent one of his younger employees, Frederick Scarlett, with an extra stagecoach and a fresh span of mules, from the inn to Fort Crittenden, the next station west. As Scarlett crossed the Jordan River Bridge at Lehi, a Mrs. William Ball told him a band of Indians had stopped to boast that they planned to kill the first stage driver they saw. Thus alerted, Scarlett warily covered the twelve miles to Crittenden; he failed to sight a single brave. Passing the incident off as insignificant, the youngster changed his team and rode out the following morning without mentioning the warning. Unfortunately, the eastbound stage had left for Point of the Mountain before Scarlett awakened and was three to four miles ahead. On the stage were the driver, Wood Reynolds, and another Overland employee, Thomas O'Shonnison.

Jogging along in a half-sleep, Scarlett was startled out of his lethargy by the sound of rapid rifle fire cracking through the warm morning air. He whipped his mules into a full gallop toward the shots, but the miles passed slowly beneath the huge Concord's churning wheels. Then, northwest of Cold Springs, he saw the stage, apparently without a team, standing like a silent monument in high brush about a quarter-mile from the road. Great splashes of blood marked the prairie in front of him — too much to be human, Scarlett decided. As he approached the solitary coach he could see that two horses in its team were dead, a third was dying, and the fourth missing. He found Reynolds' scalped and naked body pierced by arrows and lying in a clutter of mail sacks and scattered letters. Scarlett turned away and vomited. In a final outrage, the frenzied Indians, honoring Reynolds' courage and bravery, had torn out his heart and eaten it in the belief that somehow his gallantry would pass on to them.[18]

[16] *Utah Historical and Genealogical Magazine*, Vol. XXVI, p. 156.

[17] Journal History, May 19, 1863.

[18] Hamilton Gardner, *History of Lehi* (Salt Lake City, 1913), pp. 163–164.

O'Shonnison's nude and mutilated corpse was lying on the other side of the coach. Even the stage, pocked by bullets and arrows, had not been spared. Before leaving, the hostiles had partially dismantled it. While Scarlett further surveyed the horror, he was unaware that twelve-year-old George Kirkham was racing to Lehi with word of the massacre. Herding cattle near Cold Springs, the boy had been a reluctant eyewitness to the Indian attack and butchery which followed.[19]

Rockwell was the first to respond and arrive at the scene. Ordering the bodies and mail to be placed in the damaged coach, he drove the grisly cargo to Great Salt Lake City and Overland Stage headquarters, then reported the murders to the army. Efforts to track down the culprits were unsuccessful. A month later the tribes signed a treaty at Brigham City ending hostilities.

Reynolds' horrible death deeply affected Mary Ann. She had treated the young driver as one of the family, and his loss could not have struck her more cruelly had he been a son or a brother. Finally, she told her husband that she no longer would stay at the ranch, even though a temporary peace had been negotiated with the tribes. Abiding by her wish, Rockwell shuttered the home and moved the family into Great Salt Lake City. Once they were relocated, he saw to it that operations returned to normal at the stage station, then joined several friends — Adam Sharp, Hat Shurtliff, Sam Bennion, and Job Harker — in scouting Skull Valley for ranch lands.[20] Zion was growing and Rockwell calculated that a decent spread soon would be hard to find for a man who wanted to raise livestock. Six days later each man had selected a piece of ground which suited him. Rockwell filed on a section called Government Creek west of the Sheeprock Mountains near the Tooele–Juab line.[21] It was exactly what he wanted. He visualized a comfortable cabin, a few thousand head of good horses, and seclusion. Rockwell was now fifty years old and looked forward to spending his days in peace and quiet, contentedly commuting between the city and the projected summer ranch at Government Creek.

[19] The massacre was detailed in the *Deseret News*, June 17, 1863. See also Journal History, June 17, 1863. George Kirkham's eyewitness version is related in Gardner, *History of Lehi*, pp. 163–64.

[20] Bennion, "Journal." Book 3, p. 19.

[21] In 1874 Rockwell was able to secure a land patent on the section. See Patent Record Book 1, Patent 1311, p. 442, Tooele County Recorder's Office.

But anonymity was not to be his. In the East he had gained a certain notoriety through highly flavored newspaper accounts of the Utah War and interviews with apostate Mormons and Gentiles fresh from the "abominations" of Zion. Many of the men in Johnston's Army and Connor's command had written of "the Destroying Angel of Mormondom" and "the Danite Chieftain" in their letters home. In journalistic jargon, Rockwell was hot copy. And because of this, a one-time hashish-eater, Fitz Hugh Ludlow, now a roving correspondent for *The Atlantic Monthly*, rolled into the territory in late June of 1863.[22] Ludlow was planning an article for the literary magazine which would depict for its readers the Mormon "Way of Life," and high on his list of persons to interview was Orrin Porter Rockwell.[23] Ludlow may not have planned it that way, but the piece ultimately would expand into a book of adventures in crossing the plains. However, for the time being he was interested only in the man he later would label the "Destroying Angel."

Ludlow was relaxing on the veranda of the Townsend House one sunny morning soon after his arrival, when the landlord brought Rockwell over and introduced him. Ludlow reflected mild surprise at the Mormon's warm greeting and good-natured jibe that the author-traveler had shown poor taste in not scheduling a longer visit, a remark which prompted Ludlow's response that Utah had a reputation for dissuading outsiders who considered making the land of Zion a place of permanent residence. Rockwell countered with a promise to halt Ludlow's stage as it passed his door, stable his horses, carry the writer to a table, and "inflict upon us the penalty of a real Mormon dinner."[24]

According to Ludlow, Rockwell laughingly added:

> "Bless yer soul, but we're savage! . . . Once drew a sassige on a Yankee Gentile myself — crammed it right down his throat with scalding hot gravy and pancakes. We Mormons torture 'em awful. The Gentile I drew the sassige on bore it like a man, and is livin' yet. Well, I'll soon see ye agin." So he shook hands with us, jumped on his mustang, and ambled away as gently as if, instead of being a destroying angel, he were a colporteur of peace tracts, or a peddler of Winslow's Soothing Syrup.

[22] Robert S. de Ropp, *Drugs and the Mind* (New York, 1957), pp. 77–78.

[23] Ludlow, "Among the Mormons," *The Atlantic Monthly*, Vol. XIII, p. 492.

[24] Fitz Hugh Ludlow, *The Heart of the Continent: A Record of Travel Across the Plains and in Oregon, With an Examination of the Mormon Principle* (New York, 1870), pp. 353–54.

... Next to Brigham Young, he was the most interesting man and problem that I encountered in Utah. His personal appearance in itself was very striking. His figure was of the middle height, and very strongly made; broad across the shoulders, and set squarely on the legs. His arm was of large girth, his chest round as a barrel, and his hand looked as powerful as a grizzly bear's. His face was of the mastiff type, and its expression, fidelity, fearlessness, ferocity. A man with his massive lower jaw, firm mouth, and good-humored but steady and searching eyes of steel-blue, if his fanaticism takes the Mormon form, must infallibly become like Porter Rockwell. Organization and circumstances combine to make any such man a destroying angel. Having always felt the most vivid interest in supernatural characters of that species, I was familiar with most of them from the biblical examples of those who smote Egypt, Sodom, and Sennacherib, to the more modern Arab, Azrael, and that famous one who descended, all white-bearded and in shining raiment from the Judges' Cave, to lead the van of Quinnipiack's forlorn hope and smite the red-skinned Philistines. Out of this mass of conflicting and particular angels I had abstracted an ideal and general angel; but when I suddenly came on a real one, in Porter Rockwell, I was surprised at his unlikeness to my thought. His hair, black and iron-gray in streaks, was gathered into a cue, just behind the apex of the skull, and twisted into a hard round bunch, confined with a comb — in nearly the same fashion as was everywhere prevalent among Eastern ladies twenty years ago. He was very obliging in his manners; placable, jocose, never extravagant when he conversed, save in burlesque. If he had been converted to Methodism in its early times, instead of Mormonism, he might have been a second Peter Cartwright, preaching and pummeling his enemies into the Kingdom instead of shooting them to Kingdom Come. No one ignorant of his career would take him on sight for a man of bad disposition in any sense. But he was that most terrible instrument which can be handled by fanaticism; a powerful physical nature welded to a mind of very narrow perceptions, intense convictions, and a changeless tenacity. In his build he was a gladiator; in his humor, a Yankee lumberman; in his memory, a Bourbon; in his vengeance, an Indian. A strange mixture, only to be found on the American Continent.[25]

Bright and early on the Fourth of July a flaming vermillion nine-passenger stagecoach braked to a halt in front of the Townsend House in a cloud of dust and noise. It was driven by a stable boy and contained a solitary passenger, Rockwell, who, incidentally, owned the conveyance.

[25] Ibid., pp. 354–55. Certainly Ludlow's thumbnail sketch of Rockwell is the best of those left behind by writers who observed the Mormon first-hand.

He had come to take Ludlow on a tour of the valley.[26] As the landscape bounced by, the writer filled his notebooks with commentary on such important data as the temperature of natural hot springs at the city's northern limits, geological observations of interesting rock forms, and the salinity of the great lake. Rockwell studiously avoided any serious discussion of Mormonism, instead describing in pantomime the way he had seen a Gosiute family feast on a dinner of grasshoppers. "It seemed strange," Ludlow wrote as he watched the Mormon's gestures, "to be riding in the carriage and by the side of a man, who, if universal report among the Gentiles were correct, would not hesitate to cut my throat at the Church's orders. It was like an Assyrian taking an airing in the chariot of the Angel of Death. I was not likely to become obnoxious to the Church: I certainly did not mean to be if I could help it."

From Ludlow's own account it is apparent that his treatment at Rockwell's hands was more than fair, yet Ludlow insisted on laying an apocryphal homicide at the feet of his gracious host.

> [Rockwell] had the reputation of having killed many men — forty, report said; and there are not lacking those who suspect him of still more. From an eye-witness I received, while in Utah, the following account of one of his *vendette*. A Gentile doing business in Salt Lake City during Johnston's occupation of Camp Floyd, suffered oppressive exaction from the Church authorities; and after failing, as might have been expected, to get a decision in his favor from a local Mormon judge and jury before whom he brought his petition for relief, he retired in a most exasperated state of mind to the United States encampment — partly with a view to obtaining redress through Johnston, and partly for self-protection from the Danites, with whom his prosecution of the Church had made him a marked man. One day Porter Rockwell rode into Camp Floyd. At no time during Johnston's

[26] Ludlow's reaction to the coach was one of ridicule: "It was just the chariot for a large family of angelic beings, whose wings had not been sent home yet. You could have piled all the old masters' cherubim, plus the supplementary legs, into the cavern of Porter's vast coach, without their troubling each other more than the souls in the old scholastic thesis who dance on the point of a needle, besides leaving room for the parental destroyers on top and box." Ibid., p. 356.

Perhaps Ludlow's sarcasm reached Rockwell, for a year later the Mormon ordered a custom-made buggy constructed to his personal specifications by Gen. B. M. Hughes of Atchison, Kansas. Its description indicates that the carriage was not inexpensive: "One Concord Buggy — Leather top (which can be taken off), Side Springs — Steel tire (*heavy* say ½ inch), Fellowes — deep say ½ inch, Hub — large [say] 5½ [inch] and capped at both ends (to Keep out Sand), Pole — no shafts." Feramorz Little, "Letterbook, 1863–1877," p. 39.

occupation was there anything but the merest farcical show of hostilities. . . . In accordance with habitual usage, Porter Rockwell, on the occasion mentioned, rode up to headquarters at Camp Floyd, and was sitting undismounted in conversation with one of the officers at the door, when the aggrieved plaintiff in the late suit espied him, and approached in a violent passion.

For several minutes this man publicly addressed Porter Rockwell in every term of vituperation and insult which an outraged nature could suggest, furthermore characterizing Brigham as a swindling old scoundrel, and the entire Church as his nice little game of thimblerig. Not a muscle of Porter's face moved till this harangue was finished. Then he very quietly replied, "O! you shoot your mouth at *me*, do ye? Well, I'll remember you some time," and rode away.

A few days after that some officers came up to Salt Lake City on all night's leave, and, thinking himself amply protected by their escort, the exiled trader accompanied them. During the evening he separated from his party, and went alone into a side street to call on a Gentile friend. The officers never saw him again till he lay in their presence with a revolver hole from temple to temple, having been picked up dead a little while after he left them. Of whose pistol killed him, there is no eye-witness, and as little doubt.[27]

Fitz Hugh Ludlow continued to the Pacific Coast, took a ship to New York, and eventually wrote his story, "Among the Mormons," after which he produced a book, *The Heart of the Continent*. In the *Atlantic Monthly* article Ludlow accused Rockwell of being a "heaven-elected assassin of Mormonism" and a butcher "by divine right." Wallowing in blood for his delighted Eastern readers, Ludlow wrote, "Porter Rockwell has slain his forty men. This is historical. His probable private victims amount to as many more. . . . [I] found him one of the pleasantest murderers I ever met." [28]

While Ludlow's imaginative pen poured out its melodramatic prose for posterity, the unsuspecting subject of his sensationalism was diligently attending to business. Ludlow likely would have been disappointed to learn that of all Rockwell's particular irons in the fire at the moment, none was of the shooting variety. Stage operations at Point of the Mountain maintained a steady schedule, Mary Ann and the youngsters enjoyed the comforts of their new home in the church's Fourteenth Ward area, and an apartmented cabin was under construction on the Government Creek property. Livestock raised by Rockwell under the OP and Cedar

[27] Ludlow, *Heart of the Continent*, pp. 361–64.
[28] Ludlow, "Among the Mormons," *The Atlantic Monthly*, Vol. XIII, p. 492.

Tree brands ranked with the finest. His horses, in fact, were the best, but the old scout knew how to raise other animals as well. As Salt Lakers passed Jennings' Meat Market on Main Street on Christmas Eve of 1864, they were treated to the sight of a huge hog on display in the window. The value of the hog was $500; the owner was Orrin Porter Rockwell of Salt Lake and Tooele counties.[29]

One of the highlights of the summer of '65 was the visit to Zion of Schuyler Colfax, speaker of the House of Representatives. Colfax's appearance in Utah was publicized as merely part of a sight-seeing tour, but prominent Mormons believed that he was on at least a semi-official inspection trip of the West. Accompanying the speaker were Lieutenant Governor William Bross of Illinois, Samuel Bowles, editor of the *Springfield* (Massachusetts) *Republican*, and Albert D. Richardson of the *New York Tribune*. During their eight-day stay in Great Salt Lake City that June the three men addressed the Saints from the balcony of the Salt Lake House and in the Bowery and later were permitted two lengthy interviews with Brigham Young.

At one point in the cordialities the party was introduced to Rockwell, whom Bowles was quick to describe as the "accredited leader of the Danites or 'Avenging Angels' of the church." With good-natured neighborliness Rockwell invited the four Easterners to visit his ranch and share a luxury of the plains — strawberries and cream. However, the tourists gracefully declined his offer because of a suddenly unyielding schedule. "Though given to heavy whiskey drinking of late years, he is as mild a mannered man as ever scuttled ship or murdered crews; and I really do not think that any anxiety for our lives entered into our declination of his hospitality, inexplicable as it may seem that for any less reason we should have omitted any opportunity at strawberries."

Bowles recognized that a difference of opinion existed even among Gentiles as to Rockwell's "real share in the mysterious and terrible takings-off of parties in bad odor with the saints of the church . . . ." The newspaper editor was unwilling to regard the Mormon as the utter blackguard he had been painted; however, Bowles chuckled, should Fitz Hugh Ludlow cross Rockwell's path again there might not be murder, but the correspondent "would certainly feel the sharp vengeance of the injured and irate 'Avenger.' " This because: "Mr. Ludlow tells the worst stories about Rockwell, such as that he had committed about fifty murders for the

[29] Journal History, December 24, 1864; *Deseret News*, December 28, 1864.

342

church and as many more on private account, as if accepted, proved facts; at the same time that he acknowledges being his guest, and availing himself of his courtesies to see the country. Porter shuts his teeth hard when the subject is now mentioned, and mutters that he supposes "it is all wheat," this being Utah idiom for all right. Which means, of course, that he don't suppose any such thing." [30]

Colfax and his entourage left Great Salt Lake City and continued their journey westward. The speaker was destined to return in four years and again address the Saints,[31] this time as vice president of the United States. Again he would be accompanied by Bross and Bowles, but Richardson had seen all the Mormon country he cared to during the first trip. In fact, the *Tribune* writer had very nearly met with a fatal calamity when he rode into the city alone, his three friends having decided to take the sea route home.

It was late in September when Richardson arrived in Zion for a five-week respite before heading eastward. His published letters to the *Tribune* had preceded him, and his outspoken criticism of plural marriage won only enemies among the Mormons in Utah. Although the journalist defended his right to disapprove of spiritual wifery, in print or otherwise, he nonetheless was greeted with disdain by the Saints. To make matters worse, he bore a resemblance to Fitz Hugh Ludlow, and in less time than it took to tell, an ashen-faced Richardson was being closely questioned by a stern-visaged Rockwell.

> [Rockwell had] confused me [Richardson recounted] . . . with Fitz Hugh Ludlow, who had passed through two years before, and given an unflattering description of him for the *Atlantic Monthly*. Some one told Porter, or he dreamed it, that I had characterized him as the murderer of one hundred and fifty men; and he significantly remarked that if I had said it he believed he would make it one hundred and fifty-one! He finally concluded it a mistake and contented himself with complaining to me that he had been cruelly slandered by Ludlow, and afterward while in his cups, assuring me that he *would* kill any journalist who should publish such falsehoods about him. . . .[32]

---

[30] Bowles, *Across the Continent*, pp. 128–29.

[31] During a speech from the portico of the Townsend House on West Temple Street on October 3, 1869, Colfax was repeatedly interrupted by "Port Rockwell, a Mormon ruffian in liquor," who shouted, "I never killed anyone who didn't need killing." See O. J. Hollister, *Life of Schuyler Colfax* (New York, 1886), p. 342.

[32] Albert D. Richardson, *Beyond the Mississippi* (Hartford, 1867), pp. 468–69.

Congratulating himself on emerging with a whole skin, Richardson bade Great Salt Lake City farewell and returned to the more civilized environs of New York.

By autumn of 1866, Rockwell was about to become a father once again, and on August 24 Mary Ann gave birth to their sixth child, a boy, Joseph Neff Rockwell. But there were complications, and the mother's condition grew steadily worse, until finally, on September 28, her heart gave out and she passed away. The infant died two weeks later.

Rockwell was in mourning for his wife and child when he found himself thrust into the public spotlight during a particularly sensational murder investigation. Victim of the brutal and senseless crime was Dr. John King Robinson, who had come to Utah with Connor's command and was in charge of the Camp Douglas hospital until the winter of 1865–1866. Robinson was mustered out, and taking a Mormon girl for his wife, settled down to practice in Great Salt Lake City. He also became superintendent of the first Gentile Sunday school in the Territory and was considered one of the community's most upstanding non-Mormon citizens.[33] But all was not serene in the Robinson household, for the doctor became entangled in a property dispute with Brigham Young and the city police. On October 22, 1866, Robinson left home about midnight to treat an accident victim and minutes later was killed within sight and sound of his front door.[34]

During inquest proceedings the following morning, Rockwell's name entered into the case when his whereabouts at the time of the murder came under discussion during examination of Andrew H. Burt, chief of police.[35] Burt's vague answers disclosed little of interest, and he was quickly dismissed as a witness. Rockwell was at no time directly linked to the physician or accused of complicity in the killing, yet it seemed that everyone felt a little safer for having asked. Ultimately, rewards for the arrest of Robinson's killers rose to $9,000, but the money was never

[33] *Union Vedette*, October 25, 1866. His bride was the daughter of John Kay, a prominent Latter-day Saint.

[34] For complete details of the homicide, see *Investigation Into the Murder of Dr. J. K. Robinson, Who Was Assassinated On the Night of October 22d, 1866, near the corner of East Temple and 3d South or Emigration Streets, had before Jeter Clinton, Coroner for the County of Great Salt Lake, Chief Justice Titus, and Judge McCurdy, commencing Tuesday, October 23d, at 11 o'clock A.M.* [Salt Lake City, 1866].

[35] Ibid., pp. 7–8.

344

claimed. While the surgeon's murder caused a wave of excitement in the community, another homicide six weeks later barely raised an eyebrow and rated only two inches of space in the newspapers. There was a story behind the story, though.

Police officers and spectators reacted with mixed emotions when the mutilated body of a black, Thomas Colbourn,[36] also known as Thomas Coleman[37] and Nigger Tom,[38] was found behind the old arsenal two miles east of the city on the night of December 11. His throat had been cut so deeply from ear to ear that the head had nearly been severed; a sign pinned to the victim's bare chest warned: "Notice To All Niggers! Warning!! Leave White Women Alone!!!"[39] At face value, the note seemed to dispel any doubts as to a motive for the slaying; even Achilles agreed:

> "Nigger Tom" was accused of being a practical believer in the doctrine of miscegenation, and was consequently condemned by the authorities of the church, and it was assumed that he had practically carried out his belief. His death was decreed under the blood atonement. The clerk of the hotel[40] decoyed "Tom" out in the suburbs of the city in conformity with a plot to administer Mormon justice. He wandered out on a mission to about half a mile from the Salt Lake House, in the rear of the old arsenal building. The negro always carried a knife and a pistol, and was prepared for any plot that might be made against him. . . . The errand that he was sent on was in the night. He was met by Rockwell and two others. He was seized and held down by Rockwell's companions, and Rockwell cut his throat from ear to ear with Tom's knife. As soon as he was dead, he was laid upon the ground, and when found, there was a note under his body containing a warning to all other negroes not to do likewise. It was never proved that Tom was guilty of the act of which he was accused . . . .[41]

So much for Achilles' version of the slaying. Within certain circles in the community it was whispered that Colbourn had signed his death

[36] *Union Vedette*, December 13, 1866.

[37] Salt Lake County Death Records, No. 2897.

[38] Ibid. See also Bancroft, *History of Utah*, p. 629n; Beadle, *Life in Utah*, p. 212; Achilles, *Destroying Angels of Mormondom*, p. 34.

[39] *Union Vedette*, December 13, 1866.

[40] He was employed in the Salt Lake House as a "make-shift and do-all," and according to the *Vedette* of December 13, 1866, was a member of the Mormon Church.

[41] Achilles, *Destroying Angels of Mormondom*, p. 34.

warrant by seeking out several federal officials and volunteering "important evidence" concerning various homicides in the Territory, one of which was supposed to have been the Robinson murder.[42] The "White Women" sign was a decoy to divert suspicion from the real motive, it was said. Colbourn at one time had been a slave owned by Thomas S. Williams, prominent attorney and an ex-Mormon. In April of 1859 Colbourn fought and killed another slave over the affections of a black woman. Charged with manslaughter, he was sentenced to serve a year in prison and fined $100.[43] Whatever ramifications and intrigues were involved in his vicious slaying, the coroner considered the matter too insignificant to justify the expense of an inquest, and, as in the case of John Gheen, neglected even to list the case in his register of violent deaths. As far as officialdom was concerned, no crime had been committed; the body was unceremoniously dumped into an unmarked grave and forgotten.

With Mary Ann gone, Rockwell decided to close down the Point of the Mountain station and move his operation into the city. On December 19, 1866, he paid Wells Fargo & Co. $7,500 for an acre and a quarter of property on Second East between South Temple and First South, and ran the mail from there.[44] In March of 1867 a freighter named Alexander Toponce appeared in Great Salt Lake City after scoring a business coup by selling six wagonloads of eggs in Helena, Montana, for $2 a dozen. Toponce claimed he knew Rockwell intimately: "for some reason he took quite a fancy to me." According to the freighter, Rockwell had helped him out of a tight spot:

> I had a room at the old Salt Lake house and Rockwell liked to come up there and sit and smoke and talk over the news of the min-

<hr />

[42] Bancroft, *History of Utah*, p. 629n.

[43] *Valley Tan*, April 19, 1859; Hosea Stout "Journal," Vol. 8, p. 21, and Brooks, *On The Mormon Frontier*, Vol. II, pp. 695, 702.

[44] That is, two blocks east and a half-block south of the Temple. See Salt Lake County Abstracts, Plats and Surveys, Book A2, p. 73; Salt Lake County Deeds and Transfers, Book C, pp. 579–80.
His wife's unexpected death had a deep effect on Rockwell. An army officer in Great Salt Lake City about this time observed: "Porter Rockwell has become exceedingly fond of whiskey in these latter days, and but seldom visits the city without getting drunk. On such occasions he manifests none of that violence which one might suppose would then almost certainly exhibit itself in one so desperate as he is represented to be. When drunk he is perfectly harmless, and the exuberance of vitality on such occasions is relieved by loud shouts, which may be heard for squares. He is well-behaved even when drunk." [William Elkanah Waters], *Life Among the Mormons, and A March to Their Zion* (New York, 1868), p. 187.

ing camps, and we got along fine together. I would also invite him to go down to the dining room with me.

Once I had started my wagon train to Montana and the driver of the stage from Ogden handed me a letter, that had been given to him by my wagon boss stating that at Farmington, seventeen miles north of Salt Lake eighteen head of oxen had strayed, or been stolen, from the camp during the night. . . .

Porter was in my room at the time the letter was given to me. After I read it, I had "a hunch" and threw it across the table to Rockwell.

After he read it,[45] I said, "Porter, do you think you could find those cattle for me?"

He laughed, "Old wheat in the mill," he said. That was his favorite expression, "Old wheat in the mill." "They will be at your train tomorrow night."

He put on his hat and went out at once. I did not see him again for some days, but I got a letter from the wagon boss, dated two days later telling me that, while camped on the sand ridge west of Ogden, the missing cattle had come back to the herd. He found them all present at roll call that morning. When I tried to talk to Porter about it and thank him he just laughed.[46]

Whether or not Rockwell interceded for Toponce and recovered the missing oxen is anyone's guess — and of minor importance, in any case. Of greater interest was Rockwell's insatiable curiosity about the latest mining news; the days at Murderer's Bar and Buckeye Flat had left their indelible mark, one which the scout had never been able to erase, if, in fact, he ever tried.

Tom Ryan was known around Great Salt Lake City as a truthful man. He had been a member of the California–Nevada Volunteers, and as such, found himself in the South Pass country of Dakota Territory during the summer of '65. For years there had been talk of fabulous gold deposits in the region.[47] Beyond that, no one had located anything big enough to shout about, partly because of the natural disadvantages of the high country, but mostly because the Sioux strenuously objected to trespassers. Ryan, a former miner, kept poking around during off-duty hours

[45] Rockwell could not read or write, nor did he smoke. Toponce was simply spinning a yarn here, or had confused his facts.

[46] Alexander Toponce, *Reminiscences of Alexander Toponce, Pioneer, 1839–1923* (Salt Lake City, 1923), pp. 142–43.

[47] A fur company employee first reported finding gold near South Pass in 1842. Scattered mining activity occurred during 1855, 1858, and in the early 1860s.

until finally he found what he had been looking for, a shelf of liberally gold-flecked quartz in a place called Carissa Gulch. He was unable to develop his discovery immediately or to keep quiet about it. Consequently, when his unit marched through Zion for Nevada the following year Ryan told of his good fortune to all who would listen. Because of his reputation for honesty, the soldier unwittingly sparked the beginnings of a full-scale gold rush. During the winter of 1866–1867 a large party of Mormons and Gentiles organized in Great Salt Lake City for the sole purpose of helping themselves to the precious ore before news of the find reached California. The most prominent Mormon members of the group were Rockwell and Bill Hickman.[48] "Just wanted a look-see," Hickman said.

As soon as weather permitted, about May of 1867, the party made its way to South Pass and began prospecting the gulch Ryan had described. By now the once-isolated terrain was as busy as New York's Bowery; somehow word had gotten out, and half the miners in Montana had come to strike it rich at South Pass. June 8 turned into a hot, steamy day, but no one cared. Rockwell, Hickman, H. S. Reedall, Harry Hubbel, J. W. Lawrence, Frank Marshall, John Smith, Homer Roberts, and Richard Grace, of the Utah group, discovered the Carissa lode, a ledge of rock "rich beyond anything that any of the party had before seen; the walls were well defined, and there was every probability that a great producer had been discovered." [49] News of the find spread through the camp before the sun had set, and the stampede was on. But Rockwell, remembering the grand and glorious days of California, at once recognized the problems facing those who staked claims on the Carissa. In 1849 prospectors at Coloma had only to pluck nuggets from pockets in the earth. At South Pass the ore was located in quartz deposits and called for pulverization, a necessarily large-scale, long-range operation to be truly profitable. It was a program holding little interest for either Rockwell or Hickman, and by July the two men were on their way back home.

For a man who had the reputation of being Lord High Executioner of the Mormon Church, it was a paradox of the times that men in trouble would turn to Rockwell for help, especially when circumstances placed them at his mercy. Herman Francis Reinhart, for example, was a huge bear of a man who made his living hauling passengers and supplies to

48 C. G. Coutant, *The History of Wyoming* (Laramie, 1899), two volumes, Vol. I, p. 647. See also Hickman, *Brigham's Destroying Angel*, pp. 174–75.

49 Coutant, *History of Wyoming*, Vol. I, p. 648.

Montana. Reinhart awoke one morning in early 1868 at his camp near Stockton, Tooele County, and found that his string of fourteen horses had been stolen. A friendly federal judge told him that only an experienced hunter or mountaineer could find his animals in Utah, so Reinhart went to the one man he felt could recommend such a person, Brigham Young. The church leader listened to the Gentile's tale of woe and suggested that he do business with Rockwell. Reinhart was more than disturbed by Young's advice, for he had heard — and was convinced — that Rockwell had played a principal part in the Mountain Meadows massacre. On the other hand he wanted his horses back. To the teamster's great relief, Rockwell struck him as being a reasonably honest soul. Said Reinhart:

> He made me a fair offer, better than any Gentile or white man in Salt Lake City. He said he would take one of his horses, let me have one, and we could put a pack of blankets and provisions on the third, and he would go with me to his place at [Government Creek], 180 miles, and hunt all the way there, and then get his herders to start from there to hunt my horses. He would be to all expense and if we got the horses I was to let him have a choice of two horses for his trouble. He seemed to act perfectly square and like a liberal gentleman (if he was a Mormon). I was to let him know in a few days if I should conclude to take his offer so as to prepare him for our trip.[50]

But in the long run Reinhart had no need to avail himself of Rockwell's talents; a message arrived from Fillmore reporting that two men had been captured in possession of a stolen herd of horses. Reinhart recovered his animals, paid a $25 reward for their return, settled his bills, and left for more peaceable parts of the country. He took with him a vastly revised concept of the man called Danite.

About this time Rockwell is supposed to have figured in an incident which amplified his already legendary exploits as a manhunter and scout. It came about when one of the Overland stages on the Great Salt Lake route from California was relieved at gunpoint of its cargo, gold bullion in the amount of $40,000, near Riverbed, west of Rockwell's Government Creek ranch. The lone bandit escaped while the stage driver pushed on to Faust Station in Rush Valley, where, coincidentally, Rockwell waited to board the coach as a special Wells Fargo shotgun guard to Fort Bridger. Outfitting himself with cold rations, the Mormon set out alone to capture the highwayman and recover the loot.

[50] Herman Francis Reinhart, *The Golden Frontier; The Recollections of Herman Francis Reinhart, 1851–1869*, edited by Doyce B. Nunis, Jr. (Austin, Texas, 1962), pp. 280–81.

It was a difficult trail to follow, since the fugitive had taken great pains to avoid leaving tracks, but after two days he located the man camped on the sinks at Cherry Creek, about sixty miles south of Lookout Pass. From a vantage point, Rockwell could see that the outlaw had succeeded in caching the bullion until the right moment came to haul it away. For days the suspect's movements followed the same unvaried routine of watching for sign that he was being pursued; and all the while Rockwell doggedly kept him in sight, waiting for him to make for the gold. Then one morning nearly a week after the holdup, the man rode out and dug up the bullion. When the last bar had been exhumed, Rockwell stepped in and made his arrest. He took prisoner and bullion to Government Creek, placing a guard over both while he went to bed for some solid sleep. But Rockwell's slumber was short-lived; his foreman, Hat Shurtliff, dozed on guard duty and awakened only in time to see the robber escaping on horseback. Scrambling for a gun, he yelled the alarm. Rockwell, bleary-eyed and half asleep, rushed to the door of his cabin, squinted at the fleeing rider, and snapped off a long shot without apparent effect.

The following day Rockwell turned the bullion over to stage officials in Great Salt Lake City with an explanation of why the culprit was missing. Several days later an unsigned and somewhat rambling telegraph message from Fort Bridger to Wells Fargo announced that Rockwell had stolen the gold from the original bandit and kept it for himself. It appeared that the fugitive had made one last effort to implicate the man who had cheated him of a fortune. Like the robbery, it failed, too.[51] The

[51] This episode is related by Glynn Bennion in "Suggestion and Quick Draw," *Salt Lake Tribune*, February 24, 1924. See also James Sharp, "The Old Man's Story," *Improvement Era*, Vol. XLVI (1943), pp. 85, 100–1. In one version a former telegraph operator in the Riverbed area was supposed to have had prior knowledge of the gold shipment and disappeared just before the holdup. Still another tale tells of a gunshot victim riding into Fort Bridger a day or so before the mysterious telegraph message was received at the Wells Fargo office in Great Salt Lake City. He wandered off, it is said, and later was found dead at the foot of a telegraph pole with a makeshift transmitting "bug" clutched in his hand. See James Sharp, "Singing Wires," *Improvement Era*, Vol. XLVII (1944), pp. 754, 794. Despite all these leads, I have never been able to verify any part of the story, includ-

Case of the Great Bullion Robbery is only one of the scores of accounts, some true, others not so true, which have blended through the years to create the perplexing and always controversial Rockwell image.[52]

Of all the men Orrin Porter Rockwell set out to catch, probably the most cold-blooded was a boy with the rather unpretentious name of Chauncey W. Millard. At age eighteen Millard was a real frontier hardcase, a transplanted New York street arab who drifted West after serving a short hitch in the Union Army and signed on as a teamster in Great Salt Lake City for a couple of freighters named Harlem P. Swett[53] and

---

ing the original bullion robbery. The incident is included here simply because it is one of the most widespread and popular of the Rockwell legends.

[52] How frustrating some of these will-o'-the-wisp stories can be is illustrated by W. G. Tittsworth's description of activity near Diamond Peak, scene of the great diamond hoax of the 1870s. Tittsworth writes that "Hank Langford, from Park City, Utah, . . . was in camp, hale and hearty, after being disembowelled on the streets of Salt Lake City by Porter Rockwell, one of Brigham Young's notorious destroying angels . . . ." With that tantalizing sentence, Tittsworth leaves us to wonder what the Rockwell–Langford scrape was all about and when, precisely, it occurred. See W. G. Tittsworth, *Outskirt Episodes* (Des Moines, Iowa, 1927), pp. 31–32.

Two other yarns about Rockwell are deserving of mention, if for no other reason than that they make good reading. But most important, even legends have a place in biography. Both stories have to do with his unshorn locks and reputed immortality. The first concerns a gunfight in which Rockwell is alleged to have withstood the savage fire of several desperadoes and ultimately put them to flight. When the smoke cleared, the story goes, he shook himself like a great shaggy bear and several pistol balls of various calibers fell from the folds of his ill-fitting homespun coat, thus offering witnesses additional evidence of the fulfillment of Joseph Smith's prophecy protecting Rockwell from harm. A similar anecdote is mentioned by James T. Harwood in his manuscript autobiography, "A Basket of Chips (1860–1940)," in which Harwood recalls: "The year that the railroad reached Lehi, and when I was twelve years old, Porter Rockwell met a man whom he had quarreled with in a saloon near my father's harness shop. This man emptied every chamber of his six-shooter at Porter, and the balls splattered all around him, but not one touched him . . . ."

The second tale tells of a bet made by a gunslinger in California who claimed that he could add Rockwell to his collection of notches. The killer rode to Utah, they say, waylaid Rockwell on the trail one afternoon, and, poking a heavy revolver in his face, told the Mormon to say his prayers. "You wouldn't try and shoot a man without a cap on your pistol, would you?" Rockwell is supposed to have replied. The gunman's eyes flickered from target to weapon, and in that instant he was shot from the saddle by Rockwell, who fired his own gun through a coat pocket. The outlaw was dead when he struck the ground. Bennion, "Suggestion and Quick Draw," *Salt Lake Tribune*, February 24, 1924.

[53] Gardner, *History of Lehi*, p. 205.

Chauncey Mayfield. On December 11, 1868, Millard, Swett, and May-field passed along the west side of Utah Lake and camped at a stone house near J. C. Naile's home. Swett and Mayfield were sitting on the front seat of the wagon with Millard in back. All at once an explosion roared at Mayfield's side. He turned in time to see Swett topple from the seat, dead, a gaping hole in his back.

"What the hell are you doing!" Mayfield shouted as Millard whipped a smoking revolver in his direction.[54] Millard thumbed back the hammer and fired point-blank. The ball smashed through the bones of Mayfield's hand as he tried vainly to protect himself. With a scream the wounded man leaped from the wagon and ran for his life while Millard pumped four shots at him. Finally, the hammer smacked flatly on an empty chamber.[55] Mayfield stumbled down the road to Lehi, his torn hand throbbing with pain. Millard ran on foot toward Cedar Valley to the west and pushed his way into the cabin of John Irvin, begging Irvin to let him stay "until the weather clears."[56]

Posses combed the region without success, and by December 16 Mil-lard was ready to make a break for it. Waiting until Irvin left the cabin, he stripped the premises, taking with him a coat, a blanket, Irvin's double-barrelled shotgun, ammunition, food, field glasses, and a horse. When Irvin returned and found his home looted, he galloped to Lehi for the law, and while changing mounts, learned for the first time that he had been harboring a killer. Late in the afternoon of the sixteenth Irvin and three other men started in search of the young desperado. They returned the next day, empty-handed. Then, when everyone had given up hope of finding Millard, a teamster from American Fork reported seeing the youngster in the West Mountains north of Cedar Fort.[57] This time pro-fessionals were called in.

Rockwell and Deputy Sheriff Henry Heath quietly saddled up and slipped out of town on the night of December 17. By sundown of the next day Chauncey W. Millard, sidewalk tough, ex-soldier, teamster, and murderer, was led handcuffed into Lehi. Wrote the correspondent for the *Deseret News*: "He seems utterly indifferent about his position. He says he has tried to make money by stealing and killing and having failed, would sooner die than live." Sadly enough, Millard would get his wish.

---

54 *Deseret News*, December 12, 1868.
55 Ibid.
56 Ibid., December 17, 1868.
57 Ibid., December 18, 1868.

Justice moved swiftly for the teen-ager. By January 16, 1869, scarcely a month after his capture, a district court jury had brought in a verdict of guilty of murder in the first degree. The youth was sentenced to be executed on the morning of January 29.

> At 25 minutes to 11 o'clock a.m., Chauncey W. Millard was taken to the place of execution, on the west side of the court house. He walked with the irons on his hands and feet. A chair was got for him, in which he sat for a few minutes, and then rose to his feet, and read in a clear, full, firm voice, the 7th Chapter of Matthew. He made no further remarks, but spoke something with the Sheriff and the police and Dr. Roberts, who stood nearby, and then sat down. The Sheriff then took the irons off his wrists, he placing himself in position; the Sheriff moved a few paces off and then gave the signal. Two bullets passed through his left breast. He raised his right hand a little, the testament from which he read falling out of his hand, and all was over with him. . . .[58]

Rockwell was in the crowd of more than four hundred spectators who watched the firing squad snuff out the life of the condemned youth. Whether he heard Millard's last conversation with the sheriff and the physician is not known, but it would have startled even the implacable Rockwell to know that the boy had sold his body to the Provo surgeon for a pound of candy . . . and was eating the sweets at the moment the shots ended his life.[59]

Although Millard's execution may have distressed his captor in many respects, it had no apparent effect on Rockwell's unrelenting war on rustlers. In July of '69 he helped a Hamilton, Nevada, rancher named Nelson run down and apprehend a pair of the Nevadan's hired hands who had stolen ten of his best horses. Young or old, Rockwell had no use for rustlers; to a man of his breed, horses and cattle represented property no one tampered with. He may have taken a measure of satisfaction when the Hamilton *Empire* wrote an article thanking him for assisting Nelson in time of need,[60] but his greatest pleasure came when the *Deseret News* mentioned that he had been awarded a premium for the best four-year-old filly and year-old mule colt entered in the ninth annual Deseret Agricultural and Manufacturing Society exhibit in Great Salt Lake City on October 4, 1869.[61]

[58] Ibid., January 29, 1869.

[59] Gardner, *History of Lehi*, p. 206n.

[60] The account was picked up and published in the *Deseret News*, July 8. 1869.

[61] Journal History, October 5, 1869, p. 5. Record of the Deseret Agricultural and Manufacturing Society, p. 109, shows that he was awarded a $5 prize for the filly and $10 for the mule colt.

Chapter Nineteen

THE GATHERING TWILIGHT

FOR THE SAME REASON THE TRANSCONTINENTAL RAILROAD held the key to the future of the West, it posed a threat to the security of the Latter-day Saints, who had thrice abandoned their homes rather than suffer Gentile neighbors. Largely as the result of General Connor's reports concerning Utah's potential mineral wealth, in 1868 the Mormons anticipated that the railroad would bring an army of adventurers and spoilers to their land. It did not come as a surprise to many, therefore, when stories floated about that Daniteism had been resurrected for the purpose of "defending the Saints" against the dreaded Gentile invasion.[1]

But true or not, Rockwell was no longer interested in such intrigues. Gradually the old-time stronghearts of the church found themselves seeking less turbulent existences. Lot Smith was on a mission to Great Britain, Robert T. Burton was fulfilling a similar obligation in the eastern states, George W. Bean could be found herding sheep near Santaquin, Bill Hickman had been disfellowshiped, and John D. Lee was headed for excommunication. Outside of a brief change of pace in May of 1870 when he

---

[1] Wyl, *Mormon Portraits*, pp. 191–92, quotes Mrs. Sarah Pratt, widow of Apostle Orson Pratt, as having a conversation in 1868 with Heber C. Kimball in which Kimball said, " '. . . we have just reorganized the Danite Band in the Endowment House. Fifty brethren have joined and been sworn in!' " He added, Mrs. Pratt said, " 'We'll have plenty of work for them to do pretty soon.' "

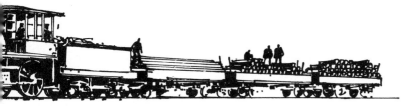

was called to head a posse in search of Albert H. Haws, a Nevada bad-man who had shot down a United States marshal, Rockwell led the peaceful life he sought.[2]

There were, of course, scattered occasions when he disagreed with some of the habitués of Whisky Street. (A man could not be expected to stop enjoying life entirely.) And at least once it cost him money. Rock-well was sampling a drop or two of warmth in the Salt Lake House — to keep out the nip of night air — when the bartender passed a remark which, though unrecorded, was sufficient to arouse the disputatious instincts of the old scout. In the ensuing argument the offender was catapulted the length of his tavern and sent crashing through the front window. Glassware and furniture also suffered in the melee. While the vanquished bartender conceded the point under discussion, he retaliated by having Rockwell brought up on charges of drunkenness and disturbing the peace. Rockwell was ordered to post a $500 peace bond when his explanation failed to impress Jeter Clinton, the local magistrate.[3] The

[2] At least three posses had undertaken to capture Haws for the murder of Marshal William R. Storey. When the wanted man was finally cornered, he resisted and was shot to death on May 4, 1870. Two citizens were killed and a third wounded in the struggle to capture Haws. Details can be found in the *Deseret News*, May 3 and 4, 1870. See also *Tullidge's Histories*, Vol. II, p. 101.

[3] *Salt Lake Herald*, October 9, 1870.

size of the bond may seem excessive, but only two months earlier, Rockwell and a few friends had filed notice of location on a three thousand foot stretch of ground in the Ophir Mining District. The claim was rich in silver and carried the name of its discoverer — the Rockwell Lode of the Rockwell Mining Company.[4]

As a thriving metropolis, Great Salt Lake City was experiencing growing pains of agonizing proportions. Political machinations abounded as never before in the city. The Utah Liberal party was born, a woman's suffrage bill was passed, and a full-scale anti-Mormon crusade was in progress. In Congress, powerful influences were pushing legislation intended to crush the last of the "twin relics of barbarism," polygamy.[5] Excitement over passage of the Cullom Bill in the House caused great agitation in Zion, though the measure ultimately was shelved by the Senate. Through it all, the rallying cry for anti-Mormons rang clear: Destroy Brigham Young!

As winter surrendered to spring in 1871, the combined efforts of Gentiles and apostates had failed to unsettle the church or its leadership. But in a sheepherder's shack west of Nephi a confrontation was taking place which soon would have violent repercussions. At a table cluttered with dirty dishes sat two men — one a federal marshal, the other a desperado reputed to have killed literally scores of men. Marshal Sam Gilson spoke earnestly and convincingly to the man he had spent weeks attempting to contact. What the lawman wanted was a full confession of the outlaw's misdeeds. He especially wanted knowledge of a major crime which could be linked to the Mormon hierarchy. In return, Gilson promised to use his

---

[4] Others involved in the venture included his son, Orrin [DeWitt] Rockwell, Brigham H. Young, J. R. Walker, George W. Boyd, Vincent Shurtliff, Alex Mayus, James Crossly, G. W. Cooly, S. D. Burnett, G. McConnell, W. McConnell, and M. McConnell. See Ophir Mining District, Record Book A, p. 182, Tooele County Recorder's office.

For other mining transactions concerning Rockwell, consult Tooele County Deeds, Book D, p. 445; Book E, pp. 153–54, and p. 429. On July 24 and August 14, 1877, Rockwell purchased property from Henry J. Faust and Seth Fletcher, respectively, for which he paid a sum total of eight thousand dollars in cash. Deed Book X, pp. 494–95, 517–18.

[5] The other being slavery. See the Republican Party Platform for 1856. Women first won the vote in Wyoming Territory in 1869, and a few weeks later women in Utah Territory won the franchise, which they lost in 1887 by an act of Congress aimed at punishing Mormon plural marriage practices. Utah, however, came into the Union in 1896 with woman suffrage.

influence in the informer's behalf. The marshal's impassioned arguments eventually prevailed, and the desperado nodded his assent. William A. "Bill" Hickman had decided to "unbosom myself where it would do some good." [6]

If Hickman is to be believed, he had been bordering on open conflict with the church for years because of his audacity in asking for a share of the spoils from the murder of Richard Yates during the Utah War of 1857. Since then, he said, he had been accused of "talking" to General Connor and being friendly with "Josephites." [7] Finally, Hickman claimed, the breach became irreconcilable and he was disfellowshiped for refusing to kill Connor on orders of Brigham Young. Before they parted company that evening, Gilson and Hickman agreed that the Yates murder was "the one on which we could with the greatest safety rely for prosecuting Brigham Young." [8]

On the last day of September, Gilson formally arrested Hickman on a charge of murder, took him before Chief Justice James B. McKean for arraignment, and hustled him off to the confines of Camp Douglas for safekeeping. In the two weeks following his arrest, Hickman wrote a full confession, which was presented to a grand jury at the camp. On October 28, United States Marshal M. T. Patrick arrested Salt Lake City Mayor Daniel H. Wells and a prominent Mormon attorney, Hosea Stout, on indictments alleging complicity in the Yates killing. William H. Kimball was arrested the same day on a warrant charging him with being an accessory to the murder of the last member of the Aiken Party near Hot Springs. [9] Hickman was named co-defendant in each case. Brigham Young, who was out of the city on his annual visit to the southern settle-

---

[6] Hickman, *Brigham's Destroying Angel*, p. 191.

[7] Followers of Joseph Smith III.

[8] Hickman, *Brigham's Destroying Angel*, p. 191. Hickman's confession implicating Brigham Young brought a bitter denunciation from the Saints. With the Nauvoo Legion in the field against the Utah Expedition was Daniel W. Jones, into whose camp Hickman had ridden after the slaying of Richard Yates. In retrospect Jones challenged Hickman's statement as the work of a liar. "Now if Yates had been killed as Hickman related in his book he would not have manifested so much interest in what President Young would say . . . . Hickman killed Yates for his money and horse the same as any other thief and murderer would have done, and then excused himself by telling he was counseled to do these things. I know positively that Governor Young's orders were to avoid bloodshed in every way possible." Jones, *Forty Years Among the Indians*, p. 130.

[9] *Salt Lake Tribune*, October 30, 1871.

ments, was named jointly in the indictment with William Kimball.[10] Since the court had been assured that Brigham Young would appear for trial, his case was set over until the March term. Wells was freed on $50,000 bail, but Stout and Kimball were denied the same privilege and were confined with their accuser, Hickman, at Camp Douglas.

In the confusion following the first indictment, many Mormons scrambled for hiding places. They feared that an all-out drive on ranking churchmen was in the offing under the pretext of law enforcement. For a brief period, two stalwarts came out of retirement to protect their leaders. One, George Washington Bean, had always been a quiet man, having developed an inexhaustible patience in decades of dealing with stolid Indians. But he was disposed to comment somewhat vitriolically about this latest turn of events. Referring to Judge McKean, whom he considered a sectarian bigot: "It fired some of us to action when he permitted falsehoods to bring fine men and even Brigham Young to trial. It kept some of us busy at times to keep the brethren out of the clutches of his merciless Myrmidons. Many of the brethren had to be guarded safely through and between settlements and again O. P. Rockwell and George W. Bean were on duty. . . ." [11]

After the first scare passed, Rockwell availed himself of the opportunity of spending a few comfortable nights in the city. While touring the taverns he chanced to meet George Alfred Townsend, a newspaperman of renown, who was in Zion to cover the trial of Brigham Young on earlier charges of "lewd and lascivious cohabitation" stemming from his plural marriages. Townsend had established himself as a reporter of worth during the Civil War while writing under the pen name of "Gath." Over a drink, the correspondent had time to study the noted frontiersman, and came away singularly unimpressed. In an October 27 letter to the *Cincinnati Commercial*, Townsend observed, somewhat cynically:

> Human life in Utah is safer than probably anywhere in civilization. The motives and causes of murder exist in a less degree — as avarice, liquor, gambling, quarrelsomeness and prostitution. The industrious political vagabonds who write letters from Utah to the East have created the band of "Danites" and other hob-goblins out of air and foolscap.
> I talked to Porter Rockwell, the alleged leader of the "Danites,"

[10] Walker, "Journal," p. 541.

[11] Bean, *Autobiography*, p. 158.

a fat, curly-haired, good-natured chap, fond of a drink, a talk, and a wild venture. The United States authorities have several times used him to make arrests of lawless characters.[12]

Gath also had some thoughts about Bill Hickman: ". . . a Judas and a Joab in one . . . . Hickman is a Missouri border ruffian, a polygamist, and a human hyena."

Legal proceedings against Brigham Young took a surprising twist in late November when prosecutor R. N. Baskin, confident that the Mormon president was out of reach and unavailable in remote southern Utah, demanded that the cohabitation trial be convened at once and that the defendant appear or forfeit his $5,000 bond. While the church's legal counsel argued for a postponement, Rockwell saddled his fastest pony and rode south to track down Young and his retinue. Time meant everything, for Mormon attorneys could obtain a continuance only until January 9, 1872; decisive action alone could forestall forfeiture of Young's bond and his arrest. After days of searching, Rockwell located Brigham in Cedar City on December 20. They began the return trip the same day. According to one Mormon historian, the party met General Connor in Beaver, and he readily agreed not to mention seeing Young so that the appearance in court would be entirely voluntary.[13] (Connor, en route from Pioche to Great Salt Lake City, is supposed to have offered to post further bail for Young, "even if it amounts to a million dollars.") Because of Rockwell's efforts, the president was able to arrive in the city well ahead of the appointed hour and thwart Baskin's attempt to discredit him.[14]

Three months later the United States Supreme Court handed down a decision in the Engelbrecht case which set aside all legal proceedings in Utah during the previous eighteen months and declared null and void indictments found against nearly one hundred and forty persons. The

---

[12] Townsend's articles from Zion made excellent reading with their clean, biting wit — especially his descriptions of prominent Gentiles and anti-Mormons found in *Mormon Trials at Salt Lake City*, pp. 17–19, and 39.

[13] Whitney, *History of Utah*, Vol. II, p. 658n.

[14] Orson F. Whitney, who put forth the claim that General Connor had offered a million dollars in bail for President Young, was exaggerating. That the old soldier did, indeed, make such a gesture is corroborated by Brigham H. Roberts and entries in the Church's history, but the figure is conceded to have been $100,000. Still, a not inconsiderable amount. See Manuscript History of Brigham Young, 1871, Vol. II, pp. 2101–2.

landmark opinion resulted in all charges against Young, Wells, Stout, Kimball, and, ironically, Hickman himself, being dropped.[15]

While the Saints basked in the warmth of their victory, Rockwell was scrapping with another branch of the federal government; the Treasury Department refused to pay on his mail contract. According to his figures, the post office owed him $1,310.63 for services rendered, and he intended to collect one way or another. Since everyone else seemed to be doing things "legal-like," Rockwell retained the services of a lawyer. Contacting bankers in Washington through friends, the Mormon told them to "get my money!" J. D. T. McAllister was a witness as Rockwell scratched his mark on the authorization. Rockwell did get his money, "legal-like," right down to the sixty-three cents.[16]

Some time in 1870 or 1871 Rockwell had slowed down long enough to take a fourth wife. The bride's name was Christine Olsen. She had been his housekeeper. On July 27, 1872, Rockwell, at fifty-nine, and Christine, at thirty-four, became the parents of a daughter, Irene, who died the same day of complications incident to birth.[17] The infant was Rockwell's twelfth offspring. There would be two more, both girls — Elizabeth Christine, born June 3, 1873, and Ida May, born October 4, 1878.[18]

Elijah Averett remembered Rockwell during these days as a hearty, robust fellow, still protecting Brigham Young when the occasion de-

---

[15] Even though he was despised as a traitor, Hickman continued for several years to reside near Fort Crittenden. One traveler who spied him on the road had this comment:

> Why the fiend is permitted to live is a mystery. His confessions of bloody deeds, if true, should expose him to the vengeance of Gentiles whose friends he has slain; if false, the wonder is that he is not riddled by Mormon bullets. It is a mark of the astonishing forbearance of this people that, believing him to be a malignant liar, they allow him to go about the country unmolested, and the only accountable reason for his safety from the wrath of the Gentiles is, that they hope at some future day to use him as a witness to prove the murders committed by him at the bidding of the church. . . . He walks the streets by day armed with two revolvers and a belt of cartridges, looking furtively about him to see if some avenger is not nigh. . . . And thus he lives in a continual hell.

John Codman, *The Round Trip, by Way of Panama Through California, Oregon, Nevada, Utah, Idaho and Colorado* (New York, 1879), pp. 195–96. Hickman died in Lander City, Wyoming, August 21, 1883.

[16] William Clayton, "Letterbook, 1860–1879," p. 287. Dated June 22, 1873. (Microfilm at Utah State Historical Society.)

[17] *Utah Genealogical and Historical Magazine*, Vol. XXVI, p. 156.

[18] Ibid.

manded. During one of the president's last visits to Utah's Dixie, Averett recollected: "Porter Rockwell was along for a bodyguard to Brigham, and while at Pipe [Springs] on the way back Port got rather drunk, and as they left Pipe Brigham and the driver of the team were sitting in the front seat looking solemnly ahead and Port was shouting and waving his hat . . . ." [19]

Rockwell's conduct may have had a bearing on subsequent events, for the puritanical Brigham Young was not one to tolerate indecorum in his presence. Whatever the reason, Rockwell was sent on a mission on June 1, 1873. It was the last time his services would be requested by the church to which he had devoted a lifetime. The call came after George W. Bean, reporting on the Fish Lake region of central Utah, had waxed enthusiastic upon the merits of Grass Valley, near the lake. Young's instructions to Bean and Rockwell were succinct: "Colonize the straggling bands of natives in the vicinity . . . teach them honesty, industry, morality and religion."

By the first of August, Bean, his family, Rockwell, and a Gentile volunteer named Clark were on their way south.[20] Mrs. Bean, who braided Rockwell's hair when it needed it, was miffed at her husband for telling church authorities "too good a story" about the valley; she did not relish the prospect of leaving a comfortable farm to start life anew among wild Indians. Her feelings could well have reflected the attitude of the entire group, but they held their peace.

In ten days the company reached Cedar Grove in Grass Valley and bent to the task of raising cabins and storing feed for the approaching winter.[21] Word of this choice land south of Thistle and Sanpete valleys reached other ears in Great Salt Lake City, and before long the colony began to grow. Bean and A. K. Thurber cut a road to a mountain top on which Joseph A. Young located a sawmill. Thirty tons of hay were up and prospects were excellent. Satisfied that he was no longer needed, Rockwell packed his gear and rode alone back to the ranch and livestock at Government Creek.[22]

[19] Elijah Averett, "Journal." MS, p. 21.

[20] Bean, *Autobiography*, p. 171.

[21] Gottfredson, *Indian Depredations in Utah*, p. 330.

[22] No sooner had Rockwell taken his leave than a fracas broke out between a party of Navajos and a family named McCarty. Three braves were killed and a fourth wounded in the shooting which erupted over a calf the Indians had butchered. See ibid., pp. 330–32.

Chapter Twenty

TRAIL'S END

There was something about Orrin Porter Rockwell that so unmanned his opponents that they would not, could not, and did not outface him. Even if it were possible to escape his lightning wit, eye and hand. Was it the word of the Prophet of the Lord that he should not be harmed?[1]

DURING THE THREE YEARS SUBSEQUENT to his Grass Valley mission, Rockwell poured his strength and enthusiasm into the one thing which had replaced the church as a motivating force in his life — the ranch. Stock bearing his brands swarmed over Tooele County, south into Juab County, and west into Nevada.[2] On those increasingly rare days when he rode into the city, Rockwell contented himself with the quiet corner of a saloon; then he either spent the night at home with Christine on Second West Street or repaired to the Colorado Stables, where he kept a small office.[3] Rockwell learned that while he could change his pattern of living,

[1] Israel Bennion in the "Church Section," *Deseret News*, August 31, 1935.

[2] Rockwell horses were marked with the Cedar Tree brand on the right thigh; cattle carried a three-inch-high OP on the right hip. Records of Marks and Brands, Utah Territory, December 29, 1849, to December 9, 1874, pp. 37, 113.

[3] *Salt Lake Herald*, June 11, 1878.

his name remained Porter Rockwell, and nothing could erase that. Greenhorns sat around many a campfire on the emigrant trail and listened wide-eyed to tales of Indian massacres and to ballads of fighting men. There were at least two about Rockwell. One opens:

Have you heard of Porter Rockwell, the Mormon Triggerite,
They say he hunts down outlaws when the moon is shining bright,
So if you rustle cattle, I'll tell you what to do,
Get the drop on Porter Rockwell, or he'll get the drop on you.[4]

The other goes:

Old Port Rockwell looks like a man,
With a beard on his face and his hair in a braid,
But there's none in the West but Brigham who can
Look in his eyes and not be afraid.

For Port is a devil in a human shape,
Though he calls himself "Angel," say vengeance is sweet;
But he's black, bitter death, and there's no escape,
When he wails through the night his dread war cry, "Wheat!"
Wheat!
Somewhere a wife with her babes kneels to pray,
For she knows she's a widow and orphans are they.[5]

These are words and images of another day and another time. But Zion was full of fresh new faces in 1876, a new generation anxious, even eager, to dredge up old memories and lay them bare. It was an all-Mormon jury which finally convicted John D. Lee of murder in the first degree for his role in the Mountain Meadows affair, a crime perpetrated nineteen years earlier. Rockwell's reaction to the verdict is not found in history, but when Brigham Young made no effort to save Lee from the firing squad — and it was whispered openly that a deal had been struck to protect others from a similar fate — Rockwell must surely have realized that an era had passed.[6] Emboldened by their success in the Mountain

[4] *Utah, A Guide to the State*, compiled by workers of the Writers' Program of the Work Projects Administration for the State of Utah (New York, 1941), p. 288.

[5] Olive W. Burt, *American Murder Ballads*, collected and edited by Olive Woolley Burt (New York, 1958), p. 115. Used by permission of Olive W. Burt.

[6] Lee was executed March 23, 1877, at Mountain Meadows, and his remains were buried in Panguitch.

Meadows prosecution, the anti-Mormon faction pressed for revival of old charges against church members accused of crimes committed during the early days of Utah's colonization. All at once, names long since forgotten were resurrected — among them, the Aiken Party.

Cholera morbus was the diagnosis of doctors who examined the pain-racked and suffering Brigham Young. For six days they hovered at his bedside. But despite their struggle to save him, the church president died August 29, 1877.

Anti-Mormons impatiently waited for the church to crumble and for its membership to divide and fall in the fight for succession to the Mormon throne now that the iron-fisted leader was dead. When chaos failed to erupt, the Gentiles proceeded with plans to prosecute Mormons for capital crimes, regardless of the passage of time and the obvious scarcity of witnesses. An unusually cooperative grand jury began handing down indictments with unrestrained zeal.

The first to be arrested was ailing Jeter Clinton, justice of the peace. He was accused of killing John Banks during the "Morrisite" uprising of 1862.[7] Shortly thereafter the grand jury issued indictments against Orrin Porter Rockwell and Sylvanus Collett in regard to the Aiken affair; the two men specifically were accused of the murder of John Aiken.[8] When Rockwell was arrested on September 29, 1877, the *Salt Lake Tribune* made no effort to conceal its pleasure in reporting: "Another one of 'our best society,' O. P. Rockwell, was jugged yesterday. This man has been one of the chief murderers of the Mormon Church, opening his career of blood in Nauvoo, under the regime of the Prophet. He was indicted a day or two ago by the grand jury of the First District Court, for participation in the horribly atrocious murder of the Aiken party, in 1858, on the Sevier. He was arrested, yesterday, by the United States marshal, in this city, and sent to the penitentiary for safekeeping. . . ."[9]

After a week in prison Rockwell was admitted to bail. Three friends — Sam McIntyre, J. A. Cunningham, and Orin Dix — posted $15,000 in bonds in his behalf.[10] Associate Judge Philip H. Emerson set trial for the

---

[7] The case against Clinton was disposed of in April 1879, when U.S. Attorney Philip T. Van Zile was forced to move for dismissal on grounds of insufficient evidence.

[8] See Utah County and Territorial Criminal Records, Files 81, 82 (The People vs. O. P. Rockwell et al.), Utah County Clerk's Office, Provo, Utah.

[9] *Salt Lake Tribune*, September 30, 1877.

[10] Ibid., October 6, 1877.

October term of district court the following year. Rockwell engaged the firm of Frank Tilford and A. Hagan to represent him, but each time the lawyers attempted to discuss the case with their client, he would shrug off questions with "Wheat! Wheat!" [11] While they fretted over his defense, Rockwell went unconcernedly about his business.

The months passed quickly, and with the advent of summer came a special occasion. Thespian Denman Thompson had consented to play the starring role in *Joshua Whitcomb* for two nights only, June 7 and 8, in the Salt Lake Theatre. The bill promised to attract standing-room-only audiences and was considered the highlight of the season. Rockwell was one of the fortunate who obtained tickets to the final performance, Saturday night, June 8. As expected, the theater was jammed, and it was only after some little exertion that Rockwell and his daughter Mary found seats. After the final curtain Rockwell escorted Mary home, then dropped into a nearby tavern to spend an hour before retiring.

He left the saloon at Main and First South, a block west of the theater, and walked to the Colorado Stables three blocks away, arriving between midnight and one o'clock in the morning. According to the hostler who saw him come in, Rockwell flopped on a bed in his office and slept soundly for several hours. Upon awakening he complained of being cold. And within minutes he was seized by a wave of nausea. Later in the afternoon he again suffered a congestive chill and violent vomiting. During the hours between the two attacks Rockwell spoke freely with the

[11] Ibid., June 12, 1878. Rockwell also paid a Provo lawyer, Warren N. Dusenberry, $250 to defend him on the murder charges. The Dusenberry receipt is dated January 31, 1878.

hostler and, after the second chill and nausea had subsided, he insisted on getting up.

He sat on the edge of the bed and pulled on his boots,[12] then suddenly lurched backward and lapsed into unconsciousness.[13] A physician was hastily summoned to the scene and attempted mouth-to-mouth resuscitation, but it was too late. Orrin Porter Rockwell — Mormon, pioneer, scout, and accused assassin — was dead. For a Sunday afternoon the news spread quickly, and within an hour a crowd of several hundred curious citizens gathered at the stable for a final glimpse of the man who had been regarded as immortal. The atmosphere was one of disbelief. At sixty-five another man would have been considered a patriarch, but so widespread and accepted were the stories of Rockwell's invincibility that an autopsy and an inquest were ordered.[14]

A three-man coroner's jury heard four physicians testify that a post-mortem operation had disclosed: ". . . failure of the heart's action, caused by a suspension of the nervous power. There were no evidences of injury, nor any symptoms of poisoning." [15] Soon afterward the jury brought in a verdict of death from natural causes.[16] Funeral services were scheduled for the following morning.

Meanwhile the *Tribune* was having a field day. Rockwell's passing had provided its editors with an opportunity to attack the church for the first time in months, and they made the most of it. In his obituary, the newspaper commented: "Thus the gallows was cheated of one of the fittest candidates that ever cut a throat or plundered a traveler." They accused him of "at least a hundred murders for the Church . . ." and added that he "had a decided objection to sleeping in the dark." [17] (Presumably because Rockwell's conscience troubled him.) Hinting that there was "strong evidence" against Rockwell in the Aiken murder, the paper

[12] Thus disproving the old wives' tale that in the minutes before his death Rockwell struggled to remove them so that he would not die with his boots on.

[13] Rockwell's last hours are reported in the *Salt Lake Tribune*, June 11, 1878. Compare with the *Salt Lake Herald*, June 11, 1878. Oddly, the *Deseret News* on June 10, 1878, notes his passing with only the barest of details in a story headlined "An Old Citizen Departed."

[14] At the time of his baptism when he was sixteen, Rockwell was the youngest member of the Church. When he died, he was the oldest Mormon in terms of fellowship.

[15] *Salt Lake Tribune*, June 12, 1878. In essence, death was due to a heart attack.

[16] *Salt Lake Herald*, June 12, 1878.

[17] *Salt Lake Tribune*, June 11, 1878.

nevertheless suggested: ". . . it is extremely doubtful whether a jury could have been empaneled that would convict him on proof of the crime charged." In one paragraph he was described as "an extremely ignorant, illiterate man, being unable to write his own name, and was superstitious as a savage"; then, in the same story, the writer explained that Rockwell's ranches and stock were worth an estimated $30,000. But the most critical remarks were saved for the editorial columns:

Porter Rockwell is another of the long list of Mormon criminals whose deeds of treachery and blood have reddened the soil of Utah, and who has paid no forfeit to offended law. When he was commissioned by the Prophet Joseph Smith, avenger-in-chief for the Lord, the Latter-day Saints were living a troublous life on the border; and it was give and take between the elect and their unconverted enemies. Wherever the former settled they stirred up strife with their neighbors, until they became so generally hated, that they were compelled to seek a home in the inaccessible wilderness in order to get away from the human race. Arrived in this Territory with the savage Indian only to dispute possession with them, and escape from these rocky fastnesses almost an impossibility, the fanatical hate of the inspired leaders of the Church suffered no restraint, and the avenging angels were made bloody instruments of these holy men's will. Porter Rockwell was chosen as a fitting agent to lead in these scenes of blood. Brutal in his instincts, lawless in his habits, and a fanatical devotee of the Prophet, the commands of this gloomy despot he received as the will of the Lord, and with the ferocity born of mistaken zeal, he grew to believe that the most acceptable service he could render the Almighty, was, as Lear expresses it, to "kill, kill, kill, kill, kill!" He killed unsuspecting travelers, whose booty was coveted by his prophet-master. He killed fellow Saints who held secrets that menaced the safety of their fellow criminals in the priesthood. He killed Apostates who dared to wag their tongues about the wrongs they had endured. And he killed mere sojourners in Zion merely to keep his hand in.

When the railroad was opened to Utah and the officers of the law began to make their weight felt, murder was no longer practiced as a fine art, and those who had followed the profession sought other avenues of usefulness. The Danite Rockwell retired from the avenging business, and for some years past has been extensively engaged in raising horses and cattle. But the recollection of his evil deeds haunted him, and conscience preyed upon his soul like the undying worm. To gain escape from this fiery torment he sought the intoxicating bowl, and whenever he appeared in the streets of Salt Lake, it was generally in the character of a vociferating maniac.

He died in time to escape the hand of the law. Being indicted in the First District for participating in the Aiken murder, District

Attorney [Philip T.] Van Zile was gathering together a mass of evidence which must have convicted him of the crime charged, and brought him to the same fate as was visited upon the "butcher Lee." Death steps in to save these destroyers of their race from the penalty they so richly deserve, but their evil deeds live after them, and of this aged criminal it can be truly said:

> He left a name at which the world grows pale,
> To paint a moral and adorn a tale.

Nearly a thousand persons filled the Fourteenth Ward assembly rooms on June 12 for Rockwell's funeral. Joseph F. Smith, a member of the Council of Twelve Apostles, delivered the eulogy. Elder Smith said: "He had his little faults, but Porter's life on earth, taken altogether, was one worthy of example, and reflected honor upon the Church. Through all his trials he had never once forgotten his obligations to his brethren and his God." The words were saluted by the *Tribune* as a "fitting tribute of one outlaw to the memory of another . . . ." Even in death Rockwell was the center of controversy.

At the graveside in Salt Lake City Cemetery the mourners departed, and workers shoveled dirt on the coffin of a man whose life on the frontier would be as misunderstood and as perplexing to outsiders as the epitaph on his headstone:

> *He was brave & loyal to his faith,*
> *true to the prophet Jos. Smith,*
> *a promise made him by the prophet*
> *thro. obedience it was fulfilled.*

BIBLIOGRAPHY

ABBREVIATIONS

CSmH   Henry E. Huntington Library, San Marino, California
CSt   Stanford University Libraries, Stanford, California
CtY   Yale University, Coe Collection of Western Americana,
        Beinecke Library, New Haven, Connecticut
CU-B   University of California, H. H. Bancroft Library,
        Berkeley, California
DLC   U.S. Library of Congress, Washington, D.C.
DNA   National Archives, Washington, D.C.
GS   Genealogical Society of Utah, Salt Lake City, Utah
InU   Indiana University, Lilly Library, Bloomington, Indiana
NN   New York Public Library, New York, New York
UHi   Utah State Historical Society, Salt Lake City, Utah
ULA   Utah State University, Logan, Utah
UPB   Brigham Young University, Harold B. Lee Library,
        Provo, Utah
USlC   Church Historical Department, Church of Jesus Christ
        of Latter-day Saints, Salt Lake City, Utah
UU   University of Utah, Marriott Library, Salt Lake City, Utah

DOCUMENTS

"A Record of Marriages (Solemnized) (Alphabetically Arranged) 1853–1856." This restricted list of marriages is on microfilm in GS.

"Abstract of the Census of 1840, Jackson County, Missouri." Copy on file in GS.

BULLOCK, THOMAS. "List of Saints in Jackson County [Missouri]." On file in USlC.

Circuit Court Records, Richmond, Missouri, 1843.

"Civil Marriages Performed in Nauvoo, Illinois, 1842–1843." GS.

Document Containing the Correspondence, Orders, etc., in Relation to the Disturbances With the Mormons; and the Evidence Given Before the Hon. Austin A. King, Judge of the Fifth Judicial Circuit of the State of Missouri, at the Court-House in Richmond, In a Criminal Court of Inquiry, Begun November 12, 1838. On The Trial of Joseph Smith, Jr., and Others, for High Treason and Other Crimes Against the State (Published by order of the General Assembly, Fayette, Missouri, 1841). Also printed as *Senate Document 189*, 26th Congress, 2nd Session, 1840.

"Engagement Between United States Troops and Sioux Indians," *House of Representatives Report No. 63*, 33rd Congress, 2nd Session, 1855.

INGALLS, CAPTAIN RUFUS. "Report to the Quartermaster General," *Senate Executive Document No. 1*, 34th Congress, 1st Session, 1855. DNA.

"Jackson County, Missouri, Marriage Records, 1827–1910." GS.

"Massacre at Mountain Meadows," *Senate Executive Document No. 42*, 36th Congress, 1st Session, 1860.

Office of Indian Affairs Records, DNA.

"Petition of the Mormons to Congress," *House Document No. 22*, 26th Congress, 2nd Session, December 21, 1840. DNA.

Records of Marks and Brands, Utah Territory, December 29, 1849, to December 9, 1874. UHi.

"Reports Relating to the Fort Kearny, South Pass, and Honey Lake Wagon Road, 1857–1861," Records of the Secretary of Interior, DNA.

"Report of the Secretary of the Interior," *Senate Executive Document No. 5*, 34th Congress, 3rd Session, 1856. DNA.

———, *House Executive Document No. 1*, 34th Congress, 3rd Session, 1856. DNA.

———, *House Executive Document No. 2*, 35th Congress, 1st Session, 1857. DNA.

———, *House Executive Document No. 2*, 35th Congress, 2nd Session, 1858. DNA.

ROCKWELL, ORRIN PORTER. Affidavit contained in evidence submitted by the Church of Jesus Christ of Latter-day Saints to the U.S. House of Representatives on May 10 and 21, 1842 (previously submitted to the Senate Judiciary Committee, 26th Congress, 1st Session, December 2, 1839–July 21, 1840), to substantiate claims against the State of Missouri for damages allegedly inflicted by residents of that State against the Mormons from 1833 to 1838. DNA.

Salt Lake City Death Records, 1848–1884. Department of Vital Statistics.

Salt Lake County Abstracts, Plats, and Surveys, Book A-2. Recorder's Office.

———, Coroner's Register, 1858–1880. Department of Vital Statistics.

———, Deeds and Transfers, Books A, B, and C. Recorder's Office.

———, Mortgage Records, Book B. Recorder's Office.

SIMPSON, CAPTAIN J. H., *Report of Explorations Across the Great Basin of the Territory of Utah, For a Wagon-Route From Camp Floyd to Genoa, in Carson Valley* (Washington, D.C., 1876). DNA.

Orrin Porter Rockwell
circa 1855
(Daughters of Utah Pioneers)

Tooele County Agreements, Book A. Tooele County Recorder's Office, Tooele, Utah.

———, Deeds, Book X.

———, Land Patents, Book 1.

———, Ophir Mining District Records, Books, A, D, and E.

U.S. Population Census, Sixth (1840), Illinois. DNA.

———, Seventh (1850), Utah. DNA.

———, Eighth (1860), Utah. DNA.

U.S. State Department, Territorial Papers, Utah Series, April 30, 1853–December 24, 1859. DNA.

Utah County Deeds, Book G. Utah County Recorder's Office, Provo, Utah.

Utah Executive Papers, 1856–1858. Utah State Archives, Salt Lake City, Utah.

"Utah Expedition," *House Executive Document No. 71*, 35th Congress, 1st Session, 1858. DNA.

Utah Military Records, Utah State Archives, Salt Lake City, Utah.

Vital Historical Records of Jackson County, Missouri, 1826–1876, collected, compiled, and published by the Kansas City Chapter, Daughters of the American Revolution (Kansas City, 1933–1934).

AVERETT, ELIJAH. "Journal." UHi (Man A 34); UU (ACC 359).

BALLARD, HENRY. "Private Journal." UHi (Man A 18).

BELNAP, GILBERT. "Journal." UHi (Man A 169); UPB; USlC; UU (ACC 399).

BENNION, JOHN. "Journal." Five volumes. UHi; UPB (MSS 981).

BIGLER, JACOB GATES. "Diary." UPB.

BOGGS, WILLIAM M. "Short Sketch of My 'History' of Crossing the 'Plains,' to California in the Year, 1846." Owned by Mrs. Thomas Kongsgaard, Napa, California.

BONNEY, EDWARD. "The Banditti of the Prairies." Two manuscripts, one entirely different, the other containing occasional variations, from the 1850 book based on them. InU.

BOYLE, HENRY G. "Diary." UPB; UU (ACC 384).

BROWN, LORENZO. "Journal, 1823–1900." UPB (MSS 497); USlC.

BROWN, THOMAS D. "Journal of the Southern Indian Mission." UHi, UPB.

CALL, ANSON. "Life and Record." UHi, UPB.

CHEESMAN, PAUL R. "An Analysis of the Accounts Relating Joseph Smith's Early Visions." M.A. Thesis, Brigham Young University, 1965. UPB.

CLAYTON, WILLIAM. "Letterbook, 1860–1879." UHi.

CONOVER, PETER WILSON. "Autobiography." UHi (Man A 240); UPB.

CROSBY, CAROLINE BARNES. "Journal." UHi; USlC.

CROSBY, JONATHAN. "Biographical Sketch." UHi.

DUNCAN, CHAPMAN. "Biography." UPB.

GINN, JOHN I. "Mormon and Indian Wars, the Mountain Meadows Massacre and Other Tragedies and Transactions Incident to the Mormon Rebellion of 1857, Together With the Personal Recollections of a Civilian Who Witnessed Many of the Thrilling Scenes Described. UHi (Man A 77).

GOVE, JESSE A. "Journal of the March of the Utah Expedition from Fort Bridger to Fort Leavenworth, August 9 to October 6, 1861." This is MS 226 of the Coe Collection. CtY.

GRIFFIN, CHARLES E. "History." DLC; UHi (Man A 1565); USlC.

HAIGHT, ISAAC CHAUNCEY. "Biographical Sketch and Diary." UHi; UPB; USlC; UU.

HAMMOND, MILTON D. "Journal." UHi; USlC; UU.

LILBURN W. BOGGS
(California State Library)

HARKER, JOSEPH. "History." UPB; USIC.

HARMON, APPLETON MILO. "Diary." DLC; UHi; UPB; USIC.

HARWOOD, JAMES T. "A Basket of Chips, 1860–1940." Autobiography. UU.

HEYWOOD, JOSEPH L. "Diary." UPB (MSS 179).

HOGAN, GOUDY E. "History." UHi (Man A 164); UPB; USIC.

HUNTINGTON, OLIVER BOARDMAN. "Diary." Three volumes. UHi (Man A 858); UPB.

Interviews with living Utah Pioneers in 1935, conducted under the Writers' Program of the Works Project Administration. See interviews with David McMullin, Heber Naegle, and Moroni Spillsbury. UHi; UPB.

JEPSON, JAMES. "Memories and Experiences." UHi (Man A 1389); ULA; UPB; USIC.

JOHNSON, JOEL HILLS. "Journal." UHi (Man A 26-2); UPB; USIC.

JOHNSTON, COLONEL ALBERT SIDNEY. Letter to Major Irvin McDowell, assistant adjutant general, September 11, 1857. This is MS 276 of the Coe Collection, CtY.

JONES, RICHARD WILDS. "Travel Diary." UHi.

Journal History of the Church of Jesus Christ of Latter-day Saints. A daily account of the activities of the church, incorporating transcripts of letters, journal excerpts, editorial notations, and other published and unpublished material. USIC.

KANE, THOMAS L. Papers. CSt.

KARTCHNER, WILLIAM DECATUR. "Expedition of the Emmett Company." UHi; UPB (MSS 904); USIC.

LAUB, GEORGE. "Diary." Three volumes. UHi (Man A 171); UPB; USIC.

LEAVITT, SARAH STURDEVANT. "Memoirs." CSmH.

LITTLE, FERAMORZ. "Letterbook, 1863–1877." In possession of Mrs. Juanita Brooks, St. George, Utah.

LONG, M. M., AND O. H. O'NEILL. "Journals of the Eastern and Central Divisions of the Fort Kearny, South Pass, and Honey Lake Wagon Road, June 4, 1857, to October 8, 1859." Records of the Secretary of the Interior, DNA.

LOVE, ANDREW. "Journal." UHi (Man A 506); UPB (MSS 474).

LYMAN, AMASA M. "Journal." USIC.

LYMAN, ELIZA MARIE PARTRIDGE [SMITH]. "Autobiography and Diary, 1820–1885." UHi; UPB; USIC.

MACE, WANDLE. "Journal." UHi; UPB; USIC.

MOORE, DAVID. "Salmon River Mission Journal." CU-B; UHi, USIC.

MORRIS, GEORGE. "Autobiography." UPB.

NEFF, JOHN. "Mill Account Book." UHi.

PECK, REED. "Mormons So Called" (Quincy, Adams County, Illinois, September 18, 1839). CSmH.

PETTEGREW, DAVID. "History and Journal." UHi (Man A 109-1); UPB (MSS 473); USIC.

PHELPS, JOHN WOLCOTT. "Diary." NN; UHi.

PITCHFORTH, SAMUEL. "Diary." UPB; USIC.

RIDD, JAY DONALD. "Almon Whiting Babbitt, Mormon Emissary." M.A. Thesis, University of Utah, 1953. UHi; UPB; UU.

ROCKWELL, ORRIN PORTER. Letter to Colonel Thomas Leiper Kane. November 20, 1858. CtY.

ROUNDY, ELIZABETH D. E., Letter to LDS Church Historian (undated). USIC.

SHURTLIFF, LUMAN ANDROS. "Biographical Sketch." UHi (Man A 557); UPB.

SMITH, ELIAS. "Journal, January 1, 1859–August 24, 1864." Published in part as "Elias Smith, Journal of a Pioneer Editor, March 6, 1859–September 23, 1863," edited by A. R. Mortensen, *Utah Historical Quarterly*, Vol. XXI (1953).

ALMON WHITING BABBITT
(Utah Historical Society)

SMOUT, EDWIN WARD. "Journal." CSmH; UPB.

SNOW, ELIZA R. "Diary." UPB; USlC.

STOUT, ALLEN JOSEPH. "Journal." UHi (Man A 428); UPB; USlC.

STOUT, HOSEA. "Journal." Eight volumes. UHi; USlC.

TAYLOR, JOHN. "Reminiscences." UHi; UPB.

VAN ALFEN, NICHOLAS. "Porter Rockwell and the Mormon Frontier."
M.S. Thesis, Brigham Young University, 1938. UHi; UPB.

VAN SICKLE, H. "Utah Desperadoes." CU-B.

WALKER, CHARLES L. "Journal." Twelve volumes. UHi; ULA; UPB.

YOUNG, BRIGHAM. "Manuscript History." USlC.

YOUNG, BRIGHAM. Excerpts from the "Manuscript History of Brigham
Young." Abstracted from records of the LDS Church for Hubert
Howe Bancroft. This collection contains three volumes catalogued as
"Early Records of Utah" [1847–1851]; "Incidents in Utah History"
[1852–1854]; and "Utah Historical Incidents" [1855–1867]. CU-B;
UHi; UPB.

BOOKS, PAMPHLETS, ARTICLES

ACHILLES [SAMUEL D. SIRRINE]. *The Destroying Angels of Mormondom;
or a Sketch of the Life of Orrin Porter Rockwell, the Late Danite
Chief* (San Francisco, 1878). CU-B

Ackley, Richard Thomas. "Across the Plains in 1858," edited by J. Cecil Alter, annotated by Dale L. Morgan, *Utah Historical Quarterly*, Vol. IX (July, October 1941).

Aitkin, W. *A Journey Up the Mississippi River, From Its Mouth to Nauvoo, the City of the Latter-day Saints* (Ashton-Under-Lynne, England [1845]).

An Appeal to the American People: Being An Account of the Persecutions of the Church of Latter Day Saints; and of the Barbarities Inflicted on Them by the Inhabitants of the State of Missouri (Cincinnati, 1840).

Austin, Emily M. *Mormonism; or, Life Among the Mormons* (Madison, Wisconsin, 1882).

Bancroft, Hubert Howe. *History of California* (San Francisco, 1886–1890), seven volumes.

———. *History of Utah, 1540–1887* (San Francisco, 1890).

Bandel, Eugene. *Frontier Life in the Army, 1854–1861*, translated by Olga Bandel and Richard Jente; edited by Ralph P. Bieber (Glendale, 1932).

Baskin, R. N. *Reminiscences of Early Utah* ([Salt Lake City,] 1914).

Beadle, J. H. *Life in Utah, or the Mysteries and Crimes of Mormonism* (Philadelphia, 1870).

———. *Polygamy, or the Mysteries and Crimes of Mormonism* (Philadelphia, 1883).

Bean, George W. *Autobiography*, compiled by Flora Diana Bean Horne (Salt Lake City, 1945).

Bennett, John C. *The Accoucheur's Vade Mecum* (Buffalo, 1837).

———. *The History of the Saints; or an Exposé of Joe Smith and Mormonism* (Boston, 1842).

———. *The Poultry Book. A Treatise on Breeding and General Management of Domestic Fowl; With Numerous Original Descriptions, and Portraits From Life* (Boston, 1854).

Bennett, William P. *The Sky-Sifter* ([Gold Hill, Nevada,] 1892).

Bennion, Glynn. "Suggestion and Quick Draw," *The Salt Lake Tribune*, February 24, 1924.

Bigler, Henry W. "Incidents (1857–1858)." A series of reminiscences published in the St. George *Union* from August 22 to December 12, 1896.

———. "Extracts from the Journal of Henry W. Bigler," *Utah Historical Quarterly*, Vol. V (1932).

Biographical History of Northeastern Ohio, Embracing the Counties of Ashtabula, Geauga and Lake (Chicago, 1893).

BLUTH, JOHN V. "The Salmon River Mission," *Improvement Era,* Vol. III, Nos. 11 and 12 (1900).

BOGGS, WILLIAM M. "Sketch of Lilburn W. Boggs," *Missouri Historical Review,* Vol. IV (January 1910).

BONNEY, EDWARD. *The Banditti of the Prairies; A Tale of the Mississippi Valley* (Chicago, 1850).

BOWLES, SAMUEL. *Across the Continent; A Summer's Journey to the Rocky Mountains, the Mormons, and the Pacific States, with Speaker Colfax* (Springfield, 1866).

———. *Our New West; Records of Travel Between the Mississippi River and Pacific Ocean* (Hartford, 1869).

BRITTON, ROLLIN J. "Early Days on Grand River and the Mormon War," *The Missouri Historical Review,* a series of six articles appearing from Vol. XIII, No. 2 (July 1919) through Vol. XIV, Nos. 3–4 (April–July 1920) inclusive.

BROOKS, JUANITA. *The Mountain Meadows Massacre* (Stanford, 1950, and Norman, Oklahoma, 1962).

BROWN, J. ROBERT. *Journal of a Trip Across the Plains of the U.S. From Missouri to California, in the Year 1856* (Columbus, Ohio, 1860).

BROWN, JAMES S. *California Gold, An Authentic History of the First Find* (Oakland, 1894).

———. *Life of a Pioneer, Being an Autobiography* (Salt Lake City, 1900).

BROWNE, ALBERT G. "The Utah Expedition," *The Atlantic Monthly, A Magazine of Literature, Art, Science, and Politics,* Vol. III (1859).

BURNETT, PETER H. *Recollections and Opinions of an Old Pioneer* (New York, 1880).

BURT, OLIVE W. *American Murder Ballads* (New York, 1958).

BURTON, RICHARD F. *The City of the Saints and Across the Rocky Mountains to California* (London, 1861).

CAIN, JOSEPH, AND ARIEH C. BROWER. *Mormon way-bill to the gold mines, from the Pacific Springs, by the northern & southern routes, viz. Fort Hall, Salt Lake. and Los Angelos, including Sublet's, Hudspeth's, and the various cut-offs; also — from Los Angelos to St. Francisco, by coast route, with the distances to the different rivers in California; — together with important information to emigrants* (G. S. L. City, Deseret, 1851).

CARVALHO, S. N. *Incidents of Travel and Adventure in the Far West; with Col. Frémont's Last Expedition* (New York, 1857).

CHAMBERLIN, RALPH V. *The University of Utah; A History of Its First Hundred Years, 1850–1950* (Salt Lake City, 1960).

CHANDLESS, WILLIAM. *A Visit to Salt Lake, Being a Journey Across the Plains and a Residence in the Mormon Settlements at Utah* (London, 1857).

CLAMPITT, JOHN W. *Echoes from the Rocky Mountains* (Chicago, 1890).

CLARK, JAMES R. "The Kingdom of God, The Council of Fifty and the State of Deseret," *Utah Historical Quarterly*, Vol. XXVI (April 1958).

CLARK, JOHN A. *Gleanings By The Way* (New York, 1842).

CLAYTON, WILLIAM. *The Latter-Day Saints' Emigrants' Guide, Being a Table of Distances Showing all the Springs, Creeks, Rivers, Hills, Mountains, Camping Places, and all other Notable Places, from Council Bluffs, to the Valley of the Great Salt Lake* (St. Louis, 1848).

———. *William Clayton's Journal, A Daily Record of the Journey of the Original Company of "Mormon" Pioneers from Nauvoo, Illinois, to the Valley of the Great Salt Lake* (Salt Lake City, 1921).

CLYMAN, JAMES. *James Clyman, American Frontiersman, 1792–1881*, edited by Charles L. Camp (San Francisco, 1928).

CODMAN, JOHN. *The Round Trip, By Way of Panama Through California, Oregon, Nevada, Utah, Idaho, and Colorado* (New York, 1879).

CODY, WILLIAM F. *The Life of Hon. William F. Cody, Known as Buffalo Bill, the Famous Hunter, Scout, and Guide. An Autobiography* (Hartford, 1879).

CORRILL, JOHN. *A Brief History of the Church of Christ of Latter Day Saints (Commonly Called Mormons); Including An Account Of Their Doctrine and Discipline; With the Reasons of the Author for Leaving the Church* (St. Louis, 1839).

COUTANT, C. G. *The History of Wyoming* (Laramie, 1899). Two volumes.

COWDERY, OLIVER. *Defence in a Rehearsal of My Grounds for Separating Myself from the Latter Day Saints* (Norton, Ohio, 1839).

CRADLEBAUGH, JOHN. *Utah and the Mormons; Speech of Hon. John Cradlebaugh, of Nevada, on the Admission of Utah as a State. Delivered in the House of Representatives, February 7, 1863.*

378

GENERAL PATRICK EDWARD CONNOR
(Utah Historical Society)

CRARY, C. G. *Pioneer and Personal Reminiscences* (Marshalltown, Iowa, 1893).

CROSBY, JESSE W. "The History and Journal of the Life and Travels of Jesse W. Crosby," *Annals of Wyoming*, Vol. XI (July 1939).

CUMMINGS, HORACE. "Conspiracy of Nauvoo," *The Contributor*, Vol. V (April 1884).

DANIELS, WILLIAM M. *A Correct Account of the Murder of Generals Joseph and Hyrum Smith, at Carthage, on the 27th Day of June, 1844* (Nauvoo, 1845).

DAVIS, W. J. *An Illustrated History of Sacramento County, California* (Chicago, 1890).

DEROPP, ROBERT S. *Drugs and the Mind* (New York, 1957).

DERUPERT, A. E. D. *Californians and Mormons* (New York, 1881).

DILKE, CHARLES W. *Greater Britain: A Record of Travel in English-Speaking Countries During 1866 and 1867* (London, 1868). Two volumes.

Doctrine and Covenants of the Church of the Latter Day Saints, Carefully Selected From the Revelations of God, and Compiled by Joseph Smith, Jr., Oliver Cowdery, Sidney Rigdon, Frederick G. Williams (Kirtland, Ohio, 1835).

DRUM, GEN. RICHARD C. "Reminiscences of the Indian Fight at Ash Hollow, 1855," *Nebraska State Historical Society Collections* Vol. XVI (1911).

DRURY, WELLS. *An Editor on the Comstock Lode* (Palo Alto, 1948).

DUNN, J. P., JR. *Massacres of the Mountains, A History of the Indian Wars of the Far West, 1815–1875* (New York, 1886).

EGAN, HOWARD. *Pioneering The West, 1846 to 1878. Major Howard Egan's Diary, also Thrilling Experiences of Pre-Frontier Life Among Indians; Their Traits, Civil and Savage, and Part of Autobiography, Inter-Related to His Father's, By Howard R. Egan.* Edited, Compiled, and Connected In Nearly Chronological Order By Wm. M. Egan (Richmond, Utah, 1917).

ELLSWORTH, S. GEORGE. *Dear Ellen. Two Mormon Women and Their Letters* (Salt Lake City, 1974).

ESSHOM, FRANK. *Pioneers and Prominent Men of Utah* (Salt Lake City, 1913).

FERRIS, BENJAMIN G. *Utah and the Mormons* (New York, 1854).

FERRIS, MRS. B. G. *The Mormons At Home; With Some Incidents of Travel From Missouri to California, 1852–53, In a Series of Letters* (New York, 1856).

FIELD, MATTHEW C. *Prairie and Mountain Sketches*, collected by Clyde and Mae Reed Porter, edited by Kate L. Gregg and John Francis McDermott (Norman, Oklahoma, 1957).

FLINT, THOMAS. "Diary of Dr. Thomas Flint," *Annual Publications of the Historical Society of Southern California*, Vol. XII (1923).

FORD, THOMAS. *History of Illinois* (Chicago, 1854).

GARDNER, HAMILTON. *History of Lehi* (Salt Lake City, 1913).

GIBBS, JOSIAH F. "Gunnison Massacre — 1853 — Millard County, Utah — Indian Mareer's Version of the Tragedy — 1894," *Utah Historical Quarterly*, Vol. I (July 1928).

GOLDER, FRANK ALFRED. *The March of the Mormon Battalion, from Council Bluffs to California, Taken From the Journal of Henry Standage* (New York, 1928).

GOTTFREDSON, PETER. *History of Indian Depredations in Utah* (Salt Lake City, 1919).

GOVE, JESSE A. *The Utah Expedition, 1857–1858; Letters of Capt. Jesse A. Gove, 10th Inf., U.S.A., of Concord, N.H., to Mrs. Gove, and special correspondence of the New York Herald*, edited by Otis G. Hammond (Concord, 1928).

LOT SMITH
(Utah Historical Society)

GREELEY, HORACE. *An Overland Journey from New York to San Francisco in the Summer of 1859* (New York, 1860).

GREEN, NELSON WINCH. *Fifteen Years Among the Mormons, Being the Narrative of Mrs. Mary Ettie V. Smith* (New York, 1860).

GREENE, JOHN P. *Facts Relative to the Expulsion of the Mormons From the State of Missouri, Under the "Exterminating Order"* (Cincinnati, 1839).

GREGG, THOMAS. *History of Hancock County, Illinois, Together With an Outline History of the State and a Digest of State Law* (Chicago, 1880).

———. *The Prophet of Palmyra* (New York, 1890).

GUNNISON, JOHN W. *The Mormons, or Latter-day Saints in the Valley of the Great Salt Lake* (Philadelphia, 1852).

HALL, WILLIAM. *The Abominations of Mormonism Exposed; Containing Many Facts and Doctrines Concerning That Singular People, During Seven Years' Membership With Them; From 1840 to 1847* (Cincinnati, 1852).

HAMILTON, HENRY S. *Reminiscences of a Veteran* (Concord, 1897).

HANKS, SIDNEY ALVARUS, AND EPHRAIM K. HANKS. *Scouting for the Mormons on the Great Frontier* (Salt Lake City, 1948).

HARDY, JOHN. *History of the Trials of Elder John Hardy, Before the Church of "Latter Day Saints" in Boston, For Slander, in Saying that G. J. Adams, S. Brannan and William Smith Were Licentious Characters* (Boston, 1844).

HARMON, APPLETON MILO. *Appleton Milo Harmon Goes West*, edited by Maybelle Harmon Anderson (Berkeley, 1946).

HARPENDING, ASBURY. *The Great Diamond Hoax and Other Stirring Incidents In The Life Of Asbury Harpending*, edited by James H. Wilkins (San Francisco, 1913).

HARRIS, SARAH HOLLISTER. *An Unwritten Chapter of Salt Lake 1851–1901* (New York, 1901). Privately printed.

HAY, JOHN. "The Mormon Prophet's Tragedy," *The Atlantic Monthly*, Vol. XXIV (December 1869).

HEITMAN, FRANCIS B. *Historical Register and Dictionary of the United States Army, From Its Organization, September 29, 1789, to March 2, 1903* (Washington, D.C., 1903). Two volumes.

HICKMAN, WILLIAM A. *Brigham's Destroying Angel, Being the Life, Confession, and Startling Disclosures of the Notorious Bill Hickman, the Danite Chief of Utah, edited by J. H. Beadle* (New York, 1872).

HICKMAN, W. Z. *History of Jackson County, Missouri* (Topeka, 1920).

Historical Encyclopedia of Illinois, edited by Newton Bateman, J. Seymour Currey, Paul Selby, and *History of Hancock County*, edited by Charles J. Scofield (Chicago, 1921). Three volumes.

History of Caldwell and Livingston Counties, Missouri (St. Louis, 1886).

History of Jackson County, Missouri (Kansas City, 1881).

"History of the Las Vegas Mission," *Nevada State Historical Society Papers*, Vol. V (1926).

History of Sacramento County, California (Oakland, 1880).

History of Santa Clara County, California (San Francisco, 1881).

History of Santa Clara County, California (Los Angeles, 1922).

HOLLISTER, O. J. *Life of Schuyler Colfax* (New York, 1886).

HOWE, EBER D. *Mormonism Unvailed* (Painesville, Ohio, 1834).

HUNT, JAMES R. *Mormonism; Embracing the Origin, Rise and Progress of the Sect, With an Examination of the Book of Mormon; also, Their Troubles In Missouri, and Final Expulsion From the State* (St. Louis, 1844).

HUNTINGTON, O. B. "A Trip to Carson Valley," *Eventful Narratives* (Salt Lake City, 1887).

HYDE, JOHN, JR. *Mormonism: Its Leaders and Designs* (New York, 1857).

382

WILLIAM A. HICKMAN
(Utah Historical Society)

HYDE, ORSON. *Speech of Elder Orson Hyde, Delivered Before the High Priests' Quorum, in Nauvoo, April 27, 1845, Upon the Course and Conduct of Mr. Sidney Rigdon, and Upon the Merits of His Claims to the Presidency of the Church of Jesus Christ of Latter-day Saints* (Liverpool and New York, 1845).

Investigation Into the Murder of Dr. J. K. Robinson, Who Was Assassinated On the Night of October 22d, 1866, near the corner of East Temple and 3d South or Emigration Streets, had before Jeter Clinton, Coroner for the County of Great Salt Lake, Chief Justice Titus, and Judge McCurdy, commencing Tuesday, October 23d, at 11 o'clock, A.M. [Salt Lake City, 1866].

JACKSON, JOSEPH H. *A Narrative of the Adventures and Experience of Joseph H. Jackson; Disclosing the Depths of Mormon Villainy Practiced in Nauvoo* (Warsaw, Illinois, 1844).

JACKSON, W. TURRENTINE. *Wagon Roads West, A Study of Federal Road Surveys and Construction in the Trans-Mississippi West, 1846–1869* (Berkeley, 1952).

JAQUES, JOHN. "Some Reminiscences." A series of letters to the *Salt Lake Herald* from December 1 to December 29, 1878.

JARMAN, WILLIAM. *U.S.A. Uncle Sam's Abscess, or Hell Upon Earth For U.S. Uncle Sam* (Exeter, England, 1884).

JENSON, ANDREW. *Church Encyclopaedia*, Book I, edited by Andrew Jenson, containing Volumes V, VI, VII, and VIII of *The Historical Record*, a monthly periodical (Salt Lake City, 1889).

————. *Church Chronology; A Record of Important Events Pertaining to the History of the Church of Jesus Christ of Latter-day Saints*, compiled by Andrew Jenson (Salt Lake City, 1914).

————. *Latter-Day Saint Biographical Encyclopedia* (Salt Lake City, 1901–1936). Four volumes.

JOHNSTON, WILLIAM PRESTON. *The Life of Gen. Albert Sidney Johnston* (New York, 1878).

JONES, DANIEL W. *Forty Years Among the Indians, A True Yet Thrilling Narrative of the Author's Experiences Among the Natives* (Salt Lake City, 1890).

Journal of Discourses, by Brigham Young, President of the Church of Jesus Christ of Latter-day Saints, His Two Counselors, the Twelve Apostles, and Others (Liverpool, 1854–1886). Twenty-six volumes.

KELLY, CHARLES. "Holy Murder," the biography of Orrin Porter Rockwell. Unpublished galley proofs of the original book as written by Charles Kelly. (In the collection of Alfred L. Bush, Princeton, N. J.) Kelly pulled this single set of proofs in his Western Printing Co. plant in Salt Lake City about 1931. Shortly afterward, Hoffman Birney arrived in Utah to complete research for his *Zealots of Zion* (Philadelphia, 1931), and persuaded him to allow a revision of Kelly's work using these proofs. When a publisher for the resulting biography — which appeared under their joint authorship in 1934 (see below) and which bears little resemblance to the book Kelly contemplated — was found, the type of the original text was melted, leaving this set of proofs as the only copy of the book ever printed. The title suggested by Birney was "The Sword of the Prophet," but Kelly preferred "Holy Murder."

KELLY, CHARLES, AND HOFFMAN BIRNEY. *Holy Murder, the Story of Porter Rockwell* (New York, 1934).

KNIGHT, NEWEL. "Journal," *Scraps of Biography* (Salt Lake City, 1883).

KORNS, J. RODERICK. "West From Fort Bridger. The Pioneering of the Immigrant Trails Across Utah 1846–1850," *Utah Historical Quarterly*, Vol. XIX (1951).

Latter-day Saints Millennial Star (Liverpool, 1840, *et seq.*)

LEARY, A. J. *The Crimes of the Latter Day Saints in Utah; By a Mormon of 1831* (San Francisco, 1884).

LEE, JOHN D. *Mormonism Unveiled; Including the Remarkable Life and Confessions of the Late Mormon Bishop John D. Lee* (St. Louis, 1877).

———. *Journals of John D. Lee, 1846–47 and 1859*, edited by Charles Kelly (Salt Lake City, 1938).

———. *A Mormon Chronicle: The Diaries of John D. Lee, 1848–1876*, edited and annotated by Robert Glass Cleland and Juanita Brooks (San Marino, California, 1955). Two volumes.

Lee, Trial! (The). *An Exposé of the Mountain Meadows Massacre, Being a Condensed Report of the Prisoner's Statement, Testimony of Witnesses, Charge of the Judge, Arguments of Counsel, and Opinions of the Press Upon the Trial.* By the *Salt Lake Daily Tribune* Reporter (Salt Lake City, 1875).

LETTS, JOHN M. *California Illustrated: Including a Description of the Panama and Nicaragua Routes. By a Returned Californian* (New York, 1852).

LINGENFELTER, RICHARD E. *1858–1958 The Newspapers of Nevada. A History and Bibliography*, with an introduction by David F. Myrick (San Francisco, 1964).

LINN, WILLIAM ALEXANDER. *The Story of the Mormons* (New York, 1902).

LITTLE, JAMES A. *Jacob Hamblin, A Narrative of His Personal Experience, As A Frontiersman, Missionary to the Indians and Explorer* (Salt Lake City, 1881).

LITTLE, JAMES A. "Biography of Lorenzo Dow Young," *Utah Historical Quarterly*, Vol. XIV (1946).

LUDLOW, FITZ HUGH. "Among the Mormons," *The Atlantic Monthly*, Vol. XIII (April 1864).

———. *The Heart of the Continent; A Record of Travel Across the Plains and in Oregon, With an Examination of the Mormon Principle* (New York, 1870).

MAJORS, ALEXANDER. *Seventy Years on the Frontier, Being Memoirs of of Lifetime on the Border* (Chicago, 1893).

MAJORS, JOHN. *Common Sense; or Thoughts of a Plain Man, in Regard to Several Things of Importance* (n.p., 1878).

MARCY, RANDOLPH B. *Thirty Years of Army Life on the Border* (New York, 1866).

MARSDEN, WILLIAM. "Journal and Diary of William Marsden," *Daughters of Utah Pioneers, Lesson for January, 1951.* Separately printed in *Heart Throbs of the West* (Salt Lake City, 1951), Vol. XII.

MARSHALL, WALTER GORE. *Through America* (London, 1882).

McCLURE, A. K. *Three Thousand Miles Through the Rocky Mountains* (Philadelphia, 1869).

McLAWS, MONTE B. "The Attempted Assassination of Missouri's Ex-Governor, Lilburn W. Boggs," *Missouri Historical Review*, Vol. LX (October 1965).

METCALF, ANTHONY. *Ten Years Before the Mast. Shipwrecks and Adventures at Sea! Religious Customs of India and Burman's Empire. How I Became a Mormon and Why I Became an Infidel* [Malad City, Idaho, 1888].

MILLER, GEORGE. Letters to the *Northern Islander*, Beaver Island, Wisconsin. Published August 9, 1855, to October 18, 1855. Printed separately by H. W. Mills in "De Tal Palo Tal Astilla," *Annual Publications of the Historical Society of Southern California* (1917).

MORGAN, DALE L. "The State of Deseret," *Utah Historical Quarterly*, Vol. VIII (April, July, October 1940).

————. *The Humboldt: Highroad of the West* (New York, 1943).

————. *The Great Salt Lake* (Indianapolis, 1947).

————. "A Bibliography of the Church of Jesus Christ of Latter Day Saints [Strangite]," *The Western Humanities Review*, Vol. V (Winter 1950–51).

————. "Miles Goodyear and the Founding of Ogden," *Utah Historical Quarterly*, Vol. XXI (July, October 1953).

————. "The Reminiscences of James Holt; A Narrative of the Emmett Company," edited by Dale L. Morgan, *Utah Historical Quarterly*, Vol. XXIII (1955).

————. *Overland in 1846, Diaries and Letters of the California–Oregon Trail*, edited by Dale L. Morgan (Georgetown, California, 1963). Two volumes.

NELSON, JOHN YOUNG. *Fifty Years on the Trail, the Adventures of John Young Nelson*, as described to Harrington O'Reilly (London, 1889).

NEWTON, JOSEPH H., WILLIAM RICHARDS, AND WILLIAM STANLEY. *An Appeal to the Latter-day Saints* (Philadelphia, 1863).

NOALL, CLAIRE. "Mormon Midwives," *Utah Historical Quarterly*, Vol. X (1942).

OAKS, DALLIN H., AND MARVIN S. HILL. *Carthage Conspiracy; The Trial of the Accused Assassins of Joseph Smith* (Urbana, Illinois; Chicago, London, 1975).

OLNEY, OLIVER H. *The Absurdities of Mormonism Portrayed, a Brief Sketch* (Hancock County, Illinois, March 3, 1843).

ORTON, RICHARD M. *Records of California Men in the War of the Rebellion, 1861 to 1867* (Sacramento, 1890).

PALMER, LYMAN L. *History of Napa and Lake Counties, California* (San Francisco, 1881).

Pearl of Great Price, Being a Choice Selection From the Revelations, Translations, and Narrations of Joseph Smith (Liverpool, 1851).

PRATT, LOUISA BARNES. "The Journal of Louisa Barnes Pratt," *Heart Throbs of the West* (Salt Lake City, 1947), Vol. VIII.

PRATT, ORSON. "Extracts from Orson Pratt's Private Journal," *Millennial Star* (Liverpool, 1849–1850), Vols. XI, XII passim.

PRATT, PARLEY PARKER. *Autobiography*, edited by Parley P. Pratt (New York, 1874).

————. "A Mormon Mission to California in 1851, From the Diary of Parley Parker Pratt," edited by Reva Holdaway Stanley, *California Historical Quarterly*, Vol. XIV (June 1935).

Proceedings of a Convention, Held at Carthage, in Hancock County, Ill., on Tuesday and Wednesday, October 1st and 2nd, 1845 (Quincy, 1845).

REID, J. M. *Sketches and Anecdotes of the Old Settlers and New Comers, The Mormon Bandits and Danite Band* (Keokuk, 1876).

REINHART, HERMAN FRANCIS. *The Golden Frontier, the Recollections of Herman Francis Reinhart, 1851–1869*, edited by Doyce B. Nunis, Jr. (Austin, 1962).

REMY, JULES. *A Journey to Great-Salt-Lake City* (London, 1861). Two volumes.

RICHARDS, ROBERT. *The California Crusoe; or, The Lost Treasure Found* (London, 1854).

RICHARDSON, ALBERT D. *Beyond the Mississippi* (Hartford, 1867).

ROBERTS, B. H. *The Missouri Persecutions* (Salt Lake City, 1900).

————. *The Rise and Fall of Nauvoo* (Salt Lake City, 1900).

————. *Comprehensive History of the Church of Jesus Christ of Latter-day Saints* (Salt Lake City, 1930). Six volumes.

————. *History of the Church of Jesus Christ of Latter-day Saints. Period II. Apostolic Interregnum. From the Manuscript History of Brigham Young and Other Original Documents.* Introduction and notes by B. H. Roberts (Salt Lake City, 1932). A one-volume addition to the six-volume *History of the Church, Period I*, by Joseph Smith, this is considered to be Vol. VII of the entire work.

RHODEHAMEL, JOSEPHINE DEWITT, AND RAYMUND FRANCIS WOOD. *Ina Coolbrith, Librarian and Laureate of California* (Provo, 1973).

ROBIE, WENDALL. "Murderer's Bar and Gold Rush on the Middlefork," *The Pony Express*, Vol. XXV (July 1958).

ROBINSON, EBENEZER. "Items of Personal History of the Editor," *The Return* (Davis City, Iowa, 1889–1890).

ROGERS, FRED. *Soldiers of the Overland, Being Some Account of the Services of General Patrick Edward Connor & His Volunteers in the Old West* (San Francisco, 1938).

SCOTT, CHARLES A. "Diary of the Utah Expedition, 1857–1861," edited by Robert E. Stowers and John M. Ellis, *Utah Historical Quarterly*, Vol. XXVII (1960).

SHARP, JAMES. "The Old Man's Story," *Improvement Era*, Vol. XLVI (1943).

———. "Singing Wires," *Improvement Era*, Vol. XLVII (1944).

SHERMAN, GENERAL WILLIAM T. *Memoirs* (New York, 1875). Two volumes.

SHOOK, CHARLES A. *The True Origin of Mormon Polygamy* (Cincinnati, 1914).

SIOLI, PAOLA. *Historical Souvenir of El Dorado County, California* (Oakland, 1883).

SLATER, NELSON. *Fruits of Mormonism* (Coloma, California, 1851).

SMITH, CLARK. *Mystery and Crime in the Land of the Ute; An Exposé of Mormonism* (Cornelius, Oregon, 1878).

SMITH, JOSEPH, JR. *History of the Church of Jesus Christ of Latter-day Saints. Period I. History of Joseph Smith, the Prophet, by Himself.* Introduction and notes by B. H. Roberts (Salt Lake City, 1902–1912). Six volumes.

SMITH, JOSEPH, III. *Joseph Smith III and the Restoration*, edited by Mary Audentia Smith Anderson, and condensed by Bertha Audentia Anderson Holmes (Independence, 1952).

SMITH, LUCY MACK. *Biographical Sketches of Joseph Smith the Prophet, and His Progenitors for many Generations* (Liverpool, 1853).

SMITH, PAGE, AND CHARLES DANIEL. *The Chicken Book* (Boston, Toronto, 1975).

SMITH, PAULINE UDALL. *Captain Jefferson Hunt of the Mormon Battalion* (Salt Lake City, 1958).

SORENSEN, CAROLE GATES. *Henry Gates Family of Upper Canada, 1791–1981, With Genealogies of Allied Families* (n.p. 1981).

SOUTHERN, WILLIAM, JR. "Lilburn W. Boggs," *Messages and Proclamations of the Governors of the State of Missouri*, compiled and edited by Buel Leopard and Floyd C. Shoemaker. Vol. I (Columbia, 1922).

Orrin Porter Rockwell
Circa 1878
(Utah Historical Society)

Stenhouse, T. B. H. *The Rocky Mountain Saints: A Full and Complete History of the Mormons, From the First Vision of Joseph Smith to the Last Courtship of Brigham Young* (New York, 1873).

Stout, Hosea. *On the Mormon Frontier: The Diary of Hosea Stout, 1844–1861,* edited by Juanita Brooks (Salt Lake City, 1965). Two volumes.

Swartzell, William. *Mormonism Exposed, Being a Journal of a Residence in Missouri From the 28th of May to the 20th of August, 1838* (Pekin, Ohio, 1840).

Switzler, William F. *Illustrated History of Missouri From 1541 to 1877* (St. Louis, 1879).

Tanner, Joseph M. *John Riggs Murdock, A Biographical Sketch* (Salt Lake City, 1909).

Taylor, Lillie Jane Orr. *Life History of Thomas Orr Jr., Pioneer Stories of California and Utah* ([Placerville], 1930).

Thompson, Thomas H., and Albert A. West. *History of Nevada with Illustrations and Biographical Sketches of Its Prominent Men and Pioneers* (Oakland, California, 1881).

Tittsworth, W. G. *Outskirt Episodes* (Des Moines, 1927).

Toponce, Alexander. *Reminiscences of Alexander Toponce, Pioneer, 1839–1923* (Salt Lake City, 1923).

TOWNSEND, GEORGE ALFRED. *The Mormon Trials at Salt Lake City* (New York, 1871). A series of letters to the *Cincinnati Commercial*, from October 20 to 27, 1871.

TRACY, ALBERT. "Journal of Captain Albert Tracy," edited by J. Cecil Alter and Robert J. Dwyer, *Utah Historical Quarterly*, Vol. XIII (1945).

Transactions of the Kansas State Historical Society, Embracing the Fifth and Sixth Biennial Reports, 1886–1888 (Topeka, 1890), Vol. IV.

TUCKER, POMEROY. *Origin, Rise and Progress of Mormonism* (New York, 1867).

TULLIDGE, EDWARD W. *Life of Brigham Young* (New York, 1876).

————. *History of Salt Lake City* (Salt Lake City, 1886).

————. *Tullidge's Histories. Vol. II. Containing the History of all the Northern, Eastern and Western Counties of Utah; Also the Counties of Southern Idaho* (Salt Lake City, 1889).

TULLIDGE, EDWARD W., ED. *Tullidge's Quarterly Magazine* (Salt Lake City, 1880–1885), three volumes.

TUTTLE, NEWTON. "A Territorial Militiaman in the Utah War; Journal of Newton Tuttle," edited by Hamilton Gardner, *Utah Historical Quarterly*, Vol. XXII (October 1954).

TYLER, DANIEL. *A Concise History of the Mormon Battalion in the Mexican War, 1846–1847* (Salt Lake City, 1881).

Utah, A Guide to the State, compiled by workers of the Writers' Program of the Work Projects Administration for Utah (New York, 1941).

Utah Genealogical and Historical Magazine, Vol. XXVI (1935).

VAUX [JUNIUS F. WELLS]. "The Echo Canyon War," *The Contributor*, Vols. III, IV (1882–1883).

VERITE. A series of three letters by this otherwise unidentified correspondent for the San Francisco *Daily Alta California*, dated February 7 and 9, 1863, detailing the battle at Bear River. Reprinted in *Tullidge's Quarterly Magazine*, Vol. I (January 1881).

WAITE, MRS. C. V. *The Mormon Prophet and His Harem* (Chicago, 1867).

[WATERS, WILLIAM E.]. *Life Among the Mormons, and A March to Zion* (New York, 1868).

WERNER, M. R. *Brigham Young* (New York, 1925).

WHITMER, DAVID. *An Address to All Believers in Christ* (Richmond, Missouri, 1887).

WHITMER, JOHN. "History of the Church of the Latter Day Saints From 1831 to 1846," including the suppressed chapters xx, xxi and xxii, and the unpublished portion of Chapter xix. The Reorganized Church of Jesus Christ of Latter Day Saints published all but these entries in its *Journal of History*, Vol. I (1908). The suppressed material was published in 1964 in Salt Lake City by Modern Microfilm Co.

WHITNEY, ORSON F. *History of Utah* (Salt Lake City, 1892–1904). Four volumes.

WILLIS, WILLIAM L. *History of Sacramento County, California* (Los Angeles, 1913).

WOODRUFF, WILFORD. "Autobiography," *Tullidge's Quarterly Magazine* (Salt Lake City, 1885), Vol. III.

————. *History of His Life and Labors as Recorded in His Daily Journals*, edited by Matthias F. Cowley (Salt Lake City, 1909).

WOOLLEY, CATHARINE E. MEHRING. "Diary," as excerpted by J. Cecil Alter in his series, "In the Beginning," the *Salt Lake Tribune*, September 6, 1934, to March 30, 1935.

WYL [WYMETAL], WILHELM W. *Mormon Portraits, Joseph Smith, the Prophet, His Family and His Friends* (Salt Lake City, 1886).

YOUNG, ANN ELIZA. *Wife No. 19, or the Story of a Life in Bondage, Being a Complete Exposé of Mormonism, and Revealing the Sorrows, Sacrifices and Sufferings of Women in Polygamy* (Hartford, 1876).

ZUFELT, HARMON. "The Battle of Bear River," *The Utah Monthly Magazine*, Vol. IX (December 1892).

NEWSPAPERS

Burlington Hawkeye, Burlington, Iowa.

Daily Alta California, San Francisco, California.

Daily Missouri Republican, St. Louis, Missouri.

Deseret News, Salt Lake City, Utah.

Elders' Journal of the Church of Latter Day Saints, Kirtland, Ohio, and Far West, Missouri.

Ensign, The, Buffalo, Scott County, Iowa T.

Evening and Morning Star, Independence, Missouri, and Kirtland, Ohio.

Frontier Guardian, Kanesville, Iowa.

Jeffersonian Republican, Jefferson City, Missouri.

Latter Day Saints' Messenger and Advocate, Kirtland, Ohio.

Missouri Whig, Palmyra, Missouri.

Mormon, The, New York, New York.

Mountaineer, The, Salt Lake City, Utah.

Naked Truths About Mormonism, Oakland, California.
Nauvoo Expositor, Nauvoo, Illinois.
Nauvoo Neighbor, Nauvoo, Illinois.
New York Daily Herald, New York, New York.
New York Times, The, New York, New York.
New York Weekly Tribune, New York, New York.
People's Daily Organ, The, St. Louis, Missouri.
Quincy Whig, Quincy, Illinois.
St. Louis American, St. Louis, Missouri.
St. Louis Daily New Era, St. Louis, Missouri.
Salt Lake Herald, Salt Lake City, Utah.
Salt Lake Tribune, Salt Lake City, Utah.
Seer, The, Washington, D.C., and Liverpool.
Times and Seasons, Commerce and Nauvoo, Illinois.
Union Vedette, Camp Douglas, Utah.
Valley Tan, Salt Lake City, Utah.
Wasp, The, Nauvoo, Illinois.
Western Monitor, Fayette, Missouri.

INDEX

Achilles, identified, xvi; on Orrin Porter
Rockwell, 222–23; on death of Almon W.
Babbitt, 236n41; on John Tobin, 289; on
slaying of Henry Jones and mother,
290n15; on death of John Gheen, 301; on
death of [   ] Davidson, 304n20; on
shooting of McRae brothers, 313; on
murder of Thomas Colbourn, 345–46

Adam-ondi-Ahman, "stake of Zion," 41n45

Aiken, John, California gambler, 268;
wounded, 275; killed, 278; indictment in
death of, 364

Aiken Party, 268–69; *Placerville Index* on,
269n5; gambling paraphernalia of, 270;
arrested, 270–71; freed, 273; attacked,
276; property of, 278; mentioned, 357

Aiken, Thomas, California gambler, 268;
money belt of, 271, 271n18, 274; disappearance of, 274; alleged death of, 276

Aldrich, Mark, Hancock County militia
officer, accused of Joseph and Hyrum
Smith murders, 136n13

Alexander, Colonel Edmund B., and Utah
Expedition, 254; and Pacific Springs raid,
255–57

Alexander, Horace, scout, 175–76

Allen, Charles, tarred and feathered, 13

Allen, John, anti-Mormon, 136n13

Allred's Settlement (Spring City), 211

Alton Telegraph, mentioned, 134

"Amicus Curiae," pseudonym, 242n57.
See also W. W. Drummond

Andrus, Milo, Mormon guerila, 261, 262

Angell, Truman O., journey east of, 226n5

anti-Mormons, organize in Illinois, 117–18;
demand Mormon expulsion, 131; meeting
of, attacked, 137–38

Appleby, W. I., journey east of, 226n5; on
W. W. Drummond, 243n59

Archambault, Auguste, and Almon W.
Babbitt death, 235n35

Archer, John, Illinois militiaman, 146

Armstrong, S., mentioned, 80

Army of Israel, 46n55

Arnold, Orson P., wounded, 262n29

Ashmore, [   ], California outlaw, 302n16.
See also Joachim Johnston

Austin, Emily M., on suffering Mormons,
22n2; account of drowning incident, 24n3

Avard, Sampson, forms secret society, 30;
as Danite officer, 30–31; accuses Joseph
Smith, Jr., 32; excommunication of,
32n19; addresses Danite captains, 36–37;
on consecration of property, 40; threatens
Adam Black, 42; proposes wholesale poisoning, 44; as Danite surgeon, 47; testifies in court, 54

"Avenging Angels." *See* Danites

Averett, Elijah, on OPR, 360–61; at Pipe
Springs, 361

Babbitt, Almon W., in Nauvoo, 141; defends
OPR, 148–49; and legal fee, 151; drunk
in court, 214n60; advocates express company, 225; in Washington, D.C., 230;
quarrels with Brigham Young, 230; disfellowshiped, 230n14; description of,
231; funds carried by, 231n7; hires OPR,
232; last letter of, 234n32; killed by Indians, 233–35; Achilles on death of,
236n41; W. W. Drummond on, 241

Babbitt, Julia Ann (Mrs. Almon W.), and
husband's death, 235n35; absolves Mormons, 244

Backenstos, [   ], marries niece of Joseph
Smith, Jr., 130n3

Backenstos, Jacob B., Mormon sympathizer,
130; Hancock County sheriff, 138; attempt on life of, 138–39; and death of
Frank Worrell, 139–40; arrest, trial, acquittal of, in shooting, 142; protects
Chauncey L. Higbee, 146–47; subsequent
adventures of, 150n4

Baldwin, Caleb, jailed, 55–56; flees to Illinois, 57

Ball, Mrs. William, sounds Indian alarm, 336

Ballard, Henry, Mormon guerila, 261

Banks, John, death of, 364

Bannock Indians, in peace talks, 335

Baptiste, John, grave robber, and Moroni
Clawson, 318n64

Bardsley, Mrs. Alice, flees Utah, 192n28

Baskin, R. N., federal prosecutor, 359

Bateman, Sam, and pistol accident, 262n29;
as posse member, 316

Battiese, Ute sub-chief, 209

Battle Creek, Indian fight at, 330n23

Baum, Jacob, and shooting of Frank Worrell,
140

Baxter, John, acquitted of robbery-murder, 134n8

Beadle, John Hanson, writer, and William A. Hickman, 33n22; and Danites, 33n22; on Aiken Party, 276n30

Bean, Elizabeth (Mrs. George Washington), braids OPR's hair, 181; and Grass Valley mission, 361

Bean, George Washington, on shooting of Frank Worrell, 140n22; as Indian interpreter, 181; and OPR, 181–82; and Walkara, 202–7; loses arm in cannon accident, 204, 210n47; and Gunnison massacre, 213; explores new route, 217–18; herds sheep, 354; as bodyguard, 358; on Chief Justice James B. McKean, 358; to Grass Valley mission, 361

Bean, Henry, killed by Indians, 325

Bear Hunter, Shoshone chief, 326; killed in Bear River battle, 330

Bear River battle, 326–331; and white renegades, 328n18; casualties of, 330–31; spoils of, sold at public auction, 331n25

Bear River ferry crossing, 324

Bear-Scratch, Ute sub-chief, 209

Beaverads, Ute sub-chief, slashed with knife, 204–5

Beaver Creek, mentioned, 173

Beck, David J. C., sued by John Gheen, 299

Beckwith, Lieutenant E. G., mentioned, 218

Beebe, George, beaten by mob, 15; home of, destroyed, 15n41

Beebe, Isaac, settles in Independence, Mo., 8

Beebe, Luana. See Luana Hart Beebe Rockwell

Beebe, Olive, in Independence, Mo., 8

Bell, William, merchant, interview with in New York Herald, 241–42; as postmaster, 272n20

Benedict, Dr. J. M., court testimony of, 278n37

Bennett, David, shot by mob, 16

Bennett, Dr. John Cook, joins Mormons, 62; as brigadier general of Invincible Dragoons of Illinois, 62; and Nauvoo City Charter, 62; named mayor of Nauvoo, 63; resigns, 70; letters of, to Sangamo Journal, 70; threats upon, 70n12; confrontation of, with OPR, 71–72; and plural marriage, 71n13; mentioned, 76; and Joseph O. Boggs, 77; as poultry farmer and expert, 78, 78n37; and Sidney Rigdon, 97

Bennett, Wallace F., Utah senator, mentioned, 11

Bennett, William P., on OPR, 192n28

Bennion, John, seeks grazing privileges, 220; reports horse theft, 316

Bennion, Sam, organizes posse, 316; scouts Skull Valley, 337

Benson, Ezra T., sent to meet migration, 167; mentioned, 168; sawmill of, 193; and Lorenzo D. Custer, 193; in wagon train, 226; arms of, 227n8

Bentz, Lewis, arrest warrant for, 295–96

Bernhisel, Dr. John M., territorial delegate to Congress, 230; announces mail contract, 238n47

Bevins, William, miner, affidavit of, 326n13

Big Blue District, Jackson County, Mo., described, 7; mob violence erupts in, 14; Mormons expelled from, 19

Big Fan. See Danites

Bigler, Henry W., and letter on Aiken Party, 270n11

Birch, Robert H., account of Davenport murder, 134n8

Black, Adam, justice of the peace, and the Mormons, 41–42

"Blackfoot Mission," as observation corps, 251

"Blackhawk, Captain." See Jonathan Dunham

Black's Fork, Utah Expedition winter camp near, 283–84

Blennarhasset, R. S., Missouri lawyer, mentioned, 86, 86n3

Blood Atonement, mentioned, 299, 299n5

Bloody Chief, leader of White Knife Snakes, 215n64; and secret handshake, 215–16

Bogart, Samuel, Methodist minister, as leader of militia at Crooked River, 45–47

Boggs, Dr. Joseph O., brother of L. W. Boggs, 69; on L. W. Boggs, 70n11; and John C. Bennett, 77–78; on OPR, 78n36

Boggs, Lilburn W., lieutenant governor of Missouri, warns Mormons, 13; urges militia call, 19; cursed by Joseph Smith, Jr., 21; as governor of Missouri, 42; issues "Exterminating Order," 48–49; political background of, 50n63; mentioned, 61; death of, prophesied, 64; attempted assassination of, 67–68; as state senator, 69n11; death of, 70n11; journey west of, 75n27, 158; as alcalde of Sonoma, 188; men-

Coleman, Thomas. *See* Thomas Colbourn

Colesville Branch, Jackson County, Mo., 7; Missourians attack, 15

Colfax, Schuyler, Utah visit of, 342; and OPR, 343n31

Collett, Sylvanus, trial of, 268n1; escorts Aiken Party, 274; charged with murder, 275; court testimony of, 276n31; indictment of, in John Aiken death, 364

Colorado Stables, mentioned, 306, 362, 365

Commerce, Ill. *See* Nauvoo

Comstock, Captain Nehemiah, attacks Haun's Mill, 50

Conditt, Lilace W., killed in Iowa, 299, 299n7

Connor, Colonel Patrick Edward, and shooting of L. W. Boggs, 73, 332; ordered to protect mail routes, 322–26; founds Camp Douglas, 323; and Bear River battle, 326–31; as "Father of Utah Mining," 332n1; promoted to brigadier general, 334; at Pleasant Grove, 335; and William A. Hickman, 357; offers to post Brigham Young's bail, 359n14

Conover, A. H., on Indian attacks, 325

Conover, Peter Wilson, on death of Frank Worrell, 139n21; explores new route, 218

Cooke, Colonel Philip St. George, Dragoon officer, escorts governor, 253

Coolbrith, Ina, mentioned, 220n78

Cooly, G. W., and Rockwell Mining Company, 356n4

Cooper, Colonel S., U.S. adjutant general, 214

Cornogg, William B., and southern route expedition, 170–72

Corrill, John, colonizes Jackson County, 8; arrested, 16; jailed, 18–19; on dissenters, 26; warns John Whitmer, 27; and the Danites, 33n23; on Sampson Avard, 38; mentioned, 39n38; testifies in court, 54

Council Bluffs, Iowa, Mormon camp at, 150n3; and malarial fever, 152

Council Bluffs Bugle, and Joseph Ellis Johnson, 234n32

Council House, Brigham Young, Governor Cumming, and OPR in, 291

Council of Fifty, legislature of the Kingdom of God, founding of, in secrecy, 136; conceives western expedition, 137; names OPR messenger, 146; mentioned, 150, 152, 169; at prayer, 158; members among pioneers, 158n22; in daily session, 177–80;

sanctity of proceedings, 179; proceedings described, 180n40; John D. Lee code for, 180n40; and Ira E. West, 180n40

Council Point, Iowa, Mormon camp at, 150n3

Cowdery, Oliver, and Joseph Smith, Jr., 4; and organization of church, 5; colonizes Jackson County, 8; leaves for Ohio, 13; excommunication of, 25; mentioned, 32n19

Cradlebaugh, Judge John, judicial crusade of, 288n13; letter from Peter K. Dotson to, 295–96; mentioned, 306

crime, in Great Salt Lake City, 297ff

Crooked River, Mo., battle at, 45–47

Crosby, Caroline, in California, 189

Crosby, Jesse W., on burning Fort Supply, 260

Crosby, Jonathan, in California, 189

Crossly, James, and Rockwell Mining Company, 356n4

Cullom Bill, and suppression of polygamy, 356

Cumming, Alfred, governor of Utah, 253; and Thomas L. Kane, 286–87; and OPR, 287–88; at Cache Cave, 287; and Echo Canyon, 287; end of term as governor, 315

Cummings, James W., Nauvoo Legion officer, 251

Cunningham, Andrew, and "Blackfoot Mission," 251

Cunningham, J. A., posts OPR's bail, 364

Custer, Lorenzo D., killed by Indians, 193–95

Cutler, Alpheus, president of High Council, marries Luana Beebe Rockwell, 145; Rockwell children sealed to, 145; organizes new church, 145n40

Cutler, Orson, posse member, 316

Cutler's Park, Neb., handcart companies rendezvous at, 231–32

Dalton, Simon, indicted for murder, 280n42

Daniels, William M., and death of Joseph Smith, Jr., 126n43

Danites, secret society, charter members of, 28n12; "Daughter of Zion," 30–31, 36, 74n25; "Brother of Gideon," 30; "Sons of Dan," 32, 35; inner workings of, 33–34; covenant of, 35–36; attack of, on Gallatin, Millport, Grindstone Fork, 43; Destruction Company, exposed, 54; mentioned,

399

Gravelly Ford, emigrants killed at, 323

Great Salt Lake, and Jim Bridger, 160

Great Salt Lake City, named 168; ordered put to torch, 284; abandonment of, 290–91; crime in, 297ff

Great Salt Lake Valley, described by Moses (Black) Harris, 160; arrival of first Mormons in, 164–65; described, 166

Greeley, Horace, on Mormons, 298

Green, Evan M., sells land to OPR, 294

Green River, Mormon encampment at, 161

Greene, John P., at Crooked River battle, 46–47; as Nauvoo city marshal, 112; and Augustine Spencer arrest, 112; destroys *Nauvoo Expositor* press, 116; charged with riot, 117; warns Governor Ford, 124

Greene, John Y., and southern route expedition, 170–72

Greenwood Valley, Calif., mentioned, 184n1

Gregg, Thomas, on the Danites, 134n7

Greys, Carthage, Illinois militia company, 121; to guard Mormon leaders, 124–25; Mormons obtain roster of, 130; flee volunteer army, 133

Grindstone Fork, Daviess County, Mo., raided, 43

Grosepene, Ute Indian, contracts venereal disease, 211

Grover, William N., anti-Mormon lawyer, accused of murders of Joseph and Hyrum Smith, 136n13

Gunnison, Lieutenant John W., on L. W. Boggs, 65n17; slain by Indians, 202; W. W. Drummond on, 241; mentioned, 289

Gunnison massacre, circumstances of, 201–2; Mormons blamed, 241

Haden, Joel H., letter of Daniel Dunklin to, 14n37

Hagen, A., lawyer, 365

Haight, Isaac, emigrant company captain, 176

Half-Way House, Mormon, in goldfields, 186, 189–90

Hall, J., on Joseph Smith, Jr., and OPR, 93n13

Hall, William, on shooting of Lilburn W. Boggs, 73; on shooting of Frank Worrell, 140n22

Hamilton's Hotel, Carthage, Ill., 115

Hamilton, William R., member of Carthage Greys, 126n42

Hanks, Ebenezer, authorized to trade with Indians, 169

Hanks, Ephraim, mentioned by Richard F. Burton, 308; as stage station operator, 315

Hardin, Brigadier General J. J., commands volunteer army, 133; on governor's Nauvoo committee, 141; orders arrest of Jacob Backenstos, 142

Harding, Stephen S., governor of Utah, ouster of, sought, 333

Harker, Job, scouts Skull Valley, 337

Harker, Joseph, court testimony of, 276; journal of, 276n32

Harmon, Appleton Milo, pioneer company captain, 152; constructs odometer, 156n18

Harney, Brigadier General William S., and Ash Hollow fight, 226n7; as "Squaw-killer," 226n7; and Utah Expedition, 252

Harper, John, and Frank Worrell, 138n18; court testimony of, 139n21

Harris, Broughton D., Secretary of Utah Territory, quarrels with Brigham Young, 230

Harris, Martin, baptized, 6

Harris, Moses (Black), mountaineer, scout, trapper, and the Mormons, 160

Harris, Sarah Hollister (Mrs. Broughton D.), on Almon W. Babbitt, 230n15

Hastings Cutoff, mentioned, 161; pioneers use, 163

Haun, Jacob, disregards counsel, 50. *See also* Haun's Mill

Haun's Mill, massacre at, 50–51; mentioned, 100

Hawley, W. J., emigrant train captain, on Almon W. Babbitt, 235n34

Haws, Albert H., Nevada outlaw, killed by posse, 355n2

Haws, Alpheus, on Humboldt River, 216n66

Haws, Peter, counterfeiter, 216n66

Heath, Henry, deputy sheriff, captures Chauncey W. Millard, 352

Hempstead, Captain Charles H., on Bear River battle, 326–31

Hereford, Robert, mountaineer, and Hot Springs Brewery Hotel, 294n29; in barroom argument, 303–4

Heywood, Joseph L., on OPR, 219; in wagon train, 226; arms of, 227n8

Hickman, William A. (Bill), and the Danites, 33n22; hunts Jim Bridger, 200; description of, 200n18; and mountaineer difficulties, 201; mentioned, 220; carries mail, 238; describes mail trip, 239n51; on W. W. Drummond, 243; as Mormon guerilla leader, 251; burns Utah Expedition supply train, 259; and cattle raid, 262–63; brothers of, captured, 262n33; admits slaying Richard Yates, 279n39; tells of killing "Buck," 279–81; indicted for murder, 280n42; indicted for treason, 284; heads gang, 302; wounded in gunfight, 302–3; mentioned by Richard F. Burton, 308; buys military stores, 311; on Utah Expedition, 312; on death of fugitives, 318; and General Patrick Edward Connor, 323n9; and Carissa Gulch gold, 348; disfellowshiped, 354; writes confession, 357; arrested on murder charges, 357; George Alfred Townsend on, 358; criminal charges against dropped, 360; John Codman on, 360n15; death of, 360n15

Hickok, James B., with Utah Expedition, 258n19

Higbee, Chauncey L., and Nauvoo conspiracy, 110; harassment of, 111; arrested, 112; struck by OPR, 115; mentioned, 117; seen in Carthage mob, 130; threatened by OPR, 146–47

Higbee, Elias, and Missouri affidavits, petitions, 11n32; appointed Danite captain general, 31n17, 38n35; journey of, to Washington, D.C., 59; and pressing of Mormon claims, 60n6

Higbee, Francis, and Nauvoo conspiracy, 110; harassment of, 111; attacked by OPR, 122–23; seen in Carthage mob, 130

Higbee, Isaac, arms of, 227n8

Higbee, John, arrest warrant for, 295–96

Higgins, Alfred, outlaw, 309n37

High Council of Church of Jesus Christ of Latter-day Saints, 169n5; organized, 170n7; approves southern route expedition, 170; sends epistle to California Mormons, 170–71; and OPR, 175

Hill Cumorah, golden plates in, 4

Hinkle, George M., and the Danites, 31n17; as "The Thunderbolt," 44n54; accusation of, as traitor, and rebuttal of, 52, 52n66

Hirons, James, and southern route expedition, 170–72

Hoffman, Captain William, Fort Laramie commanding officer, 236n39

Hogan, Goudy E., goldseeker, 191

Holcombe, Major Reburn S., Haun's Mill historian, 51n64; as "Burr Joyce," 51n64

Hollingshead, Joseph, and Indians, 305–6

Honeyman, Lieutenant Francis, and Indian skirmish, 334

Host of Israel, 46n55

Hot Springs Brewery Hotel, and OPR, 294; and Charles Mogo, 294n29; and David H. Burr, 294n29; fight at, 303–4; closing of, 346

Hubbel, Harry, at Carissa Gulch, 348

Humboldt River, Indian troubles at, 215–16, 216n66

Hunt, Gilbert, and southern route expedition, 170–72

Hunt, Jefferson, and the Danites, 31n17; and Mormon Battalion, 169; and southern route expedition, 169–72; dispute with OPR; as messenger to Brigham Young, 174–75; at Mormon Tavern, 188

Hunt, Joe, on Aiken Party, 271–72

Hunt, John, and southern route expedition, 170–72; describes adventure, 171–72

Huntington, Clark Allen, Indian interpreter, 214; and White Knife Snakes, 215–16

Huntington, Dimick B., on the Danites, 31n17; as Indian interpreter, 206

Huntington, Lot, arrested, 302; wounded in gunfight, 302–3; charged with assaulting governor, 316; wanted for burglary, horse theft, 316–17; killed, 317–18

Huntington, Oliver Boardman, and the Danites, 35; describes Far West surrender, 54n68; charts western route, 213–17; and Alpheus Haws, 216n66; incurs Army disfavor, 217

Hyde, John, on the Danites in Utah, 225n3

Hyde, Orson, apostatizes, 44–45; and Mormon western migration, 137n16

Independence, Mo., mob violence at, 13n34

Independence Rock, Mormon pioneers at, 160; mentioned, 168

Indians, negotiation with, 152; Timpanogos Utes, 180–82, 193; Little Chief, 181n42; Sowiette, 182; Walkara, 182; whites killed by, 191, 323, 336–37; attack Fort Utah,

Johnston, 285; description of, 285–86; meets Alfred Cumming, 286; escorted by OPR, 287; letter from OPR to, 295

Kanosh, Pahvant Indian chief, 213; and Gunnison massacre, 202n26, 213–14

Karrick, Frank, livestock stolen from, 314–15

Kartchner, William Decatur, and Mormon western migration, 137n17

Kay, John, prominent Mormon, 344n33

Kearny, Colonel Stephen W., Army of the West commander, and Mormon Battalion, 150

Kelly, Joseph, Springville citizen, 199

Kennedy, Charles, messenger, 151

Kimball, Ellen Sanders (Mrs. Heber C.), on Great Salt Lake Valley, 166

Kimball, Heber C., signs Far West covenant, 56; mentioned, 151; and Council of Fifty, 158n22, 179; leads emigrant company, 174; named to First Presidency, 175; as judge, 184; and endowment ceremonies, 197n11; denouncement of, by W. W. Drummond, 241; on approaching Army, 248–49; indicted for treason, 284; disfellowships Israel Evans, 311; and Danites in Utah, 354n1

Kimball, Hiram, wins mail contract, 238; thrashed by OPR, 238n48; mail contract of, cancelled, 246–47, 247n65

Kimball, William H., mentioned, 151; as captain of Nauvoo Legion Life Guards, 193n1; asked by OPR to trail Indians, 196; as Nauvoo Legion officer, 251; indicted for murder, 280n42; named in murder indictment, 357; charges against, dismissed. 359–60

King, Austin A., judge, presides at trial, 54; and OPR, 99; brother-in-law of Hugh Brazeale, 89n23

King, John, mentioned, 78n36

Kinkead, John Henry, merchant, character of, 272n20

Kinney, Chief Justice J. F., journey of, east, 226n5; Brigham Young appears before, 333

Kirkham, George, witnesses Indian attack, 337

Kirtland, Ohio, branch of Mormon church, emigrates to Missouri, 22

Knight, Newel, mentioned, 22n2

Lamb, Alice, court testimony of, 277

Lamoreaux, Andrew L., mentioned, 59n4

Lander, Frederick W., engineer, and Pacific Wagon Road Company, 265n38

Laney, Isaac, wounded at Haun's Mill, 51

Lanford, Hank, "disembowelled" by OPR, 351n52

LaRamie, Jacques, 158n24

Larson, Thurston, and southern route expedition, 170–72

Las Vegas, mentioned, 173

Lathrop, Asahel A., and southern route expedition, 170–72

Laub, George, and Seventies trial, 311

Law, Jane (Mrs. William), excommunicated, 111

Law, William, member of the First Presidency, on L. W. Boggs shooting, 73; and "drowned woman" story, 105n4; breach of, with Joseph Smith, Jr., 108; and Nauvoo conspiracy, 110; excommunicated, 111; as "prophet," 113; seen in Carthage mob, 130

Law, Wilson, Nauvoo Legion officer, and secret guns, 76; breach of, with Joseph Smith, Jr., 108; and Nauvoo conspiracy, 110; excommunicated, 111; seen in Carthage mob, 130

Lawrence, J. W., at Carissa Gulch, 348

Leach, Dr. W. H., court testimony of, 278n37

Lee, John D., mentioned, 39, 52, 342; in election-day fracas, 40–41; and Crooked River battle, 46–48; defends Far West, 50; signs Far West covenant, 56; on Nauvoo home, 144–45; crosses plains, 175–76; wife of, dies, 176; on cattle and horse committee, 178; as co-captain of predator hunt, 179; arrest warrant for, 295–96; and Mountain Meadows massacre, 305; as Yauguts, 305n24; excommunication mentioned, 354; convicted in Mountain Meadows massacre, 363; executed, 363n6

Lehi, Shoshone sub-chief, killed in Bear River battle, 330

Liberty Jail, Clay County, Mo., 55–56, 95–96

Life Guards, in Nauvoo, Ill., 101, 106; in Utah, 193n1

Lima, Ill., Mormon settlement at, destroyed, 138

Lincoln, Abraham, relationship of, to OPR, 3; authorizes Mormon cavalry, 322

McConnell, M., and Rockwell Mining Company, 356n4

McConnell, W., and Rockwell Mining Company, 356n4

McCullough, Major Ben, peace commissioner to Utah, 291

McDougal, T. A., Illinois attorney general, on governor's Nauvoo committee, 141

McGarry, Major Edward, executes Indians, 324–25; and Bear River battle, 328–31

McIntyre, Sam, posts OPR's bail, 364

McKean, James B., chief justice, arraigns William A. Hickman, 357

McKean, Theodore, posts bail for Brigham Young, 333

McKenzie, David, engraver, 306; and counterfeiting scheme, 306–7

McNeill, Frank, and John Gheen, 300

McQuary, Fountain, and Frank Worrell, 138n18

McRae, Alexander, Sr., and the Danites, 31n17; jailed, 55–56; flees to Illinois, 57; sons of, sought by law, 312–13; sons of, killed, 313

McRae, Alexander, Jr., wanted for robbery, 312–13, killed by posse, 313, 313n50

McRae, Kenneth, wanted for robbery, 312–13; killed by posse, 313, 313n50

Meacham, Morris, indicted for murder, 280n42

Metcalf, Anthony, on Aiken Party, 269n5

meteor shower, description of, 21; taken for godly sign, 22

Miles, Calvin, on death of Frank Worrell, 139n21

Miles, Josiah, on death of Frank Worrell, 139n21

Millard, Chauncey W., teamster, commits murder, 351–52; captured, 352; executed, 353; sells body for candy, 353

Miller, George, and Nauvoo conspiracy, 110n13

Miller, John, murder of, 153n12

Miller, William, and "Bogus Brigham" incident, 144n36; journey of, east, 226n5

Millport, Daviess County, Mo., raided, 43

Mills, George, and mock trial, 157

Mississippi Saints, mentioned, 167

mock trials, 157

Mogo, Charles, buys property from OPR,

177n28; and Hot Springs Brewery Hotel, 294n29

Mojave Desert, mentioned, 173

Monroe, Marcellus, and Mormon scouts, 251

Morgan, Dale L., western historian, and Missouri affidavits and petitions, 11n32; copies Peck manuscript, 26n7

Morgan, William, Missouri sheriff, 56; attacked by citizens, 57n73

Morley, Ill., Mormon settlement, destroyed, 138

Morley, Isaac, colonizes Jackson County, jailed by mob, 18–19

Mormon, The, newspaper, refutes W. W. Drummond charges, 243n59, 244

Mormon Battalion, call for, 150; sick detachment of, 167; mentioned, 168; members counseled not to re-enlist, 170–71; and Daniel Davis, 173; and Boyd Stewart, 190

Mormon camps, in Iowa, 150n3

Mormon Grove, mentioned, 229

Mormon Island, William Tecumseh Sherman at, 185n2; and "half-way" house, 186

Mormon Tavern, in goldfields, 188

Mormons, seek godly sign, 21; expelled from Missouri, 51–54; appeal to Congress, 60; and Grattan massacre, 226n7; amnesty granted to, 288; abandon Great Salt Lake City, 290–91; express system of, 254n9, 292; return to Great Salt Lake City, 293; petition Abraham Lincoln, 333

Morrell, H. F., and sale of Fort Bridger, 260n25

Morris, Captain [R. M.], mentioned, 214, 289; route named for, 218n75

Morrisites, mentioned, 364

Mottin, Giles, reports burglary, 316

mountain fever, strikes pioneers, 161; description of, 161n32; and Brigham Young, 164

Mountain Meadows massacre, mentioned, 288n13, 296

Mt. Pisgah, Iowa, Mormon camp at, 150n3

"Move South," Mormon exodus, 290–91; mentioned, 290n16; ends, 293

Murderer's Bar, in goldfields, 186; and Round Tent Saloon, 187

Murdock, George, recognizes Aiken Party property, 278

Murdock, John Riggs, called for Indian duty, 207–8; reputation of, as wagonmaster, 207n39; carries mail, 240; brings word of Utah Expedition, 246; and Israel Evans, 311

Naile, J. C., mentioned, 295, 312, 352; bids on government surplus, 311
Natsab, Ute Indian, guide, 214
Nauvoo, Ill., founded by Joseph Smith, Jr., 58; city charter granted, 62–63; as haven for freebooters, coiners, 106; as a "lawless city," 134; city charter of, revoked, 135
Nauvoo Expositor, newspaper, prospectus of, 113; suppression of, 115–17
Nauvoo House, mentioned, 130, 135
Nauvoo Legion, authorized, 62; hunts emigrant thieves, 193n1; officers of, 251; at Fort Bridger and Cache Cave, 254; casualties of, 258n20; warned of Aiken Party, 270
Nauvoo Neighbor, newspaper, on OPR, 103; as *The Wasp*, 103n1; mentioned, 134
Nauvoo Temple, construction of, 133; "sealings" in, 145
Navajoes, in Grass Valley, 361n22
Nease, Peter, on southern route expedition, 170–72
Nebeker, John, in exploring party, 218
Neff, Amos, and Walkara, 202–5
Neff, Franklin, and canyon tollgate, 203n27
Neff, John, buys canyon property, 197; mill of, 214
Neff, Mary Ann. *See* Mary Ann Neff Rockwell
Neff's Canyon, 197n10
Neibaur, [Isaac], arrested, 302; charged with assault on governor, 316
Nelson, [ ], Nevada rancher, horses stolen from, 353
Nephi (Salt Creek), wall constructed around, 208
New Harmony, and Southern Indian Mission, 203
New Jerusalem, site of, 7
Nielsen, Frederic, shoots friend, 258n20
Nigger Tom. *See* Thomas Colbourn
Niobrara River, Mormon camp at, 152
North Platte, Mormon ferry on the, 160
Norton, Eli, and Nauvoo police, 108
Norton, John, called Danite leader, 200n18

Norton, Wiley, called Danite leader, 200n18
Nowland, Smallwood, anti-Mormon, 90

Oats, Martin, teamster, killing of, 303–4
O'Banion, Patterson, killed in Crooked River battle, 45–46
odometer, pioneers' use of, 156n18
Olney, Oliver H., on L. W. Boggs shooting, 69
Olsen, Christine. *See* Christine Olsen Rockwell
Omaha Indians, chief council of, called, 152
OP, cattle brand, 341–42, 362n2
Ophir Mining District, 356
Oregon, as possible Zion, 141; and Jacob Backenstos, 150n4
Orr, Thomas J., Jr., and OPR's assumed identity, 189
Osborne, Dr. *See* Thomas L. Kane
O'Shonnison, Thomas, killed by Indians, 336–37
Ousley, Mrs. S. M. *See* Electa Rockwell

Pace, William B., Nauvoo Legion officer, 251
Pacific Springs, pioneers at, 160; raid at, 255–57; mentioned, 262
Pacific Wagon Road Survey, 239; mentioned, 265
Pack, John, among first in Great Salt Lake Valley, 165; co-captain of predator hunt, 179; angers Council of Fifty, 179–80; angers Brigham Young, 180
Page, Hiram, beaten by mob, 15; home of, destroyed, 15n41
Pahvant Indians, massacre Gunnison party, 202
Paiute Indians, and OPR, 305
Parashont, Indian sub-chief, 213
Parker, Elias, arrests OPR, 83; mentioned, 85
Parks, Brigadier General [ ], Missouri militia, 49
Parrish, Orrin, teamster, survives Indian attack, 232; and Potter-Parrish murders, 232n20
Partridge, Edward, bishop, 7; colonizes Jackson County, 8; tarred and feathered, 12; signs petition to governor, 14
passports, Brigham Young issues, 272–73

Patrick, M. T., U.S. marshal, arrests Daniel H. Wells, 357

Patten, David W., leads Danite raid, 43; as "Captain Fearnaught," 44n54; and Crooked River battle, 45–46; killed, 47

Pawpaw Grove, Ill., Joseph Smith, Jr., preaches at, 92–93

peace commission, in Ill., 141; in Utah, 288

Peacock, William, and southern route expedition, 170–72

Pearson, Elias F., and southern route expedition, 170–72

Peck, Reed, on dissenters, 26; manuscript of, 26n7; on the Danites, 30, 33n23; as Danite adjutant, 31; negotiates Far West surrender, 51–52; testifies in court, 54

peepstone, and Joseph Smith, Jr., 5n10

Peltro, Colonel [   ], government surveyor, attacked, 289

penitentiary, site selected for, 203

Perry, Box Elder County, Utah, 220n80

Peters, Lyman, court testimony of, 268n1, 270n6

Pettegrew, David, on Jackson County troubles, 14n39; mentioned, 17

Phelps, Captain John W., Army officer, on Thomas L. Kane, 285–86

Phelps, Morris, testifies in court, 54–55

Phelps, William Wines, editor of *Evening and Morning Star*, 8; colonizes Jackson County, 8; on Negroes, 10; mobbed, 12; founder of Far West, Mo., 22; excommunicated, 25; calms Nauvoo Mormons, 131; and endowment ceremonies, 197n11

Pierce, Eli Harvey, and southern route expedition, 170–72

Pierce, Franklin, U.S. President, 212

Pike, Dr. Walter R., court testimony of, 278n37

pistols, and speculators, 107; smuggled into Carthage Jail, 123; pepperbox, 124; of OPR, described, 315n52

Pitcher, Colonel Thomas, disarms Mormons, 19

Pizarro, a play, in Nauvoo, 113; OPR as player in, 113; staged in Social Hall, 197–98

Platte River ferry, mentioned, 184n1

plural marriage, doctrine of, 110

Pocatello, Shoshone chief, 326

polygamy, public abhorrence of, 243n61;

investigation of, 288n13; and Richard F. Burton, 308; legislation against, 356

Pony Express, mentioned, 308; brings news of Fort Sumter, 311; Elias Smith on, 311n43

Poorets. *See* George W. Bean

Pope, Nathaniel, judge, 81

Porter, Irene, grandmother of OPR, 3

Porter, John, ancestor of OPR, 3

Porter's Spring, Weber County, Utah, 220n80

Potter-Parrish murders, mentioned, 232n20, 288n13

Powell, Senator Lazarus E., peace commissioner to Utah, 291

Prairie Settlement, Mo., Mormons expelled from, 19

Pratt, Louisa Barnes, and OPR, 188n16

Pratt, Orson, mentioned, 151; designs odometer, 156n18; and Council of Fifty, 158n22; leads advance party, 164–65; first in Great Salt Lake Valley, 164–65; advocates express company, 225; journeys east, 226; suffers snowblindness, 228

Pratt, Parley P., meets OPR's mother, 3n5; captures spies, 15; describes meteor shower, 21–22; at Crooked River battle, 46–47; surrenders at Far West, 53

Pratt, Sarah M., and John C. Bennett, 74n25; on revival of Daniteism, 354n1

predator hunt, captains of, named, 179; birds and animals destroyed, 179

Price, Captain George F., and Bear River battle, 328–31; and Indian skirmish, 334

priesthood, Aaronic, OPR ordained to, 31; Melchizedek, OPR holds, 151n42, 197

prophecies, of Joseph Smith, Jr., on L. W. Boggs and Thomas Carlin, 64–65; on OPR, 102

Quincy Whig, mentioned, 134; on arrest of OPR, 146; on Mormon Battalion, 150n4

Ramus, Ill., bandit gangs in, 106n5

Rancho Santa Ana del Chino, and southern route expedition, 171–73

Ray, John, named in robbery, 134n8

Ray, John A., journey east of, 226n5

Redden, Return Jackson, named in robbery, 134n8; accused of killing "Arvine Hodges," 134n8; and death of Frank Worrell, 138–40; joins pioneers, 153; discovers cave, 164; fears assassination, 179; on Humboldt River, 216n66

Redden's Cave. *See* Cache Cave

Reedall, H. S., at Carissa Gulch, 348

Rees, Amos, mentioned, 49

Reese, Enoch, advocates express company, 225; posts bail for Brigham Young, 333

Reese, Colonel John, and exploring party, 215

Reformation, Mormons, and Jedediah M. Grant, 298–99

Reinhart, Herman Francis, on OPR, 348–49

Remy, Jules, French scientist, wounded by Indians, 220–21; on Brigham Young, 221; on OPR, 221–22; on W. W. Drummond, 243n61

revelations, of Joseph Smith, Jr., on western Missouri, 6; on Zion's Camp, 24; on consecration of property, 40; on Far West Temple site, 65

Reynolds, J. H., Missouri sheriff, at shooting of L. W. Boggs, 67–68; mentioned, 85; foils escape, 89–90; writes to Joseph Smith, Jr., 91; arrests Joseph Smith, Jr., 92–93; and Sidney Rigdon, 97

Reynolds, Major John L., Army officer, 213

Reynolds, Wood, charged with assault on governor, 316; killed by Indians, 336–37

Rich, Charles Coulson, at Crooked River battle, 47n58; at Far West, 52; letter for, 167; mentioned, 168; with Amasa Lyman, 187–91

Richards, Franklin D., at Fort Kearny, 232; on hostile Indians, 233n28; at Fort Laramie, 236; on Almon W. Babbitt, 236n41

Richards, Silas, and W. W. Drummond, 243n59

Richards, Willard, mentioned, 110n13, 119, 151, 153, 154; in Carthage Jail, 123–25; names attackers, 130; and Council of Fifty, 158n22; leads emigrant company, 174; named to First Presidency, 175; as Secretary of Utah Territory *pro tem*, 230

Richardson, Albert D., *New York Tribune* correspondent, visits Utah Territory, 342; and OPR, 343

Richardson's Point, Iowa, Mormon camp at, 150n3

Ricks, Thomas, wounded by Indians, 176

Rigdon, Sidney, mentioned, 6n18; describes Big Blue district, 7; in Far West, 25; "Salt Sermon" of, 27; ultimatum of, to

dissenters, 28; and Danites, 29–30; acknowledges Danites, 33n23; and Danite covenant, 35–36; Fourth of July oration of, 38–39; on consecration of property, 40; vows death to apostates, 45; surrenders at Far West, 53; jailed, 55; flees to Illinois, 56; journeys to Washington, D.C., 59; named Nauvoo city councilman, 63; denounced by Joseph Smith, Jr., 97–98; as Nauvoo postmaster, 97; and Nauvoo conspiracy, 110n13; returns from Pittsburgh, 131; seeks to succeed Joseph Smith, Jr., 132; excommunicated, 133

Riverbed, Utah, stagecoach robbery at, 349–51, 350n51

Roberts, Dr. [   ], Provo surgeon, and execution of Chauncey W. Millard, 353

Roberts, Homer, at Carissa Gulch, 348

Roberts, Wilson, on Jackson County, Mo., citizens' committee, 78n36

Robie, Wendell, mentioned, 186n7

Robinson, Ebenezer, and dissenters, 28n12

Robinson, George W., forms secret society, 30; as Danite officer, 31, 32; surrender of, at Far West, 53

Robinson, Dr. John King, property dispute with Brigham Young of, and murder of, 344; and OPR, 344; marriage of, to a Mormon, 344n33

Robison, Lewis, scout, 175–76; burns Fort Bridger, 260; and purchase of Fort Bridger, 260n25

Rockwell, Alvira, sister of OPR, 3n2

Rockwell, Caroline (Mrs. M. C. R. Smith), sister of OPR, 3n2; mentioned, 3n4, 16n46, 60; on Book of Mormon, 4n9; baptism of, 6

Rockwell, Caroline Stewart, daughter of OPR, 24, 24n5

Rockwell, Christine Olsen, wife of OPR, receives patriarchal blessing, 105n4; bears children, 360; mentioned, 362

Rockwell, David Porter, son of OPR, 304

Rockwell, Electa (Mrs. S. M. Ousley), sister of OPR, 3n2; baptism of, 6; terrorized by mob, 16–17; marries, 24n4

Rockwell, Elizabeth Christine, daughter of OPR, 360

Rockwell, Emily (Mrs. Christopher Stafford), sister of OPR, 3n2; mentioned, 16n46

Rockwell, Emily Amanda (Mrs. Emily Amanda Gates Brizzee Tyrrell), daughter

of OPR, 24; named in indenture, 24n5;
kidnapped, 184; and Hiram Gates and
Levi Fifield, 184; elopement and later life
of, 184n1

Rockwell, Horace, brother of OPR, 3n2

Rockwell Ferry, on Big Blue River, 9; commandeered by mob, 17

Rockwell, Ida May, daughter of OPR, 360

Rockwell, Irene, infant daughter of OPR,
dies at birth, 360

Rockwell, John Orrin, son of OPR, 294

Rockwell, Joseph Neff, infant son of OPR,
dies, 344

Rockwell, Letitia, daughter of OPR, 335

Rockwell, Luana Hart Beebe, wife of OPR,
8; terrorized by mob, 17; leaves OPR, 79;
endowments, remarriage, and sealing of,
145; later life of, in Utah, 145n40

Rockwell, Mary, sister of OPR, 3n2

Rockwell, Mary Amanda, daughter of OPR,
217, 336, 365

Rockwell, Mary Ann Neff, wife of OPR,
197; gives birth, 217, 238, 304, 335, 344;
mentioned, 293; death of, 344

Rockwell, Merritt, brother of OPR, 3n2

Rockwell Mining Company, organized, 356

Rockwell, Orin, father of OPR, 3; mentioned, 6; receives patriarchal blessing,
6n16; operates ferry, 9; home of, destroyed, 16–17; death of, 58n1; claims of,
60

Rockwell, Orrin DeWitt, son of OPR, 60;
changes name, 60n7; and mining claim,
356n4

Rockwell, Orrin Porter, en route to Kirtland, Ohio, 2; birthplace and genealogy
of, 3, 3n3; and golden plates, 4; and Book
of Mormon, 4; descriptions of, 5, 61,
88n10, 90, 146–47, 181, 221–22, 309,
335, 338–39; leg injury of, 5; baptized, 6;
marries, 8, 205, 360; operates ferry, 9;
and grand jury presentment, 9n28; affidavits of, 11n32, 60n6; signs petition to
governor, 14; home of, destroyed, 17;
ferry of, commandeered, 17; driven from
Jackson County, 22; in Far West, 23;
signs ultimatum to dissenters, 28; joins
Danites, 36; ordained a deacon, 39; at Far
West surrender, 52; signs Far West covenant, 55–56; aids in jailbreak, 56; journey
of, to Washington, D.C., to seek indem-
nity, 59–60; and Cyrus Ward, 65; uses
alias, 66, 188, 188n16, 190; called "The

Destroying Angel," 71, 74n25, 190,
200n18, 236; confronts John C. Bennett,
71–72; and John Stephenson slaying,
71n15; arrested in shooting of L. W.
Boggs, 74; reward offered for, 77; named
in Book of the Law of the Lord, 79; Philadelphia letter of, 80; arrested, 82–83; and
Joseph H. Jackson, 87–88; attempts jail
escape, 89–90, 98–99; and dove incident,
94; attempt on life of, 95–96; mother
visits, 96; freed from jail, 99; prophecy
concerning, 102; as bartender, 103; and
"drowned woman" story, 105n4; as
Joseph Smith, Jr.'s, bodyguard, 105n4;
and Augustine Spencer, 111; subdues
Charles Foster, 112; acts in *Pizarro*, 113;
strikes Chauncey L. Higbee, 115; charged
with riot, 117; attacks Francis Higbee,
122–23; interrupts Governor Thomas
Ford, 127–28; brings news of martyrdom,
128; named in robbery, 134n8; sought on
counterfeiting charges, 136; as member of
Council of Fifty, 136n16; shoots Frank
Worrell, 138–41; meets Joseph Smith III,
149; as Camp of Israel messenger, 150;
as bodyguard to Brigham Young, 151; as
pioneer scout and hunter, 152; mail- and
freight-carrying ventures of, 153, 225, 232,
236, 295, 320, 360; and Indians, 153,
168–69, 182–83, 191, 195–96, 208–10;
on buffalo-hunting, 155; and Brigham
Young's spyglass, 156; and mock trials,
157; and Council of Fifty, 158, 158n22,
179–80; and James Bordeaux, 159; scouts
Miles Goodyear route, 164; among first
Mormons in Great Salt Lake Valley, 165;
as escort for Ezra T. Benson, 167–68; as
escort for Brigham Young, 168; and
southern route expedition, 170–72; dispute of, with Jefferson Hunt, 172; aids
emigrant companies, 175–76; property of,
177, 177n27, 177n28, 197, 294, 294n27,
294n29, 320, 332n1, 337n21, 346, 356n4;
on cattle and horse committee, 178; and
predator hunt, 179; and Platte River
ferry, 179; named deputy sheriff, 179n37;
as escort for Amasa Lyman, 180; daughter
of, abducted, 184; at gold diggings, 186;
in rifle matches, 186n8, 190; confronts
Sam Brannan, 187; trained dog of, 188,
188n18; and death of James M. Flake,
188n15; accused of murder, 192; in endowment ceremonies, 197; called Danite
leader, 200n18, 342; selects site for penitentiary, 203; and Walkara, 202–7; visits
southern settlements, 205–7; "wheat" as
catchword, 206n34, 309, 342–43, 347,

365; and Gunnison massacre investigation, 213; advertisement for stolen mare of, 214; as Army guide and explorer, 217–19; cuts hair for wig, 219–20; visit of, with French scientists, 221; Achilles on, 222–23; guides wagon train, 226–30; weapons of, 227n8, 315n52; suffers snow-blindness, 228; and Hill Cumorah treasures, 228n11; thrashes Hiram Kimball, 238n48; brings word of Utah Expedition, 246–48; as guerilla leader, 251; as escort for Capt. Van Vliet, 253; leads Pacific Springs raid, 255–57; and cattle raid, 262–64; and John I. Ginn, 265–67; and Aiken Party, 273–80, 288; delivers captured livestock, 267; indicted for murder, 280n42; watches troops, 282; takes pulpit, 283n1; indicted for treason, 284; escorts official party, 287–88; and John Tobin, 288, 289; and death of Henry Jones and mother, 288–90, 290n15; guards new governor, 291; brings word of Army move, 291; and family, 293; receives whisky license, 294n28, 310; arrest warrant for, 295; and John Gheen death, 298–301; arrests rustlers, 302; and killing of Martin Oats, 303–4; and death of Joachim Johnston and Myron Brewer, 308; and Richard F. Burton, 308–10; threatened by Alfred Higgins, 309n37; rumored dead, 310; ordains members of Seventies, 310n41; and Seventies' trial of Israel Evans, 310–11; and shooting of McRae brothers, 313; tracks horsethieves, 313–16; kills Lot Huntington, 317–18; hosts Brigham Young, 320–21; as guide for Army, 326–27; in Bear River battle, 327–31; and shooting of L. W. Boggs, 332–33; gold mine of, 332n1; posts bail for Brigham Young, 333; with troops at Pleasant Grove, 335; scouts Skull Valley, 337; and Fitz Hugh Ludlow, 338–39, 341; orders special buggy, 340n26; livestock brands and awards of, 341–42, 353, 353n61, 362n2; wife of, dies, 344; and murder of Thomas Colbourn, 345–46; and Alexander Toponce, 346; drinking habits of, 346n44; and Carissa Gulch gold, 348; and Herman Francis Reinhart, 348–49; and Riverbed stage robbery, 349–51; legends about, 350n51, 351n52; captures Chauncey W. Millard, 352; recovers stolen horses, 353; leads posse after Albert H. Haws, 355; jailed after brawl, 355; files silver claim, 356n4; and George A. Townsend, 358; searches for Brigham Young, 359; at Pipe Springs, 361; colo-

nizes Grass Valley, 361; ballads about, 363; indicted for murder, 364; death of, 365–66; obituary of, 367–68; funeral of, 368; epitaph of, 368

Rockwell, Orrin Porter, Jr. *See* Orrin DeWitt Rockwell

Rockwell, Peter, brother of OPR, 3n2; baptized, 6

Rockwell, Sarah, daughter of OPR, 66, 238

Rockwell, Sarah Witt, mother of OPR, 3; and buried treasure, 5n10; receives patriarchal blessing, 6n14; sets baptismal record, 6n17; terrorized by mob, 16; jail visit of, 96; mentioned, 100

Rockwell, deacon William, ancestor of OPR, 3

Rockwood, Albert P., mentioned, 153; as Nauvoo Legion officer, 251

Rollings, James, sells canyon property, 197

Rollins, Joseph, mentioned, 178

Round Tent, saloon in goldfields, 187, 189

Roundy, Mrs. Elizabeth D. E., and biography of OPR, 4n6, 102n26, 219–20

Rowland, Frank, teamster, killed by Indians, 233–35

Ruby Valley, named, 215n63; mentioned, 317; Indian treaty signed at, 335

runaway officials, and Utah Expedition, 243n61

Rupe, [James], civilian teamster, 264

Rushton, Richard, and "drowned woman" story, 105n4

Ryan, Tom, and Carissa Gulch gold, 347–48

Ryland, John F., Missouri Circuit Court judge, 94

Sagwitch, Shoshone chief, 326; shot by soldiers, 330n23

Salmon River, mentioned, 276

Salt Creek, mentioned, 173

Salt Lake Tribune, on OPR, 364, 366–68

"Salt Sermon," of Sidney Rigdon, 27, 27n9

San Pitch, Shoshone chief, venereal disease of, 211; and Bear River battle, 326

Sangamo Journal, publishes John C. Bennett letters, 74

Scarlett, Frederick, stage driver, and Indian attack, 336–37

Scofield, [   ], alias of OPR, 188n16

Scofield, Quincy, scout, 175–76

Scotts Bluff, Neb., on Mormon trail, 156

118–19; jailed, 122; killed by mob, 124–27; burial of, 130; Council of Fifty organized by, 136
Smith, Joseph, III, and bartending incident, 104n3; meets OPR, 149
Smith, Joseph, Sr., settles in Manchester, N.Y., 3; confers patriarchal blessing, 6n16
Smith, Joseph F., delivers eulogy, 368
Smith, Josephine Donna, daughter of Don Carlos Smith, 220n78; takes name Ina Coolbrith, 220n78
Smith, Lot, Nauvoo Legion officer, as guerilla leader, 251; burns government supply wagons, 261; and pistol accident, 262n29; and cattle raid, 262–64; on OPR, 263, 264; and Aiken Party, 270–71; indicted for treason, 284; protects mail, 322; on British mission, 354
Smith, Lucy Mack, move of, to Kirtland, Ohio, 6
Smith, M. C., mentioned, 16n46, 60
Smith, Mrs. M. C. R. See Caroline Rockwell
Smith, General Persifor F., Army officer, 289
Smith, Samuel, brother of Joseph Smith, Jr., 5
Smith, Sardius, killed at Haun's Mill, 51
Smith, William, brother of Joseph Smith, Jr., 69n10
Smoot, A. O., wagon train captain, 226; arms of, 227n8; at Fort Kearny, 232; brings word of Utah Expedition, 246
Snow, Erastus, first to enter Great Salt Lake Valley, 164–65; journey of east, 226n5; arms of, 227n8
Snow, Warren S., Nauvoo Legion officer, 251
Snow, Zerubbabel, and endowment ceremonies, 197n11
Social Hall, in Great Salt Lake City, 197
Soda Springs, mentioned, 251
"Sons of Dan." See Danites
South Pass, Mormon pioneers at, 160
Southern Indian Mission, at New Harmony, 203–4
southern route, expedition along, 170–73
Sowiette, Ute chief, 182
Spaniards, death of, 210–11
Spanish Fork River, mentioned, 173
Spanish Trail. See southern route
Spencer, Augustine, warrant for arrest of, 111

Spencer, Daniel, at Fort Kearny, 232; mule stolen from, 296
Spencer, Orson, quarrel of, 111
Sprague, Samuel L., and endowment ceremonies, 197n11
Stafford, Christopher M., affidavit of, 5n10; mentioned, 6n14, 16n46
Stafford, Mrs. C. M. See Emily Rockwell
Staines, William C., and endowments, 197n11
Stansbury, Captain Howard, topographical survey expedition of, 288n14
Stanton, Charles T., letter of, 75n27
Stanton, Sidney, mentioned, 75n27
stealing in Nauvoo, 106n6
Stenhouse, T. B. H., on lawlessness, 298; excommunication of, 298n4; on death of John Gheen, 300; on deaths of fugitives, 319n65; on Camp Douglas, 323
Stephenson, John, slaying of, 71n15
Steptoe, Lieutenant Colonel Edward Jenner, declines post as Utah military governor, 212; investigates Gunnison massacre, 212; to chart new Carson Valley route, 212–13; drunk in court, 214n60; leaves Utah, 219
Stevenson, Colonel Jonathan, and OPR, 173
Stewart, Boyd, in shooting match, 190; and Mormon Battalion, 190n23; mission of, to Oregon, 190n24; as delinquent taxpayer, 190n24
Stewart, James, and Frank Worrell, 138n18
Stewart, Riley, in election-day fracas, 40–41
Stewart, Sir William Drummond, 88n9
Stiles, George P., associate justice, advocates express company, 225
Stoddard, Judson, and "Jack Smith," 187; asked to trail Indians, 196; brings word of Utah Expedition, 246
Storey, William R., U.S. marshal, killed, 355
Stout, Allen Joseph, and Danites, 35; set free, 55; on Jonathan Dunham and Nauvoo Legion, 123; on deaths of Joseph and Hyrum Smith, 129–30
Stout, Hosea, at Far West, 52; on OPR's arrest, 147n43; on Richard Yates, 279n39; on Henry Jones and mother, 290n15; represents OPR, 294n29; on death of John Gheen, 300; on crime and violence, 303; arrested on murder complicity charge, 357
Sublette, William, and Fort William, 158n24

suffrage, women's, in Utah, 356n5

Sutherland, Thomas, shotgun guard, 231; as disillusioned Mormon, 232n19; killed by Indians, 233–35

Sutter's Fort, mentioned, 169; Mormons at, 186

Sutter's Mill, and gold discovery, 211

Swartzell, William, describes Danite session, signs, and passwords, 34; on voting bloc, 40

Swett, Harlem P., freighter, killed, 351–52

Taylor, John, in Carthage Jail, 123–25; and Territorial Convention, 226; letter from John M. Bernhisel to, 238n47; indicted for treason, 284

Taylor, Joseph M., court testimony of, 270n8, 271n14

Taylor, Stephen, escorts Captain Stewart Van Vliet, 253

Thayer, brother [   ], on Danites, 34; on consecration of property, 40

Thompson, Denman, actor, 365

Thompson, Robert, at Crooked River battle, 46

Thresher, secret society. *See* Danites

"Thunderbolt, The," Danite leader, 44n54

Thurber, A. K., and Grass Valley road, 361

Tilford, Frank, lawyer, 365

Times and Seasons, on OPR, 77; on Joseph Smith, Jr., 105n4

Timpanogos Utes, and Mormons, 180–82; mentioned, 193

Tintic, Ute sub-chief, 209; quarrels of, with Walkara, 211

Tobin, John, attempted murder of, 288; background of, 288n14

Tompkins, [   ], silversmith, suspect in shooting of L. W. Boggs, 78n36

Toponce, Alexander, freighter, and OPR, 346–47

Town, David, and Joseph Smith, Jr., 92–93; mentioned, 93n13

Townsend, George Alfred, newspaper correspondent, as "Gath," 358; on OPR, 358–59

Townsend House, and Gentiles, 267; and Aiken Party, 271–72

Tracy, Captain Albert, Army officer, on Echo Canyon fortifications, 293

Treasure City *White Pine News*, and John I. Ginn, 273n22

True Church of Latter-day Saints, The, organized by Alpheus Cutler, 145n40

Twiss, Thomas, Indian agent, 235–36; powwow of, with Cheyenne chiefs, 237; letter of, 243n61

Tyrrell, Emily Amanda. *See* Emily Amanda Rockwell

Tyrrell, David, marriage of, 184n1

Uhlinger, Philip, storekeeper, mentioned, 68, 68n4

Uinta, Ute Indian, quarrels with Walkara, 211

Union Vedette, at Camp Douglas, 327

Unionville *Silver State*, and John I. Ginn, 273n22

University of the City of Nauvoo, authorized by Nauvoo City Charter, 58

Ure, James, journeys east, 226n5; as clerk of wagon train company, 226n6

Urim and Thummim, 4

Utah Expedition, ordered to Utah, 242; units of, 250; and Brigadier General William S. Harney, 252; and Colonel Albert Sidney Johnston, 252; and Colonel Edmund B. Alexander, 254; attacked at Pacific Springs, 255–56; Mormon harassment of, 258; supplies for, 258n18; casualties of, 258n20; supply trains of, destroyed, 259; cattle herd of, lost to Mormon raiders, 262–64; and prisoners, 264n33; verges on collapse, 282–83; ordered to Fort Bridger, 283–84; losses of, to guerilla action, 284n2; and amnesty proclamation, 291; march of, to Great Salt Lake City, 291; establishes Camp Floyd, 293; returns east, 311

Utah Liberal Party, 356

Utah War. *See* Utah Expedition,

Utes, mentioned, 193

Valley Tan, on death of John Gheen, 300

valley tan, local whisky, 309; 309n36

Van Buren County, Mo., Mormons driven from, 13

Van Buren, President Martin, interview with Joseph Smith, Jr., 59, 59n5

Van Buren, Captain Michael E., Army officer, mentioned, 289

Van Etten, [E. W.], express rider, 256n16

Van Vliet, Captain Stewart, Army emissary, 252; interview of, with Brigham Young, 252–53; and Mormon escort, 253; on Mormons, 253–54

by mob, 20; and Zion's Camp, 24; and the Danites, 34; threatens Adam Black, 41–42; leads raids, 43; as "The Intrepid," 44n54; defends Far West, 50; surrenders at Far West, 53; jailed, 55–56; flees to Illinois, 57

Williams, Isaac, owner of Rancho Santa Ana del Chino, 172

Williams, Colonel Levi, anti-Mormon minister, and deaths of Joseph and Hyrum Smith, 136n13

Williams, Thomas S., authorized to trade with Indians, 169; buys property from OPR, 177n28; mentioned, 216n66; as slave owner, 346

Williams, Wiley, mentioned, 49

Willie, James G., handcart company captain, 232n19

Willis, [   ], and exploring party, 215

Willis, John, and John Tobin shooting, 288n14

Willock, Major General [   ], Missouri militia, 49

Wills, John, anti-Mormon, 136n13

Wilcox, Phineas, missing in Nauvoo, 141n27

Wilson, Mrs. [   ], and child, killed by Indians, 231–32

Wilson, Harmon T., Carthage constable, sends spy to Nauvoo, 87; arrests Joseph Smith, Jr., 92–93

Wilson's Grocery, mobbers' rendezvous, 17

Winter Quarters, Neb., Mormon camp at, 150n3, 152

Wolf, John A., arrest warrant for, 295–96

Wood, E. B., Illinois militiaman, 146

Wood, Joseph, Missouri lawyer, 86

Woodruff, Wilford, and OPR, 3n3; on Haun's Mill, 51; mentioned, 151; and Great Salt Lake Valley, 166; on Pacific Springs raid, 255

Woods, Sashiel, mentioned, 48n60

Woodson, Samuel H., neighbor of L. W. Boggs, 67; mentioned, 78n36

Woolley, Mrs. Catharine E. Mehring, mentioned, 178, 197

Workman, Jackson, and southern route expedition, 170–72

Workman, Jake, and southern route expedition, 170–72

Worrell, Frank, member of Carthage Greys, 128; testimony of, 135–36; killed, 138–40; OPR arrested in death of, 146–47

Wright, Tuck, as member of Aiken Party, 268; wounded, 274; killed, 278

Wright, W. B., and Alice Young, 289; called to Sandwich Islands, 289

Wyl [Wymetal], Wilhelm, German author, and "drowned woman" story, 105n4

Yates, Richard, trader, killed, 279n39; William A. Hickman confesses killing of, 357; Daniel W. Jones on death of, 357n8

Yauguts. See John D. Lee

Yellow Creek, Mormon camp at, 266

Yelrome, Ill., Mormon settlement, attacked, 138

Young, Alice, daughter of Brigham Young, 289; and John Tobin, 289; and W. B. Wright, 289; and Hiram Clawson, 289

Young, Brigham, on the Danites, 32n18; signs Far West covenant, 56; as lieutenant general of Nauvoo Legion, 63n14; on William Law, 113; on church succession, 132; imitates Joseph Smith, Jr., 132n5; implicated in Hodge killing, 134n8; and Amos Davis, 142n31; and counterfeiting charges, 144; and "Bogus Brigham" incident, 144n36; administers to William Clayton, 150; OPR as bodyguard to, 151; and Emmeline Free, 151, 151n6; loses spyglass, 155–56; criticizes pioneers, 157; and Council of Fifty, 158n22; orders pioneer ferry, 160; stricken with mountain fever, 164; enters Great Salt Lake Valley, 165; and Sam Brannan, 167–68; returns to Winter Quarters, 168; named prophet, seer, and revelator, 175; is "boss of these prairies," 176; on gold craze, 177; denounces John Pack, 180; letter of, to Sam Brannan, 184–85; and Indian affairs, 196; on Jim Bridger, 196, 200–1; on Walkara, 201–4; visits southern settlements, 205–6; parleys with Walkara, 206–8; on being governor, 212; advocates express company, 224–26; hears of Hill Cumorah treasures, 228n11; quarrels with Almon W. Babbitt, 230; quarrels with Broughton D. Harris, 230; urges investigation into Almon W. Babbitt death, 236n41; wins mail contract, 238; denounced by W. W. Drummond, 241; on A. W. Babbitt, 247n63; ousted as governor, 248; on being U.S. president, 248; meets Captain Stewart Van Vliet, 252; succeeded by Alfred Cumming, 253; and "scorched earth" policy, 253–54; ultimatum of, to Gentiles, 272; issues "passports," 272–73; and Aiken Party, 280;

416

indicted for murder, 280n42; alerted to Army move, 282; and "Move South," 284; indicted for treason, 284; and Thomas L. Kane, 284n6; recognizes successor, 288; meets with U.S. Peace Commission to Utah, 291; sets limit for Army camp, 292; hears of lawlessness, 298; and death of John Gheen, 301; and counterfeit plates, 306–7; disfellowships Israel Evans, 311; buys military stores, 311; visits OPR, 320; orders mail routes protected, 321–22; charged with polygamy, 333; acquitted, 333n4; as anti-Mormon target, 356; named in murder indictment, 358; and illegal cohabitation charges, 359–60; at Pipe Springs, 360; and John D. Lee conviction, 363; death of, 364

Young, Brigham H., and Rockwell Mining Company, 356n4

Young, Harriet Page Wheeler, wife of Brigham Young, and Great Salt Lake Valley, 166

Young, John R., letter of, on Aiken Party, 270n11; 271n18

Young, Joseph A., at Fort Laramie, 236; as Nauvoo Legion officer, 251; mentioned, 310n41; and Grass Valley sawmill, 361

Young, Lorenzo Dow, on Sampson Avard, 38n34; at Crooked River battle, 46–47; home of, as a meeting place, 184; posts bail for Brigham Young, 333

Young, Phineas H., journeys east, 226n5

YX Company. *See* Brigham Young Express and Carrying Company

Zion, holy city of, site of, 7; in Great Salt Lake Valley, 137, 137n17; Oregon and Vancouver Island considered for, 141

Zion's Camp, debacle of, 24